Praise for *Implementing Domain-Driven Design*

"With *Implementing Domain-Driven Design*, Vaughn has made an important contribution not only to the literature of the Domain-Driven Design community, but also to the literature of the broader enterprise application architecture field. In key chapters on Architecture and Repositories, for example, Vaughn shows how DDD fits with the expanding array of architecture styles and persistence technologies for enterprise applications—including SOA and REST, NoSQL and data grids—that has emerged in the decade since Eric Evans' seminal book was first published. And, fittingly, Vaughn illuminates the blocking and tackling of DDD—the implementation of entities, value objects, aggregates, services, events, factories, and repositories—with plentiful examples and valuable insights drawn from decades of practical experience. In a word, I would describe this book as *thorough*. For software developers of all experience levels looking to improve their results, and design and implement domain-driven enterprise applications consistently with the best current state of professional practice, *Implementing Domain-Driven Design* will impart a treasure trove of knowledge hard won within the DDD and enterprise application architecture communities over the last couple decades."

—Randy Stafford, Architect At-Large, Oracle Coherence Product Development

"Domain-Driven Design is a powerful set of thinking tools that can have a profound impact on how effective a team can be at building software-intensive systems. The thing is that many developers got lost at times when applying these thinking tools and really needed more concrete guidance. In this book, Vaughn provides the missing links between theory and practice. In addition to shedding light on many of the misunderstood elements of DDD, Vaughn also connects new concepts like Command/Query Responsibility Segregation and Event Sourcing that many advanced DDD practitioners have used with great success. This book is a must-read for anybody looking to put DDD into practice."

—Udi Dahan, Founder of NServiceBus

"For years, developers struggling to practice Domain-Driven Design have been wishing for more practical help in actually implementing DDD. Vaughn did an excellent job in closing the gap between theory and practice with a complete implementation reference. He paints a vivid picture of what it is like to do DDD in a contemporary project, and provides plenty of practical advice on how to approach and solve typical challenges occurring in a project life cycle."

—Alberto Brandolini, DDD Instructor, Certified by Eric Evans and
   Domain Language, Inc.

"*Implementing Domain-Driven Design* does a remarkable thing: it takes a sophisticated and substantial topic area in DDD and presents it clearly, with nuance, fun and finesse. This book is written in an engaging and friendly style, like a trusted advisor giving you expert counsel on how to accomplish what is most important. By the time you finish the book you will be able to begin applying all the important concepts of

DDD, and then some. As I read, I found myself highlighting many sections . . . I will be referring back to it, and recommending it, often."

—Paul Rayner, Principal Consultant & Owner, Virtual Genius, LLC., DDD Instructor, Certified by Eric Evans and Domain Language, Inc., DDD Denver Founder and Co-leader

"One important part of the DDD classes I teach is discussing how to put all the ideas and pieces together into a full blown working implementation. With this book, the DDD community now has a comprehensive reference that addresses this in detail. *Implementing Domain-Driven Design* deals with all aspects of building a system using DDD, from getting the small details right to keeping track of the big picture. This is a great reference and an excellent companion to Eric Evans seminal DDD book."

—Patrik Fredriksson, DDD Instructor, Certified by Eric Evans and Domain Language, Inc.

"If you care about software craftsmanship—and you should—then Domain-Driven Design is a crucial skill set to master and *Implementing Domain-Driven Design* is the fast path to success. *IDDD* offers a highly readable yet rigorous discussion of DDD's strategic and tactical patterns that enables developers to move immediately from understanding to action. Tomorrow's business software will benefit from the clear guidance provided by this book."

—Dave Muirhead, Principal Consultant, Blue River Systems Group

"There's theory and practice around DDD that every developer needs to know, and this is the missing piece of the puzzle that puts it all together. Highly recommended!"

—Rickard Öberg, Java Champion and Developer at Neo Technology

"In *IDDD*, Vaughn takes a top-down approach to DDD, bringing strategic patterns such as bounded context and context maps to the fore, with the building block patterns of entities, values and services tackled later. His book uses a case study throughout, and to get the most out of it you'll need to spend time grokking that case study. But if you do you'll be able to see the value of applying DDD to a complex domain; the frequent sidenotes, diagrams, tables, and code all help illustrate the main points. So if you want to build a solid DDD system employing the architectural styles most commonly in use today, Vaughn's book comes recommended."

—Dan Haywood, author of *Domain-Driven Design with Naked Objects*

"This book employs a top-down approach to understanding DDD in a way that fluently connects strategic patterns to lower level tactical constraints. Theory is coupled with guided approaches to implementation within modern architectural styles. Throughout the book, Vaughn highlights the importance and value of focusing on the business domain all while balancing technical considerations. As a result, the role of DDD, as well as what it does and perhaps more importantly doesn't imply, become ostensibly clear. Many a time, my team and I would be at odds with the friction encountered in applying DDD. With *Implementing Domain-Driven Design* as our luminous guide we were able to overcome those challenges and translate our efforts into immediate business value."

—Lev Gorodinski, Principal Architect, DrillSpot.com

Implementing
Domain-Driven Design

Implementing Domain-Driven Design

Vaughn Vernon

♠ Addison-Wesley

Upper Saddle River, NJ • Boston • Indianapolis • San Francisco
New York • Toronto • Montreal • London • Munich • Paris • Madrid
Capetown • Sydney • Tokyo • Singapore • Mexico City

The publisher offers excellent discounts on this book when ordered in quantity for bulk purchases or special sales, which may include electronic versions and/or custom covers and content particular to your business, training goals, marketing focus, and branding interests. For more information, please contact:

> U.S. Corporate and Government Sales
> (800) 382-3419
> corpsales@pearsontechgroup.com

For sales outside the United States, please contact:

> International Sales
> international@pearsoned.com

Visit us on the Web: informit.com/aw

Library of Congress Control Number: 2012954071

ISBN-13: 978-0-321-83457-7
ISBN-10:   0-321-83457-7
Printed and bound in Great Britain by Bell & Bain Ltd, Glasgow
First printing, January 2013
24
27

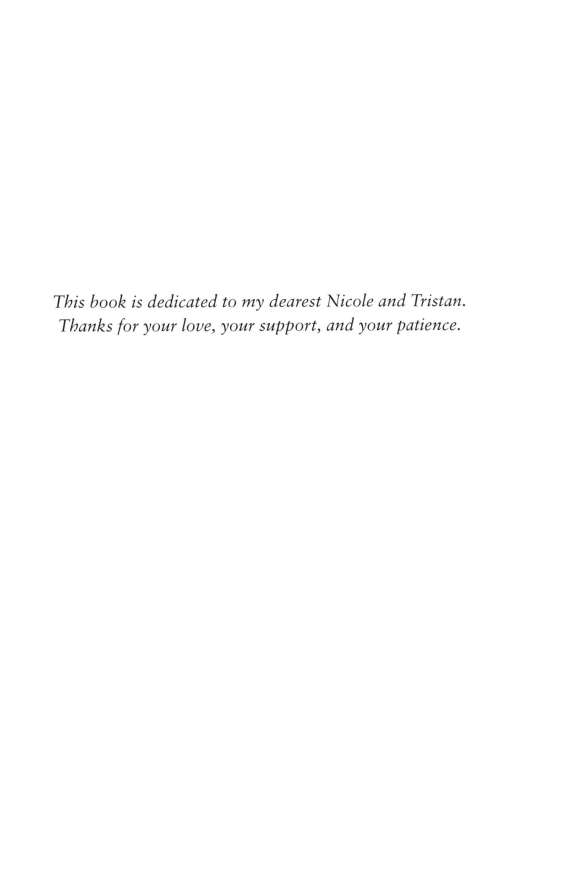

This book is dedicated to my dearest Nicole and Tristan.
Thanks for your love, your support, and your patience.

Contents

Foreword

In this new book, Vaughn Vernon presents the whole of Domain-Driven Design (DDD) in a distinctive way, with new explanations of the concepts, new examples, and an original organization of topics. I believe this fresh, alternative approach will help people grasp the subtleties of DDD, particularly the more abstract ones such as Aggregates and Bounded Contexts. Not only do different people prefer different styles—subtle abstractions are hard to absorb without multiple explanations.

Also, the book conveys some of the insights of the past nine years that have been described in papers and presentations but have not appeared in a book before now. It places Domain Events alongside Entities and Value Objects as the building blocks of a model. It discusses the Big Ball of Mud and places it into the Context Map. It explains the hexagonal architecture, which has emerged as a better description of what we do than the layered architecture.

My first exposure to the material in this book came almost two years ago (although Vaughn had been working on his book for some time by then). At the first DDD Summit, several of us committed to writing about certain topics about which we felt there were fresh things to say or there was a particular need in the community for more specific advice. Vaughn took up the challenge of writing about Aggregates, and he followed through with a series of excellent articles about Aggregates (which became a chapter in this book).

There was also a consensus at the summit that many practitioners would benefit from a more prescriptive treatment of some of the DDD patterns. The honest answer to almost any question in software development is, "It depends." That is not very useful to people who want to learn to apply a technique, however. A person who is assimilating a new subject needs concrete guidance. Rules of thumb don't have to be right in all cases. They are what usually works well or the thing to try first. Through their decisiveness, they convey the philosophy of the approach to solving the problem. Vaughn's book has a good mix of straightforward advice balanced with a discussion of trade-offs that keep it from being simplistic.

Not only have additional patterns, such as Domain Events, become a mainstream part of DDD—people in the field have progressed in learning how to apply those patterns, not to mention adapting them to newer architectures and technologies. Nine years after my book, *Domain-Driven Design: Tackling Complexity in the Heart of Software*, was published, there's actually a lot to say about DDD that is new, and there are new ways to talk about the fundamentals. Vaughn's book is the most complete explanation yet of those new insights into practicing DDD.

—Eric Evans
  Domain Language, Inc.

Preface

All the calculations show it can't work. There's only one thing to do: make it work.

—Pierre-Georges Latécoère,
early French aviation entrepreneur

And make it work we shall. The Domain-Driven Design approach to software development is far too important to leave any capable developer without clear directions for how to implement it successfully.

Getting Grounded, Getting Airborne

When I was a kid, my father learned to pilot small airplanes. Often the whole family would go up flying. Sometimes we flew to another airport for lunch, then returned. When Dad had less time but longed to be in the air, we'd go out, just the two of us, and circle the airport doing "touch-and-goes."

We also took some long trips. For those, we always had a map of the route that Dad had earlier charted. Our job as kids was to help navigate by looking out for landmarks below so we could be certain to stay on course. This was great fun for us because it was a challenge to spot objects so far below that exhibited little in the way of identifying details. Actually, I'm sure that Dad always knew where we were. He had all the instruments on the dashboard, and he was licensed for instrument flight.

The view from the air really changed my perspective. Now and then Dad and I would fly over our house in the countryside. At a few hundred feet up, this gave me a context for home that I didn't have before. As Dad would cruise over our house, Mom and my sisters would run out into the yard to wave at us. I knew it was them, although I couldn't look into their eyes. We couldn't converse. If I had shouted out the airplane window, they would never have heard me. I could see the split-rail fence in the front dividing our property from the road. When on the ground I'd walk across it as if on a balance beam. From the air, it looked like carefully woven twigs. And there was the huge yard that I circled row by row on our riding lawn mower every summer. From the air, I saw only a sea of green, not the blades of grass.

I loved those moments in the air. They are etched in my memory as if Dad and I were just taxiing in after landing to tie down for the evening. As much as I loved those flights, they sure were no substitute for being on the ground. And as cool as they were, the touch-and-goes were just too brief to make me feel grounded.

Landing with Domain-Driven Design

Getting in touch with Domain-Driven Design (DDD) can be like flight to a kid. The view from the air is stunning, but sometimes things look unfamiliar enough to prevent us from knowing exactly where we are. Getting from point A to point B appears far from realistic. The DDD grownups always seem to know where they are. They've long ago plotted a course, and they are completely in tune with their navigational instruments. A great number of others don't feel grounded. What is needed is the ability to "land and tie down." Next, a map is needed to guide the way from where we are to where we need to be.

In the book *Domain-Driven Design: Tackling Complexity in the Heart of Software* [Evans], Eric Evans brought about what is a timeless work. It is my firm belief that Eric's work will guide developers in practical ways for decades to come. Like other pattern works, it establishes flight far enough above the surface to give a broad vision. Yet, there may be a bit more of a challenge when we need to understand the groundwork involved in implementing DDD, and we usually desire more detailed examples. If only we could land and stay on the surface a bit longer, and even drive home or to some other familiar place.

Part of my goal is to take you in for a soft landing, secure the aircraft, and help you get home by way of a well-known surface route. That will help you make sense of implementing DDD, giving you examples that use familiar tools and technologies. And since none of us can stay home all the time, I will also help you venture out onto other paths to explore new terrain, taking you to places that perhaps you've never been before. Sometimes the path will be steep, but given the right tactics, a challenging yet safe ascent is possible. On this trip you'll learn about alternative architectures and patterns for integrating multiple domain models. This may expose you to some previously unexplored territory. You will find detailed coverage of strategic modeling with multiple integrations, and you'll even learn how to develop autonomous services.

My goal is to provide a map to help you take both short jaunts and long, complicated treks, enjoying the surrounding detail, without getting lost or injured along the way.

Mapping the Terrain and Charting for Flight

It seems that in software development we are always mapping from one thing to another. We map our objects to databases. We map our objects to the user interface and then back again. We map our objects to and from various application representations, including those that can be consumed by other systems and applications. With all this mapping, it's natural to want a map from the higher-level patterns of Evans to implementation.

Even if you have already landed a few times with DDD, there is probably more to benefit from. Sometimes DDD is first embraced as a technical tool set. Some refer to this approach to DDD as *DDD-Lite*. We may have homed in on Entities, Services, possibly made a brave attempt at designing Aggregates, and tried to manage their persistence using Repositories. Those patterns felt a bit like familiar ground, so we put them to use. We may even have found some use for Value Objects along the way. All of these fall within the catalog of *tactical design* patterns, which are more technical. They help us take on a serious software problem with the skill of a surgeon with a scalpel. Still, there is much to learn about these and other places to go with tactical design as well. I map them to implementation.

Have you traveled beyond tactical modeling? Have you visited and even lingered with what some call the "other half" of DDD, the *strategic design* patterns? If you've left out the use of Bounded Context and Context Maps, you have probably also missed out on the use of the Ubiquitous Language.

If there is a single "invention" Evans delivers to the software development community, it is the Ubiquitous Language. At a minimum he brought the Ubiquitous Language out of the dusty archives of design wisdom. It is a team pattern used to capture the concepts and terms of a specific core business domain in the software model itself. The software model incorporates the nouns, adjectives, verbs, and richer expressions formally spoken by the development team, a team that includes one or more business domain experts. It would be a mistake, however, to conclude that the Language is limited to mere words. Just as any human language reflects the minds of those who speak it, the Ubiquitous

Language reflects the mental model of the experts of the business domain you are working in. Thus, the software and the tests that verify the model's adherence to the tenets of the domain both capture and adhere to this Language, the same conceived and spoken by the team. The Language is equally as valuable as the various strategic and tactical modeling patterns and in some cases has a more enduring quality.

Simply stated, practicing DDD-Lite leads to the construction of inferior domain models. That's because the Ubiquitous Language, Bounded Context, and Context Mapping have so much to offer. You get more than a team lingo. The Language of a team in an explicit Bounded Context expressed as a domain model adds true business value and gives us certainty that we are implementing the correct software. Even from a technical standpoint, it helps us create better models, ones with more potent behaviors, that are pure and less error prone. Thus, I map the strategic design patterns to understandable example implementations.

This book maps the terrain of DDD in a way that allows you to experience the benefits of both strategic and tactical design. It puts you in touch with its business value and technical strengths by peering closely at the details.

It would be a disappointment if all we ever did with DDD is stay on the ground. Getting stuck in the details, we'd forget that the view from flight teaches us a lot, too. Don't limit yourself to rugged ground travel. Brave the challenge of getting in the pilot's seat and see from a height that is telling. With training flights on strategic design, with its Bounded Contexts and Context Maps, you will be prepared to gain a grander perspective on its full realization. When you reward yourself with DDD flight, I will have reached my goal.

Summary of Chapters

The following highlights the chapters of this book and how you can benefit from each one.

Chapter 1: Getting Started with DDD

This chapter introduces you to the benefits of using DDD and how to achieve the most from it. You will learn what DDD can do for your projects and your teams as you grapple with complexity. You'll find out how to score your project to see if it deserves the DDD investment. You will consider the common alternatives to DDD and why they often lead to problems. The chapter lays the foundations of DDD as you learn how to take the first steps on your project, and it even gives you some ways to sell DDD to your management, domain experts, and technical team members. That will enable you to face the challenges of using DDD armed with the knowledge of how to succeed.

You are introduced to a project case study that involves a fictitious company and team, yet one with real-world DDD challenges. The company, with the charter to create innovative SaaS-based products in a multitenant environment, experiences many of the mistakes common to DDD adoption but makes vital discoveries that help the teams solve their issues and keep the project on track. The project is one that most developers can relate to, as it involves developing a Scrum-based project management application. This case study introduction sets the stage for subsequent chapters. Each strategic and tactical pattern is taught through the eyes of the team, both as they err and as they make strides toward maturity in implementing DDD successfully.

Chapter 2: Domains, Subdomains, and Bounded Contexts

What is a Domain, a Subdomain, and a Core Domain? What are Bounded Contexts, and why and how should you use them? These questions are answered in the light of mistakes made by the project team in our case study. Early on in their first DDD project they failed to understand the Subdomain they were working within, its Bounded Context, and a concise Ubiquitous Language. In fact, they were completely unfamiliar with strategic design, only leveraging the tactical patterns for their technical benefits. This led to problems in their initial domain model design. Fortunately, they recognized what had happened before it became a hopeless morass.

A vital message is conveyed, that of applying Bounded Contexts to distinguish and segregate models properly. Addressed are common misapplications of the pattern along with effective implementation advice. The text then leads you through the corrective steps the team took and how that resulted in the creation of two distinct Bounded Contexts. This led to the proper separation of modeling concepts in their third Bounded Context, the new Core Domain, and the main sample used in the book.

This chapter will strongly resonate with readers who have felt the pain of applying DDD only in a technical way. If you are uninitiated in strategic design, you are pointed in the right direction to start out on a successful journey.

Chapter 3: Context Maps

Context Maps are a powerful tool to help a team understand their business domain, the boundaries between distinct models, and how they are currently, or can be, integrated. This technique is not limited to drawing a diagram of your system architecture. It's about understanding the relationships between the various Bounded Contexts in an enterprise and the patterns used to map objects cleanly from one model to another. Use of this tool is important to succeeding with Bounded Contexts in a complex business enterprise. This chapter takes you through the process used by the project team as they applied Context Mapping to understand the problems they created with their first Bounded Context (Chapter 2). It then shows how the two resulting clean Bounded Contexts were leveraged by the team responsible for designing and implementing the new Core Domain.

Chapter 4: Architecture

Just about everyone knows the Layers Architecture. Are Layers the only way to house a DDD application, or can other diverse architectures be used? Here we consider how to use DDD within such architectures as Hexagonal (Ports and Adapters), Service-Oriented, REST, CQRS, Event-Driven (Pipes and Filters, Long-Running Processes or Sagas, Event Sourcing), and Data Fabric/Grid-Based. Several of these architectural styles were put to use by the project team.

Chapter 5: Entities

The first of the DDD tactical patterns treated is Entities. The project team first leaned too heavily on these, overlooking the importance of designing with Value Objects when appropriate. This led to a discussion of how to avoid widespread overuse of Entities because of the undue influence of databases and persistence frameworks.

Once you are familiar with ways to distinguish their proper use, you see lots of examples of how to design Entities well. How do we express the Ubiquitous Language with an Entity? How are Entities tested, implemented, and persisted? You are stepped through how-to guidance for each of these.

Chapter 6: Value Objects

Early on the project team missed out on important modeling opportunities with Value Objects. They focused too intensely on the individual attributes of Entities when they should have been giving careful consideration to how multiple related attributes are properly gathered as an immutable whole. This chapter looks at Value Object design from several angles, discussing how to identify the special characteristics in the model as a means to determine when to use a Value rather than an Entity. Other important topics are covered, such as the role of Values in integration and modeling Standard Types. The chapter then shows how to design domain-centric tests, how to implement Value types, and how to avoid the bad influence persistence mechanisms can have on our need to store them as part of an Aggregate.

Chapter 7: Services

This chapter shows how to determine when to model a concept as a fine-grained, stateless Service that lives in the domain model. You are shown when you should design a Service instead of an Entity or Value Object, and how Domain Services can be implemented to handle business domain logic as well as for technical integration purposes. The decisions of the project team are used to exemplify when to use Services and how they are designed.

Chapter 8: Domain Events

Domain Events were not formally introduced by Eric Evans as part of DDD until after his book was published. You'll learn why Domain Events published by the model are so powerful, and the diverse ways that they can be used, even in supporting integration and autonomous business services. Although various kinds of technical events are sent and processed by applications, the distinguishing characteristics of Domain Events are spotlighted. Design and implementation guidance is provided, instructing you on available options and trade-offs. The chapter then teaches how to create a Publish-Subscribe mechanism, how Domain Events are published to integrated subscribers across the enterprise, ways to create and manage an Event Store, and how to properly deal with common messaging challenges faced. Each of these areas is discussed in light of the project team's efforts to use them correctly and to their best advantage.

Chapter 9: Modules

How do we organize model objects into right-sized containers with limited coupling to objects that are in different containers? How do we name these containers so they reflect the Ubiquitous Language? Beyond packages and namespaces, how can we use the more modern modularization facilities, such as OSGi and Jigsaw, provided by languages and frameworks? Here you will see how Modules were put to use by the project team across a few of their projects.

Chapter 10: Aggregates

Aggregates are probably the least well understood among DDD's tactical tools. Yet, if we apply some rules of thumb, Aggregates can be made simpler and quicker to implement. You will learn how to cut through the complexity barrier to use Aggregates that create consistency boundaries around small object clusters. Because of putting too much emphasis on the less important aspects of Aggregates, the project team in our case study stumbled in a few different ways. We step through the team's iterations with a few modeling challenges and analyze what went wrong and what they did about it. The result of their efforts led to a deeper understanding of their Core Domain. We look in on how the team corrected their mistakes through the proper application of transactional and eventual consistency, and how that led them to design a more scalable and high-performing model within a distributed processing environment.

Chapter 11: Factories

[Gamma et al.] has plenty to say about Factories, so why bother with treating them in this book? This is a simple chapter that does not attempt to reinvent the wheel. Rather, its focus is on understanding *where* Factories should exist. There are, of course, a few good tips to share about designing a worthy Factory in a DDD setting. See how the project team created Factories in their Core Domain as a way to simplify the client interface and protect the model's consumers from introducing disastrous bugs into their multitenant environment.

Chapter 12: Repositories

Isn't a Repository just a simple Data Access Object (DAO)? If not, what's the difference? Why should we consider designing Repositories to mimic collections rather than databases? Learn how to design a Repository that is used with an ORM, one that supports the Coherence grid-based distributed cache, and one that uses a NoSQL key-value store. Each of these optional persistence mechanisms was at the disposal of the project team because of the power and versatility behind the Repository building block pattern.

Chapter 13: Integrating Bounded Contexts

Now that you understand the higher-level techniques of Context Mapping and have the tactical patterns on your side, what is involved in actually implementing the integrations between models? What integration options are afforded by DDD? This chapter uncovers a few different ways to implement model integrations using Context Mapping. Instruction is given based on how the project team integrated the Core Domain with other supporting Bounded Contexts introduced in early chapters.

Chapter 14: Application

You have designed a model per your Core Domain's Ubiquitous Language. You've developed ample tests around its usage and correctness, and it works. But how do other members of your team design the areas of the application that surround the model? Should they use DTOs to transfer data between the model and the user interface? Or are there other options for conveying model state up to the presentation components? How do the Application Services and infrastructure work? This chapter addresses those concerns using the now familiar project to convey available options.

Appendix A: Aggregates and Event Sourcing: A+ES

Event Sourcing is an important technical approach to persisting Aggregates that also provides the basis for developing an Event-Driven Architecture. Event Sourcing can be used to represent the entire state of an Aggregate as a sequence of Events that have occurred since it was created. The Events are used to rebuild the state of the Aggregate by replaying them in the same order in which they occurred. The premise is that this approach simplifies persistence and allows capturing concepts with complex behavioral properties, besides the far-reaching influence the Events themselves can have on your own and external systems.

Java and Development Tools

The majority of the examples in this book use the Java Programming Language. I could have provided the examples in C#, but I made a conscious decision to use Java instead.

First of all, and sad to say, I think there has been a general abandonment of good design and development practices in the Java community. These days it may be difficult to find a clean, explicit domain model in most Java-based projects. It seems to me that Scrum and other agile techniques are being used as substitutes for careful modeling, where a product backlog is thrust at developers as if it serves as a set of designs. Most agile practitioners will leave their daily stand-up without giving a second thought to how their backlog tasks will affect the underlying model of the business. Although I assume this is needless to say, I must assert that Scrum, for example, was never meant to stand in place of design. No matter how many project and product managers would like to keep you marching on a relentless path of continuous delivery, Scrum was not meant only as a means to keep Gantt chart enthusiasts happy. Yet, it has become that in so many cases.

I consider this a big problem, and a major theme I have is to inspire the Java community to return to domain modeling by giving a reasonable amount of thought to how sound, yet agile and rapid, design techniques can benefit their work.

Further, there are already some good resources for using DDD in a .NET environment, one being *Applying Domain-Driven Design and Patterns: With Examples in C# and .NET* by Jimmy Nilsson [Nilsson]. Due to Jimmy's good work and that of others promoting the Alt.NET mindset, there is a high tide of good design and development practices going on in the .NET community. Java developers need to take notice.

Second, I am well aware that the C#.NET community will have no problem whatsoever understanding Java code. Due to the fact that much of the DDD community uses C#.NET, most of my early book reviewers are C# developers, and I never once received a complaint about their having to read Java code. So, I have no concern that my use of Java in any way alienates C# developers.

I need to add that at the time of this writing there was a significant shift toward interest in using document-based and key-value storage over relational databases. This is for good reason, for even Martin Fowler has aptly nicknamed these "aggregate-oriented storage." It's a fitting name and well describes the advantages of using NoSQL storage in a DDD setting.

Yet, in my consulting work I find that many are still quite married to relational databases and object-relational mapping. Therefore, I think that in practical terms there has been no disservice to the community of NoSQL enthusiasts by my including guidance on using object-relational mapping techniques for domain models. I do acknowledge, however, that this may earn me some scorn from those who think that the object-relational impedance mismatch makes it unworthy of consideration. That's fine, and I accept the flames, because there is a vast majority who must still live with the drudgeries of this impedance mismatch on a day-to-day basis, however unenlightened they may seem to the minority.

Of course, I also provide guidance in Chapter 12, "Repositories," on the use of document-based, key-value, and Data Fabric/Grid-Based stores. As well, in several places I discuss where the use of a NoSQL store would tend to influence an alternative design of Aggregates and their contained parts. It's quite likely that the trend toward NoSQL stores will continue to spur growth in that sector, so in this case object-relational developers need to take notice. As you can see, I understand both sides of the argument, and I agree with both. It's all part of the ongoing friction created by technology trends, and the friction needs to happen in order for positive change to happen.

Acknowledgments

I am grateful to the fine staff at Addison-Wesley for giving me the opportunity to publish under their highly respected label. As I have stated before in my classes and presentations, I see Addison-Wesley as a publisher that understands the value of DDD. Both Christopher Guzikowski and Chris Zahn (Dr. Z) have supported my efforts throughout the editorial process. I will not forget the day that Christopher Guzikowski called to share the news that he wanted to sign me as one of his authors. I will remember how he encouraged me to persevere through the doubts that most authors must experience, until publication was in sight. Of course, it was Dr. Z who made sure the text was put into a publishable state. Thanks to my production editor, Elizabeth Ryan, for coordinating the book's publication details. And thanks to my intrepid copyeditor, Barbara Wood.

Going back a ways, it was Eric Evans who devoted a major portion of five years of his career to write the first definitive work on DDD. Without his efforts, the wisdom that grew out of the Smalltalk and patterns communities, and that Eric himself refined, many more developers would just be hacking their way to delivering bad software. Sadly, this problem is more common than it should be. As Eric says, the poor quality of software development, and the uncreative joylessness of the teams that produce the software, nearly drove him to exit the software industry for good. We owe Eric hearty thanks for concentrating his energy into educating rather than into a career change.

At the end of the first DDD Summit in 2011, which Eric invited me to attend, it was determined that the leadership should produce a set of guidelines by which more developers could succeed with DDD. I was already far along with this book and was in a good position to understand what developers were missing. I offered to write an essay to provide the "rules of thumb" for Aggregates. I determined that this three-part series entitled "Effective Aggregate Design" would form the foundation for Chapter 10 of this book. Once released on dddcommunity.org, it became quite clear how such sound guidance was greatly needed. Thanks to others among the DDD leadership who reviewed that essay and thus provided valuable feedback for this book. Eric Evans and Paul Rayner did several detailed reviews of the essay. I also received feedback from Udi Dahan, Greg Young, Jimmy Nilsson, Niclas Hedhman, and Rickard Öberg.

Special thanks go to Randy Stafford, a longtime member of the DDD community. After attending a DDD talk I gave several years ago in Denver, Randy urged me to become more involved in the larger DDD community. Sometime later, Randy introduced me to Eric Evans so I could pitch my ideas about drawing the DDD community together. While my ideas were a bit grander and possibly less achievable, Eric convinced us that forming a smaller contingent composed of clear DDD leadership would have more near-term value. From these discussions the DDD Summit 2011 was formed. Needless to say, without Randy's coaxing me to push forward with my views of DDD, this book would not exist, and perhaps not even a DDD Summit. Although Randy was too busy with Oracle Coherence work to contribute to this book, perhaps we will get the chance to write something in the future in a combined effort.

A huge thank-you goes to Rinat Abdullin, Stefan Tilkov, and Wes Williams for contributing sections about specialized topics to the text. It's nearly impossible to know everything about everything related to DDD, and absolutely impossible to be an expert in all areas of software development. That's why I turned to experts in specific areas to write a few sections of Chapter 4 and Appendix A. Thanks go to Stefan Tilkov for his uncommon knowledge of REST, to Wes Williams for his GemFire experience, and to Rinat Abdullin for sharing his continually expanding experience with Event Sourcing for Aggregate implementation.

One of my earliest reviewers was Leo Gorodinsk, and he stuck with the project. I first met Leo at our DDD Denver meetup. He provided a lot of great feedback on this book based on his own struggles while implementing DDD with his team in Boulder, Colorado. I hope my book helped Leo as much as his critical reviews helped me. I see Leo as part of DDD's future.

Many others provided feedback on at least one chapter of my book, and some on several chapters. Some of the more critical feedback was provided by Gojko Adzic, Alberto Brandolini, Udi Dahan, Dan Haywood, Dave Muirhead, and Stefan Tilkov. Specifically, Dan Haywood and Gojko Adzic delivered much of the early feedback, which was based on the most-painful-to-read content I produced. I am glad they endured and corrected me. Alberto Brandolini's insights into strategic design in general, and Context Mapping specifically, helped me focus on the essence of that vital material. Dave Muirhead, with an abundance of experience in object-oriented design, domain modeling, as well as object persistence and in-memory data grids—including GemFire and Coherence—influenced my text regarding some of the history and finer details of object persistence. Besides his REST contribution, Stefan Tilkov supplied additional insights into architecture in general, and SOA and Pipes and Filters specifically. Finally, Udi Dahan validated and helped me clarify some of the concepts of CQRS, Long-Running Processes (aka Sagas), and messaging with NServiceBus. Other reviewers who provided valuable feedback were Rinat Abdullin, Svein Arne Ackenhausen, Javier Ruiz Aranguren, William Doman, Chuck Durfee, Craig Hoff, Aeden Jameson, Jiwei Wu, Josh Maletz, Tom Marrs, Michael McCarthy, Rob Meidal, Jon Slenk, Aaron Stockton, Tom Stockton, Chris Sutton, and Wes Williams.

Scorpio Steele produced the fantastic illustrations for the book. Scorpio made everyone on the IDDD team the superheroes that they truly are. At the other end of the spectrum was the nontechnical editorial review by my good friend Kerry Gilbert. While everyone else made sure I was technically correct, Kerry put me "under the grammar hammer."

My father and mother have provided great inspiration and support throughout my life. My father—AJ in the "Cowboy Logic" humor throughout this book—is not *just* a cowboy. Don't get me wrong. Being a great cowboy would be enough. Besides loving flight and piloting airplanes, my father was an accomplished civil engineer and land surveyor, and a talented negotiator. He still loves math and studying the galaxies. Among many other things he taught me, my Dad imparted to me how to solve a right triangle when I was around ten years old. Thanks, Dad, for giving me a technical bent at a young age. Thanks also go to my mom, one of the nicest people you could ever know. She has always encouraged and supported me through my personal challenges. Besides, what stamina I have comes from her. I could go on, but I could never say enough good things about her.

Although this book is dedicated to my loving wife, Nicole, and our marvelous son, Tristan, my thanks would not be complete without a special mention here. They are the ones who allowed me to work on and complete the book. Without their support and encouragement my task would not have been possible. Thanks so much, my dearest loved ones.

About the Author

Vaughn Vernon is a veteran software craftsman with more than twenty-five years of experience in software design, development, and architecture. He is a thought leader in simplifying software design and implementation using innovative methods. He has been programming with object-oriented languages since the 1980s and applying the tenets of Domain-Driven Design since his Smalltalk domain modeling days in the early 1990s. His experience spans a wide range of business domains, including aerospace, environmental, geospatial, insurance, medical and health care, and telecommunications. He has also succeeded in technical endeavors, creating reusable frameworks, libraries, and implementation acceleration tools. He consults and speaks internationally and has taught his Implementing Domain-Driven Design classes on multiple continents. You can read more about his latest efforts at www.VaughnVernon.co and follow him on Twitter here: @VaughnVernon.

Guide to This Book

The book *Domain-Driven Design* by Eric Evans presents what is essentially a large *pattern language*. A pattern language is a set of software patterns that are intertwined because they are dependent on each other. Any one pattern references one or more other patterns that it depends on, or that depend on it. What does this mean for you?

It means that as you read any given chapter of this book, you could run into a DDD pattern that isn't discussed in that chapter and that you don't already know. Don't panic, and please don't stop reading out of frustration. The referenced pattern is very likely explained in detail in another chapter of the book.

In order to help unravel the pattern language, I used the syntax found in Table G.1 in the text.

Table G.1   The Syntax Used in This Book

When You See This . . .	It Means This . . .
Pattern Name (#)	1. It is the first time the pattern is referenced in the chapter that you are reading, or 2. It is an important additional reference to a pattern that was already mentioned in the chapter, but it's essential to know where to locate more information about it at that point in the text.
Bounded Context (2)	The chapter you are reading is referencing Chapter 2 for you to find out deep details about Bounded Contexts.
Bounded Context	It is the way I reference a pattern already mentioned in the same chapter. I don't want to irritate you by making every reference to a given pattern bold, with a chapter number.
[REFERENCE]	It is a bibliographic reference to another work.

continues

Table G.1   The Syntax Used in This Book (*Continued*)

When You See This . . .	It Means This . . .
[Evans] or [Evans, Ref]	I don't cover the specific referenced DDD pattern extensively, and if you want to know more, you need to read these works by Eric Evans. (They're always recommended reading!)
	[Evans] means his classic book, *Domain-Driven Design.*
	[Evans, Ref] means a second publication that is a separate, condensed reference to the patterns in [Evans] that have been updated and extended.
[Gamma et al.] and [Fowler, P of EAA]	[Gamma et al.] means the classic book *Design Patterns.*
	[Fowler, P of EAA] means Martin Fowler's *Patterns of Enterprise Application Architecture.*
	I reference these works frequently. Although I reference several other works as well, you will tend to see these a bit more than others. Examine the full bibliography for details.

If you start reading in the middle of a chapter and you see a reference such as Bounded Context, remember that you'll probably find a chapter in this book that covers the pattern. Just glance at the index for a richer set of references.

If you have already read [Evans] and you know its patterns to some degree, you'll probably tend to use this book as a way to clarify your understanding of DDD and to get ideas for how to improve your existing model designs. In that case you may not need a big-picture view right now. But if you are relatively new to DDD, the following section will help you see how the patterns fit together, and how this book can be used to get you up and running quickly. So, read on.

Big-Picture View of DDD

Early on I take you through one of the pillars of DDD, the **Ubiquitous Language (1)**. A Ubiquitous Language is applicable within a single **Bounded Context (2)**. Straightaway, you need to familiarize yourself with that critical domain modeling mindset. Just remember that whichever way your software models are designed *tactically*, *strategically* you'll want them to reflect the following: a clean Ubiquitous Language modeled in an explicitly Bounded Context.

Strategic Modeling

A Bounded Context is a conceptual boundary where a domain model is applicable. It provides a context for the Ubiquitous Language that is spoken by the team and expressed in its carefully designed software model, as shown in Figure G.1.

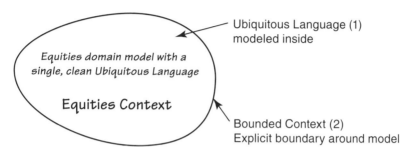

Figure G.1   A diagram illustrating a Bounded Context and relevant Ubiquitous Language

As you practice strategic design, you'll find that the **Context Mapping** (3) patterns seen in Figure G.2 work in harmony. Your team will use Context Maps to understand their project terrain.

We've just considered the big picture of DDD's strategic design. Understanding it is imperative.

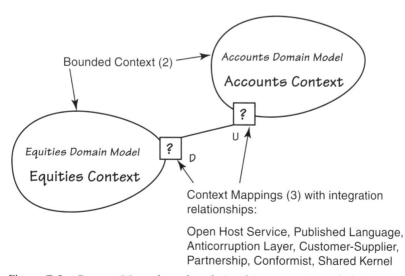

Figure G.2   Context Maps show the relationships among Bounded Contexts.

Architecture

Sometimes a new Bounded Context or existing ones that interact through Context Mapping will need to take on a new style of **Architecture (4)**. It's important to keep in mind that your strategically and tactically designed domain models should be architecturally neutral. Still, there will need to be some architecture around and between each model. A powerful architectural style for hosting a Bounded Context is **Hexagonal,** which can be used to facilitate other styles such as **Service-Oriented, REST** and **Event-Driven,** and others. Figure G.3 depicts a Hexagonal Architecture, and while it may look a little busy, it's a fairly simplistic style to employ.

Sometimes we may be tempted to place too much emphasis on architecture rather than focusing on the importance of carefully crafting a DDD-based model. Architecture is important, but architectural influences come and go. Remember to prioritize correctly, placing more emphasis on the domain model, which has greater business value and will be more enduring.

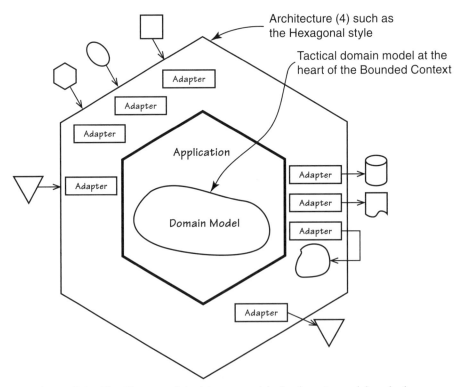

Figure G.3   The Hexagonal Architecture with the domain model at the heart
of the software

Tactical Modeling

We model tactically inside a Bounded Context using DDD's building block patterns. One of the most important patterns of tactical design is **Aggregate** (**10**), as illustrated in Figure G.4.

An Aggregate is composed of either a single **Entity** (**5**) or a cluster of Entities and **Value Objects** (**6**) that must remain transactionally consistent throughout the Aggregate's lifetime. Understanding how to effectively model Aggregates is quite important and one of the least well understood techniques among DDD's building blocks. If they are so important, you may be wondering why Aggregates are placed later in the book. First of all, the placement of tactical patterns in this book follows the same order as is found in [Evans]. Also, since Aggregates are based on other tactical patterns, we cover the basic building blocks—such as Entities and Value Objects—before the more complex Aggregate pattern.

An instance of an Aggregate is persisted using its **Repository** (**12**) and later searched for within and retrieved from it. You can see an indication of that in Figure G.4.

Use stateless **Services** (**7**), such as seen in Figure G.5, inside the domain model to perform business operations that don't fit naturally as an operation on an Entity or a Value Object.

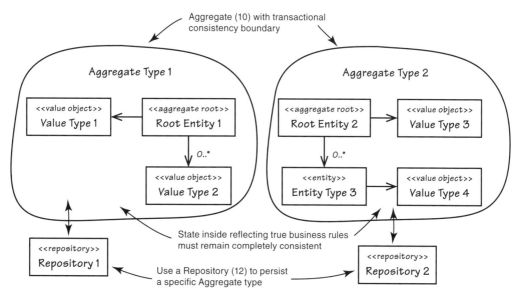

Figure G.4 Two Aggregate types with their own transactional consistency boundaries

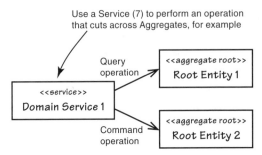

Figure G.5   Domain Services carry out domain-specific operations, which may involve multiple domain objects.

Use **Domain Events** (8) to indicate the occurrence of significant happenings in the domain. Domain Events can be modeled a few different ways. When they capture occurrences that are a result of some Aggregate command operation, the Aggregate itself publishes the Event as depicted in Figure G.6.

Although often given little thought, it's really important to design **Modules** (9) correctly. In its simplest form, think of a Module as a package in Java or a namespace in C#. Remember that if you design your Modules mechanically rather than according to the Ubiquitous Language, they will probably do more harm than good. Figure G.7 illustrates how Modules should contain a limited set of cohesive domain objects.

Of course, there's much more to implementing DDD, and I won't try to cover it all here. There's a whole book ahead of you that does just that. I think this Guide gets you off on the right foot for your journey through implementing DDD. So, enjoy the journey!

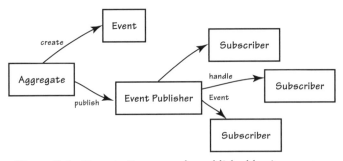

Figure G.6   Domain Events can be published by Aggregates.

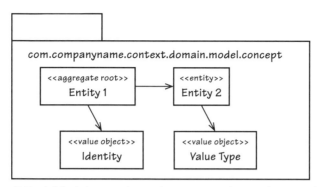

Figure G.7 A Module contains and organizes cohesive domain objects.

Oh, and just to get you familiarized with Cowboy Logic, here's one for the trail:

Cowboy Logic

AJ: "Don't worry about bitin' off more than you can chew. Your mouth is probably a whole lot bigger than you think." ;-)

LB: "You meant to say 'mind,' J. Your mind is bigger than you think!"

Chapter 1

Getting Started with DDD

Design is not just what it looks like and feels like.
Design is how it works.
—*Steve Jobs*

We strive to produce quality in the software we develop. We achieve some quality by using tests to help us avoid delivering software with a fatal number of bugs. Yet, even if we could produce completely bug-free software, that in itself does not necessarily mean that a quality software model is designed. The software model—the *way* the software expresses the solution to the business goal being sought—could still suffer greatly. Delivering software with few defects is obviously good. Still, we can reach higher for a well-designed software model that explicitly reflects the intended business objective, and our work may even reach the level of *great*.

The software development approach called *Domain-Driven Design*, or *DDD*, exists to help us more readily succeed at achieving high-quality software model designs. When implemented correctly, DDD helps us reach the point where *our design is exactly how the software works*. This book is about helping you correctly implement DDD.

You may be completely new to DDD, you may have tried it and struggled, or you may have already succeeded with it before. Regardless, you no doubt are reading this book because you want to improve your ability to implement DDD, and you can. The chapter road map helps you target your specific needs.

Road Map to This Chapter

- Discover what DDD can do for your projects and your teams as you grapple with complexity.
- Find out how to score your project to see if it deserves the DDD investment.
- Consider the common alternatives to DDD and why they often lead to problems.
- Grasp the foundations of DDD as you learn how to take the first steps on your project.
- Learn how to sell DDD to your management, domain experts, and technical team members.

continues

- Face the challenges of using DDD armed with knowledge of how to succeed.
- Look in on a team that is learning how to implement DDD.

What should you expect from DDD? Not a heavy, dense, ceremonial process that blocks your way to progress. Rather, expect to use the agile development techniques you probably already have come to trust. Beyond agile, anticipate the acquisition of methods that help you gain deep insight into your business domain, with the prospect of producing testable, malleable, organized, carefully crafted, high-quality software models.

DDD gives you both the *strategic and tactical modeling tools* necessary to design high-quality software that meets core business objectives.

Can I DDD?

You can implement DDD if you have

- A passion for creating excellent software every day, and the tenacity to achieve that goal

- The eagerness to learn and improve, and the fortitude to admit you need to

- The aptitude to understand software patterns and how to properly apply them

- The skill and patience to explore design alternatives using proven agile methods

- The courage to challenge the status quo

- The desire and ability to pay attention to details, to experiment and discover

- A drive to seek ways to code smarter and better

I'm not going to tell you that there isn't a learning curve. To put it bluntly, the learning curve can be steep. Yet, this book has been put together to help flatten the curve as much as possible. My goal is to help you and your team implement DDD with the greatest potential for success.

DDD isn't first and foremost about technology. In its most central principles, DDD is about discussion, listening, understanding, discovery, and business value, all in an effort to centralize knowledge. If you are capable of *under-standing the business* in which your company works, you can at a minimum participate in the software model discovery process to produce a **Ubiquitous Language**. Sure, you're going to have to learn more about the business, lots more. Still, you are on your way to succeeding with DDD already because you can comprehend the concepts of your business, you revel in developing great software, and that gives you the proper footing to take DDD all the way.

Won't having years, even a decade or two, of software development experience help? It might. Nevertheless, software development experience doesn't give you the ability to listen and learn from *domain experts*, the people who know the most about some high-priority area of the business. You are at a greater advantage if you can engage with those who seldom, if ever, express themselves using technical lingo. You're going to have to listen and listen carefully. You're going to have to respect their viewpoint and trust that they know a lot more than you do.

> **There Are Big Advantages to Engaging with Domain Experts**
> You are at a greater advantage if you can engage with those who seldom, if ever, express themselves using technical lingo. Just as you are going to learn from them, there is a high probability that they are also going to learn from you.

What you may like best about DDD is that the domain experts are also going to *have to listen to you*. You are on the team just as they are. As strange as it may seem, the domain experts don't know everything about their business, and they are also going to learn more about it. Just as you are going to learn from them, there is a high probability that they are also going to learn from you. Your questions about what they know will most likely also uncover what they don't know. You'll be directly involved in helping everyone on the team discover a deeper understanding of the business, *even shaping the business*.

It's great when a team learns and grows together. If you give it a chance, DDD makes that possible.

> **But We Don't *Have* Domain Experts**
> A domain expert is not one by job title. These are the people who know the line of business you are working in really well. They probably have a lot of background in the business domain, and they might be product designers or even your salespeople.
> Look past the job title. The people you are looking for know more about what you are working on than anyone else, and for sure way more than you know. *Find them. Listen. Learn. Design in code.*

So far we're off to a pretty reassuring start. Still, I am also not going to tell you that technical ability isn't important, that somehow you can get by without it. You will have to grasp some advanced software *domain modeling* concepts. Even so, it doesn't necessarily mean you are going to be in over your head. If you have abilities somewhere between grasping *Head First Design Patterns* [Freeman et al.] and grokking the original *Design Patterns* [Gamma et al.] text, or even more advanced patterns, you stand a really good chance of succeeding with DDD. You can bank on this: I'm going to do everything I can to make that happen by lowering the bar, no matter what your level of experience.

What's a Domain Model?

It's a software model of the very specific business domain you are working in. Often it's implemented as an object model, where those objects have both data and behavior with literal and accurate business meaning.

Creating a unique, carefully crafted domain model at the heart of a core, strategic application or subsystem is essential to practicing DDD. With DDD your domain models will tend to be smallish, very focused. Using DDD, you never try to model the whole business enterprise with a single, large domain model. Phew, that's good!

Consider the following perspectives of the people who can benefit from DDD. I know you fit in here somewhere:

- *Newbie, junior developer*: "I'm young, with fresh ideas, I've got pent-up energy to code, and I'm going to have an impact. What's got me miffed is one of the projects I sprint on. I didn't expect that my first gig off campus would mean shoveling data back and forth using lots of almost identical yet redundant 'objects.' Why is this architecture so complex if that's all that's happening? What's up with *that*? The code breaks a lot when I try to change it. Does anyone actually understand what it's supposed to do? Now there are some complex new features I have to add. I regularly slap an *adapter* around legacy classes to shield me from the goo. *No joy.* I'm sure there's something I can do besides code and debug all day and night just to finish iterations. Whatever that is, I'm going to track it down and own it. I heard some of the others talking about DDD. *It sounds like Gang of Four, but tuned for the domain model.* Nice."

Gotcha covered.

- *Midlevel developer*: "Over the past few months I've been included on the new system. It's my turn to make a difference. I get it, but what I'm missing are profound insights when I'm meeting with the senior developers. Sometimes things seem whacked, but I'm not sure why. I'm going to help change the way things are done around here. I know that throwing technology at a problem only takes you so far, and that's basically not far enough. What I need is *a sound software development technique* that's going to help me become a wise and experienced software practitioner. One of the senior architects, the new guy, made a pitch for something called DDD. I'm listening."

You're sounding senior already. Read on. Your forward-thinking attitude will be rewarded.

- *Senior developer, architect*: "I've used DDD on a few projects, but not since landing this new position. I like the power of the *tactical patterns*, but there's a lot more I could apply, with *strategic design* being one. What I found most insightful when reading [Evans] was the Ubiquitous Language. *That's powerful stuff.* I've had discussions with a number of my teammates and management, trying to influence DDD's adoption here. One of the new kids and a few of the midlevel and senior members are jazzed about the prospects. Management isn't so excited. I recently joined this company, and although I was brought in to lead, it seems that the organization is less interested in disruptive advancements than I thought. Whatever. I'm not giving up. With other developers psyched about it, *I know we can make it happen.* The payoffs are going to be much greater than anticipated. We'll draw the pure business people—the domain experts—closer to our technical teams, and *we'll actually invest in our solutions*, not just grunt them out iteration after iteration."

Now *that's* what a leader does. This book has lots of guidance that shows how to succeed with *strategic design*.

- *Domain expert*: "I've been involved in specifying the IT solutions to our business challenges for a long time now. Maybe it's too much to expect, but I wish the developers understood better what we do here. They're always talking down to us like we're stupid. What they don't understand is, if it wasn't for us there wouldn't be jobs here for them to mess around with computers. The developers always have some strange way of talking about what our software does. If we talk about A, they say it's really called B. *It's like we have to have some sort of dictionary and road map on hand every time we try to communicate what we need.* If we don't let them have their way by calling B what we know is A, they don't cooperate. We waste so much time in this mode. *Why can't the software just work the way the real experts think about the business?*"

You've got that right. One of the biggest problems is the false need for translation between business people and techies. This chapter is for you. As you're going to see, *DDD puts you and developers on level ground.*

And, surprise! You've got some developers already leaning your way. Help them here.

- *Manager*: "We are shipping software. It's not always with the greatest result, and changes seem to take longer than they should. The developers keep talking about some domain something-or-another. I'm not sure we need to get high centered on yet another technique or methodology, like it's some kind of silver bullet. I've heard all that a thousand times before. We try, the fad dies, and we are right back to the same-old same-old. I keep saying that we need to stay the course and stop dreaming, but the team keeps hounding me. They've worked hard, so I owe them a listen. *They are smart people and they all deserve a chance to improve things* before they get torqued and move on. I could allow them some time to learn and adjust if I can get backing from upper management. I think I could get that approval if I can convince my boss of the team's claims of *achieving critical software investment and a centralization of business knowledge*. Truth is, it will make my job easier if *I can do something to inspire trust and cooperation between my teams and business experts*. Anyway, that's what I am hearing I can do."

Good manager!

Whoever you are, here's an important heads-up. To succeed with DDD *you are going to have to learn something*, and actually a lot of somethings. That shouldn't be a big deal, though. You are smart and you have to learn all the time. Yet we all face this challenge:

> Personally I'm always ready to learn, although I do not always like being taught.
> —Sir Winston Churchill

That's where this book comes in. I've tried to make the teaching as pleasant as possible while delivering the vital understanding you need to implement DDD with success.

Your question, though, is: "Why should I do DDD?" That's fair.

Why You Should Do DDD

Actually, I've already given you some pretty good reasons why DDD makes so much practical sense. At the risk of breaking the DRY principle ("Don't repeat yourself"), I reiterate them here and also add to the earlier reasons. Does anyone hear an echo?

- Put domain experts and developers on a level playing field, which produces software that makes perfect sense to the business, not just the coders. This doesn't mean merely tolerating the opposite group. It means becoming one cohesive, tight-knit team.

- That "makes sense to the business" thing means investing in the business by making software that is as close as possible to what the business leaders and experts would create if they were the coders.

- You can actually teach the business more about itself. No domain expert, no C-level manager, no one, ever knows every single thing about the business. It's a constant discovery process that becomes more insightful over time. With DDD, everybody learns because everybody contributes to discovery discussions.

- Centralizing knowledge is key, because with that the business is capable of ensuring that understanding the software is not locked in "tribal knowledge," available only to a select few, who are usually only the developers.

- There are zero translations between the domain experts, the software developers, and the software. That doesn't mean maybe some few translations. It means zero translations because your team develops a common, shared language that everyone on the team speaks.

- The design is the code, and the code is the design. The design is how it works. Knowing the best code design comes through quick experimental models using an agile discovery process.

- DDD provides sound software development techniques that address both strategic and tactical design. Strategic design helps us understand what are the most important software investments to make, what existing software assets to leverage in order to get there fastest and safest, and who must be involved. Tactical design helps us craft the single elegant model of a solution using time-tested, proven software building blocks.

Like any good, high-yielding investment, DDD has some up-front cost of time and effort for the team. Considering the typical challenges encountered by every software development effort will reinforce the need to invest in a sound software development approach.

Delivering Business Value Can Be Elusive

Developing software that delivers true business value is not the same thing as developing ordinary business software. Software that delivers true business value aligns with the business strategic initiatives and bears solutions with clearly identifiable competitive advantage—software that is not about technology, but about the business.

Business knowledge is never centralized. Development teams have to balance and prioritize among the needs and requests of multiple stakeholders and engage with many people having diverse skill sets, all with the goal of uncovering software functional and nonfunctional requirements. After gathering all that information, how can teams be certain that any given requirement delivers true business value? In fact, what are the business values being sought, and how do you uncover them, prioritize them, and realize them?

One of the worst disconnects of a business software development effort is seen in the gap between domain experts and software developers. Generally speaking, true domain experts are focused on delivering business value. On the other hand, software developers are typically drawn to technology and technical solutions to business problems. It's not that software developers have wrong motivations; it's just what tends to grab their attention. Even when software developers engage with domain experts, the collaboration is largely at a surface level, and the software that gets developed often results in a translation/mapping between how the business thinks and operates and how the software developer interprets that. The resulting software generally does not reflect a recognizable realization of the mental model of the domain experts, or perhaps it does so only partially. Over time this disconnect becomes costly. The translation of domain knowledge into software is lost as developers transition to other projects or leave the company.

A different, yet related problem is when one or more domain experts do not agree with each other. This tends to happen because each expert has more or less experience in the specific domain being modeled, or they are simply experts in related but different areas. It's also common for multiple "domain experts" to have no expertise in a given domain, where they are more of a business analyst, yet they are expected to bring insightful direction to discussions. When this situation goes unchecked, it results in blurred rather than crisp mental models, which lead to conflicting software models.

Worse still is when the technical approach to software development actually wrongly changes the way the business functions. While a different scenario, it is well known that enterprise resource planning (ERP) software will often change the overall business operations of an organization to fit the way the ERP functions. The total cost of owning the ERP cannot be fully calculated in terms of license and maintenance fees. The reorganization and disruption to the business can be far more costly than either of those two tangible factors. A similar dynamic is at play as your software development teams interpret what the business needs into what the newly developed software actually does. This can be both costly and disruptive to the business, its customers, and its partners. Furthermore, this technical interpretation is both unnecessary and avoidable with the use of proven software development techniques. The solution is a key investment.

How DDD Helps

DDD is an approach to developing software that focuses on these three primary aspects:

1. DDD brings domain experts and software developers together in order to develop software that reflects the mental model of the business experts. This does not mean that effort is spent on modeling the "real world." Rather, DDD delivers a model that is the most useful to the business. Sometimes useful and realistic models happen to intersect, but to the degree that they diverge, DDD chooses useful.

   With this aspect the efforts of domain experts and software developers are devoted to jointly developing a Ubiquitous Language of the areas of the business that they are focused on modeling. The Ubiquitous Language is developed with full team agreement, is spoken, and is directly captured in the model of the software. It is worth reiterating that the team is composed of both domain experts and software developers. It's never "us and them." It's always *us*. This is a key business value that allows business know-how to outlive the relatively short initial development efforts that deliver the first few versions of the software, and the teams that produce it. It's the point where the cost of developing software is a justifiable business investment, not just a cost center.

   This entire effort unifies domain experts who initially disagree with each other, or who simply lack core knowledge of the domain. Further, it strengthens the close-knit team by spreading deep domain insight among all team members, including software developers. Consider this the hands-on training that every company should invest in its knowledge workers.

2. DDD addresses the strategic initiatives of the business. While this strategic design approach naturally includes technical analysis, it is more concerned with the strategic direction of the business. It helps define the best inter-team organizational relationships and provides early-warning systems for recognizing when a given relationship could cause software and even project failure. The technical aspects of strategic design have the goal of cleanly bounding systems and business concerns, which protects each *business-level service*. This provides meaningful motivations

for how an overall *service-oriented architecture* or *business-driven architecture* is achieved.

3. DDD meets the real technical demands of the software by using tactical design modeling tools to analyze and develop the executable software deliverables. These tactical design tools allow developers to produce software that is a correct codification of the domain experts' mental model, is highly testable, is less error prone (a provable statement), performs to service-level agreements (SLAs), is scalable, and allows for distributed computing. DDD best practices generally address a dozen or more higher-level architectural and lower-level software design concerns, with a focus on recognizing true business rules and data invariants, and protecting the rules from error situations.

Using this approach to software development, you and your team can succeed in delivering true business value.

Grappling with the Complexity of Your Domain

We primarily want to use DDD in the areas that are most important to the business. You don't invest in what can be easily replaced. *You invest in the nontrivial, the more complex stuff, the most valuable and important stuff that promises to return the greatest dividends.* That's why we call such a model a **Core Domain (2)**. It is these, and in second priority the *significant* **Supporting Subdomains (2)**, that deserve and get the biggest investment. Rightly, then, we need to grasp what *complex* means.

> **Use DDD to Simplify, Not to Complicate**
> Use DDD to model a complex domain in the simplest possible way. Never use DDD to make your solution more complex.

What qualifies as complex will differ from business to business. Different companies have different challenges, different levels of maturity, and different software development capabilities. So rather than determining what is *complex*, it may be easier to determine what is *nontrivial*. Thus, *your team and management will have to determine if a system you are planning to work on deserves the cost of making a DDD investment.*

DDD Scorecard: Use Table 1.1 to determine whether your project qualifies for an investment in DDD. If a row on the scorecard describes your project, place the corresponding number of points in the right-hand column. Tally all the points for your project. If it's 7 or higher, seriously consider using DDD.

Table 1.1 The DDD Scorecard

Does Your Project Score a Total of 7 Points or Higher?

If Your Project . . .	Points	Supporting Thoughts	Your Score
If your application is completely data-centric and truly qualifies for a pure CRUD solution, where every operation is basically a simple database query to Create, Read, Update, or Delete, you don't need DDD. Your team just needs to put a pretty face on a database table editor. In other words, if you can trust your users to insert data directly into a table, update it, and sometimes delete it, you wouldn't even need a user interface. That's not realistic, but it's conceptually relevant. If you could even use a simple database development tool to create a solution, don't waste your company's time and money on DDD.	0	This seems like a no-brainer, but it's not usually that easy to determine simple versus complex. It's not as if every application that isn't pure CRUD deserves the time and effort of using DDD. So maybe we could come up with other metrics to help us draw a line between what is complex and what is not . . .	
If your system requires just 30 or fewer business operations, it's probably pretty simple. This would mean that your application would have no more than 30 total user stories or use case flows, with each of those flows having only minimal business logic. If you could quickly and easily develop such an application using Ruby on Rails or Groovy and Grails and not feel the pain of lacking power and control over complexity and change, your system probably doesn't need to use DDD.	1	To be clear, I am talking about 25 to 30 single business methods, not 25 to 30 whole service interfaces, each with multiple methods. The latter might be complex.	
So let's say that somewhere in the range of 30 to 40 user stories or use case flows could be creeping toward complexity. Your system might be getting into DDD territory.	2	*Caveat emptor:* Very often complexity is not recognized soon enough. *We software developers are really, really good at underestimating complexity and level of effort.* Just because we might want to code up a Rails or Grails application doesn't mean we should. In the long run those could hurt more than help.	

continues

11

Table 1.1 The DDD Scorecard (*Continued*)

Does Your Project Score a Total of 7 Points or Higher?

If Your Project . . .	Points	Supporting Thoughts	Your Score
Even if the application is not going to be complex now, will it grow in complexity? You may not know this for sure until real users start working with it, but there is a step in the "Supporting Thoughts" column that may help uncover the true situation. Be careful here. If there is any hint at all that the application has even moderate complexity—here's a good time to be paranoid—that may be sufficient indication that it will actually be more than moderately complex. Lean toward DDD.	3	Here it pays off to walk through the more complex usage scenarios with domain experts and see where it leads. Are domain experts . . . 1. . . . already asking for more complex features? If so, it's likely an indication that the application is already or will soon become too complex to use a CRUD approach. 2. . . . so bored with the features that they can hardly bear discussing them? It's probably not complex.	
The application's features are going to change often over a number of years, and you can't anticipate that the kinds of changes will be simple.	4	DDD can help you manage the complexity of refactoring your model over time.	
You don't understand the **Domain (2)** because it's new. As far as you and your team know, nobody has done this before. That most likely means it's complex, or at least deserves due diligence with analytical scrutiny to determine the level of complexity.	5	You are going to need to work with domain experts and experiment with models to get it right. You certainly also scored on one or more of the previous criteria, so use DDD.	

This scoring exercise may have led your team to these conclusions:

It's too bad that we can't shift gears quickly and easily when we discover we are on the wrong side of complexity, no matter if the wrong side is more or less complex than we thought.

Sure, but that just means that we need to become much better at determining simplicity versus complexity early on in our project planning. That would save us a lot of time, expense, and trouble.

Once we make a major architectural decision and get several use cases deep in development, we are usually stuck with it. We had better choose wisely.

If any of these observations resonates with your team, you are making good use of critical thought.

Anemia and Memory Loss

Anemia can be a serious health ailment with dangerous side effects. When the name **Anemic Domain Model** [Fowler, Anemic] was first coined, *it wasn't meant to be a complimentary term*, as if to say that a domain model that is weak, without the power of inherent behavioral qualities, could possibly be a good thing. Strangely enough, Anemic Domain Models have popped up left and right in our industry. The trouble is that most developers seem to think this is quite normal and would not even acknowledge that a serious condition exists when employed in their systems. It's a real problem.

Are you wondering if your model is feeling tired, listless, forgetful, clumsy, needing a good shot in the arm? If you're suddenly experiencing technical hypochondria, here's a good way to perform a self-examination. You'll either put yourself at ease or confirm your worst fears. Use the steps in Table 1.2 to perform your checkup.

Table 1.2 Determine Your Domain Model Health History

	Yes / No
Does the software you call a "domain model" have mostly public getters and setters, and no business logic or almost none at all—you know, objects that are mostly attribute value holders?	
Are the software components that frequently use your "domain model" the ones that house most of the business logic of your system, and do those heavily invoke the public getters and setters on the "domain model"? You probably call this particular client layer of the "domain model" a **Service Layer** or **Application Layer (4, 14)**. If instead this describes your user interface, answer "Yes" to this question and write a thousand times on a whiteboard that you'll never, ever do that again.	
Hint: The correct answers are either "Yes" to both questions or "No" to both questions.	

How did you do?

If you answered "No" to both questions, your domain is doing well.

If you answered "Yes" to both questions, your "domain model" is very, very ill. It's anemic. The good news is that you can get help for it by reading on.

If you answered "Yes" to one question and "No" to the other question, you are either in denial or suffering from delusions or another neurological issue that could be caused by anemia. What should you do if you have conflicting answers? Go straight back to the first question and run the self-examination once again. Take your time, but remember that your answer to both questions must be an emphatic "Yes!"

As [Fowler, Anemic] says, an Anemic Domain Model is a bad thing because you pay most of the high cost of developing a domain model, but you get little or none of the benefit. For example, because of the object-relational impedance mismatch, developers of such a "domain model" spend a lot of time and effort mapping objects to and from the persistence store. That's a high price to pay while getting little or no benefit in return. I'll add that what you have is not a domain model at all, but just a data model projected from a relational model (or other database) into objects. It's an impostor that may actually be closer to the definition of **Active Record** [Fowler, P of EAA]. You can probably simplify your architecture by not being pretentious and just admit that you are really using a form of **Transaction Script** [Fowler, P of EAA].

Reasons Why Anemia Happens

So if an Anemic Domain Model is the sickly outcome of a poorly executed design effort, why do so many use it while thinking that their model is experiencing fine health? Certainly it does reflect a procedural programming mentality, but I don't think that's the primary reason. A good portion of our industry is made up of sample code followers, which isn't bad as long as the samples are quality ones. Often, however, sample code is purposely focused on demonstrating some concept or application programming interface (API) feature in the simplest possible way, without concern for good design principles. Yet oversimplified sample code, which usually demonstrates with a lot of getters and setters, is copied every day without a second thought about design.

There is another, older influence. The ancient history of Microsoft's Visual Basic had much to do with where we are today. I'm not saying that Visual Basic was a bad language and integrated development environment (IDE), because it's always been a highly productive environment and in some ways influenced the industry for the good. Of course, some may have avoided its direct influence altogether, but Visual Basic indirectly caught up with just about every software developer eventually. Just note the timeline shown in Table 1.3.

Table 1.3 The Timeline from Behavior Rich to Infamous Anemia

1980s	1991	1992–1995	1996	1997	1998–
Objects make an impact due to Smalltalk and C++	Visual Basic properties and property sheets	Visual tools and IDEs become prolific	Java JDK 1.0 released	JavaBean specification	Explosion of reflection-based tools for Java and .NET platforms based on properties

What I am talking about is the influence of properties and property sheets, both backed by property getters and setters that were made so popular by the original Visual Basic forms designer. All you had to do was place a few custom control instances on a form, fill out their property sheets, and *voilà!* You had a fully functioning Windows application. It took just a few minutes to do that compared to the few days required to program a similar application directly against the Windows API using C.

So what does all that have to do with Anemic Domain Models? *The Java-Bean standard was originally specified to assist in the creation of visual programming tools for Java.* Its motivation was to bring the Microsoft ActiveX capabilities to the Java platform. It offered the hope of creating a market full of third-party custom controls of various kinds, just like Visual Basic's. Soon almost every framework and library jumped on the JavaBean bandwagon. This included much of the Java SDK/JDK as well as libraries such as the popular Hibernate. Specific to our DDD concerns, *Hibernate was introduced to persist domain models*. The trend continued as the .NET platform reached us.

Interestingly, any domain model that was persisted using Hibernate in the early days had to expose public getters and setters for every persistent simple attribute and complex association in every domain object. This meant that even if you wanted to design your POJO (Plain Old Java Object) with a behavior-rich interface, you had to expose your internals publicly so that Hibernate could persist and reconstitute your domain objects. Sure, you could do things to hide the public JavaBean interface, but by and large most developers didn't bother or even understand why they should have.

Should I Be Concerned about Using Object-Relational Mappers with DDD?

The preceding critique of Hibernate is from a historical perspective. For quite a while now Hibernate has supported the use of hidden getters and setters, and even direct field access. I demonstrate in later chapters how to avoid anemia in your models when using Hibernate and other persistence mechanisms. So, don't sweat it.

Most, if not all, of the Web frameworks also function solely on the JavaBean standard. If you want your Java objects to be able to populate your Web pages, the Java objects had better support the JavaBean specification. If you want your HTML forms to populate a Java object when submitted to the server side, your Java form object had better support the JavaBean specification.

Just about every framework on the market today requires, and therefore promotes, the use of public properties on simple objects. Most developers can't help but be influenced by all the anemic classes all over their enterprises. Admit it. You've been bitten by it, haven't you? As a result, we have a situation that might be best labeled *anemia everywhere*.

Look at What Anemia Does to Your Model

All right, so let's say we can agree that this is both true and vexing to us. What does *anemia everywhere* have to do with *memory loss*? When you are reading through the client code of an Anemic Domain Model (for example, the impostor **Application Service (4, 14)**, à la Transaction Script), what do we usually see? Here's a rudimentary example:

```
@Transactional
public void saveCustomer(
    String customerId,
    String customerFirstName, String customerLastName,
    String streetAddress1, String streetAddress2,
    String city, String stateOrProvince,
    String postalCode, String country,
    String homePhone, String mobilePhone,
    String primaryEmailAddress, String secondaryEmailAddress) {

    Customer customer = customerDao.readCustomer(customerId);

    if (customer == null) {
        customer = new Customer();
        customer.setCustomerId(customerId);
    }

    customer.setCustomerFirstName(customerFirstName);
    customer.setCustomerLastName(customerLastName);
    customer.setStreetAddress1(streetAddress1);
    customer.setStreetAddress2(streetAddress2);
    customer.setCity(city);
    customer.setStateOrProvince(stateOrProvince);
    customer.setPostalCode(postalCode);
    customer.setCountry(country);
    customer.setHomePhone(homePhone);
    customer.setMobilePhone(mobilePhone);
```

```
    customer.setPrimaryEmailAddress(primaryEmailAddress);
    customer.setSecondaryEmailAddress (secondaryEmailAddress);

    customerDao.saveCustomer(customer);
}
```

Example Purposely Kept Simple

Admittedly, this example is not from a very interesting domain, but it does help us examine a less-than-ideal design and determine how we can refactor it to a much better one. Let's be clear that this exercise is not leading us to a cooler way to save data. It's about crafting a software model that adds value to your business, even though this example may not seem valuable.

What did this code just do? Actually it's pretty versatile code. It saves a Customer no matter whether it is new or preexisting. It saves a Customer no matter whether the last name changed or the person moved to a new home. It saves a Customer no matter whether the person got a new home phone number or discontinued home phone service, or whether he or she got a mobile phone for the first time, or both. It even saves a Customer who switched from using Juno to using Gmail instead, or who changed jobs and now has a new work e-mail address. Wow, this is an awesome method!

Or is it? Actually, we have no idea under what business situations this saveCustomer() method is used—not exactly, anyway. Why was this method created in the first place? Does anyone remember its original intent, and all the motivations for changing it to support a wide variety of business goals? Those memories were quite likely lost only a few weeks or months after the method was created and then modified. And it gets even worse. You don't believe me? Look at the next version of this same method:

```
@Transactional
public void saveCustomer(
    String customerId,
    String customerFirstName, String customerLastName,
    String streetAddress1, String streetAddress2,
    String city, String stateOrProvince,
    String postalCode, String country,
    String homePhone, String mobilePhone,
    String primaryEmailAddress, String secondaryEmailAddress) {

    Customer customer = customerDao.readCustomer(customerId);

    if (customer == null) {
        customer = new Customer();
        customer.setCustomerId(customerId);
    }
```

```
    if (customerFirstName != null) {
        customer.setCustomerFirstName(customerFirstName);
    }
    if (customerLastName != null) {
        customer.setCustomerLastName(customerLastName);
    }
    if (streetAddress1 != null) {
        customer.setStreetAddress1(streetAddress1);
    }
    if (streetAddress2 != null) {
        customer.setStreetAddress2(streetAddress2);
    }
    if (city != null) {
        customer.setCity(city);
    }
    if (stateOrProvince != null) {
        customer.setStateOrProvince(stateOrProvince);
    }
    if (postalCode != null) {
        customer.setPostalCode(postalCode);
    }
    if (country != null) {
        customer.setCountry(country);
    }
    if (homePhone != null) {
        customer.setHomePhone(homePhone);
    }
    if (mobilePhone != null) {
        customer.setMobilePhone(mobilePhone);
    }
    if (primaryEmailAddress != null) {
        customer.setPrimaryEmailAddress(primaryEmailAddress);
    }
    if (secondaryEmailAddress != null) {
        customer.setSecondaryEmailAddress (secondaryEmailAddress);
    }

    customerDao.saveCustomer(customer);
}
```

I have to note here that this example isn't as bad as it gets. Many times the data-mapping code becomes quite complex, and a lot of business logic gets tucked away in it. I'm sparing you the worst in this example, but you've probably seen it for yourself.

Now each of the parameters other than the customerId is optional. We can now use this method to save a Customer under at least a dozen business situations, and more! But is that really a good thing? How could we actually test this method to ensure that it doesn't save a `Customer` under the wrong situations?

Without going into extensive detail, this method could function incorrectly in more ways than it could correctly. Perhaps there are database constraints that prevent a completely invalid state from being persisted, but now you have to look at the database to be sure. Almost certainly it will take you some time to mentally map between Java attributes and column names. Once you've figured out that part, you find that the database constraints are missing or incomplete.

You could look at the possibly many clients (not counting those added after the user interface was completed to manage automatic remote clients) and compare source revisions to gain some insight into why it is implemented the way it is right now. As you search for answers, you learn that nobody can explain why this one method works the way it does, or how many correct uses there are. It could take several hours or days to understand it on your own.

Cowboy Logic

AJ: "That fella's so confused, he doesn't know if he's sackin' potatoes or rollerskatin' in a buffalo herd."

Domain experts can't help here because they would have to be programmers to understand the code. Even if a domain expert or two knew enough about programming or could at least read the code, they would probably be at least equally at a loss as a developer regarding all that code is meant to support. With all these concerns in mind, do we dare change this code in any way, and if so, how?

There are at least three big problems here:

1. There is little intention revealed by the `saveCustomer()` interface.

2. The implementation of `saveCustomer()` itself adds hidden complexity.

3. The `Customer` "domain object" isn't really an object at all. It's really just a dumb data holder.

Let's call this unenviable situation *anemia-induced memory loss*. It happens all the time on projects that produce this kind of implicit, completely subjective code "design."

> **Hold On a Minute!**
>
> At this point some of you may be thinking, "Our designs never really leave the whiteboard. We just draw some structure, and once agreement on that is reached, we are set free to implement. Scary."
>
> If so, try not to distinguish design from implementation. Remember that when practicing DDD, *the design is the code and the code is the design.* In other words, whiteboard diagrams aren't the design, just a way to discuss the challenges of the model.
>
> Stay tuned, as you'll learn how to take ideas off the whiteboard and make them work for you.

By now you should be worried about this kind of code and how you can create a better design. The good news is that you can succeed in producing an explicit, carefully crafted design in your code.

How to Do DDD

Let's back away from heavy implementation discussions for a moment to consider one of the most empowering features of DDD, the Ubiquitous Language. It's one of the two primary pillars of DDD's strengths, the second being the **Bounded Context (2)**, and one cannot properly stand without the other.

> **Terms in a Context**
>
> For now think of a Bounded Context as a conceptual boundary around a whole application or finite system. The reason for this boundary is to highlight that every use of a given domain term, phrase, or sentence—the Ubiquitous Language—inside the boundary has a specific contextual meaning. Any use of the term outside that boundary could, and probably does, mean something different. Chapter 2 explains Bounded Context in depth.

Ubiquitous Language

The Ubiquitous Language is a shared team language. It's shared by domain experts and developers alike. In fact, it's shared by everyone on the project team. No matter your role on the team, since you are on the team you use the Ubiquitous Language of the project.

> **So, You Think You Know What a Ubiquitous Language Is**
>
> *Obviously it's the language of the business.*
>
> Well, no.
>
> *Surely it must be adopting industry standard terminology.*
>
> No, not really.

Clearly it's the lingo used by the domain experts.

Sorry, but no.

The Ubiquitous Language is a shared language developed by the team—a team composed of both domain experts and software developers.

That's it. Now you've got it!

Naturally, the domain experts have a heavy influence on the Language because they know that part of the business best and may be influenced by industry standards. However, the Language is *more centered on how the business itself thinks and operates.* Also, many times two or more domain experts disagree on concepts and terms, and they are actually wrong about some because they haven't thought of every case before. So, as the experts and developers work together to craft a model of the domain, they use discussion with both consensus and compromise to achieve the very *best Language for the project.* The team never compromises on the quality of the Language, just on the best concepts, terms, and meanings. Initial consensus is not the end, however. The Language grows and changes over time as tiny and large breakthroughs are achieved, much like any other living language.

This is no gimmick to get developers to be on the same page as domain experts. It's not just a bunch of business jargon being forced on developers. It's a real language that is created by the whole team—domain experts, developers, business analysts, everyone involved in producing the system. The Language may start out with terms that are the natural lingo of the domain experts, but it isn't limited to that because the Language must grow over time. Suffice it to say that when multiple domain experts are involved in creating the Language, they often disagree ever so slightly on the terms and meanings of what they thought were already ubiquitous.

In Table 1.4, we not only model the administration of flu vaccines in code, but the team must also speak the Language openly. When the team discusses this aspect of the model, they literally speak phrases such as "Nurses administer flu vaccines to patients in standard doses."

There will be some haggling and wrangling over the Language that exists in the minds of experts and what evolves from there. It's all part of the natural progression of developing the best Language that will matter a lot for a long time. This happens through open discussion, looking at existing documents, business tribal knowledge that finally surfaces, as well as referencing standards, dictionaries, and thesauruses. There's also a point reached where we come to terms with the fact that some words and phrases just don't aptly fit the business context as well as we once thought, and we realize that others fit it much better.

Table 1.4   Analyzing the Best Model for the Business

Which is better for the business?

Though the second and third statements are similar, how should the code be designed?

Possible Viewpoints	Resulting Code

"Who cares? Just code it up."
 	
Um, not even close.
	`patient.setShotType(ShotTypes.TYPE_FLU);`
	`patient.setDose(dose);`
	`patient.setNurse(nurse);`

"We give flu shots to patients." Better, but misses some important concepts.	`patient.giveFluShot();`

"Nurses administer flu vaccines to patients in standard doses."
 	
This seems like what we'd like to run with at this time, at least until we learn more.
	`Vaccine vaccine = vaccines.standardAdultFluDose();`
	
	`nurse.administerFluVaccine(patient, vaccine);`

So how do you capture this all-important Ubiquitous Language? Here are some ways that work as experimentation leads to advancement:

- Draw pictures of the physical and conceptual domain and label them with names and actions. These drawings are mostly informal but may contain some aspects of formal software modeling. Even if your team does some formal modeling with Unified Modeling Language (UML), you want to avoid any kind of ceremony that will bog down discussions and stifle the creativity of the ultimate Language being sought.

- Create a glossary of terms with simple definitions. List alternative terms, including the ones that show promise and the ones that didn't work, and why. As you include definitions, you cannot help but develop reusable phrases for the Language because you are forced to write in the Language of the domain.

- If you don't like the idea of a glossary, still capture some kind of documentation that includes the informal drawings of important software concepts. Again, the goal here is to force additional Language terms and phrases to surface.

- Since only one or a few team members may capture the glossary or other written documents, circle back with the rest of the team to review the resulting phrases. You won't always, if ever, agree on all the captured linguistics, so be agile and ready to edit heavily.

Those are some ideal first steps to coining a Ubiquitous Language that fits your specific domain. However, this is absolutely not the model that you are developing. It's only the genesis of the Ubiquitous Language that will very soon be expressed in your system's source code. We are talking Java, or C#, or Scala, or some other programming language of choice. These drawings and documents also don't address that the Ubiquitous Language will continue to expand and morph over time. The artifacts that originally led us down an inspiring path to developing a useful Ubiquitous Language that was just right for our specialized domain will very likely be rendered obsolete over time. *That's why in the end it is team speech and the model in the code that are the most enduring and the only guaranteed current denotations of the Ubiquitous Language.*

Since team speech and the code will be the lasting expression of the Ubiquitous Language, be prepared to abandon the drawings, glossary, and other documentation that will be difficult to keep up-to-date with the spoken Ubiquitous Language and source code as they are rapidly enhanced. This is not a requirement of using DDD, but it is pragmatic because it becomes impractical to keep all the documentation in sync with the system.

With this knowledge we can redesign the `saveCustomer()` example. What if we chose to make `Customer` reflect each of the possible business goals that it must support?

```
public interface Customer {
    public void changePersonalName(
        String firstName, String lastName);
    public void postalAddress(PostalAddress postalAddress);
    public void relocateTo(PostalAddress changedPostalAddress);
    public void changeHomeTelephone(Telephone telephone);
    public void disconnectHomeTelephone();
    public void changeMobileTelephone(Telephone telephone);
    public void disconnectMobileTelephone();
    public void primaryEmailAddress(EmailAddress emailAddress);
    public void secondaryEmailAddress(EmailAddress emailAddress);
}
```

We can argue that this is not the best model for a `Customer`, but when implementing DDD, questioning the design is expected. As a team we are free to haggle over what is the best model and settle only after we've discovered the Ubiquitous Language that is agreed upon. Still, the preceding interface does explicitly reflect the various business goals that a `Customer` must support, even if the Language could be improved by refinements again and again.

It's important to understand too that the Application Service would also be refactored to reflect the explicit intentions of the business goals at hand. Each Application Service method would be modified to deal with a single use case flow or user story:

```
@Transactional
public void changeCustomerPersonalName(
    String customerId,
    String customerFirstName,
    String customerLastName) {

    Customer customer = customerRepository.customerOfId(customerId);

    if (customer == null) {
        throw new IllegalStateException("Customer does not exist.");
    }

    customer.changePersonalName(customerFirstName, customerLastName);
}
```

This is different from the original example because in that code a single method was used to deal with many different use case flows or user stories. In the new example we have limited a single Application Service method to deal with changing the personal name of the Customer, and nothing more. Thus, when using DDD, it is our job to refine Application Services accordingly. This implies that the user interface likewise reflects a narrower user goal, which may have previously been true. Now, however, this specific Application Service method doesn't require its client to pass ten nulls following the first- and last-name parameters.

Doesn't this new design put your mind at ease? You can read the code and easily comprehend it. You can also test it and confirm that it does exactly what it is meant to do, and that it doesn't do anything that it shouldn't.

Thus, the Ubiquitous Language is a team pattern used to capture the concepts and terms of a specific core business domain in the software model itself. The software model incorporates the nouns, adjectives, verbs, and richer expressions formally formulated and spoken by the close-knit team. Both the software and the tests that verify the model's adherence to the tenets of the domain capture and adhere to this Language, the same one spoken by the team.

Ubiquitous, but Not Universal

Some further clarification about the reach of a Ubiquitous Language is in order. There are a few basic concepts that we need to keep carefully in mind:

- *Ubiquitous* means "pervasive," or "found everywhere," as *spoken among the team and expressed by the single domain model* that the team develops.

- The use of the word *ubiquitous* is not an attempt to describe some kind of enterprise-wide, company-wide, or worldwide, universal domain language.

- There is one Ubiquitous Language per Bounded Context.

- Bounded Contexts are relatively small, smaller than we might at first imagine. A Bounded Context is large enough only to capture the complete Ubiquitous Language of the isolated business domain, and no larger.

- The Language is ubiquitous only within the team that is working on the project that develops in an isolated Bounded Context.

- On a single project that develops a single Bounded Context, there are always one or more additional isolated Bounded Contexts with which it integrates using **Context Maps** (3). Each of the multiple Bounded Contexts that integrate has its own Ubiquitous Language, even though some terms of each may overlap.

- If you try to apply a single Ubiquitous Language to an entire enterprise, or worse, universally among many enterprises, you will fail.

When you begin a new project in which you are properly using DDD, identify the isolated Bounded Context that is being developed. This places an explicit boundary around your domain model. Discuss, research, conceptualize, develop, and speak the Ubiquitous Language of the isolated domain model within the explicit Bounded Context. Reject all concepts that are not part of the agreed-upon Ubiquitous Language of your isolated Context.

The Business Value of Using DDD

If your experience is anything like mine, you know that software developers can no longer pursue technologies and techniques just because they sound cool or intriguing. We must justify everything that we do. I think that has not always been true, but it is a good thing it is true now. I think the best justification for using any technology or technique is to provide value to the business. If we can establish real, tangible business value, why would the business ever refuse to use what we recommend?

The business case is strengthened especially if we can demonstrate that the business values are higher with our recommended approach than with other options.

> **Isn't Business Value Most Important?**
>
> Sure, and perhaps I should have put this subheading "The Business Value of Using DDD" earlier in the book. But it's done, now. This subheading could actually be "How You Can Sell DDD to Your Boss." Until you are mostly convinced that there is a real chance that you can actually implement DDD in your company, this book is just hypothetical. And I don't want you to read this book as just a theoretical exercise. Read it as a concrete reality for your company. Then you can become more excited about how your company can really benefit. So read on.

Let's consider the very realistic business value of employing DDD. Be sure to share this openly with your management, domain experts, and technical team members. The value and benefits are summarized here, then I will elaborate. I start off with the less technical benefits.

1. The organization gains a useful model of its domain.

2. A refined, precise definition and understanding of the business is developed.

3. Domain experts contribute to software design.

4. A better user experience is gained.

5. Clean boundaries are placed around pure models.

6. Enterprise architecture is better organized.

7. Agile, iterative, continuous modeling is used.

8. New tools, both strategic and tactical, are employed.

1. The Organization Gains a Useful Model of Its Domain

The emphasis of DDD is to invest our efforts in what matters most to the business. We don't over-model. We focus on the Core Domain. Other models exist to support the Core Domain and are important, too. Yet the supporting models may not be given the priority and effort of the Core Domain.

When our focus is on what distinguishes our business from all others, our mission is well understood and we have the parameters we need to keep on track. We will deliver exactly what is needed to achieve competitive advantage.

2. A Refined, Precise Definition and Understanding of the Business Is Developed

The business may actually come to understand itself and its mission better than before. I have heard others state that the Ubiquitous Language developed for the business's Core Domain has found its way into marketing materials. Certainly it should be incorporated in vision documents and mission statements.

As the model is refined over time, the business develops a deep understanding that can serve as an analysis tool. Details surface out of the minds of your domain experts as you are challenged by one another and shaped by technical team partners. These details can help your business analyze the value of the current and future direction, both strategic and tactical.

3. Domain Experts Contribute to Software Design

There is business value when the organization grows a deeper understanding of the core business. Domain experts don't always agree on concepts and terminology. Sometimes the differences are fostered by different experiences from outside before joining the organization. Sometimes it happens because of the divergent paths taken by each expert within the same organization. Yet when brought together to a DDD effort, the domain experts gain consensus among themselves. This fortifies the effort and the organization as a whole.

Developers now share a common Language as a unified team along with domain experts. They benefit further from the knowledge transfer from the domain experts they work with. As developers inevitably move on, either to a new Core Domain or out of the organization, training and handoffs are easier. The chances of developing "tribal knowledge," where only a select few understand the model, are reduced. The experts, remaining developers, and new ones continue to share a common knowledge that is available to anyone in the organization who requires it. This advantage exists because there remains an express goal to adhere to the Language of the domain.

4. A Better User Experience Is Gained

Often the end user experience can be tuned to better reflect the model of the domain. Domain-Driven is formally "baked in," influencing human use of the software.

When software leaves too much to the understanding of its users, users must be trained to make a great number of decisions. In essence the users are only transferring the understanding in their minds into data that they enter into forms. The data is then saved to a data store. If users don't understand exactly what is needed, the results are incorrect. Often this leads to guesswork with related lowered productivity until users can figure out the software.

When the user experience is designed to follow the contours of the underlying expert model, users are led to correct conclusions. The software actually trains the users, which reduces the training overhead to the business. Quicker to productivity with less training—that's business value.

We next move into more technically driven benefits to the business.

5. Clean Boundaries Are Placed around Pure Models

The technical team is discouraged from doing what might appeal more to their programming and algorithmic interests by aligning expectations with business advantage. Purity in direction allows for focus on the potency of the solution, with efforts directed to where they matter the most. Achieving this is very closely connected to understanding the Bounded Context of the project.

6. Enterprise Architecture Is Better Organized

When Bounded Contexts are well understood and carefully partitioned, all teams in the enterprise develop an acute understanding of where and why integrations are necessary. The boundaries are explicit, and the relationships between them are as well. The teams that have models that intersect by usage dependency employ Context Maps to establish formal relationships and ways to integrate. This can actually lead to a very thorough understanding of the entire enterprise architecture.

7. Agile, Iterative, Continuous Modeling Is Used

The word *design* can evoke negative thoughts in the minds of business management. However, DDD is not a heavyweight, high-ceremony design and development process. DDD is not about drawing diagrams. It is about carefully refining the mental model of domain experts into a useful model for the business. It is not about creating a real-world model, as in trying to mimic reality.

The team's efforts follow an agile approach, which is iterative and incremental. Any agile process that the team feels comfortable with can be used successfully in a DDD project. The model that is produced is the working software. It is refined continuously until it is no longer needed by the business.

8. New Tools, Both Strategic and Tactical, Are Employed

A Bounded Context gives the team a modeling boundary in which to create a solution to a specific business problem domain. Inside a single Bounded

Context is a Ubiquitous Language formulated by the team. It is spoken among the team and in the software model. Disparate teams, sometimes each responsible for a given Bounded Context, use Context Maps to strategically segregate Bounded Contexts and understand their integrations. Within a single modeling boundary the team may employ any number of useful tactical modeling tools: **Aggregates (10)**, **Entities (5)**, **Value Objects (6)**, **Services (7)**, **Domain Events (8)**, and others.

The Challenges of Applying DDD

As you implement DDD, you will encounter challenges. So has everyone else who has succeeded at it. What are the common challenges and how do we justify using DDD as we face them? I will discuss the more common ones:

- Allowing for the time and effort required to create a Ubiquitous Language

- Involving domain experts at the outset and continuously with the project

- Changing the way developers think about solutions in their domain

One of the greatest challenges in using DDD can be the time and effort required to think about the business domain, research concepts and terminology, and converse with domain experts in order to discover, capture, and enhance the Ubiquitous Language rather than coding in techno-babble. If you want to apply DDD completely, with the greatest value to the business, it's going to require more thought and effort, and it's going to take more time. That's the way it is, period.

It can also be a challenge to solicit the necessary involvement from domain experts. No matter how difficult it is, make sure you do. If you don't get commitment from at least one real expert, you are not going to uncover deep knowledge of the domain. When you do get the domain experts' involvement, the onus falls back on the developers. Developers must converse with and listen carefully to the true experts, molding their spoken language into software that reflects their mental model of the domain.

If the domain you are working in is truly distinguishing to your business, domain experts have the edge-knowledge locked up in their heads, and you need to draw it out. I've been on projects where the real domain experts are hardly around. Sometimes they travel a lot and it can be weeks between one-hour meetings with them. In a small business it can be the CEO or one of the vice presidents, and they have lots of other things to do that may seem more important.

Cowboy Logic

AJ: "If you can't rope the big steer, you're gonna go hungry."

Getting domain expert involvement may require creativity . . .

How to Involve Domain Experts in Your Project

Coffee. Use that Ubiquitous Language:

"Hi, Sally, I got you a tall half-skinny half-one-percent extra-hot split-quad-shot latte with whip. Do you have a few minutes to talk about . . . ?"

Learn to use the Ubiquitous Language of C-Level management: ". . . profits . . . revenues . . . competitive edge . . . market domination." Seriously.

Hockey tickets.

Most developers have had to *change the way they think* in order to properly apply DDD. We developers are technical thinkers. Technical solutions come easy for us. It's not that thinking technically is bad. It's just that there are times when thinking less technically is better. If it's been our habit to practice software development only in technical ways for years, perhaps now would be a good time to consider a new way of thinking. Developing the Ubiquitous Language of your domain is the best place to start.

Cowboy Logic

LB: "That fella's boots are too small. If he don't find himself another pair, his toes are gonna hurt."

AJ: "Yep. If you don't listen, you're gonna have to feel."

There's another level of thought that is required with DDD that goes beyond concept naming. When we model a domain through software, we are required to give careful thought to which model objects do what. It's about *designing the behaviors of objects*. Yes, we want the behaviors to be named properly to convey the essence of the Ubiquitous Language. But what an object does by means of a specific behavior must be considered. This is a level of effort that goes beyond creating attributes on a class and exposing getters and setters publicly to clients of the model.

Let's now look at a more interesting domain, one that is more challenging than the rudimentary one previously considered. I purposely repeat my previous guidance here to reinforce the ideas.

Again, what happens if we simply provide data accessors to our model? To reemphasize, if we only expose the data accessors for our model objects, the results will look much like a data model. Consider the following two examples and decide for yourself which of the two requires more thorough design thought, and which produces the greater benefit to its clients. The requirement is in a Scrum model, where we need to commit a backlog item to a sprint. You probably do this all the time, so it's most likely a familiar domain.

The first example, as is commonly done today, uses attribute accessors:

```
public class BacklogItem extends Entity {
    private SprintId sprintId;
    private BacklogItemStatusType status;
    ...
    public void setSprintId(SprintId sprintId) {
        this.sprintId = sprintId;
    }

    public void setStatus(BacklogItemStatusType status) {
        this.status = status;
    }
    ...
}
```

As for the client of this model:

```
// client commits the backlog item to a sprint
// by setting its sprintId and status

backlogItem.setSprintId(sprintId);
backlogItem.setStatus(BacklogItemStatusType.COMMITTED);
```

The second example uses a domain object behavior that expresses the Ubiquitous Language of the domain:

```
public class BacklogItem extends Entity {
    private SprintId sprintId;
    private BacklogItemStatusType status;
    ...

    public void commitTo(Sprint aSprint) {
        if (!this.isScheduledForRelease()) {
            throw new IllegalStateException(
                "Must be scheduled for release to commit to sprint.");
        }

        if (this.isCommittedToSprint()) {
            if (!aSprint.sprintId().equals(this.sprintId())) {
                this.uncommitFromSprint();
            }
        }

        this.elevateStatusWith(BacklogItemStatus.COMMITTED);

        this.setSprintId(aSprint.sprintId());

        DomainEventPublisher
            .instance()
            .publish(new BacklogItemCommitted(
                    this.tenant(),
                    this.backlogItemId(),
                    this.sprintId()));
    }
    ...
}
```

The client of this explicit model seems to operate on safer ground:

```
// client commits the backlog item to a sprint
// by using a domain-specific behavior

backlogItem.commitTo(sprint);
```

The first example uses a very data-centric approach. The onus is entirely on the client to know how to correctly commit the backlog item to a sprint. The model, which is not really a domain model, doesn't help at all. What if the client mistakenly changes only the sprintId but not the status, or the opposite? Or what if in the future another attribute must be set? The client code must be analyzed for correct mapping of data values to the proper attributes on the BacklogItem.

This approach also exposes the shape of the BacklogItem object and clearly focuses attention on its data attributes and not on its behaviors. Even if you argue that `setSprintId()` and `setStatus()` are behaviors, the case in point is that these "behaviors" have no real business domain value. These "behaviors" do not explicitly indicate the intentions of the scenarios that the domain software is supposed to model, that of committing a backlog item to a sprint. They do cause cognitive overload when the client developer tries to mentally select from among the `BacklogItem` attributes needed to commit a backlog item to a sprint. There could be many because it's a data-centric model.

Now consider the second example. Instead of exposing the data attributes to clients, it exposes a behavior that explicitly and clearly indicates that a client may commit a backlog item to a sprint. Experts in this particular domain discuss the following requirement of the model:

> Allow each backlog item to be committed to a sprint. It may be committed only if it is already scheduled for release. If it is already committed to a different sprint, it must be uncommitted first. When the commit completes, notify interested parties.

Thus, the method in the second example captures the Ubiquitous Language of the model in context, that is, the Bounded Context in which the `BacklogItem` type is isolated. And as we analyze this scenario, we discover that the first solution is incomplete and contains bugs.

With the second implementation clients don't need to know what is required to perform the commit, whether simple or complex. The implementation of this method has as much or as little logic as necessary. We easily added a guard to protect against committing a backlog item that is not yet scheduled for release. True, you can also place guards inside the setters of the first implementation, but the setter now becomes responsible for understanding the full context of the object's state rather than just the requirements for `sprintId` and `status`.

There's another subtle difference here, too. Note that if the backlog item is already committed to another sprint, it will first be uncommitted from the current sprint. This is an important detail, because when a backlog item is uncommitted from a sprint, a Domain Event is to be published to clients:

> Allow each backlog item to be uncommitted from a sprint. When the backlog item is uncommitted, notify interested parties.

The publication of the uncommitted notification is obtained for free just by using the domain behavior `uncommitFrom()`. Method `commitTo()` doesn't even need to know that it notifies. All it needs to know is that it must uncommit from any current sprint before committing to a new sprint. Additionally, the `commitTo()` domain behavior also notifies interested parties with an Event as its final step. Without placing this rich behavior in `BacklogItem` we would have to publish Events from the client. That would certainly leak domain logic from the model. Bad.

Clearly, more thought is needed to create the `BacklogItem` of the second example than that of the first. Yet the thought needed is not so much greater, and the benefits are so much higher. The more we learn to design in this way, the easier it becomes. In the end, there is certainly more required thought, more effort, more collaboration and orchestration of team efforts, but not so much that DDD becomes heavy. New thought is well worth the effort.

Whiteboard Time

- Using the specific domain you currently work in, think of the common terms and actions of the model.

- Write the terms on the board.

- Next, write phrases that should be used by your team when you talk about the project.

- Discuss them with a real domain expert to see how they could be refined (remember to bring the coffee).

Justification for Domain Modeling

Tactical modeling is generally more complex than *strategic modeling*. Thus, if you intend to develop a domain model using the DDD tactical patterns (Aggregates, Services, Value Objects, Events, and so forth), doing so will require more careful thought and greater investment. Since this is so, how does an organization justify tactical domain modeling? What criteria can be used to qualify a given project for the extra investment needed to properly apply DDD from top to bottom?

Picture yourself leading an expedition through unfamiliar territory. You would want to understand the surrounding landmasses and borders. Your team would study maps, maybe even draw their own, and determine their strategic approach. You would consider aspects of the terrain and how it could be used to your advantage. No matter how much planning is done, some facets of such an endeavor are going to be really difficult.

If your strategy indicated that you'd have to scale a vertical rock face, you'd need some fitting tactical tools and maneuvers for that ascent. Standing at the bottom and looking up, you might see some indication of specific challenges and perilous areas. Yet, you wouldn't see every detail until you were on the rock face. You might need to drive pitons into slick rock, but you could use various-size cams to wedge into natural cracks. To latch on to these climbing protections, you'd bring along your carabiners. You would try to take as straight a path as possible but would have to make specific determinations point by point. Sometimes you might even have to backtrack and reroute depending on what the rock dictated. Many people think of climbing as a dangerous thrill sport, but those who actually climb will tell you it's safer than driving a car or flying an airplane. Clearly, for that to be true, climbers need to understand the tools and techniques and how to judge the rock.

If developing a given **Subdomain** (2) requires such a difficult, even precarious, ascent, we'd bring the DDD tactical patterns along for the climb. A business initiative that matches the criteria of the Core Domain should not quickly dismiss the use of the tactical patterns. The Core Domain is an unknown and complex area. The team is best protected against a disastrous mid-asset fall if using the right tactics.

Here's some practical guidance. I begin with the high-level ones and progress to more details:

- If a Bounded Context is being developed as the Core Domain, it is strategically vital to the success of the business. The core model is not well understood and will require lots of experimentation and refactoring. It likely deserves commitment to longevity with continuous enhancement. It may not always be your Core Domain. Nonetheless, if the Bounded Context is complex, innovative, and needs to endure for a long time as it undergoes change, strongly consider the use of the tactical patterns as an investment in the future of your business. This assumes that your Core Domain deserves the best developer resources with a high skill level.

- A domain that may become a **Generic Subdomain** (2) or Supporting Subdomain to its consumers may actually be a Core Domain to your business. You don't always judge a domain from the viewpoint of its ultimate consumers. If you are developing a Bounded Context as your chief business initiative, it is your Core Domain regardless of how it is viewed by customers outside your business. Strongly consider the use of the tactical patterns.

- If you are developing a Supporting Subdomain that, for various reasons, cannot be acquired as a third-party Generic Subdomain, it is possible that the tactical patterns would benefit your efforts. In this case consider the skill level of the team and whether or not the model is new and innovative. It is innovative if it adds specific business value, captures special knowledge, and is not just technically intriguing. If the team is capable of properly applying tactical design, and the Supporting Subdomain is innovative and must endure for years in the future, this is a good opportunity to invest in your software using tactical design. However, this does not make this model the Core Domain since in the eyes of the business it is merely Supporting.

These guidelines may be somewhat confining if your business employs a good number of developers with vast experience in and a very high comfort level with domain modeling. Where experience is very high, and the engineers themselves believe the tactical patterns would be the best choice, it makes sense to trust their opinion. Honest developers, no matter how experienced, will indicate in a specific case that developing a domain model is, or is not, the best choice.

The type of business domain itself is not automatically the determining factor for choosing a development approach. Your team should consider important questions to help you make the final determination. Consider the following short list of more detailed decision parameters, which is more or less aligned with and expands on the preceding higher-level guidelines:

- Are domain experts available and are you committed to forming a team around them?

- Although the specific business domain is somewhat simple now, will it grow in complexity over time? There is risk in using Transaction Script[1] for complex applications. If you use Transaction Script now, will the potential for refactoring to a behavioral domain model later on be practical if/when the Context becomes complex?

- Will the use of the DDD tactical patterns make it easier and more practical to integrate with other Bounded Contexts, whether third-party or custom developed?

- Will development really be simpler and require less code if you use Transaction Script? (Experience with both approaches proves that many times Transaction Script requires as much or more code. This is probably because the complexity of the domain and the innovation of the model were not well understood during project planning. Underestimating domain complexity and the innovation involved happens often.)

- Do the critical path and timeline allow for any overhead required for tactical investment?

---

1. Here I am generalizing terms. In this list I use Transaction Script to represent several non-domain-model approaches.

- Will the tactical investment in a Core Domain protect the system from changing architectural influences? Transaction Script may leave it exposed. (Domain models are often enduring while architectural influences tend to be more disruptive to other layers.)

- Will clients/customers benefit from a cleaner, enduring design and development approach, or could their application be replaced by an off-the-shelf solution tomorrow? In other words, why would we ever develop this as a custom application/service in the first place?

- Will developing an application/service using tactical DDD be more difficult than using other approaches such as Transaction Script? (Skill level and availability of domain experts is vital to answering this question.)

- If the team's toolkit was complete with DDD enablers, would we conscientiously choose to use another approach instead? (Some enablers make model persistence practical, such as using object-relational mapping, full Aggregate serialization and persistence, an Event Store, or a framework that supports tactical DDD. There may be other enablers, too.)

This list is not prioritized for your domain, and you can probably assemble additional criteria. You understand the compelling reasons for using the best and most empowering methods possible to your advantage. You also know your business and technology landscape. In the end it is the business customer, not the object practitioners and technologists, who must be pleased. Choose wisely.

DDD Is Not Heavy

In no way do I want to imply that properly practicing DDD leads to a heavyweight process with lots of ceremony and all the crufty documentation artifacts that must be supported. That's not what DDD is about. It is meant to fit well into any agile project framework, such as Scrum, that the team desires to use. Its design tenets lean toward rather rapid test-first refinements of a real software model. If you were in need of developing a new domain object, such as an Entity or a Value Object, the test-first approach works like this:

1. Write a test that demonstrates how the new domain object should be used by a client of the domain model.

2. Create the new domain object with enough code to make the test compile.

3. Refactor both until the test properly represents the way a client would use the domain object, and the domain object has proper behavioral method signatures.

4. Implement each domain object behavior until the test passes, refactoring the domain object until no inappropriate code duplications exist.

5. Demonstrate the code to team members, including domain experts, to ensure that the test is using the domain object according to the current meaning of the Ubiquitous Language.

You may conclude that this is not any different from the test-first approach you already practice. Well, it might be a little different, but the point is that it's basically the same. This test stage is not attempting to prove with absolute certainty that the model is bulletproof. Later we will add tests to do that. First we want to focus on how the model will be used by clients, and these tests drive the model's design. The good news is that it really is an agile approach. DDD promotes lightweight development, not ceremonious, heavy, up-front design. From that standpoint it really isn't different from common agile development. So, while the preceding steps may not enlighten you about agile, I think they clarify the position of DDD, that it is meant to be used in an agile way.

Later you also add tests that verify the correctness of the new domain object from every possible (and practical) angle. At this point you are interested in the correctness of the expression of a domain concept that is embodied in the new domain object. Reading the demonstrative clientlike test code must reveal the proper expressiveness using the Ubiquitous Language. Domain experts who are nontechnical should be able, with the help of a developer, to read the code well enough to get a clear impression that the model has achieved the goal of the team. This implies that test data must be realistic and support and enhance the desired expressiveness. Otherwise, domain experts cannot make a complete judgment about the implementation.

This test-first agile methodology repeats until you have a model that is working according to the tasks outlined for the current iteration. The steps outlined previously are agile and represent what Extreme Programming originally promoted. Using agile does not eliminate any essential DDD patterns and practices. They go together quite well. Of course, you can choose to use full DDD without doing test-first development. You can always develop tests against existing model objects. However, designing from the model client's perspective adds a very desirable dimension.

Fiction, with Bucketfuls of Reality

As I contemplated how to best present implementation guidance for contemporary use of DDD, I wanted to provide justification for everything I say should be done. That meant supplying not just the how, but the why. It occurred to me that looking at a few projects as case studies would appropriately illustrate why I made a certain suggestion and demonstrate how proper use of DDD will solve the challenges commonly faced.

Sometimes it's easier to look at the problems faced by other project teams and learn from their misuse of DDD than it is to look inward. Certainly, once you recognize the flaws of others' work, you'll be able to judge whether or not you are leaning in the same precarious direction, or even standing in the thick of the same morass. Then, knowing where you are headed or where you already are, you can make the precise adjustments to correct problems and avoid the same in the future.

Rather than present a series of actual projects that I have worked on—ones that I could not discuss openly anyway—I decided to use a bit of fiction based on real-world situations that I and others have experienced. That way I could create the perfect state of affairs to demonstrate the reasons a specific implementation approach works best, or at least better, when dealing with challenges in DDD.

So it is not just fiction on which I am interested in building case studies. It is a fictitious company with a real-world business charter, fictitious teams within the company with real-world software to build and deploy, and real-world DDD challenges and resulting problems with real-world solutions to them. It's what I call "fiction with bucketfuls of reality." I have found it quite effective to write in this style. I hope you benefit from it.

When presenting any set of examples, we must limit the scope to make it practical. Otherwise, the volume will drown efforts to teach and learn. Examples cannot be overly simplistic either, or vital lessons would be lost. To balance this effort, the business situation I have chosen is largely based on greenfield development.

As we peer into the projects at various points in time, we'll see different problems and successes that the teams experience. The Core Domain that is the focus of the examples is sufficiently complex to examine DDD from various perspectives. Our Bounded Contexts use one or more others, which enables us to investigate integration with DDD. Still, the three sample models cannot possibly demonstrate every aspect of strategic design, such as occurs in a "brownfield" environment common where many legacy systems exist. I don't completely dodge those less attractive regions, as if they are irrelevant. Whenever advisable we will diverge from the main samples and study areas where DDD guidance can be used in additional advantageous ways.

Now allow me to introduce you to the company and tell you a little bit about its teams and the projects they are working on.

SaaSOvation, Its Products, and Its Use of DDD

The company is SaaSOvation. As its name implies, SaaSOvation's charter is to develop a series of software as a service, or SaaS, products. The SaaS products are hosted by SaaSOvation and accessed and used by subscribing organizations. The company's business plan includes two planned products, one to precede the other.

The flagship product is named CollabOvation. It is a corporate collaboration suite, which sports the features of leading social networks. These include forums, shared calendars, blogs, instant messaging, wiki, message boards, document management, announcements and alerts, activity tracking, and RSS feeds. All of the collaboration tools are focused on the needs of corporate businesses, helping them spike productivity in smaller projects, in larger programs, and across business units. Business collaboration is important for creating and facilitating a synergistic atmosphere in today's changing and sometimes uncertain, yet fast-paced economy. Anything that can help propel productivity forward, transfer knowledge, promote idea sharing, and associatively manage the creative process so results will not be misplaced will be a boon to the corporate success equation. CollabOvation provides a high-value proposition to customers, and the challenge will also please its developers.

The second product, named ProjectOvation, is the Core Domain of primary focus. The tool focuses on the management of agile projects, using Scrum as the iterative and incremental project management framework. ProjectOvation follows the traditional Scrum project management model, complete with product, product owner, team, backlog items, planned releases, and sprints. Backlog item estimation is provided through business value calculators that use cost-benefit analysis. If you think of Scrum at its richest, that's where ProjectOvation is headed. But SaaSOvation plans to get more bang for its buck.

CollabOvation and ProjectOvation would not go down entirely separate paths. SaaSOvation and its board of advisers envisioned innovation around weaving collaboration tools in with agile software development. Thus, CollabOvation features will be offered as an optional add-on to ProjectOvation. Without a doubt, supplying collaboration tools for project planning, feature and story discussions, team and inter-team group discussion, and support will be a popular option. SaaSOvation forecasts that more than 60 percent of ProjectOvation subscribers will add on CollabOvation features. And this kind of add-on sales often ends up leading to new full sales of the add-on product itself. Once a sales channel is established and software development teams see the power of collaboration in their project management suite, their enthusiasm will influence full corporate adoption of the complete collaboration suite. Due to this viral sales approach, SaaSOvation further forecasts that at a minimum 35 percent of all ProjectOvation sales will lead to full corporate adoption of CollabOvation. They consider this a conservative estimate, but one that will make it extremely successful.

The CollabOvation product development team is staffed first. There are a few seasoned veterans on the team, but a greater number of midlevel developers. Early meetings pointed to Domain-Driven Design as the favored design and development approach. One of the two senior developers had used a minimal set of DDD patterns on a previous project at his former employer. As he described his experience to the team, it would have been clear to a more experienced DDD practitioner that this was not full use of DDD. What he had done is sometimes referred to as DDD-Lite.

DDD-Lite is a means of picking and choosing a subset of the DDD tactical patterns, but without giving full attention to discovering, capturing, and enhancing the Ubiquitous Language. As well, this technique generally bypasses the use of Bounded Contexts and Context Mapping. Its focus is much more technical, with a desire to solve technical problems. It can have benefits, but generally not with as high a reward as including strategic modeling along with it. SaaSOvation bought into this. In its case doing so soon led to problems because the team didn't understand Subdomains and the power and safety of explicit Bounded Contexts.

Things could have been worse. SaaSOvation actually avoided some major pitfalls of using DDD-Lite, just because its two core products formed a natural set of Bounded Contexts. This tended to keep the CollabOvation model and the ProjectOvation model formally segregated. But that was just by chance. It didn't mean the team understood Bounded Context, which is why the problems they did experience happened in the first place. Well, you either learn or you fail.

It's good that we can benefit from examining SaaSOvation's incomplete use of DDD. The team eventually learned from their mistakes by acquiring a better grasp of strategic design. You will also learn from the adjustments the CollabOvation team made, as the eventual ProjectOvation team benefited from retrospectives of the early conditions of its sister and partner project. See **Subdomains** (2) and **Bounded Contexts** (2), as well as **Context Maps** (3), for the full story.

Wrap-Up

Well, that's a pretty encouraging start with DDD. I think by now you probably have gotten a good feeling that you and your team can actually succeed with an advanced software development technique. I agree.

Of course, we aren't going to oversimplify things. Implementing DDD takes real concerted effort. If it were easy, everybody would be writing great code, and we know that just doesn't happen. So get ready. It will be worth it, because your design will be exactly how your software works.

Here's what you've learned so far:

- You've discovered what DDD can do for your projects and your teams to help you grapple with domain complexity.

- You found out how to score your project to see if it deserves the DDD investment.

- You considered the common alternatives to DDD and why using those approaches often leads to problems.

- You've grasped the foundations of DDD and are prepared to take the first steps on your project.

- You've found out how to sell DDD to your management, domain experts, and technical team members.

- You are now armed with knowledge of how to succeed while facing the challenges of DDD.

Here's where we're going next. The next two chapters are on the all-important strategic design, followed by a chapter on software architectures with DDD. This is really important stuff to get a handle on before you move to the subsequent chapters on tactical modeling.

Chapter 2

Domains, Subdomains, and Bounded Contexts

There are just as many notes as I required,
neither more nor less.
—*Mozart in the film* Amadeus
(Orion Pictures, Warner Brothers, 1984)

There are three things you are going to have to understand very clearly:

- What your **Domain** is

- What your **Subdomains** are

- What your **Bounded Contexts** are

Just because all these concepts were discussed in detail in the second half of [Evans] does not mean that they are of secondary importance. To succeed in implementing DDD, you have to get these right.

> **Road Map to This Chapter**
> - Grasp the big picture of DDD by understanding Domains, Subdomains, and Bounded Contexts.
> - Learn why strategic design is so essential, and why designing without it hurts.
> - Consider a practical real-world Domain with multiple Subdomains.
> - Make sense of Bounded Contexts, both conceptually and technically.
> - See SaaSOvation's "aha!" moments as they discover strategic design.

Big Picture

A Domain, in the broad sense, is what an organization does and the world it does it in. Businesses identify a market and sell products and services. Each kind of organization has its own unique realm of know-how and way of doing things. That realm of understanding and its methods for carrying out its operations is its Domain. When you develop software for an organization, you are working in its Domain. It should be pretty obvious to you what your Domain is. You work in it.

One thing to be aware of is that the term *Domain* may be a bit overloaded. Domain can refer to both the entire domain of the business, as well as just one core or supporting area of it. I will do my best to distinguish each use of the term. When referring to just one area of the business, I will generally qualify it with the use of **Core Domain, Subdomain,** and the like.

Because the term *domain model* includes the word *domain*, we might get the idea that we should create a single, cohesive, all-inclusive model of an organization's entire business domain—you know, like an enterprise model. However, when using DDD, that is not our goal. DDD places emphasis on just the opposite. The whole Domain of the organization is composed of Subdomains. Using DDD, models are developed in Bounded Contexts. In fact, developing a Domain Model is actually one way that we focus on only one specific area of the whole business domain. Any attempt to define the business of even a moderately complex organization in a single, all-encompassing model will be at best extremely difficult and will usually fail. As is made clear in this chapter, vigorously separating distinct areas of the whole business domain will help us succeed.

So, if a domain model shouldn't be all-inclusive of what the organization does and how it does it, what should it be, exactly?

Almost every software Domain has multiple Subdomains. It really doesn't matter whether the organization is huge and extremely complex or consists of just a few people and the software they use. There are different functions that make any business successful, so it's advantageous to think about each of those business functions separately.

Subdomains and Bounded Contexts at Work

Here's a fairly simple example to introduce how Subdomains can be used. Think of a retail company that sells products online. The products it sells could be just about anything, so we won't think too carefully about them. To do business in this Domain, the company must present a catalog of products to shoppers, it must allow orders to be placed, it must collect payment for the products sold, and it must ship the products to buyers. This online retailer's Domain seems to be composed of these four primary Subdomains: *Product Catalog, Orders, Invoicing,* and *Shipping.* The upper part of Figure 2.1 shows the *e-Commerce System.*

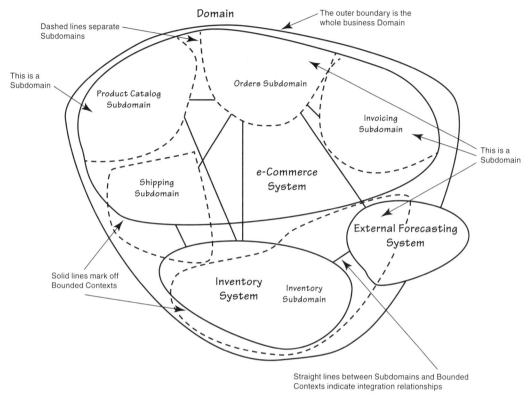

Figure 2.1 A Domain with Subdomains and Bounded Contexts

This all seems quite straightforward, and to some degree it is. However, if we introduce just one additional detail, we will make our example more complex. Consider for a moment how difficult it can be to deal with *Inventory*, an additional system and Subdomain seen in Figure 2.1. We'll get back to the increased complexity in a moment. First let's peer into the physical subsystems and logical Subdomains in the diagram.

Notice that at this time just three physical systems exist to realize this retailer's Domain, only two of which are hosted internally. Those two internal systems represent what we might think of as two Bounded Contexts. Since, unfortunately, most systems today are not created by employing a DDD approach, this ends up being a fairly typical situation, with fewer subsystems responsible for many business functions.

Inside the *e-Commerce Bounded Context* there are really multiple implicit domain models at play, even though they are not cleanly separated as such. These otherwise separate domain models are actually fused into one software model, and that's very unfortunate. It might be less of a problem for the retailer if it had purchased this Bounded Context from a third party rather than building it, but whoever maintains this system has experienced the negative consequences of the increasing complexity that results from blending the *Product Catalog*, the *Orders*, the *Invoicing*, and the *Shipping* models into one large e-commerce model. As the various logical models need to grow to facilitate new features, each of the conflicting concerns will impede the progress of each of the others. This would be especially so if another logical model—a major new feature set—must be added. It's just what happens when software concerns are not cleanly separated.

This is particularly unfortunate because a lot of software developers think it's clever to bake everything possible into one system. It's your basic all-knowing, all-doing e-commerce system, and thus it will certainly satisfy everyone's needs. This is deceiving, however, because no matter how many concerns can be piled into one subsystem, it will never address the needs of every potential consumer. Never. Add to this the fact that not separating otherwise distinct software domain models by Subdomain will make ongoing changes much more burdensome, since everything will tend to be connected to and depend on everything else.

Yet, using one of the DDD strategic design tools, we can to some degree cut through the complexity by externally dissecting these intertwined models into logically separated Subdomains according to their actual functionality. The logical Subdomain separations are indicated by the dashed lines in Figure 2.1. It's not that we have somehow refactored the third-party models into cleanly separated ones. We've just indicated what separate models should exist, at least as they apply to our specific retailer's business operations. We've also drawn some connections between logical Subdomains and even physical Bounded Contexts to show integrations.

Now let's shift from technical complexities and focus on the business complexities faced by our small company. It has limited funds and it has limited warehouse space. There's a constant juggling act going on. The company must not overspend on products that aren't selling well, and some products sell better at certain times than they do at other times. Obviously, if some products don't sell according to plans, the company's funds are tied up with products that its customers don't want, not right now anyway. The money is frozen. As a result, the company has limited room to stock products that are selling well at any given time.

That's not all. There ends up being another problem. If some products sell more quickly than anticipated, the company will not be able to inventory enough of them to fulfill customer demand. This insufficient inventory challenge could cause customers to obtain the same urgently needed products elsewhere. Sure, some product wholesalers are willing to drop-ship on behalf of the retailer, but that option costs more and introduces other undesirable consequences. There are also cost-saving strategies to stock some products nearby for local consumption and drop-ship others that sell well in distant regions. Thus, drop-shipping should be leveraged to the retailer's advantage, not as a last-minute tactic employed to rescue a sale gone bad. After all, it's not that the products that are selling the best are scarce. It's just that they are not readily available from the small retail company because it didn't optimally inventory them. If customers experience delays on a continuing basis, it will likely cost the online sales company at least a significant part of any competitive advantage it had previously earned. This example is inspired by customer problems commonly solved by Lokad.[1]

To be clear, we haven't investigated the limits of the challenges faced with inventories, and these undesirable situations are not limited to small retailers. Retailers everywhere desire to purchase and inventory precisely according to their exact needs, minimizing cost and optimizing sales fulfillment according to demand. Yet the small retailer tends to suffer the penalties of suboptimal performance more quickly than large retailers.

What would help any online retailer tremendously is a way to base future inventory and sales demands on past trends. If the retailer could use a forecasting engine, providing it with data about inventory and sales history, it could obtain demand forecasts with specific numbers for optimizing its inventory—when to reorder and how much of each product to obtain.

For the small retailer to add such forecasting capabilities would probably constitute a new **Core Domain**, because it is a nontrivial problem to solve, and succeeding would help the company establish a new competitive advantage. In fact, the third physical Bounded Context in Figure 2.1 is an *External Forecasting System*. The *Orders* Subdomain and the *Inventory* Bounded Context integrate with *Forecasting* to supply historical product sales and returns information. Additionally, we should also have the *Catalog* Subdomain provide globally recognized product bar codes, which would allow *Forecasting* to compare the small retailer's product lines to related and similar sales trends worldwide, resulting in a broader perspective. This leads to the *Forecasting* engine possessing the means to calculate the most accurate numbers needed by the small retailer to correctly stock products.

If this new solution were actually a Core Domain, and it most likely is, the team developing it would benefit greatly from understanding the surrounding

---

1. www.lokad.com/.

business terrain composed of logical Subdomains and the integrations needed. Thus, highlighting the preexisting integrations indicated on the diagram in Figure 2.1 is key to grasping the project situation at the time the project begins.

It's not always the case that Subdomains feature such distinct models of significant size and functionality. Sometimes a Subdomain can be as simple as a set of algorithms that, while essential to the business solution, are not part of the distinguished Core Domain. Applying good DDD techniques, such simple Subdomains can be separated from the Core using **Modules (9)** and need not be housed in a heavy, architecturally significant subsystem component.

When we employ DDD, we strive for each Bounded Context to mark off where the meaning of every term used by the domain model is well understood, or at least should be if we've done a good job of modeling the software. It's chiefly a *linguistic* boundary. These contextual boundaries are a key to implementing DDD.

Cowboy Logic

LB: "We get along just fine with the neighbors, until their fences break down."

AJ: "That's right. Keep your fences horse-high."

Note that a single Bounded Context does not necessarily fall within only a single Subdomain, but it may. In Figure 2.1, only one Bounded Context, *Inventory*, falls within just one Subdomain.[2] That makes it rather apparent that proper DDD was not in use when the *e-Commerce System* was developed. In that system we've identified four Subdomains, and there are probably more. On the other hand, the *Inventory System* does seem to be aligned as one Subdomain per Bounded Context by limiting its domain model to inventorying products. The *Inventory System*'s apparently clean model may be due to employing DDD, or it may be merely coincidental. We'd have to look under the hood to know for sure. Regardless, we can still make practical use of *Inventory* to develop the new Core Domain.

Linguistically, which of the Bounded Contexts in Figure 2.1 has a better design? In other words, which has an unambiguous set of domain-specific terms? When we consider that there are at least four Subdomains in the *e-Commerce*

---

2. True, the *Shipping* Subdomain uses *Inventory*, but that doesn't make *Inventory* part of the *e-Commerce System* where *Shipping* has context.

System, it's almost certain that terms and meanings collide there. For example, the term *Customer* must have multiple meanings. When a user is browsing the Catalog, Customer means one thing, but when a user is placing an Order, it means something else. Here's why. When browsing the Catalog, Customer is being used in the context of previous purchases, loyalty, available products, discounts, and shipping options. On the Order itself, however, Customer has a limited meaning. Among the few details there is a name with a ship-to address, a bill-to address, a total due, and payment terms. Just by this basic reasoning we see that in the *e-Commerce System* there is no one clean meaning for Customer. Given this situation, as we look around that system we would expect to find several other terms that have multiple meanings. It's not a clean Bounded Context with an explicit meaning for each term naming a domain concept.

Yet, there's also no guarantee that the *Inventory System* has a completely clean model, possessing wholly unambiguous domain linguistics. Even in this apparently focused Context we could face differences in meanings among the things that are being controlled in inventory. This is because there are different ways that inventoried *Items* are used. Is there a clean distinction between an Item being ordered, one being received, one in stock, and one moving out of stock? An Item on order that is not yet available for sale is called Back-Ordered Item. An Item being received is often called Goods Received. An item in stock may be called a Stock Item. An Item being consumed is often referred to as an Item Leaving Inventory. An inventoried Item that becomes spoiled or broken is often called a Wasted Inventory Item.

By looking at Figure 2.1, we don't know how well the range of inventory concepts and their accompanying linguistics are modeled. When using DDD, we'd leave none of it to guesswork. We would be certain that each of those concepts is well understood, spoken of explicitly, and modeled as such. The way domain experts describe each of these concepts could lead to separating some in different Bounded Contexts.

From outward appearances we would conclude that the *Inventory System* has better DDD health than the *e-Commerce System*. Perhaps the team that worked out its model didn't attempt to make one Item represent all inventoried item situations. Although uncertain, it's possible that the model of the *Inventory System* will be easier to integrate with than that of the *e-Commerce System*.

Speaking of integration, Figure 2.1 further shows that Bounded Contexts in an enterprise rarely if ever completely stand alone. Even when the third-party *e-Commerce System* attempts to provide a large, all-encompassing model, it can't do everything the retailer needs. The solid straight lines running between and connecting the various Subdomains in the *e-Commerce System*, the *Inventory System*, and the *External Forecasting System* show the necessary integration relationships, which proves that different models must work together. There are always specific kinds of relationships involved in integration, and you'll learn more about the possible integration options in **Contexts Maps (3)**.

That's the high-level summary of one view of a simple business domain. We've briefly encountered a Core Domain and gotten the notion that it is an important part of DDD. Now we need to understand it better.

Focus on the Core Domain

With an understanding of Subdomains and Bounded Contexts, consider an abstract view of a different Domain found in Figure 2.2. This could represent any domain, perhaps even the one you work in. I've removed the explicit names so you can mentally fill in the blanks. Naturally, our business goals are on a path of continuous refinement and expansion reflected by ever-changing

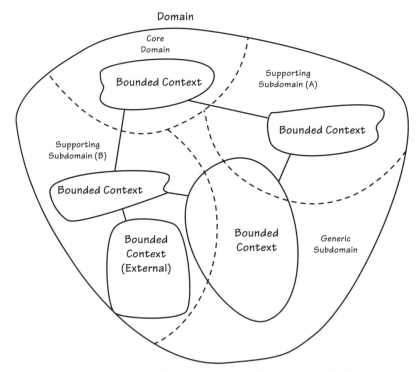

Figure 2.2   An abstract business Domain that includes Subdomains and Bounded Contexts

Subdomains and the models within. This diagram only captures the whole business Domain at a moment in time with a specific perspective, and one that could be somewhat short-lived.

Whiteboard Time

- In one column make a list of all the Subdomains that you are aware of in your daily work. In another column list the Bounded Contexts. Do Subdomains intersect with multiple Bounded Contexts? If so, it's not necessarily a bad thing, just a fact of enterprise software.

- Now, using the template in Figure 2.2, write in some of the names of the software running in your enterprise with the Subdomains, Bounded Contexts, and the integration relationships between them.

Was that difficult? Probably, because the template in Figure 2.2 likely doesn't closely reflect the existing boundaries in your Domain.

- Start over. This time you should draw a diagram that aligns with *your* Domain, Subdomains, and Bounded Contexts. Use the techniques displayed in Figure 2.2, but go ahead and fit them to your world.

Of course, you may not know about every Subdomain and Bounded Context in your entire enterprise, especially if your Domain is really large and complex. But you may be able to figure out the ones you deal with on a day-to-day basis. Anyway, give it a go. Don't be afraid of being wrong. You'll get some good practice at Context Mapping, which will be refined in the next chapter. If you want to jump to that chapter briefly for more advice, that's fine. Still, don't worry about being perfect just now. Grasp the basic ideas first.

Now look at the top of the Domain boundary in Figure 2.2 and you'll see the Subdomain labeled *Core Domain*. Introduced earlier, this is another aspect of DDD of major importance. A **Core Domain** is a part of the business Domain that is of primary importance to the success of the organization. Strategically speaking, the business must *excel* with its Core Domain. It is of utmost importance to the ongoing success of the business. That project gets the highest priority, one or more domain experts with deep knowledge of that Subdomain, the best developers, and as much leeway and leverage as possible to give the close-knit team an unobstructed success path. Most of your DDD project efforts will be focused on the Core Domain.

Two other kinds of Subdomains are found in Figure 2.2, *Supporting Subdomain* and *Generic Subdomain*. Sometimes a Bounded Context is created or acquired to support the business. If it models some aspect of the business that is essential, yet not Core, it is a **Supporting Subdomain**. The business creates a Supporting Subdomain because it is somewhat specialized. Otherwise, if it captures nothing special to the business, yet is required for the overall business solution, it is a **Generic Subdomain**. Being Supporting or Generic doesn't mean unimportant. These kinds of Subdomains are important to the success of the business, yet there is no need for the business to excel in these areas. It's the Core Domain that requires excellence in implementation, since it will provide distinct advantages to the business.

Whiteboard Time

- To make sure you grasp the significance of the Core Domain concepts, what you should do next is go back to your fresh whiteboard drawing and see if you can identify where a Core Domain is being developed in your organization.

- Next, see if you can identify the Supporting Subdomains and Generic Subdomains in your Domain.

Remember: Ask the Domain Experts!

Even if you don't get it just right the first time, this exercise will help you to think carefully about what software most distinguishes your business, what supports the distinguishing software, and what doesn't distinguish your business's success at all. Keep working at it so you become more comfortable with the thought processes and techniques.

Discuss each Subdomain and Bounded Context in your drawing with a few domain experts who specialize in the different areas.

Not only will you learn a lot from them, but you'll gain valuable experience in *listening to the experts*. That's a hallmark of implementing DDD well.

What you've just learned is the big-picture foundation of strategic design.

Why Strategic Design Is So Incredibly Essential

OK, you've learned some DDD terminology and the meaning behind it, but not much has been said about *why* this is so important. I've really just asserted that it is very important and hoped that you'd believe me. But like most statements of "fact," I'd better back my assertion now. Let's jump in on our running example, that of the projects going on at SaaSOvation. They've managed to get themselves into a real jam.

Early on in their first effort with DDD, the collaboration project team began to veer off the path to developing a clean model. This happened because they didn't understand strategic design, not even at its most basic level. As is true of most developers, their focus was on the details of **Entities**
(5) and **Value Objects (6)**, which obscured their vision of the bigger picture. *They blended their core concepts with generic ones, causing the creation of two models in one.* Before long they started to feel the pain of the design reflected in Figure 2.3. The bottom line? They had not fully achieved the goal of implementing DDD.

A few on the SaaSOvation team asserted, "So what if collaboration concepts are tightly coupled to Users and Permissions? We must track who did what!" The senior developer pointed out that it's actually not the coupling alone that the team should

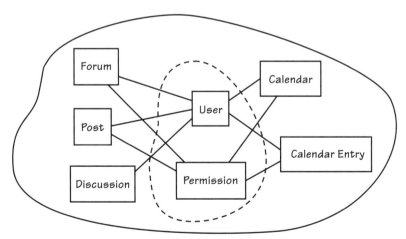

Figure 2.3   The team didn't understand basic strategic design, which led to mismatched concepts in the collaboration model. The dashes encircle the problem elements.

be concerned with. "In the end, a Forum, a Post, a Discussion, a Calendar, and a Calendar Entry will all be coupled to some kind of human *collaborator* objects. *And that's just it. The linguistics are wrong here.*" As he elaborated, he showed that Forum, Post, Discussion, and the like were all *coupled to the wrong linguistic concepts.* Users and Permissions *have nothing to do with collaboration and don't harmonize in the true Ubiquitous Language of Collaboration.* Users and Permissions are identity and access concepts—security concerns. Every concept modeled in the *Collaboration Context*—as in the Bounded Context surrounding the collaboration domain model—should have a linguistic association to collaboration, and right now they don't. "What we should be focused on are collaboration concepts, such as Author and Moderator. Those are the correct concepts and linguistic terms in a collaboration setting."

Naming a Bounded Context

Did you notice the name *Collaboration Context* used here? This is the way we name a Bounded Context, which is in the form *Name-of-Model Context*. In this case we use *Collaboration Context* because it is the Bounded Context that contains the domain model of the Collaboration project. We also have *Identity and Access Context* for the Bounded Context that contains the model of the Identity and Access project, and *Agile Project Management (PM) Context* for the Bounded Context that holds the model of the Agile Project Management project.

To reiterate, at a fundamental level, the SaaSOvation developers didn't at first understand that Users and Permissions had nothing to do with collaboration tools. Well, sure, they did have users of their software, and those users had to be distinguished one from another to determine the tasks each could perform. But collaboration tools should be interested in the roles of users, rather than who they specifically are and each little action they are permitted to perform. However, the collaboration model now had user and permission details completely intertwined. If something changed about the way users and/or permissions worked, a lot or all of the model would suffer from the ripple. In fact, this problem was right at the threshold. The team wanted to switch from a permissions approach and use role-based access management instead. When they decided to make this switch, it made them more aware of the strategic modeling problem at hand.

They now realized that a Forum should not be concerned with who can post a subject, or under what conditions that is permitted. A Forum just needs to know that an Author is doing that right now, or had done that previously. The team was now grasping that determining who can do something is the concern of a completely separate model, and the core collaboration model only needed to know that any question regarding who can do what had already been answered. The Forum just needed to be given an Author who wants to Post to a Discussion. The Forum and Author are clearly concepts of the Ubiquitous Language of the collaboration model, a Bounded Context named *Collaboration Context*. User and Permission, or some similar concepts such as Role, belonged someplace completely different. Those needed to be isolated from the *Collaboration Context*.

It would be easy for the team to conclude that they only needed to factor out the tight coupling to User and Permission. After all, there would not be anything wrong with separating User and Permission/Role into a separate Module. That could help them place these concepts in a separate logical *Security Subdomain* within the same Bounded Context. However, what made the best modeling choice stand out even more boldly was the realization that the team's next Core Domain project would have very similar role-based access needs and would lean on the use of domain-specific role characteristics. Clearly, Users and Roles were truly part of a Supporting or Generic Subdomain that had an enterprise-wide, and even customer-facing, part to play in the future.

Taking a more vigorous approach to clean modeling would help them avoid a more insidious problem. They were probably leaning toward working their way into a **Big Ball of Mud (3)**. It wasn't just that their User and Permission concepts were not properly modularized. While modularization is an essential DDD modeling tool, it doesn't fix linguistic misalignment.

The senior developer was very concerned that, if left unchecked, this situation could *easily lead to an undisciplined mindset that would allow more tangle to eventually creep in subtly.* In time, as the team faced modeling another set of noncollaboration concepts, the Core Domain would become even less clear. They could end up with only an implicit model with source code that wouldn't reflect an expressive Ubiquitous Language of Collaboration. What the team really needed to understand was their business Domain, its Subdomains, as well as the Bounded Contexts they were developing. Doing so would prevent the entry of the dastardly foe of strategic design, the muck of the Big Ball of Mud. Thus, *the team needed to gain a strategic modeling mindset.*

Oh, No! There's That Word *Design* Again!

If you think that *design* is a dirty word when agile is in practice, it's not with DDD. Using DDD with agile is completely natural. Always keep design in check with agile. Design need not be heavy.

Yeah, that was an important lesson to learn. They did manage to work their way through it with a lot of research and finally got a handle on their Domain and Subdomains. How they did that will be presented soon.

Alignment with the DDD Community

The running examples in this book are provided as three Bounded Contexts. These Bounded Contexts are likely different from those you work with. The examples present fairly typical modeling situations. However, not everyone would agree that Users and Permissions should be separated out of a given Core Domain. Perhaps in some cases it might make sense to intertwine them with your Core model. As always, that is the choice of a specific team. In my experience, however, this is one of the basic problems encountered by those new to DDD, and one that misleads their implementation efforts into an unnecessarily messy result. Another common misstep would be to meld the collaboration and agile project management models into one. These are only a few common problems. Other common modeling errors are discussed in each chapter.

At a minimum, the problems posed here, and those that follow, are *representative* of the kinds of modeling mistakes that are made when teams fail to understand the importance of linguistic drivers and Bounded Contexts. Thus, even if you disagree with the specific example problems, both the problems and solutions are still applicable in a general way to all DDD projects, because they all focus on the linguistics of a given Bounded Context.

My goal is to teach the principles of implementing DDD using the simplest, yet nontrivial, examples possible. I can't afford to allow the examples to get in the way of my teaching and your learning. If I demonstrate that identity and access management, collaboration, and agile project management all have separate linguistics, readers are well served by what the examples emphasize. Since it is each team's choice to discover the linguistic drivers that *they* find important, and that help *them* achieve the vision of their domain experts, assume that there is no mistake in the "ultimate correct" conclusions reached by the SaaSOvation developers and the modeling choices they made in their DDD implementation journey.

All of my guidance regarding Subdomains and Bounded Contexts is closely aligned with that of the broader DDD community, as it reflects my own experience. Other DDD leaders may have a slightly different focus. However, my explanations definitely provide a firm foundation for any team to move forward without ambiguity. Clearing the murky areas of DDD is the most important service to the community, and it is my primary goal. It should be your goal to put these guidelines to use in the most practical way to benefit your project.

Real-World Domains and Subdomains

I have something more to tell you about domains. They have both a *problem space* and a *solution space*. The problem space enables us to think of a strategic business challenge to be solved, while the solution space focuses on how we will implement the software to solve the problem of the business challenge. Here's how that fits into what you've already learned:

- The problem space is the parts of the Domain that need to be developed to deliver a new Core Domain. Assessing the problem space involves examining Subdomains that *already exist and those that are needed*. Thus, your problem space is the combination of the Core Domain and the Subdomains it must use. The Subdomains in the problem space are usually different from project to project since they are used to explore a current strategic business problem. This makes Subdomains a very useful tool in assessing the problem space. Subdomains allow us to rapidly view different parts of the Domain that are necessary to solve a specific problem.

- The solution space is one or more Bounded Contexts, a set of specific software models. That's because the Bounded Context *is a specific solution*, a *realization view*, once developed. The Bounded Context is used to realize a solution as software.

It is a desirable goal to align Subdomains one-to-one with Bounded Contexts. Doing so expressly segregates domain models into well-defined areas of business by objective, melding the problem space with the solution space. In practice this is not always possible, but it can work in a greenfield effort. Considering a legacy system, and probably a Big Ball of Mud, however, Subdomains often intersect Bounded Contexts, similar to what we discussed regarding Figure 2.1. In a large and complex enterprise we can employ an *assessment view* to understand our problem space, which can save us from making costly mistakes. We can conceptually divide a single, large Bounded Context using two or more Subdomains, or multiple Bounded Contexts as part of a single Subdomain. Consider an example to help clarify the difference between the problem space and the solution space.

Imagine a large, monolithic system, classified as an ERP application. Strictly speaking, an ERP may be thought of as a single Bounded Context. However, since ERP systems provide many modular business services, there's a benefit to thinking of distinct modules as different Subdomains. For example, we could divide the inventory module and purchasing module into separate, logical Subdomains. True, these modules aren't available through completely different systems. Both are part of the same ERP. Still, each provides a very different set of services to the business domain. For analytical discussions let's name these as separate Subdomains, the *Inventory Subdomain* and the *Purchasing Subdomain*. Continuing with the example, we'll see why doing so is useful.

As a core business initiative, the organization whose Domain is represented in Figure 2.4 (a concrete example using the template from Figure 2.2) starts planning the design and development of a specialized domain model to reduce the cost of doing business. The model will provide decision-making tools to be used by purchasing agents. Algorithms discovered over years of manual, human process must now be automated by software to ensure that they are always used by all purchasing agents without error. This new Core Domain *will make the*

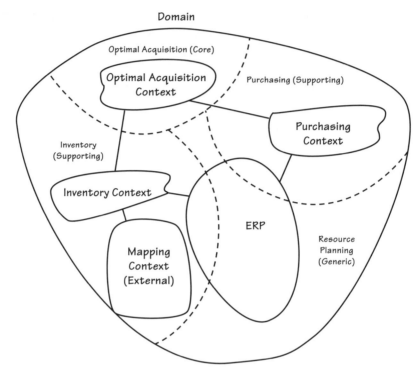

Figure 2.4   The Core Domain and other Subdomains involved in purchasing and inventory. This view is limited to select Subdomains used for specific problem space analysis, not the entire Domain.

organization more competitive by identifying better deals more quickly, and then ensuring that the needed inventories are met. To accurately stock inventory, use of the previously examined *Forecasting System* of Figure 2.1 would help here as well.

Before we can execute a specific solution, we need to make an assessment of the problem space and the solution space. Here are some questions that should be answered in order to steer your project in the right direction:

- What is the name of and vision for the strategic Core Domain?

- What concepts should be considered part of the strategic Core Domain?

- What are the necessary Supporting Subdomains and the Generic Subdomains?

- Who should do the work in each area of the domain?

- Can the right teams be assembled?

If we don't understand the vision and goals of the Core Domain and the areas of the Domain that are needed to support it, we won't be able to strategically take advantage of them and avoid associated pitfalls. Keep problem space assessment high-level, but make it thorough. Be sure that all stakeholders are aligned with and committed to successfully delivering on the vision.

Whiteboard Time

Take a moment to look at your whiteboard work and consider: What is your problem space? Recall that it is the combination of the strategic Core Domain and the Subdomains supporting it.

When you have a good understanding of the problem space, you then turn to the solution space. The first assessment will contribute knowledge to the second. The solution space will be strongly influenced by the existing systems and technologies, and those that are to be newly created. Here we really need to think in terms of cleanly separated Bounded Contexts because we are looking at the Ubiquitous Language of each. Consider these crucial questions:

- What software assets already exist, and can they be reused?

- What assets need to be acquired or created?

- How are all of these connected to each other, or integrated?

- What additional integration will be needed?

- Given the existing assets and those that need to be created, what is the required effort?

- Do the strategic initiative and all supporting projects have a high probability of success, or will any one of them cause the overall program to be delayed or even fail?

- Where are the terms of the Ubiquitous Languages involved completely different?

- Where is there overlap and sharing of concepts and data between Bounded Contexts?

- How are shared terms and/or overlapping concepts mapped and translated between the Bounded Contexts?

• Which Bounded Context contains the concepts that address the Core Domain and which of the [Evans] tactical patterns will be used to model it?

Remember, the efforts in developing the solutions in the Core Domain are a key business investment!

The specialized purchasing model described previously and pictured in Figure 2.4—the one that captures decision-making tools and algorithms—represents the solution for the Core Domain. The domain model will be implemented in an explicit Bounded Context: the *Optimal Acquisitions Context*. This Bounded Context aligns one-to-one with the Subdomain, the *Optimal Acquisitions Core Domain*. Being aligned with just one Subdomain, and its carefully crafted domain model, will make it one of the best Bounded Contexts in this business domain.

Yet another Bounded Context, the *Purchasing Context*, will be developed in order to refine some technical aspects of the purchasing process as a helper to the *Optimal Acquisitions Context*. These refinements don't reveal any special knowledge about an optimal approach to purchasing. They just make it easier for the *Optimal Acquisitions Context* to interact with the ERP at an arm's length. It's just a convenient model that operates against the ERP published interface. The new *Purchasing Context* and the preexisting ERP purchasing module fall within the *Purchasing (Supporting) Subdomain*.

The ERP purchasing module is as a whole a Generic Subdomain. That's because you could replace this Subdomain with any off-the-shelf purchasing system as long as it fulfills your basic business needs. However, being used along with the new *Purchasing Context* in the *Purchasing Subdomain* makes it work in a Supporting fashion.

> **You Can't Change the World of Bad Software Design**
>
> In a typical brownfield enterprise you are going to have undesirable situations like those illustrated in Figures 2.1 and 2.4. This means that Subdomains in poorly designed software will not align in an ideal way, one-to-one, with Bounded Contexts. You can't change the world of bad software design. You can only hope to implement proper DDD in projects you work on. In the end you will have to integrate with and even work in brownfield domains, so be prepared to exercise the techniques taught in the first one-third of this chapter as you analyze the multiple implicit models found in a single, brown Bounded Context.

Sticking with Figure 2.4, the *Optimal Acquisition Context* must also interact with the *Inventory Context*. *Inventory* manages warehousing items. It uses the ERP inventory module, which falls within the *Inventory (Supporting) Subdomain*. As a convenience to delivery contractors, the *Inventory Context* can provide maps and directions to each of its warehouses from an origin location by using an external geographical mapping service. From the *Inventory*

Context point of view, there is nothing special about mapping. There are several geographical mapping services to choose from, and there may be advantages to changing the chosen mapping system over time. The mapping service is itself a Generic Subdomain, but it is consumed by a Supporting Subdomain.

Note these key points as viewed from the perspective of the company developing the *Optimal Acquisition Context*. In the solution space the geographical mapping service is not part of the *Inventory Context*, although in the problem space it is considered part of the *Inventory Subdomain*. In the solution space, even if the mapping services are provided by a simple component-based API, it is in a different Bounded Context. The Ubiquitous Languages of *Inventory* and of *Mapping* are mutually exclusive, which means they are in different Bounded Contexts. When the *Inventory Context* uses something from the external *Mapping Context*, the data may go through at least some minimal translation to be properly consumed.

On the other hand, from the point of view of the external business organization that develops and offers the mapping service for subscription, mapping is a Core Domain. That external organization has its own domain, or realm of business operations. It must remain competitive, constantly refining its domain model in order to retain subscribers and attract new ones. If you were the CEO of the mapping organization, you'd make sure to give customers, including the one subscriber under discussion, every reason to stick with your services rather than move on to the competition. However, that doesn't change the perspective of the subscriber that is developing its inventory system. To the inventory system it is still a Generic Subdomain. It could, if it was to its advantage, subscribe to a different mapping service.

Whiteboard Time

What are the Bounded Contexts in your solution space? At this point you should be able to refer back to your whiteboard diagram for a good idea. Still, you may be a bit surprised as we dig deeper into how to properly use Bounded Contexts. So be ready for possible refinements. We are doing agile development, after all.

So, for the balance of this chapter we are going to shift gears and consider the importance of Bounded Contexts as an essential solution space modeling tool for DDD. In **Context Maps** (3) the discussion primarily stresses how to deal with mapping different, but related, Ubiquitous Languages, by integrating their Bounded Contexts.

Making Sense of Bounded Contexts

Don't forget, a Bounded Context is an explicit boundary within which a domain model exists. The domain model expresses a Ubiquitous Language as a software model. The boundary is created because each of the model's concepts inside, with its properties and operations, has a special meaning. If you are a member of such a modeling team, you'd know exactly the meaning of each of the concepts in your Context.

> **Bounded Context Is Explicit and Linguistic**
> A Bounded Context is an explicit boundary within which a domain model exists. Inside the boundary all terms and phrases of the Ubiquitous Language have specific meaning, and the model reflects the Language with exactness.

It is often the case that in two explicitly different models, objects with the same or similar names have different meanings. When an explicit boundary is placed around each of the two models individually, the meaning of each concept in each Context is certain. Thus, a Bounded Context is principally a *linguistic boundary*. You should use these points of reasoning as a touchstone to determine if you are correctly using Bounded Contexts.

Some projects fall into the trap of attempting to create an all-inclusive model, one where the goal is to get the entire organization to agree on concepts with names that have only one global meaning. Approaching a modeling effort in this way is a pitfall. First, it will be nearly impossible to establish agreement among all stakeholders that all concepts have a single, pure, and distinct global meaning. Some organizations are so large and complex that you'd never be able to get all stakeholders together, let alone establish total meaningful agreement among them. Even if you are working in a smaller company with relatively few stakeholders, establishing an enduring definition of a single global concept is still unlikely. Thus, the best position to take is to embrace the fact that differences always exist and apply Bounded Context to separately delineate each domain model where differences are explicit and well understood.

A Bounded Context does not dictate the creation of a single kind of project artifact. It's not an individual component, document, or diagram.[3] So it's not a JAR or DLL, but these can be used to deploy a Bounded Context as described later in the chapter.

Consider this sharp contrast between an Account in a *Banking Context* and an Account in a *Literary Context* as presented in Table 2.1.

---

3. You can draw a diagram of one or more Bounded Contexts as seen here and in Context Maps. However, the diagram is not the Bounded Context.

Table 2.1   The Diversity of Meanings That the Term Account Can Have

Context	Meaning	Example
Banking Context	An Account maintains a record of debit and credit transactions indicating a customer's current financial state with the bank.	Checking Account and Savings Account
Literary Context	An Account is a set of literary expressions about one or more related events over a time span.	Amazon.com sells the book *Into Thin Air: A Personal Account of the Mt. Everest Disaster.*

Looking at Figure 2.5, there is nothing characteristic of the Account types by name that distinguishes them. It is only by looking at the name of each conceptual container—its Bounded Context—that you understand the differences between the two.

These two Bounded Contexts are probably not in the same Domain. The point is to demonstrate that context is king.

Context Is King

Context is king, especially when implementing DDD.

In the financial world the word *security* is often used. The Securities and Exchange Commission (SEC) restricts the term *security* to use with equities. Now consider this: Futures contracts are commodities and not under the jurisdiction of the SEC. However, some financial firms call Futures by the name *security* as a reference but mark them with the **Standard Type (6)** `Futures`.

Is that the best Language for a Future? It depends on the Domain it's used in. Some would obviously say it is, while others would insist that it isn't. Context is also *cultural*. Inside a given firm that trades Futures, it may align best with the culture to use the term *Security* in a specific Ubiquitous Language.

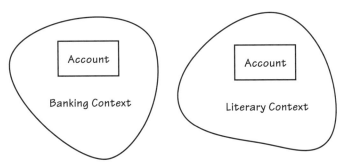

Figure 2.5   Account objects in two different Bounded Contexts have completely different meanings, but you know that only by considering the name of each Bounded Context.

It is often the subtly different meanings that are most commonly faced in your enterprise. Here's why. The name chosen by each team in each Context is always made with the Ubiquitous Language in mind. You never name a concept arbitrarily, such as to purposely distinguish it from a term in a different Context. Consider two banking Contexts, one for checking accounts and one for savings accounts.[4] We don't need to give the name Checking Account to the object in the *Checking Context* or the name Savings Account to the object in the *Savings Context*. Both concepts may safely be named Account because each Bounded Context distinguishes subtle meanings. Of course, there is no rule that says that more meaning cannot be added to these names. That's the decision of your team.

When integrations are needed, mapping must be done between Bounded Contexts. This can be a complex aspect of DDD and calls for a corresponding amount of care. We don't usually use an object instance outside its boundary, but related objects in multiple contexts may share some subset of common state.

Here's another example with a common name used in multiple Bounded Contexts, but this time within the same Domain. Consider the modeling challenges of a publishing organization that must deal with the various stages of the life cycle of books. Roughly speaking, publishers deal with similar stages as a book progresses through these different Contexts:

- Conceptualizing and proposing a book

- Contracting with authors

- Managing the book's authorship and editorial process

- Designing the book layout, including illustrations

- Translating the book into other languages

- Producing the physical print and/or electronic editions

- Marketing the book

- Selling the book to resellers and/or directly to consumers

- Shipping a physical book to resellers and consumers

Throughout each of these stages, is there one single way to properly model a Book? Absolutely not. At each of these stages the Book has different definitions. It is not until contract that the Book has a tentative title, which might

---

4. This assumes a Domain where separate Bounded Contexts are used for checking and savings accounts.

change during editing. During the authorship and editorial phases, the Book has a collection of drafts with comments and corrections, along with a final draft. Graphic designers create page layouts. Production uses the layouts and to create press images, "blue lines," and finally plates. Marketing doesn't need most of the editorial or production artifacts, perhaps just cover art and high-level descriptions. For shipping, the Book might carry only an identity, inventory location, availability count, a size, and a weight.

What would happen if you tried to design a central model for Books that facilitated all the stages in its life cycle? There would be a high degree of confusion, disagreement, and contention, and little deliverable software. Even if a correct common model could be delivered from time to time, it would likely meet the needs of all clients only occasionally and far too briefly.

To counter that kind of undesirable churn and burn, such a publisher modeling with DDD would use separate Bounded Contexts for each of the life cycle stages. In every one of the multiple Bounded Contexts, there is a type of Book. The various Book objects would share an identity across all or most of the Contexts, perhaps first established at the conceptualization stage. However, the model of a Book in each Context would be different from all others. That's fine, and in fact the way it should be. When the team of a given Bounded Context speaks about a Book, it means exactly what they require for their Context. The organization embraces the natural need for differences. This is not to say that such positive outcomes are trivial to achieve. Nonetheless, using explicit Bounded Contexts, software gets delivered regularly with incremental improvements that address the specific needs of the business.

At this point let's take a quick look at the solution used by the SaaSOvation collaboration team to solve the modeling challenge as shown in Figure 2.3.

As indicated previously, in a *Collaboration Context* domain experts don't describe the people who employ the collaboration facilities as Users with Permissions. Rather, they talk about these collaborators in terms of the roles they play in the Context, as Authors, Owners, Participants, and Moderators. Some contact information may exist there, but probably not all of it. On the other hand, it's in an *Identity and Access Context* that we talk about Users. In that Context User objects have usernames and detailed information about the individual person, including detailed ways to contact the person.

Yet, we don't create an Author object out of thin air. Every collaborator must be prequalified. We confirm the existence of a User playing the appropriate Role within the *Identity and Access Context*. The attributes of an authentication descriptor are passed with requests to the *Identity and Access Context*. To create a new collaborator object, such as a Moderator, we use a subset of User attributes and a Role name. The exact details of how we obtain object state from a separate Bounded Context is not important (although later on

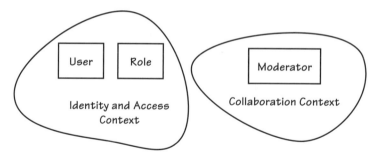

Figure 2.6   The Moderator object in its Context is based on User and Role in a different context.

it's explained extensively). What's important now is that these two different concepts are similar and different at the same time, and that the differences are determined by the Bounded Context. Figure 2.6 exemplifies User and Role in their own Context being used to create a Moderator in a different Context.

Whiteboard Time ───

- See if you can identify some subtly different concepts that exist in multiple Bounded Contexts in your Domain.

- Determine whether the concepts are properly separated, or if developers simply copied code into both.

Generally you can determine a proper separation because the similar objects have different properties and operations. In that case the boundary has separated the concepts appropriately. However, if you see the exact same objects in multiple contexts, it probably means there is some modeling error, unless the two Bounded Contexts are using a **Shared Kernel (3)**.

Room for More than the Model

A Bounded Context does not necessarily encompass only the domain model. True, the model is the primary occupant of the conceptual container. However, a Bounded Context is not limited to the model only. It often marks off a system, an application, or a business service.[5] Sometimes a Bounded Context

─────────────────

5. Admittedly the meanings of *system*, *application*, and *business service* are not always agreed upon. However, in a general sense I intend these to mean a complex set of components that interact to realize a set of significant business use cases.

houses less than this if, for example, a Generic Subdomain can be produced
without much more than a domain model. Consider portions of a system that
are typically part of a Bounded Context.

When the model drives the creation of a persistence database schema, the
database schema will live inside the boundary. This is the case because the
schema is designed, developed, and maintained by the modeling team. It means
that the database table names and column names, for example, will directly
reflect names used in the model, rather than names translated to another style.
For example, say our model has a class named `BacklogItem` and that class has
Value Object properties named `backlogItemId` and `businessPriority`:

```
public class BacklogItem extends Entity  {
    ...
    private BacklogItemId backlogItemId;
    private BusinessPriority businessPriority;
    ...
}
```

We would expect to see those mapped to the database in like manner:

```
CREATE TABLE `tbl_backlog_item` (
    ...
    `backlog_item_id_id` varchar(36) NOT NULL,
    `business_priority_ratings_benefit` int NOT NULL,
    `business_priority_ratings_cost` int NOT NULL,
    `business_priority_ratings_penalty` int NOT NULL,
    `business_priority_ratings_risk` int NOT NULL,
    ...
) ENGINE=InnoDB;
```

On the other hand, if a database schema is preexisting or if a separate team of
data modelers forces contradicting designs on the database schema, the schema
does not live within the Bounded Context occupied by the domain model.

When there are **User Interface (14)** views that render the model and drive
execution of its behavior, these are also inside the Bounded Context. However,
this does not mean that we model the Domain in the user interface, causing
domain model anemia. We want to reject the **Smart UI Anti-Pattern** [Evans]
and any temptation to drag domain concepts that belong in the model into
other areas of the system.

Users of the system/application are not always limited to humans and
may include other computer systems. Components such as Web services may
exist. We might use RESTful resources to provide interaction with the model
as an **Open Host Service (3, 13)**. Or perhaps we deploy Simple Object Access

Protocol (SOAP) or messaging service endpoints instead. In all such cases, the service-oriented components are inside the boundary.

Both user interface components and service-oriented endpoints delegate to **Application Services (14)**. These are different kinds of services, generally providing security and transaction management, and acting as **Facade** [Gamma et al.] to the model. They are task managers, transforming use case flow requests into the execution of domain logic. Application Services are also inside the boundary.

> **More on Architectural and Application Concerns**
>
> If you want to consider how DDD fits with various architectural styles, see **Architecture (4)**. Also, Application Services are treated specially in **Application (14)**. There are helpful diagrams and code snippets in both chapters.

The Bounded Context primarily encapsulates the Ubiquitous Language and its domain model, but it includes what exists to provide interaction with and support of the domain model. Pay attention to keeping the aspects of each Architectural concern in their proper place.

Whiteboard Time

- Look at each of the Bounded Contexts you identified in your whiteboard diagram. When you think of those, do you imagine components other than the domain model as being within the boundary?

- If there is a user interface and a set of Application Services, make sure they are inside the boundary. (You have flexibility in how you represent these. See Figures 2.8, 2.9, and 2.10 for some ideas for representing various components.)

- If your database schema or other persistence store was developed for your model, make sure it is also inside the boundary. (Figures 2.8, 2.9, and 2.10 provide one way to represent a database schema.)

Size of Bounded Contexts

How many **Modules (9)**, **Aggregates (10)**, **Events (8)**, and **Services (7)**—the primary building blocks of a domain model created using DDD—should a Bounded Context contain? That's a bit like asking, "How long is a piece of string?" A Bounded Context should be as big as it needs to be in order to fully express its complete Ubiquitous Language.

Extraneous concepts that are not truly part of the Core Domain should be factored out. If a concept is not in your Ubiquitous Language, it should not be introduced in your model in the first place. Still, if one or more extraneous concepts creep in, get rid of them. They probably belong in a separate Supporting or Generic Subdomain, or in no model at all.

Be careful not to mistakenly factor out concepts that do truly belong in the Core Domain. Your model must completely exhibit the richness of the Ubiquitous Language in context, leaving out nothing essential. Clearly, good judgment is needed. Tools such as **Context Maps** (3) can help shape your team's good judgment.

In the film *Amadeus*[6] there is a scene where the Austrian emperor Joseph II communicates to Mozart that the musical work Mozart had just performed was a quality piece, but one that contained "simply too many notes." Mozart aptly replies to the emperor, "There are just as many notes as I required, neither more nor less." This reply well illustrates an essential mentality to take into stepping off contextual boundaries around our models. There is a very appropriate number of domain concepts to model in a given Bounded Context, neither more nor less.

Of course this is rarely as easy for each of us to achieve as when Mozart would compose a symphony with the ease of writing a letter to a friend. At any given time we may have missed an opportunity to refine the domain model to some degree. During each iteration we challenge our assumptions about the model, which forces us to add or remove a concept or change the way concepts behave and collaborate. But the point is that *we face that challenge time and again*, and using DDD principles *we give serious consideration to what belongs and what does not*. We use Bounded Context and tools such as Context Maps to help analyze what is truly part of a Core Domain. We don't resort to applying arbitrary segregation rules based on non-DDD principles.

The Beautiful Sound of Domain Models

If our models were music, they would have the unmistakable sound of completeness, purity, power, and possibly even elegance and beauty.

If we constrain a given Bounded Context too stringently, gaping holes result from vital but missing contextual concepts. And if we keep piling concepts onto the model that don't express the core of the business problem being solved, we will muddy the waters so much that we will fail to observe and understand what is essential. Our goal? If our models were music, they would have the unmistakable sound of completeness, purity, power, and possibly even

---

6. Orion Pictures, Warner Brothers, 1984.

elegance and beauty. The number of notes—the Modules, Aggregates, Events, and Services inside—would be neither more nor less than what the correct design requires. Those "listening" in on the model would never have to ask what that strange "sound" is in the middle of an otherwise harmonious symphony. Nor would they be distracted by moments of complete silence caused by a missing page or two of musical notes.

What could lead us into creating a wrong-sized Bounded Context? We might mistakenly allow architectural influences, rather than the Ubiquitous Language, to guide us. Perhaps the way a platform, framework, or some infrastructure is typically used to package and deploy components could unduly influence the way we think about Bounded Contexts, treating them as technical rather than linguistic boundaries.

Another trap would be to divide Bounded Contexts in order to distribute tasks to available developer resources. Technical leads and project managers might think it is easier for developers to manage smaller tasks. While that might be the case, enforcing boundaries for the sake of task distribution plays false to the linguistic motivations of contextual modeling. In fact, there is no need to impose fake boundaries in order to manage technical resources.

The important question is, What does the Language of the domain experts indicate about the real contextual boundaries?

When a fake Context is formulated in order to address an architectural component or developer resources, the Language becomes fragmented and lacks expressiveness. Hence, focus on the Core Domain with the concepts that naturally fit together into a single Bounded Context, according to the Language spoken by domain experts. After you do so, you can identify the components that naturally fit in a single, cohesive model. Keep all such components in the Bounded Context.

Sometimes the problem of creating miniature Bounded Contexts can be avoided with careful application of Modules. Given an analysis of a set of services that are spread across multiple "Bounded Contexts," you will find that judicious use of Modules could reduce the total number of actual Bounded Contexts to just one. Modules can also be used as a means to divide developer responsibilities, hence managing task distribution using a more appropriate tactical approach.

Whiteboard Time ───

- Draw a Bounded Context of your current model as a big, irregularly shaped ellipse.

▌ Even if you don't yet have an explicit model, still think of the Language within.

- Inside the ellipse, write the names of the primary concepts that you are sure your code implements. See if you can spot concepts that should be there but are missing, and those that are there but shouldn't be. What should you do about each of those problems?

> **Be Careful to Practice DDD Using Linguistic Drivers**
> The bottom line: If you are not following the Language drivers, you are not working with and listening to domain experts to create the Bounded Context. Think carefully about the size of your Bounded Contexts. Don't be too quick to miniaturize them.

Aligning with Technical Components

It doesn't hurt to think about a Bounded Context in terms of the technical components that house it. Just keep in mind that technical components don't define the Context. Let's consider some common ways that they are composed and deployed.

When using an IDE such as Eclipse or IntelliJ IDEA, a Bounded Context is often housed in a single project. When using Visual Studio and .NET, you may favor dividing your user interface, Application Services, and domain model into separate projects within the same solution, or you may decide on another division. The source tree of the project may be limited to the domain model itself, or it may contain surrounding **Layers (4)** or **Hexagonal (4)** areas. There is a lot of flexibility here. Using Java, the top-level package generally defines the highest-level Module name for the Bounded Context. Using one of the preceding examples, that could be done something like this:

```
com.mycompany.optimalpurchasing
```

The source tree of this Bounded Context would be further divided according to Architectural responsibilities. Here's a view of the project's possible second-level package names:

```
com.mycompany.optimalpurchasing.presentation
com.mycompany.optimalpurchasing.application
com.mycompany.optimalpurchasing.domain.model
com.mycompany.optimalpurchasing.infrastructure
```

Even with these modular divisions, only a single team should work in a single Bounded Context.

A Single Team for a Single Bounded Context

Assigning a single team to work on a single Bounded Context is not an attempt to limit flexibility to team organization. It's not as if teams can't be arranged as needed, or that individual members of one team cannot be used on one or more other projects. A company should use people in the way that best fits its needs. This is simply stating that it is best for one well-defined, cohesive team of domain experts and developers to focus on one Ubiquitous Language modeled in an explicit Bounded Context. If you assign two or more distinct teams to one Bounded Context, each team will contribute to a divergent and ill-defined Ubiquitous Language.

There is also the possibility that two teams will cooperate in the design of a Shared Kernel, which is actually not a typical Bounded Context. This Context Mapping pattern forms an intimate relationship between two teams, which requires ongoing consultation when model changes are deemed necessary. This modeling approach is less common and is generally avoided if possible.

When using Java, we may technically house a Bounded Context in one or more JAR files, including WAR or EAR files. The desire for modularization may have an influence here. Loosely coupled parts of the domain model could be housed in separate JAR files, enabling them to be deployed independently by version. This would be especially useful with large models. Creating multiple JAR files of a single model would provide the advantage of managing versions of its elements using OSGi bundles or using Java 8 Jigsaw modules. Thus, various high-level modules, their versions, and their dependencies could be managed as bundles/modules. There are at least four such bundles/modules represented by the preceding DDD-based, second-level Modules, and possibly more.

For a native Windows Bounded Context, such as for the .NET platform, deployment would be done using separate assemblies in DLL files. Think of a DLL as having similar deployment motivations to those of JAR described previously. The model could be partitioned for deployment in similar ways. All common language runtime (CLR) modularization is managed through assemblies. The specific version of an assembly and the versions of dependent assemblies are recorded in the assembly's manifest. See [MSDN Assemblies].

Sample Contexts

Because the samples represent a greenfield development environment, the three chosen Bounded Contexts eventually align in the most desirable way, one-to-one, with their respective Subdomains. The team wasn't successful in aligning them one-to-one from the start, which teaches a crucial lesson. The ultimate outcome is shown in Figure 2.7.

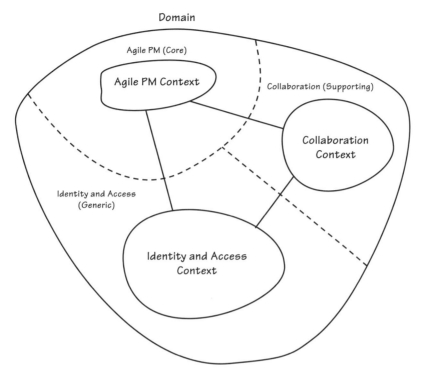

Figure 2.7 The assessment view of the sample Bounded Contexts in fully aligned Subdomains

The following material demonstrates how the three models form a realistic, modern enterprise solution. There are always multiple Bounded Contexts in any project in the real world. Integration among them is an important scenario in today's enterprise. In addition to Bounded Context and Subdomains, we must also grasp Context Mapping with **Integration (13)**.

Let's look at the three Bounded Contexts provided as sample DDD implementations.[7] They are the *Collaboration Context*, the *Identity and Access Context*, and the *Agile Project Management Context*.

Collaboration Context

Business collaboration tools are one of the most important areas for creating and facilitating a synergistic workplace in the fast-paced economy. Anything

---

7. Note that Context Maps provides more detail about the actual three sample Bounded Contexts, how they are related to each other, and how they are integrated. Still, more depth is concentrated on the Core Domain.

that can help increase productivity, transfer knowledge, promote idea sharing, and associatively manage the creative process so results will not be misplaced is a boon to the corporate success equation. Whether the software tools offer features for broad communities or for narrow audiences targeted to daily activities and projects, corporations are flocking to the best-of-breed online tools, and SaaSOvation wants a share of that market.

The core team tasked to design and implement the *Collaboration Context* was given a first-release mandate to support the following minimum suite of tools: forums, shared calendars, blogs, instant messaging, wiki, message boards, document management, announcements and alerts, activity tracking, and RSS feeds. While supporting a broad array of features, each of the individual collaboration tools in the suite can also support targeted, narrow team environments, yet they remain in the same Bounded Context because they are all part of collaboration. Unfortunately this book cannot provide the entire collaboration suite. However, we do explore parts of the domain model for the tools represented in Figure 2.8, namely, Forums and Shared Calendars.

Now, to the team experience . . .

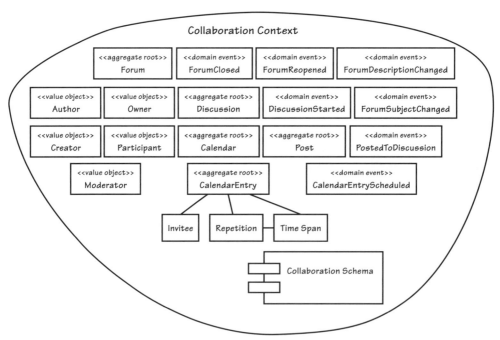

Figure 2.8 The *Collaboration Context*. Its Ubiquitous Language determines what belongs inside the boundary. For readability, some model elements are not shown. The same goes for user interface (UI) and Application Service components.

Tactical DDD was used from the inception of product development, but the team was still learning some of DDD's finer points.
In fact, they were really using what amounted to DDD-Lite,
employing the tactical patterns mostly for a technical payoff.
Sure, they were attempting to capture the Ubiquitous Language
of collaboration, but they didn't understand that the model had
clear limits that couldn't be stretched too far. As a result, they
made a mistake by baking security and permissions into the
collaboration model. The team realized well into the project that designing security and
permissions as part of their model was not as desirable as they once thought.

Early on they were not overly concerned about or fully aware of the danger of
constructing an application silo. Yet, without using a central security provider, that's
just what would happen. It constituted mixing two models in one. Soon enough they
learned that the confusing entanglement that resulted from blending security concerns into their Core Domain had backfired. Right in the middle of core business
logic, in behavioral methods, developers would check for client permissions to carry
out the request:

```
public class Forum extends Entity {
    ...
    public Discussion startDiscussion(
            String aUsername, String aSubject) {
        if (this.isClosed()) {
            throw new IllegalStateException("Forum is closed.");
        }

        User user = userRepository.userFor(this.tenantId(), aUsername);

        if (!user.hasPermissionTo(Permission.Forum.StartDiscussion)) {
            throw new IllegalStateException(
                    "User may not start forum discussion.");
        }

        String authorUser = user.username();
        String authorName = user.person().name().asFormattedName();
        String authorEmailAddress = user.person().emailAddress();

        Discussion discussion = new Discussion(
                this.tenant(), this.forumId(),
                DomainRegistry.discussionRepository().nextIdentity(),
                authorUser, authorName, authorEmailAddress,
                aSubject);

        return discussion;
    }
    ...
}
```

> **Did I Just See a Train Wreck?**
>
> Some developers consider the chaining of multiple expressions in a row, such as `user.person().name().asFormattedName()`, a "train wreck." Others consider it expressiveness in code. I am not addressing either of those viewpoints. Rather, I am focused on the muddled model. The "train wreck" is another topic entirely.

This was really bad design. Developers should not have been able to reference `User` here, let alone query a **Repository (12)** for one. Even `Permission` should have been out of reach. It was possible because these were wrongly designed as part of the collaboration model. What is more, this distortion caused them to overlook a concept that they should have modeled, namely, `Author`. Instead of gathering three related attributes into an explicit Value Object, the developers seemed to be satisfied to deal with the data elements separately. Security was on their minds rather than collaboration.

This was not an isolated case. Every collaboration object had similar issues. As the risk of creating a Big Ball of Mud was becoming imminent, the team decided the code had to change. Besides, the team also wanted to switch from a permissions approach to security and use role-based access management instead. What would they do?

Being users of agile development methodologies and eventual builders of agile project management tools, they were not afraid to employ refactoring efforts just in time. So iteratively refactor they would. Still the question remained: What were the best DDD patterns to get them out of their bad situation, a deep bog of ill-placed code?

As a few on the team spent extra hours poring over the [Evans] tactical building block patterns, they realized that these were not the answer. They had followed the guidance in those patterns to create Aggregates by composing Entities and Value Objects in a technical way. They used Repositories and **Domain Services (7)** as well. Nonetheless, they were missing something important, and possibly this pointed to the need to pay closer attention to the second half of [Evans].

Finally doing so, they noted some empowering techniques. As they pored over "Part III: Refactoring toward Deeper Insight" [Evans], it was obvious that DDD offered far more than they once thought. With the techniques gleaned from that part of [Evans], they now knew how they could improve their current model by paying closer attention to the Ubiquitous Language. By spending more quality time with their domain experts, they could produce a model that more closely resembled their mental model. But that still didn't address the security morass that distorted their vision of a pure collaboration domain model.

Further into the book there was "Part IV: Strategic Design" [Evans]. One of the team members found what proved to be crucial guidance that would eventually lead them to the realization of a Core Domain. One of the first new tools employed was Context Maps, which led to a better understanding of their current project situation. Although a simple exercise, drawing the first Context Map and formulating discussions about their predicament was a big step forward. It led to productive analysis toward a resolution, which eventually unblocked the team.

They now had a few options to make interim refinements, enabling them to stabilize their increasingly brittle model:

1. They could possibly refactor the model into **Responsibility Layers** [Evans], dividing the security and permissions features by pushing them down into a lower logical layer of the existing model. But that didn't seem like the best approach. The use of Responsibility Layers is intended to address large-scale models, or to plan for those that will eventually grow to a large scale. Each layer is meant to remain in the model because it is part of the Core Domain, even though the layers should be carefully divided. On the other hand, what the team was dealing with were misappropriated concepts—ones that didn't belong in the Core Domain.

2. Alternatively they could work toward a **Segregated Core** [Evans]. This could be accomplished by an exhaustive search for all security and permissions concerns in the *Collaboration Context*, followed by the refactoring of the identity and access components into completely separate packages in the same model. It would not produce the ultimate outcome of creating a completely separate Bounded Context, but it would move the team closer to it. This seemed to be precisely what was needed, for the pattern itself states: "The time to chop out a Segregated Core is when you have a large Bounded Context that is critical to the system, but where the essential part of the model is being obscured by a great deal of supporting capability." The supporting capability was definitely security and permissions. The team eventually realized that a separate *Identity and Access Context* would emerge out of these efforts and serve as a Generic Subdomain to their *Collaboration Context*.

The initiative to create a Segregated Core would not be simple. It could require a few weeks of unplanned work. But if they didn't take corrective action and refactor soon, they'd be paying for their lack of corrective action with bugs, coupled with a fragile code base that would not respond well to change. Business leadership helped confirm the wisdom of this direction when they determined that a successful separation into a new business service could someday lead to a new SaaS product.

Importantly, the team now understood the value of Bounded Contexts and of fighting hard to maintain a cohesive Core Domain. Using additional patterns of strategic design, they could segregate reusable models in separate Bounded Contexts and integrate as appropriate.

Likely the future *Identity and Access* Bounded Context would look different from the embedded security and permissions design. Designing for reuse would force the team to focus on a more general-purpose model, one that could be exploited by many applications as necessary. That dedicated team—different from our *Collaboration Context* team, but formed using a few members from it—could also introduce various implementation strategies. The strategies could include use of third-party products and customer-specific integrations, which had become far out of reach due to the embedded security tangle.

Since the development of the Segregated Core became an interim step, we don't focus on those results here. Briefly, it amounted to moving all security and permissions classes to segregated Modules and requiring Application Services clients to check security and permissions using those objects prior to calling into the Core Domain. That freed the Core to implement only collaboration model object compositions and behaviors. The Application Service took care of security and object translation:

```java
public class ForumApplicationService ... {
    ...
    @Transactional
    public Discussion startDiscussion(
            String aTenantId, String aUsername,
            String aForumId, String aSubject) {
        Tenant tenant = new Tenant(aTenantId);
        ForumId forumId = new ForumId(aForumId);

        Forum forum = this.forum(tenant, forumId);

        if (forum == null) {
            throw new IllegalStateException("Forum does not exist.");
        }

        Author author =
                this.collaboratorService.authorFrom(
                        tenant,
                        anAuthorId);

        Discussion newDiscussion =
                forum.startDiscussion(
                        this.forumNavigationService(),
                        author,
                        aSubject);

        this.discussionRepository.add(newDiscussion);

        return newDiscussion;
    }
    ...
}
```

The result to the `Forum` looked like this:

```java
public class Forum extends Entity {
    ...

    public Discussion startDiscussionFor(
        ForumNavigationService aForumNavigationService,
        Author anAuthor,
        String aSubject) {
        if (this.isClosed()) {
            throw new IllegalStateException("Forum is closed.");
        }
```

```
Discussion discussion = new Discussion(
        this.tenant(),
        this.forumId(),
        aForumNavigationService.nextDiscussionId(),
        anAuthor,
        aSubject);

DomainEventPublisher
    .instance()
    .publish(new DiscussionStarted(
            discussion.tenant(),
            discussion.forumId(),
            discussion.discussionId(),
            discussion.subject()));

return discussion;
}
...
}
```

This removed the `User` and `Permission` tangle and focused the model strictly on collaboration. Again, it was not a picture-perfect outcome, but it prepared the team for the future refactorings to separate and integrate Bounded Contexts. The *Collaboration Context* team would finally remove all the security and permissions Modules and types from their Bounded Context and gladly employ the new *Identity and Access Context*. Their ultimate goal to make security central and reusable was now within reach.

Granted, the team could have started out going in the other direction. They could have miniaturized Bounded Contexts by creating a number of separate ones, ending up with ten or more total—one for each collaboration facility (for example, Forum and Calendar as separate models). What could have led them in that direction? Since most of the collaboration facilities were not coupled to the others, each could be deployed as an autonomous component. By placing each facility in a separate Bounded Context, the team could create ten or so natural deployment units. True, but producing ten different domain models was unnecessary to achieve those deployment objectives and would probably only serve to work against the modeling principles of the Ubiquitous Language.

Instead, the team kept the model as one but chose to create a separate JAR file for each collaboration facility. Using Jigsaw modularization, they created a version-based deployment unit for each. Besides JAR files for the natural collaboration divisions, they also needed one for shared model objects, such as `Tenant`, `Moderator`, `Author`, `Participant`, and others. Going this route supported the development of a unified Ubiquitous Language, while meeting the deployment objectives that had architectural and application management advantages.

With this understanding we can examine how the *Identity and Access Context* came about.

Identity and Access Context

Most enterprise applications today need to have some form of security and permissions components in place to ensure that people who try to use the system are authentic users and are authorized to do what they attempt to do. As we just analyzed, a naive approach to application security builds users and permissions in with each discrete system, which creates a silo effect in every application.

Cowboy Logic

LB: "You have no locks on your barns and silos, but nobody steals your corn?"

AJ: "My dog Tumbleweed cares for access management. It's my own silo effect."

LB: "I don't think you really understand the book."

The users of one system cannot be easily associated with the users of any other systems, even though many of the people using them are the same. To prevent silos from popping up all over the business landscape, architects need to centralize security and permissions. This is done by purchasing or developing an identity and access management system. The route chosen will depend much on the level of sophistication needed, the time available, and the total cost of ownership.

Correcting the identity and access tangle in CollabOvation would be a multistep process. First the team refactored using Segregated Core [Evans]; see the "Collaboration Context" section. This step served the intended purpose at the time to ensure that CollabOvation was cleansed of security and permissions concerns. However, they figured that identity and access management should eventually occupy a context boundary of its own. That would require an even greater effort.

This constitutes a new Bounded Context—the *Identity and Access Context*—and will be used by other Bounded Contexts through standard DDD integration techniques. To the consuming contexts the *Identity and Access Context* is a Generic Subdomain. The product will be named IdOvation.

As Figure 2.9 shows, the *Identity and Access Context* provides support for multitenant subscribers. When developing an SaaS product, this goes without

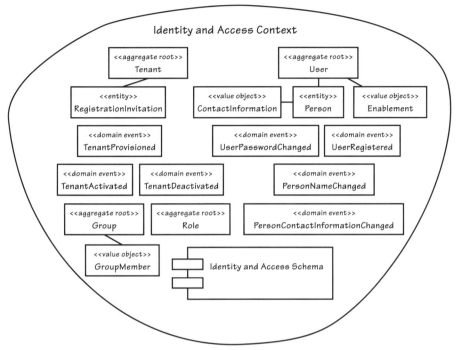

Figure 2.9 The *Identity and Access Context*. Everything inside the boundary is in context per the Ubiquitous Language. There are other components in this Bounded Context, some in the model and some in other layers, but they are not shown here for the sake of readability. The same goes for UI and Application Service components.

saying. Each tenant and every object asset owned by a given tenant would have a completely unique identity, logically isolating each tenant from all others. Users of the systems are registered via self-service by invitation only. Secured access is handled by means of an authentication service, and passwords are always highly encrypted. Groups of users and nested groups enable sophisticated identity management across the entire organization and down to the smallest of teams. Access to system resources is managed through simple, elegant, yet powerful role-based permissions.

As a more advanced step, throughout the model **Domain Events** (8) are published when model behaviors cause state transformations of special interest to observers of such occurrences. These Events are generally modeled as nouns combined with verbs in the past tense, such as `TenantProvisioned`, `UserPasswordChanged`, `PersonNameChanged`, and others as well.

The next chapter, "Context Maps," shows how the *Identity and Access Context* is used by the other two sample Contexts using DDD integration patterns.

Agile Project Management Context

The lightweight methods of agile development have propelled it to popularity, especially following the creation of the Agile Manifesto in 2001. In its vision statement, SaaSOvation has as its second primary and strategic initiative to develop an agile project management application. Here's how things went . . .

After three quarters of successful Collab-Ovation subscription sales, planned upgrades with incremental improvements per customer feedback, and better-than-expected revenues, the company's plans for ProjectOvation were launched. It's their new Core Domain, and top developers from CollabOvation will be pulled in to leverage their SaaS multitenancy and newfound DDD experience.

The tool focuses on management of agile projects, using Scrum as the iterative and incremental project management framework. ProjectOvation follows the traditional Scrum project management model, complete with product, product owner, team, backlog items, planned releases, and sprints. Backlog item estimation is provided through business value calculators that use cost-benefit analysis.

The business plan began with a two-headed vision. CollabOvation and Project-Ovation would not go down entirely separate paths. SaaSOvation and its board of directors envisioned innovation around weaving collaboration tools in with agile software development. Thus, CollabOvation features will be offered as an optional add-on to ProjectOvation. Because it provides add-on features, CollabOvation is a Supporting Subdomain to ProjectOvation. Product owners and team members will interact in product discussions, release and sprint planning, and backlog item discussions, and they will share calendars, and more. There is a future plan to include corporate resource planning with ProjectOvation, but initial agile product goals must first be met.

The technical stakeholders originally planned to develop the ProjectOvation features as an extension of the CollabOvation model by using a revision control system source branch. That actually would have been a huge mistake, although typical of those not focusing proper attention on Subdomains in their problem space and Bounded Contexts in their solution space.

Fortunately the technical staff learned from early problems with the muddled *Collaboration Context*. The lesson they learned from that experience convinced them that even starting down the path of combining the agile project management model with the collaboration model would be a major mistake. Now the teams were starting to think with a strong leaning toward DDD strategic design.

Figure 2.10 shows that as a result of *adopting a strategic design mentality*, the ProjectOvation team now appropriately thinks of their consumers as Product Owners

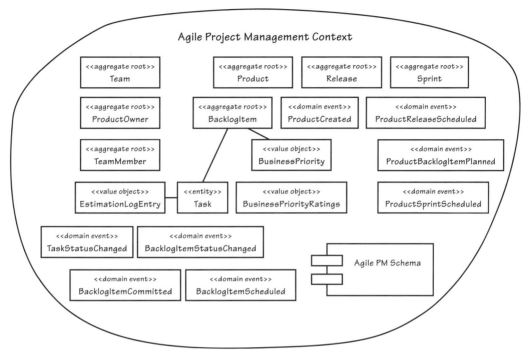

Figure 2.10   The *Agile Project Management Context*. The Ubiquitous Language of this Bounded Context is concerned with Scrum-based agile products, iterations, and releases. For readability, some components, including those from the UI and Application Services, are not shown here.

and Team Members. After all, those are the project member roles played by Scrum practitioners. The users and roles are managed inside the separate *Identity and Access Context*. By using that Bounded Context, self-service enables subscribers to manage their own personal identity. Administrative controls enable managers, such as product owners, to specify their product team members. With the roles properly managed, the Product Owners and Team Members can be created where they belong, inside the *Agile Project Management Context*. The remainder of the project's design will benefit as the team focuses on capturing the Ubiquitous Language of agile project management into a carefully crafted domain model.

One requirement calls for ProjectOvation to operate as a set of autonomous application services. The team desires to limit the dependency of ProjectOvation on other Bounded Contexts to a reasonable periodicity, or at least as much as is practical. Generally speaking, ProjectOvation will be capable of operating on its own, and if IdOvation or CollabOvation were to go offline for any number of reasons, ProjectOvation would continue to function autonomously. Of course, in that case some things might get out of sync for a while, and probably a very short while at that, but the system would continue to function.

The Context Gives Each Term a Very Specific Meaning

A Scrum-based `Product` has any number of `BacklogItem` instances that describe the software being constructed. This is far different from the products on an e-commerce site that you put in a shopping cart to purchase. How do we know? Because of the Context. We understand what our `Product` means because it is in the *Agile PM Context*. In an *Online Store Context*, `Product` means something very different. The team didn't need to name the product `ScrumProduct` in order to communicate the difference.

The Core Domain of Product, Backlog Items, Tasks, Sprints, and Releases is already off to a better start given the SaaSOvation experience gains. Still, we are interested in looking in on the big lessons they learned along the steep learning curve of carefully modeling **Aggregates (10)**.

Wrap-Up

That was a seriously intense discussion of the importance of DDD strategic design!

- You've looked into Domains, Subdomains, and Bounded Contexts.

- You've discovered how to strategically assess the current lay of the enterprise landscape using both problem space and solution space assessments.

- You peered extensively into the details of how to use Bounded Contexts to explicitly segregate models linguistically.

- You've learned what is included in Bounded Contexts, how to right-size them, and how they can be built for deployment.

- You felt the pain the SaaSOvation team experienced early on in the design of the *Collaboration Context* and how the team worked their way out of that bad situation.

- You saw the formation of the current Core Domain, the *Agile Project Management Context*, which is the focus of the design and implementation examples.

As promised, the next chapter takes a deep dive into Context Mapping. It is an essential strategic modeling tool to use in designs. You may have figured out that we've done a bit of Context Mapping already in this chapter. It was unavoidable as we assessed different domains. Still, we will go into much more detail next.

Chapter 3

Context Maps

> *Whatever course you decide upon, there is always someone to tell you
> that you are wrong. There are always difficulties arising which tempt
> you to believe that your critics are right. To map out a course of action
> and follow it to an end requires courage.*
> —*Ralph Waldo Emerson*

The **Context Map** of a project can be expressed in two ways. The easier way is to draw a simple diagram that shows the mappings between two or more existing **Bounded Contexts** (2). Understand, however, that you are just drawing a simple diagram of what already exists. The drawing illustrates how the actual software Bounded Contexts in the solution space are related to one another through integration. This means that the more detailed way to express Context Maps is as the source code implementations of the integrations. We'll look at both ways in this chapter, but for most of the implementation details see **Integrating Bounded Contexts (13)**.

At a high level, keep in mind that this chapter focuses on the *solution space assessment*, whereas the previous chapter dealt quite a bit with the *problem space assessment*.

Road Map to This Chapter

- Learn why drawing a Context Map is essential for the success of your project.
- See how easy it can be to draw a meaningful Context Map.
- Consider the common organizational and system relationships and how they affect your projects.
- Learn from the SaaSOvation teams as they produce Maps to get control of their projects.

Why Context Maps Are So Essential

When you start out on a DDD effort, first draw a visual Context Map of your *current project situation*. Produce a Context Map of the current Bounded

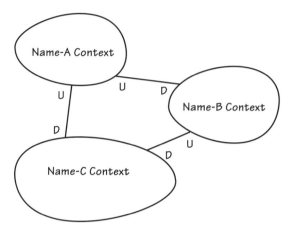

Figure 3.1   A Context Map of an abstract Domain. Three Bounded Contexts and their relationships are drawn. The U stands for Upstream and D stands for Downstream.

Contexts involved in your project and the integration relationships between them. Figure 3.1 shows an abstract Context Map. We'll be filling in the details as we progress.

This simple drawing is your team's Map. Other project teams can refer to it, but they should also create their own Maps if they are implementing DDD. Your Map is drawn primarily to give your team the solution space perspective it needs to succeed. Other teams may not be using DDD and/or they may not care about your perspective.

> **Oh, No! There's New Terminology!**
> We are introducing Big Ball of Mud, Customer-Supplier, and Conformist here. Be patient; these and other DDD team and integration relationships noted here are discussed in detail later in this chapter.

For example, when you are integrating Bounded Contexts in a large enterprise, you may need to interface with a **Big Ball of Mud**. The team maintaining the muddy monolith may not care what direction your project takes as long as you adhere to their API. So, they aren't going to gain any insight from your Map or what you do with their API. Still, your Map needs to reflect the kind of relationship you have with them, because *it will give your team needed insight and indicate areas where inter-team communication is imperative*. Having that understanding can do much to help your team succeed.

> **Communications Facility**
> Besides giving you an inventory of systems you must interact with, a Context Map serves as a catalyst for inter-team communication.

Imagine what would happen if your team assumes that the team maintaining the muddy monolith will provide new APIs that you are depending on, but they don't intend to provide them, or they don't even know what you are thinking. Your team is counting on a **Customer-Supplier** relationship with the mud. The legacy team, however, by providing only what they currently have, forces your team into an unexpected **Conformist** relationship. Depending on how late in the project you got the bad news, this unseen yet actual relationship could delay your delivery or even cause your project's failure. By drawing a Context Map early, you will be forced to think carefully about your relationships with all other projects you depend on.

> Identify each model in play on the project and define its BOUNDED CONTEXT. . . . Name each BOUNDED CONTEXT, and make the names part of the UBIQUITOUS LANGUAGE. Describe the points of contact between the models, outlining explicit translation for any communication and highlighting any sharing. [Evans, p. 345]

When the CollabOvation team first started developing its greenfield model, they should have used a Context Map. Even though they were nearly starting from scratch, stating their assumptions about the project in the form of a Map would have prompted them to think  about separate Bounded Contexts. They still could have listed significant modeling elements on a whiteboard, and then gathered them into groups of related linguistic terms. That would have forced recognition of linguistic boundaries and resulted in a simple Context Map. However, they actually didn't understand strategic modeling in the least. They first needed to attain a strategic modeling breakthrough. Later on they did make the crucial discovery of this project-saving tool, applying it to their eventual benefit. When the subsequent Core Domain project got under way, it again paid off substantially.

Let's see how you can quickly produce a useful Context Map.

Drawing Context Maps

A Context Map captures the *existing* terrain. First, you should map the present, not the imagined future. If the landscape will change as your current project progresses, you can update the Map at that time. First focus on the current situation so you can form an understanding of where you are and determine where to go next.

Creating a graphical Context Map need not be complicated. Your first option is always hand-drawn diagrams where whiteboards and dry-erase markers rule. The style used here is easily adapted as shown by [Brandolini]. If you decide to use a tool to capture the drawing, be sure to keep it informal.

Referring back to Figure 3.1, the Bounded Context names are just place-holders, as are the integration relationships. They would all be actual names in a tangible Map. The upstream and downstream relationships are shown, the meanings of which are explained later in the chapter.

Whiteboard Time

Draw a simple diagram of your current project situation that communicates at a high level where the boundaries are, the relationships between them and their teams, what kinds of integrations are involved, and the necessary translations between them.

> Remember that software implements what's in the drawing. If you need more information about what you should draw, consider the systems that your Bounded Context integrates with.

Sometimes we'll want to zoom in and add more detail to a given part of a Context Map. It's just a different perspective on the same Context(s). Besides boundaries, relationships, and translations, we may want to include other items such as **Modules (9)**, significant **Aggregates (10)**, perhaps how teams are allocated, and any other information relevant to the Contexts. These techniques are demonstrated later in the chapter.

All of the drawings and any prose can be placed into a single reference document if it has value to the team. With any such effort we should avoid ceremony and remain both simple and agile. The more ceremony you add, the fewer people will want to use the Map. Putting too much detail in diagrams won't really help the team. Open communication is the key. As conversations unveil strategic insight, add it to the Context Map.

> **No, It's Not Enterprisy**
> A Context Map is *not* an Enterprise Architecture or system topology diagram.

A Context Map is *not* an Enterprise Architecture or system topology diagram. The information is conveyed relative to interacting models and DDD organizational patterns. Still, Context Maps may be used in high-level architectural investigations, providing views of the enterprise not otherwise available. They may highlight architectural deficiencies such as integration bottlenecks. Because they exhibit an organizational dynamic, Context Maps may even help us identify sticky governance issues that could block progress, and other team and management challenges that are more difficult to uncover using other methods.

Cowboy Logic

AJ: "The missus said, 'I was out in the pasture with the cows; didn't you notice me?' I said, 'Nope.' She didn't talk to me for a week."

The diagrams deserve to be posted prominently on a wall in a team area. If the team frequents a wiki, the diagrams might also be uploaded there. If a wiki will be largely ignored, don't bother. It's been said that a wiki can be a place where information goes to die. No matter where they are displayed, Context Maps will be hidden in plain sight unless the team pays regular attention to them through meaningful discussion.

Projects and Organizational Relationships

To briefly reiterate, SaaSOvation is on a path to develop and refine three products:

1. A social collaboration suite product, CollabOvation, enables registered users to publish content of business value using popular Web-based tools such as forums, shared calendars, blogs, wikis, and the like. This is the SaaSOvation flagship product and was the company's first Core **Domain (2)** (although the team didn't know the DDD terminology at the time). It is the Context from which IdOvation's (point 2) model was eventually extracted. CollabOvation now uses IdOvation as a **Generic Subdomain (2)**. CollabOvation will itself be consumed as a **Supporting Subdomain (2)**, being an optional add-on to ProjectOvation (point 3).

2. A reusable identity and access management model, IdOvation provides secure role-based access management for registered users. These features were first combined with CollabOvation (point 1), but that implementation was limited and not reusable. SaaSOvation has refactored CollabOvation, introducing a new, clean Bounded Context. A key product feature is the

support of multiple tenants, which is vital to an SaaS application. IdOvation serves as a Generic Subdomain to its consuming models.

3. An agile project management product, ProjectOvation, is at this point in time the new Core Domain. Users of this SaaS product can create project management assets, as well as analysis and design artifacts, and track progress using a Scrum-based execution framework. As with CollabOvation, ProjectOvation uses IdOvation as a Generic Subdomain. One of the innovative features adds team collaboration (point 1) to agile project management, enabling discussions around Scrum products, releases, sprints, and individual backlog items.

Finally, the Definitions!
The organizational and integration patterns mentioned previously are defined . . .

What are the relationships between these Bounded Contexts and their individual project teams? There are several DDD organizational and integration patterns, one of which commonly exists between any two Bounded Contexts. Each of the following definitions is largely quoted from [Evans, Ref]:

- **Partnership**: When teams in two Contexts will succeed or fail together, a cooperative relationship needs to emerge. The teams institute a process for coordinated planning of development and joint management of integration. The teams must cooperate on the evolution of their interfaces to accommodate the development needs of both systems. Interdependent features should be scheduled so that they are completed for the same release.

- **Shared Kernel**: Sharing part of the model and associated code forms a very intimate interdependency, which can leverage design work or undermine it. Designate with an explicit boundary some subset of the domain model that the teams agree to share. Keep the kernel small. This explicit shared stuff has special status and shouldn't be changed without consultation with the other team. Define a continuous integration process that will keep the kernel model tight and align the **Ubiquitous Language (1)** of the teams.

- **Customer-Supplier Development**: When two teams are in an upstream-downstream relationship, where the upstream team may succeed interdependently of the fate of the downstream team, the needs of the downstream team come to be addressed in a variety of ways with a wide range of consequences. Downstream priorities factor into upstream planning. Negotiate and budget tasks for downstream requirements so that everyone understands the commitment and schedule.

- **Conformist**: When two development teams have an upstream/downstream relationship in which the upstream team has no motivation to provide for the downstream team's needs, the downstream team is helpless. Altruism may motivate upstream developers to make promises, but they are unlikely to be fulfilled. The downstream team eliminates the complexity of translation between bounded contexts by slavishly adhering to the model of the upstream team.

- **Anticorruption Layer**: Translation layers can be simple, even elegant, when bridging well-designed Bounded Contexts with cooperative teams. But when control or communication is not adequate to pull off a shared kernel, partner, or customer-supplier relationship, translation becomes more complex. The translation layer takes on a more defensive tone. As a downstream client, create an isolating layer to provide your system with functionality of the upstream system in terms of your own domain model. This layer talks to the other system through its existing interface, requiring little or no modification to the other system. Internally, the layer translates in one or both directions as necessary between the two models.

- **Open Host Service**: Define a protocol that gives access to your subsystem as a set of services. Open the protocol so that all who need to integrate with you can use it. Enhance and expand the protocol to handle new integration requirements, except when a single team has idiosyncratic needs. Then, use a one-off translator to augment the protocol for that special case so that the shared protocol can stay simple and coherent.

- **Published Language**: The translation between the models of two Bounded Contexts requires a common language. Use a well-documented shared language that can express the necessary domain information as a common medium of communication, translating as necessary into and out of that language. Published Language is often combined with Open Host Service.

- **Separate Ways**: We must be ruthless when it comes to defining requirements. If two sets of functionality have no significant relationship, they can be completely cut loose from each other. Integration is always expensive, and sometimes the benefit is small. Declare a bounded context to have no connection to the others at all, enabling developers to find simple, specialized solutions within this small scope.

- **Big Ball of Mud**: As we survey existing systems, we find that, in fact, there are parts of systems, often large ones, where models are mixed and boundaries are inconsistent. Draw a boundary around the entire mess and designate it a Big Ball of Mud. Do not try to apply sophisticated modeling within this Context. Be alert to the tendency for such systems to sprawl into other Contexts.

By integrating with the *Identity and Access Context*, both the *Collaboration Context* and the *Agile Project Management Context* avoid going their Separate Ways with respect to security and permissions. True, Separate Ways may be applied Context-wide for a specific system, but it can also be employed on a case-by-case basis. For example, one team could refuse to use a centralized security system but may still choose to integrate with some other corporate standard facilities.

The teams will cooperate with Customer-Supplier roles. There's no way that SaaSOvation's management will allow one team to force others to be Conformists. It's not that a Conformist relationship is always negative. Rather, Customer-Supplier requires commitment on the part of the Supplier to provide support for the Customer, which fosters the kind of inter-team relationships SaaSOvation thinks it needs to achieve complete success. Of course, Customers aren't always right, and so some give-and-take must exist. Overall it is the positive organizational relationship that the teams need to maintain.

The teams' integrations will make use of Open Host Service and Published Language. Perhaps surprisingly they will also employ Anticorruption Layer. This is not a contradiction, even though they are establishing open standards between their Bounded Contexts. They can still realize the benefits of isolated translation by using its fundamental principles in the downstream Contexts, but with less complexity than needed when consuming a Big Ball of Mud. The translation layers will be simple and elegant.

The Context Map drawings that follow use these abbreviations to indicate the patterns employed at each end of a relationship:

- ACL for Anticorruption Layer

- OHS for Open Host Service

- PL for Published Language

As you review the following sample Context Maps and supporting text, it may be helpful to glance back at Chapter 2, "Domains, Subdomains, and Bounded Contexts." The diagrams of each of the three sample Bounded Contexts are also useful here. Since they remain fairly high-level, those diagrams could be included as part of the Maps for each Context, although they are not repeated here.

Mapping the Three Contexts

Now let's jump into the team experience so we can learn from what they did . . .

When the CollabOvation team realized the tangle they had created, they dug into [Evans] to help find their way out of it. Among other discoveries of enormous value within the strategic design patterns, they found a practical tool named Context Maps. They also found a helpful article online by [Brandolini] expanding on this technique. Since the tool's guidance indicated that they should map the existing terrain, that's the first step they took. Figure 3.2 shows the results.

The first Map produced by the team highlights their early recognition of the existence of a Bounded Context that they named *Collaboration Context*. By the odd shape of the existing boundary they appropriately conveyed the likely existence of a second Context, but one without a clean and clear separation from the Core Domain.

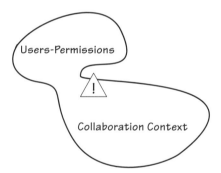

Figure 3.2 The tangle within the *Collaboration Context* caused by unwelcome concepts is exposed by this Map. The caution sign points out the area of impurity.

A narrow passage near the top allows foreign concepts to migrate back and forth almost without censure, as the caution sign indicates. It's not that Context boundaries need to be completely impenetrable. As with any boundary, the team wants the *Collaboration Context* to control with full knowledge what crosses its borders and for what purpose. Otherwise the territory becomes overrun with unknown and possibly unwelcome visitors. In the case of a model, the unwelcome visitors generally cause confusion and bugs. Modelers should be cordial and even welcoming, but under conditions that favor order and harmony. Any foreign concepts entering the boundaries need to demonstrate the right to be there, even taking on characteristics compatible with the territory within.

This analysis led to a better understanding not only of the current condition of the model, but in what direction the project needed to go. Once the project team realized that concepts such as security, users, and permissions did not belong inside the *Collaboration Context*, they responded accordingly. The team had to segregate these from the Core Domain and allow them to enter only under agreeable terms.

This is a vital DDD project commitment. The Language of each Bounded Context must be honored in order for all models to remain pure. Linguistic segregation and a strict adherence to it help each team involved in the project to focus on their own Bounded Context and keep their vision correctly focused on their own work.

Applying Subdomain analysis, or problem space assessment, led the team to the diagram shown in Figure 3.3. Two Subdomains were carved out of a single Bounded Context. Since it is a good goal to align Subdomains one-to-one with Bounded Contexts, this analysis showed the need to separate the single Bounded Context into two.

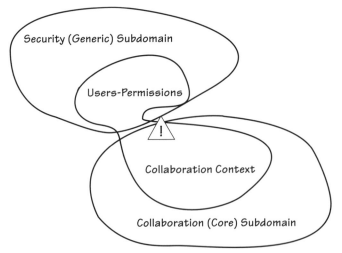

Figure 3.3   The team's Subdomain analysis led to the discovery of two, a Collaboration Core Domain and a Security Generic Subdomain.

The Subdomain and boundary analysis led to decisions. When human users of Col-labOvation interact with the available features, they do so as Participants, Authors, Moderators, and so forth. A variety of other contextual separations are discussed later, but this gives a good idea of the necessary divisions that were created. With that knowledge, the clean and crisp boundaries indicated on the high-level Context Map shown in Figure 3.4 came about. The team used **Segregated Core** [Evans] to refactor to reach this point of clarity. The recognizable shapes of the boundaries act as icons or visual cues for each Context. Keeping the same relative shapes across diagrams can help with cognition.

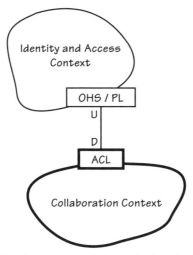

Figure 3.4 The original Core Domain is marked with a bold boundary and integration points. Here IdOvation serves as a Generic Subdomain for the downstream CollabOvation.

The Context Maps usually don't appear all at once as the various sketches may lead you to believe, although when finally understood, they are not difficult to produce. Thought and discussion help to refine a Map through rapid iterations. Some of the refinements might come in the way of integration points, which describe the relationships between Contexts.

The first two Maps indicate the gains made after applying strategic design. After the original CollabOvation project was well under way, the team had factored out identity and access concerns. As they progressed, they produced the Context Map in Figure 3.4. The team sketched only the Core Domain, *Collaboration Context*, along with the new Generic Subdomain, *Identity and Access Context*. They didn't depict any future models, such as the *Agile Project Management Context*. It wouldn't help the team to jump ahead too far. They only needed to correct flaws with what existed. Transformations supporting forthcoming systems would be needed soon enough, and that Map belonged to the future team to produce.

Whiteboard Time

- Thinking of your own Bounded Context, can you identify concepts that don't belong? If so, draw a new Context Map that shows the desired Contexts and relationships between them.

- Which of the nine DDD organizational and integration relationships would you choose, and why?

When the next project involving Project-Ovation was starting up, it was time to augment the existing Map with the new Core Domain, the *Agile Project Management Context*. The results of that mapping are seen in Figure 3.5. It was not premature to capture what was in plan-ning, even though it was not yet in code. The details inside the new Context weren't fully understood, but that would come with discussion. Applying high-level strategic design at this early stage would help all teams understand where their responsibilities lay. Since the third of the three high-level Maps is just an augmentation of the previous, we'll be focusing on it. That's where SaaSOvation is headed. The company has assigned experienced lead developers to the new project. Being the richest of the three Contexts and the current direction, the new Core Domain is where the best developers should be working.

Some essential segregations are already well understood. Similar to the *Collaboration Context*, when users of ProjectOvation create products, plan releases, schedule sprints, and work on the tasks of backlog items, they do so as Product Owners and Team Members. The *Identity and Access Context* is segregated out of the Core Domain. The same goes for their use of the *Collaboration Context*. It is now a Supporting Subdomain. Any consumption by the new model will be protected by boundaries and translations into Core Domain concepts.

Consider the finer details of these diagrams. They are not system architecture diagrams. If they were, given that *Agile Project Management Context* is

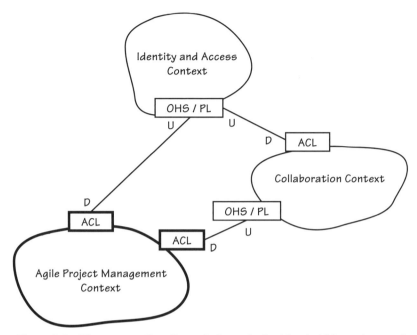

Figure 3.5 The current Core Domain is marked with a bold boundary and integration points. The CollabOvation Supporting Subdomain and IdOvation Generic Subdomain are upstream.

our new Core Domain, we would expect it to reside at the top or center of the diagram. Here, however, it is at the bottom. This possibly curious characteristic indicates visually that the core model is downstream of the others.

This nuance serves as another visual cue. Upstream models have influences on downstream models, as activities on a river that occur upstream tend to have impacts on populations downstream, whether positive or negative. Consider pollutants dumped into a river by a large city. Those pollutants may have little impact on that city, but downstream cities may face severe consequences. The vertical proximity of models on the diagram helps identify the upstream influences on downstream models. The labels *U* and *D* explicitly call this out between each associated model. These labels make vertical positioning of each Context less important, yet it is still visually appealing to employ them.

Cowboy Logic

LB: "When you get yourself a powerful thirst, always
     drink upstream from the herd."

The *Identity and Access Context* is furthest upstream. It has an impact on both the *Collaboration Context* and the *Agile Project Management Context*. Our *Collaboration Context* is also upstream to the *Agile Project Management Context* because the agile model depends on the collaboration model and services. As noted in **Bounded Contexts (2)**, ProjectOvation will operate as autonomously as is practical. Operation must continue largely independent of the availability of surrounding systems. This does not mean that autonomous services can operate entirely independently of upstream models. We must design in ways to drastically limit direct real-time dependencies. Though autonomous, our *Agile Project Management Context* is still downstream of the others.

Outfitting an application with autonomous services does not mean that databases from upstream Contexts are simply replicated into the dependent Context. Replication would force the local system to take on many undesirable responsibilities. That would require the creation of a Shared Kernel, which doesn't really achieve autonomy.

On the latest Map, note the connector boxes on the upstream side of each connection. Both of the connectors are labeled OHS/PL, an abbreviation identifying Open Host Service and Published Language. All three downstream connector boxes are labeled ACL, shorthand for Anticorruption Layer. The technical implementations are covered under **Integrating Bounded Contexts (13)**. Briefly, these integration patterns have these technical characteristics:

- **Open Host Service**: This pattern can be implemented as REST-based resources that client Bounded Contexts interact with. We generally think of Open Host Service as a remote procedure call (RPC) API, but it can be implemented using message exchange.

- **Published Language**: This can be implemented in a few different ways but is many times done as an XML schema. When expressed with REST-based services, the Published Language is rendered as representations of domain concepts. Representations may include both XML and JSON, for example. It is also possible to render representations as Google Protocol Buffers. If you are publishing Web user interfaces, it might also include HTML representations. One advantage to using REST is that each client can specify its preferred Published Language, and the resources render representations in the requested content type. REST also has the advantage of producing hypermedia representations, which facilitates HATEOAS. Hypermedia makes a Published Language very dynamic and interactive, enabling clients to navigate to sets of linked resources. The Language may be published using standard and/or custom media types. A Published Language is also used in an **Event-Driven Architecture (4)**, where **Domain Events (8)** are delivered as messages to subscribing interested parties.

- **Anticorruption Layer:** A **Domain Service** (7) can be defined in the downstream Context for each type of Anticorruption Layer. You may also put an Anticorruption Layer behind a **Repository** (12) interface. If using REST, a client Domain Service implementation accesses a remote Open Host Service. Server responses produce representations as a Published Language. The downstream Anticorruption Layer translates representations into domain objects of its local Context. This is where, for example, the *Collaboration Context* asks the *Identity and Access Context* for a User-in-Moderator-role resource. It might receive the requested resource as XML or JSON, and then translates to a `Moderator`, which is a Value Object. The new `Moderator` instance reflects a concept in terms of the downstream model, not the upstream model.

The chosen patterns are common ones. Constraining the choices helps keep the scope of integration discussed in this book manageable. We'll see, even among these select few patterns, that there is diversity in how they can be applied.

The question remains: Is that all there is to creating a Context Map? Possibly. The high-level view provides a good amount of knowledge about the project as a whole. Still, we may be curious about what goes on inside the connections and the named relationships on each Context. Curiosity among team members influences us to produce a bit more detail. When we zoom in, the somewhat blurred picture of the three integration patterns becomes clearer.

Let's take a minor step back in time. Since the *Collaboration Context* was the first Core Domain, let's peer inside it. First we introduce the zooming technique with the simpler integrations, then progress to the more advanced ones.

Collaboration Context

Now, back to the experience of the Collaboration team . . .

The *Collaboration Context* was the first model and system—the first Core Domain—and its workings are now well understood. The integrations employed here are easier yet less robust in terms of reliability and autonomy. Creating a zoomed Context Map is done with relative ease.

As a client of the REST-based services published by the *Identity and Access Context*, the *Collaboration Context* takes a traditional RPC-like approach to reaching resources. This Context doesn't permanently record any data from the *Identity and Access Context* that it can subsequently reference for local reuse. Rather, it reaches out to the remote system to request information every single time it needs it. This Context is obviously highly dependent on remote services, not autonomous. This is a fact that SaaSOvation is willing to live with for now. Integration with a Generic Subdomain was completely unexpected. To meet their demanding delivery schedule the team couldn't invest time in a more elaborate autonomous design. At the time the up-front ease-of-design perk could not be passed up. After the rollout of ProjectOvation and the experience with autonomy gained there, similar techniques may be employed for CollabOvation.

The boundary objects in the zoomed Map captured in Figure 3.6 request a resource synchronously. When the remote model's representation is received, the boundary objects grab the content of interest out of the representation and translate it, creating the appropriate Value Object instance. A Translation Map to turn the representation into a Value Object is shown in Figure 3.7. Here a `User` in the `Role` of Moderator in the *Identity and Access Context* is translated as a `Moderator` Value Object in the *Collaboration Context*.

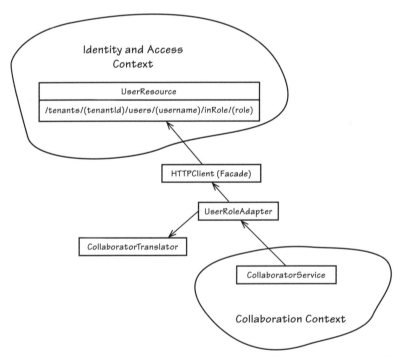

Figure 3.6 A zoom in on the Anticorruption Layer and Open Host Service of the integration between the *Collaboration Context* and the *Identity and Access Context*

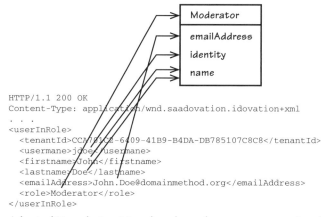

```
HTTP/1.1 200 OK
Content-Type: application/wnd.saadovation.idovation+xml
. . .
<userInRole>
  <tenantId>CCA101C2-6409-41B9-B4DA-DB785107C8C8</tenantId>
  <usermane>jdoe</usermane>
  <firstname>John</firstname>
  <lastname>Doe</lastname>
  <emailAddress>John.Doe@domainmethod.org</emailAddress>
  <role>Moderator</role>
</userInRole>
```

Figure 3.7   A logical Translation Map that shows how a representational state (XML in this case) is mapped to a Value Object in the local model.

Whiteboard Time

Create a Translation Map of one of the interesting aspects of integration found in your project's Bounded Context.

> What if you find the translations overly complex, requiring a lot of data copying and synchronization, making your translated object look a lot like the one from the other model? Perhaps you are using too much from the foreign Bounded Context, adopting too much from that model, and thus causing confusing conflict in your own model.

Unfortunately, if the synchronous request fails because the remote system is unavailable, the entire local execution must fail. The user will be informed of the problem and asked to try again later.

Systems integrations commonly rely on RPC. At a high level RPC appears to be very much like a regular programming procedure call. Libraries and tools make it attractive and easy to use. Unlike calling a procedure that resides in your own process space, however, a remote call has a higher potential for performance-degrading latency or outright failure. Network and remote system load can delay RPC completion. When the RPC target system is unavailable, a user's request to your system will not complete successfully.

While REST-based resource usage isn't really RPC, it still has similar characteristics. Although complete system failure is relatively rare, this is a potentially annoying limitation. The team looks forward to improving on this situation as soon as possible.

Agile Project Management Context

Since the *Agile Project Management Context* is the new Core Domain, let's pay particularly close attention to it. Let's zoom in on it and its connections to other models.

To achieve a greater degree of autonomy than RPC affords, the *Agile Project Management Context* team will need to carefully constrain its use. Out-of-band, or asynchronous, event processing is therefore strategically favored.

A greater degree of autonomy can be achieved when dependent state is already in place in our local system. Some may think of this as a cache of whole dependent objects, but that's not usually the case when using DDD. Instead we create local domain objects translated from the foreign model, maintaining only the minimal amount of state needed by the local model. To get the state in the first place we may need to make limited, well-placed RPC calls, or similar requests for REST-based resources. But any necessary synchronization with remote model changes can often best be achieved through message-oriented notifications published by remote systems. The notifications might be sent on a service bus or a message queue, or be published via REST.

> **Think Minimalistic**
>
> The synchronized state is the limited, minimal attributes of the remote models that are needed by the local model. It's not only to limit our need to synchronize data, it's also a matter of modeling concepts properly.

It pays to limit our use of remote state, even when considering the design of the local modeling elements themselves. We don't want, for example, a `ProductOwner` and a `TeamMember` to in reality reflect a `UserOwner` and a `UserMember` because they take on so many characteristics of the remote `User` object that a hybridization happens unwittingly.

Integration with the *Identity and Access Context*

Looking at the zoomed Map in Figure 3.8, we see that the resource URIs provide notifications about significant Domain Events that have occurred in the *Identity and Access Context*. These are made available through the `NotificationResource` provider, which publishes a RESTful resource. Notification resources are groups of published Domain Events. Every Event ever published is always available for consumption in order of occurrence, but each client is responsible for preventing duplicate consumption.

A custom media type indicates that two resources can be requested:

```
application/vnd.saasovation.idovation+json
//iam/notifications
//iam/notifications/{notificationId}
```

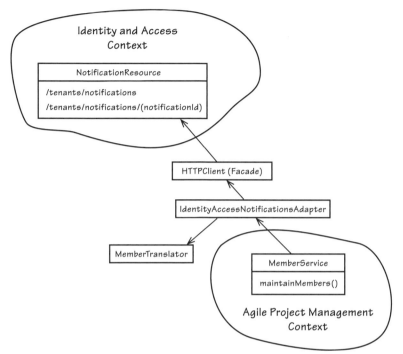

Figure 3.8 A zoom in on the Anticorruption Layer and Open Host Service of the integration between the *Agile Project Management Context* and the *Identity and Access Context*

The first resource URI enables clients to get (literally HTTP GET) the current notification log (a fixed set of individual notifications). Per the documented custom media type,

```
application/vnd.saasovation.idovation+json
```

the URI is considered minted and stable because it never changes. No matter what the current notification log consists of, this URI provides it. The current log is a set of the most recent events that have occurred in the Identity and Access model. The second resource URI enables clients to get and navigate a chain of all previous event-based notifications that have been archived. Why do we need a current log and any number of distinct archived notification logs? See **Domain Events (8)** and **Integrating Bounded Contexts (13)** for details on how feed-based notifications work.

Actually at this point the ProjectOvation team is not committed to using REST in all cases. For example, they are currently negotiating with the CollabOvation team over whether to use a messaging infrastructure instead.

Under consideration is the use of RabbitMQ. Nonetheless, at this time their integrations with the *Identity and Access Context* will be REST-based.

For now let's leave most of the technology details out of the picture and consider the role of each of the objects interacting in the zoomed Map. Here's an explanation of the integration steps visually demonstrated in the sequence diagram found in Figure 3.9:

- `MemberService` is a Domain Service that is responsible for providing `ProductOwner` and `TeamMember` objects to its local model. It is the interface of the basic Anticorruption Layer. Specifically, `maintain-Members()` is used periodically to check for new notifications from the *Identity and Access Context*. This method is not invoked by normal clients of the model. When a recurring timer interval fires, the notified component uses the `MemberService` by invoking method `maintainMembers()`. Figure 3.9 shows the timer recipient as `MemberSynchronizer`, which delegates to `MemberService`.

- The `MemberService` delegates to `IdentityAccessNotification-Adapter`, which plays the role of the Adapter between the Domain Service and the remote system's Open Host Service. The Adapter acts as a client to the remote system. The interaction with the remote `Notification-Resource` is not shown.

- Once the Adapter has received the response from the remote Open Host Service, it delegates to the `MemberTranslator` to translate the Published Language media into concepts of the local system. If the local `Member` instance already exists, the translation updates the existing domain object. This is indicated by the `MemberService` self-delegation to its internal `updateMember()`. The `Member` subclasses are `ProductOwner` and `TeamMember`, which reflect the local contextual concepts.

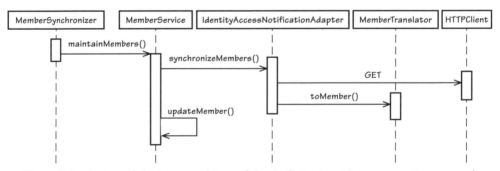

Figure 3.9   A view of the inner workings of the *Agile Project Management Context* and *Identity and Access Anticorruption Layer*

We should not focus on the technologies or integration products involved. Rather, by cleanly separating Bounded Contexts, we are able to keep each Context pure, while applying data from other Contexts to express concepts in our own.

The diagrams and supporting text exemplify how we might create Context Map documents. It need not be extensive but should provide enough background and explanation to bring a new project member up to speed. However, create a document only if it is helpful to the team.

Integration with the *Collaboration Context*   Next, let's consider how the *Agile Project Management Context* interacts with the *Collaboration Context*. Here, too, we strive for autonomy, but this raises the bar, posing some interesting challenges to accomplish the goal of system independence.

ProjectOvation has add-on features that are supplied by CollabOvation. Some include project-based forum discussions and shared calendar scheduling. Users won't directly interact with CollabOvation. ProjectOvation must determine whether the options are available to a given tenant and, if so, on its own facilitate resource creation in CollabOvation.

Consider a section of this *Create a Product* use case:

Precondition: The collaboration feature is enabled (option was purchased).

1. The user provides Product descriptive information.

2. The user indicates a desire for a team discussion.

3. The user requests that the defined Product be created.

4. The system creates the Product with a Forum and Discussion.

A Forum and a Discussion must be created in the *Collaboration Context* on behalf of the Product. In contrast, this is unlike the *Identity and Access Context* where a tenant has already been provisioned and users, groups, and roles have been defined, and notifications about those events are available. In that case the objects are preexisting. In this case the *Agile Project Management Context* needs objects that don't exist yet and won't exist until it requests them. That's a potential obstacle to autonomy because we depend on the availability of the *Collaboration Context* in order to create resources remotely. With desired autonomy, this raises an interesting challenge.

Why Is Discussion Used in Both Contexts?
This is an interesting situation because it's one where the name of the concept, Discussion, is the same in both Bounded Contexts, but they are different types, different objects, and thus have different state and different behavior.

> In the *Collaboration Context* a Discussion is an Aggregate and it manages a set of Posts—implicit children that are themselves Aggregates. In the *Agile PM Context* the Discussion is a Value Object and only holds a reference to the actual Discussion with Posts in the foreign Context. Note, however, that in Chapter 13 when the team implements the integrations, they discover that they should strongly type the different kinds of Discussions in the *Agile PM Context.*

We need to leverage eventual consistency using **Domain Events (8)** and an **Event-Driven Architecture (4)**. There's nothing that says that only remote systems can consume notifications produced by our local system. When a `ProductInitiated` Domain Event is published by our model, it is handled by our own system. The local handler requests the Forum and Discussion to be created remotely. This could be done via RPC or messaging, depending on what CollabOvation supports. If using RPC and the remote collaboration system were not available at that time, the local handler would simply keep trying on a periodic basis until it finally met with success. If messaging is supported instead of RPC, the local handler would send a message to the collaboration system. In turn, collaboration would respond with its own message when resource creation completes. When the Event handler back in ProjectOvation received this notification, it would update the `Product` with an identity reference to its newly created discussion.

What happens if the product owner or team members try to use the discussion prior to its existence? Is the unavailable discussion considered a bug in the model? Will it cause the system to exhibit an unreliable condition? Consider the fact that any given subscriber may not have paid to use the collaboration add-on in the first place. That's a nontechnical reason to design in resource unavailability. Working around eventual consistency is in no way a kludge. It's just another valid state that should be modeled.

An elegant way to handle all of the possible unavailability scenarios is to make them explicit. Consider this **Standard Type** implemented as a **State** [Gamma et al.], as described in **Value Objects (6)**:

```java
public enum DiscussionAvailability {
    ADD_ON_NOT_ENABLED, NOT_REQUESTED, REQUESTED, READY;
}

public final class Discussion implements Serializable {
    private DiscussionAvailability availability;
    private DiscussionDescriptor descriptor;
    ...
}

public class Product extends Entity {
    ...
```

```
    private Discussion discussion;
    ...
}
```

Using this design, a `Discussion` Value Object is protected from misuse because the State defined by `DiscussionAvailability` protects it. When someone attempts to participate in a discussion about the `Product`, it can safely hand off its `discussion` State. If not `READY`, the participant will be shown one of three messages:

To use team collaboration you need to purchase the add-on option.

The product owner didn't request the creation of a product discussion.

The discussion setup has not yet completed; check back soon.

If the `Discussion availability` is `READY`, we allow full team member participation.

Interestingly, as implied by the first of the unavailable state messages, the possibility exists that the business chooses to make collaboration options selectable even though they have not yet been purchased. Leaving collaboration UI options enabled could be an effective marketing tickler to encourage follow-on purchase. Who better to nag management to purchase an add-on option than those who are daily reminded that they could be using it, but cannot? Clearly, technical benefits are not the only ones realized by the use of the availability State.

At this time the team isn't certain what its actual integration with collaboration will be. For the sake of Customer-Supplier discussions, they've produced the diagram in Figure 3.10. The *Agile Project Management Context* may use a second Anticorruption Layer to manage integration between itself and the *Collaboration Context*. It would be like the one it uses for the *Identity and Access Context*. The diagram shows the primary boundary objects, which are similar to their counterparts used for identity and access management integration. Actually there is not one single `CollaborationAdapter`. It is just a placeholder for the several needed, but unknown at this time.

Shown inside the local Context are `DiscussionService` and `SchedulingService`. These represent the Domain Services that could be used to manage discussions and calendar entries in the collaboration system. The actual mechanisms will be determined by Customer-Supplier negotiations between the teams, which are implemented in **Integrating Bounded Contexts (13)**.

The team can understand part of their model now. What happens, for example, when a discussion has been created and the result is communicated

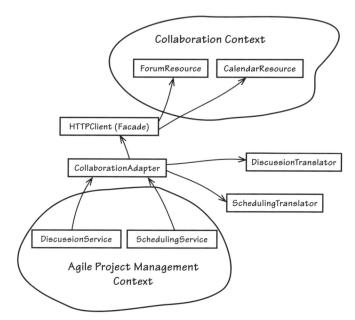

Figure 3.10   A zoom in on an Anticorruption Layer and Open Host Service of the possible integration components between *Agile Project Management Context* and *Collaboration Context*

to the local Context? The asynchronous component—either RPC client or message handler—tells the `Product` to `attachDiscussion()`, passing it a new `Discussion` Value instance. All local Aggregates with pending remote resource interests will be cared for in this fashion.

This examination has gone into some useful detail on Context Maps. We need to exercise restraint, however, as we can quickly reach the point of diminishing returns. Perhaps we could have included **Modules (9)**, but those have been placed in their own dedicated chapter. Include any relevant, high-level elements that will lead to vital team communication. On the other hand, push back when detail seems ceremonious.

Produce Context Maps that you can post on the wall. You can upload them to a team wiki as long as it's not just the project's attic where nobody ever goes. Keep discussions about the project flowing back to your Map to stimulate useful refinements.

Wrap-Up

That was definitely a productive session with Context Mapping.

- We've discussed what Context Maps are, what help they provide to your team, and how you can create them with ease.

- You took a detailed look into SaaSOvation's three Bounded Contexts and their supporting Context Maps.

- Using mapping, you zoomed in on the integrations between each of the Contexts.

- You examined the boundary objects supporting Anticorruption Layer and their interactions.

- You saw how to produce a Translation Map showing the local mapping between REST-based resources and the corresponding object in the consuming domain model.

Not every project will need the level of detail demonstrated here. Others may require more. The trick is to balance the need to understand with practicality and not pile too much detail into this level. Remember that we are likely not going to keep a very detailed graphical Map up-to-date far into the project. We'll benefit most from what can be posted on a wall, enabling team members to point at them during discussions. If we reject ceremony and embrace simplicity and agility, we'll produce useful Context Maps that help us move forward rather than bog down the project.

Chapter 4

Architecture

> *Architecture should speak of its time and place,*
> *but yearn for timelessness.*
> —*Frank Gehry*

One of the big advantages of DDD is that it doesn't require the use of any specific architecture. Since our carefully crafted **Core Domain** (**2**) resides at the heart of a **Bounded Context** (**2**), it enables one or more architectural influences to play a role in the entire application or system.[1] Some architectural influences surround the domain model and have a broad overall effect, while others address specific demands. The goal is to *use just the right choices and combinations of architecture and architecture patterns*.

The real demands for specific software qualities should drive the use of architectural styles and patterns. The ones chosen must be proven to meet or exceed required qualities. Avoiding architectural style and pattern overuse is just as important as using the right ones. Allowing real, genuine quality demands to drive what we do with architecture is a beneficial risk-driven approach [Fairbanks]. That way we use architecture only to mitigate the risk of failure, not to increase our risk of failure by using an architectural style or pattern that cannot be justified. Thus, we must be able to justify every architectural influence in use, or we eliminate it from our system.

Our ability to justify the selection of any architectural styles and patterns is limited to the available functional requirements, such as use cases or user stories, and even scenarios specific to the domain model. In other words, you cannot determine the necessary software qualities without functional requirements. Lacking these kinds of inputs, we actually cannot make sound architectural choices, which implies that employing a use-case-driven architecture approach to software development is still applicable today.

---

1. This chapter is about architectural styles, application architectures, and architecture patterns. A style describes how to implement a specific architecture, while an architecture pattern explains how to address a specific concern within an architecture but is broader than a design pattern. I suggest you not get too hung up on the differences, but just understand that DDD can reside at the heart of a lot of surrounding architectural influences.

Architecture Isn't a Coolness Factor

The following architectural styles and patterns are not a grab bag of cool tools we should apply everywhere possible. Instead, use them only where applicable, where they mitigate a specific risk that would otherwise increase the potential for project or system failure.

[Evans] focused on the Layers Architecture. That being so, SaaSOvation first concluded that DDD could only be effective using that well-known pattern. It took the teams some time to understand that DDD is considerably more adaptable than that, even though Layers was most popular at the time [Evans] was written.

The principles of a Layers Architecture can still be used to govern good decision making. We don't need to stop there, however, as we'll consider some of the more modern architectures and patterns that can be leveraged where needed. This will prove the versatility and broad applicability of DDD.

For sure, SaaSOvation did not need every architectural influence all at once, but its teams needed to choose wisely from the options available to them.

Interviewing the Successful CIO

To give a bit of a perspective on why each of the architectural influences discussed in the chapter might be used, we're going to leap a decade into the future and talk to SaaSOvation's CIO. While the company's beginnings were humble, architectural decision helped it succeed each step of the way. Let's tune in to the program *TechMoney*, with Anchor Maria Finance-Ilmundo . . .

Maria: Tonight, my exclusive interview is with Mitchell Williams, CIO of the enormously successful SaaSOvation. We're continuing our "Know Your Architectural $tyles" series. Tonight's focus is on how selecting the right architecture can bring enduring success. Welcome to the show, Mitchell, and thanks for joining us.

Mitchell: I'm glad to be here again, Maria. It's always a pleasure.

Maria: Can you take us through some of the early architectural decisions you went with, and why?

Mitchell: Of course. Believe it or not, we actually started off planning our projects around desktop deployment. Our team designed for the desktop application to persist to a central database. They chose the Layers Architecture for this approach.

Maria: Did that make sense?

Mitchell: Well, we believe it did, especially since we were only dealing with a single application tier plus the central database. It would have served us well for a simple client-server style.

Maria: But the tables soon turned, didn't they?

Mitchell: They certainly did. We actually joined forces with a business partner and decided to move forward with an SaaS subscription model. We sought some significant funding to support our efforts and landed it. We determined that our agile project management application would go on the back burner for a while until we first developed a suite of collaboration tools. This had a twofold benefit. First, we'd enter the accelerating collaboration market, but then we'd also have a natural feature add-on for the project management application. You know, collaborating on software development project deliverables.

Maria: Interesting. It all sounds quite grassroots. Where did these decisions lead you?

Mitchell: As the software complexity increased, we needed to manage quality by introducing unit and feature testing tools. To do that, we kind of turned Layers on its ear by introducing the Dependency Inversion Principle, or DIP. It was important since the team could easily test by stubbing out the UI and Infrastructure Layers and concentrate on testing the Application and

Domain. In fact, we could develop the UI in isolation and delay decisions on persistence technology for some time. And it actually wasn't a big leap away from Layers. The team had a high comfort level.

Maria: Wow, swapping out the UI *and* persistence! That seems risky. How tough was it?

Mitchell: Well, actually not so much. As it turns out, the fact that we were using the Domain-Driven Design tactical patterns didn't hurt us at all. Since we used the Aggregate pattern and Repositories, we could develop against in-memory persistence behind the Repository interfaces and swap in a persistence mechanism after we had time to consider our options.

Maria: Dude.

Mitchell: Totally.

Maria: And?

Mitchell: Bang. Things were off and running. We delivered CollabOvation and ProjectOvation, with successive profitable quarters.

Maria: Ka-ching.

Mitchell: Got that right. We then decided that we wanted to support mobile devices in addition to desktop browsers since mobile exploded and it got all over us. For that we'd use REST. Subscribers started asking for things like federated identity and security, as well as sophisticated project and time resource management tools. And then new investors wanted to see reports on their preferred business intelligence dash.

Maria: Amazing. So mobile wasn't the only thing exploding. Let me get your take on dealing with all that.

Mitchell: The team decided that migrating to a Hexagonal Architecture was an appropriate choice to handle all these additions. They found that the Ports and Adapters approach gave them the ability to add new kinds of clients almost ad hoc. The same went for new output Port types, like innovative new persistence mechanisms, such as NoSQL, and messaging capabilities. And that all spelled c-l-o-u-d.

Maria: So you had confidence in those modifications?

Mitchell: Absolutely.

Maria: Huge. If you don't buckle under all that, it probably means you made great choices that leveraged your ability to go even further.

Mitchell: Exactly. By now we were adding new tenants by many hundreds every month. We actually added a service to migrate existing data from legacy corporate collaboration tools into our cloud. The team decided that an SOA focus allowed them to aggregate this data nicely using Mule's Collection Aggregator. It could sit on the service boundary while still using the Hexagonal Architecture.

Maria: Ah, so you didn't introduce SOA because it sounded cool. You used it when it made sense. Perfect. We haven't seen good decision making like that throughout the industry.

Mitchell: Yes, Maria, and that's really the approach we took all along. It was our blueprint for success. For example, in time we added TrackOvation, our defect tracking software, which integrated with ProjectOvation. And as ProjectOvation features grew, the UI became more and more sophisticated. The Product Owner's dashboard of all Scrum products and defects in their systems updated with each application command and corresponding event. Since Product Owners across subscribing tenants had different preferred views, it made the dashboards even more complex. And, naturally, we also had to support the mobile devices. The team considered the merits of including a CQRS architecture pattern.

Maria: CQRS? Come on, Mitch, that's pretty heady. Was that one of those uncertainties that we don't know how it plays out? What about walking off the plank there?

Mitchell: No, not really. Once the team had a valid reason to use CQRS to ease the friction between the command and query universes, it was full steam ahead, and they never looked back.

Maria: Exactly. Wasn't that about the time that your subscribers starting asking for features that required distributed processing?

Mitchell: Yes; if we didn't get this one right we'd soon be drowning in complexity. Some features required running through a series of distributed processes before delivering an answer. The ProjectOvation team would not make the user wait for these potentially long-running tasks and risk timeouts. They introduced a fully Event-Driven Architecture, employing a classic Pipes and Filters pattern to manage these.

Maria: But that wasn't the end of your journey down Complexity Lane, was it? How tough was that?

Mitchell: LOL. No, no. Never would that happen, it seemed. However, when you have a smart team, it makes Complexity Lane like a stroll in the park. In actuality, the Event-Driven Architecture simplified many areas of the expanding suite of systems.

Maria: True, that. Go on. That was an *obvious* opportunity. We're getting to my favorite part of the story. You know . . . [eyes twinkle $$$]

Mitchell: Our architecture allowed us to scale so rapidly and manage change so well that RoaringCloud acquired SaaSOvation for, well . . . that's all a matter of public record.

Maria: I'd say, and *very* public. At $50 per common share that was around $3 billion worth of public record.

Mitchell: Good memory for financial facts! And that was serious incentive to get the integration right. They brought a vast number of new subscribers, and the user base actually started to stress the ProjectOvation infrastructure. It was now time to distribute and parallelize the Pipes and Filters. That called for adding in long-running processes, sometimes called Sagas.

Maria: Nice. Can you categorically say that that was fun?

Mitchell: Fun indeed, but necessary even more so.

Maria: And it seems that the fun would never end. Probably one of the least expected and even shocking chapters in your long success story came next.

Mitchell: You know it. Now that RoaringCloud had a monopoly in the marketplace due to the plethora of subscription applications and millions of users, the government took notice and began regulating the industry. A new law was passed to require RoaringCloud to track every change to a project. Actually, the best way to handle this compliance situation as a natural part of the domain model was to use Event Sourcing.

Maria: Man, you were poised. That's crazy. I mean, really, really crazy.

Mitchell: That's a crazy good problem to have, really.

Maria: What's so amazing to me is that through all these years, the core of your applications was based on DDD software models. Yet, obviously DDD didn't hurt you. You seemed to not experience hardships because of it.

Mitchell: In fact it was quite the opposite. We firmly believe that it was because we chose DDD early, and took the time to understand it thoroughly, that the business situations we could not escape—and didn't want to—were handled in stride.

Maria: Well, as I like to say, "Ka-ching!" Thanks again, Mitchell. We've learned how selecting the right architecture can bring enduring success, right here on "Know Your Architectural $tyles."

Mitchell: My pleasure, Maria. Thanks for inviting me.

That was a bit quirky, but helpful. It demonstrates how the architectural influences discussed in the following sections can be used with DDD, and how to introduce each at just the right time.

Layers

The Layers Architecture [Buschmann et al.] pattern is considered by many to be the granddaddy of all. It supports N-tier systems and is, thus, commonly used in Web, enterprise, and desktop applications. Here we rigorously separate the various concerns of our application or system into well-defined layers.

> Isolate the expression of the domain model and the business logic, and eliminate any dependency on infrastructure, user interface, or even application logic that is not business logic. Partition a complex program into layers. Develop a design within each layer that is cohesive and that depends only on the layers below. [Evans, Ref, p. 16]

Figure 4.1 shows the layers common to a DDD application that uses a traditional Layers Architecture. Here the isolated Core Domain resides in one layer

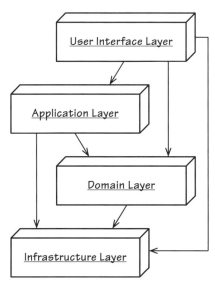

Figure 4.1 The traditional Layers Architecture in which DDD is applied

in the architecture. Above it are the **User Interface** and **Application Layers.**
Below it is the **Infrastructure Layer.**

An essential rule of this architecture is that each layer may couple only to
itself and below. There are distinctions within the style. A **Strict Layers Architecture** is one that allows coupling only to the layer directly below. A **Relaxed
Layers Architecture,** however, allows any higher-level layer to couple to any
layer below it. Since both the User Interface and the Application Services often
need to employ infrastructure, many, if not most, systems are based on Relaxed
Layers.

Lower layers may actually loosely couple to higher layers, but this is only by
means of a mechanism such as **Observer** or **Mediator** [Gamma et al.]; there is
never a direct reference from lower to higher. Using Mediator, for example, the
higher layer would implement an interface defined by the lower layer, then pass
the implementing object as an argument to the lower layer. The lower layer uses
the implementing object with no knowledge of where it resides architecturally.

The User Interface is to contain only code that addresses user view and
request concerns. It must not contain domain/business logic. Some may conclude that since validation is required by the User Interface, it must contain
business logic. The kinds of validation found in the User Interface are not the
kinds that belong in the domain model (only). As discussed in **Entities (5),** we
still want to limit coarse-grained validations that express deep business knowledge only to the model.

If the User Interface components use objects from the domain model, it is
generally limited to rendering its data on the glass. If using this approach, a
Presentation Model (14) can be used to prevent the view itself from knowing
about domain objects.

Since a user may be either a human or other systems, sometimes this layer
will provide the means to remotely invoke the services of an API in the form of
an **Open Host Service (13).**

Components in the User Interface are direct clients of the Application Layer.

Application Services (14) reside in the Application Layer. These are different from **Domain Services (7)** and are thus devoid of domain logic. They
may control persistence transactions and security. They may also be in charge
of sending Event-based notifications to other systems and/or for composing
e-mail messages to be sent to users. The Application Services in this layer are
the direct clients of the domain model, though themselves possessing no business logic. They remain very lightweight, coordinating operations performed
against domain objects, such as **Aggregates (10).** They are the primary means
of expressing use cases or user stories on the model. Hence, a common function of an Application Service is to accept parameters from the User Interface,

use a **Repository (12)** to obtain an Aggregate instance, and then execute some command operation on it:

```
@Transactional
public void commitBacklogItemToSprint(
    String aTenantId, String aBacklogItemId, String aSprintId) {
    TenantId tenantId = new TenantId(aTenantId);

    BacklogItem backlogItem =
        backlogItemRepository.backlogItemOfId(
                tenantId, new BacklogItemId(aBacklogItemId));

    Sprint sprint = sprintRepository.sprintOfId(
                tenantId, new SprintId(aSprintId));

    backlogItem.commitTo(sprint);
}
```

If our Application Services become much more complex than this, it is probably an indication that domain logic is leaking into the Application Services, and that the model is becoming anemic. So it's a best practice to keep these model clients very thin. When a new Aggregate must be created, an Application Service would use a **Factory (11)** or the Aggregate's constructor to instantiate it and then use the corresponding Repository to persist it. An Application Service may also use a Domain Service to fulfill some domain-specific task designed as a stateless operation.

When the domain model is designed to publish **Domain Events (8)**, the Application Layer may register subscribers to any number of Events. Doing so enables the Events to be stored, forwarded, and otherwise dealt with as one of the application's duties. This frees the domain model to be aware of only its own core concerns and enables the **Domain Event Publisher (8)** to remain lightweight and liberated from messaging infrastructure dependencies.

Since the domain model possessing all business logic is discussed at great length in the other chapters, it is not repeated here. Nonetheless, there are some challenges associated with the domain and the use of traditional Layers. Using Layers may require the Domain Layer to make some limited use of Infrastructure. I'm not saying that core domain objects would do this, as we should absolutely avoid that altogether. However, adhering to the definition of Layers may require implementations of some interfaces in the Domain Layer that depend on technologies provided by Infrastructure.

For example, Repository interfaces require implementations that use components, such as persistence mechanisms, housed in Infrastructure. What if we just implemented the Repository interfaces in Infrastructure? Since the Infrastructure Layer is below the Domain Layer, the references from Infrastructure upward to Domain would violate the rules of Layers Architecture. Still, avoiding that does not mean that the primary domain objects would couple to Infrastructure. To avoid that we might use implementation **Modules (9)** to hide technical classes:

```
com.saasovation.agilepm.domain.model.product.impl
```

As indicated in **Modules (9)**, `MongoProductRepository` could be housed in that package. This is not the only way to address this challenge, however. We might decide instead to implement such interfaces in the Application Layer, which would uphold the rules of Layers. Figure 4.2 provides a glimpse of this approach. But doing that may seem a bit distasteful.

There is a better way, as discussed in the section entitled "Dependency Inversion Principle."

In a traditional Layers Architecture the Infrastructure is at the bottom. Things like persistence and messaging mechanisms reside there. Messages may include those sent by enterprise messaging middleware systems or more basic e-mails (SMTP) or text messages (SMS). Think of all the technical components and frameworks that provide low-level services for the application. Those are usually considered to be part of Infrastructure. The higher-level Layers couple to the lower-level components to reuse the technical facilities provided. That being the case, again we want to reject any notion of coupling core domain model objects to Infrastructure.

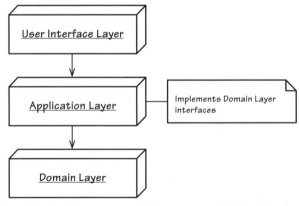

Figure 4.2   The Application Layer could house some technical implementations of interfaces defined by the Domain Layer.

The SaaSOvation teams noted that having the Infrastructure Layer at the bottom posed some disadvantages. For one it made implementing technical aspects required by the Domain Layer kind of bitter-tasting since the rules of Layers had to be violated. And actually their code was difficult to test. How could they overcome this disadvantage?

Could we whip up something a bit sweeter if we adjusted the order of Layers?

Dependency Inversion Principle

There is a way to improve on the traditional Layers Architecture by adjusting the way dependencies work. The Dependency Inversion Principle (DIP) was postulated by Robert C. Martin and described in [Martin, DIP]. The formal definition states:

> High-level modules should not depend on low-level modules. Both should depend on abstractions.

> Abstractions should not depend upon details. Details should depend upon abstractions.

The essence of this definition is communicating that a component that provides low-level services (Infrastructure, for this discussion) should depend on interfaces defined by high-level components (for this discussion, User Interface, Application, and Domain). While there are several ways to express an architecture that uses DIP, we could boil it down to the structure shown in Figure 4.3.

Does DIP Really Support All Those Layers?

Some would conclude that DIP has only two layers, one at the top and one at the bottom. The one at the top would implement interface abstractions defined in the layer at the bottom. Adjusting Figure 4.3 to fit this, the Infrastructure Layer would be the one at the top, and the User Interface Layer, Application Layer, and Domain Layer would constitute one at the bottom. You may or may not prefer this view of a DIP architecture. Don't worry; the **Hexagonal** [Cockburn] or **Ports and Adapters Architecture** is where this is all headed.

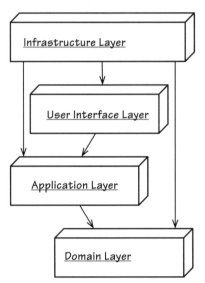

Figure 4.3   The possible Layers when the Dependency Inversion Principle is used. We move the Infrastructure Layer above all others, enabling it to implement interfaces for all Layers below.

From the architecture of Figure 4.3, we would have a Repository implemented in Infrastructure for an interface defined in Domain:

```
package com.saasovation.agilepm.infrastructure.persistence;

import com.saasovation.agilepm.domain.model.product.*;

public class HibernateBacklogItemRepository
    implements BacklogItemRepository  {
    ...
    @Override
    @SuppressWarnings("unchecked")
    public Collection<BacklogItem> allBacklogItemsComittedTo(
        Tenant aTenant, SprintId aSprintId) {
        Query query =
            this.session().createQuery(
                "from -BacklogItem as _obj_ "
                + "where _obj_.tenant = ? and _obj_.sprintId = ?");

        query.setParameter(0, aTenant);
        query.setParameter(1, aSprintId);

        return (Collection<BacklogItem>) query.list();
    }
    ...
}
```

Focusing on the Domain Layer, using DIP enables both the Domain and Infrastructure to depend on abstractions (interfaces) defined by the domain model. Since the Application Layer is the direct client of the Domain, it depends on Domain interfaces and indirectly accesses Repository and any technical Domain Service implementation classes provided by Infrastructure. It may use any one of a few ways to acquire the implementations, including **Dependency Injection**, **Service Factory**, and **Plug In** [Fowler, P of EAA]. The examples throughout the book use Dependency Injection provided by Spring Framework and sometimes the Service Factory via class `DomainRegistry`. In fact, `DomainRegistry` uses Spring to look up references to beans that implement interfaces defined by the domain model, including Repositories and Domain Services.

Interestingly enough, when we think about the influence that DIP has on this architecture, we might conclude that there are actually no longer any layers at all. Both high-level and low-level concerns are dependent only on abstractions, which seems to topple the stack. What if we actually thought of turning this architecture on its ear and adding a bit more symmetry? Let's next see how that would work.

Hexagonal or Ports and Adapters

With the **Hexagonal Architecture**[2] Alistair Cockburn codified a style to produce symmetry [Cockburn]. It advances this goal by allowing many disparate clients to interact with the system on equal footing. Need a new client? Not a problem. Just add an Adapter to transform any given client's input into that understood by the internal application's API. At the same time, output mechanisms employed by the system, such as graphics, persistence, and messaging, may also be diverse and swappable. That's possible because an Adapter is created to transform application results into a form accepted by a specific output mechanism.

As we discuss it, you may agree that this architecture has potential for timelessness.

---

2. We refer to this architecture by the name Hexagonal, even though its name seems to have changed to Ports and Adapters. Despite its changed name, the community still refers to it as Hexagonal. The Onion Architecture has also surfaced. However, it appears to many that Onion is just an (unfortunate) alternate name for Hexagonal. We can safely assume that they are the same and stick with the [Cockburn] definition.

These days many teams that say they are using a Layers Architecture are actually using Hexagonal instead. This is due, in part, to the number of projects that now use some form of Dependency Injection. It's not that Dependency Injection is automatically Hexagonal. It's just that it encourages a way of producing an architecture that leans naturally toward the development of a Ports and Adapters style. In any case, a more thorough understanding will clarify this point.

We usually think of the place where clients interact with the system as its "front end." Likewise, we consider the place where the application retrieves persisted data, stores new persistent data, or sends output as its "back end." But Hexagonal promotes a different way of looking at the areas of a system, as indicated by Figure 4.4. There are two primary areas, the *outside* and the *inside*. The outside enables disparate clients to submit input and also provides mechanisms to retrieve persisted data, store the application's output (for example, a database), or send it elsewhere along its way (for example, messaging).

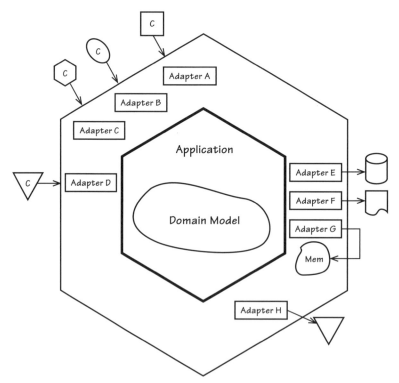

Figure 4.4   The Hexagonal Architecture is also known as Ports and Adapters. There are Adapters for each of the *outside* types. The *outside* reaches the *inside* through the application's API.

Cowboy Logic

AJ: "My horses sure do like their new hexagonal corral.
It gives 'em more corners to run to when I'm carryin'
a saddle."

In Figure 4.4 each client type has its own Adapter [Gamma et al.], which transforms input protocols into input that is compatible with the application's API—the inside. Each of the hexagon's sides represents a different kind of Port, for either input or output. Three of the clients' requests arrive via the same kind of input Port (Adapters A, B, and C), and one uses a different kind of Port (Adapter D). Perhaps the three use HTTP (browser, REST, SOAP, and so on) and the one uses AMQP (for example, RabbitMQ). There is not a strict definition of what a Port means, making it a flexible concept. In whatever way Ports are partitioned, client requests arrive and the respective Adapter transforms their input. It then invokes an operation on the application or sends the application an event. Control is thus transferred to the inside.

We Probably Are Not Implementing the Ports Ourselves

We actually normally don't implement the Ports ourselves. Think of a Port as HTTP and the Adapter as a Java Servlet or JAX-RS annotated class that receives method invocations from a container (JEE) or framework (RESTEasy or Jersey). Or we might create a message listener for NServiceBus or RabbitMQ. In that case the Port is more or less the messaging mechanism, and the Adapter is the message listener, because it is the responsibility of the message listener to grab data from the message and translate it into parameters suitable to pass into the Application's API (the client of the domain model).

Design the Application Inside per Functional Requirements

When using Hexagonal, we design the application with our use cases in mind, not the number of supported clients. Any number and type of clients may request through various Ports, but each Adapter delegates to the application using the same API.

The application receives requests by way of its public API. The application boundary, or inner hexagon, is also the use case (or user story) boundary. In other words, we should create use cases based on application functional requirements, not on the number of diverse clients or output mechanisms. When the application receives a request via its API, it uses the domain model to fulfill all requests involving the execution of business logic. Thus, the application's API is published as a set of Application Services. Here again, Application Services are the direct client of the domain model, just as when using Layers.

The following represents a RESTful resource published using JAX-RS. A request arrives through the HTTP input Port, and the handler acts as an Adapter, delegating to an Application Service:

```java
@Path("/tenants/{tenantId}/products")
public class ProductResource extends Resource {

    private ProductService productService;
    ...
    @GET
    @Path("{productId}")
    @Produces({ "application/vnd.saasovation.projectovation+xml" })
    public Product getProduct(
            @PathParam("tenantId") String aTenantId,
            @PathParam("productId") String aProductId,
            @Context Request aRequest) {

        Product product = productService.product(aTenantId, aProductId);

        if (product == null) {
            throw new WebApplicationException(
                    Response.Status.NOT_FOUND);
        }

        return product; // serialized to XML using MessageBodyWriter
    }
    ...
}
```

The various JAX-RS annotations provide a significant part of the Adapter, parsing the resource path and turning its parameters into `String` instances. The `ProductService` instance is injected and used by this request to delegate to the application inside. The `Product` is serialized to XML and placed in a `Response`, which is then sent through the HTTP output Port.

JAX-RS Isn't the Focus Here

This is just one way to use the application and domain model inside. In essence, JAX-RS is not important. We could instead use Restfulie, or create a Node.js server running the restify module. Further still, Adapters designed to handle input from other Ports would delegate to the same API, as you will see.

What about the other side of the application, to the right? Consider Repository implementations as persistence Adapters, providing access to previously stored Aggregate instances and storage for new ones. As depicted in the diagram (Adapters E, F, and G), we might have Repository implementations for relational databases, document stores, distributed cache, and in-memory stores. If the application sends Domain Event messages to the outside, it would use a different Adapter (H) for messaging. The output messaging Adapter is the opposite of the input Adapter that supports AMQP and thus goes out a different Port from the one used for persistence.

A big advantage with Hexagonal is that Adapters are easily developed for test purposes. The entire application and domain model can be designed and tested before clients and storage mechanisms exist. Tests could be created to exercise `ProductService` well before any decision is made to support HTTP/REST, SOAP, or messaging Ports. Any number of test clients can be developed before the user interface wireframes have been completed. Long before a persistence mechanism is selected for the project, in-memory Repositories can be employed to mimic persistence for the sake of testing. See **Repositories (12)** for details on developing in-memory implementations. Significant progress can be made on the core without the need for supplementary technical components.

If using true Layers, consider the advantages of toppling the structure and developing based on Ports and Adapters instead. When designed properly, the hexagon inside—the application and domain model—will not leak to the outside parts. This promotes a clean application boundary inside in which use cases are implemented. Outside any number of client Adapters can support numerous automated tests and real-world clients, as well as storage, messaging, and other output mechanisms.

When the SaaSOvation teams considered the advantages of using the Hexagonal Architecture, they decided to make the switch from Layers. It wasn't difficult, actually. It just required adopting a slightly different mindset in using the familiar Spring Framework.

Because the Hexagonal Architecture is versatile, it could well be the foundation that supports other architectures required by the system. For instance, we might factor in Service-Oriented, REST, or an Event-Driven Architecture; employ CQRS; use a Data Fabric or Grid-Based Distributed Cache; or tack on Map-Reduce distributed and parallel processing, most of which are discussed later in this chapter. The Hexagonal style forms the strong foundation for supporting any and all of those additional architectural options. There are other ways, but *for the remainder of this chapter assume that Ports and Adapters is used to assist with developing around each of the remaining topics discussed.*

Service-Oriented

The Service-Oriented Architecture, or SOA, has different meanings to different people. This can make discussions about it somewhat challenging. It's best to try to find some common ground, or at least define the ground for this discussion. Consider some principles of SOA as defined by Thomas Erl [Erl]. Besides the fact that services are always interoperable, they also possess the eight design principles presented in Table 4.1.

Table 4.1 Design Principles of Services

Service Design Principle	Description
1. Service Contract	Services express their purpose and capabilities by means of a contract in one or more description documents.
2. Service Loose Coupling	Services minimize dependency and only have an awareness of each other.
3. Service Abstraction	Services publish only their contract and hide internal logic from clients.
4. Service Reusability	Services can be reused by others in order to build more coarse-grained services.
5. Service Autonomy	Services control their underlying environment and resources to remain independent, which allows them to remain consistent and reliable.
6. Service Statelessness	Services place the responsibility of state management on consumers, where this does not conflict with what is controlled for Service Autonomy.
7. Service Discoverability	Services are described with metadata to allow discovery and to make their Service Contract understood, allowing them to be (re)usable assets.
8. Service Composability	Services may be composed within more coarse-grained services no matter the size and complexity of the composition they fall within.

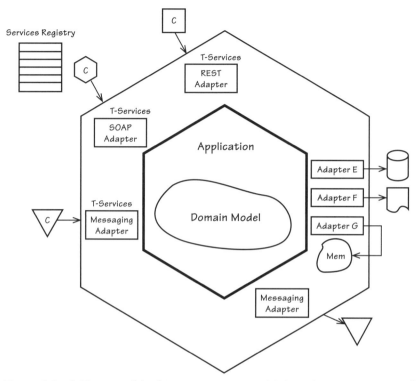

Figure 4.5   A Hexagonal Architecture supporting SOA, with REST, SOAP, and messaging services

We can combine these principles with a Hexagonal Architecture, with the service boundary at the far left and the domain model at the heart. The basic architecture is presented in Figure 4.5, where consumers reach services using REST, SOAP, and messaging. Note that one Hexagonal-based system supports multiple technical service endpoints. This has a bearing on how DDD is used within an SOA.

Since opinions vary widely on what SOA is and what value it provides, it wouldn't be surprising if you disagree with what's presented here. Martin Fowler labels this situation "service-oriented ambiguity" [Fowler, SOA]. Therefore, I won't make a valiant attempt to disambiguate SOA here. I will, however, provide a perspective on one way DDD fits into the set of *priorities* declared in the SOA Manifesto.[3]

---

3. The SOA Manifesto itself has received considerable negative criticism, but we may still glean some value from it.

First, considering the pragmatic viewpoints expressed by one of the Manifesto contributors [Tilkov, Manifesto] gives an important context. Commenting on the Manifesto, he brings us at least a step or two closer to understanding what SOA services can be:

> [The Manifesto] gives me the option to view a service as either a set of SOAP/WSDL interfaces or a collection of RESTful resources. . . . This is not [an] attempt at a definition—it's an attempt to find out what values and principles we could find that we all can agree on.

Stefan's comments are noteworthy. Finding agreement always helps, and we can probably agree that a business service can be provided by any number of technical services.

The technical services could be RESTful resources, SOAP interfaces, or message types. The business service emphasizes *business strategy*, a way to bring business and technology together. However, defining a single business service does not equate to defining a single **Subdomain (2)** or Bounded Context. No doubt as we perform both problem space and solution space assessments, we will find that a business service comprises a number of each. Thus, Figure 4.5 shows the architecture of only a single Bounded Context, one that may provide a set of technical services realized through a number of RESTful resources, SOAP interfaces, or message types—just a part of the overall business service. In the SOA solutions space we would expect to see many Bounded Contexts, whether any individual one uses a Hexagonal Architecture or another. Neither SOA nor DDD need specify how each set of technical services is designed and deployed, there being a wide variety of options.

Still, when using DDD our goal is to create a Bounded Context with a complete, linguistically well-defined domain model. As discussed in **Bounded Contexts (2)**, we don't want architecture to influence the size of the domain model. That could happen if one or a few of the technical service endpoints, such as a single REST resource, a single SOAP interface, or a system message type, were to be used to dictate the size of a Bounded Context. Doing so would force many, very small Bounded Contexts and domain models, perhaps each consisting of only one Entity acting as the Root of a single, small Aggregate. This could result in hundreds of such miniature Bounded Contexts in a single enterprise.

While that approach may be viewed as having technical advantages, it does not necessarily realize the goals of strategic DDD. It works against a clean, well-modeled domain based on a complete and comprehensive **Ubiquitous Language (1)**, actually fragmenting the Language. And, according to the SOA Manifesto, unnaturally fragmenting Bounded Contexts is not necessarily the spirit of SOA:

1. **Business value** over technical strategy

2. **Strategic goals** over project-specific benefits

Assuming we can accept these as worthy values, they align very well with strategic DDD. As explained in **Bounded Contexts (2)**, the technical component architecture drivers are less important when partitioning models.

The SaaSOvation teams had to learn a difficult and important lesson, that listening to the linguistic drivers aligns better with DDD. Each of their three Bounded Contexts reflects the goals of SOA—both for the business and in the technical services.

The three sample models discussed in **Bounded Contexts (2)**, **Context Maps (3)**, and **Integrating Bounded Contexts (13)** individually represent the single linguistically well-defined domain model. Each domain model is surrounded by a set of open services that implement an SOA that meets the business objectives.

Representational State Transfer—REST

Contributed by Stefan Tilkov

REST has become one of the most used, and abused, architecture buzzwords of the last few years. As usual, different people think about different things when they use the acronym. To some, REST means sending XML over HTTP connections without using SOAP; some equate it with using HTTP and JSON; others believe that to do REST you need to send method arguments as URI query parameters. All of these interpretations are wrong, but luckily—and vastly different from many other concepts such as "components" or "SOA"—there is an authoritative source for what REST means: the dissertation by Roy T. Fielding, which coined the term and defines it very clearly.

REST as an Architectural Style

The first thing to understand when trying to "get" REST is the concept of architectural styles. An architectural style is to architecture what a design pattern is to a specific design. It is an abstraction of those aspects that are common to different concrete implementations, enabling discussion of their relevant benefits without getting lost in technical detail. There are many different styles of distributed systems architecture, including client-server and distributed objects. The first few chapters of Fielding's thesis explain some of them, including the constraints they mandate for an architecture that adheres to each of them. The concept of architectural styles and constraints imposed by them might strike you as somewhat theoretical, and you'd be right. They form the theoretical foundation of a (then) new architectural style that Fielding introduces. This is REST, which is the architectural style that the Web's architecture is supposed to adhere to.

Of course the Web—as embodied by its most important standards, URI, HTTP, and HTML—predates Fielding's PhD work. But he had been one of the main forces in standardization of HTTP 1.1, and a huge influence on many design decisions that led to the Web as we know it.[4] Seen this way, REST is a theoretical extrapolation, created after the fact, of the Web's architecture itself.

So why do we now equate "REST" with a specific way of building systems or, even more restricting, a way to build Web services? The reason for this is, as it turns out, that like any other technology, the Web protocols can be used in many different ways. Some of them match the goals of the original designers; some of them don't. One often-used analogy highlights this using the RDBMS world familiar to many. You can use an RDBMS in line with its architectural concepts—that is, define tables with columns, foreign key relationships, views, constraints, and so on—or you can create a single table with two columns, one called "key," one called "value," and simply store serialized objects in the value column. Of course, you'd still be using an RDBMS, but many of its benefits will not be available to you (meaningful queries, joins, sorting and grouping, and so forth).

In a very similar fashion, the Web protocols can be used in line with the original ideas that made them what they are—with an architecture that conforms to the REST architectural style—or be used in a way that fails to follow it. And similar to our RDBMS example, we ignore the underlying architectural style to our peril. Thus, a different kind of distributed systems architecture might be appropriate if we don't end up exploiting any of the benefits of using HTTP in a "RESTful" way, just as a NoSQL/key-value store is the better choice for storing whole values that are associated with a single unique key.

---

4. He also happens to be the author of the very first widely used HTTP library, one of the original developers of the Apache HTTP server, and founder of the Apache Software Foundation.

Key Aspects of a RESTful HTTP Server

So what are the key aspects of a distribution architecture that uses "RESTful HTTP"? Let's look at the server side first. Note that it's entirely irrelevant whether we are talking about a server that's used by a human using a Web browser (a "Web application") or used by some other agent, such as a client written in your programming language of choice (a "Web service").

First of all, as the name implies, resources are a key concept. How so? As a system designer, you decide what are the meaningful "things" that you want to expose as accessible from the outside, and you assign each a distinct identity. In general, each resource has one URI, and more importantly, each URI should point to one resource—the "things" you expose to the outside need to be individually addressable. For example, you might decide that each customer, each product, each product listing, each search result, and maybe each change to the product catalog should be resources in their own right. Resources have representations, renditions of their state, in one or more formats. It's through representations—an XML or JSON document, an HTML form's post data, or some binary format—that clients interact with resources.

The next key aspect is the idea of stateless communication, using self-descriptive messages. Such is an HTTP request that carries all the information the server needs to handle it. Of course, the server can (and usually will) use its own persistent state to help, but it's important that the client and server don't rely on individual requests to set up an implicit context (a session). This enables access to each resource independently of other requests, an aspect that helps in achieving massive scalability.

If you view resources as objects—and it's not at all unreasonable to do so—it's valid to ask what kind of interface they should have. The answer is another very important aspect that differentiates REST from any other architectural style for distributed systems. The set of methods that you can invoke is fixed. Every object supports the same interface. In RESTful HTTP, the methods are the HTTP verbs—most importantly, `GET`, `PUT`, `POST`, `DELETE`—that can be applied to resources.

Even though it might appear so at first sight, these methods do not translate to CRUD operations. It is very common to create resources that do not represent any persistent entity but instead encapsulate behavior that is invoked once an appropriate verb is used on them. Each of the HTTP methods has a very clear definition in the HTTP specification. For example, the `GET` method is to be used only for "safe" operations: (1) it can perform actions that reflect an effect a client might not have requested; (2) it always reads data; (3) it can potentially be cached (if the server indicates that this is the case by means of appropriate response headers).

HTTP's GET method has been called "the most optimized piece of distributed systems plumbing in the world" by none other than Don Box, one of the main figures behind SOAP-style Web services. His words highlight that a lot of the Web's performance and scalability that we take for granted is due to HTTP optimizations for this particular, very common case.

Some HTTP methods are *idempotent*, meaning that they can be safely called again without problems in case of an error or unclear outcome. This is true for GET, PUT, and DELETE.

Finally, a RESTful server enables a client to discover a path through the application's possible state transitions by means of hypermedia. This is called *Hypermedia as the Engine of Application State* (HATEOAS) in Fielding's dissertation. Put more simply, the individual resources don't stand on their own. They are connected, linked to each other. This should not come as a surprise. After all, this is where the Web got its name. For the server, this means that it will embed links in its answers, enabling the client to interact with connected resources.

Key Aspects of a RESTful HTTP Client

A RESTful HTTP client moves from one resource to the next either by following links contained in resource representations or by being redirected to resources as a result of sending data for processing to the server. Server and client cooperate to influence the client's distribution behavior dynamically. As a URI contains all information necessary for dereferencing an address—including host name and port—a client following the hypermedia principle might end up talking to a resource hosted by a different application, a different host, or even a different company.

In an ideal REST setup, a client will start with a single well-known URI and continue following hypermedia controls from then on. This is exactly the model used by the browser when rendering and displaying HTML, including links and forms, to the user. Then, it uses the user's input to interact with a multitude of Web applications, without up-front knowledge about their interface or implementations.

Granted, a browser is not a self-sufficient agent. It requires a human to make the actual decisions. But a programmatic client can adopt many of the same principles, even when some logic is hard-coded. It will follow links instead of assuming specific URI structures, or even colocation of resources in one server, and it will make use of its knowledge of one or more media types.

REST and DDD

Tempting though it may be, it is not advisable to directly expose a domain model via RESTful HTTP. This approach often leads to system interfaces that are more brittle than they need to be, as each change in the domain model is directly reflected in the system interface. There are two alternative approaches for combining DDD and RESTful HTTP.

The first approach is to create a separate Bounded Context for the system's interface layer and use appropriate strategies to access the actual Core Domain from the system's interface model. This can be deemed a classic approach, as it views the system's interface as a cohesive whole that is simply exposed using resource abstractions instead of services or remote interfaces.

Consider a concrete example of this approach. We build a system that manages a workgroup, including its tasks, schedules/appointments, subgroups, and all of the processes needed to handle these. We would design a pure domain model, untainted by the infrastructure details, that captures the Ubiquitous Language and implements the necessary business logic. To publish an interface to this carefully crafted domain model, we provide a remote interface as a set of RESTful resources. These resources reflect the use cases the client needs, which is very likely different from the pure domain model. Yet each resource is built from, for example, one or more Aggregates belonging to the Core Domain.

Of course, we could simply use the domain objects as parameters to JAX-RS resource methods—let's say /:user/:task would map to a method `get-Task()` that returns a `Task` object. That's seemingly simple, but it comes with one major problem. Any change to the `Task` object structure is immediately reflected in the remote interface, possibly breaking many clients, even though we might only have changed something that's entirely irrelevant to the outside world. Not good.

So the first approach is preferred, that of decoupling the Core Domain from the system's interface model. Doing so enables us to make changes to the Core Domain and then decide in each individual case whether that change must be reflected in the system's interface model and, if so, the best mapping to use. Note that with this approach, the classes designed for the system's interface model are usually driven by those of the Core Domain, but are certainly driven by the use cases. Note: Even in this case we could define a custom media type.

Another approach is appropriate when more emphasis is placed on standard media types. If specific media types are developed to support not only a single system interface but a category of similar client-server interactions, a domain model can be created to represent each standard media type. Such a domain model might even be reused across clients and servers, although some REST and SOA proponents view this as an anti-pattern. Note: Such an approach is essentially a **Shared Kernel** (3) or **Published Language** (3) in DDD terms.

This reflects more of an outside-in, crosscutting approach. In the workgroup and task management domain mentioned previously, there are many common formats. Let's consider the *ical* format as an example. This is a generic format that can be used by many different applications. In this case we would start by selecting a media type (ical) and then creating a domain model for this format. This model could then be used by any system that needs to understand this format—our server application, for example, but also others (such as an Android client). Naturally, with this approach a server might need to deal with many different media types, and the same media type might be used by multiple servers.

Which of these two approaches is chosen depends to a large degree on the goals of the system designer in terms of reusability. The more specialized the solution, the more useful the first approach turns out to be. The more generally useful the solution is, with the extreme end of the spectrum being standardization by an official standards body, the more sense it makes to go with the second, media-type-centric approach.

Why REST?

In my experience, a system designed conforming to REST principles fulfills the promise of loose coupling. In general, it's very easy to add new resources and links to them in existing resource representations. It's also easy to add support for new formats where needed, leading to a much less brittle set of system connections. A REST-based system is much easier to understand, as it's split into smaller chunks—the resources—each of which exposes a separately testable, debuggable, and usable entry point. The design of HTTP and the maturity of the tooling with support for features such as URI rewriting and caching make RESTful HTTP a great choice for architectures that need to be both loosely coupled and highly scalable.

Command-Query Responsibility Segregation, or CQRS

It can be difficult to query from Repositories all the data users need to view. This is especially so when user experience design creates views of data that cuts across a number of Aggregate types and instances. The more sophisticated your domain, the more this situation tends to occur.

Using only Repositories to solve this can be less than desirable. We could require clients to use multiple Repositories to get all the necessary Aggregate instances, then assemble just what's needed into a **Data Transfer Object** (DTO) [Fowler, P of EAA]. Or we could design specialized finders on various Repositories to gather the disjointed data using a single query. If these solutions seem unsuitable, perhaps we should instead compromise on user experience design, making views rigidly adhere to the model's Aggregate boundaries. Most would agree that in the long run a mechanical and spartan user interface won't suffice.

Is there an altogether different way to map domain data to views? The answer lies in the oddly named architecture pattern **CQRS** [Dahan, CQRS; Nijof, CQRS]. It is the result of pushing a stringent object (or component) design principle, command-query separation (CQS), up to an architecture pattern.

This principle, devised by Bertrand Meyer, asserts the following:

> Every method should be either a command that performs an action, or a query that returns data to the caller, but not both. In other words, asking a question should not change the answer. More formally, methods should return a value only if they are referentially transparent and hence possess no side effects. [Wikipedia, CQS]

At an object level this means:

1. If a method modifies the state of the object, it is a *command*, and its method must not return a value. In Java and C# the method must be declared `void`.

2. If a method returns some value, it is a *query*, and it must not directly or indirectly cause the modification of the state of the object. In Java and C# the method must be declared with the type of the value it returns.

That's pretty straightforward guidance, and there is a practical and theoretical basis for adhering to it. Yet, as an architecture pattern when using DDD, why and how is it applied?

Visualize a domain model, such as one of those discussed under **Bounded Contexts (2)**. We'd normally see Aggregates with both command and query methods. We'd also see Repositories that have a number of finder methods that filter on certain properties. With CQRS we are going to disregard these "normalities" and design a different way to query display data.

Now think of segregating all of the pure query responsibilities traditionally found in a model from all responsibilities that execute pure commands on the same model. Aggregates would have no query methods (getters), only command methods. Repositories would be stripped down to an `add()` or `save()` method (supporting both creation and updating saves) and only a single query method, such as `fromId()`. The single query method takes the unique identity of an Aggregate and returns it. A Repository could not be used to find an Aggregate by any other means, such as by filtering on some additional properties. With all of that removed from the traditional model, we designate it a *command model*. We still need a way to display data to the user. For that we create a second model, one that is tuned for optimized queries. That's our *query model*.

Isn't This Accidental Complexity?

Your impression may be that this proposed style is a lot of work and that we are merely replacing one set of problems with another set of problems, and adding a lot more code to do it.

Don't be too quick to dismiss this style, however. Under some circumstances the added complexity is justifiable. Remember, CQRS is meant to solve a specific view sophistication problem, not to tack on as a cool new style that will strengthen your résumé.

Known by Other Names

Note that some areas/components of CQRS may be known by other names. What I call the query model is also known as the read model, and the command model is also called the write model.

As a result, the traditional domain model would be split in two. The command model is persisted in one store and the query model in another. We end up with a set of components like the one in Figure 4.6. Some more details will clarify this pattern.

Examining Areas of CQRS

Let's step through each of the major areas of this pattern. We can start with the client and query support and move through to the command model and how updates to the query model are done.

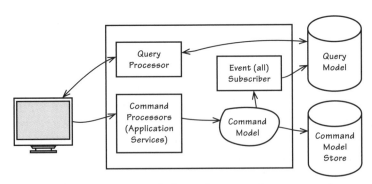

Figure 4.6   With CQRS, commands from clients travel one way to the command model. Queries are run against a separate data source optimized for presentation and delivered as user interface or reports.

Client and Query Processor

The client (at the far left in the diagram) may be a Web browser or a custom desktop user interface. It uses a set of query processors running on a server. The diagram doesn't show architecturally significant divisions between tiers on the server(s). Whatever tiers exist, the query processor represents a simple component that only knows how to execute basic queries on a database, such as a SQL store.

There are no complex layers here. At most this component runs a query against the query store database and maybe serializes the query result into some format for transport (maybe a DTO, but maybe not), if that's necessary. If the client runs Java or C#, it could query the database directly. However, that might require a large number of database client licenses, one per connection. Employing a query processor that uses pooled connections is the best choice.

If the client can consume a database result set (for example, JDBC variety), serialization is unnecessary but may be desirable anyway. There are two schools of thought here. One asserts that ultimate simplicity requires that the result set, or a very basic wire-compatible serialization of it (XML or JSON), must be consumed by the client. Others assert that DTOs should be built and consumed by the client. This may be a matter of taste, but we might agree that anytime we add DTOs and **DTO Assemblers** [Fowler, P of EAA] there is added complexity, and if not truly needed, these would be *accidental complexity*. Each team determines which approach works best for their project.

Query Model (or Read Model)

The query model is a denormalized data model. It is not meant to deliver domain behavior, only data for display (and possibly reporting). If this data model is a SQL database, each table would hold the data for a single kind of client view (display). The table can have many columns, even a superset of those needed by any given user interface display view. Table views can be created from tables, each of which is used as a logical subset of the whole.

> ### Create Support for as Many Views as Needed
>
> It's worth noting that CQRS-based views can be both cheap and disposable (for development and in maintenance). This is especially so if you use a simple form of Event Sourcing (see the section "Event Sourcing" later in the chapter and Appendix A) and save all Events into a persistent store, which can be republished at any time to create new persistent view data. Doing so, any single view could be rewritten from scratch in isolation or the entire query model be switched to completely different persistence technology. This makes it easy to create and maintain views that continuously address ongoing UI needs. This can lead to more intuitive user experiences that avoid the table paradigm but are instead much richer.

For example, a table could be designed with enough data to display user interfaces for normal users, managers, and administrators. If a corresponding database table view was created for each of those user types, the data for each security role would be divided appropriately. This builds security into the viewable data per user type. A normal user view component would select all columns from the normal user table view. A manager's view component would select all columns from the manager's table view. That way normal users would not be able to see what managers can see.

Preferably, a select statement requires only a primary key for the view being used. Here the query processor selects all columns from the normal user table view of a product:

```
SELECT * FROM vw_usr_product WHERE id = ?
```

As a side note, the table view naming convention seen here is not necessarily recommended. It just makes obvious what the sample select is doing. The primary key corresponds to the unique identity of some Aggregate type or a combined set of Aggregate types merged into a single table. In this example the `id` primary key column is the unique identity of a `Product` in the command model. The data model design should follow, as much as possible, the pattern of one table per user interface view type, with as many table views as necessary to reflect application security roles. But, be practical.

Be Practical

If there are 25 traders at a high-frequency trading desk and each one is trading securities that most of the others cannot view due to SEC compliance, would we need 25 table views? Using a trader filter would be more appropriate. Otherwise, there may be too many views to maintain to be truly practical.

In practice this may be difficult to achieve, and queries may have to join multiple tables or table views as necessarily for practical use. Joins across views/tables may be necessary or at least more practical to achieve necessary filtering. This may tend to be the case, especially when there are many user roles at play in your domain.

Don't Database Table Views Cause Overhead?

A basic database table view has no overhead when performing updates on the backing table. The view just corresponds to a query, which in this case does not even require a join. Only *materialized views* incur update overhead since the view's data must be copied into one place so it is ready for selects. Use care when designing tables and views so that query model updates perform optimally.

Client Drives Command Processing

User interface clients submit commands to the server (or indirectly execute an Application Service method) as the means of executing behavior on Aggregates, which are in the command model. The submitted command contains the name of the behavior to execute and the parameters necessary to carry it out. The command packet is a serialized method invocation. Since the command model has carefully designed contracts and behaviors, matching the commands to the contracts is a straightforward mapping.

To accomplish this the user interface must collect the data necessary to correctly parameterize the command. This implies that much thought must be given to user experience design. It must lead users toward the proper goal of submitting an explicit command. An inductive, task-driven user interface design works best [Inductive UI]. It filters out all inapplicable options, focusing on precision command execution. That said, it is possible to design a deductive user interface that generates an explicit command.

Command Processors

A command submission is received by a Command Handler/processor, which can have a few different styles. We consider those styles here, along with some advantages and disadvantages.

We can use a *categorized style* with several Command Handlers in one Application Service. This style creates an Application Service interface and implementation for a category of commands. Each Application Service could have multiple methods, one method declared for each type of command with parameters that fits the category. The primary advantage here is simplicity. This kind of handler is well understood, easy to create, and easy to maintain.

We can create a *dedicated style* handler. Each one would be a single class with one method. The method contract facilitates a specific command with parameters. This has clear advantages: There is a single responsibility per handler/processor; each handler may be redeployed independently of others; handler types can be scaled out to manage high volumes of certain kinds of commands.

This leads to the *messaging style* of Command Handler. Each command is sent as an asynchronous message and delivered to a handler designed with the dedicated style. This not only enables each command processor component to receive specifically typed messages, but processors of a given type can be added to deal with command processing load. This approach should not be used by default, as it has a more complex design. Instead, start off with either of the other two styles as synchronous command processors. Switch to asynchronous only if scalability demands require it. That said, some will conclude that an asynchronous approach providing temporal decoupling leads to more resilient systems. That viewpoint will often lead to a bias toward implementing the messaging style of Command Handlers.

Whatever kind of handler is used, decouple each one from all others. Do not allow any one handler to depend on (make use of) any others. This will allow any type of handler to be redeployed independently without impacting others.

Command Handlers generally do only a few things. If one has a creation aspect, it instantiates a new Aggregate instance and adds the new instance to its Repository. Most often it gets an Aggregate instance from its Repository and executes a command method behavior on it:

```
@Transactional
public void commitBacklogItemToSprint(
    String aTenantId, String aBacklogItemId, String aSprintId) {
    TenantId tenantId = new TenantId(aTenantId);

    BacklogItem backlogItem =
        backlogItemRepository.backlogItemOfId(
            tenantId, new BacklogItemId(aBacklogItemId));

    Sprint sprint = sprintRepository.sprintOfId(
            tenantId, new SprintId(aSprintId));

    backlogItem.commitTo(sprint);
}
```

When the Command Handler completes, a single Aggregate instance has been updated and a Domain Event has been published by the command model. This is essential to ensuring that the query model is updated. Note too that, as discussed in **Domain Events (8)** and **Aggregates (10)**, the published Event may also be used to cause the synchronization of other Aggregate instances effected by this one command, but the modification of the additional Aggregate instances would be eventually consistent with the one committed by this transaction.

Command Model (or Write Model) Executes Behavior

As each command method on the command model is executed, it completes by publishing an Event as described in **Domain Events (8)**. Using the running example, the BacklogItem would complete its command method as follows:

```
public class BacklogItem extends ConcurrencySafeEntity {
    ...
    public void commitTo(Sprint aSprint) {
        ...
```

```
        DomainEventPublisher
            .instance()
            .publish(new BacklogItemCommitted(
                    this.tenant(),
                    this.backlogItemId(),
                    this.sprintId()));
    }
    ...
}
```

What's Behind the Publisher Component?

This particular `DomainEventPublisher` is a lightweight component based on the **Observer** pattern [Gamma et al.]. See **Domain Events (8)** for details on how Events get published broadly.

This is the linchpin for updating the query model with the most recent changes to the command model. If using Event Sourcing, the Events are also necessary for persisting the state of the Aggregate that has just been modified (`BacklogItem` in this example). However, it is not a necessity to use Event Sourcing with CQRS. Unless Event logging is a requirement specified by the business, the command model can be persisted using an object-relational mapper (ORM) to a relational database or some other approach. Either way, a Domain Event must still be published to ensure that the query model is updated.

When Commands Don't Result in Event Publishing

There are circumstances when command dispatching does not lead to Events being published. For example, if a command was delivered by "at-least-once" messaging and the application ensures idempotent operations, the redelivered message is silently dropped.

Also consider the case where the application validates incoming commands. All authorized clients know about validation rules and will always pass them. However, all unauthorized clients—such as those of attackers—submitting invalid commands will fail and can be silently dropped without endangering authorized users.

Event Subscriber Updates the Query Model

A special subscriber registers to receive all Domain Events published by the command model. The subscriber uses each Domain Event to update the query model to reflect the most recent changes to the command model. This implies that each Event must be rich enough to supply all the data necessary to produce the correct state in the query model.

Should the updates be performed synchronously or asynchronously? It depends on the normal load on the system, and possibly also on where the query model database is stored. Data consistency constraints and performance requirements will influence the decision.

To update synchronously, the query model and command model would normally share the same database (or schema), and we would update the two models in the same transaction. That keeps both models completely consistent. Yet, this will require more processing time for the multiple table updates, which may not meet the service-level agreement (SLA). If the system is normally under heavy load and the query model update process is lengthy, use asynchronous updates instead. This may lead to challenges of eventual consistency, where the user interface will not immediately reflect the most recent changes in the command model. The lag time is unpredictable, but it is a trade-off that may be necessary to meet other SLAs.

What happens when a new user interface view is created but its data must be created? Design the table and any table views as described previously. Populate the new table with current state using one of a few techniques. If the command model is persisted using Event Sourcing, or if there is a full historical Event Store, replay the historical Events to produce the updates. This is possible only if the right kinds of Events already exist in the store. If they don't, the table may have to be populated as future commands enter the system. There may be another option.

If the command model is persisted using an ORM, use the backing command model store to populate the new query model table. This may employ a common data warehousing (or report database) generation technique, such as extract, transform, load (ETL). Extract the data from the command model store, transform it as needed by the user interface, and load it into the query model store.

Dealing with an Eventually Consistent Query Model

If the query model is designed to be eventually consistent—query model updates are performed asynchronously following writes to the command model store—there will be resulting idiosyncrasies in the user interface to deal with. For example, after a user submits a command, will the next user interface view have the fully updated and consistent data reflected from the query model? It may depend on system load and other factors. But we had better assume not and design for the worst case, where the user interface is never consistent.

One option is to design the user interface to temporarily display the data that was successfully submitted as parameters of the command just executed. This is a bit of a trick, but it enables the user to immediately see what will eventually be reflected in the query model. It may be the only way to ensure that the user interface does not display completely stale data just after a command is successfully executed.

What if that is not practical for a given user interface? Even if it is, there are also times when any one user executes a command and all other users viewing related data will absolutely see stale data. How can this challenge be met?

One technique suggested by [Dahan, CQRS] always explicitly displays on the user interface the date and time of the data from the query model that a user is currently viewing. To do so, each record in the query model needs to maintain the date and time of the latest update. This is a trivial step, generally supported by a database trigger. With the date and time of the latest update, the user interface can now inform the user how old the data is. If the user determines that the data is too stale to use, he or she can at that time request fresher data. Admittedly this approach is lauded by some as an effective pattern and heavily criticized by others as a hack or artifice. Certainly these opposing viewpoints indicate the need to perform user acceptance tests before this approach is employed in our own systems.

Yet, it's possible that the delayed view data synchronization is not a critical problem at all. It may also be overcome by other means, such as **Comet** (aka Ajax Push), or another form of latent update, such as some variation of **Observer** [Gamma et al.] or **Distributed Cache/Grid** (for example, Coherence or GemFire) event subscriptions. Addressing delays may even be as easy as informing users that their request has been accepted and a result will require some processing time. Carefully determine whether the eventual consistency lag time poses a problem. If so, you'll have to find the best way to address it in a given environment.

As with every pattern, CQRS introduces a number of competing forces. We must exercise a great deal of care and choose wisely. Certainly if a user interface is not overly complex or regularly cut across several different Aggregates in a single view, employing CQRS would serve to introduce accidental complexity rather than necessary complexity. CQRS is the right choice when it removes a risk that has a high probability of causing failure if ignored.

Event-Driven Architecture

> Event-driven architecture (EDA) is a software architecture promoting the production, detection, consumption of, and reaction to events. [Wikipedia, EDA]

The Hexagonal Architecture shown in Figure 4.4 can represent the notion of one system participating in an EDA by means of incoming and outgoing messages. An EDA doesn't have to use Hexagonal, but it's a decent way to present the concepts here. On a greenfield project it would be well worth it to consider using Hexagonal as the overarching style.

Examining Figure 4.4, say that the triangular client and the corresponding triangular output mechanism represent the messaging mechanism used by the Bounded Context. Input events enter on a Port separate from the one used by the other three clients. Output events likewise travel via a different Port. As proposed previously, the separate Ports could represent the message transport over AMQP, as used by RabbitMQ, rather than the more common HTTP that the other clients use. Whichever actual messaging mechanism may be in use, we will assume that events enter and exit the system by means of the symbolic triangles.

There may be a number of different kinds of events that enter and exit a hexagon. We are interested specifically in Domain Events. The application may also subscribe to system, enterprise, or other types of events as well. Perhaps those deal with system health and monitoring, logging, dynamic provisioning, and the like. Yet, it is the Domain Events that convey the happenings requiring our modeling attention.

We can replicate the system in the Hexagonal Architecture view as many times as necessary to represent the complement of systems in the enterprise that support the Event-Driven way. That's been done in Figure 4.7. Again, it's not that every system will be based on Hexagonal. The diagram just demonstrates how Event-Driven could be supported if multiple systems were Hexagonal at their foundation. Otherwise, feel free to replace the hexagons with Layers, or another style.

The Domain Events published by one such system through the output Port would be delivered to subscribers represented in the others through their input Port. The various Domain Events received have a specific meaning in each receiving

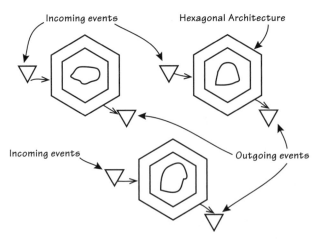

Figure 4.7   Three systems using an Event-Driven Architecture with an overarching Hexagonal style. The EDA style decouples all but the systems' dependency on the messaging mechanism itself and the Event types they subscribe to.

Bounded Context, or possibly no meaning at all.[5] If the Event type is of interest in a specific Context, its properties are adapted to the application's API and used to execute an operation there. The command operation executed on the application's API is then reflected into the domain model according to its protocol.

It's possible that a specific Domain Event received represents only one part of a multitask process. Until all anticipated Domain Events arrive, the multitask process is not considered completed. But how does the process begin? How is it distributed across the enterprise? And how do we handle tack progress through to process completion? The answers are discussed subsequently in the section on long-running processes. But first some initial groundwork is in order. Message-based systems often reflect a Pipes and Filters style.

Pipes and Filters

In one of its simplest forms, Pipes and Filters are available using a shell/console command line:

```
$ cat phone_numbers.txt | grep 303 | wc -l
3
$
```

Here a Linux command line is used to find how many contacts are in the fancy personal information manager, `phone_numbers.txt`, who have Colorado-based phone numbers. Admittedly this is not a very reliable way to implement that use case, but it does demonstrate how Pipes and Filters work:

1. The `cat` utility outputs the contents of `phone_numbers.txt` to what is called the *standard output stream*. Normally this stream is connected to the console. But when the | symbol is used, the output is piped to the input of the next utility.

2. Next, `grep` reads its input from the standard input stream, which was the result of `cat`. The argument to `grep` tells it to match lines that contain the text 303. Each line that it finds is output to its standard output stream. As with `cat`, `grep`'s output stream is now piped to the input of the next utility.

3. Finally, `wc` reads its standard input stream, which was piped from `grep`'s standard output. The command-line argument to `wc` is -1, telling it to count the number of lines it reads. It outputs the result, which in this case

---

5. If using message filters or routing keys, subscribers can avoid receiving Events that are meaningless to them.

is 3, because three lines were output by `grep`. Note that now the standard output is displayed to the console since this time there is no Pipe to an additional command.

This can be approximated using a Windows console, but with less piping:

```
C:\fancy_pim> type phone_numbers.txt | find /c "303"
3
C:\fancy_pim>
```

Consider what happens with each of the utilities. Each receives a dataset, processes it, and outputs a different dataset. The dataset that is output changes from the input because each utility acts as a Filter. By the end of the filtering process the output is completely different from the input. The input started out as a text file with individual lines of contact information and ended up being the text digit representing the number 3.

Using the basic principles from this example, how might we apply them to an Event-Driven Architecture? In fact, we can find some useful overlap. The following discussion is based on the **Pipes and Filters** messaging pattern found in [Hohpe, Woolf]. Understand, however, that a messaging Pipes and Filters approach is not exactly like the command-line version, and it is not intended to be. For example, an EDA Filter doesn't need to actually filter anything. A Filter in an EDA may be used to perform some processing while leaving the message data intact. Yet Pipes and Filters in an EDA is similar enough to the command-line type that the previous example helped lay some groundwork for what follows. If you are a more advanced reader, feel free to "filter" what follows.

Table 4.2 presents some of the basic characteristics of a message-based Pipes and Filters process.

Table 4.2   Basic Characteristics of a Message-Based Pipes and Filters Process

Characteristic	Description
Pipes are message channels	Filters receive messages on an inbound Pipe and send messages on an outbound Pipe. The Pipe is actually a message channel.
Ports connect Filters to Pipes	Filters connect to inbound and outbound Pipes through a Port. Ports make Hexagonal (Ports and Adapters) a fitting overarching style.
Filters are processors	Filters may process messages without actually filtering.
Separate processors	Each Filter processor is a separate component, and proper component granularity is achieved by careful design.

Table 4.2 Basic Characteristics of a Message-Based Pipes and Filters Process (*Continued*)

Characteristic	Description
Loosely coupled	Each Filter processor is composed into the process independent of all others. Filter processor composition may be defined by configuration.
Interchangeable	The order in which a processor receives messages may be rearranged per use case requirements, again using configured composition.
Filters may multi-Pipe	While the command-line Filters read from and write to only one Pipe, messaging Filters may read from and/or write to multiple Pipes, which implies parallel or concurrent processing.
Use same-type Filters in parallel	The busiest and possibly slowest Filters may be deployed in multiples to increase throughput.

Now, what if we were to think of each of the utilities cat, grep, and wc (or type and find) as components in an Event-Driven Architecture? What if we even implemented components to act as message senders and receivers to process telephone numbers in a similar way? (Again, I am not trying to illustrate a one-to-one command-line replacement, just a simple messaging example with the same basic goals.)

Here's how a messaging Pipes and Filters approach could work, with steps illustrated in Figure 4.8:

1. We could start off with a component named PhoneNumbersPublisher that reads all the lines in phone_numbers.txt and then creates and sends an Event message that includes all of the text lines. The Event is named AllPhoneNumbersListed. Once it is sent, the pipeline begins.

2. A message handler component named PhoneNumberFinder is configured to subscribe to AllPhoneNumbersListed and receives it. This message handler is the first Filter in the pipeline. The Filter is configured to search for the text 303. This component processes the Event by searching each line for the 303 text sequence. It then creates a new Event named PhoneNumbersMatched, placing the full lines of matching results in the Event. The Event message is sent, continuing the pipeline.

3. A message handler component named MatchedPhoneNumberCounter is configured to subscribe to PhoneNumbersMatched and receives it. This message handler is the second Filter in the pipeline. Its sole responsibility

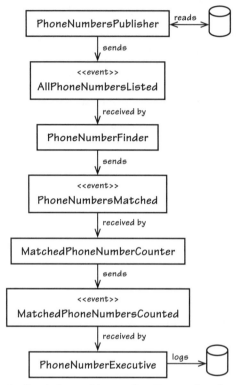

Figure 4.8   A pipeline is formed by sending Events that the Filters process.

is to count the phone numbers in the Event and then forward the results in a new Event. In this case it counts three total lines containing phone numbers. The Filter completes by creating the `MatchedPhoneNumbers-Counted` Event, setting the `count` property to 3. The Event message is sent, continuing the pipeline.

4. Finally, a message handler component subscribed to `MatchedPhone-NumbersCounted` receives it. This component is named `PhoneNumber-Executive`. Its single responsibility is to log the result, including the `count` Event property and the date and time it was received, to a file. In this case it writes

```
3 phone numbers matched on July 15, 2012 at 11:15 PM
```

The pipeline for this specific process is now completed.[6]

---

6. For simplicity I don't discuss Ports, Adapters, and the application API of the Hexagonal Architecture.

This kind of pipeline is somewhat flexible. If we wanted to add any new Filters to the pipeline, we'd create new Events that each existing Filter subscribes to and publishes. Basically we'd have to carefully change the sequential order of the pipeline via configuration. Of course, it's not as easy to change this process as with the command-line approach. Typically, however, we won't change Domain Event pipelines all that frequently. While this particular distributed process is not very useful in itself, it does demonstrate how Pipes and Filters might work in a messaging, Event-Driven Architecture.

So, would we actually expect that we'd see Pipes and Filters exploited to solve a problem like this? Well, ideally not. (In fact, if you find this example annoying, it's probably because you already know better. That's fine, but there are plenty of others who are helped by it.) This is meant only as a synthetic example, one that highlights the concepts. In a real enterprise we would use this pattern to break down a large problem into smaller steps that would make distributed processing easier to understand and manage. It would also allow multiple systems to care only for what they do well.

In an actual DDD scenario, Domain Events reflect names meaningful to the business. Step 1 could publish a Domain Event based on the behavioral outcome of an Aggregate in one Bounded Context. Steps 2 through 4 could occur in one or more different Bounded Contexts that receive the initial Event and then publish one of the subsequent ones. Those three steps could create or modify Aggregates in their respective Contexts. It does depend on the domain, but those are common outcomes of handling Domain Events in a Pipes and Filters Architecture.

As explained in **Domain Events** (8), these are not just paper-thin technical notifications. They explicitly model business process activity occurrences that are useful for domain-wide subscribers to know about, and they pack unique identity and as many knowledge-conveying properties as necessary to clearly get their point across. Yet this synchronous, step-by-step style can be extended to accomplish more than one thing at the same time.

Long-Running Processes, aka Sagas

The synthetic Pipes and Filters example can be extended to demonstrate another Event-Driven, distributed, parallel processing pattern, namely, **Long-Running Processes**. A Long-Running Process is sometimes called a Saga, but depending on your background that name may collide with a preexisting pattern. An early description of Sagas is presented in [Garcia-Molina & Salem]. In an attempt to avoid confusion and ambiguity, I have chosen to use the name Long-Running Process, and sometimes I use the name Process for brevity.

Cowboy Logic

LB: *"Dallas* and *Dynasty*, now *those* are what I call
sagas!"

AJ: "For all you German readers, y'all know *Dynasty* as
Der Denver Clan."

Extending the previous example, we could create parallel pipelines by adding
just one new Filter, `TotalPhoneNumbersCounter`, as an additional subscriber to `AllPhoneNumbersListed`. It receives the Event `AllPhone-`
`NumbersListed` virtually in parallel with the `PhoneNumberFinder`. The
new Filter has a very simple goal, counting all existing contacts. This time,
however, `PhoneNumberExecutive` both starts the Long-Running Process
and tracks it through completion. The executive may or may not reuse the
`PhoneNumbersPublisher`, but the important thing is what's new about it.
The executive, implemented as an Application Service or Command Handler,
tracks the progress of the Long-Running Process and understands when it is
completed and what to do when that happens. Refer to Figure 4.9 as we step
through the sample Long-Running Process.

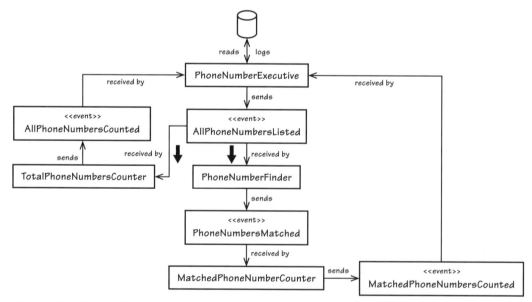

Figure 4.9   The single Long-Running Process executive initiates the parallel processing and tracks
it to completion. The wider arrows indicate where the parallelism begins when two Filters receive
the same Event.

Different Ways to Design a Long-Running Process

Here are three approaches to designing a Long-Running Process, although there may be more:

- Design the process as a composite task, which is tracked by an executive component that records the steps and completeness of the task using a persistent object. This is the approach discussed most thoroughly here.

- Design the process as a set of partner Aggregates that collaborate in a set of activities. One or more Aggregate instances act as the executive and maintain the overall state of the process. This is the approach promoted by Amazon's Pat Helland [Helland].

- Design a stateless process in that each message handler component that receives an Event-carrying message must enrich the received Event with more task progress information as it sends the next message. The state of the overall process is maintained only in the body of each message sent from collaborator to collaborator.

Since the initial Event is now subscribed to by two components, both Filters receive the same Event virtually simultaneously. The original Filter goes about as it always has, matching the specific 303 text pattern. The new Filter only counts all lines, and when it has completed, it sends the Event `AllPhone-NumbersCounted`. The Event includes the count of total contacts. If there are, for example, 15 total phone numbers, the Event `count` property is set to 15.

Now it is the responsibility of `PhoneNumberExecutive` to subscribe to two Events, both `MatchedPhoneNumbersCounted` and `AllPhone-NumbersCounted`. The parallel processing is not considered completed until both of these Domain Events are received. When completion is reached, the results of the parallel processing are merged into a single result. The executive now logs

```
3 of 15 phone numbers matched on July 15, 2012 at 11:27 PM
```

The log output is enhanced with the total count of phone numbers in addition to the previous matching, date, and time information. Although the tasks performed to yield results were really simple, they were performed in parallel. And if at least some of the subscriber components were deployed to different computing nodes, the parallel processing was also distributed.

There is a problem with this Long-Running Process, however. The `PhoneNumberExecutive` currently has no way of knowing that it has received the two completion Domain Events associated with the specific, corresponding parallel processes. If many such processes were started in parallel, and completion Events for each were received out of order, how would the executive know which parallel process was ending? For our synthetic example, logging with mismatched events is hardly tragic. But when dealing with corporate business domains, an improperly aligned Long-Running Process could be disastrous.

The first step in the solution to this troublesome situation is to *assign a unique Process identity* that is carried by each of the associated Domain Events. This could be the same identity assigned to the originating Domain Event that causes the Long-Running Process to begin (for example, `AllPhoneNumbers-Listed`). We could use a universally unique identifier (UUID) allocated specifically to the Process. See **Entities (5)** and **Domain Events (8)** for a discussion of providing unique identity. The `PhoneNumberExecutive` would now write output to the log only upon receiving completion Events with equal identities. However, we can't expect the executive to wait around until all the completion Events are received. It, too, is an Event subscriber that comes and goes with the receipt and handling of each delivery.

Executive *and* Tracker?

Some find that merging the concepts of *executive* and *tracker* into a single object—an Aggregate—to be the simplest approach. Implementing such an Aggregate as a part of the domain model that naturally tracks just a part of the overall Process can be a liberating technique. For one, we avoid developing a separate tracker as state machine, in addition to the Aggregates that must also exist. In fact, the most basic Long-Running Processes are best implemented just that way.

In a Hexagonal Architecture, a Port-Adapter message handler would simply dispatch to an Application Service (or Command Handler), which would load the target Aggregate and delegate to its appropriate command method. Since the Aggregate would in turn fire a Domain Event, the Event would be published in part as an indication that the Aggregate has completed its role in the Process.

This approach closely follows that promoted by Pat Helland, which he refers to as *partner activities* [Helland], and is the second approach described in the sidebar "Different Ways to Design a Long-Running Process." Ideally, however, discussing a separate executive and tracker is a more effective way to teach the overall technique, and a more intuitive way to learn it.

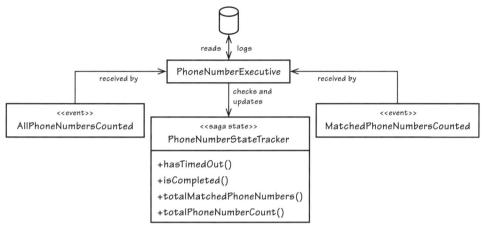

Figure 4.10   A *PhoneNumberStateTracker* serves as a Long-Running Process state object to track progress. The tracker is implemented as an Aggregate.

In an actual domain each instance of a Process executive creates a new Aggregate-like state object for tracking its eventual completion. The state object is created when the Process begins, associating the same unique identity that each related Domain Event must carry. It may also be useful for it to hold a timestamp of when the Process began (the reasons are discussed later in the chapter). The Process state tracker object is illustrated in Figure 4.10.

As each pipeline in the parallel processing completes, the executive receives a corresponding completion Event. The executive retrieves the state tracking instance by matching the unique Process identity carried by the received Event and sets a property that represents the step just completed.

The Process state instance usually has a method such as isCompleted(). As each step is completed and recorded on this state tracker, the executive checks isCompleted(). This method checks for the recorded completion of all required parallel processes. When the method answers true, the executive has the option to publish a final Domain Event if required by the business. This Event could be required if the completing Process is just a branch in a larger parallel process, for example.

A given messaging mechanism may lack features that guarantee *single delivery* of each Event.[7] If it is possible for the messaging mechanism to deliver a Domain Event message two or more times, we can use the Process state object to de-duplicate. Does this require special features to be provided by the messaging mechanism? Consider how it can be handled without them.

---

7. This does not mean guaranteed delivery, but guaranteed single delivery, or once and only once.

When each completion Event is received, *the executive checks the state object for an existing record of completion for that specific Event.* If the completion indicator is already set, the Event is considered a duplicate and is ignored, yet acknowledged.[8] Another option is to *design the state object to be idempotent.* That way, if duplicate messages are received by the executive, the state object absorbs the duplicate occurrence recordings equally. While only the second option designs the state tracker itself as idempotent, both of these approaches support idempotent messaging. See **Domain Events (8)** for further discussion of Event de-duplication.

Some Process completion tracking may be time-sensitive. We can deal with Process time-outs passively or actively. Recall that the Process state tracker can hold a timestamp of its inception. Add to this a total allowable time constant (or configuration) value and the executive can manage time-sensitive Long-Running Processes.

A passive time-out check is performed each time a parallel processing completion Event is received by the executive. The executive retrieves the state tracker and asks it if a time-out has occurred. A method such as `hasTimedOut()` can serve that purpose. If the passive time-out check indicates that the allowable time threshold has been exceeded, the Process state tracker can be marked as abandoned. It's also possible to publish a corresponding failure Domain Event. Note that a disadvantage of the passive time-out check is that the Process could remain active well past its threshold if one or more completion Events are for some reason never received by the executive. This may be unacceptable if a larger parallel process is dependent on certain success or failure of this Process.

An active Process time-out check can be managed using an external timer. For example, a JMX `TimerMBean` instance is one way to get a Java-managed timer. The timer is set for the maximum time-out threshold just as the Process begins. When the timer fires, the listener accesses the Process state tracker. If the state is not already completed (always checked in case the timer fires just as an asynchronous Event completes the Process), it is then marked as abandoned, and a corresponding failure Event is published. If the state tracker is marked as completed prior to the timer firing, the timer can then be terminated. One disadvantage of the active time-out check is that it requires more system resources, which may burden a high-traffic environment. Also, a race condition between the timer and the arriving completion Event could incorrectly cause failure.

---

8. When the messaging mechanism finally receives acknowledgment of receipt, the message will not be delivered again.

Long-Running Processes are often associated with distributed parallel processing but have nothing to do with distributed transactions. They require a mindset that embraces eventual consistency. We must enter any effort to design a Long-Running Process soberly, with the expectation that when infrastructure or the tasks themselves fail, well-designed error recovery is essential. Every system participating in a single instance of a Long-Running Process must be considered inconsistent with all other participants until the executive receives the final completion notification. True, some Long-Running Processes may be capable of succeeding with only partial completion, or they may delay for even a number of days before full completion. But if the Process runs aground and the participating systems are left in inconsistent states, compensation may be necessary. If compensation is mandatory, it could surpass the complexity of designing the success path. Perhaps business procedures could allow for failures and offer workflow solutions instead.

The SaaSOvation teams employ an Event-Driven Architecture across Bounded Contexts, and the ProjectOvation team will use the simplest form of a Long-Running Process to manage the creation of `Discussions` assigned to `Product` instances. The overarching style is Hexagonal to manage the outside messaging and publishing of Domain Events around the enterprise.

Not to be overlooked is that the Long-Running Process executive can publish one, two, or more Events to initiate the parallel processing. There may also be not only two, but three or more subscribers to any initiating Event or Events. In other words, a Long-Running Process may lead to many separate business process activities executing simultaneously. Thus, our synthetic example is limited in complexity only for the sake of communicating the basic concepts of a Long-Running Process.

Long-Running Processes are often useful when integration with legacy systems can have high latency. Even if latency and legacy are not the chief concerns, we still benefit from the distribution and parallelism with elegance, which can lead to highly scalable, highly available business systems.

Some messaging mechanisms have built-in support for Long-Running Processes, which can greatly expedite adoption. One such is [NServiceBus], which specifically calls them Sagas. Another Saga implementation is provided with [MassTransit].

Event Sourcing

Sometimes the business cares about tracking changes that occur to the objects in a domain model. There are varying levels of change tracking interest, and ways to support each level. Typically businesses have chosen to track only when some entity is created and last modified, and by whom. It's a relatively simple and straightforward approach to change tracking. This, however, doesn't provide any information about the individual changes in the model.

With an increased desire for even more change tracking, the business demands more metadata. It begins to care also about the individual operations that were executed over time. Maybe it even wants to understand how long certain operations took to execute. Those desires lead to the need to maintain an audit log or journal of the finer-grained use case metrics. But an audit log or journal has its limitations. It can convey some information about what has happened in the system, perhaps even allowing for some debugging. But it doesn't allow us to examine the state of individual domain objects before and after specific kinds of changes. What if we could stretch more out of change tracking?

As developers we have all experienced finer-grained change tracking in one form or another. The most common example is with the use of a source code repository, such as CVS, Subversion, Git, or Mercurial. What all of these variations of source revision management systems have in common is that they all know how to track changes that occur on a source file. The change tracking provided by this genre of tool enables us to go all the way back in time, to view a source code artifact from its very first revision, and then to proceed revision by revision, all the way to the very latest. When committing all source files to revision control, it can track changes of the whole development life cycle.

Now, if we think about applying this concept to a single Entity, then to an Aggregate, then to every Aggregate in the model, we can understand the power of change tracking objects and the value it can produce in our systems. With that in mind, we want to develop a means to know what occurred in the model to cause the creation of any given Aggregate instance, and also what has happened to that given Aggregate instance throughout time, operation by operation. Given the history of everything that's happened, we could even support temporal models. This level of change tracking is at the heart of a pattern named Event Sourcing.[9] Figure 4.11 shows a high-level view of this pattern.

There are varying definitions of Event Sourcing, so some clarification is fitting. We are discussing the use where every operational command executed

---

9. A discussion of Event Sourcing generally requires an understanding of CQRS, which is treated in the earlier section on that topic.

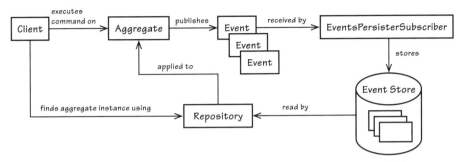

Figure 4.11 A high-level view of Event Sourcing, where Aggregates publish Events that are stored and used to track the model's state changes. The Repository reads Events from the Store and applies them to reconstitute the Aggregate's state.

on any given Aggregate instance in the domain model will publish at least one Domain Event that describes the execution outcome. Each of the events is saved to an **Event Store** (8) in the order in which it occurred. When each Aggregate is retrieved from its Repository, the instance is reconstituted by playing back the Events in the order in which they previously occurred.[10] In other words, first the very earliest Event is played back, and the Aggregate applies the Event to itself, modifying its state. Next, the second-oldest Event is played back in the same manner. This continues until all Events, from the oldest to the most recent, are completely played back and applied. At that point the Aggregate exists in the state it had upon the most recent execution of some command behavior.

A Moving Target?

The definition of Event Sourcing has undergone some scrutiny and refinement, and at the time of writing it is still not completely settled. As with most leading-edge techniques, refinement is necessary. What is described here captures the essence of the pattern as applied using DDD and probably to a large degree reflects how in general it will be used moving forward.

Over a long period of changes to any and all Aggregate instances, doesn't the playback of hundreds, thousands, or even millions of Events cause serious latency and overhead in processing the model? At least for some of the higher-traffic models that would most certainly be the case.

To avoid this bottleneck we can apply an optimization that uses Aggregate state *snapshots*. A process is developed to produce, in the background, a

---

10. The Aggregate state is a conflation of previous Events, but only by applying them in the same order in which they occurred.

snapshot of the Aggregate's in-memory state at a specific point in Event Store history. To do this, the Aggregate is loaded into memory using all previous Events to the current point in time. The Aggregate state is then serialized, and the serialized snapshot image is then saved to the Event Store. From that point forward the Aggregate is first instantiated using the most recent snapshot, and then all Events newer than that snapshot are played back on the Aggregate as described previously.

Snapshots are not created randomly. Rather, they can be created at points where a predefined number of newer Events have occurred. The team would determine a number based on domain heuristics or other observations. For example, we might find that Aggregate retrieval performs optimally when having no more than 50 or 100 or so Events between snapshots.

Event Sourcing leans heavily in the direction of technical solution. We can produce domain models that publish Domain Events without the need to support Event Sourcing. As a persistence mechanism, Event Sourcing replaces and is far different from using an ORM tool. Because Events are often persisted in an Event Store as binary representations, they cannot (optimally) be used for queries. In fact, Repositories designed for an Event Sourcing model require only a single get/find operation, and that method takes as a parameter only the Aggregate unique identity. Further, by design Aggregates don't have any query methods (getters). As a result, we need another way to query, which generally leads to employing CQRS (discussed previously) hand-in-glove with Event Sourcing.[11]

Since Event Sourcing leads us down the path of thinking differently about the way domain models are designed, we need to justify our use. At its most basic, Event history can reveal solutions to bugs in the system. Debugging with the use of explicit history of everything that has ever happened to the model has a big advantage. Event Sourcing can lead to high-throughput domain models, scaling to extremely large numbers of transactions per second. Appending to a single database table, for example, is extremely fast. Further, it enables the CQRS query model to be scaled out, because updates to that data source are performed in the background after the Event Store is updated with new Events. This can additionally allow for replicating the query model to more data source instances in support of growing numbers of clients.

But technical advantages don't always sell techniques to the business. Thus, consider just a few of the business advantages of using Event Sourcing that are afforded due to the technical implementation:

---

11. Although we can use CQRS without using Event Sourcing, the opposite is not usually practical.

- Patch the Event Store with new or modified Events that fix problems. This may have business implications, but if it is legal in a given situation, the patch can save the system from serious issues that occurred because of bugs in the model. Since the patches have a built-in audit trail, the use of patches may decrease any legal implications by making them explicit and traceable.

- Besides patching, we can also undo and redo changes in the model by replaying varying sets of Events. This may have technical implications and business implications and may not be possible to support in all cases.

- With an accurate history of everything that has occurred in the domain model, the business can consider "what if?" questions. That is, by playing back stored Events on a set of Aggregates that have experimental enhancements, the business can get accurate answers to hypothetical questions. Would the business benefit if it could simulate conceptual scenarios using real historical data? Very likely, yes. It's an alternative way to approach business intelligence.

Would the business benefit from one or more of these technical and nontechnical advantages?

Appendix A provides rich details on implementing Aggregates with Event Sourcing and discusses how views may be projected for CQRS. For further details see [Dahan, CQRS] and [Nijof, CQRS].

Data Fabric and Grid-Based Distributed Computing

Contributed by Wes Williams

As software systems become more and more complex and sophisticated, with expanding user bases and requirements centered around "big data," traditional database solutions can become performance bottlenecks. Organizations that face the realities of information systems of colossal size have no alternative but to seek solutions that are equal to the computing challenges. Data Fabrics—also sometimes called Grid Computing[12]—offer performance and elastic scalability capabilities that such business situations demand.

---

12. This is not to say that Fabrics and Grids are identical concepts, but for those looking at this architecture in a general way these labels often mean the same thing. Certainly marketing and sales often limit them to the same meaning. In any case, this section uses the term *Data Fabric* since it generally represents a richer set of capabilities than Grid Computing.

Cowboy Logic

AJ: "Would you like some information in exchange for a drink?"

LB: "Sorry, J. We only accept cache here."

One good thing about Data Fabrics is that they support domain models in a natural way, nearly eliminating any impedance mismatch. In fact, their distributed caches easily accommodate the persistence of domain objects in general and act as Aggregate Stores specifically.[13] Simply stated, an Aggregate stored in a Fabric's map-based cache[14] is the value part of a key-value pair. The key is formed from the globally unique identity of the Aggregate, and the Aggregate state itself is serialized to some binary or textual representation serving as the value:

```
String key = product.productId().id();

byte[] value = Serializer.serialize(product);

// region (GemFire) or cache (Coherence)
region.put(key, value);
```

Thus, a positive consequence of using a Data Fabric with features closely aligned with the technical aspects of a domain model is the possibility of shortened development cycles.[15]

The examples provided in this section demonstrate how a Data Fabric can host a domain model in cache and enable system functionalities at distributed scale. In doing so, we'll explore ways to support the CQRS architecture pattern and Event-Driven Architecture using Long-Running Processes.

Data Replication

Thinking of an in-memory data cache, we may immediately consider the real possibility of losing all or part of our system's state if the cache fails in some

---

13. Martin Fowler has recently promoted the term *Aggregate Store*, although the concept has existed for some time.
14. In GemFire this is called a region, but it's the same concept that Coherence calls a cache. I use *cache* for consistency.
15. Some NoSQL stores likewise act as natural "Aggregate Stores," simplifying technical aspects of implementing DDD.

way. It's a real concern, but far from troublesome when redundancy is built into the Fabric.

Consider the memory cache provided by a Fabric when using a cache-per-Aggregate strategy. In that case the Repository of a given Aggregate type is backed by a dedicated cache. A cache supporting only a single node would be quite vulnerable to failures at a single point. However, a Fabric providing multinode caches with replication would be quite reliable. You can choose the level of redundancy based on the probability of the number of nodes that may fail at any given time, which becomes very narrow as more nodes are included. You also have the latitude to trade redundancy for performance since, of course, performance can be impacted by the number of node replications required for an Aggregate to be fully committed.

Here's an example of how cache (or region, again depending on the concrete Fabric) redundancy may work. One node acts as the *primary* cache/region, and any number of others are *secondary*. If a primary store fails, a fail-over occurs and one of the secondaries becomes the new primary. When the former primary recovers, all data stored on the new primary gets replicated to the recovered node and it becomes a secondary.

An additional advantage of fail-over nodes is that they ensure guaranteed delivery of events published from the Fabric. Thus, updates to Aggregates and any Fabric events published as a result are never lost. Obviously, cache redundancy and replication are essential features for storing business-critical domain model objects.

Event-Driven Fabrics and Domain Events

A primary feature of a Fabric is the support of an Event-Driven style, with guaranteed delivery. Most Fabrics have built-in eventing of a technical nature, that is, the automatic notification of events that inform about cache-level and entry-level occurrences. Those should not be confused with Domain Events. For example, a cache-level event informs of happenings such as cache reinitialization, and an entry-level event informs about occurrences such as entry creation and updates.

Still, with a Fabric supporting an open architecture there should be a way to support publishing Domain Events directly out of Aggregates. Your Domain Events may have to subclass a specific framework event type, such as `EntryEvent` (for example, GemFire), but that's a small price to pay for the power they afford.

How might you actually use Domain Events in a Fabric? As discussed in **Domain Events (8)**, your Aggregates would use a simple `DomainEvent-Publisher` component. In the cache of a Fabric this publisher may simply put the published Events into a specific cache/region. Cached Events would then be delivered to subscribers (listeners), either synchronously or asynchronously. So as not to waste precious memory in this dedicated Event cache/region, as each Event is fully acknowledged by all subscribers, its entry would be removed from the map. Of course, each Event is only fully acknowledged once it has been published by one or more subscribers to a message queue or bus and/or used to freshen a CQRS query model.

Since Domain Event subscribers may also use the Events to carry out the synchronization of other dependent Aggregates, eventual consistency is guaranteed by means of the architecture.

Continuous Queries

Some Fabrics support a kind of event notification known as Continuous Query. This enables a client to register a query with the Fabric that will ensure that the client receives notification of changes in the cache that satisfy the query. One use of the Continuous Query is by user interface components, which enables these to listen for changes that could impact the current view.

Do you see what's coming? CQRS has a strong fit with the Continuous Query feature, assuming that the query model is maintained in the Fabric. Rather than requiring the view to chase after view table updates, the notifications delivered as registered Continuous Queries are resolved, allowing the views to update just in time. Here's an example of a client registering for Gem-Fire Continuous Query events:

```
CqAttributesFactory factory = new CqAttributesFactory();

CqListener listener = new BacklogItemWatchListener();

factory.addCqListener(listener);

String continuousQueryName = "BacklogItemWatcher";

String query = "select * from /queryModelBacklogItem qmbli "
        + "where qmbli.status = 'Committed'";

CqQuery backlogItemWatcher = queryService.newCq(
        continuousQueryName, query, factory.create());
```

The Data Fabric will now deliver CQRS query model updates based on Aggregate modifications to the client callback object provided by the `CqListener`, along with metadata that was added, updated, or destroyed when the matching criteria are met.

Distributed Processing

A powerful use of a Data Fabric is to distribute processing across the Fabric's replicated caches and return the aggregated results to the client. This enables the Fabric to fulfill Event-Driven, distributed parallel processing, perhaps using Long-Running Processes.

To illustrate this feature, we'll have to mention some concrete approaches in GemFire and Coherence. Your Process executive could be implemented as a GemFire Function or a Coherence Entry Processor. Both can serve as **Command** [Gamma et al.] handlers that execute in parallel across distributed, replicated cache. (You might instead choose to think of this concept as a Domain Service, but what it does may not be domain-centric.) For consistency let's call this feature a Function. A Function can optionally accept a filter to constrain the execution against matching Aggregate instances.

Let's look at a sample Function that implements a Long-Running Process for the previously presented Phone Number Count Process. This Process will be executed in parallel across the replicated cache using a GemFire Function:

```
public class PhoneNumberCountSaga extends FunctionAdapter {
    @Override
    public void execute(FunctionContext context) {
        Cache cache = CacheFactory.getAnyInstance();
        QueryService queryService = cache.getQueryService();

        String phoneNumberFilterQuery = (String) context.getArguments();
        ...
        // Pseudo code
        // - Execute Function to obtain MatchedPhoneNumbersCounted.
        //   - Send answer to the aggregator by invoking the
        //     aggregator.sendResult(MatchedPhoneNumbersCounted).
        // - Execute Function to obtain AllPhoneNumbersCounted.
        //   - Send answer to the aggregator by invoking the
        //     aggregator.sendResult(AllPhoneNumbersCounted).
        // - The aggregator automatically accumulates the answers
        //   from each distributed Function call and returns the
        //   single aggregated answer to the client.
    }
}
```

Here is sample code for a client that will execute a Long-Running Process in parallel against distributed replicated cache:

```
PhoneNumberCountProcess phoneNumberCountProcess =
        new PhoneNumberCountProcess();
```

```
String phoneNumberFilterQuery =
        "select phoneNumber from /phoneNumberRegion pnr "
        + "where pnr.areaCode = '303'";

Execution execution =
        FunctionService.onRegion(phoneNumberRegion)
                .withFilter(0)
                .withArgs(phoneNumberFilterQuery)
                .withCollector(new PhoneNumberCountResultCollector());

PhoneNumberCountResultCollector resultCollector =
        execution.execute(phoneNumberCountProcess);

List allPhoneNumberCountResults = (List) resultsCollector.getResult();
```

Of course, the process could be much more complex or far simpler than this one. This also demonstrates that a Process is not of necessity an Event-Driven concept, but one that can work with other concurrent, distributed processing approaches. For a full discussion of Fabric-based distributed and parallel processing, see [GemFire Functions].

Wrap-Up

We've reviewed several architectural styles and architecture patterns that can be used with DDD. This is not an exhaustive list because there are just too many possibilities, which emphasizes the versatility of DDD. For example, we haven't considered how to apply DDD when Map-Reduce is at play. That's a topic for a future discussion.

- We've discussed the traditional Layers Architecture and how it can be improved on by using the Dependency Inversion Principle.

- You've learned about the strengths of the possibly timeless Hexagonal Architecture, which provides an overarching style for application architectures.

- We've emphasized how DDD should be used in an SOA environment, with REST, and using a Data Fabric or a Grid-Based Distributed Cache.

- You got an overview of CQRS and how it can simplify some aspects of the application.

- We've taken a look at the various aspects of how Event-Driven works, including Pipes and Filters, Long-Running Processes, and even a glimpse at Event Sourcing.

We next move on to a series of chapters on DDD tactical modeling. Those chapters will help you see the finer-grained modeling options at your disposal, and how to best put them to work.

Chapter 5

Entities

> *I'm Chevy Chase . . . and you're not.*
> —*Chevy Chase*

There is a tendency for developers to focus on data rather than the domain. This can happen with those new to DDD, because of the prevailing approaches to software development that place importance on the database. Instead of designing domain concepts with rich behaviors, we might think primarily about the attributes (columns) and associations (foreign keys) of the data. Doing so reflects the data model into object counterparts, which leads to almost every concept in our "domain model" being coded as an **Entity** abounding with getter and setter methods. It's easy to find tools that will generate all that for us. Although there may be nothing wrong with property accessors, that's not the only behavior DDD Entities should have.

It's a trap that was sprung on SaaSOvation developers. Learn from their lessons in Entity design.

Road Map to This Chapter

- Consider why Entities have their proper place when we need to model unique things.
- See how unique identities may be generated for Entities.
- Look in on a design session as a team captures its **Ubiquitous Language (1)** in Entity design.
- Learn how you can express Entity roles and responsibilities.
- See examples of how Entities can be validated and how to persist them to storage.

Why We Use Entities

We design a domain concept as an Entity when we care about its individuality, when distinguishing it from all other objects in a system is a mandatory constraint. An Entity is a unique thing and is capable of being changed continuously over a long period of time. Changes may be so extensive that the object might seem much different from what it once was. Yet, it is the same object by identity.

As the object changes, we may be interested in tracking when, how, and by whom changes were made. Or we might be satisfied that its current form implies enough about its previous state transitions that explicit change tracking is unnecessary. Even if we don't decide to track every detail of its change history, we could still reason on and discuss the sequences of valid changes that could occur to these objects over their entire lifetime. It is the unique identity and mutability characteristics that set Entities apart from **Value Objects (6)**.

There are times when an Entity is not the appropriate modeling tool to reach for. Misappropriated use happens far more often than many are aware. Often a concept should be modeled as a Value. If this is a disagreeable notion, it might be that DDD doesn't fit your business needs. It is quite possible that a CRUD-based system would be more fitting. If so, that decision should save your project both time and money. The problem is that pursuing CRUD-based alternatives doesn't always save those precious resources.

Businesses regularly put too much effort into developing glorified database table editors. Without the correct tool selection, CRUD-based solutions treated elaborately are too expensive. When CRUD makes sense, languages and frameworks such as Groovy and Grails, Ruby on Rails, and the like make the most sense. If the choice is correct, it should save time and money.

Cowboy Logic

AJ: "What kinda CRUD did I just land in?"

LB: "That's a cow pie, J!"

AJ: "I know what pie is. You got your apple pie and your cherry pie. This ain't no pie."

LB: "Like they say, 'Never kick a cow pie on a hot day.' It's a good thing you didn't kick it."

On the other hand, if we apply CRUD to the wrong systems—more complex ones that deserve the precision of DDD—we may regret it. When complexity grows, we experience the limitation of poor tool selection. CRUD systems can't produce a refined business model by only capturing data.

If DDD is a justifiable investment in the business's bottom line, we use Entities as intended.

> When an object is distinguished by its identity, rather than its attributes, make this primary to its definition in the model. Keep the class definition simple and

focused on life cycle continuity and identity. Define a means of distinguishing each object regardless of its form or history. . . . The model must define what it means to be the same thing. [Evans, p. 92]

This chapter teaches how to place the proper emphasis on Entities and shows you various Entity design techniques.

Unique Identity

In the early stages of designing an Entity, we purposely focus only on those primary attributes and behaviors that are central to its unique identity, as well as those useful for querying it, and we purposely ignore all other attributes and behaviors until we settle on the primary ones.

Rather than focusing on the attributes or even the behavior, strip the Entity object's definition down to the most intrinsic characteristics, particularly those that identify it or are commonly used to find or match it. Add only behavior that is essential to the concept and attributes that are required by that behavior. [Evans, p. 93]

So that's what we'll do first. Having a range of available options for implementing identity is really important, as are those for ensuring that the uniqueness is preserved throughout time.

An Entity's unique identity may or may not also be practical for finding or matching. Using the unique identity for matching usually depends on how human-readable it is. For example, if the application makes searching for a person's name available to users, it is very unlikely that the name is used as the `Person` Entity unique identity. People very frequently have nonunique names. On the other hand, if the application makes searching for a company's tax ID possible, the tax ID may well be the primary unique identifier for the `Company` Entity. Governments issue unique tax identities.

Value Objects can serve as holders of unique identity. They are immutable, which ensures identity stability, and any behavior specific to the kind of identity is centralized. Having a focal point for identity behavior, however simple, keeps the know-how from leaking into other parts of the model and into clients.

Consider some common identity creation strategies, from the apparently simplest and most basic to those with increasing complexity:

- The user provides one or more original unique values as input to the application. The application must ensure that they are unique.

- The application internally generates an identity using an algorithm that ensures uniqueness. We can get a library or framework to do this for us, but it can be done by the application.

- The application relies on a persistence store, such as a database, to generate a unique identity.

- Another **Bounded Context (2)** (system or application) has already determined the unique identity. It is input or selected by the user from a set of choices.

Let's consider the individual strategies, along with particular challenges related to each. There are almost always side effects when considering the range of technical solutions. One such side effect occurs when we use relational databases for object persistence, which leak into our domain models. We round out identity creation concerns by addressing the impact of the timing of identity generation, the relational database's referential identity on domain objects, and how object-relational mapping (ORM) plays into this situation. We'll also consider some practical guidance on keeping unique identities stable.

User Provides Identity

It appears to be a straightforward approach to have a user manually enter the details of unique identity. The user types a recognizable value or symbol into an input field or selects from a set of available characteristics, and the Entity is created. True, it is a simple enough approach. But there can be complications.

One complication is relying on users to produce quality identities. The identity may be unique but incorrect. Most times identities must be immutable, so users shouldn't change them. This is not always the case, and there may be advantages to enabling users to correct identity values. Here's an example. If we use the titles of `Forum` and `Discussion` as unique identities, what would happen if the user spelled the title incorrectly, or later decided that the title was not as fitting as it could have been, as shown in Figure 5.1? What's the cost of change? Although user-provided identity may seem like a well-budgeted approach, it may not be. Can users be relied upon to produce both unique and correct, long-lasting identities?

Preventing this problem starts with design discussions. Teams need to consider fail-proof approaches to enable users to define unique identity. Workflow-based identity approval is not conducive to high-throughput domains but works best when human-readable identity is a must. If it takes extra time and effort to create and approve an identity that will be used pervasively throughout

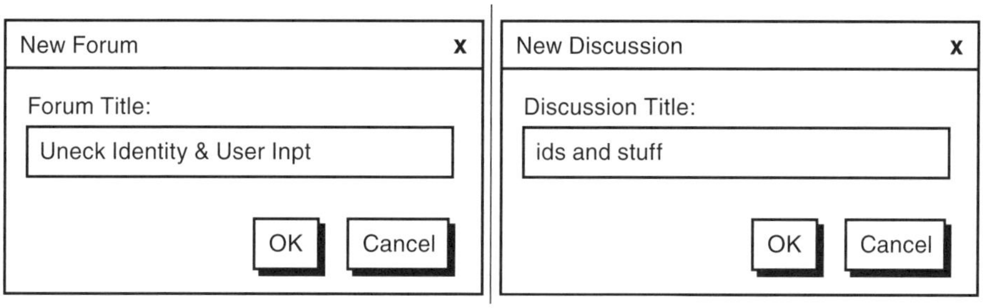

Figure 5.1 The forum title is misspelled and the discussion title is less than desirable.

the business for years to come, and supporting a workflow is possible, adding a few extra cycles to ensure the quality of the identity is a good investment.

We always have the option to include user-entered values as Entity properties available for matching, but not to use them for unique identity. Simple properties are more easily modified as part of the normal operational state of the Entity that changes over time. In that case we will need to use another means to obtain unique identity.

Application Generates Identity

There are highly reliable ways to autogenerate unique identities, although care must be taken when the application is clustered or otherwise distributed across multiple computing nodes. There are identity creation patterns that can, to a much greater degree of certainty, produce a completely unique identity. The *universally unique identifier* (UUID), or *globally unique identifier* (GUID), is one such approach. A common variation follows, where the result of each step is concatenated into a single textual representation:

1. Time in milliseconds on the computing node

2. IP address of the computing code

3. Object identity of the factory object instance within the virtual machine (Java)

4. Random number generated by the same generator within the virtual machine (Java)

This produces a 128-bit unique value. It is most often expressed as a 32-byte or 36-byte hexadecimal encoded text string. The text format is 36 bytes when you use the common hyphen segment separators in the format `f36ab21c-67dc-5274-c642-1de2f4d5e72a`. Without the hyphens it is 32 bytes. Either way, the identity is big and is not considered human-readable.

In the Java world, this formula has been replaced by a standard UUID generator available since Java 1.5. It's provided by class `java.util.UUID`. This implementation supports four different generator algorithms based on the Leach-Salz variant. Using the Java standard API, we can easily generate a pseudo-random unique identity:

```
String rawId = java.util.UUID.randomUUID().toString();
```

It uses type 4, employing a cryptographically strong pseudo-random-number generator, which is based on the `java.security.SecureRandom` generator. Type 3 employs a name encryption approach, which uses `java.security.MessageDigest`. We can get a name-based UUID like this:

```
String rawId = java.util.UUID.nameUUIDFromBytes(
        "Some text".getBytes()).toString();
```

We can also blend the pseudo-random-number generation with encryption:

```
SecureRandom randomGenerator = new SecureRandom();

int randomNumber = randomGenerator.nextInt();

String randomDigits = new Integer(randomNumber).toString();

MessageDigest encryptor = MessageDigest.getInstance("SHA-1");

byte[] rawIdBytes = encryptor.digest(randomDigits.getBytes());
```

Now we are left only with the task of converting the `rawIdBytes` array to a hexadecimal text representation. We could get that conversion for free. After generating the random number and converting it to a `String`, we pass that text to the `UUID nameUUIDFromBytes()` **Factory** [Gamma et al.] method.

There are other identity generation facilities, such as `java.rmi.server.UID` and `java.rmi.dgc.VMID`, but these seem inferior to `java.util.UUID` and are not discussed here.

UUID is a relatively fast identity to generate, requiring no interaction with the outside, such as a persistence mechanism. Even if a specific kind of Entity is created many times per second, the UUID generator can keep up the pace. For higher-performance domains we can cache any number of UUID instances, refilling the cache in the background. If cached UUID instances are lost due to server restart, there are no gaps in identities because they are all based on random, manufactured values. Refilling the cache on server restart has no negative consequences of abandoned values.

With such a large identity, its use could in rare cases be rendered impractical because of the memory overhead. In such cases an 8-byte long identity generated by the persistence mechanism would improve matters. A smaller, 4-byte integer, with two billion or so unique values, may even suffice. These approaches are discussed next.

Considering the following, understandably we don't normally want to display a UUID on our user interface views:

```
f36ab21c-67dc-5274-c642-1de2f4d5e72a
```

A full UUID is usually appropriate when it can be hidden from users and human-readable reference techniques can be used. For example, we can design hypermedia resources with URIs that can be e-mailed or sent around using other user-to-user messaging. The text relationship part of the link can be used to disguise the mysterious-looking UUID, just as the text in <a>text</a> disguises technical links in HTML.

Depending on the level of trust you have in the uniqueness of individual segments of the hexadecimal text UUID, you may decide to use just one or a few segments of the whole. The shortened identities are more trustworthy when used only as the *local identity* of Entities within the **Aggregate (10)** boundary. Local identity means that Entities held inside an Aggregate need only have uniqueness among other Entities held inside the same Aggregate. On the other hand, the Entity serving as an Aggregate Root requires global unique identity.

Our own identity generator could use one or more specific UUID segments. Consider a contrived example: `APM-P-08-14-2012-F36AB21C`. This 25-character identity represents a `Product` (P) from the *Agile Project Management Context* (APM) that was created on August 14, 2012. The extra text `F36AB21C` is the first segment of a generated UUID, which uniquely sets it apart from other `Product` Entities created on the same day. It has the benefit of human readability with a high probability for global uniqueness. Users aren't the only ones to benefit. When identities such as this one are passed between Bounded Contexts, developers immediately know where they originated. For SaaSOvation this approach could be practical since Aggregates are further segregated by tenancy.

Maintaining this kind of identity in a `String` would probably not be a good choice. A custom identity Value Object would work better:

```
String rawId = "APM-P-08-14-2012-F36AB21C"; // would be generated
ProductId productId = new ProductId(rawId);
...
Date productCreationDate = productId.creationDate();
```

A client can ask for identity details, such as the date the product was created, and it's conveniently provided. Clients need not understand the raw identity format. Now the `Product` Aggregate Root can expose its creation date without indicating to clients how it is obtained:

```
public class Product extends Entity {
    private ProductId productId;
    ...
    public Date creationDate() {
        return this.productId().creationDate();
    }
    ...
}
```

You may find identity generation in third-party libraries and frameworks. The Apache Commons project has a Commons Id (sandbox) component, which supplies five different identity generators.

Some persistence stores, such as NoSQL Riak and MongoDB, can generate identities for you. Normally to save a value in Riak, you use HTTP PUT, which takes a key:

```
PUT /riak/bucket/key

[object serialization]
```

You may instead use POST without providing a key, forcing Riak to generate a unique identity. Still, we do need to think about early versus late identity generation, as discussed later in this chapter.

What will serve as a Factory for your application-generated identities? For Aggregate Root identity generation, I like to use its **Repository (12)**:

```
public class HibernateProductRepository
        implements ProductRepository {
    ...
    public ProductId nextIdentity() {
        return new ProductId(
                java.util.UUID.randomUUID().toString().toUpperCase());
    }
    ...
}
```

This seems like a natural location for identity generation.

Persistence Mechanism Generates Identity

Delegating the generation of unique identity to a persistence mechanism has some unique advantages. If we call on the database for a sequence or incrementing value, it will always be unique.

Depending on the range needed, the database can generate a unique 2-byte, 4-byte, or 8-byte value. In Java, a 2-byte short integer would allow for up to 32,767 unique identities; a 4-byte normal integer would afford 2,147,483,647 unique values; and an 8-byte long integer would provide up to 9,223,372,036,854,775,807 distinct identities. Even zero-filled text representations of these ranges are narrow, at five, ten, and 19 characters respectively. These can also be employed to create composite identities.

One possible downside is performance. It can take significantly longer to go to the database to get each value than to generate identities in the application. Much depends on database load and application demand. One way around this is to cache sequence/increment values in the application, such as in a Repository. This can work well, but we generally count on losing a good number of unused values when server nodes must be restarted. If the gaps caused by lost cache are unacceptable, or if you have planned for only a relatively small number of values (2-byte short integer), caching preallocated values may not be a practical or necessary option. It may be possible to harvest and recover lost identities, but that may be more trouble than it is worth.

Preallocation and caching are not an issue if the model can suffice with late identity generation. Here's how it's done with Hibernate and an Oracle sequence:

```
<id name="id" type="long" column="product_id">
    <generator class="sequence">
        <param name="sequence">product_seq</param>
    </generator>
</id>
```

Here's an example of the same approach, but using a MySQL auto-increment column:

```
<id name="id" type="long" column="product_id">
    <generator class="native"/>
</id>
```

This does perform well, and it is quite easy to configure in a Hibernate mapping definition. The problem could be the timing of generation, which is discussed a bit later. The remainder of this subsection covers the early identity generation requirement.

> **Order May Matter**
>
> Sometimes it matters when the identity generation and assignment occur for an Entity.
>
> *Early* identity generation and assignment happen *before* the Entity is persisted.
>
> *Late* identity generation and assignment happen *when* the Entity is persisted.

Here a Repository supports early generation, serving the next available Oracle sequence using a query:

```
public ProductId nextIdentity() {
    Long rawProductId = (Long)
        this.session()
            .createSQLQuery(
                "select product_seq.nextval as product_id from dual")
            .addScalar("product_id", Hibernate.LONG)
            .uniqueResult();

    return new ProductId(rawProductId);
}
```

Since Oracle returns sequence values that Hibernate maps as `BigDecimal` instances, we must inform Hibernate that we want the `product_id` result converted to a `Long`.

What do we do about databases, such as MySQL, that don't support sequences? MySQL supports auto-incrementing columns. Normally the auto-increment does not occur until a row is newly inserted. Still, there is a way to make a MySQL auto-increment work like an Oracle sequence:

```
mysql> CREATE TABLE product_seq (nextval INT NOT NULL);
Query OK, 0 rows affected (0.14 sec)

mysql> INSERT INTO product_seq VALUES (0);
Query OK, 1 row affected (0.03 sec)

mysql> UPDATE product_seq SET nextval=LAST_INSERT_ID(nextval + 1);
Query OK, 1 row affected (0.03 sec)
Rows matched: 1  Changed: 1  Warnings: 0

mysql> SELECT LAST_INSERT_ID();
+------------------+
| LAST_INSERT_ID() |
+------------------+
|                1 |
+------------------+
1 row in set (0.06 sec)
```

```
mysql> SELECT * FROM product_seq;
+---------+
| nextval |
+---------+
|       1 |
+---------+
1 row in set (0.00 sec)
```

We've created a table in a MySQL database named `product_seq`. Next, we insert a single row into the table, initializing its one and only column, `nextval`, to 0. Those first two steps establish the sequence emulator for the `Product` Entity. The next two statements demonstrate a single sequence value generation. We update the one and only row by incrementing the `nextval` column by 1. The update statement uses a MySQL function, `LAST_INSERT_ID()`, to increment the column's `INT` value. The expression parameter is first executed, then the result is assigned to the `nextval` column. The result of the expression parameter `nextval + 1` remains stable in the `LAST_INSERT_ID()` function, such that when the subsequence `SELECT LAST_INSERT_ID()` statement is evaluated, the value of `nextval` that results from that exact execution is returned in the result set. Last, as a test, we can `SELECT * FROM product_seq` to prove that the current value of `nextval` is the same returned with the function result.

Hibernate 3.2.3 uses `org.hibernate.id.enhanced.SequenceStyle-Generator` to facilitate portable sequences, but that supports only late identity generation (when the Entity is inserted). To support early sequence generation in a Repository we will have to create a custom Hibernate or JDBC query. Here is a reimplementation of the `ProductRepository` method next-`Identity()` for MySQL:

```java
public ProductId nextIdentity() {
    long rawId = -1L;
    try {
        PreparedStatement ps =
            this.connection().prepareStatement(
                "update product_seq "
                + "set next_val=LAST_INSERT_ID(next_val + 1)");

        ResultSet rs = ps.executeQuery();

        try {
            rs.next();
            rawId = rs.getLong(1);
        } finally {
            try {
                rs.close();
```

```
        } catch(Throwable t) {
            // ignore
        }
    }

} catch (Throwable t) {
    throw new IllegalStateException(
            "Cannot generate next identity", t);
}

return new ProductId(rawId);
}
```

Using JDBC, there is no need to execute a second query on the database to get the results of function LAST_INSERT_ID(). The update query does it all. We get the long value from the ResultSet, using it to create the ProductId.

The last trick is to get a JDBC connection from Hibernate. This can be a bit of a pain, but it's possible:

```
private Connection connection() {
    SessionFactoryImplementor sfi =
            (SessionFactoryImplementor)sessionFactory;
    ConnectionProvider cp = sfi.getConnectionProvider();
    return cp.getConnection();
}
```

Without a Connection object we can't get a ResultSet by executing a PreparedStatement. Without that it's not possible to use a portable sequence.

Using portable sequences from Oracle, MySQL, and other databases, we have the means to generate more compact, guaranteed unique identities that support pre-insert creation.

Another Bounded Context Assigns Identity

When another Bounded Context assigns identity, we need to integrate to find, match, and assign each identity. DDD integrations are explained in **Context Maps (3)** and **Integrating Bounded Contexts (13)**.

Making an exact match is the most desirable. Users need to provide one or more attributes, such as an account number, username, e-mail address, or other unique symbol, to pinpoint the intended result.

Often, matching involves fuzzy input, resulting in multiple search results, along with some human user selection. Figure 5.2 illustrates this. The user enters the "like search" (wildcard) criterion for the sought-after Entity. We

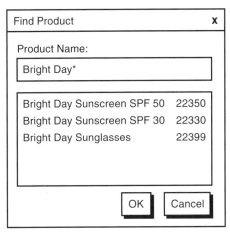

Figure 5.2 The search results from matching an external system to find an identity. The selection user interface may or may not display the identity. This example does display it.

access the API of the external Bounded Context, which resolves the search to zero, one, or multiple similarly described objects. The user then selects the specific result from among the multiple options. The identity of the selected choice is used as the local identity. Some additional state (properties) from the foreign Entity may also be copied into the local Entity.

This has synchronization implications. What happens if externally referenced objects transition in ways that affect local Entities? How will we know that the associated object changed? This problem can be solved using an **Event-Driven Architecture (4)** with **Domain Events (8)**. Our local Bounded Context subscribes to Domain Events published by external systems. When a relevant notification is received, our local system transitions its own Aggregate Entities to reflect the state of those in external systems. Sometimes synchronization must be initiated by the local Bounded Context with changes being pushed to the originating external system.

This is rarely easy to do, but it leads to more autonomous systems. When autonomy is achieved, it can actually narrow searches to local objects. This is not a matter of caching foreign objects locally. Rather, it involves translating foreign concepts into those of the local Bounded Context, as explained in **Context Mapping (3)**.

This is the most complex of identity creation strategies. The maintenance of the local Entity is dependent not only on transitions caused by local domain behaviors but possibly also on those that occur in one or more external systems. Use this approach as conservatively as possible.

When the Timing of Identity Generation Matters

Identity generation can occur either early, as part of the object's construction, or late, as part of its persistence. Sometimes it's important to time identity generation early, and other times not. If it matters, we need to understand what's involved.

Consider possibly the simplest case, that we can tolerate the late allocation of identity when a new Entity is persisted, that is, a new row is inserted in the database. This is demonstrated in the diagram in Figure 5.3. The client just instantiates a new `Product` and adds it to the `ProductRepository`. When the `Product` instance is newly created, the client doesn't need its identity. And it's a good thing, too, because the identity won't exist then. It's only after the instance is persisted that the identity is available.

Why might timing matter? Consider a scenario where the client subscribes to outgoing Domain Events. An Event occurs when a new `Product` instantiation completes. The client saves the published Event to an **Event Store (8)**. Eventually those stored Events are published as notifications that reach subscribers outside the Bounded Context. Using the approach of Figure 5.3, the Domain Event is received before the client has the opportunity to add the new `Product` to the `ProductRepository`. Thus, the Domain Event would not contain the valid identity of the new `Product`. For the Domain Event to be correctly initialized, the identity generation must be completed early. Figure 5.4 demonstrates that approach. The client queries for the next identity from the `ProductRepository`, passing it to the `Product` constructor.

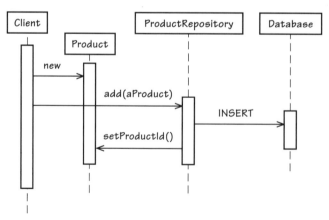

Figure 5.3 The simplest way to allocate a unique identity is to have the data store generate it the first time the object is persisted.

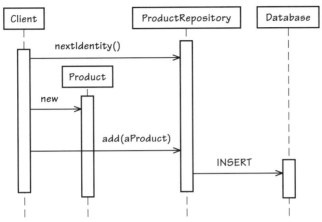

Figure 5.4 Here unique identity is queried from the *Repository* and assigned during instantiation. The complexities of identity generation are hidden behind the *Repository* implementation.

There is another problem that can occur when identity generation is delayed until the Entity is persisted. It occurs when two or more new Entities must be added to a `java.util.Set`, but their identity has not yet been assigned, making them equal to the other new ones (for example, `null`, or 0, or –1). If the Entity's `equals()` method compares identities, those newly added to the Set will appear to be the same object. Only the first object added will be contained, and all others will be excluded. This causes a dubious bug whose root cause is at first difficult to understand and fix.

To avoid this bug we must do one of two things. Either we change the design to allocate and assign identity early, or we refactor the `equals()` method to compare attributes other than the domain identity. If choosing the `equals()` method approach, it must be implemented as if the Entity is a Value Object. In that case, the same object's `hashCode()` method must harmonize with the `equals()` method:

```
public class User extends Entity  {
    ...
    @Override
    public boolean equals(Object anObject) {
        boolean equalObjects = false;
        if (anObject != null &&
                this.getClass() == anObject.getClass()) {
            User typedObject = (User) anObject;
            equalObjects =
                this.tenantId().equals(typedObject.tenantId()) &&
```

```
                    this.username().equals(typedObject.username()));
        }
        return equalObjects;
    }

    @Override
    public int hashCode() {
        int hashCode =
            + (151513 * 229)
            + this.tenantId().hashCode()
            + this.username().hashCode();

        return hashCode;
    }
    ...
}
```

In the case of a multitenancy environment, the `TenantId` instance is also considered part of unique identity. No two `User` objects under different `Tenant` subscribers must be considered equal.

More to the point, when faced with this add-to-`Set` situation, I prefer early allocation and assignment to the Value equality test approach. It is more desirable for Entities to have `equals()` and `hashCode()` methods that are based on the object's unique identity rather than other attributes.

Surrogate Identity

Some ORM tools, such as Hibernate, want to deal with object identity on their own terms. Hibernate prefers the database's native type, such as a numeric sequence, as the primary identity of each Entity. If the domain requires another kind of identity, it causes an undesirable conflict for Hibernate. To cure this, we need to use two identities. One of the identities is designed for the domain model and adheres to the requirements of the domain. The other is for Hibernate and is known as a *surrogate identity*.

Creating a surrogate identity is straightforward. Create an attribute on the Entity to hold the type of the surrogate. Generally a `long` or `int` does it. Also create a column in the database entity table to hold the unique identity, and place a primary key constraint on it. Then include in the Entity's Hibernate mapping definition an `<id>` element. Remember, in this case it has nothing to do with the domain-specific identity. It is being created only for the sake of the ORM, Hibernate.

It's best to hide the surrogate attribute from the outside world. Because the surrogate is not part of the domain model, visibility constitutes persistence leakage. Although some leakage may be unavoidable, we can take some steps to tuck it away from model developers and clients.

One safeguard employs a **Layer Supertype** [Fowler, P of EAA]:

```
public abstract class IdentifiedDomainObject
        implements Serializable  {

    private long id = -1;

    public IdentifiedDomainObject() {
        super();
    }

    protected long id() {
        return this.id;
    }

    protected void setId(long anId) {
        this.id = anId;
    }
}
```

This Layer Supertype is `IdentifiedDomainObject`, an abstract base class that hides the surrogate primary key from the view of clients using `protected` accessor methods. Clients will never have to wonder if the methods are for their use since they are not visible outside the **Module (9)** of the Entity that extends the base class. We could even declare `private` scope. Hibernate has no problems using method or field reflection with any level of visibility, `public` to `private`. Additional Layer Supertypes may add value, such as for supporting optimistic concurrency, as seen in **Aggregates (10)**.

We need to map the surrogate `id` attribute to the database column through the Hibernate definition. Here class `User` has its `id` attribute mapped to the database table column named `id`:

```
<hibernate-mapping default-cascade="all">
    <class
      name="com.saasovation.identityaccess.domain.model.identity.User"
      table="tbl_user" lazy="true">

        <id
            name="id"
            type="long"
            column="id"
            unsaved-value="-1">
```

```
        <generator class="native"/>
    </id>
    ...
</class>
</hibernate-mapping>
```

Here is the MySQL table definition to store the `User` objects:

```
CREATE TABLE `tbl_user` (
    `id` int(11) NOT NULL auto_increment,
    `enablement_enabled` tinyint(1) NOT NULL,
    `enablement_end_date` datetime,
    `enablement_start_date` datetime,
    `password` varchar(32) NOT NULL,
    `tenant_id_id` varchar(36) NOT NULL,
    `username` varchar(25) NOT NULL,
    KEY `k_tenant_id_id` (`tenant_id_id`),
    UNIQUE KEY `k_tenant_id_username` (`tenant_id_id`,`username`),
    PRIMARY KEY (`id`)
) ENGINE=InnoDB;
```

The first column, `id`, is the surrogate identity. The last column statement in the definition declares `id` as the table's primary key. We can distinguish the surrogate and the domain's identity. There are two columns, `tenant_id_id` and `username`, that provide unique identity for the domain. They are combined to form one unique key named `k_tenant_id_username`.

There is no need for the domain identity to play the role of database primary key. We allow the surrogate `id` to serve as the database primary key, which keeps Hibernate happy.

Surrogate database primary keys can be used throughout the data model as foreign keys in other tables, providing referential integrity. This may be a requirement for data management in your enterprise (for example, for audits) or for tools support. The referential integrity is important for Hibernate, too, when wiring tables together to implement the various any-to-any (such as 1:M) mappings. They also support table joins to optimize queries when reading Aggregates out of the database.

Identity Stability

In most cases unique identity must be protected from modification, remaining stable throughout the lifetime of the Entity to which it is assigned.

Trivial measures may be taken to prevent identity modification. We can hide identity setters from clients. We might also create guards in setters to prevent even the Entity itself from changing the state of the identity if it already exists. Guards are coded as assertions in Entity setters. Here's an example of an identity setter:

```
public class User extends Entity  {
    ...
    protected void setUsername(String aUsername) {
        if (this.username != null) {
            throw new IllegalStateException(
                    "The username may not be changed.");
        }
        if (aUsername == null) {
            throw new IllegalArgumentException(
                    "The username may not be set to null.");
        }
        this.username = aUsername;
    }
    ...
}
```

In this example, the username attribute, being the domain identity of the User Entity, is mutable only once, and only internally. The setter, method setUsername(), provides self-encapsulation that is hidden from clients. When an Entity public behavior self-delegates to the setter, the method checks the username attribute to see if it is already non-null. If it is already non-null, indicating an unchangeable invariant state, the IllegalStateException is thrown. The exception indicates that username must be maintained as a modify-once state.

Whiteboard Time

- Consider some true Entities from your current domain and write their names.

What are their unique identities, both domain and surrogate? Would any of the identities have been better served by a different kind of identity generation, or the timing of the identity assignment?

- Indicate next to each Entity whether you should have used a different identity assignment approach—user, application, persistence, or other Bounded Context—and why (even if you can't change it now).

- Note next to each Entity whether it needs early identity generation or can suffice with late identity generation, and explain why.

Consider the stability of each identity, which is one area you can improve on if necessary.

This setter does not get in the way of Hibernate when it needs to reconstitute object state from persistence. Since the object is first constructed with its default, zero-argument constructor, the username attribute is initially null. This enables re-initialization to occur cleanly, and the setter will enable the one-time Hibernate-initiated assignment to take place. This is completely bypassed when instructing Hibernate to use field (attribute) access for persistence and rehydration purposes, rather than accessors.

A test affirms that the modify-once guard properly protects the state of User identity:

```
public class UserTest extends IdentityTest {
    ...
    public void testUsernameImmutable() throws Exception {
        try {
            User user = this.userFixture();
            user.setUsername("testusername");
            fail("The username must be immutable after↵
initialization.");
        } catch (IllegalStateException e) {
            // expected, fall through
        }
    }
    ...
}
```

This exemplary test demonstrates how the model works. Upon successful completion it proves that method setUsername() guards existing, non-null identity from being altered. (We discuss guards and Entity tests more thoroughly as part of validation.)

Discovering Entities and Their Intrinsic Characteristics

Now let's look at some lessons learned by the SaaSOvation teams . . .

At first the CollabOvation team got caught in the trap of doing a lot of entity-relationship (ER) modeling in Java code. They put too much focus on database, tables, and columns, and how those were reflected in objects. That led to a largely **Anemic Domain Model** [Fowler, Anemic] composed of a lot of getters and setters. They should have been thinking more about DDD. By the  time they needed to factor out the security tangle, as described in **Bounded Contexts (2)**, they had learned to focus more on modeling the Ubiquitous Language. That led to good results. In this section we will see how the newer *Identity and Access Context* team gained from the lessons learned.

The Ubiquitous Language in a cleanly separated Bounded Context gives us the concepts and terms we need to design our domain model. The Language doesn't suddenly appear. It must be developed through careful discussion with domain experts and by mining requirements. Some terminology uncovered will be nouns that name things, adjectives that describe them, and verbs that indicate what the things do. It would be a mistake to think that the objects distill to only a set of nouns that name classes and verbs that name prominent operations, that we can capture deep insight by considering nothing else. Limiting ourselves in that way could stifle the fluency and richness that the model deserves. Investing in liberal amounts of discussion and reviews of specifications will help develop a Language that reflects considerable thought, effort, agreement, and compromise. In the end the team speaks the Language in complete sentences, and the model clearly reflects the spoken Language.

If it is important for these special domain scenarios to outlive team discussions, capture them in a lightweight document. In an early form, your Ubiquitous Language can take the shape of a glossary and a set of simple usage scenarios. Yet, it would be a further mistake to think of the Language as the glossary and scenarios only. In the end the Language is modeled by your code, and it may be difficult or impossible to keep documentation in sync.

Uncovering Entities and Properties

Let's take up a very basic example. In the *Identity and Access Context* the SaaSOvation team knows that it needs to model a User. True, this modeling example is not taken from the **Core Domain (2)**, but we do transition to that example later. At this time I want to clear away added complexity inherent with the Core Domain and just focus on a more basic Entity. It has enough modeling challenge to serve as an effective teaching tool.

Here's what the team knew about a User in terse software requirements (not use cases or user stories) that roughly reflected statements from the Ubiquitous Language. They did need refinement:

- Users exist in association with and under the control of a tenancy.
- Users of a system must be authenticated.
- Users possess personal information, including a name and contact information.
- User personal information may be changed by the users themselves or by a manager.
- User security credentials (passwords) may be changed.

The team had to read and listen carefully. As soon as they saw/heard different forms of the word *change* used, they were pretty sure that they were dealing with at least one Entity. True enough, "change" could also mean "replace the Value" instead of "change the Entity." Was there anything else that sealed the team's choice of which building block to use? There was. The key term was *authenticated*, which was a strong indication to the team that some kind of search resolution needed to be provided. If you have a bunch of things, and one of the things needs to be found out of many, you need unique identity to distinguish the one from all others. A search will need to resolve from many users in association with a tenant down to a single one.

But what about the statement regarding tenancy controlling users? Doesn't that imply that the real Entity here is Tenant, not User? This opens up a discussion about **Aggregates (10)**, which we save for that chapter. In short, the answer is "yes and no." Yes, there is a Tenant Entity, and no, this doesn't mean there is not a User Entity. They are both Entities. To understand why Tenant and User are the **Roots (10)** of two different Aggregates, see that chapter. And yes, both User and Tenant are ultimately types of Aggregates, but the team avoids those concerns at first.

The justification here is that each `User` must be uniquely identified, clearly distinguished from all others. A `User` must also support change over time, so it is clearly an Entity. At this time, it doesn't matter how we model the personal information inside the `User`.

The team needed to give some attention to clarifying the meaning of the first requirement:

- Users exist in association with and under the control of a tenancy.

At first the team could just add a note or change the wording of the statement in some way that would show that tenants own users, *but they don't collect and contain them*. The team needed to be careful because they didn't want to get down into the technical and tactical modeling weeds. The statements needed to make sense to the whole team. They settled on this:

- Tenants allow for the registration of many users by invitation.
- Tenants may be active or be deactivated.
- Users of a system must be authenticated but can be authenticated only if the tenant is active.
- . . .

Well, that was a surprise! Following further discussion, the team cut cleanly through the issues of word craft and at the same time gave the requirements much more meaning. They found that the original statement about users under tenancy control was incomplete. The fact is that users are registered within a tenancy, and by invitation only. It was also important to state that tenants may be active or inactive, and that users can be authenticated only when their tenancy is active. This complete restating of one requirement, the addition of another, and the clarification of a third revealed a far more accurate definition of what actually happens.

The effort did away with any possible implications about what manages the life cycle of users but made it clear that whatever owns users, some users may be unavailable under specific circumstances. Those were the important scenarios to capture at that time.

It seemed at this point that they had the beginnings of a glossary of the terms of a Ubiquitous Language. Still, they didn't have enough information to flesh out the definitions. The team will wait a while longer to make entries in the glossary.

They had a couple of known Entities, as shown in Figure 5.5. It was important to know next how they would be uniquely identified, and what additional properties might be needed to find them among many possible objects of the same type.

```
<<entity>>     <<entity>>
  Tenant         User
```

Figure 5.5   Two *Entities*, `Tenant` and `User`, following early discovery

The team decided that they would use a full UUID to identify each `Tenant` uniquely, a case where the application generates the identity. The large text value was easily justified, not only for guaranteed uniqueness, but also because it added a good measure of security to each subscriber. It would be difficult for anyone to randomly reproduce a UUID as first-level access to proprietary data. They also saw the need to explicitly segregate the Entities that belonged under each `Tenant` from those that belonged to every other. A requirement like this is stated to address additional security issues that tenant subscribers—competitive businesses—have with hosted applications and services. Thus, every Entity in all systems would be "striped" with this unique identity, and every query would require the unique identity to find any Entity, no matter what.

The unique tenant identity is not an Entity. It is a Value of some kind. The question is, Should this identity have a specialized type, or can it remain a simple `String`?

There seemed to be no need to model **Side-Effect-Free Functions (6)** on the identity. It's just a hexadecimal text representation of a large number. But the identity would be used broadly. It would be set on all other Entities in every Context. In this case strong typing could be advantageous. By defining a `TenantId` Value Object, the team could more confidently ensure that all subscriber-owned Entities were striped with the correct identity. Figure 5.6 shows how this is modeled, with both the `Tenant` and the `User` Entities.

The `Tenant` must be named. The `name` can be a simple `String` attribute because it has no special behavior. The `name` helps resolve queries. A help desk worker would need to find the `Tenant` by `name` before he or she could provide assistance. It's a necessary attribute and an "intrinsic characteristic." The `name` may also be constrained as unique among all other subscribers, but that's not important now.

Other attributes may be associated with each subscriber, such as a support contract and call activation PIN, billing and payment information, and maybe a business location along with customer contacts. But those are business concerns, not part of

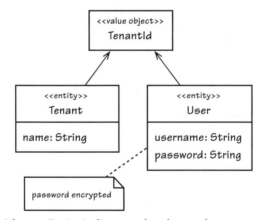

Figure 5.6 After an *Entity* is discovered and named, uncover the attributes/ properties that uniquely identify it and enable it to be found.

security. Attempting to stretch the *Identity and Access Context* too far would be a defeating effort.

Support will be managed by a different Context. After finding the tenant by name, the software can use its unique `TenantId`. It would then be used to access the *Support Context*, for example, or the *Billing Context*, or the *Customer Relationship Management Context*. Support contracts, business location, and customer contacts have little to nothing to do with security. Still, associating the name of the subscriber with the `Tenant` will help support personnel quickly provide needed support. The `name` belongs.

Having completed what appears to be the essence of `Tenant`, the team turned their attention to the `User` Entity for a while. What would serve as its unique identity? Most identity systems support a unique username. It doesn't matter much what comprises the username, as long as it is unique within the tenant. (Usernames need not be unique across tenant lines.) It will be left to the discretion of users to determine their own usernames. If the subscribing business has certain policy criteria for usernames, or if the names will be determined by a federated security integration, it will be left to the registering user to comply. The team simply declared a `username` attribute on class `User`.

One requirement states that a security credential exists. It indicates that this is a password. The team picked up on the terminology and declared a `password` attribute on class `User`. They concluded that the `password` would never be stored as clear text. A note was made that the `password` must be encrypted. Since they will need a way to encrypt each password before it is associated with the `User`, it seemed as if this called for some kind of **Domain Service (7)**. The team created a placeholder in the glossary of the Ubiquitous Language, which could now be started. The glossary would be limited, but useful:

- **Tenant:** A named organizational subscriber of identity and access services, as well as other online services. Facilitates user registration through invitation.

- **User:** A registered security principal within a tenancy, complete with personal name and contact information. The User has a unique username and an encrypted password.

- **Encryption Service:** Provides a means to encrypt passwords and other data that cannot be stored and used as clear text.

One question remained: Should the `password` be considered a part of the unique identity of a `User`? After all, it is used to find a `User`. If so, we'd probably want to combine the two attributes into a Whole Value, naming it something like `Security-Principal`. That would make this concept much more explicit. It is an interesting idea, but it overlooks an important requirement: Passwords can be changed. There may also be times when services will need to find a `User` without being provided with a password. This is not for authentication. (Consider the scenario where we need to check to see if a `User` is playing a security `Role`. We can't require a password to find a `User` every time we need to check for access permissions.) It's not identity. We can still include both the `username` and the `password` in a single authentication query.

The idea of creating a `SecurityPrincipal` Value type produced a desirable modeling proposition. It was noted for later consideration. There were also some other concepts that went unexplored, such as how registration invitations would be provided, and the details on personal name and contact information. The team would catch those in the next quick iteration.

Digging for Essential Behavior

After essential attributes were identified, the team could look into indispensable behavior . . .

After looking back at the basic requirements the team was given, they now sought the behavior of `Tenant` and `User`:

- Tenants may be active or be deactivated.

When we think of activating and deactivating a `Tenant`, we probably visualize a Boolean toggle. As true as that may be, how it is implemented is unimportant here. If we were to place `active` in the attributes compartment of `Tenant` in the class diagram, would that necessarily tell the reader anything useful? In `Tenant.java`, would the following attribute declaration reveal intentions?

```
public class Tenant extends Entity {
    ...
    private boolean active;
    ...
```

Probably not entirely. And at first we want to focus only on attributes/properties that provide identity and enable matching on queries. We add support details like that later.

The team could have decided in favor of declaring method `setActive(boolean)`, though that wouldn't really address the terminology of the requirement. It's not that public setter methods are never appropriate, but they should be used only when the Language allows for them

and usually only when you won't have to use multiple setters to fulfill a single request. The multiple setters make the intention ambiguous. They also complicate publishing a single, meaningful Domain Event as an outcome to what should actually be a single logical command.

To address the Language, the team noted that domain experts talk about activating and deactivating. To incorporate that terminology they'd assign operations such as `activate()` and `deactivate()` instead.

The following source is an **Intention Revealing Interface** [Evans] and complies with the team's growing Ubiquitous Language:

```
public class Tenant extends Entity {
    ...
    public void activate() {
        // TODO: implement
    }

    public void deactivate() {
        // TODO: implement
    }
    ...
```

To animate their ideas, the team first developed a test to see how it feels to use the new behaviors:

```
public class TenantTest ... {
    public void testActivateDeactivate() throws Exception {
        Tenant tenant = this.tenantFixture();
        assertTrue(tenant.isActive());

        tenant.deactivate();
        assertFalse(tenant.isActive());

        tenant.activate();
        assertTrue(tenant.isActive());
    }
}
```

After this test the team felt confident in the quality of the interface. Writing the test made them realize that another method, `isActive()`, was needed. They settled on these three new methods, as seen in Figure 5.7. The Ubiquitous Language glossary grew as well:

- **Activate tenant:** Facilitate the activation of a tenant using this operation, and the current state may be confirmed.
- **Deactivate tenant:** Facilitate the deactivation of a tenant using this operation. Users may not be authenticated when the tenant is deactivated.

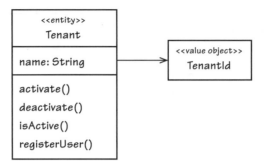

Figure 5.7 Indispensable behavior is assigned to *Tenant* during the first rapid iteration. Some behaviors are omitted due to complexity but can be added soon.

- **Authentication Service:** Coordinates the authentication of users, first ensuring that their owning tenant is active.

The last glossary entry added here indicates the discovery of another Domain Service. Before attempting to match the `User` instance, something must first check `Tenant` for `isActive()`. That understanding was gained when also considering this requirement:

- Users of a system must be authenticated but can be authenticated only if the tenant is active.

Since there is more to authentication than merely finding a `User` that matches a specific `username` and `password`, a higher-level coordinator is needed. Domain Services are good at that. Details can be added later. For now it's important that the team captured the `AuthenticationService` by name and added it to the Ubiquitous Language. The test-first approach sure paid off.

The team also considered the following requirement:

- Tenants allow for the registration of many users by invitation.

When they started analyzing this carefully, they understood it to be a bit more complex than they wanted to deal with in the first, rapid iteration. There seemed to be some kind of `Invitation` object involved. But the requirement didn't tell them enough to be understood clearly. The behavior to manage invitations wasn't clear either. So the team postponed modeling this until they could solicit more input from early domain experts and early customers. They did define the `registerUser()` method, however. It is essential to the creation of `User` instances (see "Construction" later in the chapter).

With that they ventured back into class `User`:

- Users possess personal information, including a name and contact information.
- User personal information may be changed by the users themselves or by a manager.
- User security credentials (passwords) may be changed.

User along with **Fundamental Identity**, two commonly combined security patterns, were applied.[1] From the use of the term *personal*, it is clear that a personal concept accompanies the `User`. The team worked out the composition and behavior based on the preceding statements.

`Person` is modeled as a separate class to avoid placing too much responsibility on the `User`. The word *personal* led the team to add `Person` to the Ubiquitous Language:

- **Person:** Contains and manages personal data about a `User`, including name and contact information.

Is the `Person` an Entity or a Value Object? Again here the word *change* is key. It seems unnecessary to replace the entire `Person` object just because the individual's work telephone number may change. The team made it an Entity, as indicated in Figure 5.8, which holds two Values, the `ContactInformation` and `Name`. These were currently fuzzy concepts and would stand to be refactored in time.

Managing changes to the personal name and contact information of a user resulted in some further deliberation. Should clients be given access to the `Person` object inside the `User`? One developer questioned whether a `User` would always be a person. What if it were an external system? This was not the current situation and might be rushing ahead on unknown future requirements, but the concern had merit. If clients were given access to the shape of `User`, with navigation into the `Person` in order to execute behavior, that could require client refactoring later.

If, instead, they modeled the personal behavior on `User`, making it more generalized for a security principal, they would probably avoid some of the ripple later. After they wrote some exemplary tests to explore the notion, it seemed like the right thing to do. They modeled `User` as shown in Figure 5.8.

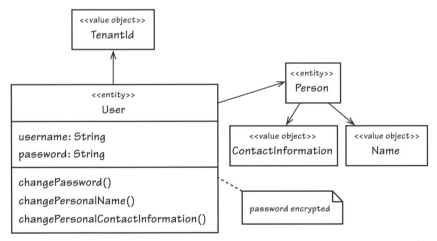

Figure 5.8   The foundational behavior of *User* drives out more associations. Without being overly specific, the team modeled a few more objects along with the operations.

---

1. See my published patterns: http://vaughnvernon.co/.

There were other considerations. Should the team expose `Person` at all, or hide it from all clients? For now they decided to leave `Person` exposed for the purpose of querying information. The accessor could later be redesigned to serve a `Principal` interface, and `Person` and `System` would each be a specialized `Principal`. The team would be able to refactor this as they gained deeper understanding.

Maintaining their cadence, the team quickly recognized the Ubiquitous Language highlighted by the final requirement currently under consideration:

- User security credentials (passwords) may be changed.

The `User` has a `changePassword()` behavior. This reflects the term used in requirements and satisfies domain experts. Access to even the encrypted password is never granted to clients. Once the password is set on `User`, it is never exposed beyond the Aggregate boundary. Anything seeking authentication has but one approach, using the `AuthenticationService`.

The team also decided that all behaviors that could cause modification, when successful, were to publish a specific Domain Event outcome. This, too, was more detail than the team wanted to address early on. But they did recognize the need for Events. Events would accomplish at least two things. First, they would enable change tracking through the life cycle of all objects (discussed later). Second, they would enable outside subscribers to synchronize with the changes, giving outsiders the potential for autonomy.

Those topics are discussed in **Events (8)** and **Integrating Bounded Contexts (13)**.

Roles and Responsibilities

An aspect of modeling is to discover the roles and responsibilities of objects. Role and responsibility analysis is applicable to domain objects in general. Here we look specifically at the roles and responsibilities of Entities.

We need some context for the term *role*. One use, when discussing the *Identity and Access Context*, is that a `Role` is an Entity and Aggregate Root that addresses a broad system security concern. Clients can ask if a user is in, or plays, a security role. That's completely different from what I am now discussing. What I am discussing in this section is how roles can be played by the objects in your model.

Domain Objects Playing Multiple Roles

In object-oriented programming, generally interfaces determine the roles of an implementing class. When designed correctly, a class has one role for each interface that it implements. If the class has no explicitly declared roles—it doesn't implement any explicit interfaces—by default it has the role of its class. That is, the class has the implicit interface of its public methods. Class `User` in the preceding examples implements no explicit interfaces, yet it plays one role, a User.

We could make one object play the role of both User and Person. Not that this is being suggested, but for now assume that we consider this a good idea. If we did, there would be no reason to aggregate a separate Person object as a referenced association of the User object. Instead, there would be just one object, one that plays two roles.

Why might we do this? Usually it's because we see both similarities and differences in two or more objects. The overlapping characteristics can be addressed by blending multiple interfaces on a single object. For example, we could have one object be both a User *and* a Person, naming the implementation class HumanUser:

```
public interface User {
    ...
}

public interface Person {
    ...
}

public class HumanUser implements User, Person {
    ...
}
```

Does this make sense? Possibly, but it may also complicate things. If both interfaces are complex, it could be difficult to implement both in one object. Also, a User may be a system, which would increase the necessary interfaces to three. Designing the single object to play the roles of User, Person, and System would be even harder. Maybe we could simplify this by creating a general-purpose Principal:

```
public interface User {
    ...
}

public interface Principal {
    ...
}

public class UserPrincipal implements User, Principal {
    ...
}
```

With this design we are attempting to determine the actual principal type at runtime (late binding). A person principal and a system principal have different implementations. Systems don't need the same kind of contact information as a person has. Still, we might try anyway, designing a forwarding delegation implementation. To do that we'd check for the existence of one type or the other at runtime and delegate to the existing object:

```java
public interface User {
    ...
}

public interface Principal {
    public Name principalName();
    ...
}

public class PersonPrincipal implements Principal {
    ...
}

public class SystemPrincipal implements Principal {
    ...
}

public class UserPrincipal implements User, Principal {
    private Principal personPrincipal;
    private Principal systemPrincipal;
    ...
    public Name principalName() {
        if (personPrincipal != null) {
            return personPrincipal.principalName();
        } else if (systemPrincipal != null) {
            return systemPrincipal.principalName();
        } else {
            throw new IllegalStateException(
                    "The principal is unknown.");
        }
    }
    ...
}
```

This design produces various problems. For one, it suffers from what is called *object schizophrenia*.[2] Behavior is delegated by a technique known

---

2. It describes an object with multiple personalities, which is not medically the definition of schizophrenia. The actual problem behind the confusing name is object identity confusion.

as forwarding or dispatching. Neither `personPrincipal` nor `system-Principal` carries the identity of Entity `UserPrincipal`, on which the behavior was originally executed. Object schizophrenia describes the situation where the objects delegated to don't know the identity of their originating object. There is confusion inside the delegates as to who they really are. It's not that every delegate method in the two concrete classes would be required to take on the base object's identity, but some could need it. We could pass in a reference to the `UserPrincipal`. But that complicates the design and actually requires the `Principal` interface to change. That's not good. As [Gamma et al.] states, "Delegation is a good design choice only when it simplifies more than it complicates."

We won't try to solve this modeling challenge here. It's used only to illustrate the challenges sometimes encountered when using object roles and to emphasize that it's a modeling style we need to be careful with. With the right tools, such as Qi4j [Öberg], we could improve things.

It might help the situation to make role interfaces finer grained, as Udi Dahan [Dahan, Roles] promotes. Here are two requirements that enable us to create fine-grained interfaces:

- Add new orders to a customer.

- Make a customer preferred (the condition for meeting this level is not stated).

Class `Customer` implements two fine-grained role interfaces: `IAddOrdersToCustomer` and `IMakeCustomerPreferred`. Each defines only a single operation, as seen in Figure 5.9. We might even implement other interfaces, such as `Ivalidator`.

As discussed in **Aggregates (10)**, we wouldn't normally collect a large number of objects, such as all its orders, on a `Customer`. So let's view this as a

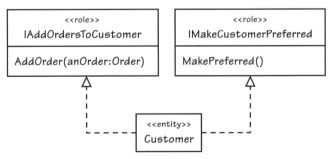

Figure 5.9 Using C#.NET naming conventions, the *Customer* Entity implements two object roles, *IAddOrdersToCustomer* and *IMakeCustomerPreferred*.

synthetic example, used solely as a means to illustrate how object roles are used.

The I interface name prefix is a style widely used in .NET programming. Besides following the .NET approach in general, some think it enhances readability: "I add orders to customer" and "I make customer preferred." Without the I prefix, the resulting verb-based names may be less desirable: AddOrders-ToCustomer and MakeCustomerPreferred. We may be more used to naming interfaces as nouns or adjectives, and that standard could certainly be applied here instead.

Consider some advantages this style promotes. The role of an Entity can change from use case to use case. When a client needs to add a new Order instance to a Customer, the role is different from when they want to make the Customer preferred. There's also a technical advantage. Different use cases may require specialized fetching strategies:

```
IMakeCustomerPreferred customer =
    session.Get<IMakeCustomerPreferred>(customerId);
customer.MakePreferred();

. . .

IAddOrdersToCustomer customer =
    session.Get<IAddOrdersToCustomer>(customerId);
customer.AddOrder(order);
```

The persistence mechanism interrogates the parameterization type name T of the Get<T>() method. It uses the type to look up an associated fetching strategy that is registered with the infrastructure. If the interface happens to have no special fetching strategy, the default is used. By executing the fetching strategy, the identified Customer object is loaded in the shape needed by the specific use case.

We may see technical merit as role marker interfaces lend a hand to enabling behind-the-scenes hooks. Other use-case-specific behavior can be associated with any given role, such as validation, enabling the execution of a specific validator as the Entity modifications are being persisted.

Fine-grained interfaces make it easier for the implementing class, such as Customer, to implement the behavior on itself. There is no need to delegate the implementation to separate classes, which helps prevent object schizophrenia.

It's fair to ask whether there is a distinct *domain modeling advantage* to separating Customer behaviors by role. Compare the previous Customer to the one in Figure 5.10; is one better than the other? Would it be easier for

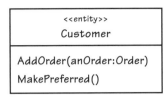

Figure 5.10   Here *Customer* is modeled with the operations that were previously on different interfaces now collapsed onto the single interface of the Entity class.

a client to mistakenly invoke the `AddOrder()` method when it should actually invoke `MakePreferred()`? Probably not. But we should not judge the approach on this alone.

Perhaps the most practical use of role interfaces is also the simplest. We can leverage interfaces to hide implementation details that we don't want leaking out of the model to clients. Design an interface to expose exactly what we want to allow clients to use, and nothing more. The implementation class can be far more complex than the interface. It might have all kinds of supporting properties with getters and setters, and implementation behavior that clients will never get a glimpse of. For example, perhaps a tool or framework forces the creation of public methods that we don't want clients to use. Even so, the domain model interface is not influenced by necessarily nasty technical implementation details. This has a definite domain modeling advantage.

Along with any design choice, ensure that the Ubiquitous Language holds sway over any technical preferences. With DDD, it's a model of the business domain that matters most.

Construction

When we newly instantiate an Entity, we want to use a constructor that captures enough state to fully identify it and enable clients to find it. When early identity generation is used, a correctly designed constructor takes as a parameter at least the unique identity. If the Entity is queried by other means, such as with a name or description, we would also include all such as constructor parameters.

Sometimes an Entity maintains one or more invariants. An invariant is a state that must stay transactionally consistent throughout the Entity life cycle. Invariants are a concern of Aggregates, but since the Aggregate Root is always an Entity, it is mentioned here. If an Entity has an invariant that is satisfied by the non-`null` state of a contained object, or calculated using some other state, that state must be provided by one or more constructor parameters.

Every User object must contain a tenantId, username, password, and person. In other words, following successful construction, references to these declared instance variables may never be null. The User constructor and its instance variable setters ensure this:

```
public class User extends Entity {
    ...
    protected User(TenantId aTenantId, String aUsername,
            String aPassword, Person aPerson) {
        this();
        this.setPassword(aPassword);
        this.setPerson(aPerson);
        this.setTenantId(aTenantId);
        this.setUsername(aUsername);
        this.initialize();
    }
    ...
    protected void setPassword(String aPassword) {
        if (aPassword == null) {
            throw new IllegalArgumentException(
                    "The password may not be set to null.");
        }
        this.password = aPassword;
    }

    protected void setPerson(Person aPerson) {
        if (aPerson == null) {
            throw new IllegalArgumentException(
                    "The person may not be set to null.");
        }
        this.person = aPerson;
    }

    protected void setTenantId(TenantId aTenantId) {
        if (aTenantId == null) {
            throw new IllegalArgumentException(
                    "The tenantId may not be set to null.");
        }
        this.tenantId = aTenantId;
    }

    protected void setUsername(String aUsername) {
        if (this.username != null) {
            throw new IllegalStateException(
                    "The username may not be changed.");
        }
        if (aUsername == null) {
            throw new IllegalArgumentException(
                    "The username may not be set to null.");
        }
```

```
        this.username = aUsername;
    }
    ...
}
```

The design of class `User` demonstrates the power of self-encapsulation. The constructor delegates instance variable assignment to its own internal attribute/property setters, which provide self-encapsulation for the variables. The self-encapsulation enables each setter to determine the appropriate contractual conditions for setting a portion of state. Each of the setters individually asserts a non-`null` constraint on behalf of the Entity, which enforces the instance contract. The assertions are called *guards* (see "Validation"). As indicated earlier in the "Identity Stability" section, the self-encapsulation techniques of these setter methods can be more complex as needed.

Use a Factory for complex Entity instantiations. This is covered in more detail in **Factories (11)**. In the preceding example, did you notice that the `User` constructor has protected visibility? The `Tenant` Entity serves as a Factory for `User` instances, and only classes in the same Module can see the `User` constructor. That way no object other than a `Tenant` may create `User` instances:

```
public class Tenant extends Entity  {
    ...
    public User registerUser(
            String aUsername,
            String aPassword,
            Person aPerson) {

        aPerson.setTenantId(this.tenantId());

        User user =
                new User(
                        this.tenantId(),
                        aUsername,
                        aPassword,
                        aPerson);

        return user;
    }
    ...
}
```

Here method `registerUser()` is the Factory. The Factory simplifies construction of the `User` default state and ensures that the `TenantId` for both the `User` and `Person` Entities is always correct. This all happens under the control of a Factory method that addresses the Ubiquitous Language.

Validation

The primary reasons to use validation in the model are to check the correctness of any one attribute/property, any whole object, or any composition of objects. We look at three levels of validation in the model. Although there are lots of ways to perform validation, including specialized frameworks/libraries, those are not examined here. Instead, general-purpose approaches are presented, but these can lead to more elaborate approaches.

Validation accomplishes different things. Just because all of the attributes/properties of a domain object are individually valid, that does not mean that the object as a whole is valid. Maybe the combination of two correct attributes invalidates the whole object. Just because a single object as a whole is valid, that does not mean that a composition of objects is valid. Perhaps the combination of two Entities, each of which has individual valid states, actually makes the composition invalid. Therefore, we may need to use one or more levels of validation to address all possible issues.

Validating Attributes/Properties

How can we protect a single attribute or property—see **Value Objects (6)** for the difference between the two—from being set to an invalid value? As discussed elsewhere in this chapter and book, I highly recommend the use of self-encapsulation. Self-encapsulation facilitates the first solution.

To quote Martin Fowler, "Self encapsulation is designing your classes so that all access to data, even from within the same class, goes through accessor methods" [Fowler, Self Encap]. Using this technique provides several advantages. It allows for the abstraction of an object's instance (and class/static) variables. It provides a way to easily derive attributes/properties from any number of others the object holds. And not least for this specific discussion, it lends support for a simple form of validation.

Actually, I don't necessarily like calling the use of self-encapsulation to protect correct object state by the name *validation*. That name puts off some developers, because validation is a separate concern and should be the responsibility of a validation class, not a domain object. I agree. Still, I am talking about something a bit different. What I'm discussing is *assertions* that follow a *design-by-contract* approach.

By definition, design by contract enables us to specify the preconditions, postconditions, and invariants of the components we design. This is advocated by Bertrand Meyer and was thoroughly expressed in his Eiffel programming language. There is some support for the Java and C# languages and a book on the subject, *Design Patterns and Contracts* [Jezequel et al.]. Here we look only at preconditions, by applying guards, as a form of validation:

```
public final class EmailAddress {

    private String address;

    public EmailAddress(String anAddress) {
        super();
        this.setAddress(anAddress);
    }
    ...
    private void setAddress(String anAddress) {
        if (anAddress == null) {
            throw new IllegalArgumentException(
                "The address may not be set to null.");
        }
        if (anAddress.length() == 0) {
            throw new IllegalArgumentException(
                "The email address is required.");
        }
        if (anAddress.length() > 100) {
            throw new IllegalArgumentException(
                "Email address must be 100 characters or less.");
        }
        if (!java.util.regex.Pattern.matches(
            "\\w+([-+.']\\w+)*@\\w+([-.]\\w+)*\\.\\w+([-.]\\w+)*",
                anAddress)) {
            throw new IllegalArgumentException(
                "Email address and/or its format is invalid.");
        }

        this.address = anAddress;
    }
    ...
}
```

There are four preconditions to the method contract of setAddress(). All of the precondition guards assert a condition of the argument anAddress:

- The parameter may not be null.

- The parameter must not be an empty string.

- The parameter must be 100 characters in length or less (but not zero characters).

- The parameter must match the basic format of an e-mail address.

If all of these preconditions pass, the address property is set to the value of anAddress. If one is not met, an IllegalArgumentException is thrown.

Class EmailAddress is not an Entity. It is a Value Object. We use it here for a few reasons. First, it is a good example of implementing various degrees of precondition guards, from null checks down to value formatting (more on this next). Second, this Value is held by the `Person` Entity as one of its properties, indirectly through the `ContactInformation` Value. So, actually, this is part of an Entity in the same way that a simple attribute declared on an Entity class is also part of it. We use the exact same kinds of precondition guards when implementing setters for simple attributes. When a Whole Value is assigned to an Entity property, there is no way to guard against setting insane state unless the smaller attributes within the Value are guarded.

Cowboy Logic

LB: "I thought I had a valid argument with the missus, but then she suddenly threw an illegal argument exception at me."

Some developers refer to these kinds of precondition checks as *defensive programming*. It certainly is defensive programming to guard against completely invalid values entering your model. Some may not agree with the increasing degree of specificity that such guards have. Some defensive programmers agree with checking for nulls, and maybe even checking for empty strings, but may shy away from checking for conditions such as string lengths, numeric ranges, value formats, and the like. Some think, for example, that leaving value size checks to the database is best. They consider things like maximum string lengths to be a concern of something other than model objects. Yet, these preconditions may be viewed as justifiable sanity checks.

There may be occasions when it is unnecessary to check for string lengths. It could make sense when using a database whose maximum `NVARCHAR` column size can never be reached. The text columns of Microsoft SQL Server can be declared using the `max` keyword:

```
CREATE TABLE PERSON (
    ...
    CONTACT_INFORMATION_EMAIL_ADDRESS_ADDRESS
        NVARCHAR(max) NOT NULL,
    ...
) ON PRIMARY
GO
```

It's not that we'd ever want an e-mail address to be 1,073,741,822 characters wide. It's just that we want to declare a column width that we will never need to worry about exceeding.

This may not be possible with some databases. With MySQL, there is a maximum *row width* of 65,535 bytes. Again, that's *row width*, not column width. If we declare even one column with the maximum VARCHAR column type width of 65,535, there is no space left for one additional column in the table. Depending on the number of VARCHAR columns in a given table, we will need to restrict each column width to some practical limit that will allow for all of the columns to fit. In cases like this we could declare character columns as TEXT, since TEXT and BLOB columns are stored in separate segments. Hence, depending on the database, there may be ways to work around column width limits and reduce the need for string length checks in the model.

If there is a potential to overflow a column, a simple string length check in the model is warranted. How impractical would it be to translate the following into a meaningful domain error?

```
ORA-01401: inserted value too large for column
```

We couldn't even determine which column was overflowed. It may be best to avoid this problem altogether by checking text widths in setter preconditions. Besides, the length check need not be only about a database column constraint. In the end, it is the domain itself that may constrain a text length for very justifiable reasons, such as constraints on legacy systems we integrate with.

We may also have to consider guarding high-low range checks, and possibly others. Even a simple formatting check, like the e-mail address format, makes sense if we want to prevent a completely insane value from being associated with an Entity. Certainly if basic values of a single Entity are sane, it will be easier to perform coarse-grained validation on whole objects and object compositions.

Validating Whole Objects

Even though we may have an Entity with completely valid attributes/properties, it does not necessarily mean the entire Entity is valid. To validate a whole Entity, we need to have access to the state of the entire object—all of its attributes/properties. We also need a **Specification** [Evans & Fowler, Spec] or **Strategy** [Gamma et al.] for the validation.

In his **Checks** pattern language, Ward Cunningham [Cunningham, Checks] addresses several approaches to validation. A useful one for whole objects is **Deferred Validation**. Ward says that this is "a class of checking that should be deferred until the last possible moment." It is deferred because it is a kind of very detailed validation, one that we would run over at least one complex object, or even a composition of objects. For that reason we discuss Deferred Validation later also as a means to address larger compositions of objects. In this subsection I limit validations to what Ward calls "the checks of simpler activities."

Because the entire state of the Entity must be available to the validation, some may see this as a good time to embed validation processing logic right in the Entity. Be cautious here. Many times the validation of a domain object changes more often than the domain object itself. Embedding validation inside an Entity also gives it too many responsibilities. It already has the responsibility to address domain behavior as it maintains its state.

A validation component has the responsibility to determine whether or not the Entity state is valid. When designing a separate validation class with Java, place it in the same Module (package) as the Entity. Assuming the use of Java, declare attribute/property read accessors with at least protected/package scope, and public is fine. Private scope will not allow the validation class to read the necessary state. If the validation class is not placed in the same Module as the Entity, all attribute/property accessors must be public, which is undesirable in many cases.

The validation class can implement the Specification pattern or the Strategy pattern. If it detects an invalid state, it informs the client or otherwise makes a record of the results that can be reviewed later (for example, after batch processing). It is important for the validation process to collect a full set of results rather than throw an exception at the first sign of trouble. Consider this reusable, abstract validator and concrete subclass:

```
public abstract class Validator {
    private ValidationNotificationHandler notificationHandler;
    ...
    public Validator(ValidationNotificationHandler aHandler) {
        super();
        this.setNotificationHandler(aHandler);
    }

    public abstract void validate();

    protected ValidationNotificationHandler notificationHandler() {
        return this.notificationHandler;
    }

    private void setNotificationHandler(
            ValidationNotificationHandler aHandler) {
        this.notificationHandler = aHandler;
    }
}
```

```
public class WarbleValidator extends Validator {

    private Warble warble;

    public Validator(
            Warble aWarble,
            ValidationNotificationHandler aHandler) {
        super(aHandler);
        this.setWarble(aWarble);
    }
    ...
    public void validate() {
        if (this.hasWarpedWarbleCondition(this.warble())) {
            this.notificationHandler().handleError(
                    "The warble is warped.");
        }
        if (this.hasWackyWarbleState(this.warble())) {
            this.notificationHandler().handleError(
                    "The warble has a wacky state.");
        }
        ...
    }
}
```

The `WarbleValidator` is instantiated with a `ValidationNotifi-cationHandler`. Whenever an invalid condition is encountered, the `Val-idationNotificationHandler` is asked to handle the condition. The `ValidationNotificationHandler` is a general-purpose implementa-tion with a `handleError()` method that takes a `String` notification mes-sage. We may instead create specialized implementations that have a different method for each kind of invalid condition:

```
class WarbleValidator extends Validator {
    ...
    public void validate() {
        if (this.hasWarpedWarbleCondition(this.warble())) {
            this.notificationHandler().handleWarpedWarble();
        }
        if (this.hasWackyWarbleState(this.warble())) {
            this.notificationHandler().handleWackyWarbleState();
        }
    }
    ...
}
```

This has the advantage of not coupling error messages, or message property keys, or anything specific to notification, to the validation process. Even better, place the notification handling inside the check method:

```
class WarbleValidator extends Validator {
    ...
    public Validator(
            Warble aWarble,
            ValidationNotificationHandler aHandler) {
        super(aHandler);
        this.setWarble(aWarble);
    }
    ...
    public void validate() {
        this.checkForWarpedWarbleCondition();
        this.checkForWackyWarbleState();
        ...
    }
    ...
    protected checkForWarpedWarbleCondition() {
        if (this.warble()...) {
            this.warbleNotificationHandler().handleWarpedWarble();
        }
    }
    ...
    protected WarbleValidationNotificationHandler
            warbleNotificationHandler() {
        return (WarbleValidationNotificationHandler)
                this.notificationHandler();
    }
}
```

In this example we use a Warble-specific ValidationNotificationHandler. It comes in as a standard type but is cast to the specific type when used internally. It is up to the model to work out the contract between itself and clients to supply the correct type.

How do clients ensure that Entity validation occurs? And where does validation processing begin?

One way places a validate() method on all Entities that require validation and may do so using a Layer Supertype:

```
public abstract class Entity
        extends IdentifiedDomainObject  {

    public Entity() {
        super();
    }
```

```
public void validate(
        ValidationNotificationHandler aHandler) {

    }
}
```

Any `Entity` subclass can safely have its `validate()` method invoked. If the concrete Entity supports specialized validation, it is executed. If not supported, the behavior is a no-op. If only some Entities validate, it may be best to declare `validate()` only on those that need it.

However, should Entities actually validate themselves? Having its own `validate()` method doesn't mean the Entity itself performs validation. Yet, it does allow the Entity to determine *what* validates it, relieving clients from that concern:

```
public class Warble extends Entity {
    ...
    @Override
    public void validate(ValidationNotificationHandler aHandler) {
        (new  WarbleValidator(this, aHandler)).validate();
    }
    ...
}
```

Each specialized `Validator` subclass performs any number of fine-grained validations, as needed. The Entity needs to know nothing about *how* it is validated, only that it can be validated. The separate `Validator` subclass also allows the validation process to change at a different pace from the Entity and enables complex validations to be thoroughly tested.

Validating Object Compositions

We can use Deferred Validation for what Ward Cunningham says are the "more complex actions requiring all of the checks of simpler activities and then some." Here we determine not only that an individual Entity is valid, but that a cluster or composition of Entities are all valid together, including one or more Aggregate instances. To do so we could instantiate the concrete `Validator` subclass with the appropriate number of instances. But it may be best to manage that kind of validation using a Domain Service. The Domain Service can use Repositories to read the Aggregate instances it needs to validate. It can then run each instance through its paces, separately or in combination with others.

Decide whether validation is appropriate at all times. On occasion an Aggregate or a set of Aggregates is in a temporary, intermediate state. Perhaps we could model a status on an Aggregate to indicate this, preventing validation at inappropriate times. When the conditions are ripe for validation, the model could inform clients by publishing a Domain Event:

```
public class SomeApplicationService ... {
    ...
    public void doWarbleUseCaseTask(...) {
        Warble warble =
            this.warbleRepository.warbleOfId(aWarbleId);

        DomainEventPublisher
            .instance()
            .subscribe(new DomainEventSubscriber<WarbleTransitioned>(){
                public void handleEvent(DomainEvent aDomainEvent) {
                    ValidationNotificationHandler handler = ...;
                    warble.validate(handler);
                    ...
                }
                public Class<WarbleTransitioned>
                        subscribedToEventType() {
                    return WarbleTransitioned.class;
                }
            });

        warble.performSomeMajorTransitioningBehavior();
    }
}
```

When received by the client, `WarbleTransitioned` indicates that validation is now appropriate. Until that time the client refrains from validating.

Change Tracking

By the definition of Entity, it is not necessary to track the changes that occur on state over its lifetime. We have to support only its continuously changing state. However, sometimes domain experts care about important occurrences in the model as time passes. When that's the case, tracking specific changes to Entities can help.

The most practical way to achieve accurate and useful change tracking is with Domain Events and an Event Store. We create a unique Event type for every important state-altering command executed against every Aggregate that domain experts care about. The combination of the Event name and its properties makes the record of change explicit. The Events are published as the command methods complete. A subscriber registers to receive every Event produced by the model. When received, the subscriber saves the Event to the Event Store.

Domain experts may not care about every change to a model, but the technical team may care anyway. This is usually for technical reasons, using a pattern named **Event Sourcing (4)**.

Wrap-Up

We've run the gamut of Entity-related topics. Here's a recap of what you've learned:

- You've covered four primary ways to generate Entity unique identities.

- You understand the importance of the timing of generation, and how to use surrogate identity.

- You now know how to ensure the stability of identities.

- We discussed how to discover the intrinsic characteristics of Entities by uncovering the Ubiquitous Language in Context. You saw how both properties and behavior are discovered.

- Along with core behavior, you looked into the strengths and weaknesses of modeling Entities using multiple roles.

- Finally, you examined the details of how to construct Entities, how to validate them, and how to track their changes when necessary.

Next, we'll be looking at a very important building block among the tactical modeling tools, Value Objects.

Chapter 6

Value Objects

Price is what you pay. Value is what you get.
—Warren Buffett

Although often overshadowed by entity-think, **Value Objects** are a vital building block of DDD. Examples of objects that are commonly modeled as Values are numbers, such as 3, 10, and 293.51; text strings, such as "hello, world!" and "Domain-Driven Design"; dates; times; more detailed objects such as a person's full name composed of first, middle, last name, and title attributes; and others such as currency, colors, phone numbers, and postal addresses. And there are more complex kinds. I'll be discussing Values that model concepts of your domain using your **Ubiquitous Language (1)**, addressing the goals of Domain-Driven Design.

> **Know the Value Advantages**
> Value types that measure, quantify, or describe things are easier to create, test, use, optimize, and maintain.

It may surprise you to learn that we should strive to model using Value Objects instead of Entities wherever possible. Even when a domain concept must be modeled as an Entity, the Entity's design should be biased toward serving as a Value container rather than a child Entity container. That advice is not based on an arbitrary preference. Value types that measure, quantify, or describe things are easier to create, test, use, optimize, and maintain.

> **Road Map to This Chapter**
> - Learn how to understand the characteristics of a domain concept to model as a Value.
> - See how to leverage Value Objects to minimize integration complexity.
> - Examine the use of domain Standard Types expressed as Values.
> - Consider how SaaSOvation learned the importance of Values.
> - Learn how the SaaSOvation teams tested, implemented, and persisted their Value types.

At first the SaaSOvation teams went over-
board with their use of Entities. This actually started to happen well before the User
and Permission concepts got intertwined
with collaboration. From project inception
they followed the popular mode of thinking
that every element of their domain model
needed to map to its own database table,
and that all their attributes should be easily

set and retrieved through public accessor methods. Since every object had a data-
base primary key, the model was tightly stitched together into a large, complex graph.
That idea primarily came from the data modeling perspective that most developers
have when unduly influenced by relational databases, where everything is normalized
and referenced using foreign keys. As they later learned, getting caught in the tide of
entity-think was not only unnecessary, it was also more costly in development time
and effort.

When designed correctly, a Value instance can be created, handed off, and
forgotten about. We don't have to worry that the consumer has somehow modified it incorrectly, or even modified it at all. A Value can have a brief or long
existence. It's just an unharmed and harmless Value that comes and goes as
needed.

This is a huge load off of our mind, similar to transitioning from a programming language without managed memory facilities to one with garbage collection. With the ease of use that Values afford, we should want as much of their
kind as we can possibly justify.

So how do we determine if a domain concept should be modeled as a Value?
We have to pay close attention to its characteristics.

> When you care only about the attributes of an element of the model, classify it as
> a VALUE OBJECT. Make it express the meaning of the attributes it conveys and
> give it related functionality. Treat the VALUE OBJECT as immutable. Don't give
> it any identity and avoid the design complexities necessary to maintain ENTI-
> TIES. [Evans, p. 99]

As easy as it may be to create a Value type, sometimes those inexperienced
with DDD face confusion when trying to choose whether to model an Entity
or a Value in a specific instance. The truth is that even experienced designers
struggle with this from time to time. Along with showing you how to implement a Value, I hope to clear up some of the mystery around the sometimes
confusing decision-making process.

Value Characteristics

As a first order of business, make certain when modeling a domain concept as a Value Object that you are addressing the Ubiquitous Language. Consider this to be an overarching principle and a characteristic that must be achieved. I imply this principle throughout the chapter.

When you are trying to decide whether a concept is a Value, you should determine whether it possesses most of these characteristics:

- It measures, quantifies, or describes a thing in the domain.

- It can be maintained as immutable.

- It models a conceptual whole by composing related attributes as an integral unit.

- It is completely replaceable when the measurement or description changes.

- It can be compared with others using Value equality.

- It supplies its collaborators with Side-Effect-Free Behavior [Evans].

It will help to understand each of these characteristics in more detail. By employing this approach to analyzing design elements in the model, you may find that you should use Value Objects far more often than you may have before.

Measures, Quantifies, or Describes

When you have a true Value Object in your model, whether you realize it or not, it is not a thing in your domain. Instead, it is actually a concept that *measures*, *quantifies*, or otherwise *describes* a thing in the domain. A person has an age. The age is not really a thing but measures or quantifies the number of years the person (thing) has lived. A person has a name. The name is not a thing but describes what the person (thing) is called.

This is closely related to the Conceptual Whole characteristic.

Immutable

An object that is a Value is unchangeable after it has been created.[1] When programming in Java or C#, for example, you use one of the Value class's

---

1. There are times when a Value Object can be designed as mutable, but the need is usually rare. I don't dwell on mutable Values here. If you are interested in when to use a mutable Value type, please see the sidebar on page 101 of [Evans].

constructors to create an instance, passing in as parameters all objects on which its state will be based. The parameters may be the objects that will directly serve as the attributes of the Value, or they may be objects that will be used to derive one or more newly constituted attributes during construction. Here's an example of a Value Object type that holds a reference to another Value Object:

```
package com.saasovation.agilepm.domain.model.product;

public final class BusinessPriority implements Serializable  {
    private BusinessPriorityRatings ratings;

    public BusinessPriority(BusinessPriorityRatings aRatings) {
        super();
        this.setRatings(aRatings);
        this.initialize();
    }
    ...
}
```

Instantiation alone does not guarantee that an object is immutable. After the object has been instantiated and initialized by means of construction, none of its methods, whether public or hidden, will from that time forward cause its state to change. In this example only the `setRatings()` and `initialize()` methods may mutate state because they are used only in the scope of construction. Method `setRatings()` is private/hidden and cannot be invoked from outside the instance.[2] Further, class `BusinessPriority` must be implemented such that none of its methods other than constructors, public or hidden, may invoke the setter. Later I will discuss how to test Value Objects for immutability.

Depending on your taste, you can at times design Value Objects that hold references to Entities. But some caution may be warranted. When the referenced Entities change state—by the Entity's behavior—the Value changes, too, which violates the quality of immutability. Thus, it may be best to employ the mindset that Entity references held by Value types are used for the sake of compositional immutability, expressiveness, and convenience. Otherwise, if Entities are held with the express purpose of mutating their state through the Value Object's interface, that's probably the wrong reason to compose them. Weigh the competing forces while considering the Side-Effect-Free Behavior characteristic discussed later in the chapter.

---

2. In some cases, frameworks such as object-relational mappers or serialization libraries (for XML, JSON, and so on) may need to use setters to reconstitute Value state from its serialized form.

Challenge Your Assumptions

If you think that the object you are designing must be mutated by its behavior, ask yourself why that is necessary. Would it be possible instead to use replacement when the Value must change? Using this approach where possible is designing toward simplification.

Sometimes it makes no sense for an object to be immutable. That's perfectly fine, and it indicates that the object should be modeled as an Entity. If your analysis leads you to that conclusion, refer to **Entities** (5).

Conceptual Whole

A Value Object may possess just one, a few, or a number of individual attributes, each of which is related to the others. Each attribute contributes an important part to a whole that collectively the attributes describe. Taken apart from the others, each of the attributes fails to provide a cohesive meaning. Only together do all the attributes form the complete intended measure or description. This is different from merely grouping a set of attributes together in an object. The grouping itself accomplishes little if the whole fails to adequately describe another thing in the model.

As Ward Cunningham illustrates in his **Whole Value** pattern[3] [Cunningham, Whole Value aka Value Object], the Value {50,000,000 dollars} has two attributes: the attribute *50,000,000* and the attribute *dollars*. Separately these attributes describe something else or nothing special. This is especially true of the number 50,000,000, but certainly also of dollars. Together these attributes are a conceptual whole that describes a monetary measure. So we would *not* expect the thing that is said to be worth 50,000,000 dollars to have two separate attributes to describe its worth, one of `amount` that is 50,000,000 and one of `currency` that is dollars. Because the thing's worth is not just 50,000,000, and not just dollars. Here's the inexplicit way to model it:

```
// incorrectly modeled thing of worth
public class ThingOfWorth {
    private String name;        // attribute
    private BigDecimal amount;  // attribute
    private String currency;    // attribute

    // ...
}
```

In this example the model and its clients have to know when and how to use `amount` and `currency` together because they don't form a conceptual whole. This begs for a better approach.

---

3. Also called Meaningful Whole.

To properly describe a thing's worth it must be treated not as two separate attributes, but as a whole value: {50,000,000 dollars}. Here it is modeled as a Whole Value:

```
public final class MonetaryValue implements Serializable  {
    private BigDecimal amount;
    private String currency;

    public MonetaryValue(BigDecimal anAmount, String aCurrency) {
        this.setAmount(anAmount);
        this.setCurrency(aCurrency);
    }
    ...
}
```

This is not to say that `MonetaryValue` is perfect and could not be improved. For sure, the use of an additional Value type such as `Currency` would help here. We'd replace the `String` type of the `currency` attribute with the much more descriptive `Currency` type. There may also be a good argument to have a **Factory** and possibly a **Builder** [Gamma et al.] to take care of that. But those topics would detract from the simple example that is meant to focus on the concept of Whole Value.

Because the wholeness of a concept in the domain is so important, the parent reference to a Value Object is not just an attribute. Rather, it is a *property* of the containing parent object/thing in the model that holds a reference to it. Granted, the type of the Value Object has one or more attributes (two in the case of `MonetaryValue`). But to the thing that holds the reference to the Value Object instance, it is a property. Therefore, the thing that is worth 50,000,000 dollars—let's call it `ThingOfWorth`—would have a property— possibly named `worth`—that holds a reference to an instance of a Value Object that has two attributes that collectively describe the measure {50,000,000 dollars}. Remember, though, that the property name—possibly `worth`—and the Value type name—possibly `MonetaryValue`—can be determined only after establishing our **Bounded Context (2)** and its Ubiquitous Language. Here's an improved implementation:

```
// correctly modeled thing of worth
public class ThingOfWorth {
    private ThingName name;     // property
    private MonetaryValue worth; // property
    // ...
}
```

As expected, I changed `ThingOfWorth` to possess a property of type `MonetaryValue` that is named `worth`. It sure cleans up the otherwise disorganized attributes. But more importantly, there is now a Value that expresses a whole.

I want to draw attention to a second change, perhaps one that you were not expecting. The `name` of the `ThingOfWorth` may be just as important to aptly describe as is its `worth`. So I also replaced the `String` type of `name` with the `ThingName` type. The use of a `String` attribute for `name` could seem thorough enough at first. But, in later iterations, you learn that the use of a plain `String` causes problems. It has allowed domain logic central to the `name` of a `ThingOfWorth` to leak out of the model. It has leaked into other parts of the model and into client code:

```
// clients deal with naming issues

String name = thingOfWorth.name();
String capitalizedName =
        name.substring(0, 1).toUpperCase()
        + name.substring(1).toLowerCase();
```

Here the client makes a feeble attempt to fix possible capitalization issues with the name. By defining a `ThingName` type instead, we can centralize all concerns dealing with the `name` of a `ThingOfWorth`. Based on this example, the `ThingName` may fully format the text name upon instantiation, relieving clients of that burden. This emphasizes the need to proliferate Values throughout the model as opposed to minimizing their significance and use. Now, rather than containing three less meaningful attributes, `ThingOfWorth` contains two properly typed and named property Values.

The constructors of a Value class play into the effectiveness of a conceptual whole. Along with immutability, we require a Value class's constructors to be the means to ensure that the Whole Value is created in one operation. You must not allow the attributes of a Value instance to be populated after construction, as if to build up the Whole Value piece by piece. Instead, the final state must be guaranteed to initialize all at once, atomically. The previously expressed `BusinessPriority` and `MonetaryValue` constructors demonstrate this.

Here's another angle on basic value type (for example, `String`, `Integer`, or `Double`) overuse. There are programming languages (such as Ruby) that allow you to effectively patch a class with new, specialized behavior. With such capabilities, you may consider using, for example, a double floating-point value to represent currency. If you need to calculate exchange rates between currencies, you could just patch class `Double` with a `convertToCurrency(Currency aCurrency)` behavior. This might seem like programming coolness, but is it really a good idea to use a language feature in this case? For one thing, this currency-specific behavior is probably lost in a sea of general-purpose floating-point responsibilities. Strike one. Likewise, there is no built-in understanding of currencies in class `Double`. So you'd have to build up the language default type to understand more about currencies. After all, you have to pass in a `Currency` to know the one to convert to. Strike two. Most importantly, class `Double` says nothing explicit about your domain. You lose track of your domain concerns by not applying the Ubiquitous Language. Big swing and a miss. Strike three.

> **Challenge Your Assumptions**
>
> If you are tempted to place multiple attributes on an Entity that as a result manifests a weakened relationship to all other attributes, the attributes should very likely be gathered into a single Value type, or multiple Value types. Each should form a conceptual whole that reflects cohesiveness, appropriately named from your Ubiquitous Language. If even one attribute is associated with a descriptive concept, it is very possible that centralizing all concerns of this concept will improve the power of the model. If one or more of the attributes must change over time, consider Whole Value replacement over maintaining an Entity through a long life cycle.

Replaceability

In your model an immutable Value should be held as a reference by an Entity as long as its constant state describes the currently correct Whole Value. If that is no longer true, the entire Value is completely replaced with a new Value that does represent the currently correct whole.

The concept of replaceability is readily understood in the context of numbers. Say that you have the concept of a `total` that is an integer in your domain. If the `total` is currently set to the value 3 but must now be the value 4, you don't, of course, modify the integer 3 itself to become the number 4. Instead you simply set the `total` to the integer 4:

```
int total = 3;

// later...

total = 4;
```

This is obvious, but it helps make a point. In this example we have just *replaced* the `total` value 3 with the value 4. This is not an oversimplification. It is exactly what replacement does even when a given Value Object type is more complex than an integer. Consider a more complex Value type:

```
FullName name = new FullName("Vaughn", "Vernon");

// later...

name = new FullName("Vaughn", "L", "Vernon");
```

The name starts out as the descriptive value of my first name and my last name. Later that Whole Value is *replaced* with the Whole Value of my first name, the first initial of my middle name, and my last name. I did not use a method on FullName to change the state of the value of name to contain the first initial of my middle name. That would violate the immutability quality of the FullName Value type. Rather we simply use Whole Value replacement, assigning the name object reference an entirely new instance of FullName. (True, this example was not an expressive way to handle replacement, and a better way is just ahead.)

Challenge Your Assumptions

If you are leaning toward the creation of an Entity because the attributes of the object must change, challenge your assumptions that it's the correct model. Would object replacement work instead? Considering the preceding replacement example, you may think that creating a new instance is impractical and lacks expressiveness. Even if the object you are dealing with is complex and changes somewhat frequently, replacement need not be an impractical, or even ugly, proposition. A later example demonstrates Side-Effect-Free Behavior for a simple and expressive way to deal with Whole Value replacement.

Value Equality

When a Value Object instance is compared to another instance, a test of object equality is employed. Throughout the system there may be many, many Value instances that are equal, and yet not the same objects. Equality is determined by comparing the types of both objects and then their attributes. If both the types and their attributes are equal, the Values are considered equal. Further, if any two or more Value instances are equal, you could assign (using replacement) any one of the equal Value instances to an Entity's property of that type and the assignment would not change the value of the property.

Here's an example of class FullName implementing a test for Value equality:

```
public boolean equals(Object anObject) {
    boolean equalObjects = false;
    if (anObject != null &&
            this.getClass() == anObject.getClass()) {
        FullName typedObject = (FullName) anObject;
```

```
        equalObjects =
            this.firstName().equals(typedObject.firstName()) &&
            this.lastName().equals(typedObject.lastName());
    }
    return equalObjects;
}
```

Each of the attributes of two `FullName` instances is compared to the others (assuming this version has only first and last names, not a middle name). If all of the attributes in both objects are equal, the two `FullName` instances are considered equal. This particular Value prevents `null firstName` and `lastName` upon construction. Thus, there is no need to protect against `null` in `equals()` comparisons of each of the corresponding properties. Further, I favor the use of self-encapsulation, so I access attributes through their query methods. This allows for derived attributes rather than requiring each attribute to exist as explicit state. Also implied is the need for a corresponding `hashCode()` implementation (demonstrated later).

Consider the combination of Value characteristics necessary to support **Aggregate (10)** unique identity. We need the Value equality capability, for example, when we query for a specific Aggregate instance by identity. Immutability is also crucial. The unique identity must never change, and this can in part be ensured through the Value immutability characteristic. We also benefit from the conceptual whole characteristic, because the identity is named per the Ubiquitous Language and holds all uniqueness-identifying attributes in one instance. However, in this specific case we don't need the replacement characteristic of a Value Object because the unique identity of an Aggregate Root will never be replaced. Yet, lacking the need for replacement characteristics does not disqualify the use of a Value here. Further, if the identity requires some Side-Effect-Free Behavior, it is implemented on the Value type.

> **Challenge Your Assumptions**
>
> Ask yourself if the concept you are designing must be an Entity identified uniquely from all other objects or if it is sufficiently supported using Value equality. If the concept itself doesn't require unique identity, model it as a Value Object.

Side-Effect-Free Behavior

A method of an object can be designed as a **Side-Effect-Free Function** [Evans]. A *function* is an operation of an object that produces output but without modifying its own state. Since no modification occurs when executing a specific operation, that operation is said to be side-effect free. The methods of an immutable Value Object must all be Side-Effect-Free Functions because they must not violate its immutability quality. You may consider this characteristic as part and parcel with immutability. It is closely tied. However, I prefer to break it out as a distinct characteristic because doing so emphasizes a huge benefit of Value Objects. Otherwise, we might see Values only as attribute containers, overlooking one of the most powerful aspects of the pattern.

The Functional Way

Functional programming languages generally enforce this characteristic. In fact, pure functional languages allow nothing but Side-Effect-Free Behavior, requiring all closures to receive and produce only immutable Value Objects.

Bertrand Meyer described Side-Effect-Free Functions as the *Query* methods of his Command-Query Separation principle, or **CQS**, as discussed by Martin Fowler in [Fowler, CQS]. A query method is one that asks an object a question. By definition, asking an object a question must not change the answer.

Here is an example of the `FullName` type's use of Side-Effect-Free Behavior to produce a new replacement value of itself:

```
FullName name = new FullName("Vaughn", "Vernon");

// later...

name = name.withMiddleInitial("L");
```

This produces the same outcome as the example discussed under "Replaceability," but in a more expressive way. This Side-Effect-Free Function is implemented as follows:

```
public FullName withMiddleInitial(String aMiddleNameOrInitial) {
    if (aMiddleNameOrInitial == null) {
        throw new IllegalArgumentException(
                "Must provide a middle name or initial.");
    }

    String middle = aMiddleNameOrInitial.trim();

    if (middle.isEmpty()) {
        throw new IllegalArgumentException(
                "Must provide a middle name or initial.");
    }

    return new FullName(
            this.firstName(),
            middle.substring(0, 1).toUpperCase(),
            this.lastName());
}
```

In this example the method `withMiddleInitial()` does not modify the state of its own Value and is, therefore, side-effect free. Instead it instantiates a new Value composed from some of its own parts and a given middle initial. This method captures important domain business logic in the model rather than allowing it to leak out into client code, which could happen in the earlier example.

When a Value References an Entity

Should a Value Object method be permitted to cause the modification of an Entity that is passed as a parameter? Without stating a rule, if such a method does cause the modification of an Entity, is it really side-effect free? Would it be easy to test that method? I say not easy or less easy. Thus, when a Value's method takes an Entity as parameter, it may be best for it to answer a result that the Entity could use to modify itself on its own terms.

Nonetheless, there are problems with such a design. Consider an example. Here a Scrum `Product`, an Entity, is used in some way by `BusinessPriority`, a Value Object, to calculate a priority:

```
float priority = businessPriority.priorityOf(product);
```

Do you see flaws in this? You have probably concluded that at least some problems exist:

- What I draw attention to is that we are forcing the Value to not only depend on a `Product`, but also to understand the shape of this Entity. Where possible, limit a Value to depend on and understand only its own type and the types of its attributes. That is not always possible, but it's a good goal.

- Someone reading the code will not know what parts of the `Product` will be used. The expression is not explicit, which weakens the clarity of the model. It would be much better if some actual or derived property of `Product` were passed.

- More important for this discussion, any Value method that takes an Entity as parameter cannot easily prove that it doesn't cause the Entity's modification, making the operation more difficult to test. So, even though a Value promises not to cause modification, no one can easily prove that it doesn't.

Given this analysis, we haven't really improved anything here. To change that and make the Value robust, you'd pass only Values as parameters to Value methods. This way you reach the greatest level of Side-Effect-Free Behavior. It is not difficult to accomplish:

```
float priority =
        businessPriority.priority(
                product.businessPriorityTotals());
```

Here we simply ask the `Product` to provide an instance of Value `Business-PriorityTotals`. You may conclude that `priority()` should return a type other than `float`. That would be especially true if expressing a priority should be a more formal part of the Ubiquitous Language, in which case a custom value type would be in order. Decisions like these come as a result of *continually* refining the model. Indeed, after some analysis the SaaSOvation team finds that the `Product` Entity should not itself calculate business priority totals at all. That would eventually be performed by a **Domain Service (7)**, and you will see the better solution in that chapter.

If you decide against designing a specialized Value Object in favor of using a basic language Value type instead (primitive or wrapper), you might be shortchanging your model. You won't have the opportunity to assign domain-specific Side-Effect-Free Functions to the basic language Value type. Any specialty behavior will be separate from the Value. And even if your programming language allows you to patch the basic type with new behavior, is that really going to enable you to capture deep domain insight?

Challenge Your Assumptions

If you think that a specific method cannot be side-effect free and must mutate the state of its own instance, challenge your assumptions. Is there a way to employ replacement rather than mutation? The preceding example provides a very simple approach to creating a new Value by reusing parts of the existing one and replacing only the specifically changed parts. Rarely would every object in the system be a Value. Some objects will almost certainly be Entities. Carefully compare the Value characteristic qualifiers against those of Entities. A reasonable amount of team thought and discussion should lead to the correct conclusions.

Once the SaaSOvation teams read the [Evans] guidance about Side-Effect-Free Functions, and other Whole Value material, they realized that they should be using Value Objects far more frequently. The teams have since come to realize that understanding the preceding Value characteristics really helped them discover more natural Value types in their domain.

Is Everything a Value Object?

By now you may have begun to think that everything looks like a Value Object. That's better than thinking that everything looks like an Entity. Where you might use a little caution is when there are truly simple attributes that really don't need any special treatment. Perhaps those are Booleans or any numeric value that is really self-contained, needing no additional functional support, and is related to no other attributes in the same Entity. On their own the simple attributes are a Meaningful Whole. Still, you could certainly make the "mistake" of unnecessarily wrapping a single attribute in a Value type with no special functionality and be better off than those who never give Value design a nod. If you find that you've overdone it a bit, you can always refactor a little.

Integrate with Minimalism

There are always multiple Bounded Contexts in every DDD initiative, which means we must find appropriate ways to integrate them. Where possible use Value Objects to model concepts in the downstream Context when objects from the upstream Context flow in. By doing so you can integrate with a priority on minimalism, that is, minimizing the number of properties that you assume responsibility for managing in your downstream model. Using immutable Values results in assuming less responsibility.

Why Be So Responsible?

Using immutable Values results in assuming less responsibility.

Reusing an example from **Bounded Contexts (2)**, recall that two Aggregates in the upstream *Identity and Access Context* have an impact on the downstream *Collaboration Context*, as illustrated in Figure 6.1. In the *Identity and Access Context* the two Aggregates are User and Role. The *Collaboration Context* is interested in whether a specific User plays a specific Role, namely,

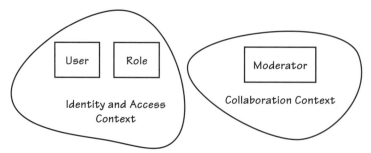

Figure 6.1   The *Moderator* object in its Context is based on the state of a *User* and *Role* in a different Context. *User* and *Role* are Aggregates, *but Moderator* is a Value Object.

Moderator. The *Collaboration Context* uses its **Anticorruption Layer (3)** to query the **Open Host Service (3)** of the *Identity and Access Context*. If the integration-based query indicates that the Moderator role is being played by the specific user, the *Collaboration Context* creates a representative object, namely, a `Moderator`.

`Moderator`, among the `Collaborator` subclasses shown in Figure 6.2, is modeled as a Value Object. Instances are statically created and associated with a `Forum` Aggregate, the important point being the minimized impact that multiple Aggregates in the upstream *Identity and Access Context*, possessing many attributes, have on the *Collaboration Context*. With just a few attributes of its own, a `Moderator` models an essential concept of the Ubiquitous Language spoken in the *Collaboration Context*. Furthermore, class `Moderator` contains no single attribute from the `Role` Aggregate. Rather, the class name itself captures the Moderator role played by a user. By choice, the `Moderator` is a statically created Value instance, and there is no goal to keep it synchronized with the remote Context of origin. This carefully chosen quality-of-service contract lifts a potentially heavy burden off the consuming Context.

Of course, there are times when an object in a downstream Context must be eventually consistent with the partial state of one or more Aggregates in a remote Context. In that case we'd design an Aggregate in the downstream consuming Context, because Entities are used to maintain a thread of continuity of change. But we should strive to avoid this modeling choice where possible. When you can, choose Value Objects to model integrations. This advice is applicable in many cases when consuming remote *Standard Types*.

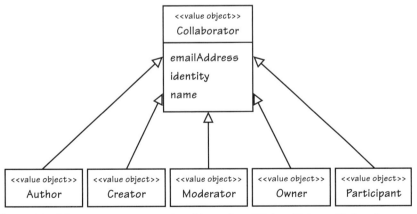

Figure 6.2   The `Collaborator` class hierarchy of Value Objects. Only a few *User* attributes are retained from the upstream Context, with class names making roles explicit.

Standard Types Expressed as Values

In many systems and applications there is a need for what I call **Standard Types**. Standard Types are descriptive objects that indicate the types of things. There is the thing (Entity) or description (Value) itself, and there are also the Standard Types to distinguish them from other types of the same thing. I am unaware of an industry standard name for this concept, but I have also heard it called a *type code* and a *lookup*. The name *type code* doesn't say much. And a *lookup* is a lookup of what? I prefer the name Standard Types because it is more descriptive. To make this concept clearer, consider a few uses. In some cases these are modeled as **Power Types**.

Your Ubiquitous Language defines a PhoneNumber (Value), which also requires you to describe the type of each one. "Is the phone number a home, mobile, work, or other type of number?" asks your domain expert. Should different types of phone numbers be modeled as a class hierarchy? Having a separate class for each type makes it more difficult for clients to distinguish among them. Here you'd likely desire to use a Standard Type to describe the type of phone, either Home, Mobile, Work, or Other. These descriptions represent the Standard Types of phones.

As I previously discussed, in a financial domain there is the possibility of having a Currency (Value) type to constrain a MonetaryValue to an amount within a specific world currency. In this case the Standard Type would provide a Value for each of the world's currencies: AUD, CAD, CNY, EUR, GBP, JPY, USD, and so on. Using a Standard Type here helps you avoid bogus currencies. Although the incorrect currency could be assigned to the MonetaryValue, a nonexistent currency could not be. If using a string attribute, you could place the model into an invalid state. Consider the misspelled *doolars* and the problems it would cause.

You might be working in the pharmaceutical field and designing for medications that have various kinds of administration routes. A specific medication (Entity) has a long life cycle and change is managed over time—it is conceptualized, researched, developed, tested, manufactured, improved, and finally discontinued. You may or may not decide to manage the life cycle stages using Standard Types. These life cycle shifts may justifiably be managed in a few different Bounded Contexts. On the other hand, the directed patient administration route of each medication can be classified by Standard Type descriptions, such as IV, Oral, or Topical.

Depending on the level of standardization, these types may be maintained at the application level only, or be escalated in importance to shared corporate databases, or be available through national or international standards bodies.

The level of standardization can sometimes influence the way Standard Types are retrieved and used inside a model.

We may think of these as Entities because they have a life of their own in a dedicated, native Bounded Context. Regardless of how they are created and maintained by any kind of standards body, if possible we should strive to treat them as Values in our consuming Context. This works well because they measure and describe the types of things, and measures and descriptions are best modeled as Values. Further, one instance of {IV}, for example, is just the same as any other instance of {IV}. They are clearly interchangeable, which also means that they are replaceable and can employ Value equality. Thus, if there is no need to maintain a continuity of change over the life cycle of descriptive types in *your* Bounded Context, model them as Values.

For the sake of maintenance it is common for Standard Types to natively reside in a separate Context from the models that consume them. There they are Entities and have a persistent life cycle with attributes such as `identity`, `name`, and `description`. There may be other attributes as well, but the ones mentioned are the most common to use in a consuming Context. We often use just one. This is in adherence to the goal to integrate with minimalism.

As a very simple example, consider a Standard Type that models a member of a group for which two types exist. There may be members that are users and members that are themselves groups (nested groups). This Java enum represents one way to support a Standard Type:

```
package com.saasovation.identityaccess.domain.model.identity;

public enum GroupMemberType {

    GROUP {
        public boolean isGroup() {
            return true;
        }
    },
    USER {
        public boolean isUser() {
            return true;
        }
    };

    public boolean isGroup() {
        return false;
    }

    public boolean isUser() {
        return false;
    }
}
```

A `GroupMember` Value instance is instantiated with a specific `Group-MemberType`. To demonstrate, when a `User` or a `Group` is assigned to a `Group`, the assigned Aggregate is asked to render a `GroupMember` corresponding to itself. Here is the `toGroupMember()` method implementation of class `User`:

```
protected GroupMember toGroupMember() {
    GroupMember groupMember =
        new GroupMember(
                this.tenantId(),
                this.username(),
                GroupMemberType.USER); // enum standard type

    return groupMember;
}
```

Use of a Java enum is a very simple way to support a Standard Type. The enum provides a well-defined finite number of Values (in this case two), it is very lightweight, and it has by convention Side-Effect-Free Behavior. But where is the Value's textual description? There are two possible answers. Often there is no need to provide a description of the type, just its name. Why? Textual descriptions are generally valid only in the **User Interface Layer (14)** and can be supplied by matching the type name to a view-centric property. Many times the view-centric property must be localized (as in multilanguage computing), making this inappropriate to support in the model. Often the name of the Standard Type alone is the best attribute to use in the model. The second answer is that there are limited descriptions built right into the enum state names GROUP and USER. You may render the descriptive names using the `toString()` behavior of each type. But if necessary, descriptive text of each type may be modeled as well.

This sample Java enum Standard Type is also, in essence, an elegant and clutter-free **State** [Gamma et al.] object. At the bottom of the enum declaration there are two methods that implement the default behavior for all States, `isGroup()` and `isUser()`. By default, both of these methods answer `false`, which is the proper basic behavior. In each of the State definitions, however, the methods are overridden to answer `true` as applicable for their specific State. When the state of the Standard Type is the GROUP, the `isGroup()` method is overridden to produce a `true` outcome. When the state of the Standard Type is the USER, the `isUser()` method is overridden to produce a `true` outcome. The state changes by replacing the current enum value with a different one.

This enum demonstrates some very basic behavior. The State pattern implementation can be more sophisticated as needed by the domain, adding more standard behaviors that are overridden and specialized by each State. As it is, this is an example of a Value type whose states are constrained to a well-defined set of constants. An important one is the `BacklogItemStatusType`, which provides `PLANNED`, `SCHEDULED`, `COMMITTED`, `DONE`, and `REMOVED` states. I use this Standard Type approach throughout the three sample Bounded Contexts. I think it keeps them as simple as possible.

State Pattern Considered Harmful?

Some consider the State pattern to be less than desirable. A common complaint is the need to create an abstract implementation of each of the behaviors supported by the type (the two methods at the bottom of `GroupMemberType`) and then to override those behaviors when the given State must provide a specialized implementation. In Java this typically requires a separate class (usually in a separate file) for the abstract type and also for each State. Like it or not, that is the way of the State pattern.

I agree that when separate State classes must be developed—one for each unique state plus an abstract type—it can become an unwieldy mess. The distinct behaviors in each class, perhaps mixed with some default behavior from the abstract class, can lead to tight coupling of subclasses and lack of readability between types. This burden is especially taxing if you have a large number of States. However, I think that the use of a Java enum is a very simple and possibly the more optimal way to use the State pattern to produce a set of Standard Types. I think you get the best of both approaches. You get a very simple Standard Type and a way to interrogate the standard for its current State. This keeps behavior cohesive to the type. Limiting the State behavior makes for practical use.

But it's still possible that you don't like even this simple implementation of State, and to each his or her own.

If you decide that you dislike the use of Java enums to support Standard Types, you can always use a unique Value instance for each type. However, if your concern is primarily that you don't like the idea of using the State pattern, you can easily use an enum for elegant Standard Type support without thinking of it as the State pattern. After all, I may be the first person to have put the enum-as-State thought into your mind. That being said, there are alternatives to implementing Standard Types other than the enum and Value approaches.

As one alternative, you can use an Aggregate as a Standard Type with one instance of the Aggregate per type. Think twice before you run with this. Standard types should generally not be maintained inside the Bounded Context that consumes them. Widely used Standard Types should normally be maintained in a separate Context with very carefully planned updates to consumers. Instead, you could choose to expose Standard Type Aggregates as immutable in consumer Contexts. But ask yourself if an immutable Entity is by definition really an Entity. If you think not, you should consider modeling it as a shared immutable Value Object instead.

A shared immutable Value Object can be obtained from a hidden persistence store. This is a viable choice if obtained from a Standard Type **Service** (7) or **Factory** (11). If employed, you should probably have one Service or Factory provider for each set of Standard Types (one for phone number types, another for postal address types, one for currency types), as depicted in Figure 6.3. In both cases the concrete implementations of a Service or Factory would access the persistence store to obtain the shared Values as needed, but clients would never know that the Values are stored in a standards database. Using either a Service or a Factory to provide the types also enables you to put a number of viable caching strategies to work easily and safely because the Values are read-only from the store and immutable in the system.

In the end, I think it is best to be biased toward enum for Standard Types whether or not you actually think of it as a State. If you have many possible Standard Type instances in a single category, consider code generation to produce the enum. A code generation approach could read through all existing Standard Types in their respective persistence store (system of record) and create a unique type/state per row, for example.

If you decide to use classical Value Objects as Standard Types, you may find it useful to introduce a Service or Factory to statically create instances as needed. This would have similar motivations as discussed previously but would be different in its implementation from those producing shared Values. In this case your Service or Factory would provide statically created immutable Value instances of each individual Standard Type. Any changes to the underlying Standard Type database entities in the system of record would not be

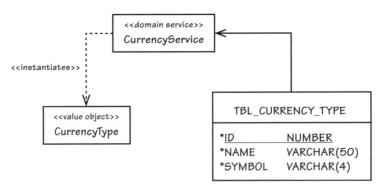

Figure 6.3 A Domain Service can be used to provide Standard Types. In this case the Service goes out to the database to read the state of a requested *CurrencyType*.

automatically reflected in the preexisting statically created representation instances. If you desired to keep such statically created Value instances synchronized with the system of record, you'd need to provide a custom solution to search for and update their state in your model. This could negate the potential usefulness of this approach.[4] Thus, you might from design inception determine that all such statically created Standard Type Values will never be updated in the consuming Bounded Context. All competing forces must be weighed.

Testing Value Objects

To emphasize test-first, I first present sample tests before I provide the Value Object implementation. These tests drive the domain model's design by providing examples of how a client will use each object.

Employing this style, we are not as interested in addressing the various aspects of unit testing, thoroughly proving that the model is completely bulletproof in every way. Rather, at this point in time there is more interest in demonstrating how various objects in the domain model will be used by clients and what those clients can expect when they use them. It is essential to assume the client's perspective when designing the model in order to capture the essential concepts. Otherwise, we could be modeling from our own perspective instead of from the business's.

> **Best Sample Code**
> Here's one way of thinking about this style of test: If we were writing a user's manual for the model, we would provide these tests as the most appropriate code samples for how clients should use this specific domain object.

This is not to say that unit tests should not be developed. All additional tests that address team standards should and must be written. However, there are different motivations for each type of test. Unit tests and behavioral tests have their place, as do the following modeling tests.

The Value Object selected is a good all-around representation taken from the latest **Core Domain** (2), the *Agile Project Management Context*.

---

4. This would be a good time to model an Aggregate in an upstream Context also as an Aggregate in the downstream Context. They wouldn't be the same class or necessarily contain all the same attributes, but modeling the downstream concept as an Aggregate would allow for eventual consistency and single point updates.

In this Bounded Context business domain experts speak of the "business priority of backlog items." To fulfill this part of the Ubiquitous Language we model the concept as a `BusinessPriority`. It provides calculated output suitable for supporting the business analysis of the value of developing each product backlog item [Wiegers]. The outputs are cost percentage, or the cost of developing a specific backlog item as compared to the cost of developing all others; total value, which is the total value gained by developing a specific backlog item; and value percentage, as in the value of developing a specific backlog item compared to the value of developing any other; and priority, which is the calculated priority the business should consider giving this backlog item when compared against all others.

These tests actually emerged over multiple brief refactoring iterations of stepwise refinements, although they are presented here as a finished set:

```
package com.saasovation.agilepm.domain.model.product;

import com.saasovation.agilepm.domain.model.DomainTest;

import java.text.NumberFormat;

public class BusinessPriorityTest extends DomainTest {

    public BusinessPriorityTest() {
        super();
    }
    ...
    private NumberFormat oneDecimal() {
        return this.decimal(1);
    }

    private NumberFormat twoDecimals() {
        return this.decimal(2);
    }

    private NumberFormat decimal(int aNumberOfDecimals) {
        NumberFormat fmt = NumberFormat.getInstance();
        fmt.setMinimumFractionDigits(aNumberOfDecimals);
        fmt.setMaximumFractionDigits(aNumberOfDecimals);
        return fmt;
    }
}
```

The class has some fixture helpers. Since the team needed to test the accuracy of various calculations, they coded methods to provide `NumberFormat` instances for fractional values that had either one or two places to the right of the decimal point. You'll see next why these are useful:

```
public void testCostPercentageCalculation() throws Exception {

    BusinessPriority businessPriority =
        new BusinessPriority(
                new BusinessPriorityRatings(2, 4, 1, 1));

    BusinessPriority businessPriorityCopy =
        new BusinessPriority(businessPriority);

    assertEquals(businessPriority, businessPriorityCopy);

    BusinessPriorityTotals totals =
        new BusinessPriorityTotals(53, 49, 53 + 49, 37, 33);

    float cost = businessPriority.costPercentage(totals);

    assertEquals(this.oneDecimal().format(cost), "2.7");

    assertEquals(businessPriority, businessPriorityCopy);
}
```

The team came up with a good idea to test for immutability. Each test first created an instance of `BusinessPriority` and then made an equivalent copy of it using the copy constructor. The first assertion in the test ensured that the copy constructor produced a copy equal to the original.

Next, they designed the test to create `BusinessPriorityTotals` and assigned it to the `totals` method variable. With `totals` they were able to use the `costPercentage()` query method and assign the results to `cost`. They then asserted that the value returned was `2.7`, which was the manually calculated correct outcome. Finally, they asserted that the behavior of method `costPercentage()` was truly side-effect free, which would be the case if `businessPriority` still had Value equality with `businessPriorityCopy`. From this test they gained a good idea of how to calculate cost percentages and what their outcome would be like.

Next, they needed to test the priority, the total value, and the value percentage calculations, using the same basic plan of attack:

```
public void testPriorityCalculation() throws Exception {

    BusinessPriority businessPriority =
        new BusinessPriority(
                new BusinessPriorityRatings(2, 4, 1, 1));

    BusinessPriority businessPriorityCopy =
        new BusinessPriority(businessPriority);
```

```
        assertEquals(businessPriorityCopy, businessPriority);

        BusinessPriorityTotals totals =
            new BusinessPriorityTotals(53, 49, 53 + 49, 37, 33);

        float calculatedPriority = businessPriority.priority(totals);

        assertEquals("1.03",
                    this.twoDecimals().format(calculatedPriority));

        assertEquals(businessPriority, businessPriorityCopy);
    }

    public void testTotalValueCalculation() throws Exception {

        BusinessPriority businessPriority =
            new BusinessPriority(
                new BusinessPriorityRatings(2, 4, 1, 1));

        BusinessPriority businessPriorityCopy =
            new BusinessPriority(businessPriority);

        assertEquals(businessPriority, businessPriorityCopy);

        float totalValue = businessPriority.totalValue();

        assertEquals("6.0", this.oneDecimal().format(totalValue));

        assertEquals(businessPriority, businessPriorityCopy);
    }

    public void testValuePercentageCalculation() throws Exception {

        BusinessPriority businessPriority =
            new BusinessPriority(
                new BusinessPriorityRatings(2, 4, 1, 1));

        BusinessPriority businessPriorityCopy =
            new BusinessPriority(businessPriority);

        assertEquals(businessPriority, businessPriorityCopy);

        BusinessPriorityTotals totals =
            new BusinessPriorityTotals(53, 49, 53 + 49, 37, 33);

        float valuePercentage =
            businessPriority.valuePercentage(totals);

        assertEquals("5.9", this.oneDecimal().format(valuePercentage));

        assertEquals(businessPriorityCopy, businessPriority);
    }
```

Nontechnical domain experts—given a bit of help—reading these example-based tests were able to understand just how `BusinessPriority` was used, the kinds of outcomes it produced, that its behavior was guaranteed to be side-effect free, and that it adhered to the concepts and intent of the Ubiquitous Language.

Importantly, the state of the Value Object was guaranteed immutable for every usage. Clients could produce results from the priority calculations of any number of product backlog items, sort them, compare them, and adjust the `BusinessPriorityRatings` of each item as needed.

Implementation

I like this `BusinessPriority` example because it demonstrates all of the Value characteristics and more. Besides showing how to design for immutability, conceptual wholeness, replaceability, Value equality, and Side-Effect-Free Behavior, it also demonstrates how you can use a Value type as a **Strategy** [Gamma et al.] (aka **Policy**).

As each test method was developed, the team understood more about how a client would use a `BusinessPriority`, enabling them to implement it to behave as the tests asserted it should. Here is the basic class definition along with constructors that the team coded:

```
public final class BusinessPriority implements Serializable  {

    private static final long serialVersionUID = 1L;

    private BusinessPriorityRatings ratings;

    public BusinessPriority(BusinessPriorityRatings aRatings) {
        super();
        this.setRatings(aRatings);
    }

    public BusinessPriority(BusinessPriority aBusinessPriority) {
        this(aBusinessPriority.ratings());
    }
```

The team decided to declare their Value types `Serializable`. There are times when a Value instance needs to be serialized, such as when it is communicated to a remote system, and may be useful for some persistence strategies.

This `BusinessPriority` itself was designed to hold a Value property named `ratings` of type `BusinessPriorityRatings` (not shown here). The `ratings` property described the business value and expense trade-off of either implementing, or not implementing, a given product backlog item. The `BusinessPriority-Ratings` type provided the `BusinessPriority` with `benefit`, `cost`, `penalty`, and `risk` ratings, which enabled a range of calculations to be performed.

Usually I support at least two constructors for each of my Value Objects. The first constructor takes the full complement of parameters necessary to derive and/or set state attributes. This primary constructor first initializes its default state. The basic attribute initialization is performed first by invoking private setters. I recommend the use of *self-delegation* and demonstrate its use here with private setters.

Keeping Values Immutable

Only the primary constructor(s) use self-delegation to set properties/attributes. No other methods shall self-delegate to setter methods. Since all setter methods in a Value Object are always private scope, there is no opportunity for attributes to be exposed to mutation by consumers. These are two important factors in maintaining the immutability of Values.

The second constructor is used to copy an existing Value to create a new one, or what is called a *copy constructor*. This constructor performs what's known as a *shallow copy* as it self-delegates to its primary constructor, passing as parameters each of the corresponding attributes of the Value being copied. We could perform a *deep copy* or *clone* where all contained attributes and properties are themselves copied to produce a completely unique object, but still equal to the value of the one copied. However, this many times proves to be both complex and unnecessary when dealing with Values. If a deep copy is ever needed, it can be added. But when dealing with immutable Values, it is never a problem to share attributes/properties between instances.

This second constructor, the copy constructor, is important for unit tests. When we test a Value Object, we want to include verification that it is immutable. As demonstrated earlier, when the unit test begins, create the new test Value Object instance and a copy of it using the copy constructor, and assert that the two instances are equal. Next, test the Value instance Side-Effect-Free Behavior. If all test goal assertions pass, the final assertion is that the tested and the copied instances are still equal.

Next, we implement the Strategy/Policy part of the Value type:

```java
public float costPercentage(BusinessPriorityTotals aTotals) {
    return (float) 100 * this.ratings().cost() /
        aTotals.totalCost();
}

public float priority(BusinessPriorityTotals aTotals) {
    return
        this.valuePercentage(aTotals) /
            (this.costPercentage(aTotals) +
                this.riskPercentage(aTotals));
}

public float riskPercentage(BusinessPriorityTotals aTotals) {
    return (float) 100 * this.ratings().risk() /
        aTotals.totalRisk();
}

public float totalValue() {
    return this.ratings().benefit() + this.ratings().penalty();
}

public float valuePercentage(BusinessPriorityTotals aTotals) {
    return (float) 100 * this.totalValue() / aTotals.totalValue();
}

public BusinessPriorityRatings ratings() {
    return this.ratings;
}
```

Some of the calculation behavior requires a parameter of type `Business-PriorityTotals`. This Value provides a description of the cost-risk totals across all product backlog items. Totals are necessary when calculating percentages and the overall business priority compared to all other backlog items. None of these behaviors modifies its own instance state. We assert this externally in tests by comparing the copied state with the current state following the execution of each behavior.

There currently is no **Separated Interface** [Fowler, P of EAA] for the Strategy because there is at present only one implementation. No doubt in time that will change, and customers of the Agile PM SaaS product will be given other business priority calculation options, each with its own Strategy implementation.

The method names of the Side-Effect-Free Functions are important. Although these methods all return Values (because they are CQS query methods), they purposely avoid the use of the `get`-prefix JavaBean naming convention. This simple but effective approach to object design keeps the Value Object faithful to the Ubiquitous Language. The use of `getValuePercentage()` is a technical computer statement, but `valuePercentage()` is a fluent human-readable language expression.

Where Did My Fluent Java Go?

I think that the JavaBean specification has had a negative impact on object design, one that doesn't promote the principles of Domain-Driven Design or good object design in general. Consider the Java API that existed prior to the JavaBean specification. Take `java.lang.String`, for one example. There are but a few query methods on the class `String` that are prefixed by `get`. Most of the query methods are named more fluently, such as `charAt()`, `compareTo()`, `concat()`, `contains()`, `endsWith()`, `indexOf()`, `length()`, `replace()`, `startsWith()`, `substring()`, and the like. There's no Java-Bean code smell there! Of course, this example alone doesn't prove my point. Nonetheless, it is true that Java APIs since the JavaBean specification have been greatly influenced and lack fluency in expression. A fluent, human-readable language expression is a very worthwhile style to embrace.

If you are concerned about tooling that depends on the JavaBean specification, there are solutions. For example, Hibernate provides support for field-level access (object attributes). Thus, as far as Hibernate is concerned, your methods can be named as desired without a negative impact on persistence.

With other tools there could be a downside to designing with expressive interfaces, however. If you desire to use the standard Java EL or OGNL, for instance, you won't be able to render such types directly. You would have to use another means, such as a **Data Transfer Object** [Fowler, P of EAA] with getters, to transfer Value Object properties to the user interface. Since DTO is a commonly used pattern, albeit often technically unnecessary, some may find this of little consequence. If DTO is not an option for you, there are others. Consider the **Presentation Model** as discussed in **Application (14)**. Since your Presentation Model can serve as an **Adapter** [Gamma et al.], it can surface getters for use by views that use EL, for example. Yet, if all else fails, you may need to grudgingly design your domain objects with getters.

If you reach that conclusion, you should still not design Value Objects with full JavaBean capabilities that would allow their state to be initialized through public setters. That would violate their essential Value immutability characteristic.

The next set of methods includes the standard object overrides `equals()`, `hashCode()`, and `toString()`:

```
@Override
public boolean equals(Object anObject) {
    boolean equalObjects = false;
    if (anObject != null &&
            this.getClass() == anObject.getClass()) {
        BusinessPriority typedObject = (BusinessPriority) anObject;
        equalObjects =
            this.ratings().equals(typedObject.ratings());
    }
    return equalObjects;
}

@Override
public int hashCode() {
    int hashCodeValue =
        + (169065 * 179)
        + this.ratings().hashCode();

    return hashCodeValue;
}

@Override
public String toString() {
    return
        "BusinessPriority"
        + " ratings = " + this.ratings();
}
```

The equals() method fulfills the Value Object requirement to check for Value equality, one of the five Value characteristics. Here we always eliminate null parameters from equality. The class of the parameter must be the same as the class of the Value. If they are the same, each of the properties/attributes is compared in both Values. If each one is affirmed as equal to its corresponding property/attribute, the Whole Values are considered equal.

Per Java standards, hashCode() has the same contract as equals() in that all Values that are equal also produce equal hash code values.

There is nothing special about toString(). It creates a human-readable representation of the Value instance state. You may design the representation format as needed.

There are a few remaining methods to review:

```
protected BusinessPriority() {
    super();
}

private void setRatings(BusinessPriorityRatings aRatings) {
    if (aRatings == null) {
```

```
        throw new IllegalArgumentException(
                "The ratings are required.");
    }
    this.ratings = aRatings;
}
}
```

The zero-argument constructor is provided for the sake of framework tools that require it, such as Hibernate. Since the zero-argument constructor is always hidden, there is no danger of model clients creating invalid instances. Hibernate functions perfectly well with hidden constructors and accessors. This constructor enables Hibernate and other tools to create instances of the type as they are being reconstituted from, for example, the persistence store. Tools use the zero-argument constructor to create an initially hollow instance and then call each property/attribute setter to hydrate the object. Optionally you can tell Hibernate to bypass setter methods and directly set attributes, as is the case with this model since it doesn't provide a complete JavaBean interface. Just to reiterate, model clients use the public constructors, never the hidden one.

Finally, the class definition ends with the property setter for ratings. One of the strengths of self-encapsulation/delegation is seen in this method. An accessor method—getter or setter—need not be limited to setting an instance field. It can also perform important **Assertions** [Evans], a key element to successful software development in general and DDD models specifically.

The Assertion for valid parameters is called a *guard*, because it guards the method from being subjected to obviously invalid data. Guards can and should be used in any method when wrong parameters would cause more serious problems later if correctness were otherwise taken for granted. Here the setter asserts that the parameter aRatings is not null, and if it happens to be, it throws an IllegalArgumentException. True, the setter is logically used only once in the Value's lifetime. Still, the Assertion is a well-placed guard. You will see the advantages of self-delegation demonstrated elsewhere, too. Specifically, **Entities** (5) explains the technique thoroughly as part of a discussion of validation.

Persisting Value Objects

There are a variety of ways to persist Value Object instances to a persistent store. In a general sense it involves serializing the object to some text or binary format and saving it to disk. However, since we are not concerned with persisting individual Value instances on their own, I won't be focusing on general-purpose persistence. Rather, we are more interested in persisting Values along with the state of the Aggregate instances that contain them. The following approaches assume that a parent Entity ultimately holds references to the Value instances that get persisted. All of the following examples are based on the assumption that an Aggregate is being added to or read from its **Repository (12)**, and its contained Values are persisted and reconstituted behind the scenes along with the Entity—such as the Aggregate Root—that contains them.

Object-relational mapping (ORM, such as Hibernate) persistence is popular and widely used. However, using an ORM to map every class to a table and every attribute to a column adds complexity, which may be unwarranted. Rising in popularity is the use of NoSQL databases and key-value stores because of their ability to provide high-performance, scalable, fault-tolerant, and highly available enterprise storage. To boot, key-value stores can greatly simplify Aggregate persistence. In this chapter I stick with ORM-based persistence. Because NoSQL, key-value stores persist Aggregates exceptionally well, I give attention to that style in **Repositories (12)**.

But before we jump into Value ORM persistence examples, there's a vital modeling commitment that must be well understood and diligently followed. So to start off, let's tackle what can happen when data modeling (as opposed to domain modeling) has an inappropriate influence on your domain model, and what can be done to reject this wrong and harmful influence.

Reject Undue Influence of Data Model Leakage

Probably most times that a Value Object is persisted to a data store (for example, using an ORM tool along with a relational database) it is stored in a denormalized fashion; that is, its attributes are stored in the same database table row as its parent Entity object. This makes the storage and retrieval of Values clean and optimized and prevents any persistence store leakage into the model. It's both a pleasure and a relief when Values can be persisted this way.

There are times, however, when a Value Object in the model will of necessity be stored as an Entity with respect to a relational persistence store. In other words, when persisted, an instance of a specific Value Object type will occupy its own row in a relational database table that exists specifically for its type, and it will have its own database primary key column. This happens, for example, when supporting a collection of Value Object instances with ORM. In such cases the Value type persistent data is modeled as a database entity.

Is this an indication that the domain model object should reflect the design of the data model and be an Entity rather than a Value? No. When you face the consequences of this impedance mismatch, it is important to maintain a domain model perspective rather than a persistence perspective. To keep your perspective on the domain model you can ask yourself these questions:

1. Is the concept I am modeling a thing in the domain or does it measure, quantify, or describe a thing as one of its properties?

2. If modeled correctly to describe an element of the domain, must this model concept possess all or most of the value characteristics outlined previously?

3. Am I considering the use of an Entity in the model only because the underlying data model must store the domain model object as an entity?

4. Am I using an Entity because the domain model requires unique identity, I care about individual instances, and I must manage a continuity of change over the object's life cycle?

If your answers are "Describes, Yes, Yes, and No," you should use a Value Object. Model the persistence store in the way necessary to deal with the storage of the object, but don't let that influence the way your team conceptualizes the Value property in the domain model.

The Data Model Should Be Subordinate
Design your data model for the sake of your domain model, not your domain model for the sake of your data model.

If at all possible, always design your data model for the sake of your domain model, not your domain model for the sake of your data model. If you do the former, you will maintain a domain model perspective. If you do the latter, you will maintain a persistence perspective and your domain model will tend to serve merely as a projection of your data model. As you discipline your mind to think in terms of the domain model—DDD-think—rather than the data model, you will avoid the negative consequences of data model leakage. See **Entities (5)** for more discussion of DDD-think.

Of course, there are times when database referential integrity matters (such as for foreign keys). Absolutely, you want key columns to be properly indexed. Sure, there certainly is the need to support business intelligence reporting tools that operate against your business data. You can enable all these facets in appropriate and necessary places. Most conclude that reporting and business intelligence should not operate against your production data and should instead have a dedicated, specially designed data model. Following this more strategic mentality frees you to design your domain model's backing data model to best support your DDD efforts.

Whatever technical facets your data model uses, its entities, primary keys, referential integrity, and indexes simply must not drive the way you model domain objects. DDD is not about structuring data in a normalized fashion. It is about modeling the Ubiquitous Language in a consistent Bounded Context. I encourage you to adhere to DDD, not to data structure. As you do so, you should wisely take every possible step to hide all vestiges of data model leakage (which will occur to at least a minimal degree when using an ORM) from your domain model and its clients. This is something I discuss in the next section.

ORM and Single Value Objects

Persisting a single Value Object instance to a database is usually very straight-forward. Here my focus is on the use of Hibernate with the MySQL relational database. The basic idea is to store each of the attributes of the Value in separate columns of the row where its parent Entity is stored. Said another way, a single Value Object is denormalized into its parent Entity's row. There are advantages to employing convention for column naming to clearly identify and standardize the way serialized objects are named. I present a persisted Value Object naming convention here.

When using Hibernate to persist a single instance of a Value Object, use the component mapping element. The component element is employed because it enables the Value to be mapped directly into the parent Entity table row in a denormalized fashion. This is an optimal serialization technique that still enables Values to be included in SQL queries. Here is the section of the Hibernate mapping document that describes the mapping of the Business-Priority Value Object held by its parent Entity, class BacklogItem:

```
<component name="businessPriority"
    class="com.saasovation.agilepm.domain.model.product.↵
        BusinessPriority">
    <component name="ratings"
        class="com.saasovation.agilepm.domain.model.product.↵
            BusinessPriorityRatings">
        <property
            name="benefit"
            column="business_priority_ratings_benefit"
            type="int"
            update="true"
            insert="true"
            lazy="false"
            />
        <property
            name="cost"
            column="business_priority_ratings_cost"
```

```
            type="int"
            update="true"
            insert="true"
            lazy="false"
            />
        <property
            name="penalty"
            column="business_priority_ratings_penalty"
            type="int"
            update="true"
            insert="true"
            lazy="false"
            />
        <property
            name="risk"
            column="business_priority_ratings_risk"
            type="int"
            update="true"
            insert="true"
            lazy="false"
            />
    </component>
</component>
```

This is a good example because it demonstrates a simple Value Object mapping, but one that contains a child Value Object instance. Recall that BusinessPriority has a single ratings Value property and no additional attributes. Thus, in the mapping description the outer component element has a nested component element. This is used to denormalize the single contained ratings Value property of type BusinessPriorityRatings. Since the BusinessPriority has no attributes of its own, there are none mapped in the outer component. Instead we immediately nest the mapping of its ratings Value property. In the end, we actually store only the four integer attributes of the BusinessPriorityRatings instance into four separate columns of table tbl_backlog_item. So we map two component element Value Objects, one that has no attributes of its own and an inner Value that has four attributes.

Note the use of standard column naming of each of the Hibernate property elements. The naming convention is based on the navigation path from the ultimate parent Value down to the individual attributes. For example, consider the navigation path from the BusinessPriority down to the benefit attribute of the ValueCostRiskRatings instance. Logically it is

businessPriority.ratings.benefit

To represent this navigation path as a single relational column name I use the following:

```
business_priority_ratings_benefit
```

Of course, you can use another representative name if you like. Perhaps you prefer one that mixes camel case with underscores:

```
businessPriority_ratings_benefit
```

To your mind this sample notation may better express the navigation. I have standardized on all underscores since it leans more toward traditional SQL column names rather than object names. The corresponding MySQL database table definition includes the following columns:

```
CREATE TABLE `tbl_backlog_item` (
    ...
    `business_priority_ratings_benefit` int NOT NULL,
    `business_priority_ratings_cost` int NOT NULL,
    `business_priority_ratings_penalty` int NOT NULL,
    `business_priority_ratings_risk` int NOT NULL,
    ...
) ENGINE=InnoDB;
```

Together, the Hibernate mapping and relational database table definition provide both an optimal and queryable persistent object. Because Value attributes are denormalized into their parent Entity's table row, there is no need for the database to use joins to retrieve even a deeply nested Value instance. When you specify an HQL query, Hibernate is able to easily map from the object expression of an object attribute into an optimal SQL query expression using a column, where

```
businessPriority.ratings.benefit
```

becomes

```
business_priority_ratings_benefit
```

Hence, although there is a clear impedance mismatch between objects and relational databases, we have realized one of the more functional and optimal mappings possible.

ORM and Many Values Serialized into a Single Column

There are unique challenges associated with mapping a collection of many Value Objects into a relational database using an ORM. To be clear, by collection I mean a List or Set that is held by an Entity and contains zero, one, or more Value instances. The challenges are not insurmountable, but the object-relational impedance mismatch becomes glaringly obvious here.

One option available with Hibernate object-relational mapping is to serialize the entire collection of objects into a textual representation and persist
the representation into a single column. This approach has some drawbacks.
However, in some cases the drawbacks are unobtrusive and may be summarily
ignored in favor of leveraging this option's advantages. In such cases you may
decide to use this Value collection persistence option. Here are the potential
drawbacks to consider:

- *Column width.* Sometimes you cannot determine the maximum number
  of Value elements in the collection, or the maximum size of each serialized Value. For example, some object collections could have any number
  of elements—an unknown upper limit. Also, each of the Value elements
  in the collection could have an indeterminate serialized representation
  character width. This can happen when one or more of the attributes of
  the Value type are of type `String` and the length in characters is many
  or open-ended. In either or both of these situations, it is possible that
  the serialized form or the entire collection would overflow the maximum
  available width of a character column. This may be further compounded
  by character columns that have a relatively narrow maximum width, or
  by the total maximum number of bytes available to store an entire row
  of data. While the MySQL InnoDB engine, for example, has a maximum `VARCHAR` width of 65,535 characters, it also has a limit of 65,535
  total bytes of storage for a single row. You must allow room for enough
  columns to store an entire Entity. Oracle Database has a maximum
  `VARCHAR2`/`NVARCHAR2` width of 4,000. If you cannot predetermine the
  maximum width required to store a serialized representation of a Value
  collection and/or your maximum column width could be overflowed, you
  should avoid this option.

- *Must query.* Since with this style Value collections are serialized into a
  flat text representation, the attributes of individual Value elements cannot
  be used in SQL query expressions. If any of the Value attributes must be
  queryable, you cannot use this option. It's possible that this is a less likely
  reason to avoid this option since the need to query one or more attributes
  out of objects in a contained collection could be rare.

- *Requires custom user type.* To use this approach you must develop a
  Hibernate custom user type that manages serialization and deserialization
  of each collection. Personally, I think this is less obtrusive than the other
  concerns because a single, well-thought-out, custom user type implementation can support collections of every Value Object type (one size fits all).

I don't provide a Hibernate custom user type here to manage collection serialization to a single column, but the Hibernate community provides plenty of guidance for you to implement your own.

ORM and Many Values Backed by a Database Entity

A very straightforward approach to persisting a collection of Value instances using Hibernate (or other ORM) and a relational database is to treat the Value type as an entity in the data model. To reiterate what I asserted in the section "Reject Undue Influence of Data Model Leakage," this approach *must not* lead to wrongly modeling a concept as an Entity in the domain model just because it is best represented as a database entity for the sake of persistence. It is the object-relation impedance mismatch that in some cases requires this approach, not a DDD principle. If there were a perfectly matched persistence style available to you, you'd model the concept as a Value type and never give database entity characteristics a second thought. It helps our domain modeling mind to think that way.

To accomplish this we can employ a **Layer Supertype** [Fowler, P of EAA]. Personally it makes me feel better to tuck away the necessary surrogate identity (primary key). However, since every Object in Java (and other languages) already has an internal unique identity that is used only by the virtual machine, you may feel justified in adding a specialized identity directly to the Value. I think whatever approach we prefer, when working around the object-relational impedance mismatch we need to formulate a convincing justification in our minds for why we make a technical choice. My preferences are addressed next.

Here's an example of my preferred approach to surrogate keys, which uses two Layer Supertype classes:

```
public abstract class IdentifiedDomainObject
        implements Serializable  {

    private long id = -1;

    public IdentifiedDomainObject() {
        super();
    }

    protected long id() {
        return this.id;
    }

    protected void setId(long anId) {
        this.id = anId;
    }
}
```

The first Layer Supertype involved is `IdentifiedDomainObject`. This abstract base class provides a basic surrogate primary key that is hidden from the view of clients. Because the accessor methods are declared `protected`, clients will never have to wonder if the methods are for their use. Of course, you can further avoid any knowledge of these methods by declaring their scope `private`. Hibernate has no problems using method or field reflection on any scope other than `public`.

Next, I provide one more Layer Supertype that is specific to Value Objects:

```
public abstract class IdentifiedValueObject
        extends IdentifiedDomainObject  {

    public IdentifiedValueObject() {
        super();
    }
}
```

You may consider class `IdentifiedValueObject` as merely a marker class, a behaviorless subclass of `IdentifiedDomainObject`. I see it as having a source code documentation benefit because it makes the modeling challenge it addresses more explicit. Along those lines, class `IdentifiedDomainObject` has a second direct abstract subclass named `Entity`, which is discussed in **Entities (5)**. I like this approach. You may prefer to eliminate these extra classes.

Now that there is a convenient and suitably hidden means to give any Value type a surrogate identity, here's a sample class that puts it to use:

```
public final class GroupMember extends IdentifiedValueObject  {
    private String name;
    private TenantId tenantId;
    private GroupMemberType type;

    public GroupMember(
            TenantId aTenantId,
            String aName,
            GroupMemberType aType) {
        this();
        this.setName(aName);
        this.setTenantId(aTenantId);
        this.setType(aType);
        this.initialize();
    }
    ...
}
```

Class `GroupMember` is a Value type that is collected by the Root Entity of the Aggregate class `Group`. The Root Entity contains any number of `Group-Member` instances. Now with each `GroupMember` instance being uniquely identified to the data model using its surrogate primary key, we are free to map its persistence as a database entity while keeping it a Value in the domain model. Here's the relevant portion of class `Group`:

```
public class Group extends Entity  {
    private String description;
    private Set<GroupMember> groupMembers;
    private String name;
    private TenantId tenantId;

    public Group(
            TenantId aTenantId,
            String aName,
            String aDescription) {
        this();
        this.setDescription(aDescription);
        this.setName(aName);
        this.setTenantId(aTenantId);
        this.initialize();
    }
    ...
    protected Group() {
        super();
        this.setGroupMembers(new HashSet<GroupMember>(0));
    }
    ...
}
```

Class `Group` will gradually build up any number of `GroupMember` instances in its `Set` of `groupMembers`. Keep in mind that if you will ever perform whole collection replacement, always use the `Collection`'s `clear()` method prior to replacement. Doing so ensures that the backing Hibernate `Collection` implementation will delete obsolete elements from the data store. The following is not an actual `Group` method, but an example provided to demonstrate how, in general, to avoid orphaned Value elements when performing whole collection replacement:

```
public void replaceMembers(Set<GroupMember> aReplacementMembers) {
    this.groupMembers().clear();
    this.setGroupMembers(aReplacementMembers);
}
```

I think this ORM leakage into the model is unobtrusive because it uses a common `Collection` facility, and besides, the client doesn't see it. Synchronizing collection contents with the database doesn't always require careful thought. A single Value data store deletion is automatically covered by the use of `Collection`'s `remove()` method, so in that case there's no ORM leakage at all.

Next, we are interested in the section of `Group`'s mapping description that maps the collection:

```
<hibernate-mapping>
    <class name="com.saasovation.identityaccess.domain.model.↵
        identity.Group"
      table="tbl_group" lazy="true">
        ...
        <set name="groupMembers" cascade="all,delete-orphan"
          inverse="false" lazy="true">
            <key column="group_id" not-null="true" />
            <one-to-many class="com.saasovation.[ccc]
                identityaccess.domain.model.identity.GroupMember" />
        </set>
        ...
    </class>
</hibernate-mapping>
```

The `Set` of `groupMembers` is mapped exactly as a database entity. Additionally we see the full `GroupMember` mapping description:

```
<hibernate-mapping>
    <class name="com.saasovation.identityaccess.domain.model.↵
          identity.GroupMember"
          table="tbl_group_member" lazy="true">
        <id
            name="id"
            type="long"
            column="id"
            unsaved-value="-1">

            <generator class="native"/>
        </id>
        <property
            name="name"
            column="name"
            type="java.lang.String"
            update="true"
            insert="true"
            lazy="false"
        />
```

```
        <component name="tenantId"
            class="com.saasovation.identityaccess.domain.model.↵
                identity.TenantId">
            <property
                name="id"
                column="tenant_id_id"
                type="java.lang.String"
                update="true"
                insert="true"
                lazy="false"
            />
        </component>
        <property
            name="type"
            column="type"
            type="com.saasovation.identityaccess.infrastructure.↵
                persistence.GroupMemberTypeUserType"
            update="true"
            insert="true"
            not-null="true"
        />
    </class>
</hibernate-mapping>
```

Note the <id> element that defines the persistence surrogate primary key. And finally, here is the corresponding MySQL tbl_group_member description:

```
CREATE TABLE `tbl_group_member` (
    `id` int(11) NOT NULL auto_increment,
    `name` varchar(100) NOT NULL,
    `tenant_id_id` varchar(36) NOT NULL,
    `type` varchar(5) NOT NULL,
    `group_id` int(11) NOT NULL,
    KEY `k_group_id` (`group_id`),
    KEY `k_tenant_id_id` (`tenant_id_id`),
    CONSTRAINT `fk_1_tbl_group_member_tbl_group`
        FOREIGN KEY (`group_id`) REFERENCES `tbl_group` (`id`),
    PRIMARY KEY (`id`)
) ENGINE=InnoDB;
```

When we look at the GroupMember mapping and database table description, we get the strong impression that we are dealing with an entity. There's the primary key named id. There's the separate table that must be joined with tbl_group. There's the foreign key back to tbl_group. By any other name we are dealing with an entity, *but only from the data model perspective.* In the domain model GroupMember is clearly a Value Object. Appropriate steps have been taken in the domain model to carefully hide any persistence concerns. I give no clue to clients of the domain model that any persistence leakage has occurred. And what is more, even developers in the model must look hard to detect any notion of persistence leakage.

ORM and Many Values Backed by a Join Table

Hibernate provides a means to persist multivalued collections in a join table without requiring the Value type itself to have any data model entity characteristics. This mapping type simply persists the collection Value elements to a dedicated table with the parent Entity domain object's database identity as a foreign key. Thus, all collection Value elements can be queried by their parent's foreign key identity and reconstituted into the model's Value collection. The strength of this mapping approach is that the Value type doesn't need to have a hidden surrogate identity in order to achieve a join. To use this Value collection mapping option you employ Hibernate's `<composite-element>` tag.

This seems like a big win, and it may be for your needs. However, there are weaknesses to this approach that you should be aware of. One downside is that a join is necessary even if your Value type requires no surrogate key because it involves normalization of two tables. True, the "ORM and Many Values Backed by a Database Entity" approach also requires a join. But that approach is not limited by the second weakness of this one, which is . . .

If your collection is a `Set`, none of your Value type's attributes may be `null`. This is the case because in order to delete (garbage collection in the data model) a given `Set` element, all attributes that make the element a unique Value must be used as a sort of composite key to find and delete it. A `null` cannot be used as a part of the required composite key. Of course, if you know that a given Value type will never have `null` attributes, this is a viable approach—that is, as long as you have no additional conflicting needs.

The third downside of using this mapping approach is that the Value type being mapped may itself not contain a collection. There is no provision for mapping with `<composite-element>` if the elements themselves contain collections. If your Value type does not hold a collection of any kind and otherwise meets the requirements for this mapping style, it is available for your use.

In the end, I find this mapping approach to be limiting enough that it deserves general avoidance. To me it is simply easier to put a well-hidden surrogate identity on the Value type that is collected into a one-to-many association and not worry about any of the `<composite-element>` constraints. You may feel differently, and it certainly can be leveraged to your benefit if all the modeling cards fall into place for you.

ORM and Enum-as-State Objects

If you find enums an effective modeling choice for Standard Types and/or State objects, you will need the means to persist them. With Hibernate, Java enums require a specialized persistence technique. Unfortunately to date, the Hibernate development community does not support enums as an out-of-the-box property type. Therefore, to persist enums in our model we have to create a Hibernate custom user type.

Recall that each `GroupMember` has a `GroupMemberType`:

```
public final class GroupMember extends IdentifiedValueObject  {
    private String name;
    private TenantId tenantId;
    private GroupMemberType type;

    public GroupMember(
            TenantId aTenantId,
            String aName,
            GroupMemberType aType) {
        this();
        this.setName(aName);
        this.setTenantId(aTenantId);
        this.setType(aType);
        this.initialize();
    }
    ...
}
```

The `GroupMemberType` enum Standard Types include `GROUP` and `USER`. Here again is the definition:

```
package com.saasovation.identityaccess.domain.model.identity;

public enum GroupMemberType {

    GROUP {
        public boolean isGroup() {
            return true;
        }
    },
    USER {
        public boolean isUser() {
            return true;
        }
    };

    public boolean isGroup() {
        return false;
    }
```

```
    public boolean isUser() {
        return false;
    }
}
```

The simple answer to persisting a Java enum Value is to store its text representation. However, the simple answer leads to the unfolding of a slightly more complex technique of creating a Hibernate customer user type. Rather than include here the various approaches to class `EnumUserType` provided by the Hibernate community, I provide the wiki article resource link: http://community.jboss.org/wiki/Java5EnumUserType.

At the time of writing, this wiki article provided a variety of approaches. There were samples for implementing a custom user type class for each enum type; a way to use Hibernate 3 parameterized types to avoid implementing a custom user for each enum type (very desirable); one that supports not only text string but numeric representations of the enum value; and even an enhanced implementation by Gavin King. Gavin King's enhanced implementation allows the enum to be used as a type discriminator or as a data table identity (`id`).

Given the selection of one choice from these options, here's an example of how the enum `GroupMemberType` is mapped:

```
<hibernate-mapping>
    <class name="com.saasovation.identityaccess.domain.model.↵
            identity.GroupMember" table="tbl_group_member" lazy="true">
        ...
        <property
            name="type"
            column="type"
            type="com.saasovation.identityaccess.infrastructure.↵
                persistence.GroupMemberTypeUserType"
            update="true"
            insert="true"
            not-null="true"
        />
    </class>
</hibernate-mapping>
```

Note that the `<property>` element's type attribute is set to class `GroupMemberTypeUserType`'s full classpath. This is just one choice, and you should choose whatever one you prefer. Recall that the MySQL table description contains the column to hold the enum:

```
CREATE TABLE `tbl_group_member` (
    . . .
    `type` varchar(5) NOT NULL,
    . . .
) ENGINE=InnoDB;
```

The `type` column is a `VARCHAR` type with a maximum size of five characters, enough to hold the widest type text representation: `GROUP` or `USER`.

Wrap-Up

In this chapter you've seen the importance of favoring the use of Value Objects whenever possible, because they are simply easier to develop, test, and maintain.

- You've learned the characteristics of Value Objects and how to use them.

- You've seen how to leverage Value Objects to minimize integration complexity.

- You examined the use of domain Standard Types expressed as Values and have a few strategies for implementing them.

- You saw why SaaSOvation now favors modeling with Values whenever possible.

- You gained experience in how to test, implement, and persist Value types through the SaaSOvation projects.

Next, we'll be looking at Domain Services, stateless operations that are actually part of the model.

Chapter 7

Services

> *Sometimes, it just isn't a thing.*
> —*Eric Evans*

A **Service** in the domain is a stateless operation that fulfills a domain-specific task. Often the best indication that you should create a Service in the domain model is when the operation you need to perform feels out of place as a method on an **Aggregate (10)** or a **Value Object (6)**. To alleviate that uncomfortable feeling, our natural tendency might be to create a static method on the class of an Aggregate Root. However, when using DDD, that tactic is a code smell that likely indicates you need a Service instead.

Road Map to This Chapter

- See how domain model refinements can lead to the realization that you need a Service.
- Learn what a Service in the domain is, and what it isn't.
- Consider a necessary caution when deciding whether or not to create a Service.
- Discover how to model Services in a domain through two examples from SaaSOvation's projects.

Smelly code? That's exactly what SaaSOvation's developers experienced because of refactoring an Aggregate. Let's consider their tactical correction. Here's what happened . . .

Early on in their project the team had modeled the collection of `BacklogItem` instances as a composed Aggregate part of `Product`. That modeling situation allowed calculating the total business priority value of all product backlog items to be a simple instance method on class `Product`:

```
public class Product extends ConcurrencySafeEntity {
    ...
    private Set<BacklogItem> backlogItems;
    ...
    public BusinessPriorityTotals businessPriorityTotals() {
        ...
    }
    ...
}
```

At that time the design made perfect sense because method business-PriorityTotals() would just iterate over the composed BacklogItem instances and come up with the queried total business priority. The design properly answered the query with a Value Object, namely, BusinessPriorityTotals.

However, it wouldn't stay that way. As the analysis found in **Aggregates (10)** showed, the large cluster Product needed to be broken up, and BacklogItem would be redesigned to stand on its own as an Aggregate. Thus, the previous design that used an instance method no longer worked.

Since Product no longer contained the BacklogItem collection, the team's first reaction was to refactor the existing instance method to use the new BacklogItem-Repository to get all the BacklogItem instances the calculation needed. Does that sound right?

Actually, the senior team mentor persuaded the team not to do that. As a rule of thumb, we should try to avoid the use of **Repositories (12)** from inside Aggregates, if at all possible. What about just making the same method static on class Product and passing in the collection of BacklogItem instances that static method would need for the calculation? That way the method would remain almost intact, except for the new parameter:

```
public class Product extends ConcurrencySafeEntity {
    ...
    public static BusinessPriorityTotals businessPriorityTotals(
            Set<BacklogItem> aBacklogItems) {
        ...
    }
    ...
}
```

Was Product really the best place to create the static method? It seemed difficult to determine where it really belonged. Since the operation actually only used the business priority values of each BacklogItem, maybe the static method belonged there. Still, the business priority being sought was that of a product, not a backlog item. Quandaries.

At that point the mentoring senior developer spoke up. He noted that the team's entire source of discomfort could be dismissed with a single modeling tool, the Domain Service. How would that work?

Let's first establish some background. Then we'll revisit this modeling situation and see what the team decided to do.

What a Domain Service Is (but First, What It Is Not)

When we hear the term *service* in a software context, we might naturally envision a coarse-grained component that enables a remote client to interact with a complex business system. That basically describes a service in a **Service-Oriented Architecture (4)**. There are different technologies and approaches for developing SOA services. In the end these kinds of services emphasize system-level *remote procedure calls* (RPCs) or *message-oriented middleware* (MoM), where other systems across the data center, or across the globe, are able to interact with the service to carry out business transactions.

None of those is a Domain Service.

Further, don't confuse a Domain Service with an **Application Service**. We don't want to house business logic in an Application Service, but we do want business logic housed in a Domain Service. If you are confused about the difference, compare with **Application (14)**. Briefly, to differentiate the two, an Application Service, being the natural client of the domain model, would normally be the client of a Domain Service. You'll see that demonstrated later in the chapter.

Just because a Domain Service has the word *service* in its name does not mean that it is required to be a coarse-grained, remote-capable, heavyweight transactional operation.[1]

Cowboy Logic

LB: "Always take a good look at what you are about to eat. It's not so important to know what it is, but it's critical to know what it was."

Services that specifically belong to the business domain are a perfect modeling tool to use when your needs intersect with their sweet spot. So, now that we know what a Domain Service *isn't*, let's consider what it *is*.

---

1. There are times when a Domain Service is concerned with remote invocations on a foreign Bounded Context (2). Yet, the focus here is different in that the Domain Service is not itself providing a remote procedure call interface but is rather the client of the RPC.

Sometimes, it just isn't a thing. . . . When a significant process or transformation in the domain is not a natural responsibility of an ENTITY or VALUE OBJECT, add an operation to the model as a standalone interface declared as a SERVICE. Define the interface in terms of the language of the model and make sure the operation name is part of the UBIQUITOUS LANGUAGE. Make the SERVICE stateless. [Evans, pp. 104, 106]

Since the domain model generally deals with finer-grained behaviors that are focused on some specific aspect of the business at hand, a Service in the domain would tend to adhere to similar tenets. Since it may be dealing with multiple domain objects in a single, atomic operation, it would have the latitude to scale up a bit in complexity.

Under what conditions would an operation not belong on an existing **Entity (5)** or Value Object? It is difficult to give an exhaustive list of reasons, but I've listed a few here. You can use a Domain Service to

- Perform a significant business process

- Transform a domain object from one composition to another

- Calculate a Value requiring input from more than one domain object

The last one—a calculation—probably falls under the "significant process" category, but I call it out to be clear. It's a very common one, and that kind of operation can require two, and possibly many, different Aggregates or their composed parts as input. And when it is just plain clumsy to place the method on any one Entity or Value, it works out best to define a Service. Make sure the Service is *stateless* and has an interface that clearly expresses the **Ubiquitous Language (1)** in its Bounded Context.

Make Sure You Need a Service

Don't lean too heavily toward modeling a domain concept as a Service. Do so only if the circumstances fit. If we aren't careful, we might start to treat Services as our modeling "silver bullet." Using Services overzealously will usually result in the negative consequences of creating an **Anemic Domain Model** [Fowler, Anemic], where all the domain logic resides in Services rather than mostly spread across Entities and Value Objects. The following analysis shows the importance of thinking carefully about the tactics you should employ for each modeling situation. Following this guidance should help you make good decisions about whether or not to model a Service.

Let's investigate an example of recognizing the need to model a Service. Think of trying to authenticate a User in our *Identity and Access Context*.

Recall that in **Entities** (5) we ran into this domain scenario that the team wanted to push off until later. Well, later is now:

- Users of a system must be authenticated but can be authenticated only if the tenant is active.

Let's consider why a Service is necessary. Could we simply place this behavior on an Entity? From a client's perspective, maybe we could model authentication like this:

```
// client finds User and asks it to authenticate itself

boolean authentic = false;

User user =
    DomainRegistry
        .userRepository()
        .userWithUsername(aTenantId, aUsername);

if (user != null) {
    authentic = user.isAuthentic(aPassword);
}

return authentic;
```

I think there are at least a few problems with this design. We require clients to understand what it means to authenticate. They have to find the User and then ask the User if a given password matches the one the User holds. Also, the Ubiquitous Language is not explicitly modeled. Here we asked the User if it "is authentic" rather than ask the model to "authenticate." If possible it would be best to model in terms of the natural expressions spoken by the team, rather than force the team to adjust their view away from what comes naturally because we failed to better model the concept. But there are worse problems than these.

This does not properly model what that team discovered about authenticating a user. A glaring omission is that there is no check to determine whether or not the tenant is active. Per the requirement, if the tenant under which the user resides is not active, the user is not authenticated. Perhaps we could solve the problem like this:

```
// maybe this way is better ...

boolean authentic = false;
```

```
Tenant tenant =
    DomainRegistry
        .tenantRepository()
        .tenantOfId(aTenantId);

if (tenant != null && tenant.isActive()) {
    User user =
        DomainRegistry
            .userRepository()
            .userWithUsername(aTenantId, aUsername);

    if (user != null) {
        authentic = tenant.authenticate(user, aPassword)
    }
}

return authentic;
```

This test does properly determine that the `Tenant` is active before carrying on with authentication. We were also able to rid `User` of method `isAuthentic()` by placing `authenticate()` on `Tenant`.

But there are problems with this. Look at the additional burden that we've heaped on the client. It now needs to understand much more about authentication than it should. We could alleviate this a bit by checking whether `Tenant` `isActive()` inside method `authenticate()`, but I'd argue that that is not an explicit model. It also produces another problem. Now `Tenant` might need to understand what to do with a password. Recall that another requirement was realized, though not specifically called out in the authentication scenario:

- Passwords must be stored encrypted, not as clear text.

With our proposed solutions, we seem to keep producing more friction in the model. With the latest proposal we have to choose one of four undesirable approaches:

1. Handle encryption in `Tenant` and pass the encrypted password to `User`. This violates `Tenant`'s **Single Responsibility** [Martin, SRP] to deal with modeling only a tenant.

2. `User` may already need to know a little bit about encryption since it must guarantee that any stored password is encrypted. If so, create a method on `User` that knows how to authenticate given a clear-text password. But in this case authentication becomes a facade on `Tenant` that is fully implemented only on `User`. Further still, `User` must have a protected authentication interface to prevent clients outside the model from directly using it.

3. `Tenant` asks `User` to encrypt the clear-text password, then it compares it with the one `User` is holding. This seems to have extra steps with an untidy set of collaborations. `Tenant` is still required to understand the details of authentication even though it doesn't quite carry it out.

4. Have the client encrypt the password and pass it in to the `Tenant`. This adds further to the responsibility that the client has, when in fact the client should need to know nothing of the need to encrypt passwords.

None of these proposals help much, and the client is still too complex. Responsibility that we've dumped on the client should instead be elegantly tucked away in the model. Knowledge that is purely domain specific should never be leaked out into clients. Even if the client is an Application Service, that component is not responsible for the domain of identity and access management.

Cowboy Logic

AJ: "When you find yourself in a hole, the first thing to do is stop digging."

Really, the only business responsibility that the client should have is to coordinate the use of a single domain-specific operation that handles all other details of the business problem:

```
// inside an Application Service client with
// only task coordination responsibility

UserDescriptor userDescriptor =
    DomainRegistry
        .authenticationService()
        .authenticate(aTenantId, aUsername, aPassword);
```

In this simple and elegant solution, the client need only obtain a reference to a stateless instance of `AuthenticationService` and then ask it to `authenticate()`. This pushes all details of authentication out of the Application Service client and into the Domain Service. Any number of domain objects may be used by the Service, as needed. This includes ensuring that password encryption is performed as appropriate. The client doesn't need to understand any of those details. The Ubiquitous Language in the Context is satisfied because the proper terms are expressed by the software that models the identity management domain, rather than partly by the model and partly by the client.

A Value Object, `UserDescriptor`, is returned from the Service method. This object is small and secure. Unlike a full `User`, it includes only a few attributes essential to referencing a `User`:

```
public class UserDescriptor implements Serializable  {
    private String emailAddress;
    private TenantId tenantId;
    private String username;

    public UserDescriptor(
            TenantId aTenantId,
            String aUsername,
            String anEmailAddress) {
        ...
    }
    ...
}
```

It is suitable for storing in a per-user Web session. The client Application Service may itself return this object to its invoker or create one more suitable for it.

Modeling a Service in the Domain

Depending on the purpose of a Domain Service, it can be quite simple to model. You'll have to decide whether or not your Service should have a **Separated Interface** [Fowler, P of EAA]. If so, this might be the interface definition:

```
package com.saasovation.identityaccess.domain.model.identity;

public interface AuthenticationService {

    public UserDescriptor authenticate(
            TenantId aTenantId,
            String aUsername,
            String aPassword);
}
```

The interface is declared in the same **Module** (9) as the identity-specific Aggregates, such as `Tenant`, `User`, and `Group`. That is done because

AuthenticationService is an identity concept, and we currently place all identity-related concepts in the identity Module. The interface definition itself is quite simple. Only one operation, authenticate(), is necessary.

A choice we have is where to place the implementation class. If you are using the **Dependency Inversion Principle (4)** or **Hexagonal (4)**, you may decide to place this somewhat technical implementation class in a location outside the domain model. Technical implementations may be housed in a Module in the Infrastructure Layer, for example.

Here is the class:

```
package com.saasovation.identityaccess.infrastructure.services;

import com.saasovation.identityaccess.domain.model.DomainRegistry;
import com.saasovation.identityaccess.domain.model.identity.↵
AuthenticationService;
import com.saasovation.identityaccess.domain.model.identity.Tenant;
import com.saasovation.identityaccess.domain.model.identity.TenantId;
import com.saasovation.identityaccess.domain.model.↵
identity.User;
import com.saasovation.identityaccess.domain.model.↵
identity.UserDescriptor;

public class DefaultEncryptionAuthenticationService
        implements AuthenticationService  {

    public DefaultEncryptionAuthenticationService() {
        super();
    }

    @Override
    public UserDescriptor authenticate(
            TenantId aTenantId,
            String aUsername,
            String aPassword) {
        if (aTenantId == null) {
            throw new IllegalArgumentException(
                    "TenantId must not be null.");
        }
        if (aUsername == null) {
            throw new IllegalArgumentException(
                    "Username must not be null.");
        }
        if (aPassword == null) {
            throw new IllegalArgumentException(
                    "Password must not be null.");
        }

        UserDescriptor userDescriptor = null;
```

```
        Tenant tenant =
            DomainRegistry
                .tenantRepository()
                .tenantOfId(aTenantId);

    if (tenant != null && tenant.isActive()) {
        String encryptedPassword =
            DomainRegistry
                .encryptionService()
                .encryptedValue(aPassword);

        User user =
            DomainRegistry
                .userRepository()
                .userFromAuthenticCredentials(
                        aTenantId,
                        aUsername,
                        encryptedPassword);

        if (user != null && user.isEnabled()) {
            userDescriptor = user.userDescriptor();
        }
    }

    return userDescriptor;
    }
}
```

The method guards against `null` parameters. Otherwise, if the authentication process fails under normal conditions, the returned `UserDescriptor` will be `null`.

To authenticate we begin by attempting to retrieve the `Tenant` from its Repository using its identity. If the `Tenant` both exists and is active, we next encrypt the clear-text password. We do that now because we will use the encrypted password to retrieve the `User`. Rather than request the `User` only from a `TenantId` and matching `username`, we also match on the encrypted password. (The result of encryption is always the same for two equal clear-text passwords.) The Repository is designed to filter on all three.

If the human user has submitted the correct tenant identity, username, and clear-text password, it will result in retrieving the matching `User` instance. Still, this does not completely prove the user's authenticity. There is one final requirement not yet handled:

- Users can be authenticated only if they are enabled.

Even if the Repository finds the filtered `User` instance, it may have been disabled. Providing the possibility of disabling a `User` allows the tenant to control user authentication at a different level. Thus, as a final step the `User` instance must be both non-`null` and enabled, which will result in a `UserDescriptor` being derived from the `User`.

Is Separated Interface a Necessity?

Since this `AuthenticationService` does not have a technical implementation, is it really necessary to create a Separated Interface and implementation class, and in separate Layers and Modules? No, it is not, in fact, an absolute necessity. We could have created this particular Service with only a single implementation class with the name of the Service:

```
package com.saasovation.identityaccess.domain.model.identity;

public class AuthenticationService {

    public AuthenticationService() {
        super();
    }

    public UserDescriptor authenticate(
            TenantId aTenantId,
            String aUsername,
            String aPassword) {
        ...
    }
}
```

There would be nothing wrong with this. You might even consider this a more fitting approach since this particular Service may never need to have multiple implementations. However, given that different tenants might eventually desire specialized security standards, it's possible that there could be multiple implementations. At this point in time, however, the team has decided to drop the use of a Separated Interface and go with the class as shown here.

▼───▼

Naming Your Implementation Class

In the Java world it's become quite common to name the implementation class with its interface's name as a prefix and `Impl` as a postfix. In our example using this approach would render the name `Authentication-ServiceImpl`. Further, the interface and implementing class are often housed in the same package. Is this a good thing?

Actually, if your implementation class is named this way, it's probably a very good indication that you don't need a Separated Interface, or that you need to think more carefully about the name of the implementing class. So, no, the `AuthenticationServiceImpl` name isn't a really good one. But then again, `DefaultEncryptionAuthenticationService` is not particularly useful either. For that reason the SaaSOvation team decided to eliminate the Separated Interface for now and go with `AuthenticationService` as a simple class instead.

If your implementation class has specific decoupling goals because you are providing multiple specific implementations, name the class according to its specialty. The need to name each specialized implementation carefully is proof that specialties exist in your domain.

Some will conclude that having the interface and implementation class similarly named makes large packages of these pairs easier to browse and navigate. However, others would conclude that such large packages are poorly designed according to the goals of Modules. Further still, those with focused modularity goals will also favor placing the interface and various implementation classes in separate packages, as we do with **Dependency Inversion Principle (4)**. For example, the `EncryptionService` interface is in the domain model, while `MD5EncryptionService` resides in infrastructure.

Eliminating the Separated Interface for nontechnical Domain Services will not weaken testability since any interfaces that the Service depends on can be injected or resolved by a test-configured Service Factory, or you could pass in as parameters instances of inbound and outbound dependencies as needed. Remember, too, that nontechnical, domain-specific Services, such as calculations, must be tested for correctness.

Understandably this is a controversial topic, and I am aware that there is a large camp that regularly names interface realizations using `Impl`. Just be aware that there is a well-informed polar opposite to that camp that has very sound reasons for avoiding that approach. As always, the choice is yours to make.

▲————————————————————————————————————▲

Using Separated Interface may be more a matter of style in cases where the Service is always domain specific and will never have a technical implementation or multiple implementations. As Fowler [Fowler, P of EAA] states, Separated Interface is useful if you have certain decoupling goals: "A client that needs the dependency to the interface can be completely unaware of the implementation." However, if you are using **Dependency Injection** or a **Factory** [Gamma et al.] of Services, even when the Service interface and class are combined, you can still prevent the client from being aware of the implementation.

In other words, the following use of the `DomainRegistry` as Service Factory will decouple the client from implementation:

```
// the registry decouples client from implementation knowledge

UserDescriptor userDescriptor =
    DomainRegistry
        .authenticationService()
        .authenticate(aTenantId, aUsername, aPassword);
```

Or if you are using Dependency Injection, you can get similar benefits:

```
public class SomeApplicationService ... {
    @Autowired
    private AuthenticationService authenticationService;
    ...
}
```

The inversion-of-control container (such as Spring) injects the Service instance. Since the client never instantiates the Service, it isn't aware that the interface and implementation are either combined or separated.

Clearly, some have utter disdain for both the Service Factory and Dependency Injection and prefer to set up inbound dependencies by way of a constructor or pass them in as method parameters. In the end that is the most explicit way to wire dependencies and make code testable, and it could even be considered easier than Dependency Injection. Some may find it beneficial to use a combination of all three depending on the situation, while preferring constructor-based dependency setup overall. Several of the samples in this chapter use `DomainRegistry` for clarity, *though not necessarily indicating a preference*. Much of the source code actually distributed online in support of this book leans toward dependency set up by way of constructors, or by passing dependencies directly to methods as parameters.

A Calculation Process

Here's another example, this time from the current **Core Domain (2)**, the *Agile Project Management Context*. This Service calculates a result from Values on any number of Aggregates of a specific type. Here I think there is no good reason to use a Separated Interface, at least not at present. The calculations are always performed the same way. Unless that situation changes, we shouldn't bother separating the interface from the implementation.

Cowboy Logic

LB: "My stallion brings $5,000 per service, and I've got the mares lined up."

AJ: "Now *that* horse is in his domain."

Recall that the SaaSOvation developers originally created fine-grained static methods on `Product` to perform the desired calculations. Here's what happened next . . .

The team's mentor also pointed to the desirability of using a Domain Service instead of a static method. The idea behind this Service would be very similar to the current design, to calculate and return a `BusinessPriorityTotals` Value instance. But the Service would have to do a bit more work. This would include finding all *outstanding* backlog items of a given Scrum product and then totaling each of their individual `BusinessPriority` Values. Here's the implementation:

```
package com.saasovation.agilepm.domain.model.product;

import com.saasovation.agilepm.domain.model.DomainRegistry;
import com.saasovation.agilepm.domain.model.tenant.Tenant;

public class BusinessPriorityCalculator {

    public BusinessPriorityCalculator() {
        super();
    }


    public BusinessPriorityTotals businessPriorityTotals(
            Tenant aTenant,
            ProductId aProductId) {
        int totalBenefit = 0;
        int totalPenalty = 0;
        int totalCost = 0;
        int totalRisk = 0;

        java.util.Collection<BacklogItem> outstandingBacklogItems =
            DomainRegistry
                .backlogItemRepository()
                    .allOutstandingProductBacklogItems(
                        aTenant,
                        aProductId);
```

```
    for (BacklogItem backlogItem : outstandingBacklogItems) {
        if (backlogItem.hasBusinessPriority()) {
            BusinessPriorityRatings ratings =
                backlogItem.businessPriority().ratings();

            totalBenefit += ratings.benefit();
            totalPenalty += ratings.penalty();
            totalCost += ratings.cost();
            totalRisk += ratings.risk();
        }
    }

    BusinessPriorityTotals businessPriorityTotals =
        new BusinessPriorityTotals(
                totalBenefit,
                totalPenalty,
                totalBenefit + totalPenalty,
                totalCost,
                totalRisk);

    return businessPriorityTotals;
    }
}
```

The `BacklogItemRepository` is used to get all *outstanding* Backlog-Item instances. An outstanding `BacklogItem` is one with a status type of *Planned*, *Scheduled*, or *Committed*, not either *Done* or *Removed*. A Service in the domain is welcome to use Repositories as needed, but accessing Repositories from an Aggregate instance is not a recommended practice.

With all outstanding items for a given product, we iterate over them and total each of the `ratings` of their `BusinessPriority`. The totals that result from iteratively calculating are used to instantiate a new `BusinessPriorityTotals`, which is returned to the client. There is no need for a Service calculation process to be complex, though it could be a necessity. This one happens to be rather simple.

Note from this example that you would *absolutely not* want this logic to reside in an Application Service. Even if you consider the summing calculation in the `for` loop to be trivial, it is still business logic. But there's another reason:

```
    BusinessPriorityTotals businessPriorityTotals =
        new BusinessPriorityTotals(
                totalBenefit,
                totalPenalty,
```

```
        totalBenefit + totalPenalty,
        totalCost,
        totalRisk);
```

As the `BusinessPriorityTotals` is instantiated, its `totalValue` attribute is derived from summing the `totalBenefit` and `totalPenalty`. This logic is domain specific and must not leak into the Application Layer. We could argue that the `BusinessPriorityTotals` constructor should itself arrange for this to be derived from the two passed-in parameters. While that might be a way to improve the model, doing so wouldn't be a justification for moving the remaining calculations into an Application Service.

Although we don't house this business logic in an Application Service, an Application Service does serve as the client to the Domain Service:

```
public class ProductService ... {
    ...
    private BusinessPriorityTotals productBusinessPriority(
            String aTenantId,
            String aProductId) {
        BusinessPriorityTotals productBusinessPriority =
                DomainRegistry
                    .businessPriorityCalculator()
                    .businessPriorityTotals(
                            new TenantId(aTenantId),
                            new ProductId(aProductId));

        return productBusinessPriority;
    }
}
```

In this case a private method in the Application Service is responsible for requesting the total business priority for the product. Here the method may be supplying just one part of the payload returned to the client of `ProductService`, such as the user interface.

Transformation Services

The more technical Domain Service implementations that definitely live in Infrastructure are often those used for integration. For that reason I have delegated such examples to **Integrating Bounded Contexts (13)**. There you'll see the Service interfaces, implementation classes, and also **Adapters** [Gamma et al.] and translators used by the implementations.

Using a Mini-Layer of Domain Services

Sometimes it may be desirable to create a "mini-layer" of Domain Services above the rest of your domain model Entities and Value Objects. As I previously indicated, this will often lead down the precarious path of Anemic Domain Model, which should be considered an anti-pattern.

Yet, there are some systems where designing in the mini-layer of Domain Services makes more sense than in others and will not lead to Anemic Domain Model. It depends on the characteristics of the domain model, and in the case of the *Identity and Access Context* this is actually quite helpful.

If you were to experience working in such a domain and you did decide to produce a mini-layer of Domain Services, remember that such are always different from Application Services in the Application Layer. Address transactions and security as application concerns in Application Services, not in Domain Services.

Testing Services

We want to test our Services to make sure we gain a client perspective on how we should model. We want our domain-focused tests to reflect the way the model should be used, while at this point ignoring some of the finer software correctness focus.

> **Isn't It a Bit Late to Test?**
>
> I have normally introduced tests before implementations. I did show some test-first code snippets earlier when analyzing the need for a Service. It's just that I found it more natural to discuss the implementation a bit earlier in this chapter, that's all. However, this does show that test-first isn't an absolute necessity, although it may limit a proper modeling focus.

These tests demonstrate how to properly use `AuthenticationService`, and we first test against the successful authentication scenario:

```
public class AuthenticationServiceTest
        extends IdentityTest {

    public void testAuthenticationSuccess() throws Exception {

        User user = this.getUserFixture();

        DomainRegistry
            .userRepository()
            .add(user);
```

```
            UserDescriptor userDescriptor =
                DomainRegistry
                    .authenticationService()
                    .authenticate(
                            user.tenantId(),
                            user.username(),
                            FIXTURE_PASSWORD);

        assertNotNull(userDescriptor);
        assertEquals(user.tenantId(), userDescriptor.tenantId());
        assertEquals(user.username(), userDescriptor.username());
        assertEquals(user.person().emailAddress(),
                    userDescriptor.emailAddress());
    }
    ...
```

This example shows how the `AuthenticationService` would be used by an Application Service client. It's a happy path where that client would successfully authenticate a user by passing expected parameters.

Note that the Repository could be the full implementation, an in-memory variety, or mocked. It works fine to test with the full implementation if it is fast enough, as long as the test ends with a rollback of the transaction, preventing the buildup of extraneous instances across tests. The kind of Repository implementation used for testing is your choice.

Next, we demonstrate a scenario under which authentication fails:

```
    public void testAuthenticationTenantFailure() throws Exception {

        User user = this.getUserFixture();

        DomainRegistry
            .userRepository()
            .add(user);

        TenantId bogusTenantId =
            DomainRegistry.tenantRepository().nextIdentity();

        UserDescriptor userDescriptor =
            DomainRegistry
                .authenticationService()
                .authenticate(
                        bogusTenantId, // bogus
                        user.username(),
                        FIXTURE_PASSWORD);

        assertNull(userDescriptor);
    }
```

This authentication test fails because we purposely pass in a `TenantId` that is different from the one in which the `User` was created. Then there is the invalid username condition to demonstrate:

```
public void testAuthenticationUsernameFailure() throws Exception {

    User user = this.getUserFixture();

    DomainRegistry
        .userRepository()
        .add(user);

    UserDescriptor userDescriptor =
        DomainRegistry
            .authenticationService()
            .authenticate(
                    user.tenantId(),
                    "bogususername",
                    user.password());

    assertNull(userDescriptor);
}
```

This authentication test scenario fails because we pass in a wrong username. There's one last failure scenario demonstrated in these tests:

```
public void testAuthenticationPasswordFailure() throws Exception {

    User user = this.getUserFixture();

    DomainRegistry
        .userRepository()
        .add(user);

    UserDescriptor userDescriptor =
        DomainRegistry
            .authenticationService()
            .authenticate(
                    user.tenantId(),
                    user.username(),
                    "passw0rd");

    assertNull(userDescriptor);
}
}
```

This test provides the wrong password, which causes it to fail. In all cases when demonstrating failure scenarios the UserDescriptor is returned as null. This is a detail that clients should take note of, as it indicates what they should expect when the user is not authenticated. It also indicates that failing authentication is not an exceptional error, just a normal possibility of this domain. Otherwise, if failing authentication were considered exceptional, we'd make the Service throw an AuthenticationFailedException.

There are actually a few tests missing. I will leave it to you to test domain scenarios that include when a Tenant is not active and a User that is disabled. After that, you can create tests for the BusinessPriorityCalculator.

Wrap-Up

In this chapter we discussed what a Domain Service is and what it is not, and we analyzed when we should use a Service rather than an operation on an Entity or Value Object. There was more:

- You learned that recognizing a legitimate need for a Service is necessary to avoid overusing Services.

- You were reminded that overuse of Domain Services leads to Anemic Domain Model, an anti-pattern.

- You saw the specific steps of general practice when implementing a Service.

- You considered the pluses and minuses of using a Separated Interface.

- You reviewed a sample calculation process from the *Agile Project Management Context*.

- Finally, you considered how to provide exemplary tests to demonstrate how to use the Services our models provide.

Next, we are going to consider one of the newer DDD tactical modeling tools to appear on the scene. It's the powerful Domain Event building block pattern.

Chapter 8

Domain Events

History is the version of past events that people
have decided to agree upon.
—*Napoleon Bonaparte*

Use a **Domain Event** to capture an occurrence of something that happened in the domain. This is an extremely powerful modeling tool. Once you get the hang of using Domain Events, you will be addicted and wonder how you survived without them until now. To get started with them, all you have to do is find agreement on what your Events actually are.

Road Map to This Chapter

- Discover what Domain Events are, and when and why you should consider using them.
- Learn how Events are modeled as objects, and when they must be uniquely identified.
- Examine a lightweight **Publish-Subscribe** [Gamma et al.] pattern and how it fits with notifying clients.
- See which components publish Events and which ones are the subscribers.
- Consider why you'd want to develop an Event Store, how it can be done, and how one is used.
- Learn from SaaSOvation how Events are published to autonomous systems in different ways.

The When and Why of Domain Events

Referencing [Evans], you will find no formal definition for Domain Events. The pattern was introduced in detail sometime after the book was published. To begin a discussion about implementing Events in the **Domain (2)**, consider the contemporary definition:

Something happened that domain experts care about.

> Model information about activity in the domain as a series of discrete events. Represent each event as a domain object. . . . A domain event is a full-fledged part of the domain model, a representation of something that happened in the domain. [Evans, Ref, p. 20]

How can we determine if something that happens in the domain is important to the domain experts? As we have discussions with them, we must listen carefully for clues. Consider a few key phrases to listen for when domain experts talk:

- "When . . ."

- "If that happens . . ."

- "Inform me if . . ." and "Notify me if . . ."

- "An occurrence of . . ."

Of course, with the "Inform me if . . ." and "Notify me if . . ." expressions it's not the notification that constitutes an Event. It's just a statement of the fact that someone in the domain *wants to be notified* as a result of an important occurrence, and that *likely means* the need to model an explicit Event. In addition, domain experts might say things such as "If *that* happens, it *isn't* important, but if *this* happens, it *is* important." (Replace *that* and *this* with something meaningful in your domain.) Depending on your organizational culture, there could be other triggering phrases.

Cowboy Logic

AJ: "In the event that I want my horse, I just yell, 'Here, Trigger!' and he comes runnin'. Of course, it never hurts to let him know I'm carryin' a cube of sugar."

There will probably be times when the spoken language of the experts doesn't lead to a clear reason to model an Event, yet the business situation may still call for it. Domain experts may or may not be aware of these kinds of requirements, and they could become known only as a result of cross-team discussions. This tends to happen when Events must be broadcast to external services, where the systems in your enterprise have been decoupled and occurrences throughout the domain must be communicated across **Bounded Contexts (2)**. Events like this get published, and subscribers are notified. As such Events are handled by subscribers, they may have far-reaching impact on local and remote Bounded Contexts.

Domain Experts and Events

Although domain experts may not initially be aware of the need for every kind of Event, they should understand the reasons for them as they are included in discussions about specific Events. Once there is clear consensus, new Events become a formal part of the **Ubiquitous Language (1)**.

When Events are delivered to interested parties, in either local or foreign systems, they are generally used to facilitate eventual consistency. This is purposeful and by design. It can eliminate the need for two-phase commits (global transactions) and support of the rules of **Aggregates (10)**. One rule of Aggregates states that only a single instance should be modified in a single transaction, and all other dependent changes must occur in separate transactions. So other Aggregate instances in the local Bounded Context may be synchronized using this approach. We also bring remote dependencies into a consistent state with latency. The decoupling helps provide a highly scalable and peak-performing set of cooperating services. It also allows us to achieve loose coupling between systems.

Figure 8.1 shows how Events may originate, how they can be stored and forwarded, and where they may be used. Events may be consumed by the local, and foreign, Bounded Contexts.

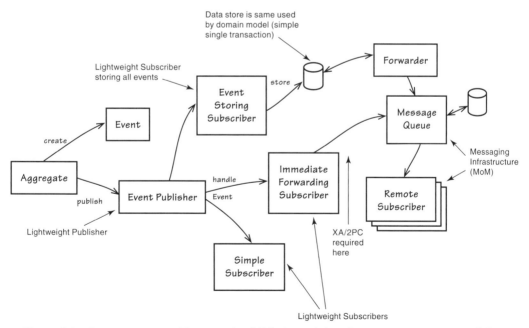

Figure 8.1 Aggregates create Events and publish them. Subscribers may store Events and then forward them to remote subscribers, or just forward them without storing. Immediate forwarding requires XA (two-phase commit) unless messaging middleware shares the model's data store.

Also, think of times when your systems normally perform batch processing. Perhaps during off-peak hours (possibly nighttime) your systems process daily maintenance of some kind, deleting obsolete objects, creating ones that are needed to support newly formed business situations, bringing some objects into agreement with others, and even notifying certain users that important things have happened. Often performing such batch processes requires you to execute some complex queries in order to determine the business situations that require attention. The calculations and procedures to address them are costly, and synchronizing all the changes requires large transactions. What if those pesky batch processes could be made redundant?

Now think of the actual occurrences that took place throughout the previous day that led to the need to play catch-up later. If each of those discrete occurrences were captured by a single Event, and published to listeners in your own system, would that simplify things? Indeed, it would eliminate the complex queries because you would know exactly what occurred and when, providing the context of *what needs to happen as a result.* You would just do it as you receive notification of each Event. The processing currently dealt with in I/O and processor-intensive batches would be spread out into short spurts throughout the day, and your business situations would be in harmony much more quickly, ready for users to take the next steps.

Does every Aggregate command result in an Event? Just as important as recognizing the *need* for an Event is knowing *when to disregard* extraneous happenings in the domain that experts or the business as a whole don't care about. Still, depending on the *technical* implementation aspects of the model or the goals of collaborating systems, it is possible that Events will be more prolific than domain experts directly require. Such is the case when using **Event Sourcing (4, Appendix A)**.

I leave some of this to **Integrating Bounded Contexts (13)**, but we'll consider the essential modeling tools here.

Modeling Events

Let's take a requirement from the *Agile Project Management Context.* The domain experts indicated the need for an Event in this way (italics added for emphasis):

Allow each backlog item to be committed to a sprint. It may be committed only if it is already scheduled for release. If it is already committed to a different sprint, it must be uncommitted first. *When the backlog item is committed, notify the sprint and other interested parties.*

When modeling Events, name them and their properties according to the Ubiquitous Language in the Bounded Context where they originate. If an Event is the result of executing a command operation on an Aggregate, the name is usually derived from the command that was executed. The command is the cause of the Event, and hence the Event's name is rightly stated in terms of the command having occurred in the past. Per the example scenario, when we commit a backlog item to a sprint, we publish an Event that explicitly models what happened in the domain:

Command operation: `BacklogItem#commitTo(Sprint aSprint)`

Event outcome: `BacklogItemCommitted`

The Event name states what occurred (past tense) in the Aggregate after the requested operation succeeded: "The backlog item was committed." The team could have modeled the name a bit more verbosely, such as `BacklogItem-CommittedToSprint`, and that would work. However, in the Ubiquitous Language of Scrum, a backlog item is never committed to anything besides a sprint. In other words, backlog items are scheduled for release, not committed to a release. There would be no doubt that this Event was published as a result of using the `commitTo()` operation. Thus, the Event is sufficiently named as it is, and the more compact name is easier to read. If your team likes a more verbose name in a specific case, however, use it.

When publishing Events from Aggregates, it is important that the Event name reflect the past nature of the occurrence. It is not occurring now. It occurred previously. The best name to choose is the one that reflects that fact.

After the right name is found, what properties should it have? For one, we need a timestamp that indicates when the Event occurred. In Java we could represent it as a `java.util.Date`:

```
package com.saasovation.agilepm.domain.model.product;

public class BacklogItemCommitted implements DomainEvent {
    private Date occurredOn;
    ...
}
```

The minimal interface `DomainEvent`, implemented by all Events, ensures support of an `occurredOn()` accessor. It enforces a basic contract for all Events:

```
package com.saasovation.agilepm.domain.model;

import java.util.Date;

public interface DomainEvent {
    public Date occurredOn();
}
```

Besides this, the team determines what other properties are necessary to represent a meaningful occurrence of what happened. Consider including whatever would be necessary to trigger the Event again. This normally includes the identity of the Aggregate instance on which it took place, or any Aggregate instances involved. Using this guidance, we might create properties of any parameters that caused the Event, if discussion proves they are useful. It's also possible that some resulting Aggregate state transition values could be helpful to subscribers.

Here's what analysis of `BacklogItemCommitted` led to:

```
package com.saasovation.agilepm.domain.model.product;

public class BacklogItemCommitted implements DomainEvent {
    private Date occurredOn;
    private BacklogItemId backlogItemId;
    private SprintId committedToSprintId;
    private TenantId tenantId;
    ...
}
```

The team decided that the identity of the `BacklogItem` and that of the `Sprint` were essential. It was the `BacklogItem` that the Event occurred on, and the `Sprint` that it occurred with. But more was involved in this decision. The requirement that drove out the need for this Event indicated specifically that the `Sprint` must be notified that a certain `BacklogItem` was committed to it. Thus, an Event subscriber in the same Bounded Context must eventually inform the `Sprint`, and it can do so only if `BacklogItemCommitted` has the `SprintId`.

Additionally, in the multitenancy environment, recording the `TenantId` is always necessary, even though it was not passed as a command parameter. It is needed for both the local and foreign Bounded Contexts. Locally the team would need the `TenantId` to query the `BacklogItem` and the `Sprint` from their respective **Repositories (12)**. Likewise, any foreign, remote systems that listen for a broadcast of this Event would need to know which `TenantId` it applies to.

How do we model the behavioral operations supplied by Events? These are generally very simple because an Event is usually designed as immutable. First and foremost, the Event's interface has the express purpose to convey the properties that reflect its cause. Most Events will have a constructor that permits only full state initialization, along with a complement of read accessors for each of its properties.

Based on that, here's what the ProjectOvation team did:

```
package com.saasovation.agilepm.domain.model.product;

public class BacklogItemCommitted implements DomainEvent {
    ...
    public BacklogItemCommitted(
            TenantId aTenantId,
            BacklogItemId aBacklogItemId,
            SprintId aCommittedToSprintId) {
        super();
        this.setOccurredOn(new Date());
        this.setBacklogItemId(aBacklogItemId);
        this.setCommittedToSprintId(aCommittedToSprintId);
        this.setTenantId(aTenantId);
    }

    @Override
    public Date occurredOn() {
        return this.occurredOn;
```

```
    }

    public BacklogItemId backlogItemId() {
        return this.backlogItemId;
    }

    public SprintId committedToSprintId() {
        return this.committedToSprintId;
    }

    public TenantId tenantId() {
        return this.tenant;
    }
    ...
}
```

With this Event published, a subscriber in the local Bounded Context can use it to notify the `Sprint` that a certain `BacklogItem` was recently committed to it:

```
MessageConsumer.instance(messageSource, false)
    .receiveOnly(
            new String[] { "BacklogItemCommitted" },
            new MessageListener(Type.TEXT) {
        @Override
        public void handleMessage(
            String aType,
            String aMessageId,
            Date aTimestamp,
            String aTextMessage,
            long aDeliveryTag,
            boolean isRedelivery)
        throws Exception {
            // first de-duplicate message by aMessageId
            ...
            // get tenantId, sprintId, and backlogItemId from JSON
            ...

            Sprint sprint =
                    sprintRepository.sprintOfId(tenantId, sprintId);

            BacklogItem backlogItem =
                    backlogItemRepository.backlogItemOfId(
                        tenantId,
                        backlogItemId);

            sprint.commit(backlogItem);
        }
    });
```

Per the system requirements, after handling the specific "BacklogItem-Committed" message, the `Sprint` is consistent with the `BacklogItem` that was recently committed to it. How the subscriber receives this Event is discussed later in this chapter.

The team realized that there might be a bit of a problem here. How is the `Sprint` updating transaction managed? We could have the message handler do that, but either way the code found in the handler needs some refactoring. It would be best for it to delegate to an

Application Service (14) to harmonize with the **Hexagonal Architecture (4)**. Doing so would allow the Application Service to manage the transaction, which is a natural application concern. In that case the handler would now look like this:

```
MessageConsumer.instance(messageSource, false)
    .receiveOnly(
            new String[] { "BacklogItemCommitted" },
            new MessageListener(Type.TEXT) {
        @Override
        public void handleMessage(
            String aType,
            String aMessageId,
            Date aTimestamp,
            String aTextMessage,
            long aDeliveryTag,
            boolean isRedelivery)
        throws Exception {
            // get tenantId, sprintId, and backlogItemId from JSON
            String tenantId = ...
            String sprintId = ...
            String  backlogItemId = ...

            ApplicationServiceRegistry
                    .sprintService()
                    .commitBacklogItem(
                            tenantId, sprintId, backlogItemId);
        }
    });
```

In this example Event de-duplication is unnecessary because committing a `BacklogItem` to a `Sprint` is an idempotent operation. If the specific

`BacklogItem` is already committed to the `Sprint`, the current request to commit it again is ignored.

It may be necessary to provide additional state and behavior if subscribers require more than the indication of the Event's cause. This could be conveyed by enriched state (more properties) or operations that derive richer state. Subscribers thus avoid querying back on the Aggregate from which the Event was published, which could be needlessly difficult or expensive. Event enrichment may be more common when using Event Sourcing because an Event used for persistence may need additional state when also published out of the Bounded Context. Examples of Event enrichment are provided in Appendix A.

Whiteboard Time

- List the kinds of Events that already occur in your domain but that aren't being captured.

- Make note of how making them an explicit part of your model would improve your design.

  It might be easiest to identify Aggregates that have dependencies on the state of other Aggregates, where eventual consistency is necessary.

To derive richer state using operations, make sure that any additional Event behaviors are **Side-Effect Free**, as discussed in **Value Objects (6)**, protecting the object's immutability.

With Aggregate Characteristics

Sometimes Events are designed to be created by direct request from clients. This is done in response to some occurrence that is not the direct result of executing behavior on an instance of an Aggregate in the model. Possibly a user of the system initiates some action that is considered an Event in its own right. When that happens, the Event can be modeled as an Aggregate and retained in its own Repository. Since it represents some past occurrence, its Repository would not permit its removal.

When Events are modeled in this way, like Aggregates they become part of the model's structure. Thus, they are not just a record of some past occurrence, although they are that also.

The Event is still designed as immutable, but it may be assigned a generated unique identity. It is possible, however, that the identity can be supported by a number of the Event's properties. Even if unique identity could be determined by a set of properties, it may be best to assign a generated unique identity as discussed in **Entities** (5). This would allow the Event to undergo various design changes over time without risking its uniqueness among all others.

When an Event is modeled in this fashion, it can be published via messaging infrastructure at the same time as it is added to its Repository. The client could call on a **Domain Service** (7) to create the Event, add it to its Repository, and then publish it over a messaging infrastructure. With this approach, both the Repository and the messaging infrastructure must be backed by the same persistence instance (data source), or a global transaction (aka XA and two-phase commit) would be necessary to guarantee that both commit successfully.

After the messaging infrastructure successfully saves the new Event message to its persistence store, it would then asynchronously send it on to any queue listener, topic/exchange subscribers, or actor if using the Actor Model.[1] If the messaging infrastructure uses a persistence store that is separate from that used by the model, and if it does not support global transactions, your Domain Service would have to see that it is first saved in the Event Store, which in this case would also act as a queue for out-of-band publishing. Each Event in the Store would be processed by a forwarding component that would send it out over the messaging infrastructure. This technique is discussed in detail later in this chapter.

Identity

Let's clarify the reasons for assigning unique identity. At times it may be necessary to distinguish Events one from another, but the need may be rare. In the Bounded Context where the Event is caused, created, and published, there will tend to be little reason to compare one Event to another, if ever. But what if, for some reason, Events must be compared? And what if an Event is designed as an Aggregate?

It may be enough to allow Event identity to be represented by its properties, as is the case with Value Objects. The Event's name/type along with the identities of the Aggregate(s) involved in the cause, as well as a timestamp of when the Event occurred, may be enough to distinguish it from others.

In cases where an Event is modeled as an Aggregate, or in other cases when Events must be compared and their combined properties do not distinguish them, we may assign an Event a formal unique identity. But there may be other reasons to assign unique identity.

---

1. See Erlang's and Scala's Actor Model of concurrency. In particular, Akka is worth considering if using Scala or Java.

Unique identity may be necessary when Events are published outside the local Bounded Context where they occur, when messaging infrastructure forwards them along. In some situations individual messages can be delivered more than once. This would happen if the message sender crashes before the messaging infrastructure confirms that the message was sent.

Whatever may cause a message's redelivery, the solution is to get the remote subscribers to detect duplicate message delivery and ignore messages already received. To help with this, some messaging infrastructures provide a unique message identity as part of the header/envelope around its body, making it unnecessary for the model to generate one. Even if the messaging system doesn't itself automatically provide a unique identity for all messages, publishers can assign one either to the Event itself or to the message. In either case, remote subscribers can use the unique identity to manage de-duplication when messages are delivered more than once.

Is there a need for `equals()` and `hashCode()` implementations? These would most often be necessary only if the local Bounded Context used them. Events sent via messaging infrastructure are sometimes not reconstituted as their native typed objects when received by subscribers but are consumed as, for example, XML, JSON, or key-value maps. On the other hand, when an Event is designed as an Aggregate and saved to its own Repository, the Event type should provide both of these standard methods.

Publishing Events from the Domain Model

Avoid exposing the domain model to any kind of middleware messaging infrastructure. Those kinds of components live only in the infrastructure. And while the domain model might at times use such infrastructure indirectly, it would never explicitly couple to it. We'll use an approach that completely avoids the use of infrastructure.

One of the simplest and most effective ways to publish Domain Events without coupling to components outside the domain model is to create a lightweight **Observer** [Gamma et al.]. For the sake of naming I use Publish-Subscribe, which is acknowledged by [Gamma et al.] as another name for the same pattern. The examples in that pattern and my use of it are lightweight because there is no network involved in subscribing to Events and publishing them. All registered subscribers execute in the same process space with the publisher and run on the same thread. When an Event is published, each subscriber is notified synchronously, one by one. This also implies that all subscribers are running within the same transaction, perhaps controlled by an Application Service that is the direct client of the domain model.

Considering the two halves of Publish-Subscribe separately helps to explain them in a DDD context.

Publisher

Perhaps the most common use of Domain Events is when an Aggregate creates an Event and publishes it. The publisher resides in a **Module (9)** of the model, but it doesn't model some aspect of the domain. Rather, it provides a simple service to Aggregates that need to notify subscribers of Events. The following is a `DomainEventPublisher`, which adheres to this definition. An abstract view of how the `DomainEventPublisher` is used can be found in Figure 8.2.

```
package com.saasovation.agilepm.domain.model;

import java.util.ArrayList;
import java.util.List;

public class DomainEventPublisher {

    @SuppressWarnings("unchecked")
    private static final ThreadLocal<List> subscribers =
            new ThreadLocal<List>();

    private static final ThreadLocal<Boolean> publishing =
            new ThreadLocal<Boolean>() {
        protected Boolean initialValue() {
            return Boolean.FALSE;
        }
    };

    public static DomainEventPublisher instance() {
        return new DomainEventPublisher();
    }

    public DomainEventPublisher() {
        super();
    }

    @SuppressWarnings("unchecked")
    public <T> void publish(final T aDomainEvent) {
        if (publishing.get()) {
            return;
        }
        try {
            publishing.set(Boolean.TRUE);
            List<DomainEventSubscriber<T>> registeredSubscribers =
                    subscribers.get();
```

```java
            if (registeredSubscribers != null) {
                Class<?> eventType = aDomainEvent.getClass();
                for (DomainEventSubscriber<T> subscriber :
                        registeredSubscribers) {
                    Class<?> subscribedTo =
                            subscriber.subscribedToEventType();
                    if (subscribedTo == eventType ||
                        subscribedTo == DomainEvent.class) {
                        subscriber.handleEvent(aDomainEvent);
                    }
                }
            }
        } finally {
            publishing.set(Boolean.FALSE);
        }
    }

    public DomainEventPublisher reset() {
        if (!publishing.get()) {
            subscribers.set(null);
        }
        return this;
    }

    @SuppressWarnings("unchecked")
    public <T> void subscribe(DomainEventSubscriber<T> aSubscriber) {
        if (publishing.get()) {
            return;
        }
        List<DomainEventSubscriber<T>> registeredSubscribers =
                subscribers.get();
        if (registeredSubscribers == null) {
            registeredSubscribers =
                    new ArrayList<DomainEventSubscriber<T>>();
            subscribers.set(registeredSubscribers);
        }
        registeredSubscribers.add(aSubscriber);
    }
}
```

Since every incoming request from users of the system is handled on a separate dedicated thread, we divide subscribers by thread. So the two Thread-Local variables, subscribers and publishing, are allocated per thread. When interested parties use the subscribe() operation to register themselves, the subscriber object reference is added to the thread-bound List. Any number of subscribers may be registered per thread.

Depending on the application server, threads may be pooled and reused request by request. We don't want subscribers registered on the thread for

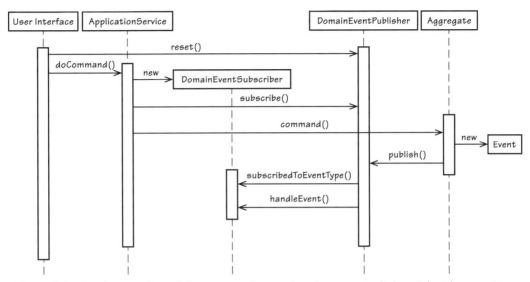

Figure 8.2   An abstract view of the sequence interactions between the lightweight Observer, **User Interface (14)**, Application Services, and the **Domain Model (1)**

a previous request to remain registered for the next request that reuses the thread. When a new user request is received by the system, it should use the `reset()` operation to clear any previous subscribers. This ensures that subscribers will be limited only to those registered from that point forward. On the presentation tier ("User Interface" in Figure 8.2), for example, we might intercept each request using a filter. The intercepting component would in some way cause a `reset()`:

```
// in a Web filter component when user request is received
DomainEventPublisher.instance().reset();

...

// later in an Application Service during same request
DomainEventPublisher.instance().subscribe(subscriber);
```

Following the execution of this code—by two separate components, as seen in Figure 8.2—there will be just one registered subscriber for the thread. From the implementation of method `subscribe()` you can see that subscribers may be registered only when the publisher is not in the process of publishing. This prevents problems such as concurrent modification exceptions on the `List`.

This problem is manifest if subscribers call back on the publisher to add new subscribers in response to a handled Event.

Next, note how an Aggregate publishes an Event. Continuing with the running example, when BacklogItem's commitTo() executes successfully, BacklogItemCommitted is published:

```
public class BacklogItem extends ConcurrencySafeEntity {
    ...
    public void commitTo(Sprint aSprint) {
        ...
        DomainEventPublisher
            .instance()
            .publish(new BacklogItemCommitted(
                    this.tenantId(),
                    this.backlogItemId(),
                    this.sprintId())));
    }
    ...
}
```

When publish() is executed on DomainEventPublisher, it iterates through all registered subscribers. Invoking subscribedToEventType() on each subscriber allows it to filter out all subscribers not subscribed to the specific Event type. Subscribers answering DomainEvent.class to this filter query will receive all Events. All qualified subscribers are sent the published Event by way of their handleEvent() method. After all subscribers have been either filtered or notified, the publisher completes.

As with subscribe(), publish() does not allow nested requests to publish Events. The thread-bound Boolean named publishing is checked and must be false for publish() to iterate and dispatch.

How is Event publishing extended to reach remote Bounded Contexts, supporting autonomous services? We'll get to that soon, but let's look closer at local subscribers.

Subscribers

What components register subscribers to Domain Events? Generally speaking, **Application Services (14)**, and sometimes Domain Services, will. The subscriber may be any component that is running on the same thread as the Aggregate that publishes the Event, and that can subscribe prior to the Event being published. This means that the subscriber is registered in the method execution path that uses the domain model.

Cowboy Logic

LB: "I want a subscription to the *The Fence Post* so I can find even more corny things to say in this book."

Since Application Services are the direct client of the domain model when using Hexagonal Architecture, they are in an ideal position to register a subscriber with the publisher before they execute Event-generating behavior on Aggregates. Here's one example of an Application Service that subscribes:

```
public class BacklogItemApplicationService ... {
    public void commitBacklogItem(
            Tenant aTenant,
            BacklogItemId aBacklogItemId,
            SprintId aSprintId) {

        DomainEventSubscriber subscriber =
                new DomainEventSubscriber<BacklogItemCommitted>() {
            @Override
            public void handleEvent(BacklogItemCommitted aDomainEvent) {
                // handle event here ...
            }
            @Override
            public Class<BacklogItemCommitted> subscribedToEventType() {
                return BacklogItemCommitted.class;
            }
        }

        DomainEventPublisher.instance().subscribe(subscriber);

        BacklogItem backlogItem =
                backlogItemRepository
                        .backlogItemOfId(aTenant, aBacklogItemId);

        Sprint sprint = sprintRepository.sprintOfId(aTenant, aSprintId);

        backlogItem.commitTo(sprint);
    }
}
```

In this (contrived) example, `BacklogItemApplicationService` is an Application Service, with a service method `commitBacklogItem()`. The method instantiates an instance of an anonymous `DomainEvent-Subscriber`. The Application Service task coordinator then registers the subscriber with the `DomainEventPublisher`. Finally, the service method uses Repositories to get instances of `BacklogItem` and `Sprint` and executes the backlog item's `commitTo()` behavior. When completed, method `commitTo()` publishes an Event of type `BacklogItemCommitted`.

What the subscriber does with the Event is not shown in this example. It could send an e-mail about the fact that a `BacklogItemCommitted`, if that made any sense. It might store the Event in an Event Store. It could forward the Event via a messaging infrastructure. Usually in these last two cases—saving to an Event Store and forwarding using messaging infrastructure—we wouldn't make a use-case-specific Application Service to handle the Event in this way. Instead we'd design a single subscriber component to do that. An example of a single-responsibility component that saves to an Event Store is found in the section "Event Store."

> **Be Careful about What the Event Handler Does**
>
> Remember, the Application Service controls the transaction. Don't use the Event notification to modify a second Aggregate instance. That breaks a rule of thumb to modify one Aggregate instance per transaction.

One thing the subscriber *should not* do is get another Aggregate instance and execute modifying command behavior on it. This would violate the *modify-single-aggregate-instance-in-single-transaction* rule of thumb, as discussed in **Aggregates (10)**. As [Evans] indicates, the consistency of all Aggregate instances other than the one used in the single transaction must be enforced by asynchronous means.

Forwarding the Event via a messaging infrastructure would allow asynchronous delivery to out-of-band subscribers. Each of those asynchronous subscribers could arrange to modify an additional Aggregate instance in one or more separate transactions. The additional Aggregate instances could be in the same Bounded Context or in others. Publishing the Event outward to any number Bounded Contexts of other **Subdomains (2)** emphasizes the word *Domain* in the term *Domain Event*. In other words, Events are a *domain-wide* concept, not just a concept in a single Bounded Context. The contract of Event publishing should have the potential to be at least as broad as the enterprise, or even broader. Yet, wide broadcast does not forbid delivery of Events by consumers in the same Bounded Context. Refer back to Figure 8.1.

Sometimes it is necessary for Domain Services to register subscribers. The motivation for doing so would be similar to the reasons that Application Services do, but in this case there would be domain-specific reasons to listen for Events.

Spreading the News to Remote Bounded Contexts

There are several possible ways for remote Bounded Contexts to become aware of Events that occur in your Bounded Context. The primary idea is that some form of messaging takes place, and an enterprise messaging mechanism is needed. To be clear, the mechanism being spoken of here goes well beyond the simple, lightweight Publish-Subscribe components just discussed. Here we are discussing what takes over where the lightweight mechanism leaves off.

There are numerous such messaging components available, and they are generally classed as middleware. From the open source ActiveMQ, RabbitMQ, Akka, NServiceBus, and MassTransit, to the various commercially licensed products, there are plenty of options. We might also home-grow a form of messaging based on REST resources, where autonomous systems are the interested parties that reach out to the publishing system, requesting all Event notifications that they have not previously consumed. All of these fall under the umbrella of **Publish-Subscribe** [Gamma et al.], with varying degrees of advantage or disadvantage. Much depends on the budget, taste, functional requirements, and nonfunctional qualities sought by the teams involved.

The use of any such messaging mechanism between Bounded Contexts requires that we adopt a commitment to eventual consistency. It can't be fought. The changes in one model that influence changes in one or more other models will not be fully consistent for some elapsed period of time. What is more, depending on the traffic to individual systems and the effects they have on others, it may be that the systems as a whole may never be fully consistent at any one instant in time.

Messaging Infrastructure Consistency

With all the chatter about eventual consistency, it might surprise you that at least two mechanisms in a messaging solution must always be consistent with each other: the persistence store used by the domain model, and the persistence store backing the messaging infrastructure used to forward the Events published by the model. This is required to ensure that when the model's changes are persisted, Event delivery is also guaranteed, and that if an Event is delivered through messaging, it indicates a true situation reflected by the model that published it. If either of these is out of lockstep with the other, it will lead to incorrect states in one or more interdependent models.

How is model and Event persistence consistency accomplished? There are three basic ways:

1. Your domain model and messaging infrastructure share the same persistence store (for example, a data source). This will allow the changes to the model and the insertion of the new message to commit under the same local transaction. It has the advantage of relatively good performance. It has the possible disadvantage that the messaging system's storage areas (such as database tables) must reside in the same database (or schema) as your model's, which may be a matter of taste. Of course, this is not a viable option if your choice of model store and your messaging mechanism's store cannot be shared.

2. Your domain model's persistence store and your messaging persistence store are controlled under a global, XA transaction (two-phase commit). This has the advantage that you can keep model and messaging storage separated from each other. It has the disadvantage that global transactions require special support, which may not be available for all persistence stores or messaging systems. Global transactions tend to be expensive and perform poorly. It is also possible that either the model's store or the messaging mechanism's store, or both, isn't XA compatible.

3. You create a special storage area (for example, a database table) for Events in the same persistence store that is used to store your domain model. This is an Event Store, as discussed later in this chapter. It is similar to option 1; however, this storage area is not owned and controlled by your messaging mechanism but instead by your Bounded Context. An out-of-band component that you create uses the Event Store to publish all stored, unpublished Events through the messaging mechanism. This has the advantage that your model and your Events are guaranteed to be consistent within a single, local transaction. It has the further advantages that are characteristic of an Event Store, including the ability to produce REST-based notification feeds. This approach allows the use of a messaging infrastructure whose message store is completely private. Given that a middleware messaging mechanism can be used after Event storage, this approach has the disadvantage that the Event forwarder must be custom-developed in order to send through the messaging mechanism, and that clients must be designed to de-duplicate incoming messages (see "Event Store").

It is the third approach that I use in my examples. While there are disadvantages to this approach, there are also several advantages that are made clear under "Event Store." My choice of this one approach in no way negates the value of selecting in favor of a different set of trade-offs. You and your team must choose from among them.

Autonomous Services and Systems

Using Domain Events allows any number of your enterprise systems to be designed as *autonomous services and systems*. I use the term *autonomous service* to represent any coarse-grained business service, possibly thought of as a system or application, that operates largely independent of other such "services" in the enterprise. The autonomous service may have a number of service interface endpoints, meaning that it offers potentially many technical service interfaces to remote clients. A high degree of independence from other systems is achieved by avoiding in-band remote procedure calls (RPCs), where a user request is satisfied only by successful completion of an API request to a remote system.

Since there may be times when the remote system is either completely unavailable or under heavy load, RPC may affect the success of the dependent system. This risk multiples as the number of systems with RPC APIs that a given system depends on increases. Thus, avoiding in-band RPC greatly eases dependency and related instances of complete failure and/or unacceptable performance caused by unavailable or low-throughput remote systems.

Rather than calling out to other systems, use asynchronous messaging to achieve a greater degree of independence between systems—autonomy. As messages carrying Domain Events from Bounded Contexts around the enterprise are received, execute behavior on your model that reflects the meaning of those Events within your Bounded Context. This does not mean that you simply replicate data or make exact copies of objects from other business services into your business service. True, some data may be copied between systems. At a minimum, copied data will include some unique identities of foreign Aggregates. But the objects in one system will seldom if ever be exact copies of objects from surrounding ones. If that probable modeling error exists, see **Bounded Contexts (2)** and **Context Maps (3)** for reasons why it is problematic and for ways to avoid it. In fact, if Domain Events are correctly designed, they will rarely if ever carry entire objects as part of their state.

The Event will hold some limited amount of command parameters and/or Aggregate state that will convey enough meaning to allow subscribing Bounded Contexts to react correctly. Certainly if any given Event does not hold enough information for any given subscriber, the *domain-wide* contract of the Event must be altered in order to supply what is needed. This probably spells designing an explicitly new version of the Event or a completely different one.

It is also true that in some cases the use of RPC cannot be easily avoided. Some legacy systems may be capable of providing only RPC. Also, when translating a concept or set of concepts from a foreign Bounded Context to your local Bounded Context is very difficult to do, extrapolating sufficient meaning from multiple Events may tend to increase complexity. If you must nearly replicate the concepts, objects, and their associations from the foreign model in your own model, you may need to consider sticking with RPC. This must be considered on a case-by-case basis, and I suggest not giving in to RPC too easily. If it can't be avoided, either surrender to RPC or try to influence the team that owns the foreign model to find a way to simplify their design. Admittedly the latter may be very difficult, if not impossible.

Latency Tolerances

Won't the potentially long latency periods before a message is received—where eventual consistency represents delays of more than a few milliseconds—cause problems? Certainly this is a matter to consider carefully, given that out-of-sync data could influence wrong and even damaging actions. We must ask how long between consistent states is acceptable, and how much delay is too great. Domain experts will likely be very much in tune with what constitutes acceptable and unacceptable delays. It may surprise developers to learn that most times, several seconds, minutes, hours, or even days between consistent states is completely tolerable. This is not to say that it is always true. But we must not assume that in any given domain, near-consistent time frames are always imperative.

Sometimes the following question will lead to an informative answer: How did the business work prior to computers, or how would it work without them now? Perhaps not even the very simplest of paper-based systems is ever immediately consistent. It would only make sense, then, that automated computer systems could also tolerate and even thrive in an eventually consistent manner. We might conclude that eventual consistency makes better business sense.

Imagine a Subdomain used to plan future team activities. As any of the individual activities becomes approved, a Domain Event is published that reflects the approval: `TeamActivityApproved`. This one follows any number of other Events that have already been published about the genesis and definition of all now-approved activities. Another Bounded Context reacts to the approval by scheduling the latest readied activity to start sometime in relation to all other approved activities.

We know that any given activity is specified and approved at least weeks before it begins. That being so, would it matter if the Event necessary to cause placement of the approved activity in the schedule were to be received minutes, hours, or possibly even days following approval? Maybe days wouldn't be acceptable. However, if the outage of a system caused the Event to be delayed for a number of hours—probably an unlikely situation—would hours without having the activity on the schedule be a completely intolerable delay? No, because it is a rare system outage that must be worked around, and the activity is still weeks off anyway. Since that is so, certainly a typical delay of perhaps as much as a few seconds—at the outer limits—for the same Event to arrive under completely normal circumstances would be not only tolerable, but acceptable. In fact any actual delays may not even be perceptible.

Cowboy Logic

AJ: "Is that a Kentucky 'shortly'?"

LB: "It might be a New York 'minute.'"

Just as much as this example may prove true, other business services will demand higher throughput. Maximum latency tolerances should be well understood and systems should have the architectural qualities to meet them and possibly even out-perform them. High availability and scalability must be designed into autonomous services and their supporting messaging infrastructure in order to dutifully fulfill stringent enterprise nonfunctional requirements.

Event Store

Maintaining a store of all Domain Events for a single Bounded Context has several potential benefits. Consider what you could do if you were to store a discrete Event for every model command behavior that is ever executed. You could

1. Use the Event Store as a queue for publishing all Domain Events through a messaging infrastructure. This is one of the primary uses in this book. It allows integrations between Bounded Contexts, where remote subscribers react to the Events in terms of their own contextual needs. (See the previous section, "Spreading the News to Remote Bounded Contexts.")

2. You may use the same Event Store to feed REST-based Event notifications to polling clients. (This is logically the same as point 1, but different in actual use.)

3. Examine a historical record of the result of every command that has ever been executed on the model. This could help trace bugs, not only in the model but also in clients. It's important to grasp that an Event Store is not just an audit log. Audit logs may helpful for debugging, but they rarely carry the complete results of each Aggregate command outcome.

4. Use the data in trending, forecasting, and for other business analytics. Many times businesses have no idea how such historical data can be used until they later realize that they need it. Unless an Event Store is maintained from the start, the historical data will be unavailable as needs arise.

5. Use the Events to reconstitute each Aggregate instance when it is retrieved from its Repository. This is a required part of what is known as Event Sourcing. It is done by applying to an Aggregate instance all previously stored Events in chronological order. You may produce snapshots of any number of stored Events (for example, groups of 100) to optimize instance reconstitution.

6. Given an application of the preceding point, undo blocks of changes to an Aggregate. This is possible by preventing (perhaps by removal or marking as obsolete) certain Events from being used to reconstitute a given Aggregate instance. You may also patch Events or insert additional Events to correct bugs in the Event stream.

Depending on your reasons to create an Event Store, it will have certain characteristics. Since the examples presented here are primarily motivated by benefits 1 and 2, our Event Store is basically concerned with holding serialized Events in the order in which they occurred. This does not mean that we couldn't use the Events to realize all of the first four benefits, because the second two are possible based on the fact that we are making a record of all significant Events in the domain. Achieving benefits 3 and 4 is, therefore, further application of what's accomplished by the first two. However, we will not be attempting to leverage the Event Store for points 5 and 6 in this chapter.

Several steps are necessary to realize benefits 1 and 2. The steps are summarized in Figure 8.3. Let's first discuss the steps covered in that sequence diagram and the components involved. We'll do so through the project experiences of SaaSOvation.

For whatever reasons we use an Event Store, one of the first things we need to do is create a subscriber that will receive every Event that is published out of the model. The team decided to do that using an aspect-oriented hook that can insert itself in the execution path of every Application Service in the system.

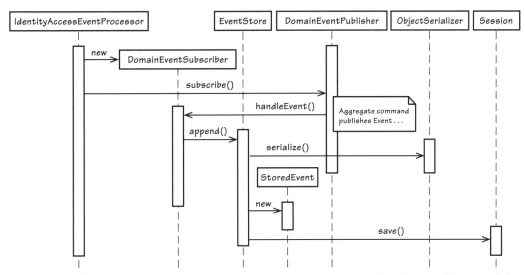

Figure 8.3 The IdentityAccessEventProcessor anonymously subscribes to all Events of the model. It delegates to EventStore, which serializes each to a StoredEvent and saves it.

Here's what the SaaSOvation team did for the *Identity and Access Context*. The following component has the single responsibility to see to it that all Domain Events get stored:

```
@Aspect
public class IdentityAccessEventProcessor {
    ...
    @Before(
    "execution(* com.saasovation.identityaccess.application.*.*(..))")
    public void listen() {
        DomainEventPublisher
            .instance()
            .subscribe(new DomainEventSubscriber<DomainEvent>() {

                public void handleEvent(DomainEvent aDomainEvent) {
                    store(aDomainEvent);
                }
```

```
              public Class<DomainEvent> subscribedToEventType() {
                  return DomainEvent.class; // all domain events
              }
          });
      }

      private void store(DomainEvent aDomainEvent) {
          EventStore.instance().append(aDomainEvent);
      }
}
```

It's a simple Event processor, and a similar one could be used by any other Bounded Context with the same mission. It's designed as an aspect (using Spring's AOP) that intercepts all Application Service method invocations. When an Application Service method is executed, this processor arranges to listen for all Domain Events that get published due to the Application Service's interaction with the model. The processor registers a subscriber with the thread-bound instance of `DomainEvent-Publisher`. This subscriber's filter is wide open, which is indicated by its answering `DomainEvent.class` from `subscribedToEventType()`. Returning that class indicates that the subscriber wants to receive all Events. When its `handleEvent()` is invoked, it delegates to `store()`, which in turn delegates to class `EventStore` to append the Event to the end of the actual Event Store.

Here's a look at the `EventStore` component's `append()` method:

```
package com.saasovation.identityaccess.application.eventStore;
...
public class EventStore ... {
    ...
    public void append(DomainEvent aDomainEvent) {

        String eventSerialization =
            EventStore.objectSerializer().serialize(aDomainEvent);

        StoredEvent storedEvent =
                new StoredEvent(
                        aDomainEvent.getClass().getName(),
                        aDomainEvent.occurredOn(),
                        eventSerialization);

        this.session().save(storedEvent);

        this.setStoredEvent(storedEvent);
    }
}
```

Method `store()` serializes the `DomainEvent` instance, places that into a new `StoredEvent` instance, and then writes that new object to the Event Store. Here is a portion of class `StoredEvent` that holds the serialized `DomainEvent`:

```
package com.saasovation.identityaccess.application.eventStore;
...
public class StoredEvent {
    private String eventBody;
    private long eventId;
    private Date occurredOn;
    private String typeName;

    public StoredEvent(
            String aTypeName,
            Date anOccurredOn,
            String anEventBody) {
        this();
        this.setEventBody(anEventBody);
        this.setOccurredOn(anOccurredOn);
        this.setTypeName(aTypeName);
    }
    ...
}
```

Each `StoredEvent` instance gets a unique sequence value autogenerated by the database and set as its `eventId`. Its `eventBody` contains the serialization of the `DomainEvent`. The serialization used here is JSON using the [Gson] library, but we could use another form. The `typeName` holds the name of the concrete class of the corresponding `DomainEvent`, and `occurredOn` is a copy of the same `occurredOn` in the `DomainEvent`.

All `StoredEvent` objects are persisted into a MySQL table. Plenty of room is reserved for Event serializations, although 65,000 characters is no doubt far more storage than will ever be needed by a single instance:

```
CREATE TABLE `tbl_stored_event` (
    `event_id` int(11) NOT NULL auto_increment,
    `event_body` varchar(65000) NOT NULL,
    `occurred_on` datetime NOT NULL,
    `type_name` varchar(100) NOT NULL,
    PRIMARY KEY (`event_id`)
) ENGINE=InnoDB;
```

That takes us through the high-level review of a few components necessary to build up the Event Store with all Event instances published by Aggregates in the domain model. We'll look at more detail later. Let's next see how these stored records of happenings in our model can be consumed by other systems.

Architectural Styles for Forwarding Stored Events

Once the Event Store is populated, it is available to provide Events to be forwarded as notifications to interested parties. We'll look at two styles of making these Events available. One style is through RESTful resources that are queried by clients, and the second style is by sending messages over a topic/exchange of a middleware messaging product.

Granted, the REST-based approach is not truly a forwarding technique. Yet, it is used to produce the same results as a Publish-Subscribe style, much as an e-mail client is a "subscriber" to e-mail messages "published" by an e-mail server.

Publishing Notifications as RESTful Resources

The REST style of Event notification works best when used in an environment that follows the basic premises of Publish-Subscribe. That is, many consumers are interested in the same events that are available from a single producer. On the other hand, if you attempt to use the REST-based style as a Queue, the approach tends to break down. Here is a summary of the good and the bad of the RESTful approach:

- If potentially many clients can go to a single well-known URI to request the same set of notifications, the RESTful approach works well. Essentially notifications are fanned out to any number of polling consumers. This follows the basic Publish-Subscribe pattern, even though it uses the *pull model* instead of the *push model*.[2]

- If one or a few consumers are required to pull from multiple producers for resources in order to get a single set of tasks to be performed in a specific sequence, you will probably quickly feel the pain of using a RESTful approach. This describes a Queue, where potentially many producers need to feed notifications to one or a few consumers, and the order of receipt may matter. A polling model is typically not a good choice for implementing Queues.

---

2. See http://c2.com/cgi/wiki?ObserverPattern for a discussion of push versus pull model in conjunction with the Observer pattern.

The RESTful approach to publishing Event notifications is quite the opposite of those published using a typical messaging infrastructure. The "publisher" does not maintain a set of registered "subscribers" because nothing gets pushed to interested parties. Instead this approach requires REST clients to pull for notifications using a well-known URI.

Consider the RESTful approach from a high level. If you are familiar with the way Atom feeds are consumed on the Web, this approach will look very familiar. It's actually based on Atom concepts.

Clients use the HTTP GET method to request what is known as the *current log.* The current log contains the very latest notifications that have been published. The client receives the current log with a number of notifications not to exceed a standard limit. Our examples use 20 as the maximum number of notifications for each log. The client navigates through each of the Events in the current log to find all that have not yet been consumed by its Bounded Context.

How does a client consume Event notifications locally? It interprets the serialized Event by type, translating any pertinent data as appropriate to the local Bounded Context. This likely includes finding related Aggregate instances in its own model and executing commands based on the interpretation of applicable Events. Of course, Events must be applied in chronological order, since the oldest Events represent operations that took place earlier than newer ones. Unless the oldest Events are applied first in the order in which they occurred, the changes that are affected on the local model could well cause bugs.

In our implementation, the current log will have at most 19 notifications. It could have somewhat fewer than 19, even as few as zero. When the current log reaches 20 total notifications, it is automatically archived. If there are no new notifications available at the time the previous current log is archived, the new current log will be empty of notifications.

What's an Archived Log All About?

There's nothing mysterious about an archived log. It just means that the specific log can no longer be altered by any action in the owning system, and clients are guaranteed that no matter how many times they ask for a particular archived log, it will always be the same.

On the other hand, the current log will change up to the point where it becomes full and is finally archived. However, the only changes that can occur to the current log would be to add new notifications until it is full.

Events previously added to any log must never change. This is so because clients must have the guarantee that once they have applied a specific Event locally, it has been applied once and for all times.

Thus, the current log may not always hold the newest or oldest notification that has yet to be applied locally. The oldest such Event may reside in the log previous to the current, or even the others before it. It's all a matter of timing based on how frequently Events fill up a given finite log (in this case with just 20 entries) and how often clients pull for the logs. Figure 8.4 shows how notification logs chain together to provide a virtual array of individual notifications.

Assuming the log state depicted by Figure 8.4, let's say that notifications 1 through 58 have already been applied locally. That means that notifications 59 through 65 have not yet been applied. If the client pulls the following URI, it will receive the current log:

```
//iam/notifications
```

The client reads from its own database a tracking record of the identity of the most recently applied notification, which in our example is 58. The onus is on the client, not the server, to track the next notification to apply. The client navigates from the top to the bottom through the current log in search of the notification with identity 58. It doesn't find it there, so it continues to navigate back to the previous log, which is an archived log. The previous log is reached by use of a hypermedia link in the current log. One style is to allow hypermedia navigation to leverage a header:

```
HTTP/1.1 200 OK
Content-Type: application/vnd.saasovation.idovation+json
...
Link: <http://iam/notifications/61,80>; rel=self
Link: <http://iam/notifications/41,60>; rel=previous
...
```

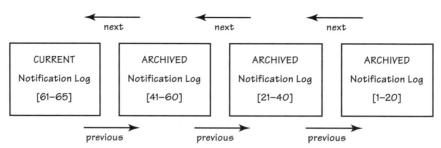

Figure 8.4   The current log and any number of linked archived logs form a virtual array of all *Events* from the most recent Event back to the very first Event. Here notifications 1 through 65 are depicted. Each of the archived logs contains the full 20-notification limit. The current log has not yet filled up and contains just five total notifications.

> **Why Doesn't the URI Reflect What's Actually in the Current Log?**
>
> Note that although the current log presently has only notifications with identities 61 through 65, its URI is composed of the full identity range, 61 through 80, for example:
>
> ```
> Link: <http://iam/notifications/61,80>; rel=self
> ```
>
> That's because the resource must remain stable over its entire lifetime. This allows for consistent access and for caching to work correctly.

From the `Link` containing `rel=previous`, the URI is used for a `GET`, which retrieves the log previous to the current one:

```
//iam/notifications/41,60
```

Using this archived log, the client now finds the sought-after notification, the one with identity 58, after three probes on individual notifications (60, 59, then 58). Since this client has already applied that notification (identity 58), it does not apply notification 58 again. Instead, it now navigates in the other direction in search of all newer notifications. In this archived log it finds identity 59 and applies it. Then it finds 60 and applies it. It has now reached the top of this archived log, so it navigates to the `rel=next` resource, which is the current log:

```
HTTP/1.1 200 OK
Content-Type: application/vnd.saasovation.idovation+json
...
Link: <http://iam/notifications/61,80>; rel=next
Link: <http://iam/notifications/41,60>; rel=self
Link: <http://iam/notifications/21,40>; rel=previous
...
```

It finds in that log notifications with identities 61, 62, 63, 64, and 65, applying each in chronological order. It reaches the end of the current log and stops processing for now, because the current log never has a link header of `rel=next`.

Sometime later the process repeats. The current log is requested by URI. Perhaps by now the activity in the source Bounded Context has caused the generation of significantly different logs by producing a number of new notifications. When the current log is now requested, it may have any number of new notifications. The client may have to navigate back one, two, or even more archived logs to find the most recently applied notification, which is presently the one with identity 65. As before, when the client finds notification 65, it will apply all newer ones in chronological order.

Any number of different client Bounded Contexts may request the notification logs. In fact, any Bounded Context that needs to know what Events have been produced by any other Bounded Context providing this kind of notification publisher may reach out to get the notifications as far back as the "beginning of time." Of course, each client Bounded Context may actually be a client only if it has proper access to the source system (for example, security rights).

But won't client polling of notification resources cause enormous amounts of unwanted traffic against your Web server? Not if your RESTful resources make effective use of caching. For example, the current log might be cached by the client itself for approximately one minute:

```
HTTP/1.1 200 OK
Content-Type: application/vnd.saasovation.idovation+json
...
Cache-Control: max-age=60
...
```

Every time the client polling precedes the one-minute caching, the client cache itself provides the previously retrieved current log. When the cache times out, the latest current log will be retrieved from the server resource. Archived logs may be cached longer since their contents never change, as demonstrated by this one-hour `max-age`:

```
HTTP/1.1 200 OK
Content-Type: application/vnd.saasovation.idovation+json
...
Cache-Control: max-age=3600
...
```

The client may use the current log `max-age` value as a timer/sleep threshold since it is unnecessary to perform `GET` requests continuously on cached resources. Sleep-induced decreased polling can benefit processing load on the client Bounded Context and on the source server. The resource provider will never receive the requests as long as the cache `max-age` has not expired. So an ill-behaved client can never hurt performance or availability of the notification producer, assuming the proper use of client caching. This highlights the benefits of using the Web and its built-in infrastructure to achieve tremendous performance and scalability benefits.

The server may also provide its own cache. Server caching of notification logs works really well because the contents of archived logs never change. Any client that requests a given archived notification log not only receives the resource, it also warms the cache for all other clients in need of the same resource. There is no need for the cache to refresh an archived log because the log is guaranteed immutable.

Wow! That was quite a bit of detail, and still more remains under **Integrating Bounded Contexts (13)**. I suggest that you reference [Parastatidis et al., RiP] for various strategies on designing efficient RESTful Event notification systems. There you will find discussions on the advantages and disadvantages of the standard media type Atom-based notification logs, as well as a few reference implementations. Also, Jim Webber provides further insight on this approach in his presentation [Webber, REST & DDD]. One of the earliest references to this approach comes from Stefan Tilkov's article on InfoQ [Tilkov, RESTful Doubts]. You can also watch my own presentation using this approach [Vernon, RESTful DDD].

Publishing Notifications through Messaging Middleware

Not surprisingly, a messaging middleware product such as RabbitMQ manages details for you that the REST style forces you to deal with on your own. The messaging system also allows you to fairly easily support both Publish-Subscribe and Queues, whichever better fits your needs. In both cases the messaging system uses a push model to send messages of Event notifications to registered subscribers or listeners.

Consider the requirements for publishing Events from our Event Store via a messaging middleware product. We are going to stick with Publish-Subscribe, using what RabbitMQ calls a *fanout exchange*. We will need a set of components that together do the following in order:

1. Query all Domain Event objects from the Event Store that have not yet been published to the specific exchange. Order the queried objects in ascending order by their sequenced unique identity.

2. Iterate over the queried objects in ascending order, sending each to the exchange.

3. When the messaging system indicates that the message was successfully published, track that Domain Event as having been published through that exchange.

We do not wait to see if subscribers confirm receipt. Subscriber systems may not even be running when the publisher sends messages through the exchange. Each subscriber is responsible for handling messages in its own time frame, ensuring that it properly carries out any necessary domain behavior on its own model. We simply allow the messaging mechanism to guarantee delivery.

Whiteboard Time

- Draw a Context Map of the Bounded Context you work on and the others you integrate with. Make sure you show connections between the Contexts that interact.

- Make notations of the kinds of relationships between them, such as **Anticorruption Layer (3)**.

- Now indicate how you would integrate these Contexts. Would you use RPC, RESTful notifications, or a messaging infrastructure? Draw those in.

Remember, you might not have much choice when integrating with a legacy system.

Implementation

Having decided on the architectural styles used for publishing Events, the SaaSOvation team is now focused on the implementation of components to accomplish that . . .

The core of notification publishing behavior is placed behind an Application Service, the `NotificationService`. That allowed the team to manage the transactional scope of changes in their own data source. It also emphasized that notification is an application concern, not a domain concern, even though the Events being published as notifications originated in the model.

There was no need for the `NotificationService` to have a **Separated Interface** [Fowler, P of EAA]. At this time there would be just one implementation of the Application Service, so the team would keep things simple. Still, every simple class has a public interface, so here it is presented as stubbed-out methods:

```
package com.saasovation.identityaccess.application;
...
public class NotificationService {
    ...
    @Transactional(readOnly=true)
    public NotificationLog currentNotificationLog() {
        ...
    }
```

```
@Transactional(readOnly=true)
public NotificationLog notificationLog(String aNotificationLogId) {
    ...
}

@Transactional
public void publishNotifications() {
    ...
}
...
}
```

The first two methods will be used for querying `NotificationLog` instances that are provided to clients as RESTful resources, and the third will be used to publish individual `Notification` instances over a messaging mechanism. The team will first tackle the query methods for getting `NotificationLog` instances, then turn their attention to the one that interacts with the messaging infrastructure.

There are some interesting implementations ahead.

Publishing the `NotificationLog`

Recall that there are two kinds of notification logs, a current log and an archived log. Thus, the `NotificationService` interface provides a query method for each type:

```
public class NotificationService {
    @Transactional(readOnly=true)
    public NotificationLog currentNotificationLog() {
        EventStore eventStore = EventStore.instance();

        return this.findNotificationLog(
                this.calculateCurrentNotificationLogId(eventStore),
                eventStore);
    }

    @Transactional(readOnly=true)
    public NotificationLog notificationLog(String aNotificationLogId) {
        EventStore eventStore = EventStore.instance();

        return this.findNotificationLog(
                new NotificationLogId(aNotificationLogId),
                eventStore);
    }
    ...
}
```

Ultimately both of these methods must "find" a `NotificationLog`. What that really means is finding a section of `DomainEvent` instances that have been serialized in the Event Store, encapsulating each one with a `Notification`, and collecting all those into a `NotificationLog`. Once a `NotificationLog` instance is created, it can be represented as a RESTful resource and provided to a requesting client.

Since the current log may be a constantly moving target, its identity must be calculated every time it is requested. Here's the calculation:

```
public class NotificationService {
    ...
    protected NotificationLogId calculateCurrentNotificationLogId(
            EventStore anEventStore) {

        long count = anEventStore.countStoredEvents();

        long remainder = count % LOG_NOTIFICATION_COUNT;

        if (remainder == 0) {
            remainder = LOG_NOTIFICATION_COUNT;
        }

        long low = count - remainder + 1;

        // ensures a minted id value even though there may
        // not be a full set of notifications at present
        long high = low + LOG_NOTIFICATION_COUNT - 1;

        return new NotificationLogId(low, high);
    }
    ...
}
```

Otherwise, for an archived log all that is needed is a `NotificationLogId` to encapsulate the low and high range of the identifier. Remember that the identifier is encoded as a textual representation of a range between low and high values, such as 21–40. Thus, the constructor for an encoded identity looks like this:

```
public class NotificationLogId {
    ...
    public NotificationLogId(String aNotificationLogId) {
        super();
        String[] textIds = aNotificationLogId.split(",");
        this.setLow(Long.parseLong(textIds[0]));
        this.setHigh(Long.parseLong(textIds[1]));
    }
    ...
}
```

Whether querying for the current log or an archived log, we now have a
NotificationLogId that describes what method findNotification-
Log() will query for:

```
public class NotificationService {
    ...
    protected NotificationLog findNotificationLog(
            NotificationLogId aNotificationLogId,
            EventStore anEventStore) {

        List<StoredEvent> storedEvents =
            anEventStore.allStoredEventsBetween(
                    aNotificationLogId.low(),
                    aNotificationLogId.high());

        long count = anEventStore.countStoredEvents();

        boolean archivedIndicator = aNotificationLogId.high() < count;

        NotificationLog notificationLog =
            new NotificationLog(
                    aNotificationLogId.encoded(),
                    NotificationLogId.encoded(
                            aNotificationLogId.next(
                                    LOG_NOTIFICATION_COUNT)),
                    NotificationLogId.encoded(
                            aNotificationLogId.previous(
                                    LOG_NOTIFICATION_COUNT)),
                    this.notificationsFrom(storedEvents),
                    archivedIndicator);

        return notificationLog;
    }
    ...
    protected List<Notification> notificationsFrom(
            List<StoredEvent> aStoredEvents) {
        List<Notification> notifications =
            new ArrayList<Notification>(aStoredEvents.size());

        for (StoredEvent storedEvent : aStoredEvents) {
            DomainEvent domainEvent =
                    EventStore.toDomainEvent(storedEvent);

            Notification notification =
                new Notification(
                        domainEvent.getClass().getSimpleName(),
                        storedEvent.eventId(),
                        domainEvent.occurredOn(),
                        domainEvent);

            notifications.add(notification);
        }
```

```
        return notifications;
    }
    ...
}
```

It's quite interesting that there is no need to actually persist any `Notification` instances or whole logs. We can just manufacture them each time they are needed. Obviously, for that reason, it helps with performance and scalability to cache `NotificationLog` resources at the points of request.

Method `findNotificationLog()` uses the `EventStore` component to query the `StoredEvent` instances it needs for a given log. Here's how the `EventStore` finds them:

```
package com.saasovation.identityaccess.application.eventStore;
...
public class EventStore ... {
    ...
    public List<StoredEvent> allStoredEventsBetween(
            long aLowStoredEventId,
            long aHighStoredEventId) {

        Query query =
            this.session().createQuery(
                    "from StoredEvent as _obj_ "
                    + "where _obj_.eventId between ? and ? "
                    + "order by _obj_.eventId");

        query.setParameter(0, aLowStoredEventId);
        query.setParameter(1, aHighStoredEventId);

        List<StoredEvent> storedEvents = query.list();

        return storedEvents;
    }
    ...
}
```

Finally, at the Web tier we publish the current log and archived logs:

```
@Path("/notifications")
public class NotificationResource {
    ...
    @GET
    @Produces({ OvationsMediaType.NAME })
    public Response getCurrentNotificationLog(
            @Context UriInfo aUriInfo) {
```

```
        NotificationLog currentNotificationLog =
            this.notificationService()
                .currentNotificationLog();

        if (currentNotificationLog == null) {
            throw new WebApplicationException(
                    Response.Status.NOT_FOUND);
        }

        Response response =
            this.currentNotificationLogResponse(
                    currentNotificationLog,
                    aUriInfo);

        return response;
    }

    @GET
    @Path("{notificationId}")
    @Produces({ OvationsMediaType.ID_OVATION_NAME })
    public Response getNotificationLog(
            @PathParam("notificationId") String aNotificationId,
            @Context UriInfo aUriInfo) {

        NotificationLog notificationLog =
            this.notificationService()
                .notificationLog(aNotificationId);

        if (notificationLog == null) {
            throw new WebApplicationException(
                    Response.Status.NOT_FOUND);
        }

        Response response =
            this.notificationLogResponse(
                    notificationLog,
                    aUriInfo);

        return response;
    }
    ...
}
```

The team could have used a `MessageBodyWriter` to generate the response, but there are some necessary minor complexities that are managed in response builder methods.

That covers the important bits used to publish both current and archived notification logs to RESTful clients.

Publishing Message-Based Notifications

The NotificationService provides a single method for publishing DomainEvent instances over a messaging infrastructure. Here is the service method:

```
public class NotificationService {
    ...
    @Transactional
    public void publishNotifications() {
        PublishedMessageTracker publishedMessageTracker =
            this.publishedMessageTracker();

        List<Notification> notifications =
            this.listUnpublishedNotifications(
                    publishedMessageTracker
                        .mostRecentPublishedMessageId());

        MessageProducer messageProducer = this.messageProducer();

        try {
            for (Notification notification : notifications) {
                this.publish(notification, messageProducer);
            }

            this.trackMostRecentPublishedMessage(
                    publishedMessageTracker,
                    notifications);
        } finally {
            messageProducer.close();
        }
    }
    ...
}
```

Method publishNotifications() first gets its PublishedMessage-Tracker. This is the object that persists the record of which Events have already been published:

```
package com.saasovation.identityaccess.application.notifications;
...
public class PublishedMessageTracker {
    private long mostRecentPublishedMessageId;
    private long trackerId;
    private String type;
    ...
}
```

Note that this class is not part of the domain model but rather belongs to the application. The `trackerId` is just this object's unique identity (essentially an Entity). The `type` attribute holds the `String` description of the type of topic/channel that the Events were published on. The attribute `mostRecent-PublishedMessageId` corresponds to the unique identity of the individual `DomainEvent` that was serialized and persisted as a `StoreEvent`. Thus, it holds the value of the `StoredEvent` `eventId` of the most recently published instance. After all new `Notification` messages have been sent, the service method ensures that the `PublishedMessageTracker` is saved with the identity of the now most recently published Event.

The Event identity along with the `type` attribute *allows us to publish the same notifications at different times to any number of topics/channels.* We just create a new instance of the `PublishedMessageTracker` with the name of the topic/channel as its `type` and start again with the first `StoredEvent`. In fact, here's how method `publishedMessageTracker()` does it:

```
public class NotificationService {
    private static final String EXCHANGE_NAME =
            "saasovation.identity_access";
    ...
    private PublishedMessageTracker publishedMessageTracker() {
        Query query =
            this.session().createQuery(
                    "from PublishedMessageTracker as _obj_ "
                    + "where _obj_.type = ?");

        query.setParameter(0, EXCHANGE_NAME);

        PublishedMessageTracker publishedMessageTracker =
            (PublishedMessageTracker) query.uniqueResult();

        if (publishedMessageTracker == null) {
            publishedMessageTracker =
                new PublishedMessageTracker(EXCHANGE_NAME);
        }

        return publishedMessageTracker;
    }
    ...
}
```

Multichannel publishing is not yet supported, but it could be added easily with a little refactoring.

Next, method `listUnpublishedNotifications()` is responsible for querying a sorted list of all unpublished `Notification` instances:

```
public class NotificationService {
    ...
    protected List<Notification> listUnpublishedNotifications(
            long aMostRecentPublishedMessageId) {
        EventStore eventStore = EventStore.instance();

        List<StoredEvent> storedEvents =
                eventStore.allStoredEventsSince(
                        aMostRecentPublishedMessageId);

        List<Notification> notifications =
                this.notificationsFrom(storedEvents);

        return notifications;
    }
    ...
}
```

In reality it's querying the EventStore for StoredEvent instances with eventId values greater than the one held by parameter aMostRecent-PublishedMessageId. Those returned from the EventStore are used to create a new collection of Notification instances.

Now, back to the main service method publishNotifications(). With the collection of DomainEvent wrapper Notification instances, it iterates and dispatches to method publish():

```
...
for (Notification notification : notifications) {
    this.publish(notification, messageProducer);
}
```

This method that publishes individual Notification instances does so through RabbitMQ, but using a very simple object library to make its interface seem more object-oriented:

```
public class NotificationService {
    ...
    protected void publish(
            Notification aNotification,
            MessageProducer aMessageProducer) {

        MessageParameters messageParameters =
            MessageParameters.durableTextParameters(
                    aNotification.type(),
                    Long.toString(aNotification.notificationId()),
                    aNotification.occurredOn());
```

```
        String notification =
            NotificationService
                .objectSerializer()
                .serialize(aNotification);

        aMessageProducer.send(notification, messageParameters);
    }
    ...
}
```

This `publish()` method creates `MessageParameters` and then sends the JSON serialized `DomainEvent` by way of a `MessageProducer`.[3] The `MessageParameters` include select properties to send along with the message body. Among these special parameters are the Event `type` string, the notification identity used as a unique message ID, and the `occurredOn` timestamp of the Event. These parameters allow subscribers to determine important facts about each message without the need to parse the JSON message body, which is the serialized Event. And the unique message ID (notification identity) supports message de-duplication, which is explained later.

Consider one more method used to fully implement publishing:

```
public class NotificationService {
    ...
    private MessageProducer messageProducer() {

        // create my exchange if nonexistent
        Exchange exchange =
            Exchange.fanOutInstance(
                    ConnectionSettings.instance(),
                    EXCHANGE_NAME,
                    true);

        // create a message producer used to forward Events
        MessageProducer messageProducer =
            MessageProducer.instance(exchange);

        return messageProducer;
    }
    ...
}
```

---

3. Classes `Exchange`, `ConnectionSettings`, `MessageProducer`, `Message-Parameters`, and others are part of a library that serves as an abstraction layer around RabbitMQ. I provide this library, which makes using RabbitMQ much more object friendly, along with the other sample code for the book.

328

Method `publishNotifications()` uses `messageProducer()` to ensure that the exchange exists and then gets the instance of `MessageProducer` used to publish. RabbitMQ supports exchange idempotence, so the first time you ask for the exchange it is created, and all subsequent times you are given the preexisting one. We don't retain an open instance of the `Message-Producer` in case a problem with the backing broker channel somehow develops. Reestablishing the connection each time publish is executed helps prevent a completely inoperable publisher. We may need to look out for possible performance issues if constant reconnection becomes a bottleneck. But for now we will count on the configured pauses between publish operations to alleviate reconnection overhead.

Speaking of pauses between publish operations, none of the preceding code indicates how Events are published to the exchange on a regular, recurring basis. That can be accomplished in a few different ways and may depend on your operational environment. For one, a JMX `TimerMBean` can be used to manage recurring time intervals.

Before presenting the following timer solution, it's important to note an important context. The Java MBean standard also uses the term *notification*, but this is not the same used by our own publishing process. In this case, a listener receives notification of each occurrence of the timer firing. Just be prepared to sort that out in your mind.

Whatever suitable interval is determined and configured for a given timer, a `NotificationListener` is registered so the `MBeanServer` can notify on each occasion when an interval is reached:

```
mbeanServer.addNotificationListener(
        timer.getObjectName(),
        new NotificationListener() {
            public void handleNotification(
                    Notification aTimerNotification,
                    Object aHandback) {
                ApplicationServiceRegistry
                        .notificationService()
                        .publishNotifications();
            }
        },
        null,
        null);
```

In this example, when method `handleNotification()` is invoked due to the timer firing, it requests the `NotificationService` to perform its `publishNotifications()` operation. That's all that's necessary. For as long as the `TimerMBean` continues to fire at regular, recurring intervals, Domain

Events will continue to be published through the exchange and consumed by subscribers across the enterprise.

Using an application-server-managed timer has the added advantage that you don't have to create a component to monitor the life cycle of your publishing process. If, for example, the `publishNotifications()` should for some reason on any given execution encounter problems and terminate with an exception, the `TimerMBean` would continue to run and fire on subsequent intervals. Administrators may need to address infrastructure errors, perhaps with RabbitMQ, but once problems are out of the way, messages would continue to be published. That said, there are other timer facilities available, such as [Quartz].

But we are still left with questions about message de-duplication. What is message de-duplication? And why is it necessary for messaging subscribers to support it?

Event De-duplication De-duplication is a necessity in environments where a single message published through a messaging system could possibly be delivered to subscribers more than once. There are various causes of duplicate messages. One way this can happen is the following:

1. RabbitMQ delivers the newly sent messages to one or more subscribers.

2. The subscribers process the messages.

3. Before subscribers can acknowledge that the messages were received and processed, they fail.

4. RabbitMQ delivers the unacknowledged messages again.

The possibility also exists when publishing out of an Event Store, and the messaging system doesn't share the Event Store's persistence mechanism, and global, XA transactions are not controlling atomic commits of Event Store and messaging persistence changes. As discussed earlier under "Publishing Notifications through Messaging Middleware," that is exactly our situation. Consider a scenario that highlights how a message could be sent more than once:

1. The `NotificationService` queries and publishes three unpublished `Notification` instances. It updates the record of this with `PublishedMessageTracker`.

2. The RabbitMQ broker receives all three messages and prepares to send them to all subscribers.

3. However, due to some exceptional condition on the application server, there is a failure of the `NotificationService`. The modification to the `PublishedMessageTracker` is not committed.

4. RabbitMQ delivers the newly sent messages to subscribers.

5. The exceptional condition on the application server is corrected. The process of publishing begins again and the `NotificationService` successfully sends messages for all unpublished Events. This includes sending (again!) messages for all Events that were previously published but unknown to the `PublishedMessageTracker`.

6. RabbitMQ delivers the newly sent messages to subscribers, at least three of which are duplicate deliveries.

In this scenario I arbitrarily use three Events. I could have used one, two, four, or many more. The number is not significant, only the fact that problems like these could cause redelivery. When you face this and other reasons for message duplication, de-duplication is necessary. See **Idempotent Receiver** [Hohpe & Woolf] for more elaborate treatment.

An Idempotent Operation

An idempotent operation is one that can be executed two or more times in succession with results identical to those of executing the same operation only once.

One way to deal with the possibility of duplicate message delivery is for subscriber model operation to be idempotent. The subscriber's response to all messages could be idempotent operations against its own domain model. The problem is that designing a domain object, or any object for that matter, to be idempotent can be difficult, impractical, or even impossible. And if we attempt to design the Event itself to carry information that reflects an idempotent action to be taken, that can also be troublesome. For one, the sender must fully understand the current business situation of all receivers relative to the Event state they will send. Further, receipt of Events that are out of sequence due to latency, retries, and so on could cause errors.

When domain object idempotence is not a viable option, you can instead design the subscriber/receiver itself to be idempotent. The receiver can be designed to refuse to execute an operation in response to a duplicate message. First, you should check to see if your messaging product supports this as a feature. If not, your receiver will need to track which messages have already been handled. One way to accomplish that is to allocate an area in the subscriber's persistence mechanism to save the name of the topic/exchange along with the unique message ID of all handled messages—yes, similar to a `Published-MessageTracker`. Then you can query for duplicates before handling each message. If the query finds that a message was already handled, the subscriber simply ignores it. The handled message tracking is not part of the domain model. It should be viewed only as a technical work-around for common messaging idiosyncrasies.

When using a typical messaging middleware product, it is not enough to save only a record of the latest handled message because messages can be received out of order. Thus, a de-duplication query that checks for message IDs less than the most recent one would cause you to ignore some messages that were received out of order. Also to be considered is that sometimes you will want to discard all handled message tracking entries that are obsolete, as in database garbage collection.

When using the REST-based notification approach, de-duplication is not really a factor. Client receivers need to save only the most recently applied notification identity since they will always be applying only the notifications of events that occurred after it. Each notification log will always be in reverse chronological order (descending) by notification identity.

In both cases—messaging middleware subscribers and REST-based notification clients—it is important that the tracking of handled message identity be committed along with any changes to the local domain model state. Otherwise, you will be unable to maintain tracking consistency in conjunction with the modifications made in response to Events.

Wrap-Up

In this chapter we looked at the definition of Domain Events and how they determine when modeling an Event would be to your advantage.

- You've learned what Domain Events are, and when and why to use them.

- You looked into how Events are modeled as objects, and when they must be uniquely identified.

- You considered when an Event should have Aggregate characteristics, and when a simple Value-based Event works best.

- You saw how lightweight Publish-Subscribe components are used in the model.

- You discovered which components publish Events and which ones subscribe to them.

- You grasped why you'd want to develop an Event Store, how it can be done, and how one is used.

- You learned about two approaches to Event publishing outside the Bounded Context: REST-based notifications and the use of messaging middleware.

- You learned some ways to de-duplicate messages in subscribing systems.

Next, we are going to change directions quite a bit and look into how domain model objects can be well organized by using Modules.

Chapter 9

Modules

The secret of all victory lies in the organization of the non-obvious.
—Marcus Aurelius

If you are using Java or C#, you are already familiar with **Modules**, though you know them by another name. Java calls them packages. C# calls them namespaces. Actually in Ruby you can use the module language construct to effect namespaces for classes. In Ruby's case the DDD pattern name matches the name of the language construct. For the sake of our DDD context I will continue to call them Modules in most cases. It will be easy for you to map that name to the programming language term you regularly use. I won't spend much time trying to explain technically what Modules do, because you probably figured that out long ago.

Road Map to This Chapter

- Learn the difference between traditional Modules and the newer deployment modularity approach.
- Consider the importance of naming Modules per the **Ubiquitous Language (1)**.
- See how designing Modules mechanically actually stifles modeling creativity.
- Learn the design choices and trade-offs made by the SaaSOvation teams.
- Find out the role Modules play outside the domain model, and when to favor new Modules over new Bounded Contexts.

Designing with Modules

In a DDD context, Modules in your model serve as named containers for domain object classes that are highly cohesive with one another. The goal should be low coupling between the classes that are in different Modules. Since Modules as used in DDD are not bland or generic storage compartments, it is also important to properly name the Modules. Their names are an important facet of the Ubiquitous Language.

Choose Modules that tell the story of the system and contain a cohesive set of concepts. This often yields low coupling among Modules, but if it doesn't, look for a way to change the model to disentangle the concepts. . . . Give Modules names that become part of the Ubiquitous Language. Modules and their names should reflect insight into the domain. [Evans, pp. 110, 111]

There are a few simple rules to keep in mind when designing Modules, as noted in Table 9.1.

Table 9.1   Simple Rules for Module Design

Module Do's and Don'ts	Why?
Do design Modules to fit modeling concepts.	Typically you'll have one Module for one or a few **Aggregates** (10) that are cohesive, if only by reference.
Do name Modules per the Ubiquitous Language.	This is a basic goal of DDD, but it will also tend to come naturally if you think about the concepts being modeled.
Don't create Modules mechanically according to a general component type or pattern being used in the model.	Our model won't benefit at all if we segregate all Aggregates into one Module, all **Services** (7) into another Module, all **Factories** (11) into yet another, for example. That misses the point of DDD Modules and will also tend to limit your creativity toward rich modeling. Instead of thinking openly about the domain, you'd tend to think only about the kinds of components or patterns you use to solve current problems.
Do design loosely coupled Modules.	Ensuring that Modules are largely independent of others has the same benefits as loosely coupled classes. This will make it easier to maintain and refactor your modeling concepts and to use larger-grained modularization facilities, such as OSGi and Jigsaw.
Do strive for acyclic dependencies on peer Modules where coupling is necessary. (Peer Modules are those at the same "level," or those with similar weight or bearing on the design.)	It's rarely possible or even practical for Modules to be completely independent of each other. After all, a domain model implies some coupling. Yet, you will reduce the coupling of components if you think in terms of making the dependency between two peer Modules only unidirectional (for example, product depends on team, but team does not depend on product).
Do relax the rules a bit between child and parent Modules. (A parent Module is one at a higher level and a child is just a level lower—parent.child, for example.)	It's really difficult to prevent dependency between parent and child Modules. If at all possible, still strive for acyclic dependencies between parents and children, but allow for circular dependencies if there's no way to avoid it (for example, a parent creates a child, and the child must reference its parent, if only by identity).

Table 9.1   Simple Rules for Module Design (*Continued*)

Module Do's and Don'ts	Why?
Don't make Modules a static concept of the model, but allow them to be molded along with the objects that they organize.	If the model's concepts are malleable and take on different shapes, behaviors, and names over time, it's very likely that the Modules that organize those same concepts should be created, renamed, and deleted in kind. It's not a necessity, but if you can see mismatched names, refactor. Yes, it can be a pain, but the pain is probably less than that experienced with poorly named Modules.

View Modules as first-class citizens of the model, and strive to create ones with as much meaning and naming consideration as is given to **Entities** (5), **Value Objects** (6), Services, and **Events** (8). This means being aggressive enough to rename existing Modules with the same boldness as when creating new ones. Always assertively place fresh and freshened domain concepts into the Modules that contemporary insight calls for.

None of us would feel good about opening a drawer in our home kitchen and finding a disorganized assortment of forks, knives, spoons, wrenches, screwdrivers, sockets, and hammers. We would probably at least refuse to eat with the silverware, even if we could gather a full place setting. We might avoid digging through the disorganized drawer to look for a particular screwdriver out of fear of being sliced by an undetected butcher's knife.

Contrast this with a kitchen drawer that has silverware neatly organized into sets of forks, knives, and spoons, and a toolbox in your garage where each type of tool has its own well-arranged drawer. We would have no problem finding what we need to use for a specific purpose, or hesitate to put it to its intended use. Everything is well organized, uncluttered. With all this modular organization in place, no one would expect to find cups and saucers in the drawer with silverware, even though both belong in the kitchen. The neat stacks of tableware would likely lead us to believe that cups and saucers have a proper place of their own. A few quick glances into nearby obvious-looking cabinets, and there they would be. We would likewise expect to find sharp cutlery in a location that promised to protect their edges and protect those intending to use them.

On the other hand, we would probably not organize our kitchen's contents using a mechanical approach, such as placing all sturdy things in one drawer and all things that might break in a high cabinet. We wouldn't want to have to remember that our flower vases are kept with our fine teacups just because both are somewhat fragile. Neither would we want to remember that we keep our stainless steel meat tenderizer with the fine cutlery just because both kinds of devices are in little danger of damage by the other sturdy ones.

If we were modeling a kitchen, it would be perfectly natural to see a Module named `placesettings`, and in it we would see objects such as `Fork`, `Spoon`, and `Knife`. Possibly we might even decide to place `Serviette` there as well, proving that it's not only being made of metal that qualifies an object to be a part of the `placesettings` Module. On the other hand, it would be less helpful to modeling place settings if we had separate Modules named `pronged`, `scooping`, and `blunt`.

Note that more recent advances in the modularization of software have led to a different level of software modularity. This approach has to do with the packaging of loosely coupled yet logically cohesive segments of software into a deployment unit by version. In a Java ecosystem we still think in terms of JAR files, but with those now assembled by version using, for example, OSGi bundles or Java 8 Jigsaw modules. Thus, various high-level modules, their versions, and their dependencies could be managed as bundles/modules. These kinds of modules/bundles are a bit different from DDD Modules, but they can complement each other. Certainly it makes sense to bundle loosely coupled parts of a domain model into the larger-grained modules according to their DDD Modules. After all, it's the loosely coupled design of your DDD Modules that will contribute to your ability to bundle with OSGi or modularize to Jigsaw.

Cowboy Logic

LB: "You gotta wonder how this gas station keeps their restrooms so neat and clean."

AJ: "Now, LB, a tornado could hit that restroom and do $10,000 in improvements."

We'll focus on how DDD Modules are used. Thinking of the *purposes of specific* Entities, Value Objects, Services, and Events of your model benefits Module design. Let's look at examples of thoughtful Module design.

Basic Module Naming Conventions

In both Java and C#, the names of Modules reflect a hierarchical form.[1] Each level in the hierarchy is separated by a dot/period. The name hierarchy

---

1. There will be some differences between Java packages and C# namespaces. If you're developing with C#, for example, you can still use this as guidance, but you'll want to adapt it to make sense for your specific programming language and platform.

generally begins with the name of the organization that produced it, composed with its Internet domain name. When the Internet domain name is used, it typically starts with the top-level domain, followed by the organizational domain name:

```
com.saasovation // Java
SaaSOvation // C#
```

Using unique top-level names prevents namespace collision with third-party Modules that are employed on your projects, or those caused when yours are consumed by others. If you have questions about the most basic conventions, you can consult the standard.[2]

Very likely your organization has already settled on a top-level Module naming convention. It's best to be consistent.

Module Naming Conventions for the Model

The next segment of the Module name identifies the Bounded Context. Basing this segment on the name of the Bounded Context is a good choice.

Here is how the SaaSOvation teams named these Modules:

```
com.saasovation.identityaccess
com.saasovation.collaboration
com.saasovation.agilepm
```

They considered using the following, but it added little if any value compared to the previous Module names. Even though they exactly name the Context, they probably produce unnecessary noise:

```
com.saasovation.identityandaccess
com.saasovation.agileprojectmanagement
```

Interestingly, too, they did not use their commercial product names (brands) in the Module names. Brand names can change, and sometimes product names have

---

2. http://java.sun.com/docs/books/jls/second_edition/html/packages.doc.html#26639.

little or no direct correlation to the underlying Bounded Contexts. It is more important to identify the Context by name since that's what the team discusses. The goal is to reflect the Ubiquitous Language. If the team were to use the following names, it wouldn't help them realize that goal:

```
com.saasovation.idovation
com.saasovation.collabovation
com.saasovation.projectovation
```

The first Module name, `com.saasovation.idovation`, has almost no correlation to its Bounded Context. The second one is fairly close. The third name is almost as deficient as the first, but slightly better. At least it has the word *project* in it. Nonetheless, the team decided that these names didn't have an intuitively obvious mental mapping to the Bounded Contexts represented. Even more, if marketing decided that any of the product names had to change—possibly for trademark infringement or cultural incompatibilities—these Module names would be completely obsolete. So the team decided to stick with the first set.

Next, they tacked on an important qualifier. It identifies that the specific Module is in the domain:

```
com.saasovation.identityaccess.domain
com.saasovation.collaboration.domain
com.saasovation.agilepm.domain
```

This convention is compatible with a traditional **Layers Architecture (4)** and a **Hexagonal Architecture (4)**. These days a system that uses Layers will generally manage them using a Hexagonal, injection style. With Hexagonal you have an "inside" part of the application, which includes the domain part. This will be similar with other architectural styles.

The `domain` compartment may be devoid of interfaces/classes and serve only as a container for lower-level Modules. Here's the next level down:

```
com.saasovation.identityaccess.domain.model
com.saasovation.collaboration.domain.model
com.saasovation.agilepm.domain.model
```

This is where model classes start to be defined. This package level can contain reusable interfaces and abstract classes.

SaaSOvation liked to place in this Module common interfaces, such as those that were used for Event publishing, and abstract base classes for Entities and Value Objects:

```
ConcurrencySafeEntity
DomainEvent
DomainEventPublisher
DomainEventSubscriber
DomainRegistry
Entity
IdentifiedDomainObject
IdentifiedValueObject
```

If you favor the style of placing Domain Services outside the `domain.model` Module, you can create a peer to it:

```
com.saasovation.identityaccess.domain.service
com.saasovation.collaboration.domain.service
com.saasovation.agilepm.domain.service
```

It is not a requirement to place Domain Services here. It is available if you consider them to be a kind of medium-grained service mini-layer above the model, or a ring surrounding it [Evans, p. 108, "Granularity"]. However, be aware that this approach can quickly lead to **Anemic Domain Model**, which is discussed in **Services (7)**.

In the case where you do not divide model and services into two packages, it is possible to drop the `model` Module and just place all model Modules directly under `domain`:

```
com.saasovation.identityaccess.domain.conceptname
```

It does eliminate one level that may seem redundant. Yet, what happens if later you do decide to place a few Domain Services into a `domain.service` sub-Module? At that point you'd probably be pretty disappointed that you failed to create a `domain.model` sub-Module.

But there's an even more important naming influence to consider. Remember that we do not develop a domain. The **Domain (2)** is some realm of know-how of the business we are working in. What we design and implement is a *model of a domain*. So when naming the ultimate Module of the model, `domain.model` seems most appropriate. Still, that's the choice of your team.

Modules of the Agile Project Management Context

SaaSOvation's current **Core Domain** (2) is the *Agile Project Management Context*, so it makes sense to see how its Modules are designed.

The ProjectOvation team chose three top-level Modules: tenant, team, and product. Here's the first:

```
com.saasovation.agilepm.domain.model.tenant
    <<value object>> TenantId
```

Its contents are a simple Value Object, TenantId, that holds the unique identity of a specific tenant, which originates in the *Identity and Access Context*. In the case of this Module, just about all others in the model will depend on it. It's essential for segregating one tenant's objects from another's. Yet, the dependency is acyclic. The tenant Module does not depend on the others.

The team Module holds Aggregates and a Domain Service that is used to manage product teams:

```
com.saasovation.agilepm.domain.model.team
    <<service>> MemberService
    <<aggregate root>> ProductOwner
    <<aggregate root>> Team
    <<aggregate root>> TeamMember
```

There are three Aggregates and one Domain Service interface. Class Team holds one ProductOwner instance and any number of TeamMember instances in a collection. The ProductOwner and TeamMember instances are created by the MemberService. All three of the Aggregate Root Entities reference the TenantId of the tenant Module:

```
package com.saasovation.agilepm.domain.model.team;
import com.saasovation.agilepm.domain.model.tenant.TenantId;
public class Team extends ConcurrencySafeEntity {
    private TenantId tenantId;
    ...
}
```

The MemberService is a front end for an **Anticorruption Layer** (3) that synchronizes product team members with identities and roles of the *Identity and Access Context*. The synchronization happens in the background, out of band with regular user requests. This Service is proactive, creating members as they are registered in the remote Context. The synchronization is eventually consistent with the remote system but lags only a short period of time from actual changes that occur remotely. It also updates member details, such as names and e-mail addresses, as needed.

The *Agile Project Management Context* has a parent Module named `product` and three children:

```
com.saasovation.agilepm.domain.model.product
    <<aggregate root>> Product
    ...
com.saasovation.agilepm.domain.model.product.backlogitem
    <<aggregate root>> BacklogItem
    ...
com.saasovation.agilepm.domain.model.product.release
    <<aggregate root>> Release
    ...
com.saasovation.agilepm.domain.model.product.sprint
    <<aggregate root>> Sprint
    ...
```

This is where the modeling of Scrum's core lives. Here you will find `Product`, `BacklogItem`, `Release`, and `Sprint` Aggregates. You'll see in **Aggregates (10)** why the concepts are modeled as separate Aggregates.

The team liked how the Modules read naturally per the Ubiquitous Language: "product," "product backlog item," "product release," and "product sprint."

With so few closely related Aggregates—only four—why didn't the team place all four in the `product` Module? Not shown here are all the other Aggregate parts, such as the `ProductBacklogItem` Entity contained by `Product`, the `Task` Entity contained by `BacklogItem`, the `ScheduledBacklogItem` contained by `Release`, and the `CommittedBacklogItem` contained

by `Sprint`. There are other Entities and Value Objects held by each Aggregate type. Too, there are a number of Domain Events published by some Aggregates. All in all, placing nearly 60 classes and interfaces in a single Module would make it quite busy, giving a definite impression of disorganization. The team opted for organization over cross-Module coupling concerns.

Like `ProductOwner`, `Team`, and `TeamMember`, all of the `Product`, `BacklogItem`, `Release`, and `Sprint` Aggregate types reference `TenantId`. And there are additional dependencies. Consider `Product`:

```
package com.saasovation.agilepm.domain.model.product;

import com.saasovation.agilepm.domain.model.tenant.TenantId;

public class Product extends ConcurrencySafeEntity {
    private ProductId productId;
    private TeamId teamId;
    private TenantId tenantId;
    ...
}
```

Also, look at `BacklogItem`:

```
package com.saasovation.agilepm.domain.model.product.backlogitem;

import com.saasovation.agilepm.domain.model.tenant.TenantId;

public class BacklogItem extends ConcurrencySafeEntity {
    private BacklogItemId backlogItemId;
    private ProductId productId;
    private TeamId teamId;
    private TenantId tenantId;
    ...
}
```

The references to `TenantId` and `TeamId` are acyclic dependencies; they go in a single direction. Yet, while the `BacklogItem` reference to `ProductId` seems to form an acyclic dependency from the `backlogItem` Module to `product`, it is actually bidirectional. Each `Product` serves as a Factory for creating `BacklogItem` (and `Release`, and `Sprint`) instances. Thus, the dependencies go in both directions. Still, the three sub-Modules are children of `product`, and we can relax the rules of dependencies a bit. Here the trade-off is organizational strengths over coupling. Again, `BacklogItem`, `Release`, and `Sprint` are all natural and expected child concepts of `Product`, so there is little sense in trying to break up these concepts beyond Aggregate boundaries.

However, couldn't the team have achieved loose coupling among these elements by the use of a generic identity type, where `BacklogItem`, `Release`, and `Sprint` would all refer to their `Product` in a nonbinding manner?

```
public class BacklogItem extends ConcurrencySafeEntity {
    private Identity backlogItemId;
    private Identity productId;
    private Identity teamId;
    private Identity tenantId;
    ...
}
```

True, the team could have achieved looser coupling. However, it would also have opened up the potential for bugs in code where each `Identity` type could not be distinguished from the others.

The *Agile Project Management Context* will continue to evolve. SaaSOvation plans to support other agile approaches and tools. Doing so will impact the current Modules, at least in driving the creation of new ones, but probably also influencing changes to existing ones. The team, having an agile mentality, was committed to refactoring Modules with due diligence.

Next, let's consider how Modules are used in other locations through the system's source code.

Modules in Other Layers

Regardless of the **Architecture (4)** you choose, you will always have to create and name the Modules of the non-model components of your architecture. Here we discuss some options for a conventional **Layered Architecture (4)**, but ones that can be applied with other architectural styles.

In a typical Layered Architecture used for an application that sports a domain model, you'd stack the layers as follows: User Interface, Application, Domain, Infrastructure. Depending on the kinds of components in each layer, as determined by your application's needs, the Modules within each layer will vary.

To start, consider the **User Interface Layer (14)** and the effect of supporting RESTful resources. It is possible that your resources will be used to service a GUI and system clients, producing representational state in XML, JSON, and HTML. However, in the case of supporting a GUI, RESTful resources will not/should not create representations that include presentation layout. They will instead produce only bland representations in a variety of markup (XML, HTML) and serialization formats (XML, JSON, Protocol Buffers). All of the graphical layouts that any of the representational state might be subjected to on the client will come from a different channel. Thus, in the User Interface Layer that supports REST you may choose to have at least two Modules that could be named like this:

```
com.saasovation.agilepm.resources
com.saasovation.agilepm.resources.view
```

RESTful resources are maintained in the `resources` package. Pure presentation concerns are provided by components in the `view` sub-package (or presentation, if you prefer). Depending on the number of REST-based resources your system requires, you may have a number of sub-Modules under each primary Module. Keeping in mind that one resource provider class can support several URIs, you may have few enough resource provider classes to keep them all in the primary Module. Whether or not to further modularize them is an easy decision to make once you determine your actual resource requirements.

The Application Layer may have other Modules, which could consist of one per service type:

```
com.saasovation.agilepm.application.team
com.saasovation.agilepm.application.product
...
com.saasovation.agilepm.application.tenant
```

Similar to the design principles of RESTful service resources, the services in the Application Layer are divided into sub-Modules only if it helps. In the *Identity and Access Context*, for example, there are only a few Application Services, and the team chose to leave them in the main Module:

```
com.saasovation.identityaccess.application
```

You could decide in favor of the more modularized design. That would also be fine. When you have more than a few services, perhaps half a dozen or so, it would probably help to modularize them more carefully.

Module before Bounded Context

We have to give careful consideration to the perceived need to divide cohesive domain model objects into separate models, or to keep them together. Sometimes the linguistics of the true, actual domain will jump out at you, and sometimes the terminology will be fuzzy. In cases where terminology is fuzzy and it is not clear if contextual boundaries should be created, first consider the possibility of keeping them together. This approach will use the thinner boundary of Module to separate, rather than the thicker one of Bounded Context.

This does not mean that we rarely use multiple Bounded Contexts. Boundaries between models are clearly justified, as the linguistics demand. You should take away that Bounded Contexts are not meant to be used as a substitute for Modules. Use Modules to modularize cohesive domain objects, and to separate those that are not cohesive or less cohesive.

Wrap-Up

We've just considered domain model modularization, why it is important, and how it is done.

- You noted the difference between traditional Modules and the newer deployment modularity approach.

- You learned about the importance of naming Modules per the Ubiquitous Language.

- You saw how designing Modules incorrectly, even mechanically, actually stifles modeling creativity.

- You considered how the Modules of the *Agile PM Context* were designed, and why certain choices were made.

- You received some helpful guidance on Modules in areas of the system outside the model.

- Finally, you got a few reminders about considering the use of Modules rather than creating new Bounded Contexts, unless the linguistics dictate the coarser-grained division.

Next, we will take a seriously deep dive into one of the least understood modeling tools of DDD, Aggregates.

Chapter 10

Aggregates

The universe is built up into an aggregate of permanent objects connected by causal relations that are independent of the subject and are placed in objective space and time.

—Jean Piaget

Clustering **Entities (5)** and **Value Objects (6)** into an **Aggregate** with a carefully crafted consistency boundary may at first seem like quick work, but among all DDD tactical guidance, this pattern is one of the least well understood.

> ### Road Map to This Chapter
>
> - Along with SaaSOvation, experience the negative consequences of improperly modeling Aggregates.
> - Learn to design by the *Aggregate Rules of Thumb* as a set of best-practice guidelines.
> - Grasp how to model true invariants in consistency boundaries according to real business rules.
> - Consider the advantages of designing small Aggregates.
> - See why you should design Aggregates to reference other Aggregates by identity.
> - Discover the importance of using *eventual consistency* outside the Aggregate boundary.
> - Learn Aggregate implementation techniques, including Tell, Don't Ask and Law of Demeter.

To start off, it might help to consider some common questions. Is an Aggregate just a way to *cluster* a graph of closely related objects under a common parent? If so, is there some practical limit to the number of objects that should be allowed to reside in the graph? Since one Aggregate instance can reference other Aggregate instances, can the associations be navigated deeply, modifying various objects along the way? And what is this concept of *invariants* and a *consistency boundary* all about? It is the answer to this last question that greatly influences the answers to the others.

There are various ways to model Aggregates incorrectly. We could fall into the trap of designing for compositional convenience and make them too large. At the other end of the spectrum we could strip all Aggregates bare and as a result fail to protect true invariants. As we'll see, it's imperative that we avoid both extremes and instead pay attention to the business rules.

Using Aggregates in the Scrum Core Domain

We'll take a close look at how Aggregates are used by SaaSOvation, and specifically within the *Agile Project Management Context* the application named ProjectOvation. It follows the traditional Scrum project management model, complete with product, product owner, team, backlog items, planned releases, and sprints. If you think of Scrum at its richest, that's where ProjectOvation is headed; this is a familiar domain to most of us. The Scrum terminology forms the starting point of the **Ubiquitous Language (1)**. Since it is a subscription-based application hosted using the software as a service (SaaS) model, each subscribing organization is registered as a *tenant*, another term of our Ubiquitous Language.

The company has assembled a group of talented Scrum experts and developers. However, since their experience with DDD is somewhat limited, the team will make some mistakes with DDD as they climb a difficult learning curve. They will grow by learning from their experiences  with Aggregates, and so can we. Their struggles may help us recognize and change similar unfavorable situations we've created in our own software.

The concepts of this domain, along with its performance and scalability requirements, are more complex than any that the team has previously faced in the initial **Core Domain (2)**, the *Collaboration Context*. To address these issues, one of the DDD tactical tools that they will employ is Aggregates.

How should the team choose the best object clusters? The Aggregate pattern discusses composition and alludes to information hiding, which they understand how to achieve. It also discusses consistency boundaries and transactions, but they haven't been overly concerned with that. Their chosen persistence mechanism will help manage atomic commits of their data. However, that was a crucial misunderstanding of the pattern's guidance that caused them to regress. Here's what happened. The team considered the following statements in the Ubiquitous Language:

- Products have backlog items, releases, and sprints.
- New product backlog items are planned.

- New product releases are scheduled.
- New product sprints are scheduled.
- A planned backlog item may be scheduled for release.
- A scheduled backlog item may be committed to a sprint.

From these they envisioned a model and made their first attempt at a design. Let's see how it went.

First Attempt: Large-Cluster Aggregate

The team put a lot of weight on the words *Products have* in the first statement, which influenced their initial attempt to design Aggregates for this domain.

It sounded to some like composition, that objects needed to be interconnected like an object graph. Maintaining these object life cycles together was considered very important. As a result the developers added the following consistency rules to the specification:

- If a backlog item is committed to a sprint, we must not allow it to be removed from the system.
- If a sprint has committed backlog items, we must not allow it to be removed from the system.
- If a release has scheduled backlog items, we must not allow it to be removed from the system.
- If a backlog item is scheduled for release, we must not allow it to be removed from the system.

As a result, `Product` was first modeled as a very large Aggregate. The Root object, `Product`, held all `BacklogItem`, all `Release`, and all `Sprint` instances associated with it. The interface design protected all parts from inadvertent client removal.

This design is shown in the following code, and as a UML diagram in Figure 10.1:

```
public class Product extends ConcurrencySafeEntity {
    private Set<BacklogItem> backlogItems;
    private String description;
    private String name;
    private ProductId productId;
    private Set<Release> releases;
```

```
    private Set<Sprint> sprints;
    private TenantId tenantId;
    ...
}
```

The big Aggregate looked attractive, but it wasn't truly practical. Once the application was running in its intended multi-user environment, it began to regularly experience transactional failures. Let's look more closely at a few client usage patterns and how they interact with our technical solution model. Our Aggregate instances employ optimistic concurrency to protect persistent objects from simultaneous overlapping modifications by different clients, thus avoiding the use of database locks. As discussed in **Entities** (5), objects carry a version number that is incremented when changes are made and checked before they are saved to the database. If the version on the persisted object is greater than the version on the client's copy, the client's is considered stale and updates are rejected.

Consider a common simultaneous, multiclient usage scenario:

- Two users, Bill and Joe, view the same `Product` marked as version 1 and begin to work on it.

- Bill plans a new `BacklogItem` and commits. The `Product` version is incremented to 2.

- Joe schedules a new `Release` and tries to save, but his commit fails because it was based on `Product` version 1.

Persistence mechanisms are used in this general way to deal with concurrency.[1] If you argue that the default concurrency configurations can be changed, reserve your verdict for a while longer. This approach is actually important to protecting Aggregate invariants from concurrent changes.

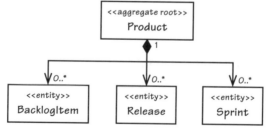

Figure 10.1   `Product` modeled as a very large Aggregate

---

1. For example, Hibernate provides optimistic concurrency in this way. The same could be true of a key-value store because the entire Aggregate is often serialized as one value, unless designed to save composed parts separately.

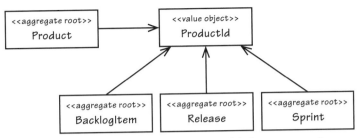

Figure 10.2 `Product` and related concepts are modeled as separate Aggregate types.

These consistency problems came up with just two users. Add more users, and you have a really big problem. With Scrum, multiple users often make these kinds of overlapping modifications during the sprint planning meeting and in sprint execution. Failing all but one of their requests on an ongoing basis is completely unacceptable.

Nothing about planning a new backlog item should logically interfere with scheduling a new release! Why did Joe's commit fail? At the heart of the issue, the large-cluster Aggregate was designed with false invariants in mind, not real business rules. These false invariants are artificial constraints imposed by developers. There are other ways for the team to prevent inappropriate removal without being arbitrarily restrictive. Besides causing transactional issues, the design also has performance and scalability drawbacks.

Second Attempt: Multiple Aggregates

Now consider an alternative model as shown in Figure 10.2, in which there are four distinct Aggregates. Each of the dependencies is associated by inference using a common `ProductId`, which is the identity of `Product` considered the parent of the other three.

Breaking the single large Aggregate into four will change some method contracts on `Product`. With the large-cluster Aggregate design the method signatures looked like this:

```
public class Product ... {
    ...
    public void planBacklogItem(
        String aSummary, String aCategory,
        BacklogItemType aType, StoryPoints aStoryPoints) {
            ...
    }
    ...
    public void scheduleRelease(
        String aName, String aDescription,
```

```
        Date aBegins, Date anEnds) {
        ...
    }

    public void scheduleSprint(
        String aName, String aGoals,
        Date aBegins, Date anEnds) {
        ...
    }
    ...
}
```

All of these methods are **CQS** commands [Fowler, CQS]; that is, they modify the state of the `Product` by adding the new element to a collection, so they have a `void` return type. But with the multiple-Aggregate design, we have

```
public class Product ... {
    ...
    public BacklogItem planBacklogItem(
        String aSummary, String aCategory,
        BacklogItemType aType, StoryPoints aStoryPoints) {
        ...
    }

    public Release scheduleRelease(
        String aName, String aDescription,
        Date aBegins, Date anEnds) {
        ...
    }

    public Sprint scheduleSprint(
        String aName, String aGoals,
        Date aBegins, Date anEnds) {
        ...
    }
    ...
}
```

These redesigned methods have a CQS query contract and act as **Factories (11)**; that is, each creates a new Aggregate instance and returns a reference to it. Now when a client wants to plan a backlog item, the transactional **Application Service (14)** must do the following:

```
public class ProductBacklogItemService ... {
    ...
    @Transactional
    public void planProductBacklogItem(
```

```
        String aTenantId, String aProductId,
        String aSummary, String aCategory,
        String aBacklogItemType, String aStoryPoints) {

    Product product =
        productRepository.productOfId(
                new TenantId(aTenantId),
                new ProductId(aProductId));

    BacklogItem plannedBacklogItem =
        product.planBacklogItem(
                aSummary,
                aCategory,
                BacklogItemType.valueOf(aBacklogItemType),
                StoryPoints.valueOf(aStoryPoints));

    backlogItemRepository.add(plannedBacklogItem);
    }
    ...
}
```

So we've solved the transaction failure issue *by modeling it away.* Any number of `BacklogItem`, `Release`, and `Sprint` instances can now be safely created by simultaneous user requests. That's pretty simple.

However, even with clear transactional advantages, the four smaller Aggregates are less convenient from the perspective of client consumption. Perhaps instead we could tune the large Aggregate to eliminate the concurrency issues. By setting our Hibernate mapping `optimistic-lock` option to `false`, we make the transaction failure domino effect go away. There is no invariant on the total number of created `BacklogItem`, `Release`, or `Sprint` instances, so why not just allow the collections to grow unbounded and ignore these specific modifications on `Product`? What additional cost would there be for keeping the large-cluster Aggregate? The problem is that it could actually grow out of control. Before thoroughly examining why, let's consider the most important modeling tip the SaaSOvation team needed.

Rule: Model True Invariants in Consistency Boundaries

When trying to discover the Aggregates in a **Bounded Context (2)**, we must understand the model's true invariants. Only with that knowledge can we determine which objects should be clustered into a given Aggregate.

An invariant is a business rule that must always be consistent. There are different kinds of consistency. One is *transactional consistency,* which is considered immediate and atomic. There is also *eventual consistency. When discussing invariants, we are referring to transactional consistency.* We might have the invariant

```
c = a + b
```

Therefore, when a is 2 and b is 3, c must be 5. According to that rule and conditions, if c is anything but 5, a system invariant is violated. To ensure that c is consistent, we design a boundary around these specific attributes of the model:

```
AggregateType1 {

    int a;

    int b;

    int c;

    operations ...

}
```

The consistency boundary logically asserts that everything inside adheres to a specific set of business invariant rules no matter what operations are performed. The consistency of everything outside this boundary is irrelevant to the Aggregate. Thus, *Aggregate* is synonymous with *transactional consistency boundary.* (In this limited example, AggregateType1 has three attributes of type int, but any given Aggregate could hold attributes of various types.)

When employing a typical persistence mechanism, we use a single transaction[2] to manage consistency. When the transaction commits, everything inside one boundary must be consistent. *A properly designed Aggregate is one that can be modified in any way required by the business with its invariants completely consistent within a single transaction.* And a properly designed Bounded Context modifies only one Aggregate instance per transaction in all cases. What is more, *we cannot correctly reason on Aggregate design without applying transactional analysis.*

Limiting modification to one Aggregate instance per transaction may sound overly strict. However, it is a rule of thumb and should be the goal in most cases. It addresses the very reason to use Aggregates.

---

2. The transaction may be handled by a **Unit of Work** [Fowler, P of EAA].

Whiteboard Time

- List on your whiteboard all large-cluster Aggregates in your system.

- Make a note next to each of those Aggregates why it is a large cluster and any potential problems caused by its size.

- Next to that list, name any Aggregates that are modified in the same transaction with others.

- Make a note next to each of those Aggregates whether true or false invariants caused the formation of poorly designed Aggregate boundaries.

The fact that Aggregates must be designed with a consistency focus implies that the user interface should concentrate each request to execute a single command on just one Aggregate instance. If user requests try to accomplish too much, the application will be forced to modify multiple instances at once.

Therefore, Aggregates are chiefly about consistency boundaries and not driven by a desire to design object graphs. Some real-world invariants will be more complex than this. Even so, typically invariants will be less demanding on our modeling efforts, making it possible to *design small Aggregates*.

Rule: Design Small Aggregates

We can now thoroughly address this question: What additional cost would there be for keeping the large-cluster Aggregate? Even if we guarantee that every transaction would succeed, a large cluster still limits performance and scalability. As SaaSOvation develops its market, it's going to bring in lots of tenants. As each tenant makes a deep commitment to ProjectOvation, SaaS-Ovation will host more and more projects and the management artifacts to go along with them. That will result in vast numbers of products, backlog items, releases, sprints, and others. Performance and scalability are nonfunctional requirements that cannot be ignored.

Keeping performance and scalability in mind, what happens when one user of one tenant wants to add a single backlog item to a product, one that is years old and already has thousands of backlog items? Assume a persistence mechanism capable of lazy loading (Hibernate). We almost never load all backlog items, releases, and sprints at once. Still, thousands of backlog items would be loaded into memory just to add one new element to the already large collection. It's worse if a persistence mechanism does not support lazy loading. Even being memory conscious, sometimes we would have to load multiple collections, such as when scheduling a backlog item for release or committing one to a sprint; all backlog items, and either all releases or all sprints, would be loaded.

To see this clearly, look at the diagram in Figure 10.3 containing the zoomed composition. *Don't let the 0..* fool you; the number of associations will almost never be zero and will keep growing over time.* We would likely need to load thousands and thousands of objects into memory all at once, just to carry out what should be a relatively basic operation. That's just for a single team member of a single tenant on a single product. We have to keep in mind that this could happen all at once with hundreds or thousands of tenants, each with multiple teams and many products. And over time the situation will only become worse.

This large-cluster Aggregate will never perform or scale well. It is more likely to become a nightmare leading only to failure. It was deficient from the start because the false invariants and a desire for compositional convenience drove the design, to the detriment of transactional success, performance, and scalability.

If we are going to design small Aggregates, what does "small" mean? The extreme would be an Aggregate with only its globally unique identity and one

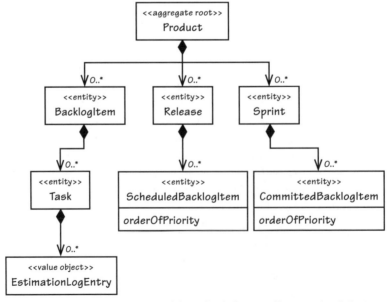

Figure 10.3   With this `Product` model, multiple large collections load during many basic operations.

additional attribute, which is *not* what's being recommended (unless that is truly what one specific Aggregate requires). Rather, limit the Aggregate to just the Root Entity and a minimal number of attributes and/or Value-typed properties.[3] The correct minimum is however many are necessary, and no more.

Which ones are necessary? The simple answer is: those that must be consistent with others, even if domain experts don't specify them as rules. For example, `Product` has `name` and `description` attributes. We can't imagine `name` and `description` being inconsistent, modeled in separate Aggregates. When you change the `name`, you probably also change the `description`. If you change one and not the other, it's probably because you are fixing a spelling error or making the `description` more fitting to the `name`. Even though domain experts will probably not think of this as an explicit business rule, it is an implicit one.

What if you think you should model a contained part as an Entity? First ask whether that part must itself change over time, or whether it can be completely replaced when change is necessary. Cases where instances can be completely replaced point to the use of a Value Object rather than an Entity. At times Entity parts are necessary. Yet, if we run through this design exercise on a case-by-case basis, many concepts modeled as Entities can be refactored to Value Objects. Favoring Value types as Aggregate parts doesn't mean the Aggregate is immutable since the Root Entity itself mutates when one of its Value-typed properties is replaced.

There are important advantages to limiting internal parts to Values. Depending on your persistence mechanism, Values can be serialized with the Root Entity, whereas Entities can require separately tracked storage. Overhead is higher with Entity parts, as, for example, when SQL joins are necessary to read them using Hibernate. Reading a single database table row is much faster. Value objects are smaller and safer to use (fewer bugs). Due to immutability it is easier for unit tests to prove their correctness. These advantages are discussed in **Value Objects (6)**.

On one project for the financial derivatives sector using Qi4j [Öberg], Niclas Hedhman[4] reported that his team was able to design approximately 70 percent of all Aggregates with just a Root Entity containing some Value-typed properties. The remaining 30 percent had just two to three total Entities. This doesn't indicate that all domain models will have a 70/30 split. It does indicate that a high percentage of Aggregates can be limited to a single Entity, the Root.

---

3. A Value-typed property is an attribute that holds a reference to a Value Object. I distinguish this from a simple attribute such as a string or numeric type, as does Ward Cunningham when describing **Whole Value** [Cunningham, Whole Value].

4. See also www.jroller.com/niclas/

The [Evans] discussion of Aggregates gives an example where having multiple Entities makes sense. A purchase order is assigned a maximum allowable total, and the sum of all line items must not surpass the total. The rule becomes tricky to enforce when multiple users simultaneously add line items. Any one addition is not permitted to exceed the limit, but concurrent additions by multiple users could collectively do so. I won't repeat the solution here, but I want to emphasize that most of the time the invariants of business models are simpler to manage than that example. Recognizing this helps us to model Aggregates with as few properties as possible.

Smaller Aggregates not only perform and scale better, they are also biased toward transactional success, meaning that conflicts preventing a commit are rare. This makes a system more usable. Your domain will not often have true invariant constraints that force you into large-composition design situations. Therefore, it is just plain smart to limit Aggregate size. When you occasionally encounter a true consistency rule, add another few Entities, or possibly a collection, as necessary, but continue to push yourself to keep the overall size as small as possible.

Don't Trust Every Use Case

Business analysts play an important role in delivering use case specifications. Much work goes into a large and detailed specification, and it will affect many of our design decisions. Yet, we mustn't forget that use cases derived in this way don't carry the perspective of the domain experts and developers of our close-knit modeling team. We still must reconcile each use case with our current model and design, including our decisions about Aggregates. A common issue that arises is a particular use case that calls for the modification of multiple Aggregate instances. In such a case we must determine whether the specified large user goal is spread across multiple persistence transactions, or if it occurs within just one. If it is the latter, it pays to be skeptical. No matter how well it is written, such a use case may not accurately reflect the true Aggregates of our model.

Assuming your Aggregate boundaries are aligned with real business constraints, it's going to cause problems if business analysts specify what you see in Figure 10.4. Thinking through the various commit order permutations, you'll see that there are cases where two of the three requests will fail.[5] What

---

5. This doesn't address the fact that some use cases describe modifications to multiple Aggregates that span transactions, which would be fine. A user goal should not be viewed as synonymous with a transaction. We are concerned only with use cases that actually indicate the modification of multiple Aggregate instances in one transaction.

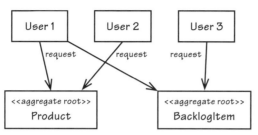

Figure 10.4 Concurrency contention exists among three users who are all trying to access the same two Aggregate instances, leading to a high number of transactional failures.

does attempting this indicate about your design? The answer to that question may lead to a deeper understanding of the domain. Trying to keep multiple Aggregate instances consistent may be telling you that your team has missed an invariant. You may end up folding the multiple Aggregates into one new concept with a new name in order to address the newly recognized business rule. (And, of course, it might be only parts of the old Aggregates that get rolled into the new one.)

So a new use case may lead to insights that push us to remodel the Aggregate, but be skeptical here, too. Forming one Aggregate from multiple ones may drive out a completely new concept with a new name, yet if modeling this new concept leads you toward designing a large-cluster Aggregate, that can end up with all the problems common to that approach. What different approach may help?

Just because you are given a use case that calls for maintaining consistency in a single transaction doesn't mean you should do that. Often, in such cases, the business goal can be achieved with eventual consistency between Aggregates. The team should critically examine the use cases and challenge their assumptions, especially when following them as written would lead to unwieldy designs. The team may have to rewrite the use case (or at least re-imagine it if they face an uncooperative business analyst). The new use case would specify *eventual consistency and the acceptable update delay*. This is one of the issues taken up later in this chapter.

Rule: Reference Other Aggregates by Identity

When designing Aggregates, we may desire a compositional structure that allows for traversal through deep object graphs, but that is not the motivation of the pattern. [Evans] states that one Aggregate may hold references to the Root of other Aggregates. However, we must keep in mind that this does not place the referenced Aggregate inside the consistency boundary of the one referencing it. The reference does not cause the formation of just one whole Aggregate. There are still two (or more), as shown in Figure 10.5.

In Java the association would be modeled like this:

```
public class BacklogItem extends ConcurrencySafeEntity  {
    ...
    private Product product;
    ...
}
```

That is, the `BacklogItem` holds a direct object association to `Product`.

In combination with what's already been discussed and what's next, this has a few implications:

1. Both the referencing Aggregate (`BacklogItem`) and the referenced Aggregate (`Product`) *must not* be modified in the same transaction. Only one or the other may be modified in a single transaction.

2. If you are modifying multiple instances in a single transaction, it may be a strong indication that your consistency boundaries are wrong. If so, it is possibly a missed modeling opportunity; a concept of your Ubiquitous Language has not yet been discovered although it is waving its hands and shouting at you (see earlier in this chapter).

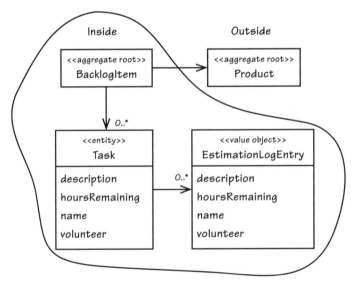

Figure 10.5   There are two Aggregates, not one.

3. If you are attempting to apply point 2, and doing so influences a large-cluster Aggregate with all the previously stated caveats, it may be an indication that you need to use eventual consistency (see later in this chapter) instead of atomic consistency.

If you don't hold any reference, you can't modify another Aggregate. So the temptation to modify multiple Aggregates in the same transaction could be squelched by avoiding the situation in the first place. But that is overly limiting since domain models always require some associative connections. What might we do to facilitate necessary associations, protect from transaction misuse or inordinate failure, and allow the model to perform and scale?

Making Aggregates Work Together through Identity References

Prefer references to external Aggregates only by their globally unique identity, not by holding a direct object reference (or "pointer"). This is exemplified in Figure 10.6.

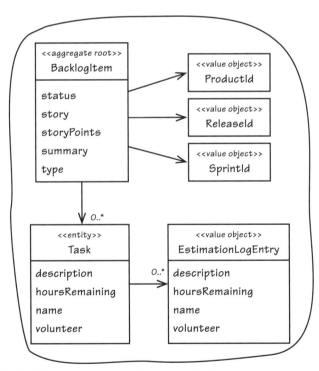

Figure 10.6 The `BacklogItem` Aggregate, inferring associations outside its boundary with identities

We would refactor the source to

```
public class BacklogItem extends ConcurrencySafeEntity {
    ...
    private ProductId productId;
    ...
}
```

Aggregates with inferred object references are thus automatically smaller because references are never eagerly loaded. The model can perform better because instances require less time to load and take less memory. Using less memory has positive implications for both memory allocation overhead and garbage collection.

Model Navigation

Reference by identity doesn't completely prevent navigation through the model. Some will use a **Repository (12)** from inside an Aggregate for lookup. This technique is called **Disconnected Domain Model,** and it's actually a form of lazy loading. There's a different recommended approach, however: Use a Repository or **Domain Service (7)** to look up dependent objects ahead of invoking the Aggregate behavior. A client Application Service may control this, then dispatch to the Aggregate:

```
public class ProductBacklogItemService ... {
    ...
    @Transactional
    public void assignTeamMemberToTask(
        String aTenantId,
        String aBacklogItemId,
        String aTaskId,
        String aTeamMemberId) {

        BacklogItem backlogItem =
            backlogItemRepository.backlogItemOfId(
                new TenantId(aTenantId),
                new BacklogItemId(aBacklogItemId));

        Team ofTeam =
            teamRepository.teamOfId(
                backlogItem.tenantId(),
                backlogItem.teamId());

        backlogItem.assignTeamMemberToTask(
                new TeamMemberId(aTeamMemberId),
```

```
            ofTeam,
            new TaskId(aTaskId));
    }
    ...
}
```

Having an Application Service resolve dependencies frees the Aggregate from relying on either a Repository or a Domain Service. However, for very complex and domain-specific dependency resolutions, passing a Domain Service into an Aggregate command method can be the best way to go. The Aggregate can then *double-dispatch* to the Domain Service to resolve references. Again, in whatever way one Aggregate gains access to others, referencing multiple Aggregates in one request does not give license to cause modification on two or more of them.

Cowboy Logic

LB: "I've got two points of reference when I'm navigating at night. If it smells like beef on the hoof, I'm heading to the herd. If it smells like beef on the grill, I'm heading home."

Limiting a model to using only reference by identity could make it more difficult to serve clients that assemble and render **User Interface (14)** views. You may have to use multiple Repositories in a single use case to populate views. If query overhead causes performance issues, it may be worth considering the use of *theta joins* or CQRS. Hibernate, for example, supports theta joins as a means to assemble a number of referentially associated Aggregate instances in a single join query, which can provide the necessary viewable parts. If CQRS and theta joins are not an option, you may need to strike a balance between inferred and direct object reference.

If all this advice seems to lead to a less convenient model, consider the additional benefits it affords. Making Aggregates smaller leads to better-performing models, plus we can add scalability and distribution.

Scalability and Distribution

Since Aggregates don't use direct references to other Aggregates but reference by identity, their persistent state can be moved around to reach large scale. *Almost-infinite scalability* is achieved by allowing for continuous repartitioning of Aggregate data storage, as explained by Amazon.com's Pat Helland in his position paper "Life beyond Distributed Transactions: An Apostate's Opinion" [Helland]. What we call *Aggregate*, he calls *entity*. But what he describes is still an Aggregate by any other name: a unit of composition that has transactional consistency. Some NoSQL persistence mechanisms support the Amazon-inspired distributed storage. These provide much of what [Helland] refers to as the lower, scale-aware layer. When employing a distributed store, or even when using a SQL database with similar motivations, reference by identity plays an important role.

Distribution extends beyond storage. Since there are always multiple Bounded Contexts at play in a given Core Domain initiative, reference by identity allows distributed domain models to have associations from afar. When an Event-Driven approach is in use, message-based **Domain Events (8)** containing Aggregate identities are sent around the enterprise. Message subscribers in foreign Bounded Contexts use the identities to carry out operations in their own domain models. Reference by identity forms remote associations or *partners*. Distributed operations are managed by what [Helland] calls *two-party activities*, but in **Publish-Subscribe** [Buschmann et al.] or **Observer** [Gamma et al.] terms it's *multiparty* (two or more). Transactions across distributed systems are not atomic. The various systems bring multiple Aggregates into a consistent state eventually.

Rule: Use Eventual Consistency Outside the Boundary

There is a frequently overlooked statement found in the [Evans] Aggregate pattern definition. It bears heavily on what we must do to achieve model consistency when multiple Aggregates must be affected by a single client request:

> Any rule that spans AGGREGATES will not be expected to be up-to-date at all times. Through event processing, batch processing, or other update mechanisms, other dependencies can be resolved within some specific time. [Evans, p. 128]

Thus, if executing a command on one Aggregate instance requires that additional business rules execute on one or more other Aggregates, use eventual consistency. Accepting that all Aggregate instances in a large-scale, high-traffic enterprise are never completely consistent helps us accept that eventual consistency also makes sense in the smaller scale where just a few instances are involved.

Ask the domain experts if they could tolerate some time delay between the modification of one instance and the others involved. Domain experts are sometimes far more comfortable with the idea of delayed consistency than are developers. They are aware of realistic delays that occur all the time in their business, whereas developers are usually indoctrinated with an atomic change mentality. Domain experts often remember the days prior to computer auto-mation of their business operations, when various kinds of delays occurred all the time and consistency was never immediate. Thus, domain experts are often willing to allow for reasonable delays—a generous number of seconds, min-utes, hours, or even days—before consistency occurs.

There is a practical way to support eventual consistency in a DDD model. An Aggregate command method publishes a Domain Event that is in time delivered to one or more asynchronous subscribers:

```
public class BacklogItem extends ConcurrencySafeEntity {
    ...
    public void commitTo(Sprint aSprint) {
        ...
        DomainEventPublisher
            .instance()
            .publish(new BacklogItemCommitted(
                    this.tenantId(),
                    this.backlogItemId(),
                    this.sprintId()));
    }
    ...
}
```

Each of these subscribers then retrieves a different yet corresponding Aggre-gate instance and executes its behavior based on it. Each of the subscribers executes in a separate transaction, obeying the rule of Aggregates to modify just one instance per transaction.

What happens if the subscriber experiences concurrency contention with another client, causing its modification to fail? The modification can be retried if the subscriber does not acknowledge success to the messaging mechanism. The message will be redelivered, a new transaction started, a new attempt made to execute the necessary command, and a corresponding commit made. This retry process can continue until consistency is achieved, or until a retry limit is reached.[6] If complete failure occurs, it may be necessary to compensate, or at a minimum to report the failure for pending intervention.

What is accomplished by publishing the BacklogItemCommitted Domain Event in this specific example? Recalling that BacklogItem already holds the identity of the Sprint it is committed to, we are in no way interested in

---

6. Consider attempting retries using Capped Exponential Back-off. Rather than defaulting to a retry every N fixed number of seconds, exponentially back off on retries while capping waits with an upper limit. For example, start at one second and back off exponentially, doubling until success or until reaching a 32-second wait-and-retry cap.

maintaining a meaningless bidirectional association. Rather, the Event allows for the eventual creation of a `CommittedBacklogItem` so the `Sprint` can make a record of work commitment. Since each `CommittedBacklogItem` has an `ordering` attribute, it allows the `Sprint` to give each `BacklogItem` an ordering different from those of `Product` and `Release`, and that is not tied to the `BacklogItem` instance's own recorded estimation of `Business-Priority`. Thus, `Product` and `Release` hold similar associations, namely, `ProductBacklogItem` and `ScheduledBacklogItem`, respectively.

Whiteboard Time

- Return to your list of large-cluster Aggregates and the two or more modified in a single transaction.

- Describe and diagram how you will break up the large clusters. Circle and note each of the true invariants inside each of the new small Aggregates.

- Describe and diagram how you will keep separate Aggregates eventually consistent.

This example demonstrates how to use eventual consistency in a single Bounded Context, but the same technique can also be applied in a distributed fashion as previously described.

Ask Whose Job It Is

Some domain scenarios can make it very challenging to determine whether transactional or eventual consistency should be used. Those who use DDD in a classic/traditional way may lean toward transactional consistency. Those who use CQRS may tend toward eventual consistency. But which is correct? Frankly, neither of those tendencies provides a domain-specific answer, only a technical preference. Is there a better way to break the tie?

Cowboy Logic

LB: "My son told me that he found on the Internet how to make my cows more fertile. I told him that's the bull's job."

Discussing this with Eric Evans revealed a very simple and sound guideline. When examining the use case (or story), ask whether it's the job of the user executing the use case to make the data consistent. If it is, try to make it transactionally consistent, but only by adhering to the other rules of Aggregates. If it is another user's job, or the job of the system, allow it to be eventually consistent. That bit of wisdom not only provides a convenient tie breaker, but it helps us gain a deeper understanding of our domain. It exposes the real system invariants: the ones that must be kept transactionally consistent. That understanding is much more valuable than defaulting to a technical leaning.

This is a great tip to add to the Aggregate Rules of Thumb. Since there are other forces to consider, it may not always lead to the final choice between transactional and eventual consistency but will usually provide deeper insight into the model. This guideline is used later in the chapter when the team revisits their Aggregate boundaries.

Reasons to Break the Rules

An experienced DDD practitioner may at times decide to persist changes to multiple Aggregate instances in a single transaction, but only with good reason. What might some reasons be? I discuss four reasons here. You may experience these and others.

Reason One: User Interface Convenience

Sometimes user interfaces, as a convenience, allow users to define the common characteristics of many things at once in order to create batches of them. Perhaps it happens frequently that team members want to create several backlog items as a batch. The user interface allows them to fill out all the common properties in one section, and then one by one the few distinguishing properties of each, eliminating repeated gestures. All of the new backlog items are then planned (created) at once:

```
public class ProductBacklogItemService ... {
    ...
    @Transactional
    public void planBatchOfProductBacklogItems(
        String aTenantId, String productId,
        BacklogItemDescription[] aDescriptions) {

        Product product =
            productRepository.productOfId(
                new TenantId(aTenantId),
                new ProductId(productId));
```

```
for (BacklogItemDescription desc : aDescriptions) {
    BacklogItem plannedBacklogItem =
        product.planBacklogItem(
            desc.summary(),
            desc.category(),
            BacklogItemType.valueOf(
                    desc.backlogItemType()),
            StoryPoints.valueOf(
                    desc.storyPoints())));

    backlogItemRepository.add(plannedBacklogItem);
    }
  }
  ...
}
```

Does this cause a problem with managing invariants? In this case, no, since it would not matter whether these were created one at a time or in batch. The objects being instantiated are full Aggregates, which maintain their own invariants. Thus, if creating a batch of Aggregate instances all at once is semantically no different from creating one at a time repeatedly, it represents one reason to break the rule of thumb with impunity.

Reason Two: Lack of Technical Mechanisms

Eventual consistency requires the use of some kind of out-of-band processing capability, such as messaging, timers, or background threads. What if the project you are working on has no provision for any such mechanism? While most of us would consider that strange, I have faced that very limitation. With no messaging mechanism, no background timers, and no other home-grown threading capabilities, what could be done?

If we aren't careful, this situation could lead us back toward designing large-cluster Aggregates. While that might make us feel as if we are adhering to the single transaction rule, as previously discussed it would also degrade performance and limit scalability. To avoid that, perhaps we could instead change the system's Aggregates altogether, forcing the model to solve our challenges. We've already considered the possibility that project specifications may be jealously guarded, leaving us little room for negotiating previously unimagined domain concepts. That's not really the DDD way, but sometimes it does happen. The conditions may allow for no reasonable way to alter the modeling circumstances in our favor. In such cases project dynamics may force us to modify two or more Aggregate instances in one transaction. However obvious this might seem, such a decision should not be made too hastily.

Cowboy Logic

AJ: "If you think that rules are made to be broken, you'd better know a good repairman."

Consider an additional factor that could further support diverging from the rule: *user-aggregate affinity*. Are the business workflows such that only one user would be focused on one set of Aggregate instances at any given time? Ensuring user-aggregate affinity makes the decision to alter multiple Aggregate instances in a single transaction more sound since it tends to prevent the violation of invariants and transactional collisions. Even with user-aggregate affinity, in rare situations users may face concurrency conflicts. Yet each Aggregate would still be protected from that by using optimistic concurrency. Anyway, concurrency conflicts can happen in any system, and even more frequently when user-aggregate affinity is not our ally. Besides, recovering from concurrency conflicts is straightforward when encountered at rare times. Thus, when our design is forced to, sometimes it works out well to modify multiple Aggregate instances in one transaction.

Reason Three: Global Transactions

Another influence considered is the effects of legacy technologies and enterprise policies. One such might be the need to strictly adhere to the use of global, two-phase commit transactions. This is one of those situations that may be impossible to push back on, at least in the short term.

Even if you must use a global transaction, you don't necessarily have to modify multiple Aggregate instances at once in your local Bounded Context. If you can avoid doing so, at least you can prevent transactional contention in your Core Domain and actually obey the rules of Aggregates as far as you are able. The downside to global transactions is that your system will probably never scale as it could if you were able to avoid two-phase commits and the immediate consistency that goes along with them.

Reason Four: Query Performance

There may be times when it's best to hold direct object references to other Aggregates. This could be used to ease Repository query performance issues. These must be weighed carefully in the light of potential size and overall performance trade-off implications. One example of breaking the rule of reference by identity is given later in the chapter.

Adhering to the Rules

You may experience user interface design decisions, technical limitations, stiff policies, or other factors in your enterprise environment that require you to make some compromises. Certainly we don't go in search of excuses to break the Aggregate Rules of Thumb. In the long run, adhering to the rules will benefit our projects. We'll have consistency where necessary, and support for optimally performing and highly scalable systems.

Gaining Insight through Discovery

With the rules of Aggregates in use, we'll see how adhering to them affects the design of the SaaSOvation Scrum model. We'll see how the project team rethinks their design again, applying newfound techniques. That effort leads to the discovery of new insights into the model. Their various ideas are tried and then superseded.

Rethinking the Design, Again

After the refactoring iteration that broke up the large-cluster `Product`, the `BacklogItem` now stands alone as its own Aggregate. It reflects the model presented in Figure 10.7. The team composed a collection of `Task` instances inside the `BacklogItem` Aggregate. Each `BacklogItem` has a globally unique identity, its `BacklogItemId`. All associations to other Aggregates are inferred through identities. That means its parent `Product`, the `Release` it is scheduled within, and the `Sprint` to which it is committed are referenced by identities. It seems fairly small.

   With the team now jazzed about designing small Aggregates, could they possibly overdo it in that direction?

Despite the good feeling coming out of that previous iteration, there was still some concern. For example, the `story` attribute allowed for a good deal of text. Teams developing agile stories won't write lengthy prose. Even so, there is an optional editor component that supports writing rich use case definitions. Those could be many thousands of bytes. It was worth considering the possible overhead.

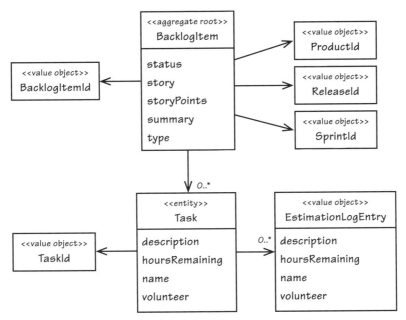

Figure 10.7   The fully composed `BacklogItem` Aggregate

Given this potential overhead and the errors already made in designing the large-cluster `Product` of Figures 10.1 and 10.3, the team was now on a mission to reduce the size of every Aggregate in the Bounded Context. Crucial questions arose. Was there a true invariant between `BacklogItem` and `Task` that this relationship must maintain? Or was this yet another case where the association could be further broken apart, with two separate Aggregates being safely formed? What would be the total cost of keeping the design as is?

A key to their making a proper determination lay in the Ubiquitous Language. Here is where an invariant was stated:

- When progress is made on a backlog item task, the team member will estimate task hours remaining.

- When a team member estimates that zero hours are remaining on a specific task, the backlog item checks all tasks for any remaining hours. If no hours remain on any tasks, the backlog item status is automatically changed to done.

- When a team member estimates that one or more hours are remaining on a specific task and the backlog item's status is already done, the status is automatically regressed.

This sure seemed like a true invariant. The backlog item's correct status is automatically adjusted and is completely dependent on the total number of hours remaining on all its tasks. If the total number of task hours and the backlog item status are to remain consistent, it seems as if Figure 10.7 does stipulate the correct Aggregate consistency boundary. However, the team should still determine what the current cluster could cost in terms of performance and scalability. That would be weighed against what they might save if the backlog item status could be eventually consistent with the total task hours remaining.

Some will see this as a classic opportunity to use eventual consistency, but we won't jump to that conclusion just yet. Let's analyze a transactional consistency approach, then investigate what could be accomplished using eventual consistency. We can then draw our own conclusion as to which approach is preferred.

Estimating Aggregate Cost

As Figure 10.7 shows, each `Task` holds a collection of `EstimationLogEntry` instances. These logs model the specific occasions when a team member enters a new estimate of hours remaining. In practical terms, how many `Task` elements will each `BacklogItem` hold, and how many `EstimationLogEntry` elements will a given `Task` hold? It's hard to say exactly. It's largely a measure of how complex any one task is and how long a sprint lasts. But some back-of-the-envelope (BOTE) calculations might help [Bentley].

Task hours are usually reestimated each day after a team member works on a given task. Let's say that most sprints are either two or three weeks in length. There will be longer sprints, but a two- to three-week time span is common enough. So let's select a number of days somewhere between ten and 15. Without being too precise, 12 days works well since there may actually be more two-week than three-week sprints.

Next, consider the number of hours assigned to each task. Remembering that tasks must be broken down into manageable units, we generally use a number of hours between four and 16. Normally if a task exceeds a 12-hour estimate, Scrum experts suggest breaking it down further. But using 12 hours as a first test makes it easier to simulate work evenly. We can say that tasks are worked on for one hour on each of the 12 days of the sprint. Doing so favors more complex tasks. So we'll figure 12 reestimations per task, assuming that each task starts out with 12 hours allocated to it.

The question remains: How many tasks would be required per backlog item? That too is a difficult question to answer. What if we thought in terms of there being two or three tasks required per **Layer (4)** or **Hexagonal Port-Adapter (4)** for a given feature slice? For example, we might count three for the **User Interface Layer (14)**, two for the **Application Layer (14)**, three for the Domain Layer, and three for the **Infrastructure Layer (14)**. That would bring us to 11 total tasks. It might be just right or a bit slim, but we've already erred on the side of numerous task estimations. Let's bump it up to 12 tasks per backlog item to be more liberal. With that we are allowing for 12 tasks, each with 12 estimation logs, or *144 total collected objects per backlog item*. While this may be more than the norm, it gives us a chunky BOTE calculation to work with.

There is another variable to be considered. If Scrum expert advice to define smaller tasks is commonly followed, it would change things somewhat. Doubling the number of tasks (24) and halving the number of estimation log entries (6) would still produce 144 total objects. However, it would cause more tasks to be loaded (24 rather than 12) during all estimation requests, consuming more memory on each. The team will try various combinations to see if there is any significant impact on their performance tests. But to start they will use 12 tasks of 12 hours each.

Common Usage Scenarios

Now it's important to consider common usage scenarios. How often will one user request need to load all 144 objects into memory at once? Would that ever happen? It seems not, but the team needs to check. If not, what's the likely high-end count of objects? Also, will there typically be multiclient usage that causes concurrency contention on backlog items? Let's see.

The following scenarios are based on the use of Hibernate for persistence. Also, each Entity type has its own optimistic concurrency version attribute. This is workable because the changing status invariant is managed on the `BacklogItem` Root Entity. When the status is automatically altered (to done or back to committed), the Root's version is bumped. Thus, changes to tasks can happen independently of each other and without impacting the Root each time one is modified, unless the result is a status change. (The following analysis could need to be revisited if using, for example, document-based storage, since the Root is effectively modified every time a collected part is modified.)

When a backlog item is first created, there are zero contained tasks. Normally it is not until sprint planning that tasks are defined. During that meeting tasks are identified by the team. As each one is called out, a team member adds it to the corresponding backlog item. There is no need for two team members to contend with each other for the Aggregate, as if racing to see who can enter new tasks more quickly. That would cause collision, and one of the two requests would fail (for the same reason simultaneously adding various parts to `Product` previously failed). However, the two team members would probably soon figure out how counterproductive their redundant work is.

If the developers learned that multiple users do indeed regularly want to add tasks together, it would change the analysis significantly. That understanding could immediately tip the scales in favor of breaking `BacklogItem` and `Task` into two separate Aggregates. On the other hand, this could also be a perfect time to tune the Hibernate mapping by setting the `optimistic-lock` option to `false`. Allowing tasks to grow simultaneously could make sense in this case, especially if they don't pose performance and scalability issues.

If tasks are at first estimated at zero hours and later updated to an accurate estimate, we still don't tend to experience concurrency contention, although this would add one additional estimation log entry, pushing our BOTE total to 13. Simultaneous use here does not change the backlog item status. Again, it advances to done only by going from greater than zero to zero hours, or regresses to committed if already done and hours are changed from zero to one or more—two uncommon events.

Will daily estimations cause problems? On day one of the sprint there are usually zero estimation logs on a given task of a backlog item. At the end of day one, each volunteer team member working on a task reduces the estimated hours by one. This adds a new estimation log to each task, but the backlog item's status remains unaffected. There is never contention on a task because just one team member adjusts its hours. It's not until day 12 that we reach the point of status transition. Still, as each of any 11 tasks is reduced to zero hours, the backlog item's status is not altered. It's only the very last estimation, the 144th on the 12th task, that causes automatic status transition to the done state.

This analysis led the team to an important realization. Even if they altered the usage scenarios, accelerating task completion by double (six days) or even mixing it up completely, it wouldn't change anything. It's always the final estimate that transitions the status, which modifies the Root. This seemed like a safe design, although memory overhead was still in question.

Memory Consumption

Now to address the memory consumption. Important here is that estimates are logged by date as Value Objects. If a team member reestimates any number of times on a single day, only the most recent estimate is retained. The latest Value of the same date replaces the previous one in the collection. At this point there's no requirement to track task estimation mistakes. There is the assumption that a task will never have more estimation log entries than the number of days the sprint is in progress. That assumption changes if tasks were defined one or more days before the sprint planning meeting, and hours were reestimated on any of those earlier days. There would be one extra log for each day that occurred.

What about the total number of tasks and estimates in memory for each reestimation? When using lazy loading for the tasks and estimation logs, we would have as many as 12 plus 12 collected objects in memory at one time per request. This is because all 12 tasks would be loaded when accessing that collection. To add the latest estimation log entry to one of those tasks, we'd have to load the collection of estimation log entries. That would be up to another 12 objects. In the end the Aggregate design requires one backlog item, 12 tasks, and 12 log entries, or 25 objects maximum total. That's not very many; it's a small Aggregate. Another factor is that the higher end of objects (for example, 25) is not reached until the last day of the sprint. During much of the sprint the Aggregate is even smaller.

Will this design cause performance problems because of lazy loads? Possibly, because it actually requires two lazy loads, one for the tasks and one for the estimation log entries for one of the tasks. The team will have to test to investigate the possible overhead of the multiple fetches.

There's another factor. Scrum enables teams to experiment in order to identify the right planning model for their practices. As explained by [Sutherland], experienced teams with a well-known velocity can estimate using story points rather than task hours. As they define each task, they can assign just one hour to each task. During the sprint they will reestimate only once per task, changing one hour to zero when the task is completed. As it pertains to Aggregate design, using story points reduces the total number of estimation logs per task to just one and almost eliminates memory overhead.

Later on, ProjectOvation developers will be able to analytically determine (on average) how many actual tasks and estimation log entries exist per backlog item by examining real production data.

The foregoing analysis was enough to motivate the team to test against their BOTE calculations. After inconclusive results, however, they decided that there were still too many variables for them to be confident that this design dealt well with their concerns. There were enough unknowns to consider an alternative design.

Exploring Another Alternative Design

Is there another design that could contribute to Aggregate boundaries more fitting to the usage scenarios?

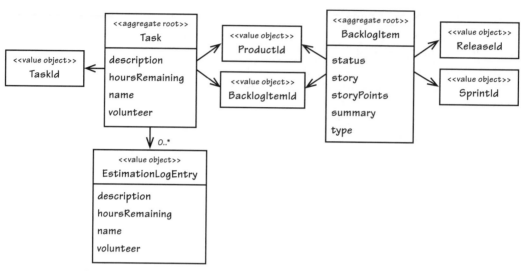

Figure 10.8   `BacklogItem` and `Task` modeled as separate Aggregates

To be thorough, the team wanted to think through what they would have to do to make `Task` an independent Aggregate, and if that would actually work to their benefit. What they envisioned is seen in Figure 10.8. Doing this would reduce part composition overhead by 12 objects and reduce lazy load overhead. In fact, this design gave them the option to eagerly load estimation log entries in all cases if that would perform best.

The developers agreed not to modify separate Aggregates, both the `Task` and the `BacklogItem`, in the same transaction. They had to determine if they could perform a necessary automatic status change within an acceptable time frame. They'd be weakening the invariant's consistency since the status couldn't be consistent by transaction. Would that be acceptable? They discussed the matter with the domain experts and learned that some delay between the final zero-hour estimate and the status being set to done, and vice versa, would be acceptable.

Implementing Eventual Consistency

It looks as if there could be a legitimate use of eventual consistency between separate Aggregates. Here is how it could work.

When a `Task` processes an `estimateHoursRemaining()` command, it publishes a corresponding Domain Event. It does that already, but the team would now leverage the Event to achieve eventual consistency. The Event is modeled with the following properties:

```
public class TaskHoursRemainingEstimated implements DomainEvent {
    private Date occurredOn;
    private TenantId tenantId;
    private BacklogItemId backlogItemId;
    private TaskId taskId;
    private int hoursRemaining;
    ...
}
```

A specialized subscriber would now listen for these and delegate to a Domain Service to coordinate the consistency processing. The Service would

- Use the `BacklogItemRepository` to retrieve the identified `BacklogItem`.
- Use the `TaskRepository` to retrieve all `Task` instances associated with the identified `BacklogItem`.
- Execute the `BacklogItem` command named `estimateTaskHoursRemaining()`, passing the Domain Event's `hoursRemaining` and the retrieved `Task` instances. The `BacklogItem` may transition its status depending on parameters.

The team should find a way to optimize this. The three-step design requires all `Task` instances to be loaded every time a reestimation occurs. When using our BOTE estimate and advancing continuously toward done, 143 out of 144 times that's unnecessary. This could be optimized pretty easily. Instead of using the Repository to get all `Task` instances, they could simply ask it for the sum of all `Task` hours as calculated by the database:

```
public class HibernateTaskRepository implements TaskRepository {
    ...
    public int totalBacklogItemTaskHoursRemaining(
            TenantId aTenantId,
            BacklogItemId aBacklogItemId) {

        Query query = session.createQuery(
            "select sum(task.hoursRemaining) from Task task "
            + "where task.tenantId = ? and "
            + "task.backlogItemId = ?");
        ...
    }
}
```

Eventual consistency complicates the user interface a bit. Unless the status transition can be achieved within a few hundred milliseconds, how would the user interface display the new state? Should they place business logic in the view to determine the current status? That would constitute a smart UI anti-pattern. Perhaps the view would just display the stale status and allow users to deal with the visual inconsistency. That could easily be perceived as a bug, or at least be very annoying.

The view could use a background Ajax polling request, but that could be quite inefficient. Since the view component could not easily determine exactly when checking for a status update is necessary, most Ajax pings would be unnecessary. Using our BOTE numbers, 143 of 144 reestimations would not cause the status update, which is a lot of redundant requests on the Web tier. With the right server-side support the clients could instead depend on Comet (aka Ajax Push). Although a nice challenge, that would introduce a completely new technology that the team had no experience using.

On the other hand, perhaps the best solution is the simplest. They could opt to place a visual cue on the screen that informs the user that the current status is uncertain. The view could suggest a time frame for checking back or refreshing. Alternatively, the changed status will probably show on the next rendered view. That's safe. The team would need to run some user acceptance tests, but it looked hopeful.

Is It the Team Member's Job?

One important question has thus far been completely overlooked: Whose job is it to bring a backlog item's status into consistency with all remaining task hours? Do team members using Scrum care if the parent backlog item's status transitions to done just as they set the last task's hours to zero? Will they always know they are working with the last task that has remaining hours? Perhaps they will and perhaps it is the responsibility of each team member to bring each backlog item to official completion.

On the other hand, what if there is another project stakeholder involved? For example, the product owner or some other person may desire to check the candidate backlog item for satisfactory completion. Maybe someone wants to use the feature on a continuous integration server first. If others are happy with the developers' claim of completion, they will manually mark the status as done. This certainly changes the game, indicating that neither transactional nor eventual consistency is necessary. Tasks could be split off from their parent backlog item because this new use case allows it. However, if it is really the team members who should cause the automatic transition to done, it would mean that tasks should probably be composed within the backlog item to allow for transactional consistency. Interestingly, there is no clear answer here either, which probably indicates that it should be an optional application preference.

Leaving tasks within their backlog item solves the consistency problem, and it's a modeling choice that can support both automatic and manual status transitions.

This valuable exercise uncovered a completely new aspect of the domain. It seems as if teams should be able to configure a workflow preference. They won't implement such a feature now, but they will promote it for further discussion. *Asking "whose job is it?" led them to a few vital perceptions about their domain.*

Next, one of the developers made a very practical suggestion as an alternative to this whole analysis. If they were chiefly concerned with the possible overhead of the `story` attribute, why not do something about that specifically? They could reduce the total storage capacity for the `story` and in addition create a new `useCaseDefinition` property. They could design it to lazy load, since much of the time it would never be used. Or they could even design it as a separate Aggregate, loading it only when needed. With that idea they realized this could be a good time to break the rule to reference external Aggregates only by identity. It seemed like a suitable modeling choice to use a direct object reference and declare its object-relational mapping so as to lazily load it. Perhaps that made sense.

Time for Decisions

This level of analysis can't continue all day. There needs to be a decision. It's not as if going in one direction now would negate the possibility of going another route later. Open-mindedness is now blocking pragmatism.

Based on all this analysis, currently the team was shying away from splitting `Task` from `BacklogItem`. They couldn't be certain that splitting it now was worth the extra effort, the risk of leaving the true invariant unprotected, or allowing users to experience a possible stale status in the view. The current Aggregate, as they understood it, was fairly small. Even if their common worst case loaded 50 objects rather than 25, it would still be a reasonably sized cluster. *For now they planned around the specialized use case definition holder.* Doing that was a quick win with lots of benefits. It added little risk, because it will work now, and it will also work in the future if they decide to split `Task` from `BacklogItem`.

The option to split it in two remained in their hip pocket just in case. After further experimentation with the current design, running it through performance and load tests, as well investigating user acceptance with an eventually consistent status, it will become clearer which approach is better. The BOTE numbers could prove to be wrong if in production the Aggregate is larger than imagined. If so, the team will no doubt split it into two.

If you were a member of the ProjectOvation team, which modeling option would you have chosen? Don't shy away from discovery sessions as demonstrated in the case study. That entire effort would require 30 minutes, and perhaps as much as 60 minutes at worst. It's well worth the time to gain deeper insight into your Core Domain.

Implementation

The more prominent factors summarized and highlighted here can make implementations more robust but should be investigated more thoroughly in **Entities (5)**, **Value Objects (6)**, **Domain Events (8)**, **Modules (9)**, **Factories (11)**, and **Repositories (12)**. Use this amalgamation as a point of reference.

Create a Root Entity with Unique Identity

Model one Entity as the Aggregate Root. Examples of Root Entities in the preceding modeling efforts are `Product`, `BacklogItem`, `Release`, and `Sprint`. Depending on the decision made to split `Task` from `BacklogItem`, `Task` may also be a Root.

The refined `Product` model finally led to the declaration of the following Root Entity:

```
public class Product extends ConcurrencySafeEntity  {
    private Set<ProductBacklogItem> backlogItems;
    private String description;
    private String name;
    private ProductDiscussion productDiscussion;
    private ProductId productId;
    private TenantId tenantId;
    ...
}
```

Class `ConcurrencySafeEntity` is a **Layer Supertype** [Fowler, P of EAA] used to manage surrogate identity and optimistic concurrency versioning, as explained in **Entities (5)**.

A `Set` of `ProductBacklogItem` instances not previously discussed has been, perhaps mysteriously, added to the Root. This is for a special purpose. It's not the same as the `BacklogItem` collection that was formerly composed here. It is for the purpose of maintaining a separate ordering of backlog items.

Each Root must be designed with a globally unique identity. The `Product` has been modeled with a Value type named `ProductId`. That type is the domain-specific identity, and it is different from the surrogate identity provided by `ConcurrencySafeEntity`. How a model-based identity is designed, allocated, and maintained is further explained in **Entities (5)**. The implementation of `ProductRepository` has `nextIdentity()` generate `ProductId` as a UUID:

```
public class HibernateProductRepository implements ProductRepository  {
    ...
    public ProductId nextIdentity() {
        return new ProductId(java.util.UUID.randomUUID()↵
.toString().toUpperCase());
    }
    ...
}
```

Using `nextIdentity()`, a client Application Service can instantiate a `Product` with its globally unique identity:

```
public class ProductService ... {
    ...
    @Transactional
    public String newProduct(
        String aTenantId, aProductName, aProductDescription) {
        Product product =
            new Product(
                new TenantId(aTenantId),
                this.productRepository.nextIdentity(),
                "My Product",
                "This is the description of my product.",
                new ProductDiscussion(
                        new DiscussionDescriptor(
                            DiscussionDescriptor.UNDEFINED_ID),
                        DiscussionAvailability.NOT_REQUESTED));

        this.productRepository.add(product);

        return product.productId().id();
    }
    ...
}
```

The Application Service uses `ProductRepository` to both generate an identity and then persist the new `Product` instance. It returns the plain `String` representation of the new `ProductId`.

Favor Value Object Parts

Choose to model a contained Aggregate part as a Value Object rather than an Entity whenever possible. A contained part that can be completely replaced, if its replacement does not cause significant overhead in the model or infrastructure, is the best candidate.

Our current `Product` model is designed with two simple attributes and three Value-typed properties. Both `description` and `name` are `String` attributes that can be completely replaced. The `productId` and `tenantId` Values are maintained as stable identities; that is, they are never changed after construction. They support reference by identity rather than direct to object. In fact, the referenced `Tenant` Aggregate is not even in the same Bounded Context and thus should be referenced only by identity. The `productDiscussion` is an eventually consistent Value-typed property. When the `Product` is first instantiated, the discussion may be requested but will not exist until sometime later. It must be created in the *Collaboration Context*. Once the creation has been completed in the other Bounded Context, the identity and status are set on the `Product`.

There are good reasons why `ProductBacklogItem` is modeled as an Entity rather than a Value. As discussed in **Value Objects (6)**, since the backing database is used via Hibernate, it must model collections of Values as database entities. Reordering any one of the elements could cause a significant number, even all, of the `ProductBacklogItem` instances to be deleted and replaced. That would tend to cause significant overhead in the infrastructure. As an Entity, it allows the `ordering` attribute to be changed across any and all collection elements as often as a product owner requires. However, if we were to switch from using Hibernate with MySQL to a key-value store, we could easily change `ProductBacklogItem` to be a Value type instead. When using a key-value or document store, Aggregate instances are typically serialized as one value representation for storage.

Using Law of Demeter and Tell, Don't Ask

Both **Law of Demeter** [Appleton, LoD] and **Tell, Don't Ask** [PragProg, TDA] are design principles that can be used when implementing Aggregates, both of which stress information hiding. Consider the high-level guiding principles to see how we can benefit:

- *Law of Demeter*: This guideline emphasizes the *principle of least knowledge*. Think of a *client* object and another object the client object uses to execute some system behavior; refer to the second object as a *server*. When the client object uses the server object, it should know as little as possible about the server's structure. The server's attributes and properties—its shape—should remain completely unknown to the client. The client can ask the server to perform a command that is declared on its surface interface. However, the client must not reach into the server, ask the server for some inner part, and then execute a command on the part. If the client needs a service that is rendered by the server's inner parts, the client must not be given access to the inner parts to request that behavior. The server should instead provide only a surface interface and, when invoked, delegate to the appropriate inner parts to fulfill its interface.

  Here's a basic summary of the Law of Demeter: Any given method on any object may invoke methods only on the following: (1) itself, (2) any parameters passed to it, (3) any object it instantiates, (4) self-contained part objects that it can directly access.

- *Tell, Don't Ask*: This guideline simply asserts that objects should be told what to do. The "Don't Ask" part of the guideline applies to the client as follows: A client object should not ask a server object for its contained parts, then make a decision based on the state it got, and then make the server object do something. Instead, the client should "Tell" a server what to do, using a command on the server's public interface. This guideline has very similar motivations as Law of Demeter, but Tell, Don't Ask may be easier to apply broadly.

Given these guidelines, let's see how we apply the two design principles to Product:

```
public class Product extends ConcurrencySafeEntity  {
    ...
    public void reorderFrom(BacklogItemId anId, int anOrdering) {
        for (ProductBacklogItem pbi : this.backlogItems()) {
            pbi.reorderFrom(anId, anOrdering);
        }
    }

    public Set<ProductBacklogItem> backlogItems() {
        return this.backlogItems;
    }
    ...
}
```

The `Product` requires clients to use its method `reorderFrom()` to execute a state-modifying command in its contained `backlogItems`. That is a good application of the guidelines. Yet, method `backlogItems()` is also public. Does this break the principles we are trying to follow by exposing `ProductBacklogItem` instances to clients? It does expose the collection, but clients may use those instances only to query information from them. Because of the limited public interface of `ProductBacklogItem`, clients cannot determine the shape of `Product` by deep navigation. Clients are given *least knowledge*. As far as clients are concerned, the returned collection instances may have been created only for the single operation and may represent no definite state of `Product`. Clients may never execute state-altering commands on the instances of `ProductBacklogItem`, as its implementation indicates:

```
public class ProductBacklogItem extends ConcurrencySafeEntity  {
    ...
    protected void reorderFrom(BacklogItemId anId, int anOrdering) {
        if (this.backlogItemId().equals(anId)) {
            this.setOrdering(anOrdering);
        } else if (this.ordering() >= anOrdering) {
            this.setOrdering(this.ordering() + 1);
        }
    }
    ...
}
```

Its only state-modifying behavior is declared as a hidden, protected method. Thus, clients can't see or reach this command. For all practical purposes, only `Product` can see it and execute the command. Clients may use only the `Product` public `reorderFrom()` command method. When invoked, the `Product` delegates to all its internal `ProductBacklogItem` instances to perform the inner modifications.

The implementation of `Product` limits knowledge about itself, is more easily tested, and is more maintainable, due to the application of these simple design principles.

You will need to weigh the competing forces between use of Law of Demeter and Tell, Don't Ask. Certainly the Law of Demeter approach is much more restrictive, disallowing all navigation into Aggregate parts beyond the Root. On the other hand, the use of Tell, Don't Ask allows for navigation beyond the Root but does stipulate that modification of the Aggregate state belongs to the Aggregate, not the client. You may thus find Tell, Don't Ask to be a more broadly applicable approach to Aggregate implementation.

Optimistic Concurrency

Next, we need to consider where to place the optimistic concurrency `version` attribute. When we contemplate the definition of Aggregate, it could seem safest to version only the Root Entity. The Root's version would be incremented every time a state-altering command is executed *anywhere inside* the Aggregate boundary, no matter how deep. Using the running example, `Product` would have a `version` attribute, and when any of its `describeAs()`, `initiateDiscussion()`, `rename()`, or `reorderFrom()` command methods are executed, the `version` would always be incremented. This would prevent any other client from simultaneously modifying any attributes or properties anywhere inside the same `Product`. Depending on the given Aggregate design, this may be difficult to manage, and even unnecessary.

Assuming we are using Hibernate, when the `Product name` or `description` is modified, or its `productDiscussion` is attached, the `version` is automatically incremented. That's a given, because those elements are directly held by the Root Entity. However, how do we see to it that the `Product version` is incremented when any of its `backlogItems` are reordered? Actually, we can't, or at least not automatically. Hibernate will not consider a modification to a `ProductBacklogItem` part instance as a modification to the `Product` itself. To solve this, perhaps we could just change the `Product` method `reorderFrom()`, dirtying some flag or just incrementing the `version` on our own:

```
public class Product extends ConcurrencySafeEntity {
    ...
    public void reorderFrom(BacklogItemId anId, int anOrdering) {
        for (ProductBacklogItem pbi : this.backlogItems()) {
            pbi.reorderFrom(anId, anOrdering);
        }
        this.version(this.version() + 1);
    }
    ...
}
```

One problem is that this code always dirties the `Product`, even when a reordering command actually has no effect. Further, this code leaks infrastructural concerns into the model, which is a less desirable domain modeling choice if it can be avoided. What else can be done?

Cowboy Logic

AJ: "I'm thinkin' that marriage is a sort of optimistic concurrency. When a man gets married, he is optimistic
that the gal will never change. And at the same time,
she's optimistic that he will."

Actually in the case of the `Product` and its `ProductBacklogItem` instances, it's possible that we don't need to modify the Root's version when any `backlogItems` are modified. Since the collected instances are themselves Entities, they can carry their own optimistic concurrency `version`. If two clients reorder any of the same `ProductBacklogItem` instances, the last client to commit changes will fail. Admittedly, overlapping reordering would rarely if ever happen, because it's usually only the product owner who reorders the product backlog items.

Versioning all Entity parts doesn't work in every case. Sometimes the only way to protect an invariant is to modify the Root version. This can be accomplished more easily if we can modify a legitimate property on the Root. In this case, the Root's property would always be modified in response to a deeper part modification, which in turn causes Hibernate to increment the Root's `version`. Recall that this approach was described previously to model the status change on `BacklogItem` when all of its `Task` instances have been transitioned to zero hours remaining.

However, that approach may not be possible in all cases. If not, we may be tempted to resort to using hooks provided by the persistence mechanism to manually dirty the Root when Hibernate indicates a part has been modified. This becomes problematic. It can usually be made to work only by maintaining bidirectional associations between child parts and the parent Root. The bidirectional associations allow navigation from a child back to the Root when Hibernate sends a life cycle event to a specialized listener. Not to be forgotten, though, is that [Evans] generally discourages bidirectional associations in most cases. This is especially so if they must be maintained only to deal with optimistic concurrency, which is an infrastructural concern.

Although we don't want infrastructural concerns to drive modeling decisions, we may be motivated to travel a less painful route. When modifying the Root becomes very difficult and costly, it could be a strong indication that we need to break down our Aggregates to just a Root Entity, containing only simple attributes and Value-typed properties. When our Aggregates consist of only a Root Entity, the Root is always modified when any part is modified.

Finally, it must be acknowledged that the preceding scenarios are not a problem when an entire Aggregate is persisted as one value and the value itself prevents concurrency conflict. This approach can be leveraged when using MongoDB, Riak, Oracle's Coherence distributed grid, or VMware's GemFire. For example, when an Aggregate Root implements the Coherence `Versionable` interface and its Repository uses the `VersionedPut` entry processor, the Root will always be the single object used for concurrency conflict detection. Other key-value stores may provide similar conveniences.

Avoid Dependency Injection

Dependency injection of a Repository or Domain Service into an Aggregate should generally be viewed as harmful. The motivation may be to look up a dependent object instance from inside the Aggregate. The dependent object could be another Aggregate, or a number of them. As stated earlier under "Rule: Reference Other Aggregates by Identity," preferably dependent objects are looked up before an Aggregate command method is invoked, and passed in to it. The use of Disconnected Domain Model is generally a less favorable approach.

Additionally, in a very high-traffic, high-volume, high-performance domain, with heavily taxed memory and garbage collection cycles, think of the potential overhead of injecting Repositories and Domain Service instances into Aggregates. How many extra object references would that require? Some may contend that it's not enough to tax their operational environment, but theirs is probably not the kind of domain being described here. Still, take great care not to add unnecessary overhead that could be easily avoided by using other design principles, such as looking up dependencies before an Aggregate command method is invoked, and passing them in to it.

This is only meant to warn against injecting Repositories and Domain Services into Aggregate instances. Of course, dependency injection is quite suitable for many other design situations. For example, it could be quite useful to inject Repository and Domain Service references into Application Services.

Wrap-Up

We've examined how crucial it is to follow the Aggregate Rules of Thumb when designing Aggregates.

- You experienced the negative consequences of modeling large-cluster Aggregates.

- You learned to model true invariants in consistency boundaries.

- You considered the advantages of designing small Aggregates.

- You now know why you should favor referencing other Aggregates by identity.

- You discovered the importance of using eventual consistency outside the Aggregate boundary.

- You saw various implementation techniques, including how you might use Tell, Don't Ask and Law of Demeter.

If we adhere to the rules, we'll have consistency where necessary and support optimally performing and highly scalable systems, all while capturing the Ubiquitous Language of our business domain in a carefully crafted model.

Chapter 11

Factories

I can't abide ugliness in factories! In we go, then!
But do be careful, my dear children!
Don't lose your heads! Don't get overexcited!
Keep very calm!
—*Willy Wonka*

Of all the patterns used in DDD, **Factory** is probably one of the better known. Highly publicized in *Design Patterns* [Gamma et al.] are **Abstract Factory, Factory Method**, and **Builder**. I won't in any way attempt to overshadow the advice given there, or that provided by [Evans]. The focus here is to provide examples of how you can use Factories in the domain model.

Road Map to This Chapter

- Learn why the use of Factories can produce expressive models that adhere to the **Ubiquitous Language (1)**.
- See how SaaSOvation uses Factory Methods as **Aggregate (10)** behaviors.
- Consider how to use Factory Methods to create Aggregate instances of other types.
- Learn how Domain Services can be designed as Factories while interacting with other **Bounded Contexts (2)** and translating foreign objects to local types.

Factories in the Domain Model

Consider the primary motivations for using Factories:

> Shift the responsibility for creating instances of complex objects and AGGRE-GATES to a separate object, which may itself have no responsibility in the domain model but is still part of the domain design. Provide an interface that encapsulates all complex assembly and does not require the client to reference the concrete classes of the objects being instantiated. Create entire AGGREGATES as a piece, enforcing their invariants. [Evans, p. 138]

A Factory may or may not have additional responsibilities in the domain model other than object creation. An object that has the purpose only of instantiating a specific Aggregate type will have no other responsibilities and will not even be considered a first-class citizen of the model. It is only a Factory. An Aggregate Root that provides a Factory Method for producing instances of another Aggregate type (or inner parts) will have the primary responsibility of providing its main Aggregate behavior, the Factory Method being just one of those.

The latter is what tends to occur more frequently in my examples. The Aggregates I demonstrate have mostly non-complex construction. Yet, some important details of Aggregate construction must be protected against the production of wrong state. Consider the demands of a multitenancy environment. If an Aggregate instance were created under the wrong tenant, giving it the wrong `TenantId`, it could be disastrous. There is a high degree of accountability to keep all data of each tenant segregated and secure from all others. Placing a carefully designed Factory Method on specific Aggregate Roots can ensure that tenancy and other association identities are created correctly. It simplifies clients, requiring them to pass only basic parameters, often **Value Objects (6)** only, by hiding the construction details from them.

Further, Factory Methods on Aggregates allow you to express the Ubiquitous Language in ways not possible through constructors alone. When the behavioral method name is expressive with respect to the Ubiquitous Language, you've made an additional powerful case for using a Factory Method.

Cowboy Logic

LB: "I used to work in a fire hydrant factory. You couldn't park anywhere near the place."

The sample Bounded Contexts do in some cases require complex construction. These situations occur when **Integrating Bounded Contexts (13)**. At those times **Services (7)** function as Factories producing Aggregates or Value Objects of various types.

One case where you would find an Abstract Factory of great benefit is when creating objects of different types in a class hierarchy, which is a classic use. The client is required to pass in only some basic parameters from which the Factory can determine the concrete type that must be created. I don't have any domain-specific class hierarchies among my examples, so I won't be demonstrating this usage here. If you see class hierarchies in your future domain modeling efforts, I suggest that you look at the related discussion under **Repositories (12)**. It will help you enter such an effort with eyes wide open. If you decide to use class hierarchies in your design, be prepared for the potential for pain that could result.

Factory Method on Aggregate Root

Throughout the three sample Bounded Contexts there are Factory sites on Aggregate Root Entities, of which Table 11.1 provides a summary.

I discuss the `Product` Factory Methods under **Aggregates (10)**. For example, its method `planBacklogItem()` creates a new `BacklogItem`, which is an Aggregate that is subsequently returned to the client.

To demonstrate the design of Factory Methods, let's look at the three in the *Collaboration Context*.

Table 11.1   Sites of Factory Methods on Aggregates

Bounded Context	Aggregate	Factory Method
Identity and Access Context	Tenant	offerRegistrationInvitation()
		provisionGroup()
		provisionRole()
		registerUser()
Collaboration Context	Calendar	scheduleCalendarEntry()
	Forum	startDiscussion()
	Discussion	post()
Agile PM Context	Product	planBacklogItem()
		scheduleRelease()
		scheduleSprint()

Creating CalendarEntry Instances

Let's look at the design. The Factory we are considering now has its site on Calendar and is used to create CalendarEntry instances. The Collab-Ovation team takes us through the implementation.

Here's a test developed to demonstrate how the Calendar Factory Method should be used:

```
public class CalendarTest extends DomainTest {
    private CalendarEntry calendarEntry;
    private CalendarEntryId calendarEntryId;
    ...
    public void testCreateCalendarEntry() throws Exception {

        Calendar calendar = this.calendarFixture();

        DomainRegistry.calendarRepository().add(calendar);

        DomainEventPublisher
            .instance()
            .subscribe(
                new DomainEventSubscriber<CalendarEntryScheduled>() {
                public void handleEvent(
                        CalendarEntryScheduled aDomainEvent) {
                    calendarEntryId = aDomainEvent.calendarEntryId();
                }
                public Class<CalendarEntryScheduled>
                        subscribedToEventType() {
                    return CalendarEntryScheduled.class;
                }
            });

        calendarEntry =
            calendar.scheduleCalendarEntry(
                    DomainRegistry
                        .calendarEntryRepository()
                        .nextIdentity()
```

```
                        new Owner(
                            "jdoe",
                            "John Doe",
                            "jdoe@lastnamedoe.org"),
                        "Sprint Planning",
                        "Plan sprint for first half of April 2012.",
                        this.tomorrowOneHourTimeSpanFixture(),
                        this.oneHourBeforeAlarmFixture(),
                        this.weeklyRepetitionFixture(),
                        "Team Room",
                        new TreeSet<Invitee>(0));

        DomainRegistry.calendarEntryRepository().add(calendarEntry);

        assertNotNull(calendarEntryId);
        assertNotNull(calendarEntry);
        ...
    }
}
```

Nine parameters are passed in to `scheduleCalendarEntry()`. Yet, as seen later, the `CalendarEntry` constructor requires a total of 11 parameters. We'll consider the benefits of this in a moment. After a new `CalendarEntry` is successfully created, the client must add it to its Repository. Failing to do so will release the new instance to be swept by the garbage collector.

The first assertion demonstrates that the `CalendarEntryId` published with the Event must be non-`null`, confirming that the Event was successfully published. It's not that the direct client of `Calendar` will actually subscribe to that Event, but the test demonstrates that the Event `CalendarEntryScheduled` is in fact published.

The new `CalendarEntry` instance must also be non-`null`. We could make additional assertions, but the two just shown are most important to documenting the Factory Method design and the client's use of it.

Now let's take a look at the implementation of the Factory Method:

```
package com.saasovation.collaboration.domain.model.calendar;

public class Calendar extends Entity  {
    ...
    public CalendarEntry scheduleCalendarEntry(
            CalendarEntryId aCalendarEntryId,
            Owner anOwner,
            String aSubject,
            String aDescription,
            TimeSpan aTimeSpan,
            Alarm anAlarm,
            Repetition aRepetition,
            String aLocation,
            Set<Invitee> anInvitees) {
```

```
        CalendarEntry calendarEntry =
            new CalendarEntry(
                    this.tenant(),
                    this.calendarId(),
                    aCalendarEntryId,
                    anOwner,
                    aSubject,
                    aDescription,
                    aTimeSpan,
                    anAlarm,
                    aRepetition,
                    aLocation,
                    anInvitees);

        DomainEventPublisher
            .instance()
            .publish(new CalendarEntryScheduled(...));

        return calendarEntry;
    }
    ...
}
```

The `Calendar` instantiates a new Aggregate, namely, `CalendarEntry`. The new instance is returned to the client following the Event `CalendarEntryScheduled` being published. (The details of the Event published are not significant to this discussion.) You may note the lack of guards at the top of this method. It is unnecessary to guard the Factory Method itself since the constructors of each of the Value parameters and the `CalendarEntry` constructor, as well as the setter methods that the constructor self-delegates to, provide all the needed guards. (See **Entities (5)** for more details on self-delegation and guards.) If you'd like to be doubly cautious, you could add guards here as well.

The team designed the method name to adhere to the Ubiquitous Language. Domain experts, along with the rest of the team, discussed the following scenario:

Calendars schedule calendar entries.

If our design were to support only a public constructor on `CalendarEntry`, it would reduce the expressiveness of the model and we would not be able to explicitly model that part of the Language of the domain. Using this design requires the full Aggregate constructor to be hidden from

clients. We declare the constructor with protected scope, which forces clients to make use of the `scheduleCalendarEntry()` Factory Method on `Calendar`:

```
public class CalendarEntry extends Entity  {
    ...
    protected CalendarEntry(
        Tenant aTenant, CalendarId aCalendarId,
        CalendarEntryId aCalendarEntryId, Owner anOwner,
        String aSubject, String aDescription, TimeSpan aTimeSpan,
        Alarm anAlarm, Repetition aRepetition, String aLocation,
        Set<Invitee> anInvitees) {
        ...
    }
    ...
}
```

While having the upside of careful construction, the lowered usage burden on clients, and an expressive model, using the `Calendar` Factory Method does have the downside of a bit more performance overhead. As is the case with any such Aggregate Factory Method, the `Calendar` will have to be acquired from its persistence store before it can be used to create the `CalendarEntry`. This extra hit may be well worth it, but as the traffic in this Bounded Context increases, the team will have to weigh the consequences carefully.

Germane to the benefits of using Factories is that two of the `CalendarEntry` constructor parameters are not passed in by clients. Given that there are 11 required constructor parameters, this design unburdens clients, requiring them to supply only nine. Most of the nine required parameters are fairly easily created by clients. (Admittedly the `Set` of `Invitee` instances is more involved, but that's not the fault of the Factory Method. The team should think in terms of designing a facility to more conveniently provide this `Set`, which may be pointing toward the creation of a dedicated Factory.)

Still, the `Tenant` and associated `CalendarId` are strictly provided only by the Factory Method. This is where we guarantee that `CalendarEntry` instances are created only for the correct `Tenant` and in association with the correct `Calendar`.

Let's now consider one more example from the *Collaboration Context*.

Creating `Discussion` Instances

Look at the Factory Method on `Forum`. It has the same motivation and very similar implementation as the one on `Calendar`, so there is no need to dive into great detail on it. Yet, there is an additional advantage of using the Factory Method here, as the team demonstrates.

Consider the Language-specific `startDiscussion()` Factory Method on `Forum`:

```
package com.saasovation.collaboration.domain.model.forum;

public class Forum extends Entity  {
    ...
    public Discussion startDiscussion(
            DiscussionId aDiscussionId,
            Author anAuthor,
            String aSubject) {
        if (this.isClosed()) {
            throw new IllegalStateException("Forum is closed.");
        }

        Discussion discussion = new Discussion(
                this.tenant(),
                this.forumId(),
                aDiscussionId,
                anAuthor,
                aSubject);

        DomainEventPublisher
            .instance()
            .publish(new DiscussionStarted(...));

        return discussion;
    }
    ...
}
```

Besides creating a `Discussion`, this Factory Method also guards against creating one if the `Forum` is closed. The `Forum` supplies the `Tenant` and associated `ForumId`. Thus, only three of five parameters required to instantiate a new `Discussion` must be supplied by the client.

This Factory Method also expresses the Ubiquitous Language of the *Collaboration Context*. The team used `Forum`'s `startDiscussion()` to design in just what the domain experts said it should do:

Authors start discussions on forums.

This allows the client to be just this simple:

```
Discussion discussion = agilePmForum.startDiscussion(
    this.discussionRepository.nextIdentity(),
    new Author("jdoe", "John Doe", "jdoe@saasovation.com"),
    "Dealing with Aggregate Concurrency Issues");
```

```
assertNotNull(discussion);
...
this.discussionRepository.add(discussion);
```

Simple, indeed, which is always a goal of a domain modeler.

This Factory Method pattern can repeat as often as necessary. I think it has been duly demonstrated how effectively Factory Methods on Aggregates can be used to express the Language in Context, reduce the burden on clients when creating new Aggregate instances, and ensure instantiations with correct state.

Factory on Service

Since much of how I use Services as Factories is related to **Integrating Bounded Contexts (13)**, I leave the bulk of the discussion to that chapter. In that chapter my focus is more on integrating with **Anti-Corruption Layer (3)**, **Published Language (3)**, and **Open Host Service (3)**. Here I want to emphasize the Factory itself and how a Service can be designed as one.

The team now provides another example from the *Collaboration Context*. It's a Factory in the form of `CollaboratorService`, producing `Collaborator` instances from tenant and user identity:

```
package com.saasovation.collaboration.domain.model.collaborator;

import com.saasovation.collaboration.domain.model.tenant.Tenant;

public interface CollaboratorService {

    public Author authorFrom(Tenant aTenant, String anIdentity);

    public Creator creatorFrom(Tenant aTenant, String anIdentity);

    public Moderator moderatorFrom(Tenant aTenant, String anIdentity);

    public Owner ownerFrom(Tenant aTenant, String anIdentity);
```

```
public Participant participantFrom(
        Tenant aTenant,
        String anIdentity);
}
```

This Service provides object translation from the *Identity and Access Context* to the *Collaboration Context*. As shown in **Bounded Contexts (2)**, the CollabOvation team doesn't speak of users when discussing collaboration. It is more to the point that humans in the collaborative media domain are authors, creators, moderators, owners, and participants. To accomplish this, the team will need to interact with the *Identity and Access Context* behind a Service and transform user and role objects from that model into corresponding collaborator objects of their own model's Context.

Since new objects that are derived from the abstract base `Collaborator` are created by the Service, it actually functions as a Factory. Taking a look at one of the interface method implementations reveals some of the detail involved:

```
package com.saasovation.collaboration.infrastructure.services;

public class UserRoleToCollaboratorService
        implements CollaboratorService {

    public UserRoleToCollaboratorService() {
        super();
    }

    @Override
    public Author authorFrom(Tenant aTenant, String anIdentity) {
        return
            (Author)
                UserInRoleAdapter
                    .newInstance()
                    .toCollaborator(
                            aTenant,
                            anIdentity,
                            "Author",
                            Author.class);
    }
    ...
}
```

Because it is a technical implementation, the class is housed in a **Module (9)** in the Infrastructure Layer.

The implementation hitches to the `UserInRoleAdapter` to morph a `Tenant` and an identity—the user's username—into an instance of class `Author`. This **Adapter** [Gamma et al.] interacts with the Open Host Service of the *Identity and Access Context* to confirm that the given user is in the role named Author. If that is true, the Adapter delegates to class `CollaboratorTranslator` to translate the Published

Language integration response to an instance of class `Author` in the local model. The `Author`, as well as the other `Collaborator` subclasses, is a simple Value Object:

```
package com.saasovation.collaboration.domain.model.collaborator;

public class Author extends Collaborator  {
    ...
}
```

Other than constructors, `equals()`, `hashCode()`, and `toString()`, each of the subclasses receives all state and behavior from `Collaborator`:

```
package com.saasovation.collaboration.domain.model.collaborator;

public abstract class Collaborator implements Serializable  {
    private String emailAddress;
    private String identity;
    private String name;

    public Collaborator(
            String anIdentity,
            String aName,
            String anEmailAddress) {
        super();
        this.setEmailAddress(anEmailAddress);
        this.setIdentity(anIdentity);
        this.setName(aName);
    }
    ...
}
```

The *Collaboration Context* uses the username as the `Collaborator` identity attribute. The `emailAddress` and `name` are simple `String` instances. In this model the team has chosen to keep each of these concepts as simple as possible. The user's name, for example, is kept as the full name in text. We've managed to separate the life cycles and conceptual terminologies from the two Bounded Contexts by means of a Service-Based Factory.

There is a measure of complexity in `UserInRoleAdapter` and `Collaborator-Translator`. In a nutshell the `UserInRoleAdapter` is responsible only for communicating with the foreign Context. The `CollaboratorTranslator` is responsible only for translation that results in creation. See **Integrating Bounded Contexts (13)** for details.

Wrap-Up

We examined the reasons for using Factories in DDD and how they often fit into the model.

- You now understand why the use of Factories can produce expressive models that more closely adhere to the Ubiquitous Language in context.

- You've seen two different Factory Methods implemented as Aggregate behaviors.

- This helped you learn how to use Factory Methods to create Aggregate instances of other types, all while ensuring the correct production and use of sensitive data.

- You also learned how Domain Services can be designed as Factories, even interacting with other Bounded Contexts and translating foreign objects to local types.

Next, we'll take a look at how Repositories can be designed for two primary styles of persistence, along with other implementation choices that must be considered.

Chapter 12

Repositories

Your eyes are the same color as my storage unit.
—Overheard at a redneck bar

A repository commonly refers to a storage location, usually considered a place of safety or preservation of the items stored in it. When you store something in a repository and later return to retrieve it, you expect that it will be in the same state as it was in when you put it there. At some point you may choose to remove the stored item from the repository.

This basic set of principles applies to a DDD **Repository**. Placing an **Aggregate (10)** instance in its corresponding Repository, and later using that Repository to retrieve the same instance, yields the expected whole object. If you alter a preexisting Aggregate instance that you retrieve from the Repository, its changes will be persisted. If you remove the instance from the Repository, you will be unable to retrieve it from that point forward.

> For each type of object that needs global access, create an object that can provide the illusion of an in-memory collection of all objects of that type. Set up access through a well-known global interface. Provide methods to add and remove objects. . . . Provide methods that select objects based on some criteria and return fully instantiated objects or collections of objects whose attribute values meet the criteria. . . . Provide repositories only for aggregates. . . . [Evans, p. 151]

These collection-like objects are all about persistence. Every persistent Aggregate type will have a Repository. Generally speaking, there is a one-to-one relationship between an Aggregate type and a Repository. However, sometimes when two or more Aggregate types share an object hierarchy, the types may share a single Repository. Both of these approaches are discussed in this chapter.

Road Map to This Chapter

- Learn about the two different kinds of Repositories and why to use one or the other.
- See how to implement Repositories for Hibernate, TopLink, Coherence, and MongoDB.

continues

- Understand why you might need additional behavior on a Repository's interface. Consider how transactions play into the use of Repositories.
- Become familiar with the challenges of designing Repositories for type hierarchies.
- Look at some fundamental differences between Repositories and **Data Access Objects** [Crupi et al.].
- Consider some ways to test Repositories and how to test using Repositories.

Strictly speaking, only Aggregates have Repositories. If you are not using Aggregates in a given **Bounded Context (2)**, the Repository pattern may be less useful. If you are retrieving and using **Entities (5)** directly in an ad hoc fashion rather than crafting Aggregate transactional boundaries, you may prefer to avoid Repositories. However, those less concerned with the tenets of DDD, only using some of its patterns in a technical way, may prefer Repositories over Data Access Objects. Still others will think that direct use of a persistence mechanism's **Session** or **Unit of Work** [P of EAA] makes more sense. This is not to suggest that you should avoid the use of Aggregates. In fact, the opposite is true. Still, it is an option that some will employ.

In my estimation there are two kinds of Repository designs, a *collection-oriented* design and a *persistence-oriented* design. There are circumstances under which a collection-oriented design will work for you, and circumstances when it is best to use a persistence-oriented design. I first discuss when to use and how to create a collection-oriented Repository and follow that with a treatment of persistence-oriented ones.

Collection-Oriented Repositories

We can consider a collection-oriented design a traditional approach because it adheres to the basic ideas presented in the original DDD pattern. These very closely mimic a collection, simulating at least some of its standard interface. Here you design a Repository interface that does not hint in any way that there is an underlying persistence mechanism, avoiding any notion of saving or persisting data to a store.

Because this design approach requires some specific capabilities of the underlying persistence mechanism, it's possible that it won't work for you. If your persistence mechanism prevents or hampers your ability to design with a collection perspective, see the following subsection. I address the conditions under which I think collection-oriented design works best. To do so I need to establish some foundational background.

Consider how a standard collection works. In Java, C#, or most any other object-oriented language, objects are added to a collection, and they remain in the collection until they are removed. There is no need to do anything special to get the collection to recognize changes to the objects that it contains, other than to ask the collection to hand you a reference to a specific object and then ask that object to do something to itself, which modifies its own state. The same object is still held by the collection, and now the state of that contained object is different from what it was prior to the modification.

Let's look at this a bit closer by stepping through a few examples. Using `java.util.Collection` as an example, here, in part, is the standard interface:

```
package java.util;

public interface Collection ... {
    public boolean add(Object o);
    public boolean addAll(Collection c);
    public boolean remove(Object o);
    public boolean removeAll(Collection c);
    ...
}
```

If we want to add an object to a collection, we use `add()`. If we want to remove the same object, we pass its reference to `remove()`. The following test assumes a newly instantiated collection of some kind that can contain `Calendar` instances:

```
assertTrue(calendarCollection.add(calendar));

assertEquals(1, calendarCollection.size());

assertTrue(calendarCollection.remove(calendar));

assertEquals(0, calendarCollection.size());
```

Simple enough. One special kind of collection, `java.util.Set`, and its implementing `java.util.HashSet`, provides the kind of collection that a Repository mimics. Every object added to a `Set` must be unique. If you attempt to add an object already contained by the `Set`, it will not be added because it is already contained. Thus, you never need to add the same object twice, as if adding it again somehow saves changes that you have asked the object to make to itself. The following test assertions prove that adding the same object more than once has no effect, positive or negative:

```
Set<Calendar> calendarSet = new HashSet<Calendar>();

assertTrue(calendarSet.add(calendar));

assertEquals(1, calendarSet.size());

assertFalse(calendarSet.add(calendar));

assertEquals(1, calendarSet.size());
```

All of these assertions succeed because, although the same `Calendar` instance is added twice, the second attempt to add the object does not change the state of the `Set`. The same goes for a Repository designed using a collection orientation. If we add the Aggregate instance `calendar` to a `CalendarRepository` designed with a collection orientation, adding `calendar` a second time is benign. Each Aggregate has a globally unique identity that is associated with the **Root Entity (5, 10)**. It is this unique identity that allows the `Set`-like Repository to prevent adding the same Aggregate instances more than once.

It is important to understand the kind of collection—a `Set`—that a Repository should mimic. Whatever the backing implementation with a specific persistence mechanism, you must not allow instances of the same object to be added twice.

Another key takeaway is that you don't need to "re-save" modified objects already held by the Repository. Consider again how you'd go about modifying an object that is held by a collection. It's really simple, actually. You'd just retrieve from the collection the reference to the object you desire to modify, and then ask the object to execute some state-transitioning behavior by invoking a command method.

> **Take-aways for Collection-Oriented Repositories**
>
> A Repository should mimic a `Set` collection. Whatever the backing implementation with a specific persistence mechanism, you must not allow instances of the same object to be added twice. Also, when retrieving objects from a Repository and modifying them, you don't need to "re-save" them to the Repository.

To illustrate, say we extend (subclass) a standard `java.util.HashSet` and create a method on the new type that allows us to find a specific object instance by unique identity. We'll give the extending class a name that identifies it as a Repository, but it's just an in-memory `HashSet`:

```
public class CalendarRepository extends HashSet {
    private Set<CalendarId, Calendar> calendars;
```

```
    public CalendarRepository() {
        this.calendars = new HashSet<CalendarId, Calendar>();
    }

    public void add(Calendar aCalendar) {
        this.calendars.add(aCalendar.calendarId(), aCalendar);
    }

    public Calendar findCalendar(CalendarId aCalendarId) {
        return this.calendars.get(aCalendarId);
    }
}
```

We don't normally subclass `HashSet` in order to create a typical Repository. Here we do so just for the sake of example. So, back to the example. Now we can add a `Calendar` instance to the specialized `Set` and later find the instance and ask it to modify itself:

```
CalendarId calendarId = new CalendarId(...);
Calendar calendar =
    new Calendar(calendarId, "Project Calendar", ...);
CalendarRepository calendarRepository = new CalendarRepository();
calendarRepository.add(calendar);

// later ...

Calendar calendarToRename =
    calendarRepository.findCalendar(calendarId);

calendarToRename.rename("CollabOvation Project Calendar");

// even later still ...

Calendar calendarThatWasRenamed =
    calendarRepository.findCalendar(calendarId);

assertEquals("CollabOvation Project Calendar",
    calendarThatWasRenamed.name());
```

Note that the instance of `Calendar`, referenced by `calendarToRename`, is modified by asking it to rename itself. Much later, after the rename is performed, the name is still what it was changed to. This was accomplished without asking the `HashSet` subclass `CalendarRepository` to save changes to the `Calendar` instance, which wouldn't make any sense. `CalendarRepository` doesn't have a `save()` method because there is no need for one. There is no reason to save changes to the `Calendar` instance that `calendarToRename` references, because the collection still holds a reference to the object being modified, and the modifications are made directly on that object.

The bottom line, then, is that a traditional collection-oriented Repository truly mimics a collection in that no parts of the persistence mechanisms are surfaced to the client by its public interface. Therefore, it is our goal to design and implement such a collection-oriented Repository with the characteristics demonstrated by a `HashSet`, but with a persistent data store instead.

As you can imagine, this requires some specific capabilities of the backing persistence mechanism. The persistence mechanism must in some way support the ability to implicitly track changes made to each persistent object that it manages. This may be accomplished in various ways, including the following two:

1. **Implicit Copy-on-Read** [Keith & Stafford]: The persistence mechanism implicitly copies each persistent object on read when it is reconstituted from the data store and compares its private copy to the client's copy on commit. Stepping through this, when you ask the persistence mechanism to read an object from the data store, it does so and immediately makes a copy of the entire object (minus any lazy-loaded parts, which also may be loaded and copied later). When a transaction created through the persistence mechanism is committed, the persistence mechanism checks for modifications on the copied objects it has loaded (or reattached to) by comparing them. All objects with detected changes are flushed to the data store.

2. **Implicit Copy-on-Write** [Keith & Stafford]: The persistence mechanism manages all loaded persistent objects through a proxy. As each object is loaded from the data store, a thin proxy is created and handed to the client. Clients unknowingly invoke behavior on the proxy object, which reflects the behavior onto the real object. When the proxy first receives a method invocation, it makes a copy of the managed object. The proxy tracks changes made to the state of the managed object and marks it dirty. When a transaction created through the persistence mechanism is committed, it checks for dirty objects and all such are flushed to the data store.

The advantages and differences between these approaches may vary, and if your system stands to suffer the negative consequences of choosing one over the other, you should measure them carefully. Of course, you can decide to go with your favorite rather than doing your homework, but that may not be the safest decision.

Still, the overall advantage to either of these approaches is that persistent object changes are tracked implicitly, requiring no explicit client knowledge or intervention to make changes known to the persistence mechanism. The bottom line here is that using a persistence mechanism like this, such as Hibernate, *allows you to employ a traditional, collection-oriented* Repository.

That said, it is possible even if you have the latitude to use such an implicit-copying change-tracking persistence mechanism, such as Hibernate, that it may be undesirable or inappropriate to use. If your requirements demand a very high-performance domain with many, many objects in memory at any given time, this sort of mechanism is going to add gratuitous overhead, in both memory and execution. You will have to consider and decide carefully whether or not this works for you. Certainly there are many domains in which Hibernate does work. So don't take my call to attention as an attempt to declare a taboo. The use of any tool should be with full awareness of trade-offs.

Cowboy Logic

LB: "When my dog got a case of worms, the veterinarian prescribed some repositories."

This could lead you to consider the use of a more optimally performing object-relational mapping tool that can support a collection-oriented Repository. One such tool is Oracle's TopLink, and its nearest relative, EclipseLink. TopLink provides a Unit of Work, which is not entirely unlike Hibernate's Session. However, TopLink's Unit of Work does not make an implicit copy-on-read. Instead, it makes an **Explicit Copy-before-Write** [Keith & Stafford]. Here the term *explicit* means that the client must inform the Unit of Work that changes are about to take place. This gives the Unit of Work the opportunity to clone the given domain object in preparation for modifications (what it calls *edits*, discussed later in this chapter). The key point is that TopLink consumes memory only when it must.

Hibernate Implementation

There are two primary steps to creating either orientation of a Repository. You need to define a public interface and at least one implementation.

Specifically in the case of a collection-oriented design, in the first step you define an interface that mimics a collection. The second step provides an implementation that addresses the use of the backing primary storage mechanism, such as Hibernate. The interface, like a collection, will often have common methods such as are found in the following example:

```
package com.saasovation.collaboration.domain.model.calendar;

public interface CalendarEntryRepository {
    public void add(CalendarEntry aCalendarEntry);
    public void addAll(
            Collection<CalendarEntry> aCalendarEntryCollection);
    public void remove(CalendarEntry aCalendarEntry);
    public void removeAll(
            Collection<CalendarEntry> aCalendarEntryCollection);
    ...
}
```

Place the interface definition in the same **Module (9)** as the Aggregate type that it stores. In this case interface `CalendarEntryRepository` is placed in the same Module (Java package) as `CalendarEntry`. The implementation class goes in a separate package, as discussed later.

Interface `CalendarEntryRepository` has methods that are very much like those provided by collections, such as the standard `java.util.Collection`. One new `CalendarEntry` may be added to this Repository using `add()`. Multiple new instances may be added using `addAll()`. Once the instances have been added, they will be persisted to some sort of data store and be retrievable by unique identity from that point forward. The antithesis of those methods is `remove()` and `removeAll()`, allowing for the removal of one or multiple instances from the collection.

I personally don't like these methods to answer Boolean results as do full-fledged collections. That's because in some cases answering `true` to an add-type operation does not guarantee success. The `true` results may still be subject to a transaction commit on the data store. Thus, `void` may be the more accurate return type in the case of a Repository.

There may be cases where adding and/or removing multiple Aggregate instances in one transaction isn't appropriate. When that is true of a given case in your domain, don't include methods `addAll()` and `removeAll()`. However, these methods are provided only for convenience. A client can always use a loop to invoke `add()` or `remove()` multiple times when iterating over a collection on its own. So eliminating the `addAll()` and `removeAll()` methods is only symbolic of a policy that can't actually be enforced by design, unless you also build in a means to detect adding and removing multiple objects in a single transaction. Doing so would likely require such a Repository to be instantiated for every transaction, which is a potentially costly proposal. I won't discuss this further.

It is possible that instances of some Aggregate types must never be removed through normal application use cases. It may be necessary to retrain the instance long after it is no longer usable in the application, possibly for refer-ential and/or historical purposes. Referentially it may actually be very difficult or impossible to remove some objects. From a business perspective it may be unwise, ill advised, or even illegal to remove some objects. In those cases you may decide to simply mark the Aggregate instance *disabled*, *unusable*, or, in some other domain-specific way, *logically removed*. If so, you may determine not to include any removal methods on the Repository public interface, or you may decide to implement the removal methods to set the unusable state of the Aggregate instance. You may instead prevent full object removal through code reviews, where clients are carefully inspected to ensure that no such uses of removal behavior exist. It's a decision to ponder, but you may find it easier to disallow removal altogether. After all, any methods on public interfaces are generally considered available for use. If removal is publicly available when logically disallowed, you probably want to consider implementing logical rather than physical removal.

Another important part of the Repository interface is the definition of finder methods:

```
public interface CalendarEntryRepository {
    ...
    public CalendarEntry calendarEntryOfId(
            Tenant aTenant,
            CalendarEntryId aCalendarEntryId);

    public Collection<CalendarEntry> calendarEntriesOfCalendar(
            Tenant aTenant,
            CalendarId aCalendarId);

    public Collection<CalendarEntry> overlappingCalendarEntries(
            Tenant aTenant,
            CalendarId aCalendarId,
            TimeSpan aTimeSpan);
}
```

The first method definition, `calendarEntryOfId()`, allows you to retrieve a specific instance of the `CalendarEntry` Aggregate by unique identity. This type uses an explicit identity type, namely, `CalendarEntryId`. The second method definition, `calendarEntriesOfCalendar()`, allows you to retrieve a collection of all `CalendarEntry` instances for a specific `Calendar` by its unique identity. Finally, the third finder method definition, `overlapping-CalendarEntries()`, provides a collection of all `CalendarEntry` instances for a specific `Calendar` over a specific `TimeSpan`. In particular, this method supports retrieving what is scheduled over a particular contiguous period of dates and times.

Finally, you may be wondering how a `CalendarEntry` is assigned its globally unique identity. This also can be conveniently provided by the Repository:

```
public interface CalendarEntryRepository  {
    public CalendarEntryId nextIdentity();
    ...
}
```

Any code responsible for instantiating new `CalendarEntry` instances uses `nextIdentity()` to get a new instance of `CalendarEntryId`:

```
CalendarEntry calendarEntry =
    new CalendarEntry(tenant, calendarId,
            calendarEntryRepository.nextIdentity(),
            owner, subject, description, timeSpan, alarm,
            repetition, location, invitees);
```

See **Entities (5)** for an exhaustive discussion of identity creation techniques, the use of domain-specific and surrogate identities, and the importance of properly timing the assignment of identity.

Let's now look at the implementation class for this traditional Repository. There are a few options for selecting the Module in which to place the class. Some like to use a Module (Java package) directly under the Aggregate and Repository Module. In this case that would mean

```
package com.saasovation.collaboration.domain.model.calendar.impl;

public class HibernateCalendarEntryRepository
        implements CalendarEntryRepository  {
    ...
}
```

Placing the class here allows you to manage the implementation in the Domain Layer, but in a special package for implementations. That way you keep the domain concepts cleanly separated from those that directly deal with persistence. This style of declaring interfaces in a richly named package, and their implementations in a sub-package named `impl` directly under it, is widely practiced in Java projects. However, in the case of the *Collaboration Context* the team has chosen to locate all technical implementation classes in the Infrastructure Layer:

```
package com.saasovation.collaboration.infrastructure.persistence;

public class HibernateCalendarEntryRepository
        implements CalendarEntryRepository {
    ...
}
```

This uses the **Dependency Inversion Principle (4)**, or **DIP**, for layering infrastructure concerns. The Infrastructure Layer is logically above all others, making references unidirectional and downward to the Domain Layer.

Class `HibernateCalendarEntryRepository` is a registered Spring bean. It has a zero-argument constructor and has another infrastructure bean object dependency injected:

```
import com.saasovation.collaboration.infrastructure
        .persistence.SpringHibernateSessionProvider;

public class HibernateCalendarEntryRepository
        implements CalendarEntryRepository {

    public HibernateCalendarEntryRepository() {
        super();
    }
    ...
    private SpringHibernateSessionProvider sessionProvider;

    public void setSessionProvider(
            SpringHibernateSessionProvider aSessionProvider) {
        this.sessionProvider = aSessionProvider;
    }

    private org.hibernate.Session session() {
        return this.sessionProvider.session();
    }
}
```

Class `SpringHibernateSessionProvider` is also housed in the Infrastructure Layer in the `com.saasovation.collaboration.infrastructure.persistence` Module and is injected into each Hibernate-based Repository. Each method that uses Hibernate's `Session` object self-invokes method `session()` to get it. Method `session()` uses the dependency-injected `sessionProvider` instance to get the thread-bound `Session` instance (seen later in this chapter).

Methods add(), addAll(), remove(), and removeAll() are implemented as follows:

```
package com.saasovation.collaboration.infrastructure.persistence;

public class HibernateCalendarEntryRepository
        implements CalendarEntryRepository {
    ...
    @Override
    public void add(CalendarEntry aCalendarEntry) {
        try {
            this.session().saveOrUpdate(aCalendarEntry);
        } catch (ConstraintViolationException e) {
            throw new IllegalStateException(
                    "CalendarEntry is not unique.", e);
        }
    }

    @Override
    public void addAll(
            Collection<CalendarEntry> aCalendarEntryCollection) {
        try {
            for (CalendarEntry instance : aCalendarEntryCollection) {
                this.session().saveOrUpdate(instance);
            }
        } catch (ConstraintViolationException e) {
            throw new IllegalStateException(
                    "CalendarEntry is not unique.", e);
        }
    }

    @Override
    public void remove(CalendarEntry aCalendarEntry) {
        this.session().delete(aCalendarEntry);
    }

    @Override
    public void removeAll(
            Collection<CalendarEntry> aCalendarEntryCollection) {
        for (CalendarEntry instance : aCalendarEntryCollection) {
            this.session().delete(instance);
        }
    }
    ...
}
```

These methods have rather simplistic implementations. Each method self-
invokes session() to get its Hibernate Session instance (as just previously
explained).

Perhaps curiously, methods add() and addAll() use the Session's method saveOrUpdate(). This is further support for Set-like adds. If a client happens to add the same CalendarEntry more than once, the saveOrUpdate() behavior makes it appear as a benign no-op. In fact, since Hibernate version 3 any form of update is a no-op since, as previously noted, updates are tracked implicitly by object state modifications. Therefore, unless the objects added by these two methods are entirely new, the behavior does nothing.

Adding can cause a ConstraintViolationException. Rather than allowing Hibernate exceptions to trickle out to clients, those exceptions are caught and wrapped by the more client-friendly IllegalStateException. We could also declare domain-specific exceptions and throw those. That is a choice for each project team. The main point is that since we are going to the trouble of abstracting away the implementation details of the underlying persistence framework, we want to insulate clients from all such details, including exceptions.

Methods remove() and removeAll() are quite simple. They only need to use the Session delete() to facilitate removal from the underlying data store. There is one additional detail regarding the removal of Aggregates that use one-to-one mappings, which is true in one case in the *Identity and Access Context*. Because you cannot cascade changes on such relationships, you will need to explicitly delete objects on both sides of the association:

```
package com.saasovation.identityaccess.infrastructure.persistence;

public class HibernateUserRepository implements UserRepository {
    ...
    @Override
    public void remove(User aUser) {
        this.session().delete(aUser.person());
        this.session().delete(aUser);
    }

    @Override
    public void removeAll(Collection<User> aUserCollection) {
        for (User instance : aUserCollection) {
            this.session().delete(instance.person());
            this.session().delete(instance);
        }
    }
    ...
}
```

The inner Person object must first be deleted, and then the User Aggregate Root. If you do not delete the inner Person object, it will be orphaned in its corresponding database table. In general this is a good reason to avoid one-to-one associations and instead use a constrained singular many-to-one unidirectional association. However, I chose to implement the one-to-one bidirectional association purposely in order to demonstrate what working with the more troublesome mappings involves.

Note that there are different preferred approaches for dealing with such situations. Some may choose to depend on ORM life cycle events to cause part object cascading deletes. I have purposely avoided such approaches because I am a strong opponent of Aggregate-managed persistence, and I strongly advocate Repository-only persistence. The arguments are passionate and never-ending, ad nauseam. You should make an informed choice, but understand that DDD experts avoid Aggregate-managed persistence as a rule of thumb.

Now back to `HibernateCalendarEntryRepository` and its finder method implementations:

```
public class HibernateCalendarEntryRepository
        implements CalendarEntryRepository {
    ...
    @Override
    @SuppressWarnings("unchecked")
    public Collection<CalendarEntry> overlappingCalendarEntries(
        Tenant aTenant, CalendarId aCalendarId, TimeSpan aTimeSpan) {
        Query query =
            this.session().createQuery(
                "from CalendarEntry as _obj_ " +
                "where _obj_.tenant = :tenant and " +
                  "_obj_.calendarId = :calendarId and " +
                  "((_obj_.repetition.timeSpan.begins between " +
                     ":tsb and :tse) or " +
                  " (_obj_.repetition.timeSpan.ends between " +
                     ":tsb and :tse))");

        query.setParameter("tenant", aTenant);
        query.setParameter("calendarId", aCalendarId);
        query.setParameter("tsb", aTimeSpan.begins(), Hibernate.DATE);
        query.setParameter("tse", aTimeSpan.ends(), Hibernate.DATE);

        return (Collection<CalendarEntry>) query.list();
    }

    @Override
    public CalendarEntry calendarEntryOfId(
            Tenant aTenant,
            CalendarEntryId aCalendarEntryId) {
        Query query =
            this.session().createQuery(
                "from CalendarEntry as _obj_ " +
                "where _obj_.tenant = ? and _obj_.calendarEntryId = ?");
```

```
        query.setParameter(0, aTenant);
        query.setParameter(1, aCalendarEntryId);

        return (CalendarEntry) query.uniqueResult();
    }

    @Override
    @SuppressWarnings("unchecked")
    public Collection<CalendarEntry> calendarEntriesOfCalendar(
        Tenant aTenant, CalendarId aCalendarId) {
        Query query =
            this.session().createQuery(
                "from CalendarEntry as _obj_ " +
                "where _obj_.tenant = ? and _obj_.calendarId = ?");

        query.setParameter(0, aTenant);
        query.setParameter(1, aCalendarId);

        return (Collection<CalendarEntry>) query.list();
    }
    ...
}
```

Each of the three finders creates a `Query` through its `Session`. As is common with Hibernate queries, the team uses HQL to describe the criteria and then loads up the parameter objects. The query is then run, asking for either a singular, unique result or a list collection of objects. The more sophisticated of the thread queries is that of `overlappingCalendarEntries()`, in which case we must find all `CalendarEntry` instances that overlap a specific date and time range, or `TimeSpan`.

Last we look at the implementation of method `nextIdentity()`:

```
public class HibernateCalendarEntryRepository
        implements CalendarEntryRepository  {
    ...
    public CalendarEntryId nextIdentity() {
        return new CalendarEntryId(
                UUID.randomUUID().toString().toUpperCase());
    }
    ...
}
```

This particular implementation does not use the persistence mechanism or data store to generate a unique identity. Rather, the relatively fast and very reliable `UUID` generator is used.

Considerations for a TopLink Implementation

TopLink has both a Session and a Unit of Work. This differs somewhat from Hibernate in that Hibernate's Session is also a Unit of Work.[1] Let's look at a perspective on the use of Unit of Work as separate from Session, and then ease into how to use them in a Repository implementation.

Without the benefit of a Repository abstraction, you'd use TopLink in this way:

```
Calendar calendar = session.readObject(...);

UnitOfWork unitOfWork = session.acquireUnitOfWork();

Calendar calendarToRename = unitOfWork.registerObject(calendar);

calendarToRename.rename("CollabOvation Project Calendar");

unitOfWork.commit();
```

The `UnitOfWork` provides a much more efficient use of memory and processing power since you must explicitly inform the `UnitOfWork` that you intend to modify the object. It is not until that time that a clone, or editing copy, of your Aggregate is made. As shown previously, method `register-Object()` answers a clone of the original `Calendar` instance. It is this clone object, referenced by `calendarToRename`, that must be edited/modified. As you cause modifications on the object, TopLink is able to track the changes that occur. When method `commit()` on `UnitOfWork` is invoked, all modified objects are committed to the database.[2]

Adding new objects to a TopLink Repository can be facilitated easily enough:

```
    ...
    public void add(Calendar aCalendar) {
        this.unitOfWork().registerNewObject(aCalendar);
    }
    ...
```

1. I am not measuring TopLink's value in terms of Hibernate. In fact, TopLink has a very long history of success, which was established long before Oracle picked up the product as a result of the WebGain debacle and subsequent "fire sale." *Top* is an acronym for "The Object People," which was the original company behind the tool that is approaching two decades of proven success. Here I am merely contrasting the way the two tools work.
2. This assumes that the Unit of Work is not nested inside a parent. If it is nested inside a parent Unit of Work, changes from the committed Unit of Work are merged with its parent. Ultimately the outermost is committed to the database.

The use of `registerNewObject()` stipulates that aCalendar is a new instance. This would enforce failure if `add()` was invoked with aCalendar that is actually preexisting. We could also use the vanilla `registerObject()` here, which would be similar to using Hibernate's `saveOrUpdate()` method (discussed earlier). Either way we satisfy the need for a workable collection-oriented interface.

But we still need a way to acquire a clone when we have to modify a pre-existing Aggregate. The trick is to find a convenient way to register such an Aggregate instance with a `UnitOfWork`. So far our discussion hasn't provided a Repository interface to do that because we've been trying to mimic a `Set` and avoid any inference to persistence in the interface. Still, we could accomplish this in a way that doesn't necessarily influence a persistence frame of mind. Consider using one of two approaches:

```
public Calendar editingCopy(Calendar aCalendar);

// or

public void useEditingMode();
```

With the first approach `editingCopy()` would acquire a `UnitOfWork`, register the given `Calendar` instance, get its clone, and answer it:

```
    ...
    public Calendar editingCopy(Calendar aCalendar) {
        return (Calendar) this.unitOfWork().registerObject(aCalendar);
    }
    ...
```

This reflects the underlying `registerObject()` way of doing things. Understandably this may not be desirable, but it is a clean approach and doesn't reflect a persistence frame of mind.

The second approach is to place the Repository into editing mode with `useEditingMode()`. After this is done, all subsequent finder methods will automatically register all objects they query with a backing `UnitOfWork` and answer the clones. It does more or less lock the Repository into use for Aggregate modifications. That is, nonetheless, how Repositories tend to be used, either read-only or read for modification. It also reflects the use of a Repository for Aggregates that have well-crafted boundaries that reflect a bias toward transactional success.

There may be other ways to design a collection-oriented repository for TopLink, but this provides a few options worth considering.

Persistence-Oriented Repositories

For times when a collection-oriented style doesn't work, you will need to employ a persistence-oriented, save-based Repository. This will be the case when your persistence mechanism doesn't implicitly or explicitly detect and track object changes. This happens to be the case when using an in-memory **Data Fabric (4)**, or by any other name a NoSQL key-value data store. Every time you create a new Aggregate instance or change a preexisting one, you will have to put it into the data store by using save() or a save-like Repository method.

There is another consideration for choosing a persistence-oriented approach, even if you are using an object-relational mapper that supports a collection-oriented approach. What would happen if you designed collection-oriented Repositories and then decided to swap out your relational database with a key-value store? You'd have a lot of ripple through your Application Layer as it would have to be changed to use save() in all places where Aggregate updates occur. You'd also want to rid your Repositories of add() and addAll(), because those would no longer pertain. In cases where it is a very realistic possibility that your persistence mechanism will shift in the future, it might be best to design with the more flexible interface in mind. The downside is that your current object-relational mapper may cause you to leave out necessary uses of save() that you may catch only later when there is no longer a backing Unit of Work.[3] The upside is that the Repository pattern will allow you to completely replace your persistence mechanism with potentially little impact on your application.

> **Take-aways for Persistence-Oriented Repositories**
> We must explicitly put() both new and changed objects into the store, effectively replacing any value previously associated with the given key. Using these kinds of data stores greatly simplifies the basic writes and reads of Aggregates. For this reason they are sometimes called Aggregate Stores or Aggregate-Oriented Databases.

When using an in-memory Data Fabric, such as GemFire or Oracle Coherence, the storage is an in-memory Map implementation mimicking java.util.HashMap, where each mapped element is considered an *entry*. Similarly, when using a NoSQL store such as MongoDB or Riak, object persistence gives the illusion of something like a collection, instead of tables, rows, and columns.

---

3. You could create Application Service (14) tests that account for updating saves as necessary. An in-memory Repository implementation (see the main text later in the chapter) could be designed to audit the thoroughness of saves.

These store key-value pairs. This is effectively a `Map`-like store, but it uses disk rather than memory as its primary persistence medium.

Although both of these styles of persistence mechanisms roughly mimic a `Map` collection, we must unfortunately explicitly `put()` both new and changed objects into the store, effectively replacing the value previously associated with the given key. That's true even when a changed object is logically the same object that is already stored, because these typically don't provide a Unit of Work to track changes or support transaction demarcation to control atomic writes. Rather, each `put()` and `putAll()` represents a separate logical transaction.

Using either of these kinds of data stores greatly simplifies the basic writes and reads of Aggregates. For example, consider the simplicity of adding this `Product` (*Agile Project Management Context*) to a Coherence data grid, and then reading it back again:

```
cache.put(product.productId(), product);

// later ...

product = cache.get(productId);
```

Here the `Product` instance is automatically serialized to the `Map` using standard Java serialization. This simplistic interface can be a bit deceptive, however. If you want really high-performing domains, there is a bit more to do. Coherence supports standard Java serialization when a custom serialization provider is not registered. Using the standard Java serialization is not generally the best option. It requires a premium of bytes to represent each object, and it performs relatively poorly.[4] You don't want to purchase a high-performance Data Fabric and then hamstring it by reducing the number of objects it can cache and reduce the overall throughput using slow serialization. So keep in mind that when using a Data Fabric, for example, distribution is introduced into your system. That will often bring a new force into domain model design, namely, custom or at least specialized serialization. That can cause you to make different decisions, at least at an implementation level.

So when using the GemFire or Coherence caches, the MongoDB or Riak key-value stores, or some other kind of NoSQL persistence, you will probably want to use a fast and compact means to convert Aggregates to their serialized/

---

4. It also limits your Coherence clients to Java only, when .NET and C++ clients could also use the grid data if you were to provide Portable Object Format (POF) serialization.

document form and then back again to their object form. Granted, attacking these challenges isn't that difficult. For instance, creating an optimal serialization for an Aggregate persisted by GemFire or Coherence is no more challenging than creating mapping descriptions for an object-relational mapper. But it's not as easy as just using put() and get() on a Map.

Next, I demonstrate how a persistence-oriented Repository can be created for Coherence, and following that I highlight some techniques for doing the same for MongoDB.

Coherence Implementation

As we did with the collection-oriented Repository, we first define an interface and then its implementation. Here's a persistence-oriented interface that defines save-based methods that are used for the Oracle Coherence data grid:

```
package com.saasovation.agilepm.domain.model.product;

import java.util.Collection;

import com.saasovation.agilepm.domain.model.tenant.Tenant;

public interface ProductRepository {
    public ProductId nextIdentity();
    public Collection<Product> allProductsOfTenant(Tenant aTenant);
    public Product productOfId(Tenant aTenant, ProductId aProductId);
    public void remove(Product aProduct);
    public void removeAll(Collection<Product> aProductCollection);
    public void save(Product aProduct);
    public void saveAll(Collection<Product> aProductCollection);
}
```

This `ProductRepository` is not entirely unlike the `CalendarEntryRepository` from the previous section. It differs only in the way it allows Aggregate instances to be included in the mimicked collection. In this case we have save() and saveAll() methods rather than add() and addAll() methods. Both method styles logically do similar things. The main difference is how the client uses the methods. To reiterate, when using a collection-oriented style, Aggregate instances are added only when they are created. When using a persistence-oriented style, Aggregate instances must be saved both when they are created and when they are modified:

```
Product product = new Product(...);

productRepository.save(product);
```

```
// later ...

Product product =
    productRepository.productOfId(tenantId, productId);

product.reprioritizeFrom(backlogItemId, orderOfPriority);

productRepository.save(product);
```

Other than that, the details are in the implementation. So let's dive right into that. First take a look at the Coherence infrastructure we need to make the leap to the data grid cache:

```
package com.saasovation.agilepm.infrastructure.persistence;

import com.tangosol.net.CacheFactory;
import com.tangosol.net.NamedCache;

public class CoherenceProductRepository
        implements ProductRepository {
    private Map<Tenant,NamedCache> caches;

    public CoherenceProductRepository() {
        super();
        this.caches = new HashMap<Tenant,NamedCache>();
    }
    ...
    private synchronized NamedCache cache(TenantId aTenantId) {
        NamedCache cache = this.caches.get(aTenantId);

        if (cache == null) {
            cache = CacheFactory.getCache(
                    "agilepm.Product." + aTenantId.id(),
                    Product.class.getClassLoader());

            this.caches.put(aTenantId, cache);
        }

        return cache;
    }
    ...
}
```

In the case of the *Agile Project Management Context*, the team has chosen to place Repository technical implementations in the Infrastructure Layer.

Along with a simple zero-argument constructor, there is the Coherence linchpin, the NamedCache. Among other imports, note those that are specific to creating or attaching to and using a cache, CacheFactory and Named-Cache. Both of these classes are in package com.tangosol.net.

The private method `cache()` is the means by which a `NamedCache` is obtained. The method lazily gets the cache on the Repository's first attempt to use it. This is primarily because each cache is named for the specific `Tenant` and the Repository must wait for a public method to be invoked before it has access to a `TenantId`. There are various Coherence named cache strategies that could be designed. In this case the team has chosen to cache using the following namespace:

1. First level by the Bounded Context short name: `agilepm`

2. Second level by the Aggregate simple name: `Product`

3. Third level by the unique identity of each tenant: `TenantId`

This has a few benefits. First, the model of each Bounded Context, Aggregate, and tenant that is managed by Coherence can be tuned and scaled separately. Also, each tenant is completely segregated from all others, so there is no way that queries for one tenant can accidentally include the objects of other tenants. This is the same motivation used when "striping" each entity table with the tenant identity in a MySQL persistence solution, yet it is even cleaner in this case. Further, anytime a finder method is required to answer all Aggregate instances for a given tenant, there is actually no query required. The finder method just asks Coherence for all entries in the cache. You'll see this optimization later with the implementation of `allProductsOfTenant()`.

As each `NamedCache` is created or attached to, it is placed into the `Map` associated with the `caches` instance variable. This allows each cache to be looked up quickly by `TenantId` on all uses subsequent to the first.

There are far too many Coherence configuration and tuning considerations to address here. It's an entire discussion on its own, and the literature already goes into this. I'll leave it to Aleks Seović to cover this topic [Seović]. Now on with the implementation:

```
public class CoherenceProductRepository
        implements ProductRepository {
    ...
    @Override
    public ProductId nextIdentity() {
        return new ProductId(
                java.util.UUID.randomUUID()
                    .toString()
                    .toUpperCase());
    }
    ...
}
```

The `nextIdentity()` method of the `ProductRepository` is implemented in the same fashion as that of the `CalendarEntryRepository`. It
grabs a UUID and uses it to instantiate a `ProductId`, which it then answers:

```
public class CoherenceProductRepository
        implements ProductRepository {
    ...
    @Override
    public void save(Product aProduct) {
        this.cache(aProduct.tenantId())
                .put(this.idOf(aProduct), aProduct);
    }

    @Override
    public void saveAll(Collection<Product> aProductCollection) {
        if (!aProductCollection.isEmpty()) {
            TenantId tenantId = null;

            Map<String,Product> productsMap =
                new HashMap<String,Product>(aProductCollection.size());

            for (Product product : aProductCollection) {
                if (tenantId == null) {
                    tenantId = product.tenantId();
                }
                productsMap.put(this.idOf(product), product);
            }

            this.cache(tenantId).putAll(productsMap);
        }
    }
    ...
    private String idOf(Product aProduct) {
        return this.idOf(aProduct.productId());
    }

    private String idOf(ProductId aProductId) {
        return aProductId.id();
    }
}
```

To persist a single new or modified `Product` instance to the data grid, use
`save()`. The `save()` method uses `cache()` to get the `NamedCache` instance
for the `TenantId` of the `Product`. It then puts the `Product` instance into the
`NamedCache`. Note the use of method `idOf()`, which has two editions, one
for a `Product` and the other for a `ProductId`. In both cases these methods
answer the `String` form of the `Product`'s unique identity, or `ProductId`. So

the put() method of the NamedCache, which implements java.util.Map, is given a String-based key and the Product instance as the value.

Method saveAll() may be a bit more complex than you expected. Why not just iterate over aProductCollection, invoking save() for each element? We could do so. However, depending on the specific Coherence cache in use, each invocation of put() requires a network request. Therefore, it's best to batch up all Product instances to be persisted in a simple local HashMap and submit them with putAll() instead. This reduces the network latency to the lowest possible delay by using a single request, which is the most optimal.

```java
public class CoherenceProductRepository
        implements ProductRepository {
    ...
    @Override
    public void remove(Product aProduct) {
        this.cache(aProduct.tenant()).remove(this.idOf(aProduct));
    }

    @Override
    public void removeAll(Collection<Product> aProductCollection) {
        for (Product product : aProductCollection) {
            this.remove(product);
        }
    }
    ...
}
```

The implementation of remove() works exactly as expected. However, given the implementation of saveAll(), removeAll() may be as big a surprise. After all, isn't there a way to remove a batch of entries? Well, no, the standard java.util.Map interface doesn't provide that, and thus neither does Coherence. So in this case we do just iterate over aProductCollection and use remove() for each element. Considering the possible consequences of removing only some of the given collection due to Coherence failure, this may seem dangerous. Of course, you will have to weigh the forces of providing a removeAll(), but remember that a major strength of Data Fabrics such as GemFire and Coherence is redundancy and high availability.

Finally, we arrive at interface method implementations that provide a few ways of finding Product instances:

```java
public class CoherenceProductRepository
        implements ProductRepository {
    ...
```

```
@SuppressWarnings("unchecked")
@Override
public Collection<Product> allProductsOfTenant(Tenant aTenant) {
    Set<Map.Entry<String, Product>> entries =
        this.cache(aTenant).entrySet();

    Collection<Product> products =
        new HashSet<Product>(entries.size());

    for (Map.Entry<String, Product> entry : entries) {
        products.add(entry.getValue());
    }

    return products;
}

@Override
public Product productOfId(Tenant aTenant, ProductId aProductId) {
    return (Product) this.cache(aTenant).get(this.idOf(aProductId));
}
...
}
```

Method `productOfId()` only has to do a basic `get()` on the Named-Cache, providing the identity of the `Product` instance being requested.

Method `allProductsOfTenant()` is the one I previously referred to. Rather than having to employ a more sophisticated Coherence filter entry process, all it needs to do is ask the data grid for all `Product` instances in the specific `NamedCache`. Because each cache is segregated down to the individual tenant, every Aggregate instance in the cache satisfies the query.

That wraps up class `CoherenceProductRepository`. This implementation shows how an abstract interface is fulfilled using Coherence as a client to persist data on the grid cache and then find it later. It doesn't show everything involved in configuring and tuning Coherence, or what it takes to create indexes for each cache, or design a compacting, high-performance serializer for each domain object. That's not the Repository's responsibility. See [Seović] for extensive coverage of those topics.

MongoDB Implementation

As with the other Repository implementations, there are some basic implementation considerations. The MongoDB implementation is actually similar to the Coherence version. Here is the high-level overview of what we need:

1. A means to serialize Aggregate instances to the MongoDB format, and then deserialize from that format and reconstitute the Aggregate instance.

MongoDB uses a special form of JSON called BSON, which is a binary JSON format.

2. A unique identity generated by MongoDB and assigned to the Aggregate.

3. A reference to the MongoDB node/cluster.

4. A unique collection in which to store each Aggregate type. All instances of each Aggregate type must be stored as a set of serialized documents (key-value pairs) in their own collection.

Let's take this step by step as we look through a Repository implementation. Since we'll use the `ProductRepository` again, you can compare the implementation to that for Coherence (previous section).

```
public class MongoProductRepository
        extends MongoRepository<Product>
        implements ProductRepository {

    public MongoProductRepository() {
        super();

        this.serializer(new BSONSerializer<Product>(Product.class));
    }
    ...
}
```

This implementation holds an instance of a `BSONSerializer`, which is used to serialize and deserialize all `Product` instances (actually held by superclass `MongoRepository`). I won't go into deep detail about `BSONSerializer`. It's a custom-developed solution for producing MongoDB `DBObject` instances from `Product` instances (and any other Aggregate types) and back to `Product` instances. This class is provided along with other sample code.

There are a few notable things you can do with a `BSONSerializer`. Basic serialization and deserialization are handled using direct field access. This frees your domain objects from having to implement JavaBean getters and setters, which tends to steer you away from an **Anemic Domain Model** [Fowler, Anemic]. Since you won't use methods to access fields, you will at some point need to migrate from one version of an Aggregate type to another version. To do so you can specify override mappings for each field on deserialization:

```
public class MongoProductRepository
        extends MongoRepository<Product>
        implements ProductRepository {
```

```
    public MongoProductRepository() {
        super();

        this.serializer(new BSONSerializer<Product>(Product.class));

        Map<String, String> overrides = new HashMap<String, String>();
        overrides.put("description", "summary");
        this.serializer().registerOverrideMappings(overrides);
    }
    ...
}
```

In this example we'll assume that a previous version of class `Product` had a field named `description`. In a subsequent version this field was renamed `summary`. To solve this problem we could run a migration script across all MongoDB collections used to store `Product` instances for each tenant. However, that could be a difficult and very lengthy set of operations, rendering it an impractical approach. As an alternative, we'll simply ask the `BSONSerializer` to map any BSON field on `Product` named `description` to the field named `summary`. Then, when the migrated `Product` is serialized back to a `DBObject` and saved in the MongoDB collection, the new serialization will contain a field named `summary` rather than `description`. Of course, it also means that any `Product` instances never read and saved back to the store will remain with the obsolete `description` field names. You'll have to weigh the trade-offs of this lazy migration approach.

Next, we need a way for MongoDB to generate a unique identity for each Aggregate instance to use:

```
public class MongoProductRepository
        extends MongoRepository<Product>
        implements ProductRepository {
    ...
    public ProductId nextIdentity() {
        return new ProductId(new ObjectId().toString());
    }
    ...
}
```

We still use method `nextIdentity()`, but in this implementation we initialize the `ProductId` with the `String` value of a new `ObjectId`. The main reason for this is that we want MongoDB to use the same unique identity that we hold in the Aggregate instance itself. Thus, when we serialize a `Product` (or another type in a different Repository implementation), we can ask the `BSONSerializer` to map that identity to the special MongoDB `_id` key:

```
public class BSONSerializer<T> {
    ...
    public DBObject serialize(T anObject) {
        DBObject serialization = this.toDBObject(anObject);

        return serialization;
    }

    public DBObject serialize(String aKey, T anObject) {
        DBObject serialization = this.serialize(anObject);

        serialization.put("_id", new ObjectId(aKey));

        return serialization;
    }
    ...
}
```

The first `serialize()` method supports no such `_id` mapping, giving clients the option to retain the matching identities, or not. Next, look at how the `save()` method is implemented:

```
public class MongoProductRepository
        extends MongoRepository<Product>
        implements ProductRepository {
    ...
    @Override
    public void save(Product aProduct) {
        this.databaseCollection(
                this.collectionName(aProduct.tenantId()))
            .save(this.serialize(aProduct));
    }
    ...
}
```

Similar to the Coherence implementation of the same Repository interface, we get a tenant-specific collection in which to store the `Product` instances for a given `TenantId`. This yields a Mongo `DBCollection` from a `DB`. To get the `DBCollection` object we have the following in the `MongoRepository` abstract base class:

```
public abstract class MongoRepository<T> {
    ...
    protected DBCollection databaseCollection(
            String aDatabaseName,
            String aCollectionName) {
```

```
        return MongoDatabaseProvider
                .database(aDatabaseName)
                .getCollection(aCollectionName);
    }
    ...
}
```

We use a `MongoDatabaseProvider` to get a connection to the database instance, which answers with a `DB` object. From the returned `DB` object we ask for a `DBCollection`. As seen in the concrete Repository implementation, the collection is named by the combination of the text `"product"` and the full identity of the tenant. The *Agile PM Context* uses a dedicated database named `agilepm`, much like the way the Coherence implementation names its cache:

```
public class MongoProductRepository
        extends MongoRepository<Product>
        implements ProductRepository {
    ...
    protected String collectionName(TenantId aTenantId) {
        return "product" + aTenantId.id();
    }

    protected String databaseName() {
        return "agilepm";
    }
    ...
}
```

Similar to the `SpringHibernateSessionProvider` presented previously, the `MongoDatabaseProvider` is the means to retrieve an application-wide instance of `DB`.

The same `DBCollection` is used for `save()` and for finding instances of `Product`:

```
public class MongoProductRepository
        extends MongoRepository<Product>
        implements ProductRepository {
    ...
    @Override
    public Collection<Product> allProductsOfTenant(
            TenantId aTenantId) {
        Collection<Product> products = new ArrayList<Product>();

        DBCursor cursor =
            this.databaseCollection(
                    this.databaseName(),
                    this.collectionName(aTenantId)).find();
```

```
        while (cursor.hasNext()) {
            DBObject dbObject = cursor.next();

            Product product = this.deserialize(dbObject);

            products.add(product);
        }

        return products;
    }

    @Override
    public Product productOfId(
            TenantId aTenantId, ProductId aProductId) {
        Product product = null;

        BasicDBObject query = new BasicDBObject();

        query.put("productId",
                new BasicDBObject("id", aProductId.id()));

        DBCursor cursor =
            this.databaseCollection(
                    this.databaseName(),
                    this.collectionName(aTenantId)).find(query);

        if (cursor.hasNext()) {
            product = this.deserialize(cursor.next());
        }

        return product;
    }
    ...
}
```

The implementation of `allProductsOfTenant()` is, again, very similar to that for Coherence. We simply ask the tenant-based `DBCollection` to `find()` all instances. As for `productOfId()`, this time we give the `DBCollection` method `find()` a `DBObject` describing the specific `Product` instance to retrieve. In both finder methods we use the returned `DBCursor` to get all, and get only the first instance, respectively.

Additional Behavior

Sometimes it is beneficial to provide additional behavior on a Repository interface, besides the typical kinds presented in the previous sections. One behavior that comes in handy is to answer the count of all instances in the collection of

Aggregates. You might think of this behavior as having the name *count*. However, since a Repository should mimic a collection as closely as possible, you might consider instead using the following method:

```
public interface CalendarEntryRepository {
    ...
    public int size();
}
```

Method `size()` is exactly what a standard `java.util.Collection` supplies. When using Hibernate, the implementation would work like this:

```
public class HibernateCalendarEntryRepository
        implements CalendarEntryRepository {
    ...
    public int size() {
        Query query =
            this.session().createQuery(
                "select count(*) from CalendarEntry");

        int size = ((Integer) query.uniqueResult()).intValue();

        return size;
    }
}
```

There may be other calculations that must be performed in the data store (database or grid included) in order to meet some stringent nonfunctional requirement. This can be the case if moving the data from its store to where the business logic executes is too slow. Instead you may have to move the code to the data. This can be accomplished using database stored procedures or data grid entry processors, such as are available with Coherence. However, such implementations are often best placed under the control of **Domain Services** (7), since those are used to house stateless, domain-specific operations.

It may at times be advantageous to query Aggregate parts out of the Repository without directly accessing the Root itself. This might be so if an Aggregate holds a large collection of some Entity type, and you need to get access only to the instances that match a certain criterion. Of course, this might make sense only if the Aggregate allows for such access by navigation through the Root. You wouldn't design a Repository to provide access to parts that the Aggregate Root would not otherwise allow access to by way of navigation. Doing so would violate the Aggregate contract. I suggest that you would also not design the Repository to provide this kind of access as a mere shortcut for client convenience. I think this should be used primarily to address performance concerns under conditions where navigation through the Root would cause an unacceptable bottleneck. The methods that address such optimal access would have the same basic characteristics as other finders (see earlier in this chapter) but would answer instances of the contained parts rather than Root Entities. Again, use with caution.

Another reason might influence you to design in special finder methods. Certain use cases of your system may not follow the exact contours of a single Aggregate type when rendering views of domain data. They may instead cut across types, possibly composing just certain parts of one or more Aggregates. In situations like this you might choose not to, in a single transaction, find whole Aggregate instances of various types and then programmatically compose them into a single container, and supply that payload container to a client. You might instead use what is called a *use case optimal query*. This is where you specify a complex query against the persistence mechanism, dynamically placing the results into a **Value Object (6)** specifically designed to address the needs of the use case.

It should not seem strange for a Repository to in some cases answer a Value Object rather than an Aggregate instance. A Repository that provides a `size()` method answers a very simple Value in the form of an integer count of the total Aggregate instances it holds. A use case optimal query is just extending this notion a bit to provide a somewhat more complex Value, one that addresses more complex client demands.

If you find that you must create many finder methods supporting use case optimal queries on multiple Repositories, it's probably a code smell. First of all, this situation could be an indication that you've misjudged Aggregate boundaries and overlooked the opportunity to design one or more Aggregates of different types. The code smell here might be called *Repository masks Aggregate mis-design*.

However, what if you encounter this situation and your analysis indicates that your Aggregate boundaries are well designed? This could point to the need to consider using **CQRS (4)**.

Managing Transactions

The domain model and its encompassing Domain Layer is never the correct place to manage transactions.[5] The operations associated with a model are

---

5. Note that for some persistence mechanisms transaction management is either non-existent or works differently from ACID transactions common with relational databases. Both Coherence and many NoSQL stores differ in that way, and this material is generally not applicable to such data storage mechanisms.

usually too fine grained to themselves manage transactions and shouldn't be aware that transactions play a part in their life cycle. If you are to avoid placing transactional concerns in the model, just where do they belong?

A common architectural approach to facilitating transactions on behalf of persistence aspects of the domain model is to manage them in the **Application Layer (14)**.[6] Generally, we create one **Facade** [Gamma et al.] there for each major use case grouping addressed by the application/system. The Facade is designed with coarse-grained business methods, usually one for each use case flow (which may be limited to one for a given use case). Each such business method coordinates a task as required by the use case. When a Facade's business method is invoked by the **User Interface Layer (14)**, whether on behalf of a human or another system, the business method begins a transaction and then acts as a client to the domain model. After all necessary interaction with the domain model is successfully completed, the Facade's business method commits the transaction it started. If an error/exception occurs that prevents completion of the use case task, the transaction is rolled back by the same managing business method.

The transaction may be managed declaratively or explicitly by developer code. Whether or not your transactions are declarative or user managed, what I have described here logically works as follows:

```
public class SomeApplicationServiceFacade {
    ...
    public void doSomeUseCaseTask()  {
        Transaction transaction = null;

        try {
            transaction = this.session().beginTransaction();

            // use the domain model ...

            transaction.commit();

        } catch (Exception e) {
            if (transaction != null) {
                transaction.rollback();
            }
        }
    }
}
```

---

6. There are other concerns managed by the Application Layer, such as security, but I don't discuss those here.

To enlist changes to the domain model in a transaction, ensure that Repository implementations have access to the same Session or Unit of Work for the transaction that the Application Layer started. That way the modifications made in the Domain Layer will be properly committed to the underlying database or rolled back.

There is such a variety in how this can be accomplished that I cannot address all possibilities. What I will do is note that enterprise Java containers and inversion-of-control containers, such as Spring, provide the means to do what I have described, and it is generally well understood. The emphasis here is to use what is appropriate for your environment. As an example, here's how you might do so using Spring:

```xml
<tx:annotation-driven transaction-manager="transactionManager"/>

<bean
    id="sessionFactory"
    class="org.springframework.orm.hibernate3.LocalSessionFactoryBean">
    <property name="configLocation">
        <value>classpath:hibernate.cfg.xml</value>
    </property>
</bean>

<bean
    id="sessionProvider"
    class="com.saasovation.identityaccess.infrastructure
            .persistence.SpringHibernateSessionProvider"
    autowire="byName">
</bean>

<bean
    id="transactionManager"
    class="org.springframework.orm.hibernate3
            .HibernateTransactionManager">
    <property name="sessionFactory">
        <ref bean="sessionFactory"/>
    </property>
</bean>

<bean
    id="abstractTransactionalServiceProxy"
    abstract="true"
    class="org.springframework.transaction.interceptor
            .TransactionProxyFactoryBean">
    <property name="transactionManager">
        <ref bean="transactionManager"/>
    </property>
    <property name="transactionAttributes">
```

```
        <props>
            <prop key="*">PROPAGATION_REQUIRED</prop>
        </props>
    </property>
</bean>
```

The configured sessionFactory bean provides the means to obtain a
Hibernate Session. The bean named sessionProvider is used to associate
a Session obtained from the sessionFactory with the current Thread
of execution. The sessionProvider bean can be used by Hibernate-based
Repositories when they need to get the Session instance for the Thread
they are running under. The transactionManager uses the session-
Factory to get and manage Hibernate transactions. The one remaining bean,
abstractTransactionalServiceProxy, is used optionally as a proxy for
declaring transactional beans using Spring configuration. The topmost declaration allows transactions to be declared via Java annotations, which may be
more convenient than using configuration:

```
<tx:annotation-driven transaction-manager="transactionManager"/>
```

With this wired you can now declare a given Facade business method transactional using a simple annotation:

```
public class SomeApplicationServiceFacade {
    ...
    @Transactional
    public void doSomeUseCaseTask()  {

        // use the domain model ...
    }
}
```

Compared to the previous example of managing a transaction, this certainly
cuts down on clutter in the business method and allows you to focus on the task
coordination itself. By means of this annotation, when the business method is
invoked, Spring automatically starts a transaction, and when the method completes, the transaction is either committed or rolled back as appropriate.

Here is a look at the source code of the sessionProvider bean as it is
implemented for the *Identity and Access Context*:

```
package com.saasovation.identityaccess.infrastructure.persistence;

import org.hibernate.Session;
import org.hibernate.SessionFactory;
```

436

```
public class SpringHibernateSessionProvider {

    private static final ThreadLocal<Session> sessionHolder =
            new ThreadLocal<Session>();

    private SessionFactory sessionFactory;

    public SpringHibernateSessionProvider() {
        super();
    }

    public Session session() {
        Session threadBoundsession = sessionHolder.get();
        if (threadBoundsession == null) {
            threadBoundsession = sessionFactory.openSession();
            sessionHolder.set(threadBoundsession);
        }
        return threadBoundsession;
    }

    public void setSessionFactory(SessionFactory aSessionFactory) {
        this.sessionFactory = aSessionFactory;
    }
}
```

Since the `sessionProvider` is a Spring bean that is declared with `autowire="byName"`, when the bean is instantiated as a singleton its `setSessionFactory()` method is invoked to inject the `sessionFactory` bean instance. To save you looking back through the chapter in search of how a Hibernate-based Repository uses this, here's a brief reminder:

```
package com.saasovation.identityaccess.infrastructure.persistence;

public class HibernateUserRepository
        implements UserRepository  {

    @Override
    public void add(User aUser) {
        try {
            this.session().saveOrUpdate(aUser);
        } catch (ConstraintViolationException e) {
            throw new IllegalStateException("User is not unique.", e);
        }
    }
    ...
    private SpringHibernateSessionProvider sessionProvider;

    public void setSessionProvider(
            SpringHibernateSessionProvider aSessionProvider) {
        this.sessionProvider = aSessionProvider;
    }
```

```
    private org.hibernate.Session session() {
        return this.sessionProvider.session();
    }
}
```

This snippet is from the `HibernateUserRepository` of the *Identity and Access Context*. This class, too, is a Spring bean that is autowired by name, which means its method `setSessionProvider()` is automatically invoked upon creation so that it gets a reference to the `sessionProvider` bean, which is an instance of `SpringHibernateSessionProvider`. When the `add()` method (or any other method that provides persistence) is invoked, it asks for a `Session` through its `session()` method. In turn, `session()` uses the injected `sessionProvider` to obtain the thread-bound `Session` instance.

While I have demonstrated how transactions are managed only when using Hibernate, all of these principles carry over to TopLink, JPA, and other persistence mechanisms. With any such persistence mechanism you must find a way to provide access to the same Session, Unit of Work, and transaction that the Application Layer is managing. Dependency injection works well for this if it is available. If it isn't available, there are other creative ways to facilitate the necessary wiring, even going as far as manually binding such objects to the current thread.

A Warning

I feel obligated to provide a parting warning about overuse of transactions in conjunction with the domain model. Aggregates must be designed carefully in order to ensure correct consistency boundaries. Be careful not to overuse the ability to commit modifications to multiple Aggregates in a single transaction just because it works in a unit test environment. If you aren't careful, what works well in development and test can fail severely in production because of concurrency issues. If need be, revisit **Aggregates (10)** for vital reminders to precisely define consistency boundaries in order to ensure transactional success.

Type Hierarchies

When using an object-oriented language to develop a domain model, it can be tempting to leverage inheritance to create type hierarchies. We might think of this as an opportunity to place default state and behavior in a base class and then extend that using subclasses. And why not? It seems like a perfect way to avoid repeating yourself.

Creating Aggregates that have a common ancestry and yet stand apart from their relatives with a separate Repository is a different use of inheritance from creating Aggregates with the same ancestry that share a single Repository. So this section does not discuss the situation where all Aggregate types in a single domain model extend a **Layer Supertype** [Fowler, P of EAA] to provide domain-wide common state and/or behavior.[7]

Rather, here I am referring to creating a relatively small number of Aggregate types that extend a common domain-specific superclass. These are designed in order to form a hierarchy of closely related types that have interchangeable, polymorphic characteristics. These kinds of hierarchies use a single Repository to store and retrieve instances of the separate types, because the client should use the instances interchangeably, and clients rarely if ever have to be aware of the specific subclass that they are dealing with at any given time, which reflects the **Liskov Substitution Principle** (LSP) [Liskov].

Here's what I mean. Say your business uses external businesses to provide various kinds of services, and you need to model the relationships. You decide to have a common abstract base class `ServiceProvider`, but for some good reason you need to divide various concrete types of these because the services each provides are both common and yet distinctly different. You might have a `WarbleServiceProvider` and a `WonkleServiceProvider`. You design these types such that you can schedule a service request in a generic way:

```
// client of domain model
serviceProviderRepository.providerOf(id)
        .scheduleService(date, description);
```

With this context, it is clear that the creation of domain-specific Aggregate type hierarchies will probably have limited usefulness in many domains. Here's why. As demonstrated previously, most times the common Repository will be designed with finder methods that retrieve instances of any of the subclasses. That means that the method will answer instances of the common superclass, in this case a `ServiceProvider`, not instances of the specific subclasses, `WarbleServiceProvider` and `WonkleServiceProvider`. Think of what would happen if finders were designed to return specific types. Clients would have to know which identities or other descriptive attributes of the Aggregates would lead to specific typed instances. Otherwise it could lead to an unmatched find or a `ClassCastException` when a matched instance of the wrong type

---

7. I discuss the benefits of using a Layer Supertype in the design of **Entities** (5) and **Value Objects** (6). See the respective chapters.

is returned. Even if you could design in a good way to find instances of the correct types, clients would also have to know which subclasses could perform specifically different operations, given that the Aggregates could not be entirely designed for LSP.

To solve the first problem of segregating types by identity, you might conclude that you could safely detect instances by encoding Aggregate type information as a discriminator in the class of the unique identity. You could do so. But that also leads to two additional problems. The client must take on the responsibility of resolving and mapping identities to types. The other new problem is coupling clients to the distinct operations by type. It leads to this kind of client type dependencies:

```
// client of domain model

if (id.identifiesWarble()) {
    serviceProviderRepository.warbleOf(id)
            .scheduleWarbleService(date, warbleDescription);
} else if (id.identifiesWonkle()) {
    serviceProviderRepository.wonkleOf(id)
            .scheduleWonkleService(date, wonkleDescription);
} ...
```

If this kind of interaction becomes the norm rather than the exception, it indicates a code smell. Granted, if the benefits gained from creating a hierarchy are so great, a rare one-off usage like this may be a worthwhile trade-off. However, in this contrived example a more discerning design of the implied `ServiceDescription` type and the internal implementation of `schedule-Service()` would probably suffice. Otherwise, I think we'd have to ask if we could gain some benefits from using inheritance while assigning each type a separate Repository. In the case where only two or a few such concrete subclasses are necessary, it may be best to create separate Repositories. When the number of concrete subclasses grows to several or many, most of which can be used completely interchangeably (LSP), it is worthwhile for them to share a common Repository.

Most of the time, this kind of situation can be completely avoided by designing type descriptive information as a property of the Aggregate (not in the identity). See the discussion about Standard Types under **Value Objects (6)**. This way a single Aggregate type could internally implement different behavior based on an explicitly determined Standard Type. Using an explicit Standard Type, we could have a single concrete `ServiceProvider` Aggregate and design its `scheduleService()` to dispatch based on its type. To shield clients from the decisions based on the type we ensure that such is not leaked out to them. Instead, `scheduleService()` and other `ServiceProvider` methods properly enclose such domain-specific decisions, as can be seen here:

```
public class ServiceProvider {
    private ServiceType type;
    ...
    public void scheduleService(
            Date aDate,
            ServiceDescription aDescription) {
        if (type.isWarble()) {
            this.scheduleWarbleService(aDate, aDescription);
        } else if (type.isWonkle()) {
            this.scheduleWonkleService(aDate, aDescription);
        } else {
            this.scheduleCommonService(aDate, aDescription);
        }
    }
    ...
}
```

If the internal dispatching becomes messy, we can always design another smaller hierarchy to deal with that. In fact, the Standard Type itself could be designed as a **State** [Gamma et al.], assuming you like that approach. In that case the various types would implement specialized behavior. This, of course, also means that we'd have a single `ServiceProviderRepository`, which addresses the desire to store different types in one Repository and use them with common behavior.

The situation could also be sidestepped with the use of role-based interfaces. Here we might have decided to design a `SchedulableService` interface that multiple Aggregate types would implement. See the discussion about roles and responsibilities under **Entities (5)**. Even if inheritance is used, Aggregate polymorphic behavior can most often be carefully designed such that no special cases are surfaced to clients.

Repository versus Data Access Object

Sometimes the idea of a Repository is considered synonymous with Data Access Object, or DAO. Both provide an abstraction over a persistence mechanism. This is true. However, an object-relational mapping tool also provides an abstraction over a persistence mechanism, but it is neither a Repository nor a DAO. Thus, we wouldn't call just any persistence abstraction a DAO. We must rather determine if the DAO pattern is being implemented.

I think there are generally differences between Repositories and DAOs. Basically, a DAO is expressed in terms of database tables, providing CRUD interfaces to them. Martin Fowler in [Fowler, P of EAA] separates the uses of DAO-like facilities from those that are used with a domain model. He identifies **Table Module, Table Data Gateway,** and **Active Record** as patterns that would typically be used in a **Transaction Script** application. That's because DAO and related patterns tend to serve as wrappers around database tables. On the other hand, Repository and **Data Mapper,** having object affinity, are typically the patterns that would be used with a domain model.

Since you can use DAO and related patterns to perform fine-grained CRUD operations on data that would otherwise be considered parts of an Aggregate, this would be a pattern to avoid with a domain model. Under normal conditions you want the Aggregate itself to manage its business logic and other internals and keep everyone else out.

I did indicate previously that at times a stored procedure or a data grid entry processor is essential to meet some demanding nonfunctional requirement. Depending on your domain, this may be more the rule than the exception. If a system nonfunctional requirement is not driving this, however, I suggest that you should avoid it. Housing and executing business logic in the data store many times runs orthogonal to DDD. I would conclude that the use of a Data Fabric Function/Entry Processor is not really disruptive to the goals of domain modeling. The Function/Entry Processor implementation would be written in Java, for example, and would adhere to the **Ubiquitous Language** (1) and goals of the domain. The only difference from the core model is where the Function/Entry Processor is executed, which is not disruptive. On the other hand, prolific use of stored procedures is potentially very disruptive to DDD because the programming language is generally not well understood by the modeling team and implementations are generally "safely" tucked away from their view. If so, that is exactly the opposite of what DDD is trying to accomplish.

You may choose to think of a Repository as a DAO in a general sense. The primary thing to keep in mind is that as much as possible you should try to design your Repositories with a collection orientation rather than a data access orientation. That will help keep you focused on the domain as a model rather than on data and any CRUD operations that may be used behind the scenes to manage its persistence.

Testing Repositories

There are two ways to look at testing Repositories. You have to test the Repositories themselves in order to prove that they work correctly. You also must test code that uses Repositories to store the Aggregates that they create and to find preexisting ones. For the first kind of test you must use the full production-quality implementations. Otherwise you won't know if your production code will work. For the second kind of test, either you can use your production implementations, or you can use in-memory implementations instead. I discuss the production implementation tests now and defer the in-memory tests to just a bit later.

Let's take a look at the tests for the Coherence implementation of the `ProductRepository` presented previously:

```
public class CoherenceProductRepositoryTest extends DomainTest {

    private ProductRepository productRepository;
    private TenantId tenantId;

    public CoherenceProductRepositoryTest() {
        super();
    }
    ...
    @Override
    protected void setUp() throws Exception {
        this.setProductRepository(new CoherenceProductRepository());
        this.tenantId = new TenantId("01234567");
        super.setUp();
    }

    @Override
    protected void tearDown() throws Exception {
        Collection<Product> products =
            this.productRepository()
                    .allProductsOfTenant(tenantId);

        this.productRepository().removeAll(products);
    }

    protected ProductRepository productRepository() {
        return this.productRepository;
    }

    protected void setProductRepository(
            ProductRepository aProductRepository) {
        this.productRepository = aProductRepository;
    }
}
```

There are some general setup and tear-down operations to prepare for and clean up after each test. To set up we create an instance of class `Coherence-ProductRepository` and then create a fake instance of `TenantId`.

To tear down we remove all `Product` instances that may have been added to the backing cache by each test. For Coherence this is an important cleanup step. If you don't remove all cached instances, they will remain during subsequent tests, which may cause failure for certain assertions such as persisted instance counts.

Next, we test the Repository behavior:

```
public class CoherenceProductRepositoryTest extends DomainTest {
    ...
    public void testSaveAndFindOneProduct() throws Exception {

        Product product =
            new Product(
                    tenantId,
                    this.productRepository().nextIdentity(),
                    "My Product",
                    "This is the description of my product.");

        this.productRepository().save(product);

        Product readProduct =
            this.productRepository()
                .productOfId(tenantId, product.productId());

        assertNotNull(readProduct);
        assertEquals(readProduct.tenantId(), tenantId);
        assertEquals(readProduct.productId(), product.productId());
        assertEquals(readProduct.name(), product.name());
        assertEquals(readProduct.description(), product.description());
    }
    ...
}
```

As the test method name states, here we save a single `Product` and attempt to find it. The first task is to instantiate a `Product` and then save it to the Repository. If no exception is thrown by the infrastructure, we may think that the `Product` was correctly saved. However, there is only one way to know for certain. We have to find the instance and compare it to the original. To find the instance we pass its globally unique identity to method `productOfId()`. If the instance was found, we can successfully assert that it is not `null`, that its `tenantId` is the same, its `productId` is the same, its `name` is the same, and its `description` is the same as the one that was stored.

Next, we test saving and finding multiple instances:

```
public class CoherenceProductRepositoryTest extends DomainTest {
    ...
    public void testSaveAndFindMultipleProducts() throws Exception {
```

```
        Product product1 =
            new Product(
                    tenantId,
                    this.productRepository().nextIdentity(),
                    "My Product 1",
                    "This is the description of my first product.");

        Product product2 =
            new Product(
                    tenantId,
                    this.productRepository().nextIdentity(),
                    "My Product 2",
                    "This is the description of my second product.");

        Product product3 =
            new Product(
                    tenantId,
                    this.productRepository().nextIdentity(),
                    "My Product 3",
                    "This is the description of my third product.");

        this.productRepository()
            .saveAll(Arrays.asList(product1, product2, product3));

        assertNotNull(this.productRepository()
            .productOfId(tenant, product1.productId()));
        assertNotNull(this.productRepository()
            .productOfId(tenant, product2.productId()));
        assertNotNull(this.productRepository()
            .productOfId(tenant, product3.productId()));

        Collection<Product> allProducts =
            this.productRepository().allProductsOfTenant(tenant);

        assertEquals(allProducts.size(), 3);
    }
    ...
}
```

First we instantiate three `Product` instances and then save them at once
using `saveAll()`. Next, we again use `productOfId()` to find individual
instances. If all three instances are not `null`, we are convinced that all three
instances were correctly persisted.

Cowboy Logic

AJ: "My sister told me her husband asked her to sell all
the stuff in his storage unit when he dies. My sister
asked him why. He said he didn't want some jerk to
have his stuff when she remarries. She told him not to
worry since she wasn't going to marry another jerk."

There is one Repository method, `allProductsOfTenant()`, that has not yet been tested. Given that the Repository cache was completely empty when the test started, we should be able to successfully read three `Product` instances from it. So we attempt to find all of them. The returned `Collection` should never be `null`, even if you don't find what you expected. So the last step in the test is to assert that the full number of expected `Product` instances, or three, was in fact found.

Now that we have a test that demonstrates how clients can use the Repository and proves its correctness, we can look at how you can more optimally test clients that use Repositories.

Testing with In-Memory Implementations

If it is very difficult to set up the full persistent implementation of a Repository for test, or too slow to use it, you can leverage another approach. You may also face undesirable conditions early on during domain modeling, perhaps when your persistence mechanisms, including the database schema, are not yet available. When you face any of these situations, it works best to implement an in-memory edition of Repositories.

Creating in-memory editions can be quite simple, but it may also pose some challenges. The simple part is creating a `HashMap` to back your interface. It is straightforward to `put()` entries to and `remove()` them from the `Map`. We just use the globally unique identity of each Aggregate instance as the key. The Aggregate instance itself serves as the value. The `add()` or `save()` methods and the `remove()` methods are quite trivial. In fact, in the case of the ProductRepository the entire implementation is fairly simple:

```
package com.saasovation.agilepm.domain.model.product.impl;

public class InMemoryProductRepository implements ProductRepository {

    private Map<ProductId,Product> store;

    public InMemoryProductRepository() {
        super();
        this.store = new HashMap<ProductId,Product>();
    }

    @Override
    public Collection<Product> allProductsOfTenant(Tenant aTenant) {
        Set<Product> entries = new HashSet<Product>();

        for (Product product : this.store.values()) {
            if (product.tenant().equals(aTenant)) {
                entries.add(product);
            }
        }
```

```
        return entries;
    }

    @Override
    public ProductId nextIdentity() {
        return new ProductId(java.util.UUID.randomUUID()
                .toString().toUpperCase());
    }

    @Override
    public Product productOfId(Tenant aTenant, ProductId aProductId) {
        Product product = this.store.get(aProductId);

        if (product != null) {
            if (!product.tenant().equals(aTenant)) {
                product = null;
            }
        }

        return product;
    }

    @Override
    public void remove(Product aProduct) {
        this.store.remove(aProduct.productId());
    }

    @Override
    public void removeAll(Collection<Product> aProductCollection) {
        for (Product product : aProductCollection) {
            this.remove(product);
        }
    }

    @Override
    public void save(Product aProduct) {
        this.store.put(aProduct.productId(), aProduct);
    }

    @Override
    public void saveAll(Collection<Product> aProductCollection) {
        for (Product product : aProductCollection) {
            this.save(product);
        }
    }
}
```

There is actually only a single special case for productOfId(). To correctly implement this finder, after getting a matching Product by the given ProductId, we must also check that the TenantId of the Product matches the Tenant parameter. If it doesn't, we set the Product instance to null.

We can actually make a near-identical copy of CoherenceProduct-RepositoryTest named InMemoryProductRepositoryTest to test this in-memory implementation. The only change that needs to be made is in setUp():

```
public class InMemoryProductRepositoryTest extends TestCase {
    ...
    @Override
    protected void setUp() throws Exception {
        this.setProductRepository(new InMemoryProductRepository());
        this.tenantId = new TenantId("01234567");

        super.setUp();
    }
    ...
}
```

Just instantiate InMemoryProductRepository rather than the Coherence implementation. Other than that the test methods themselves are identical.

The possible difficult challenges are generally related to implementing more advanced finders, where parameter criteria are complex to resolve. If the criteria and resolution logic becomes too complex, you may have to find a way to work around the situation. It might mean prepopulating the Repository with instances that will resolve the search while making the finder method itself return only the instance or instances that are prepopulated. You can prepopulate using the test's setUp() method.

Another advantage to implementing in-memory editions of your Repositories is when you need to test for proper uses of save() with a persistence-oriented interface. You can implement the save() methods to count invocations. After each test is run, you can assert that the invocation count matches the number required by the client of the specific Repository. Generally, you could use this approach when testing Application Services that must explicitly save() changes to an Aggregate.

Wrap-Up

In this chapter we looked in depth at implementing Repositories.

- You learned about collection-oriented and persistence-oriented Repositories, and why to use one or the other.

- You saw how to implement Repositories for Hibernate, TopLink, Coherence, and MongoDB.

- You investigated why you might need additional behavior on a Repository's interface.

- You considered how transactions play into the use of Repositories.

- You are now familiar with the challenges of designing Repositories for type hierarchies.

- You looked at some fundamental differences between Repositories and Data Access Objects.

- You saw how to test Repositories and different ways to test using Repositories.

Next, we'll shift gears and take a careful look at integrating Bounded Contexts.

Chapter 13

Integrating Bounded Contexts

> *Making mental connections is our most crucial learning tool,*
> *the essence of human intelligence; to forge links; to go beyond the given;*
> *to see patterns, relationships, context.*
>
> *—Marilyn Ferguson*

There are always multiple **Bounded Contexts (2)** in any project of significance, and two or more of those Bounded Contexts will need to integrate. Using **Context Maps (3)**, we discussed the relationships that commonly exist between Bounded Contexts, and we examined some ways that those relationships can be managed correctly according to the principles of DDD. If you don't have a fairly strong grasp of **Domains (2)**, **Subdomains (2)**, and Bounded Contexts, or of Context Maps, you should obtain that before continuing. The material presented here builds on those fundamental concepts.

As previously discussed, Context Maps have two primary forms. One form is a simple drawing that is used to illustrate the kinds of relationships that exist between any two or more Bounded Contexts. The second and far more concrete form is the code that actually implements those relationships. That's what we are considering now.

Road Map to This Chapter

- Review some of the basics of integration, and develop the proper mindset necessary to succeed in integrating systems in a distributed computing environment.
- See how you can approach integration using RESTful resources, and consider some of its advantages and disadvantages.
- Learn how to integrate when using messaging.
- Understand the challenges you will face when you decide to duplicate information across Bounded Contexts.
- Study examples that provide increasing maturity in design approaches.

Integration Basics

When two Bounded Contexts need to integrate, there are a few reasonably straightforward ways this can be done in code.

One such straightforward approach is for a Bounded Context to expose an application programming interface (API), and another Bounded Context to use that API via remote procedure calls (RPCs). The API could be made available using SOAP or simply support sending XML requests and responses over HTTP (not the same as REST). Actually, there are several ways to create a remotely accessible API. This is one of the more popular ways to integrate, and since it supports a procedure call style, it is easily understood by programmers used to calling procedures or methods. That's pretty much all of us.

A second straightforward way to integrate Bounded Contexts is through the use of a messaging mechanism. Each of the systems that need to interact do so through the use of a message queue or a **Publish-Subscribe** [Gamma et al.] mechanism. Of course, these messaging gateways can well be thought of as an API, but we may find broader acceptance if we simply refer to them as service interfaces instead. There are a large number of integration techniques that may be employed when using messaging, many of them discussed in [Hohpe & Woolf].

A third way to integrate Bounded Contexts is by using RESTful HTTP. Some think of this as a kind of RPC approach, but it really is not. It has some similar properties in that one system makes a request of another system, but these requests are not made using procedures that take parameters. As discussed in **Architecture (4)**, REST is a means of exchanging and modifying resources that are uniquely identified using a distinct URI. Various operations can be performed on each resource. RESTful HTTP provides methods, primarily GET, PUT, POST, and DELETE. Even though these may seem to support only CRUD operations, using a little imagination allows us to actually categorize operations with explicit intent within one of the four method categories. For example, GET can be used to categorize various kinds of query operations, and PUT can be used to encapsulate a command operation that executes on an **Aggregate (10)**.

Of course, this in no way means that there are only three ways to integrate applications. You can, for example, use file-based integration and shared-database integration, but doing so could make you old before your time.

Cowboy Logic

AJ: "You better take a low seat in your saddle. That horse is a tough one and it'll make you feel old before your time."

Although I've highlighted three common ways that are used to integrate Bounded Contexts, we'll actually stick with just two of those in this chapter. We will mostly focus on integrating with messaging mechanisms but will see how to use RESTful HTTP as well. We'll avoid examples using RPC because you can easily imagine creating procedural APIs that could be used to replace the other two approaches. Also, RPC has less resilience when our goal is to support autonomous services (aka autonomous applications). A failed system that would normally provide an RPC-based API will prevent dependent systems from succeeding in their own operations.

This brings up a topic of vital importance, which requires the attention of every integration developer.

Distributed Systems Are Fundamentally Different

Problems always arise with integration when developers who are unfamiliar with the principles of distributed systems gloss over its inherent complexity. This can be especially true when using RPC, because those inexperienced with distribution commonly imagine that any one remote call is as good as an in-process call. Such assumptions can cause cascading failure across any number of systems when just one system or one of its components becomes unavailable, even temporarily so. Thus, all developers working within distributed systems will succeed or fail by the following Principles of Distributed Computing:

- The network is not reliable.

- There is always some latency, and maybe a lot.

- Bandwidth is not infinite.

- Do not assume that the network is secure.

- Network topology changes.

- Knowledge and policies are spread across multiple administrators.

- Network transport has cost.

- The network is heterogeneous.

These are purposely stated differently from the "Fallacies of Distributed Computing" [Deutsch]. I call them *principles* to emphasize the challenges that must be worked around and complexities that must be planned for, rather than the mistakes commonly made by the naive.

Exchanging Information across System Boundaries

Most of the time when we need a foreign system to provide a service for our own system, we need to pass informational data to the service. The services we use sometimes need to provide responses. Thus, we need a reliable way to pass informational data between systems. This data needs to be exchanged between disparate systems in a structure that is easily consumed by all involved. Most of us would choose to use some standard way to do that.

Informational data sent as parameters or messages constitutes just machine-readable structures that can be generated in one of many formats. We must also create some form of contract between the data-exchanging systems, and possibly even the mechanisms to parse or interpret those structures, so they can be consumed.

There are several ways to generate the structures used to exchange information between systems. One technical implementation simply relies on the programming language facilities to serialize objects into a binary format and deserialize them on the consumer's side. This works well as long as all systems support the same language facilities, and if the serialization is actually compatible or interchangeable between disparate hardware architectures. It also requires you to deploy all the interfaces and classes of objects that are used across systems to each system that uses the specific object type.

Another approach to building exchangeable information structures is to use some standard intermediate format. Some options are to use XML, JSON, or a specialized format such as Protocol Buffers. Each of these approaches has advantages and disadvantages, some of which include richness and compactness factors, performance of type conversions, support for flexibility between object versions, and ease of use. Some of these can have costly impacts when considering the Principles of Distributed Computing listed earlier (for example, "Network transport has cost").

Using this intermediate format approach, you may still desire to deploy all the interfaces and classes of objects that are used across systems, and use a tool to place the data of the intermediate format into your type-safe objects. This has the advantage that you can use objects the same way in the consuming system as you would in the source system.

Of course, deploying these interfaces and classes also has related complexity, and it typically means that the consuming system will need to be recompiled to maintain compatibility with the latest versions of interface and class definitions. There is also the danger of using the foreign objects freely in the consuming system as if they were our very own, which would tend to violate the very DDD strategic design principles we have been fighting so hard to follow. Some may think that by declaring this as a **Shared Kernel** (3), it indemnifies the approach. However, be aware that the convenience of objects that are shared between systems can lead you down a slippery slope. Yet, regardless of the complexity and potential danger of polluted models, many believe that any strong typing afforded by this tactic is a suitable trade-off for the required complexity.

Still, I encounter those who struggle with this for various reasons, and they often wish for an easier and safer approach, but one that doesn't entirely discard type safety. Let's consider such an approach.

What if we could define a contract between the systems that produce the exchangeable information structures and those that consume them in such a way that the consumers could confidently use the data without deserializing it into object instances of specific classes? We can define such a reliable contract using a standards-based approach, which actually forms a **Published Language** (3). One such standard approach is to define a custom media type, or the semantic equivalent. Whether or not you have good reason to register such a media type using the guidelines from RFC 4288, it is the actual specification that matters. The specification defines the binding contract between producers and consumers and offers a foolproof means to exchange such media without sharing the interface and class binaries.

This does require some trade-offs, as always. You will not be able to navigate using property accessors as you would if you had the interfaces/classes for each object, and with associated type safety. You would also lack some IDE support, such as the ability to use code completion. This isn't really a big disadvantage. Further, you would have no operational function/method support that having the Event class could provide. However, I do not see the lack of Event operational functions/methods as a disadvantage, but rather as a protection. The consuming Bounded Context should be interested only in the data properties and should never be tempted to use functionality that is part of a different model. The consumer's **Port Adapters** (4) should shield its domain model from any such dependencies and must instead pass needed Event data as appropriate parameters with types as defined only in its own Bounded Context. Any necessary calculations or processing should be performed by the producing Bounded Context and provided as enriching Event data attributes.

Consider an example. SaaSOvation needs to exchange media between its various Bounded Contexts. It will do so using RESTful resources and by sending messages containing **Events** (8) between services. In fact, one kind of RESTful resource is a *notification*, and Event-based messages are also sent to subscribers as Notification objects. In other words, in both cases the Notification holds an Event, and the two are formatted into a single structure. The custom media type specification for notifications and Events could indicate a contract that includes

- Type: `Notification` format: JSON

- `notificationId`: long integer unique identity

- `typeName`: text `String` type of notification, an example type name being `com.saasovation.agilepm.domain.model.product.`↵`backlogItem.BacklogItemCommitted`

- `version`: integer version of the notification

- `occurredOn`: date/time when the notification's contained Event happened

- `event`: JSON payload details; see specific Event types

Using the fully qualified class name (package name included) for the `typeName` allows subscribers to precisely differentiate various `Notification` types. The notification specification would be followed by the various Event type specifications. For one example, consider a familiar Event named `BacklogItemCommitted`:

- Event type: `com.saasovation.agilepm.domain.model.product.`↵`backlogItem.BacklogItemCommitted`

- `eventVersion`: integer version of the Event, which is the same as the `Notification` version

- `occurredOn`: date/time when the Event occurred, which is the same as `Notification` `occurredOn`

- `backlogItemId`: `BacklogItemId`, which contains the `id` text string attribute

- `committedToSprintId`: `SprintId`, which contains the `id` text string attribute

- `tenantId`: `TenantId`, which contains the `id` text string attribute

- Event details: see specific Event types

We would, of course, specify the Event details for every Event type. With the `Notification` and all Event types specified, we can safely use a `NotificationReader` as demonstrated by this test:

```
DomainEvent domainEvent = new TestableDomainEvent(100, "testing");

Notification notification = new Notification(1, domainEvent);

NotificationSerializer serializer =
    NotificationSerializer.instance();
```

```
String serializedNotification = serializer.serialize(notification);

NotificationReader reader =
    new NotificationReader(serializedNotification);

assertEquals(1L, reader.notificationId());
assertEquals("1", reader.notificationIdAsString());
assertEquals(domainEvent.occurredOn(), reader.occurredOn());
assertEquals(notification.typeName(), reader.typeName());
assertEquals(notification.version(), reader.version());
assertEquals(domainEvent.eventVersion(), reader.version());
```

The test shows how the `NotificationReader` can provide type-safe standard parts for every serialized `Notification` object.

The next test shows how the special parts of each Event's details can also be read out of a `Notification` payload. Event object navigation is provided using XPath-like syntax, or dot-separated properties, or you may use attribute names separated by commas (Java varargs). You can see that each attribute can be read as a `String` value or as its actual primitive type (`int`, `long`, `boolean`, `double`, and so on) if the type is other than `String`:

```
TestableNavigableDomainEvent domainEvent =
    new TestableNavigableDomainEvent(100, "testing");

Notification notification = new Notification(1, domainEvent);

NotificationSerializer serializer = NotificationSerializer.instance();

String serializedNotification = serializer.serialize(notification);

NotificationReader reader =
    new NotificationReader(serializedNotification);

assertEquals("" + domainEvent.eventVersion(),
    reader.eventStringValue("eventVersion"));
assertEquals("" + domainEvent.eventVersion(),
    reader.eventStringValue("/eventVersion"));
assertEquals(domainEvent.eventVersion(),
    reader.eventIntegerValue("eventVersion").intValue());
assertEquals(domainEvent.eventVersion(),
    reader.eventIntegerValue("/eventVersion").intValue());

assertEquals("" + domainEvent.nestedEvent().eventVersion(),
    reader.eventStringValue("nestedEvent", "eventVersion"));
assertEquals("" + domainEvent.nestedEvent().eventVersion(),
    reader.eventStringValue("/nestedEvent/eventVersion"));
assertEquals(domainEvent.nestedEvent().eventVersion(),
    reader.eventIntegerValue("nestedEvent", "eventVersion").intValue());
assertEquals(domainEvent.nestedEvent().eventVersion(),
    reader.eventIntegerValue("/nestedEvent/eventVersion").intValue());
```

```
assertEquals("" + domainEvent.nestedEvent().id(),
    reader.eventStringValue("nestedEvent", "id"));
assertEquals("" + domainEvent.nestedEvent().id(),
    reader.eventStringValue("/nestedEvent/id"));
assertEquals(domainEvent.nestedEvent().id(),
    reader.eventLongValue("nestedEvent", "id").longValue());
assertEquals(domainEvent.nestedEvent().id(),
    reader.eventLongValue("/nestedEvent/id").longValue());

assertEquals("" + domainEvent.nestedEvent().name(),
    reader.eventStringValue("nestedEvent", "name"));
assertEquals("" + domainEvent.nestedEvent().name(),
    reader.eventStringValue("/nestedEvent/name"));

assertEquals("" + domainEvent.nestedEvent().occurredOn().getTime(),
    reader.eventStringValue("nestedEvent", "occurredOn"));
assertEquals("" + domainEvent.nestedEvent().occurredOn().getTime(),
    reader.eventStringValue("/nestedEvent/occurredOn"));
assertEquals(domainEvent.nestedEvent().occurredOn(),
    reader.eventDateValue("nestedEvent", "occurredOn"));
assertEquals(domainEvent.nestedEvent().occurredOn(),
    reader.eventDateValue("/nestedEvent/occurredOn"));
assertEquals("" + domainEvent.occurredOn().getTime(),
    reader.eventStringValue("occurredOn"));
assertEquals("" + domainEvent.occurredOn().getTime(),
    reader.eventStringValue("/occurredOn"));
assertEquals(domainEvent.occurredOn(),
    reader.eventDateValue("occurredOn"));
assertEquals(domainEvent.occurredOn(),
    reader.eventDateValue("/occurredOn"));
```

The `TestableNavigableDomainEvent` holds a `TestableDomain-Event`, which allows us to test navigation to deeper attributes. The various attributes are read using XPath-like syntax with varargs attribute navigation. We also test reading each attribute value as various types.

Since `Notification` and Event instances always have a version number, you can key off of the version to read specialized attributes in a specific version. Consumers that specialize in a given version can pick out the special parts that they need. However, it is also possible for consumers to receive any given Event-containing `Notification` as if it were version 1.

Thus, if we carefully consider how each Event type is designed, we can protect most consumers from incompatibility when all they need is version 1 of a given Event. Such consumers never have to change or be recompiled when an Event changes. Still, you really have to think in terms of the version compatibility and plan for smart modifications to new versions so you don't break most consumers. Sometimes it's impossible to achieve, but in many cases it is entirely possible.

This approach has the added advantage that Events can hold more than just primitive attributes and strings. Events may also safely hold instances of more sophisticated **Value Objects (6)**, which is especially effective when their Value types tend to be stable. This is certainly the case with `BacklogItemId`, `SprintId`, and `TenantId`, as demonstrated by the following code, this time using dot-separated property navigation:

```
NotificationReader reader =
        new NotificationReader(backlogItemCommittedNotification);

String backlogItemId = reader.eventStringValue("backlogItemId.id"));

String sprintId = reader.eventStringValue("sprintId.id"));

String tenantId = reader.eventStringValue("tenantId.id"));
```

The fact that any held Value instances are frozen in the structure allows Events to be not only immutable, but also eternally fixed. New versions of Value Object types contained by Events do not impact your ability to read older versions of those Values from preexisting `Notification` instances. Certainly, Protocol Buffers can be far easier to use when Event versions change significantly and often, and dealing with those changes becomes unwieldy for consumers that use the `NotificationReader`.

Understand that this is simply an option for gracefully handling deserialization without deploying Event types and dependencies everywhere. Some will find this approach quite elegant and liberating, while others will find it risky, inept, or downright dangerous. The opposite approach of deploying interfaces and classes everywhere the serialized objects are consumed is well known. Here I provide some food for thought by pointing out a less traveled road.

Cowboy Logic

LB: "You know, J, when a cowboy's too old to set a bad example, he hands out good advice."

It is possible that each approach—deploying classes to exchange serializations versus defining a media type contract—has an advantage at different stages of a project. For example, depending on the number of teams, Bounded

Contexts, change ratio, and other factors, it might work out to share classes and interfaces when your project is starting, but it could be better to use a more decoupled, custom media type contract in the production stage. In practice this may or may not work for a particular team or set of teams. Sometimes what a team starts out with ends up being what they live with ongoing, and they never take the time to make a 180-degree change.

To keep our running examples simple and understandable, in the remainder of the chapter I use the `NotificationReader` throughout. Whether or not to use a custom media type contract and `NotificationReader` in your Bounded Contexts is your choice to make.

Integration Using RESTful Resources

When a Bounded Context provides a rich set of RESTful resources through URIs, it is a kind of **Open Host Service (3)**:

> Define a protocol that gives access to your subsystem as a set of services. Open the protocol so that all who need to integrate with you can use it. Enhance and expand the protocol to handle new integration requirements. [Evans]

We can well think of the HTTP methods—GET, PUT, POST, and DELETE—combined with resources on which they operate, as a set of open services. HTTP and REST certainly form an open protocol allowing all who need to integrate with the subsystem to do so. The fact that a virtually unlimited number of resources—each with a unique identity through a URI—can be created allows the protocol to handle new integration requirements as needed. It is a very versatile way to allow clients to integrate with your Bounded Context.

Even so, since the RESTful service provider must be directly interacted with whenever a resource is operated on, this style does not permit clients to be completely autonomous. If the REST-based Bounded Context becomes unavailable for some reason, dependent client Bounded Contexts will be unable to carry out necessary integration operations during any downtime.

Still, we can overcome this to some extent by making dependence on RESTful resources a lesser obstacle to consumer autonomy. Even when RESTful (or RPC for that matter) is your only means to integrate, you can create the illusion of temporal decoupling by using timers or messaging in your own system. That way your system will reach out to any remote systems only when a timer elapses or when a message is received. If the remote system is unavailable, the timer threshold can be backed off, or if using messaging the message can be negatively acknowledged to the broker and redelivered. This naturally places more of a burden on your team to make the systems loosely coupled, but that's a price you may have to pay to achieve autonomy.

When the SaaSOvation team developing the *Identity and Access Context* needed to create a way for integrators to use their Bounded Context, they determined that RESTful HTTP would be one of the best ways to open their system for integration without directly exposing the  structural and behavioral details of their domain model. For them this meant designing a set of RESTful resources that would provide representations of identity and access concepts on a tenant-by-tenant basis.

Much of their design would allow integrating Bounded Contexts to GET resources that convey user and group identity, and also indicate role-based security permissions for those identity types. For example, if an integration client needs to know if a user within a given tenant could play a specific access role, the client should GET a resource using this URI format:

```
/tenants/{tenantId}/users/{username}/inRole/{role}
```

If the tenant's user is in the role, the resource representation is included in the successful 200 response. Otherwise, the response is a 204 No Content status code if the user does not exist or does not play that named role. It's a simple RESTful HTTP design.

Let's look at how the team exposed the access resources and how integration clients could consume them in terms of the **Ubiquitous Language (1)** of their own Bounded Context.

Implementing the RESTful Resource

As SaaSOvation started applying REST principles to one of their Bounded Contexts, they learned some important lessons. Let's look in on their journey.

As the SaaSOvation team working in the *Identity and Access Context* considered how to provide an Open Host Service for integrators, they considered simply exposing their domain model as a set of RESTful linked resources. That would mean allowing HTTP clients to GET a unique tenant resource and navigate through its users, groups, and roles. Was that a good idea? It seemed natural at first. After all, that would afford clients with the greatest flexibility. Clients could know everything about the domain model and just make decisions in their own Bounded Context.

Which DDD Context Mapping pattern best describes this design approach? In reality that is not an Open Host Service, but depending on the size of the shared model it would instead be a Shared Kernel or a **Conformist (3)**. Publishing a Shared Kernel or accepting a Conformist relationship puts consumers into a tightly coupled integration with the consumed domain model. Those kinds of relationships should be avoided if at all possible since they tend to run counter to the most fundamental goals of DDD.

It was a good thing that along the way the team found some good advice to avoid exposing their model to clients in that way. They learned to think of the use cases (or user stories) that integrators needed. That was in harmony with this part of the Open Host Service definition: "Enhance and expand the protocol to handle new integration requirements." That means that you provide only what integrators need at present, and you understand those needs only by considering a range of use case scenarios.

When the team followed that advice, they realized that, for example, what integrators are really interested in is whether or not a given user can play a specific role. Shielding the integrators from the details of understanding the domain model would ultimately increase their productivity and make their dependent Bounded Contexts more maintainable. In terms of design it meant that their User RESTful resource could include the following design:

```
@Path("/tenants/{tenantId}/users")
public class UserResource {
    ...
    @GET
    @Path("{username}/inRole/{role}")
    @Produces({ OvationsMediaType.ID_OVATION_TYPE })
    public Response getUserInRole(
            @PathParam("tenantId") String aTenantId,
            @PathParam("username") String aUsername,
            @PathParam("role") String aRoleName) {

        Response response = null;

        User user = null;

        try {
            user = this.accessService().userInRole(
                        aTenantId, aUsername, aRoleName);
        } catch (Exception e) {
            // fall through
        }

        if (user != null) {
            response = this.userInRoleResponse(user, aRoleName);
        } else {
            response = Response.noContent().build();
        }
```

```
        return response;
    }
    ...
}
```

In the **Hexagonal (4)** or Ports and Adapters architecture, class User-Resource is an Adapter for the RESTful HTTP Port provided by the JAX-RS implementation. A consumer makes a request in the form

```
GET /tenants/{tenantId}/users/{username}/inRole/{role}
```

The Adapter delegates to the AccessService, an **Application Service (14)** that provides an API at the inner hexagon. Being a direct client of the domain model, the AccessService manages the use case task and transaction. The task includes finding whether or not the User exists at all, and if so, whether or not it plays the named role:

```java
package com.saasovation.identityaccess.application;
...
public class AccessService ... {
    ...
    @Transactional(readOnly=true)
    public User userInRole(
            String aTenantId,
            String aUsername,
            String aRoleName) {

        User userInRole = null;

        TenantId tenantId = new TenantId(new TenantId(aTenantId));

        User user =
            DomainRegistry
                .userRepository()
                .userWithUsername(tenantId, aUsername);

        if (user != null) {
            Role role =
                DomainRegistry
                    .roleRepository()
                    .roleNamed(tenantId, aRoleName);

            if (role != null) {
                GroupMemberService groupMemberService =
                        DomainRegistry.groupMemberService();

                if (role.isInRole(user, groupMemberService)) {
                    userInRole = user;
                }
            }
        }
```

```
        return userInRole;
    }
    ...
}
```

The Application Service finds both the `User` and the named `Role` Aggregate. When the `Role` query method `isInRole()` is called, a `GroupMember-Service` is passed in. This is not an Application Service, but rather a **Domain Service (7)** that helps the `Role` perform certain domain-specific checks and queries that the `Role` itself should not be responsible for.

The `Response` from the `UserResource` is formed from the resolved `User` and the specific role name, using one of the custom media types:

```
package com.saasovation.common.media;

public class OvationsMediaType {
    public static final String COLLAB_OVATION_TYPE =
            "application/vnd.saasovation.collabovation+json";

    public static final String ID_OVATION_TYPE =
            "application/vnd.saasovation.idovation+json";

    public static final String PROJECT_OVATION_TYPE =
            "application/vnd.saasovation.projectovation+json";
    ...
}
```

When the user is in the named role, the `UserResource` Adapter produces an HTTP response with a JSON representation like the following:

```
HTTP/1.1 200 OK
Content-Type: application/vnd.saasovation.idovation+json
...
{
    "role":"Author","username":"zoe",
    "tenantId":"A94A8298-43B8-4DA0-9917-13FFF9E116ED",
    "firstName":"Zoe","lastName":"Doe",
    "emailAddress":"zoe@saasovation.com"
}
```

As you will see next, the integrating consumer of this RESTful resource can translate it into the specific kind of domain object needed by its Bounded Context.

Implementing the REST Client Using an Anticorruption Layer

Although the JSON representation produced by the *Identity and Access Context* is quite useful to the client integrators, when we are focused on the goals of DDD, the representation will not be consumed as is in the client Bounded Context. As discussed in previous chapters, if the consumer is the *Collaboration Context*, the team is not interested in primitive users and their roles. Instead, the team developing in the collaboration model is interested in the domain-specific roles. The fact that in some other model there is a set of User objects that can be assigned to one or more roles as modeled by a Role object is really not in the collaboration sweet spot.

So, then, how do we make the user-in-role representation serve our specific collaboration purposes? Let's take another look at a previously drawn Context Map, this time found in Figure 13.1. The important parts of the User-Resource Adapter were shown in the previous subsection. This leaves the interfaces and classes to be developed specifically for the *Collaboration Context*. These are the CollaboratorService, the UserInRoleAdapter, and

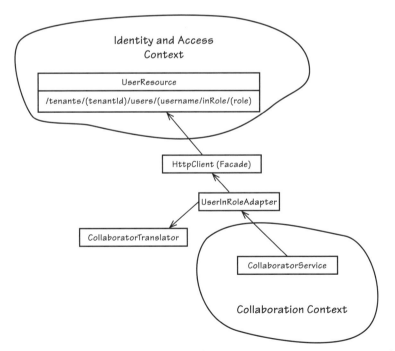

Figure 13.1 The Open Host Service of the Identity and Access Context and the Anticorruption Layer of the Collaboration Context used for integration between the two

the `CollaboratorTranslator`. There is also the `HttpClient`, but that is provided by the JAX-RS implementation through the classes `ClientRequest` and `ClientResponse`.

The trio of `CollaboratorService`, `UserInRoleAdapter`, and `CollaboratorTranslator` is used to form an **Anticorruption Layer (3)**, the means by which the *Collaboration Context* will interact with the *Identity and Access Context* and translate the user-in-role representation into a Value Object for a specific kind of `Collaborator`.

Here's interface `CollaboratorService`, which forms the simple operations of the Anticorruption Layer:

```
public interface CollaboratorService  {
    public Author authorFrom(Tenant aTenant, String anIdentity);
    public Creator creatorFrom(Tenant aTenant, String anIdentity);
    public Moderator moderatorFrom(Tenant aTenant, String anIdentity);
    public Owner ownerFrom(Tenant aTenant, String anIdentity);
    public Participant participantFrom(
            Tenant aTenant, String anIdentity);
}
```

From the viewpoint of the clients of `CollaboratorService`, the interface completely abstracts away the complexity of the remote system access and subsequent translations from the Published Language to objects that adhere to the local Ubiquitous Language. In this particular case we do use a **Separated Interface** [Fowler, P of EAA] and an implementation class because the implementation is technical and should not reside in the Domain Layer.

All of these **Factories (11)** are very similar to each other. They all create a subclass of the abstract `Collaborator` Value type, but only if the user within `aTenant` and having `anIdentity` plays the security role within one of the five types: `Author`, `Creator`, `Moderator`, `Owner`, and `Participant`. Since they are so similar, let's look at just one of the method implementations, `authorFrom()`:

```
package com.saasovation.collaboration.infrastructure.services;

import com.saasovation.collaboration.domain.model.collaborator.Author;
...
public class TranslatingCollaboratorService
        implements CollaboratorService  {
    ...
    @Override
    public Author authorFrom(Tenant aTenant, String anIdentity) {
        Author author =
```

```
                this.userInRoleAdapter
                    .toCollaborator(
                            aTenant,
                            anIdentity,
                            "Author",
                            Author.class);

        return author;
    }
    ...
}
```

First note that `TranslatingCollaboratorService` is in a **Module (9)** of the Infrastructure. We create the Separated Interface in the inner hexagon as part of the domain model. Yet, the implementation is technical and is housed at the outside of the Hexagonal architecture, where the Ports and Adapters reside.

As part of the technical implementation, generally an Anticorruption Layer will have a specialized **Adapter** [Gamma et al.] and a translator. Looking again at Figure 13.1, you can see that our specific Adapter is `UserInRoleAdapter`, and the translator is the `CollaboratorTranslator`. The specialized `User-InRoleAdapter` of this Anticorruption Layer is responsible for reaching out to the remote system, requesting the necessary user-in-role resource:

```
package com.saasovation.collaboration.infrastructure.services;

import org.jboss.resteasy.client.ClientRequest;
import org.jboss.resteasy.client.ClientResponse;
...
public class UserInRoleAdapter {
    ...
    public <T extends Collaborator> T toCollaborator(
            Tenant aTenant,
            String anIdentity,
            String aRoleName,
            Class<T> aCollaboratorClass) {

        T collaborator = null;

        try {
        ClientRequest request =
                this.buildRequest(aTenant, anIdentity, aRoleName);

        ClientResponse<String> response =
                request.get(String.class);

        if (response.getStatus() == 200) {
            collaborator =
                new CollaboratorTranslator()
```

```
                        .toCollaboratorFromRepresentation(
                            response.getEntity(),
                            aCollaboratorClass);
            } else if (response.getStatus() != 204) {
                throw new IllegalStateException(
                        "There was a problem requesting the user: "
                        + anIdentity
                        + " in role: "
                        + aRoleName
                        + " with resulting status: "
                        + response.getStatus());
            }

        } catch (Throwable t) {
            throw new IllegalStateException(
                    "Failed because: " + t.getMessage(), t);
        }

        return collaborator;
    }
    ...
}
```

If the response to the GET request is successful (status 200), it means that
the UserInRoleAdapter has received a user-in-role resource, which can now
be translated into our Collaborator subclass:

```
package com.saasovation.collaboration.infrastructure.services;

import java.lang.reflect.Constructor;
import com.saasovation.common.media.RepresentationReader;
...
public class CollaboratorTranslator {
    public CollaboratorTranslator() {
        super();
    }

    public <T extends Collaborator> T toCollaboratorFromRepresentation(
            String aUserInRoleRepresentation,
            Class<T> aCollaboratorClass)
    throws Exception {

        RepresentationReader reader =
                new RepresentationReader(aUserInRoleRepresentation);

        String username = reader.stringValue("username");
        String firstName = reader.stringValue("firstName");
        String lastName = reader.stringValue("lastName");
        String emailAddress = reader.stringValue("emailAddress");
```

```
        T collaborator =
            this.newCollaborator(
                    username,
                    firstName,
                    lastName,
                    emailAddress,
                    aCollaboratorClass);

        return collaborator;
    }

    private <T extends Collaborator> T newCollaborator(
            String aUsername,
            String aFirstName,
            String aLastName,
            String aEmailAddress,
            Class<T> aCollaboratorClass)
    throws Exception {

        Constructor<T> ctor =
            aCollaboratorClass.getConstructor(
                    String.class, String.class, String.class);

        T collaborator =
            ctor.newInstance(
                    aUsername,
                    (aFirstName + " " + aLastName).trim(),
                    aEmailAddress);

        return collaborator;
    }
}
```

This translator takes a user-in-role representation text String and the Class to be used to create the Collaborator subclass instance. First the RepresentationReader—quite similar to the NotificationReader introduced previously—is used to read four attributes out of the JSON representation. Again, we can confidently and reliably do this because the SaaSOvation custom media type forms a binding contract between producers and consumers. After the translator has the necessary String values, it uses them to instantiate the Collaborator Value Object and, in the case of this example, an Author:

```
package com.saasovation.collaboration.domain.model.collaborator;

public final class Author
        extends Collaborator  {
```

```
    public Author(
            String anIdentity,
            String aName,
            String anEmailAddress) {
        super(anIdentity, aName, anEmailAddress);
    }
    ...
}
```

There is no effort made to keep `Collaborator` Value instances synchronized with the *Identity and Access Context*. They are immutable and can only be fully replaced, not modified. Here's how an `Author` is obtained by an Application Service and then given to a `Forum` to start a new `Discussion`:

```
package com.saasovation.collaboration.application;
...
public class ForumService ... {
    ...
    @Transactional
    public Discussion startDiscussion(
            String aTenantId,
            String aForumId,
            String anAuthorId,
            String aSubject) {

        Tenant tenant = new Tenant(aTenantId);
        ForumId forumId = new ForumId(aForumId);

        Forum forum = this.forum(tenant, forumId);

        if (forum == null) {
            throw new IllegalStateException("Forum does not exist.");
        }

        Author author =
                this.collaboratorService.authorFrom(
                        tenant, anAuthorId);

        Discussion newDiscussion =
                forum.startDiscussion(
                        this.forumNavigationService(),
                        author,
                        aSubject);

        this.discussionRepository.add(newDiscussion);

        return newDiscussion;
    }
    ...
}
```

If a `Collaborator` name or e-mail address changes in the *Identity and Access Context*, such changes won't be automatically updated in the *Collaboration Context*. Those kinds of changes rarely occur, so the team made the decision to keep this particular design simple and not attempt to synchronize changes in the remote Context with objects in their local Context. We will see, however, that the *Agile Project Management Context* has different design goals.

There are other ways to implement an Anticorruption Layer, such as by means of a **Repository (12)**. However, since Repositories are typically used to persist and reconstitute Aggregates, creating Value Objects by that means seems misplaced. If our goal is to produce an Aggregate from an Anticorruption Layer, a Repository may be a more natural source.

Integration Using Messaging

A message-based approach to integration can allow any one system to achieve a higher degree of autonomy from systems it depends on. As long as the messaging infrastructure remains operational, messages can be sent and delivered even when any one system is unavailable.

One of the ways that DDD can be leveraged to make systems autonomous is through the use of Domain Events. When something of significance happens in one system, it produces an Event about it. There will tend to be several or even many such Events that occur in each system, and you will create a unique kind of Event as a means to record each. As Events occur, they are published to interested parties by means of a messaging mechanism. That's just a big-picture review. In case you bypassed the details of this topic in earlier chapters, you may be better off getting some background from **Architecture (4)**, **Domain Events (8)**, and **Aggregates (10)** before continuing here.

Staying Informed about Product Owners and Team Members

The *Agile Project Management Context* needs to manage a pool of Scrum product owners and team members for each tenant that subscribes to the service. At any time a product owner can create a new product and then assign team members to the team. How can the Scrum project management application know who plays each of these roles? The answer is that it won't go it alone.

Actually, the *Agile Project Management Context* is going to allow those roles to be managed by the *Identity and Access Context*, a natural and fitting choice. In that system each tenant that subscribes to the Scrum service will have two Role instances created: ScrumProductOwner and ScrumTeam-Member. Each User who needs to play one of those roles will be assigned to it. Here's the Application Service method in the *Identity and Access Context* that manages the task of assigning a User to a Role:

```
package com.saasovation.identityaccess.application;
...
public class AccessService ... {
    ...
    @Transactional
    public void assignUserToRole(AssignUserToRoleCommand aCommand) {

        TenantId tenantId =
                new TenantId(aCommand.getTenantId());

        User user =
                this.userRepository
                    .userWithUsername(
                            tenantId,
                            aCommand.getUsername());

        if (user != null) {
            Role role =
                    this.roleRepository
                        .roleNamed(
                                tenantId,
                                aCommand.getRoleName());

            if (role != null) {
                role.assignUser(user);
            }
        }
    }
    ...
}
```

Great, but how does this help the *Agile Project Management Context* know who is in the role of a ScrumTeamMember or ScrumProductOwner? Here's how. When method assignUser() of the Role completes, its last responsibility is to publish an Event:

```
package com.saasovation.identityaccess.domain.model.access;
...
public class Role extends Entity {
    ...
    public void assignUser(User aUser) {
```

```
            if (aUser == null) {
                throw new NullPointerException("User must not be null.");
            }
            if (!this.tenantId().equals(aUser.tenantId())) {
                throw new IllegalArgumentException(
                        "Wrong tenant for this user.");
            }

            this.group().addUser(aUser);

            DomainEventPublisher
                .instance()
                .publish(new UserAssignedToRole(
                        this.tenantId(),
                        this.name(),
                        aUser.username(),
                        aUser.person().name().firstName(),
                        aUser.person().name().lastName(),
                        aUser.person().emailAddress()));
        }
        ...
}
```

Event `UserAssignedToRole`, enriched with `User` name and e-mail address properties, is eventually delivered to all interested parties. When the *Agile Project Management Context* receives the Event, it will use it to ensure that a new `TeamMember` or `ProductOwner` is established in its model. This is not a terribly difficult use case. Yet, there are more details to manage than may at first meet the eye. Let's break these down.

As it turns out, there are some highly reusable aspects to listening for notifications from RabbitMQ. We already have a simple object-oriented library that helps make the RabbitMQ Java client easier to use. Now we're going to add one more simple class to make becoming an exchange queue consumer really simple:

```
package com.saasovation.common.port.adapter.messaging.rabbitmq;
...
public abstract class ExchangeListener {

    private MessageConsumer messageConsumer;
    private Queue queue;

    public ExchangeListener() {
        super();

        this.attachToQueue();
```

```java
            this.registerConsumer();
    }

    protected abstract String exchangeName();

    protected abstract void filteredDispatch(
            String aType, String aTextMessage);

    protected abstract String[] listensToEvents();

    protected String queueName() {
        return this.getClass().getSimpleName();
    }

    private void attachToQueue() {
        Exchange exchange =
                Exchange.fanOutInstance(
                        ConnectionSettings.instance(),
                        this.exchangeName(),
                        true);

        this.queue =
                Queue.individualExchangeSubscriberInstance(
                        exchange,
                        this.exchangeName() + "." + this.queueName());
    }

    private Queue queue() {
        return this.queue;
    }

    private void registerConsumer() {
        this.messageConsumer =
                MessageConsumer.instance(this.queue(), false);

        this.messageConsumer.receiveOnly(
                this.listensToEvents(),
                new MessageListener(MessageListener.Type.TEXT) {

            @Override
            public void handleMessage(
                    String aType,
                    String aMessageId,
                    Date aTimestamp,
                    String aTextMessage,
                    long aDeliveryTag,
                    boolean isRedelivery)
            throws Exception {
                filteredDispatch(aType, aTextMessage);
            }
        });
    }
}
```

The `ExchangeListener` is an abstract base class that concrete listener subclasses reuse. A concrete subclass need add only a little bit of code in addition to extending the abstract base class. First, it just ensures that the default base class constructor is invoked, which always happens anyway. Then all that's left is to implement three abstract methods, two of which are very simple to implement: `exchangeName()`, `filteredDispatch()`, and `listensToEvents()`.

To implement `exchangeName()` all that is needed is to return the `String` name of the exchange for which the concrete listener consumes notifications. To implement the abstract method `listensToEvents()` you must answer a `String[]` of notification types that you want to receive. Many listeners will consume only one type of notification and so would answer an array with only one element. The one remaining method, `filteredDispatch()`, is the most complex of the three because it is responsible for the heavy lifting of handling received messages. To see how it works, let's take a look at the listener of Event-carrying notifications for `UserAssignedToRole`:

```
package com.saasovation.agilepm.infrastructure.messaging;
...
public class TeamMemberEnablerListener extends ExchangeListener {

    @Autowired
    private TeamService teamService;

    public TeamMemberEnablerListener() {
        super();
    }

    @Override
    protected String exchangeName() {
        return Exchanges.IDENTITY_ACCESS_EXCHANGE_NAME;
    }

    @Override
    protected void filteredDispatch(
                String aType,
                String aTextMessage) {
        NotificationReader reader =
                new NotificationReader(aTextMessage);

        String roleName = reader.eventStringValue("roleName");

        if (!roleName.equals("ScrumProductOwner") &&
            !roleName.equals("ScrumTeamMember")) {
            return;
        }
```

```
    String emailAddress = reader.eventStringValue("emailAddress");
    String firstName = reader.eventStringValue("firstName");
    String lastName = reader.eventStringValue("lastName");
    String tenantId = reader.eventStringValue("tenantId.id");
    String username = reader.eventStringValue("username");
    Date occurredOn = reader.occurredOn();

    if (roleName.equals("ScrumProductOwner")) {
        this.teamService.enableProductOwner(
                new EnableProductOwnerCommand(
                    tenantId,
                    username,
                    firstName,
                    lastName,
                    emailAddress,
                    occurredOn));
    } else {
        this.teamService.enableTeamMember(
                new EnableTeamMemberCommand(
                    tenantId,
                    username,
                    firstName,
                    lastName,
                    emailAddress,
                    occurredOn));
    }
}

@Override
protected String[] listensToEvents() {
    return new String[] {
            "com.saasovation.identityaccess.domain.model.↵
access.UserAssignedToRole"
            };
}
}
```

The `ExchangeListener` default constructor is properly invoked, `exchangeName()` answers the name of the exchange published to by the *Identity and Access Context*, and method `listensToEvents()` answers a one-element array with the fully qualified class name of Event `User-AssignedToRole`. Note that publishers and subscribers should consider the use of fully qualified class names, which includes the Module name and the class name. This removes all possible collision or ambiguity that could exist with same or similarly named Events from different Bounded Contexts.

Again, it is `filteredDispatch()` that contains the bulk of the behavior. The method is named as it is because it can further filter the notification before it dispatches to the Application Service API. In this case it does filter before dispatching, by ignoring all notifications of type `UserAssignedToRole` that are not conveying Events about the roles named `ScrumProductOwner` and `ScrumTeamMember`. On the other hand, if the roles are the ones we are interested in receiving Events about, we get the `UserAssignedToRole` details out of the notification and dispatch to the Application Service named `TeamService`. Each of the Service methods `enableProductOwner()` and `enableTeamMember()` takes a command object, either `EnableProductOwnerCommand` or `EnableTeamMemberCommand`, respectively.

At first it might seem that a member would just be created as a result of one of these Events. However, since it is possible that each `User` could be assigned to one of these `Roles`, and then later unassigned, and then reassigned, it's possible that the member represented by the `User` in the received notification already exists. Here's how the `TeamService` deals with that situation:

```
package com.saasovation.agilepm.application;
...
public class TeamService ... {

    @Autowired
    private ProductOwnerRepository productOwnerRepository;

    @Autowired
    private TeamMemberRepository teamMemberRepository;

    ...

    @Transactional
    public void enableProductOwner(
            EnableProductOwnerCommand aCommand) {
        TenantId tenantId = new TenantId(aCommand.getTenantId());

        ProductOwner productOwner =
                this.productOwnerRepository.productOwnerOfIdentity(
                        tenantId,
                        aCommand.getUsername());

        if (productOwner != null) {
            productOwner.enable(aCommand.getOccurredOn());
        } else {
            productOwner =
                    new ProductOwner(
                            tenantId,
                            aCommand.getUsername(),
                            aCommand.getFirstName(),
                            aCommand.getLastName(),
                            aCommand.getEmailAddress(),
                            aCommand.getOccurredOn());
```

```
                    this.productOwnerRepository.add(productOwner);
          }
      }
}
```

For example, Service method `enableProductOwner()` deals with the possibility that the specific `ProductOwner` already exists. If it does exist, we assume that it may need to be enabled again, so we dispatch to the corresponding command operation. If the `ProductOwner` does not yet exist, we instantiate a new Aggregate and add it to its Repository. Actually, we deal with the `TeamMember` in the same way, so `enableTeamMember()` is implemented in the same way.

Can You Handle the Responsibility?

This all seems fine and good. It appears simple enough. We have `Product-Owner` and `TeamMember` Aggregate types, and we've designed them so that each holds some information about the backing `User` from the foreign Bounded Context. But did you realize how much responsibility we've just assumed by designing these Aggregates that way?

Recall that in the *Collaboration Context* the team decided to just create immutable Value Objects that hold similar information (see "Implementing the REST Client Using an Anticorruption Layer"). Because the Values are immutable, the team will never have to worry about keeping the shared information up-to-date. Of course, the downside to that advantage is that if some of the shared information is updated, the *Collaboration Context* will never update the related objects that it created in the past. So the Agile Project Management team went for the opposite trade-off.

Now, however, there are a few challenges to keeping the Aggregates up-to-date. Why? Can't we just listen for additional Event-carrying notifications that reflect changes to the `User` instances that correspond to our `ProductOwner` and `TeamMember` instances? Yes, indeed, we can and must do so. But the fact that we are using a messaging infrastructure makes this just a bit more challenging than might be obvious.

For example, what would happen if in the *Identity and Access Context* a manager mistakenly unassigns Joe Johnson from the `ScrumTeamMember` role? Well, we receive an Event-carrying notification that indicates that fact, so we use the `TeamService` to disable the `TeamMember` corresponding to Joe Johnson. Wait. Seconds later the manager realizes that she has unassigned the wrong user from the `ScrumTeamMember` role, and that she should have unassigned Joe Jones instead. So she quickly assigns Joe Johnson back to the role and unassigns Joe Jones. Next, the *Agile Project Management Context* receives the corresponding notifications, and everyone is happy (except maybe Joe Jones). Or, is everything *actually* OK?

We could be making a bad assumption about this use case. We are assuming that we receive the notifications in the order in which they actually occurred in the *Identity and Access Context*. Yet, things might not always work out so well. What would happen if, for whatever reason, the notifications about Joe Johnson were received in this order, `UserAssignedToRole` and then `User-UnassignedFromRole`? What will happen is that the `TeamMember` corresponding to Joe Johnson will be stuck in a disabled state, and at best someone will have to patch the data in the Agile PM database, or the manager will have to play some tricks to get the right Joe reenabled. This can happen, and ironically, it seems to always happen when we overlook the fact that it could happen. So, how do we prevent this?

Let's take a closer look at the command objects that we pass as parameters to the `TeamService` APIs. For example, consider the commands `Enable-TeamMemberCommand` and `DisableTeamMemberCommand`. Each of these requires a `Date` object, namely, `occurredOn`, to be provided. In fact, all of our command objects are designed this way. We will use the `occurredOn` values to ensure that our `ProductOwner` and `TeamMember` Aggregates deal with the command operations in a time-aware way. Thinking back to the use case that could have caused us trouble before, let's see what would happen if we dealt with the possibility of the `UserUnassignedFromRole` arriving after `UserAssignedToRole`, even though they occurred in the opposite order:

```
package com.saasovation.agilepm.application;
...
public class TeamService ... {
    ...
    @Transactional
    public void disableTeamMember(DisableTeamMemberCommand aCommand) {
        TenantId tenantId = new TenantId(aCommand.getTenantId());

        TeamMember teamMember =
                this.teamMemberRepository.teamMemberOfIdentity(
                        tenantId,
                        aCommand.getUsername());

        if (teamMember != null) {
            teamMember.disable(aCommand.getOccurredOn());
        }
    }
}
```

Note that when we dispatch to the `TeamMember disable()` command method, we are required to pass an `occurredOn` value from the command object. The `TeamMember` will use this internally to make certain that disabling takes place only if it should:

```
package com.saasovation.agilepm.domain.model.team;
...
public abstract class Member extends Entity  {
    ...
    private MemberChangeTracker changeTracker;
    ...
    public void disable(Date asOfDate) {
        if (this.changeTracker().canToggleEnabling(asOfDate)) {
            this.setEnabled(false);
            this.setChangeTracker(
                    this.changeTracker().enablingOn(asOfDate));
        }
    }

    public void enable(Date asOfDate) {
        if (this.changeTracker().canToggleEnabling(asOfDate)) {
            this.setEnabled(true);
            this.setChangeTracker(
                    this.changeTracker().enablingOn(asOfDate));
        }
    }
    ...
}
```

Note that this Aggregate behavior is provided by a common abstract base class, `Member`. Both the `disable()` and the `enable()` methods are designed to query a `changeTracker` to determine whether the requested operation can be carried out according to the `asOfDate` parameter (the command's `occurredOn` value). The `MemberChangeTracker` Value Object maintains the occurrence of the most recent related operation and uses that to answer the query:

```
package com.saasovation.agilepm.domain.model.team;
...
public final class MemberChangeTracker implements Serializable  {
    private Date emailAddressChangedOn;
    private Date enablingOn;
    private Date nameChangedOn;
    ...
    public boolean canToggleEnabling(Date asOfDate) {
        return this.enablingOn().before(asOfDate);
    }
    ...
```

```
    public MemberChangeTracker enablingOn(Date asOfDate) {
        return new MemberChangeTracker(
                asOfDate,
                this.nameChangedOn(),
                this.emailAddressChangedOn());
    }
    ...
}
```

If the operation is permitted and carried out, a replacement MemberChange-Tracker instance is obtained by using the corresponding enablingOn() method. Since we can expect PersonNameChanged and PersonContact-InformationChanged changes to possibly arrive out of order, the same kinds of facilities are available with emailAddressChangedOn and name-ChangedOn. In fact, there is one additional check for the case of e-mail address changes. It's possible that PersonContactInformationChanged Events are indicating a change of telephone number or postal address rather than a less common e-mail address change:

```
package com.saasovation.agilepm.domain.model.team;
...
public abstract class Member extends Entity  {
    ...
    public void changeEmailAddress(
        String anEmailAddress,
        Date asOfDate) {

        if (this.changeTracker().canChangeEmailAddress(asOfDate) &&
            !this.emailAddress().equals(anEmailAddress)) {
            this.setEmailAddress(anEmailAddress);
            this.setChangeTracker(
                this.changeTracker().emailAddressChangedOn(asOfDate));
        }
    }
    ...
}
```

Here we check to see if in fact the e-mail address has changed. If it has not, we don't want to track it as changed. If we did so, an out-of-order Event of the same type that did in fact carry a changed e-mail address would be ignored.

The MemberChangeTracker also serves to make Member subclass command operations idempotent, such that when the same notification is delivered multiple times by the messaging infrastructure, redundant deliveries are ignored.

We might argue that introducing the MemberChangeTracker in the Aggregate design is a mistake. We might conclude that this has nothing to do with the Ubiquitous Language of Scrum-based teams. That is true. However, we never expose the `MemberChangeTracker` outside the Aggregate boundary. It is an implementation detail, and clients will never know it exists. The only detail that clients are aware of is that they must supply the `occurredOn` value for when the corresponding fact of a modification took place. What is more, this is exactly the kind of implementation detail that Pat Helland calls for as he describes how partner relationships are managed in his treatment of scalable, distributed systems that are eventually consistent. In that paper [Helland], specifically see section 5, "Activities: Coping with Messy Messages."

Now, back to dealing with our new responsibilities . . .

Although this is a very basic example of maintaining changes to duplicate information originating in a foreign Bounded Context, it is not a trivial responsibility to take on, at least not if you are using a messaging mechanism that could deliver messages out of order and more than once.[1] Further, when we realize all of the possible operations in the *Identity and Access Context* that could have some kind of impact on just the few attributes that we maintain in `Member`, it can be a wake-up call:

- `PersonContactInformationChanged`

- `PersonNameChanged`

- `UserAssignedToRole`

- `UserUnassignedFromRole`

And then we realize that there are a few other Events that could be just as important to react to:

- `UserEnablementChanged`

- `TenantActivated`

- `TenantDeactivated`

These facts emphasize that, if at all possible, it is best to minimize or even completely eliminate information duplication across Bounded Contexts. It may not be possible to entirely avoid the duplication of information. SLAs may make it impractical to retrieve remote data every time it is needed. That's one

---

1. This could be a case where using the RESTful approach to notification consumption could be a distinct advantage since the notifications are guaranteed to be delivered in the same order in which they were appended to the **Event Store** (**4, Appendix A**). The notifications, from first to last, can be consumed over and over again for different reasons with the same order guarantees each time.

of the motivations the team had to hold the personal name of the `User` and the user's e-mail address locally. However, having the goal to reduce the amount of foreign information we take responsibility for will make our jobs much easier. It's integrating with a minimalist's mindset.

Of course, there is no way to avoid duplication of tenant and user identity, and identity duplication across Bounded Contexts is necessary in general. That is one of the primary ways that Bounded Contexts can integrate at all. Besides, identity is safe to share because it is immutable. We can even use Aggregate disabling and soft deletions to ensure that referenced objects never disappear, as we do, for example, with `Tenant`, `User`, `ProductOwner`, and `TeamMember`.

This call to attention doesn't mean that Domain Events should not be enriched with information-conveying properties. Certainly, Events must provide enough information to inform consumers of the kinds of steps that they must take in response to past facts. Still, it is possible for Event data to be used to perform calculations and derive state in consuming foreign Bounded Contexts while not actually holding on to and assuming the responsibility for keeping it synchronized with its official state located in the system of record.

Long-Running Processes, and Avoiding Responsibility

If we likened what we described in the previous section to being a responsible adult, we might compare this section to an attempt to return to our teenage years. You know, adults have to assume all kinds of responsibility. Parents have to buy cars, insure them, pay to put gasoline in the tank, and spend their money to repair them. As teens we just want to use our parents' car, but not pay for any of its expenses. There's no way teenagers are going to make a car payment for their parents, fill the tank with gasoline, pay for a mechanic, or cover the cost of insurance. They just allow their parents to take care of that horrible *R*-word stuff so they can have all the fun.

What we are doing in this section is having fun with **Long-Running Processes (4)**, but making sure we refuse to accept any of the painful responsibilities required when we duplicate information from other Bounded Contexts. We will just let the system of record deal with its own information after we've had all the fun making that foreign Bounded Context create and maintain data for us.

In **Context Maps (3)** we were presented with the *Create a Product* use case:

Precondition: The collaboration feature is enabled (option was purchased).

1. The user provides Product descriptive information.

2. The user indicates a desire for a team discussion.

3. The user requests that the defined Product be created.

4. The system creates the Product with a Forum and Discussion.

Here's where the fun begins, and where we kick responsibility across the network.

In **Context Maps** (3) the team proposed using a RESTful approach to integration between these two Bounded Contexts. However, the team finally settled on a message-based solution instead.

Also, one of the first things that you may notice is that the proposed concept originally added to the Ubiquitous Language as `Discussion` (in Chapter 3) has been refined. The Agile Project Management team saw the need to differentiate between the types of discussions, so there are now two different types: `ProductDiscussion` and `BacklogItemDiscussion`. (In this section we are concerned only with `ProductDiscussion`.) Both Value Objects have the same basic state and behavior, but the distinction adds type safety to help developers avoid attaching the wrong discussions to `Product` and `Backlog-Item`. For all practical purposes, they are the same. Each of these two discussion types just holds its availability and, if a discussion was established, the identity of the actual `Discussion` Aggregate instance in the *Collaboration Context.*

It is worth stating that the original proposal in the *Agile Project Management Context* to name one Value Object the same as the Aggregate in the *Collaboration Context* was not an error in judgment. Thus, to be completely clear, the Value Object's name was not changed from `Discussion` to `Product-Discussion` in order to distinguish it from the Aggregate in the *Collaboration Context.* From the standpoint of Context Mapping it would have been perfectly fine to leave the Value Object's name as it was, because the Context is what distinguished the two objects. The decision to create two distinct Value types in the *Agile Project Management Context* was made only from the requirements of the isolated local model.

To dive in, let's first take a look at the Application Service (API) that is used to create a `Product`:

```
package com.saasovation.agilepm.application;
...
public class ProductService ... {

    @Autowired
    private ProductRepository productRepository;

    @Autowired
    private ProductOwnerRepository productOwnerRepository;
    ...
```

```
    @Transactional
    public String newProductWithDiscussion(
                NewProductCommand aCommand) {

        return this.newProductWith(
                aCommand.getTenantId(),
                aCommand.getProductOwnerId(),
                aCommand.getName(),
                aCommand.getDescription(),
                this.requestDiscussionIfAvailable());
    }
    ...
}
```

There are actually two ways to create a new `Product`. The first method, not shown here, creates a `Product` without a `Discussion`, while the one seen here does attempt to cause a `ProductDiscussion` to eventually be created and attached to the `Product`. The two internal methods, `newProduct-With()` and `requestDiscussionIfAvailable()`, are not shown here. The latter method is used to check whether or not the CollabOvation add-on is enabled. If it is, the availability state `REQUESTED` is returned; otherwise, the state return value is `ADD_ON_NOT_ENABLED`. Method `newProductWith()` invokes the `Product` constructor, so let's look at the constructor next:

```
package com.saasovation.agilepm.domain.model.product;
...
public class Product extends ConcurrencySafeEntity {
    ...
    public Product(
                TenantId aTenantId,
                ProductId aProductId,
                ProductOwnerId aProductOwnerId,
                String aName,
                String aDescription,
                DiscussionAvailability aDiscussionAvailability) {

        this();

        this.setTenantId(aTenantId);
        this.setProductId(aProductId);
        this.setProductOwnerId(aProductOwnerId);
        this.setName(aName);
        this.setDescription(aDescription);

        this.setDiscussion(
                ProductDiscussion.fromAvailability(
                        aDiscussionAvailability));
```

```
            DomainEventPublisher
                .instance()
                .publish(new ProductCreated(
                    this.tenantId(),
                    this.productId(),
                    this.productOwnerId(),
                    this.name(),
                    this.description(),
                    this.discussion().availability().isRequested()));
    }
    ...
}
```

The client is required to pass a DiscussionAvailability, which may convey one of the following states: ADD_ON_NOT_ENABLED, NOT_REQUESTED, or REQUESTED. The READY state is reserved as a completion state. Either of the first two states results in the creation of a Product-Discussion with that exact state, which means there won't be an associated discussion, at least not as a result of construction. Given a request with the third state, REQUESTED, the ProductDiscussion will be created with a PENDING_SETUP state. Here's the ProductDiscussion Factory Method used by the Product constructor:

```
package com.saasovation.agilepm.domain.model.product;
...
public final class ProductDiscussion implements Serializable {
    ...
    public static ProductDiscussion fromAvailability(
            DiscussionAvailability anAvailability) {

        if (anAvailability.isReady()) {
            throw new IllegalArgumentException(
                    "Cannot be created ready.");
        }

        DiscussionDescriptor descriptor =
                new DiscussionDescriptor(
                        DiscussionDescriptor.UNDEFINED_ID);

        return new ProductDiscussion(descriptor, anAvailability);
    }
    ...
}
```

As long as the request is not for the READY state, which would be a problem, we get a ProductDiscussion with one of the three other states and an undefined descriptor. If the state is REQUESTED, a Long-Running Process will manage the creation of the collaborative discussion and its subsequent initiation with the `Product`. How? Recall that the last thing the `Product` constructor does is publish the `ProductCreated` Event:

```
package com.saasovation.agilepm.domain.model.product;
    ...
    public Product(...) {
        ...
        DomainEventPublisher
            .instance()
            .publish(new ProductCreated(
                this.tenantId(),
                this.productId(),
                this.productOwnerId(),
                this.name(),
                this.description(),
                this.discussion().availability().isRequested()));
    }
    ...
}
```

If the state of the discussion availability is REQUESTED, the last parameter to the Event constructor will be true, which is exactly what is needed to start the Long-Running Process.

Think back to **Domain Events** (8); every single Event instance, including those of type `ProductCreated`, is appended to an Event Store for the specific Bounded Context in which the Event occurred. All newly appended Events are then forwarded from the Event Store to interested parties by means of a messaging mechanism. In the case of SaaSOvation, the teams have decided to use RabbitMQ for that purpose. We need to create a simple Long-Running Process to manage the creation of the discussion and then attach it to the `Product`.

Before moving on to the details of the Long-Running Process, let's consider one more possible way that a discussion is requested. What if when a given `Product` instance is first created, either a discussion is not requested, or the collaboration add-on is only enabled? Later on the product owner decides to add a discussion, and the add-on is now available. The product owner can now use this command method on the `Product`:

```
package com.saasovation.agilepm.domain.model.product;
...
public class Product extends ConcurrencySafeEntity {
    ...
    public void requestDiscussion(
            DiscussionAvailability aDiscussionAvailability) {
```

```
        if (!this.discussion().availability().isReady()) {
            this.setDiscussion(
                    ProductDiscussion.fromAvailability(
                            aDiscussionAvailability));

            DomainEventPublisher
                .instance()
                .publish(new ProductDiscussionRequested(
                    this.tenantId(),
                    this.productId(),
                    this.productOwnerId(),
                    this.name(),
                    this.description(),
                    this.discussion().availability().isRequested())));
        }
    }
    ...
}
```

Method `requestDiscussion()` takes the familiar `Discussion-Availability` parameter, because the client must prove to the `Product` that the collaboration add-on is enabled. Of course, the client could cheat here and always pass `REQUESTED`, but that would just end up in a dead-end bug if the add-on is actually not available. Here, too, if the state of the discussion availability is `REQUESTED`, the last parameter to the Event constructor will be true, which is exactly what is needed to start the Long-Running Process:

```
package com.saasovation.agilepm.domain.model.product;
...
public class ProductDiscussionRequested implements DomainEvent {
    ...
    public ProductDiscussionRequested(
            TenantId aTenantId,
            ProductId aProductId,
            ProductOwnerId aProductOwnerId,
            String aName,
            String aDescription,
            boolean isRequestingDiscussion) {
        ...
    }
    ...
}
```

This Event has exactly the same properties as `ProductCreated`, which will allow both Event types to be handled by the same listener.

We might ask whether publishing this Event makes any sense if the availability state is not `REQUESTED`. It does make sense, because whether or not the request can be fulfilled, the request was still made, unless it is currently in READY state. It is the responsibility of listeners to determine whether or not to actually do something in response to the Event. Perhaps receiving this Event with isRequestingDiscussion set to false indicates a problem, or setup of the add-on is in progress but still not done. Therefore, some intervention may be necessary. The process may need to send an e-mail to the administrator group, for example.

The classes used to manage the Long-Running Process on the *Agile Project Management Context* side are similar to those used to manage the creation and maintenance of the ProductOwner and TeamMember Aggregates (see the previous section). Each of the listeners presented here is wired using Spring such that it is instantiated as the Spring application context is created for this Bounded Context. The first listener registers itself to receive two kinds of notifications on the AGILEPM_EXCHANGE_NAME, ProductCreated, and ProductDiscussionRequested:

```
package com.saasovation.agilepm.infrastructure.messaging;
...
public class ProductDiscussionRequestedListener
        extends ExchangeListener {
    ...
    @Override
    protected String exchangeName() {
        return Exchanges.AGILEPM_EXCHANGE_NAME;
    }
    ...

    @Override
    protected String[] listensToEvents() {
        return new String[] {
                "com.saasovation.agilepm.domain.model↵
.product.ProductCreated",
                "com.saasovation.agilepm.domain.model↵
.product.ProductDiscussionRequested"
                };
    }
    ...
}
```

The COLLABORATION_EXCHANGE_NAME is the interest of the second listener, and specifically for notification DiscussionStarted:

```
package com.saasovation.agilepm.infrastructure.messaging;
...
public class DiscussionStartedListener extends ExchangeListener {
    ...
```

```
    @Override
    protected String exchangeName() {
        return Exchanges.COLLABORATION_EXCHANGE_NAME;
    }
    ...
    @Override
    protected String[] listensToEvents() {
        return new String[] {
                "com.saasovation.collaboration.domain.model.↵
forum.DiscussionStarted"
                };
    }
    ...
}
```

You can probably see where this is going. If either `ProductCreated` or
`ProductDiscussionRequested` is received by the first listener, it will dispatch a command to the *Collaboration Context* to have a new `Forum` and
`Discussion` created on behalf of the `Product`. When that request is fulfilled
by the components in the *Collaboration Context*, the `DiscussionStarted`
notification is published and, once received, the corresponding discussion
identity will be initiated on the `Product`. That's the long and short of this
Long-Running Process. Here is how the `filteredDispatch()` works in the
first listener:

```
package com.saasovation.agilepm.infrastructure.messaging;
...
public class ProductDiscussionRequestedListener
        extends ExchangeListener {
    private static final String COMMAND =
            "com.saasovation.collaboration.discussion.↵
CreateExclusiveDiscussion";
    ...
    @Override
    protected void filteredDispatch(
                String aType,
                String aTextMessage) {
        NotificationReader reader =
                new NotificationReader(aTextMessage);

        if (!reader.eventBooleanValue("requestingDiscussion")) {
            return;
        }

        Properties parameters = this.parametersFrom(reader);
        PropertiesSerializer serializer =
                PropertiesSerializer.instance();
        String serialization = serializer.serialize(parameters);
        String commandId = this.commandIdFrom(parameters);
```

```
        this.messageProducer()
            .send(
                serialization,
                MessageParameters
                    .durableTextParameters(
                            COMMAND,
                            commandId,
                            new Date())))
            .close();
    }
    ...
}
```

In the case of either Event type, `ProductCreated` or `Product-DiscussionRequested`, if the `requestingDiscussion` attribute is false, we ignore the Event. Otherwise, we build up a `CreateExclusive-Discussion` command from the Event's state and send the command to the message exchange of the *Collaboration Context*.

This is a good time to pause and reflect on how this process is designed. Should the *Agile Project Management Context* really set up a listener to an Event published by a local Aggregate? Would it be better to create a listener for the `ProductCreated` Event in the *Collaboration Context* instead? If we did so, we could simply have the listener in the *Collaboration Context* manage the creation of the exclusive `Forum` and `Discussion`, and it would eliminate a bit of code from the *Agile Project Management Context*. To determine which is the better approach requires the consideration of a few factors.

Does it make sense that an upstream Bounded Context listens for Events published from a downstream Context? Or, in an **Event-Driven Architecture** **(4)**, are systems really upstream and downstream to each other? Need they be cast in that mold? Possibly the more important factor to consider is whether it would be correct for a `ProductCreated` Event to be interpreted in the *Collaboration Context* as indicating that an exclusive `Forum` and `Discussion` should be created. In fact, does `ProductCreated` actually have any meaning at all to the *Collaboration Context*? How many other Contexts may eventually desire similar automatic support for this very feature given their own unique Event types? Is it best to place such a burden to support any number of foreign Events as creation commands on the *Collaboration Context*? Yet, there is another factor to consider, which requires us to more carefully manage the success of Long-Running Processes. This topic, discussed just a bit later, may help to settle why we've approached it in this particular way.

Now, back to the example . . . Once received in the *Collaboration Context*, the command is adapted to pass to the `ForumService`, which is an

Application Service. Note that this API has not yet been designed to use command parameters but rather takes individual attribute parameters:

```
package com.saasovation.collaboration.infrastructure.messaging;
...
public class ExclusiveDiscussionCreationListener
        extends ExchangeListener {

    @Autowired
    private ForumService forumService;
    ...
    @Override
    protected void filteredDispatch(
                String aType,
                String aTextMessage) {
        NotificationReader reader =
                new NotificationReader(aTextMessage);

        String tenantId = reader.eventStringValue("tenantId");
        String exclusiveOwnerId =
                reader.eventStringValue("exclusiveOwnerId");
        String forumSubject = reader.eventStringValue("forumTitle");
        String forumDescription =
                reader.eventStringValue("forumDescription");
        String discussionSubject =
                reader.eventStringValue("discussionSubject");
        String creatorId = reader.eventStringValue("creatorId");
        String moderatorId = reader.eventStringValue("moderatorId");

        forumService.startExclusiveForumWithDiscussion(
            tenantId,
            creatorId,
            moderatorId,
            forumSubject,
            forumDescription,
            discussionSubject,
            exclusiveOwnerId);
    }
    ...
}
```

That makes sense, but shouldn't this `ExclusiveDiscussionCreation-Listener` send a response message back to the *Agile Project Management Context*? Well, not exactly. Both the `Forum` and `Discussion` Aggregates publish an Event in response to their respective creation: `ForumStarted` and `DiscussionStarted`. This Bounded Context publishes all its Domain Events though its exchange, defined by `COLLABORATION_EXCHANGE_NAME`. That's why the `DiscussionStartedListener` in the *Agile Project Management*

Context receives the `DiscussionStarted` Event. And here's what that listener does when it receives the Event:

```
package com.saasovation.agilepm.infrastructure.messaging;
...
public class DiscussionStartedListener extends ExchangeListener {

    @Autowired
    private ProductService productService;
    ...
    @Override
    protected void filteredDispatch(
                String aType,
                String aTextMessage) {
        NotificationReader reader =
                new NotificationReader(aTextMessage);

        String tenantId = reader.eventStringValue("tenant.id");
        String productId = reader.eventStringValue("exclusiveOwner");
        String discussionId =
                reader.eventStringValue("discussionId.id");

        productService.initiateDiscussion(
                new InitiateDiscussionCommand(
                    tenantId,
                    productId,
                    discussionId));
    }
    ...
}
```

This listener adapts the received notification's Event properties to pass as a command to the `ProductService` Application Service. This `initiateDiscussion()` service method works like this:

```
package com.saasovation.agilepm.application;
...
public class ProductService ... {

    @Autowired
    private ProductRepository productRepository;
    ...
    @Transactional
    public void initiateDiscussion(
                InitiateDiscussionCommand aCommand) {
        Product product =
                productRepository
                    .productOfId(
                        new TenantId(aCommand.getTenantId()),
                        new ProductId(aCommand.getProductId()));
```

```
        if (product == null) {
            throw new IllegalStateException(
                    "Unknown product of tenant id: "
                    + aCommand.getTenantId()
                    + " and product id: "
                    + aCommand.getProductId());
        }

        product.initiateDiscussion(
                new DiscussionDescriptor(
                        aCommand.getDiscussionId())));
    }
    ...
}
```

Ultimately the `Product` Aggregate's `initiateDiscussion()` behavior is executed:

```
package com.saasovation.agilepm.domain.model.product;
...
public class Product extends ConcurrencySafeEntity  {
    ...
    public void initiateDiscussion(DiscussionDescriptor aDescriptor) {
        if (aDescriptor == null) {
            throw new IllegalArgumentException(
                    "The descriptor must not be null.");
        }

        if (this.discussion().availability().isRequested()) {
            this.setDiscussion(this.discussion()
                        .nowReady(aDescriptor));
            DomainEventPublisher
                .instance()
                .publish(new ProductDiscussionInitiated(
                        this.tenantId(),
                        this.productId(),
                        this.discussion()));
        }
    }
    ...
}
```

If the `Product` `discussion` property is still in the REQUESTED state, it is transitioned to the READY state with the `DiscussionDescriptor`, which holds an identity reference to the exclusive `Discussion` in the *Collaboration Context*. The request for a `Forum` and `Discussion` to be created for and associated with the `Product` has just become consistent, although it happened eventually.

However, if `discussion` is in the `READY` state at the time of this command invocation, it is not further transitioned. Is this a bug? No. It is one way to ensure that `initiateDiscussion()` is an idempotent operation. The assumption must be made that if the state is currently `READY`, the Long-Running Process has already completed. Perhaps any subsequent command invocation is due to a notification redelivery, since the team chose to use a messaging mechanism that delivers messages at least once. Whatever the case, we need not be concerned because the idempotent operation allows for any number of infrastructure and architectural influences to be harmlessly ignored when they should be. Further, in this specific case we didn't need to design with a `ProductChangeTracker` as we did for the `Member` subclasses and their `MemberChangeTracker`. The simple fact that the `discussion` is `READY` tells us all we need to know.

There could be a problem with this overall approach, however. What happens if the Long-Running Process experiences some sort of problem due to the messaging mechanism? How would we ensure that the process is run completely to its finish? Well, it's probably time for the teenager to grow up a little.

Process State Machines and Time-out Trackers

We can make this process more mature by adding a concept similar to that described under **Long-Running Processes (4)**. The SaaSOvation developers created a reusable concept that they named `TimeConstrainedProcessTracker`. A tracker watches for processes whose allotted time for completion has expired, and those that can be retried any number of times prior to expiring. The tracker design allows for retries at fixed intervals if desired and can eventually completely time-out after no retries at all, or after a determined number of retries.

To clarify, the tracker is not part of the Core Domain. It is rather part of a technical Subdomain that any SaaSOvation project can reuse. This means that in some cases we aren't overly concerned with the rules of Aggregates when persisting trackers and later causing their modification. Trackers are relatively isolated and won't tend to face concurrency conflicts since there is a one-to-one relationship with the associated process. However, if there are conflicts, we can count on messaging retries to help our cause. Any exception in the context of a notification delivery will cause the listener to NAK the message, which in turn causes RabbitMQ to redeliver. Still, we don't anticipate the necessity of a great number of retries.

It is the `Product` that holds the current state of the process, and in that context a tracker will publish the following Event when a retry interval is reached, or when the observed process completely times out:

```
package com.saasovation.agilepm.domain.model.product;

import com.saasovation.common.domain.model.process.ProcessId;
import com.saasovation.common.domain.model.process.ProcessTimedOut;

public class ProductDiscussionRequestTimedOut extends ProcessTimedOut {

    public ProductDiscussionRequestTimedOut(
            String aTenantId,
            ProcessId aProcessId,
            int aTotalRetriesPermitted,
            int aRetryCount) {

        super(aTenantId, aProcessId,
            aTotalRetriesPermitted, aRetryCount);
    }
}
```

Events that subclass `ProcessTimedOut` are used by the tracker when retry intervals or full time-outs have been reached. Event listeners can use Event method `hasFullyTimedOut()` to determine whether the Event signifies a full time-out or is just a retry. If retries are permitted, assuming listeners have use of the `ProcessTimedOut` class, they can ask the Event for indicators and values such as `allowsRetries()`, `retryCount()`, `totalRetriesPermitted()`, and `totalRetriesReached()`.

Armed with the ability to receive notifications about retries and time-outs, we can make the `Product` participate in a better process. First, we need to start the process, and we can do that from our existing `ProductDiscussionRequestedListener`:

```
package com.saasovation.agilepm.infrastructure.messaging;
...
public class ProductDiscussionRequestedListener
        extends ExchangeListener {
    @Override
    protected void filteredDispatch(
                String aType,
                String aTextMessage) {
        NotificationReader reader =
                new NotificationReader(aTextMessage);

        if (!reader.eventBooleanValue("requestingDiscussion")) {
            return;
        }

        String tenantId = reader.eventStringValue("tenantId.id");
        String productId = reader.eventStringValue("product.id");
```

```
        productService.startDiscussionInitiation(
                new StartDiscussionInitiationCommand(
                        tenantId,
                        productId));

        // send command to Collaboration Context
        ...
    }
    ...
}
```

The `ProductService` creates the tracker and persists it, and it associates the process with the given `Product`:

```
package com.saasovation.agilepm.application;
...
public class ProductService ... {
    ...
    @Transactional
    public void startDiscussionInitiation(
            StartDiscussionInitiationCommand aCommand) {

        Product product =
                productRepository
                    .productOfId(
                        new TenantId(aCommand.getTenantId()),
                        new ProductId(aCommand.getProductId()));

        if (product == null) {
            throw new IllegalStateException(
                    "Unknown product of tenant id: "
                    + aCommand.getTenantId()
                    + " and product id: "
                    + aCommand.getProductId());
        }

        String timedOutEventName =
                ProductDiscussionRequestTimedOut.class.getName();

        TimeConstrainedProcessTracker tracker =
                new TimeConstrainedProcessTracker(
                        product.tenantId().id(),
                        ProcessId.newProcessId(),
                        "Create discussion for product: "
                            + product.name(),
                        new Date(),
                        5L * 60L * 1000L, // retries every 5 minutes
                        3, // 3 total retries
                        timedOutEventName);

        processTrackerRepository.add(tracker);
```

```
            product.setDiscussionInitiationId(
                    tracker.processId().id());
    }
    ...
}
```

The `TimeConstrainedProcessTracker` is instantiated to retry three times every five minutes, if necessary. True, we may not normally hard-code these values, but doing so allows us to see clearly how the tracker is created.

Did You Detect a Possible Problem Here?
The retry specification we are using could contribute to problems if we aren't careful, but we'll leave the design as is for now and act as if we think it's all right.

It is this approach of creating a tracker on behalf of the `Product` that may best address the reason we have handled the `ProductCreated` Event locally, rather than having it interpreted in the *Collaboration Context*. This gives our own system the opportunity to set up process management and decouple the `ProductCreated` Event from the command in the *Collaboration Context*, namely, `CreateExclusiveDiscussion`.

A background timer will fire regularly to check on process elapsed times. The timer will delegate to method `checkForTimedOutProcesses()` in the `ProcessService`:

```
package com.saasovation.agilepm.application;
...
public class ProcessService ... {
    ...
    @Transactional
    public void checkForTimedOutProcesses() {
        Collection<TimeConstrainedProcessTracker> trackers =
            processTrackerRepository.allTimedOut();

        for (TimeConstrainedProcessTracker tracker : trackers) {
            tracker.informProcessTimedOut();
        }
    }
    ...
}
```

It's the tracker's method `informProcessTimedOut()` that confirms the need to retry or time-out a process and, if confirmed, publishes the `Process-TimedOut` Event subclass.

Next, we need to add a new listener to handle retries and time-outs. Up to three retries may occur every five minutes as needed. It's the `Product-DiscussionRetryListener`:

```
package com.saasovation.agilepm.infrastructure.messaging;
...
public class ProductDiscussionRetryListener extends ExchangeListener {

    @Autowired
    private ProcessService processService;
    ...
    @Override
    protected String exchangeName() {
        return Exchanges.AGILEPM_EXCHANGE_NAME;
    }

    @Override
    protected void filteredDispatch(
                String aType,
                String aTextMessage) {
        Notification notification =
            NotificationSerializer
                .instance()
                .deserialize(aTextMessage, Notification.class);

        ProductDiscussionRequestTimedOut event =
                notification.event();

        if (event.hasFullyTimedOut()) {
            productService.timeOutProductDiscussionRequest(
                    new TimeOutProductDiscussionRequestCommand(
                            event.tenantId(),
                            event.processId().id(),
                            event.occurredOn())));
        } else {
            productService.retryProductDiscussionRequest(
                    new RetryProductDiscussionRequestCommand(
                            event.tenantId(),
                            event.processId().id())));
        }
    }

    @Override
    protected String[] listensToEvents() {
        return new String[] {
                "com.saasovation.agilepm.process.↵
ProductDiscussionRequestTimedOut"
                };
    }
}
```

This listener is interested only in `ProductDiscussionRequestTimedOut`
Events and is designed to work with any number of retry and time-out permutations. It's the process and tracker that determine how many times it could

possibly be notified. Events will be sent under one of two possible conditions. The process may have completely timed out, or it may be a notification to retry the operation. In both cases the listener dispatches to the new Product-Service. If a complete time-out has occurred, the Application Service handles the situation:

```
package com.saasovation.agilepm.application;
...
public class ProductService ... {
    ...
    @Transactional
    public void timeOutProductDiscussionRequest(
            TimeOutProductDiscussionRequestCommand aCommand) {

        ProcessId processId =
                ProcessId.existingProcessId(
                        aCommand.getProcessId());

        TenantId tenantId = new TenantId(aCommand.getTenantId());

        Product product =
                productRepository
                    .productOfDiscussionInitiationId(
                            tenantId,
                            processId.id());

        this.sendEmailForTimedOutProcess(product);

        product.failDiscussionInitiation();
    }
    ...
}
```

First an e-mail is sent to the product owner indicating that the discussion setup has failed, and then the Product is marked as failing discussion initiation. As seen from the new Product method failDiscussionInitiation(), we needed to declare an additional FAILED state as a DiscussionAvailability. Method failDiscussionInitiation() deals with the simple compensation necessary to keep the Product in a sound state:

```
package com.saasovation.agilepm.domain.model.product;
...
public class Product extends ConcurrencySafeEntity  {
    ...
    public void failDiscussionInitiation() {
        if (!this.discussion().availability().isReady()) {
            this.setDiscussionInitiationId(null);
```

```
        this.setDiscussion(
                ProductDiscussion
                    .fromAvailability(
                            DiscussionAvailability.FAILED));
        }
    }
    ...
}
```

What may be missing here is a new `DiscussionRequestFailed` Event being published by `failDiscussionInitiation()`. The team will have to consider the possible advantages of doing that. In fact, it could be that the e-mails sent to product owners and other administrative resources would be best handled as a result of just that Event. After all, what would happen if the `ProductService` method `timeOutProductDiscussionRequest()` encountered problems sending the e-mail? Things could get tedious. (Aha!) The team has made note of this and will return to address it later.

On the other hand, if the Event indicates that a retry should be attempted, the listener delegates to the following operation in the `ProductService`:

```
package com.saasovation.agilepm.application;
...
public class ProductService ... {
    ...
    @Transactional
    public void retryProductDiscussionRequest(
            RetryProductDiscussionRequestCommand aCommand) {

        ProcessId processId =
                ProcessId.existingProcessId(
                        aCommand.getProcessId());

        TenantId tenantId = new TenantId(aCommand.getTenantId());

        Product product =
                productRepository
                    .productOfDiscussionInitiationId(
                            tenantId,
                            processId.id());

        if (product == null) {
            throw new IllegalStateException(
                    "Unknown product of tenant id: "
                    + aCommand.getTenantId()
                    + " and discussion initiation id: "
                    + processId.id());
        }
```

```
        this.requestProductDiscussion(
                new RequestProductDiscussionCommand(
                        aCommand.getTenantId(),
                        product.productId().id())));
    }
    ...
}
```

The `Product` is retrieved from its Repository by means of the associated `ProcessId`, which is set on the `Product` attribute `discussionInitiationId`. After the `Product` is obtained, it is used by the `ProductService` (self-delegation) to request the discussion again.

Ultimately we get the desired outcome. When the discussion is started successfully, the *Collaboration Context* publishes the `DiscussionStarted` Event. Shortly following this our `DiscussionStartedListener` in the *Agile Project Management Context* receives the notification and dispatches to the `ProductService` as it did previously. This time, however, there's new behavior:

```
package com.saasovation.agilepm.application;
...
public class ProductService ... {
    ...
    @Transactional
    public void initiateDiscussion(
                InitiateDiscussionCommand aCommand) {
        Product product =
                productRepository
                    .productOfId(
                            new TenantId(aCommand.getTenantId()),
                            new ProductId(aCommand.getProductId()));

        if (product == null) {
            throw new IllegalStateException(
                    "Unknown product of tenant id: "
                    + aCommand.getTenantId()
                    + " and product id: "
                    + aCommand.getProductId());
        }

        product.initiateDiscussion(
                new DiscussionDescriptor(
                        aCommand.getDiscussionId()));

        TimeConstrainedProcessTracker tracker =
                this.processTrackerRepository.trackerOfProcessId(
                        ProcessId.existingProcessId(
                                product.discussionInitiationId()));
```

```
        tracker.completed();
    }
    ...
}
```

The `ProductService` now provides the finishing behavior for the process, informing the tracker that it is `completed()`. From this point forward the tracker will no longer be selected as a retry or time-out notifier. The process is done.

Although we're probably feeling good about the results, there could be a bit of a problem with this design. The way things stand, retrying requests to create a `Product` discussion could lead to some issues if we were to leave the design of the *Collaboration Context* as it is. The basic problem is that the operations in the *Collaboration Context* are currently not idempotent. Here is a breakdown of the minor design flaw and what should be done about it:

- Since guaranteed, at least once, delivery of messages is in use, as soon as a message is sent to the exchange, it is sure to reach its listener(s) in a matter of time. If there is some delay in creating the new collaboration objects and it causes even one retry, the retry will in turn cause multiple sends of the same `CreateExclusiveDiscussion` command. All such commands will eventually be delivered. Thus, any retries will make the *Collaboration Context* attempt to create the same `Forum` and `Discussion` multiple times. We won't actually end up with duplicates since uniqueness constraints are already imposed on `Forum` and `Discussion` properties. Thus, the multiple creation attempt errors will end up being benign. Yet, from the perspective of error logs the failed attempts will appear to be caused by bugs. The question is, While we still want to stipulate a complete process time-out, should the periodic retries be disabled?

- While it might seem that the solution is to disable retries in the *Agile Project Management Context*, the bottom line is that we need to make the *Collaboration Context* operations idempotent. Remember that RabbitMQ guarantees *delivery at least once* and thus may deliver the same command message multiple times, even if it is sent only once. Making the collaboration operations idempotent will prevent any attempt to create the same `Forum` and `Discussion` multiple times and will stifle logging of benign failures.

- It is possible for the *Agile Project Management Context* to fail when attempting to send the `CreateExclusiveDiscussion` command. If there is a problem with the message send, care must be taken to ensure that a resend is attempted until it succeeds. Otherwise, a request for creation of the `Forum` and `Discussion` will never be made. We can ensure command resend attempts in a few ways. If the message send fails, we can throw an exception from `filteredDispatch()`, which will cause a message NAK. As a result, RabbitMQ will consider it necessary to redeliver the `ProductCreated` or `ProductDiscussionRequested` Event notification, and our `ProductDiscussionRequestedListener` will receive it again. The other way to handle this is to simply retry the send until it succeeds, perhaps using a Capped Exponential Back-off. In the case of an offline RabbitMQ, retries could fail for quite a while. Thus, using a combination of message NAKs and retries could be the best approach. Still, if our process retries three times every five minutes, it could be all we need. After all, a complete process time-out results in an e-mail requesting human intervention.

In the end, if the *Collaboration Context*'s `ExclusiveDiscussionCreationListener` could delegate to an idempotent Application Service operation, it would solve many of our problems:

```
package com.saasovation.collaboration.application;
...
public class ForumService ... {
    ...
    @Transactional
    public Discussion startExclusiveForumWithDiscussion(
            String aTenantId,
            String aCreatorId,
            String aModeratorId,
            String aForumSubject,
            String aForumDescription,
            String aDiscussionSubject,
            String anExclusiveOwner) {

        Tenant tenant = new Tenant(aTenantId);

        Forum forum =
                forumRepository
                    .exclusiveForumOfOwner(
                            tenant,
                            anExclusiveOwner);

        if (forum == null) {
            forum = this.startForum(
                    tenant,
                    aCreatorId,
                    aModeratorId,
                    aForumSubject,
```

```
                    aForumDescription,
                    anExclusiveOwner);
    }

    Discussion discussion =
            discussionRepository
                .exclusiveDiscussionOfOwner(
                        tenant,
                        anExclusiveOwner);

    if (discussion == null) {
        Author author =
                collaboratorService
                    .authorFrom(
                            tenant,
                            aModeratorId);

        discussion =
                forum.startDiscussion(
                        forumNavigationService,
                        author,
                        aDiscussionSubject);

        discussionRepository.add(discussion);
    }

    return discussion;
}
...
}
```

By trying to find the `Forum` and `Discussion` from their unique exclusive owner attribute, we prevent attempting to create two Aggregate instances that may already exist. Wow, just a few lines of code make our Event-Driven processing so much better!

Designing a More Sophisticated Process

Still, we may desire to design a more sophisticated process. In cases where multiple completion steps are necessary, it works best to have a more elaborate state machine. To address such needs, here's the definition of a `Process` interface:

```
package com.saasovation.common.domain.model.process;

import java.util.Date;

public interface Process {
```

```
public enum ProcessCompletionType {
    NotCompleted,
    CompletedNormally,
    TimedOut
}

public long allowableDuration();
public boolean canTimeout();
public long currentDuration();
public String description();
public boolean didProcessingComplete();
public void informTimeout(Date aTimedOutDate);
public boolean isCompleted();
public boolean isTimedOut();
public boolean notCompleted();
public ProcessCompletionType processCompletionType();
public ProcessId processId();
public Date startTime();
public TimeConstrainedProcessTracker
        timeConstrainedProcessTracker();
public Date timedOutDate();
public long totalAllowableDuration();
public int totalRetriesPermitted();
}
```

The following are some of the more significant operations available with a
Process:

- allowableDuration(): If the Process can time-out, answers either
  the total duration or the duration between retries.

- canTimeout(): If the Process can time-out, this method answers
  true.

- timeConstrainedProcessTracker(): If the Process can time-out,
  answers a new unique TimeConstrainedProcessTracker.

- totalAllowableDuration(): Answers the total allowable duration
  of the Process. If retries are not permitted, the answer is allowable-
  Duration(). If retries are permitted, the answer is allowableDuration()
  multiplied by totalRetriesPermitted().

- totalRetriesPermitted(): If the Process permits time-outs and
  retries, this method answers the total number of retries that may be
  attempted.

Implementers of Process may be observed for time-out and retries under
the control of the now familiar TimeConstrainedProcessTracker. Once

we create our `Process`, we can ask it for a unique tracker. This test shows how the two objects work together, which is much the same way that `Product` worked with its tracker:

```
Process process =
    new TestableTimeConstrainedProcess(
            TENANT_ID,
            ProcessId.newProcessId(),
            "Testable Time Constrained Process",
            5000L);

TimeConstrainedProcessTracker tracker =
    process.timeConstrainedProcessTracker();

process.confirm1();

assertFalse(process.isCompleted());
assertFalse(process.didProcessingComplete());
assertEquals(process.processCompletionType(),
        ProcessCompletionType.NotCompleted);

process.confirm2();

assertTrue(process.isCompleted());
assertTrue(process.didProcessingComplete());
assertEquals(process.processCompletionType(),
        ProcessCompletionType.CompletedNormally);
assertNull(process.timedOutDate());

tracker.informProcessTimedOut();

assertFalse(process.isTimedOut());
```

The `Process` created by this test must complete (without retries) within five seconds (5000L milliseconds), which it always will do. The `Process` will be marked as completed, with fully completed processing, only after both `confirm1()` and `confirm2()` have been invoked. Internally the `Process` knows that both states must be confirmed:

```
public class TestableTimeConstrainedProcess extends AbstractProcess {
    ...
    public void confirm1() {
        this.confirm1 = true;

        this.completeProcess(ProcessCompletionType.CompletedNormally);
    }

    public void confirm2() {
        this.confirm2 = true;
```

```
        this.completeProcess(ProcessCompletionType.CompletedNormally);
    }
    ...
    protected boolean completenessVerified() {
        return this.confirm1 && this.confirm2;
    }

    protected void completeProcess(
            ProcessCompletionType aProcessCompletionType) {

        if (!this.isCompleted() && this.completenessVerified()) {
            this.setProcessCompletionType(aProcessCompletionType);
        }
    }
    ...
}
```

Even when this `Process` self-invokes `completeProcess()`, the `Process` cannot be marked as completed until `completenessVerified()` answers `true`. That method will answer `true` only when both `confirm1` and `confirm2` have been set to `true`. In other words, both the `confirm1()` and `confirm2()` operations must have been executed. Thus, method `completenessVerified()` allows for multiple processing steps to be confirmed as completed before the entire `Process` is considered completed, and every specialized kind of `Process` can have its own definition of `completenessVerified()`.

Yet, what will happen when the final step of this test is run?

```
...

tracker.informProcessTimedOut();

assertFalse(process.isTimedOut());
```

From its internal state the tracker knows that the `Process` has actually not timed out. Thus, the assertion in the next line of code will always be false. (Of course, it is assumed that the entire test will complete in less than five seconds, and it is strongly believed that it always will under normal test conditions.)

An `AbstractProcess` base class implements `Process`, serving as an Adapter, and provides a really easy way to develop a more sophisticated Long-Running Process. Since `AbstractProcess` extends the `Entity` base class, it's easy to design an Aggregate as a `Process`. For example, we could make `Product` subclass `AbstractProcess`, although it doesn't need that level of sophistication. Still, we can imagine leveraging this approach to accommodate a more complex process and require method `completeness-Verified()` to determine whether or not all required steps have completed.

When Messaging or Your System Is Unavailable

No single approach to developing complex software systems is a panacea. There are always issues and drawbacks with any approach, some of which we have already discussed. One problem with a messaging system is that it can become unavailable for a period of time. This may be an infrequent situation, but when it does happen, there are a few things to keep in mind.

When a messaging mechanism is offline for some time, notification publishers will be unable to send messages through it. Since this situation may be detected by the publishing client, it would likely work best to back off attempts to send notifications until the messaging system is available once again. This will be evident when any one send succeeds. But until that time, make sure that attempts to send occur less frequently than when everything is working well. It could make sense to back off as much as 30 seconds or a minute between retries. Remember, if your system has an Event Store, your Events will continue to be queued in your live system and can be sent as soon as messaging is available again.

Certainly listeners will not receive new Event-carrying notifications if the messaging infrastructure goes away for a period of time. When the messaging mechanism becomes available again, will your client listeners be automatically reactivated, or will it be necessary to subscribe to your consumer-side client mechanism again? If automatic recovery of consumers is not supported, you will need to be certain that your consumers are reregistered. Otherwise, you will eventually make the unwanted discovery that your Bounded Context isn't receiving the notifications that are necessary to keep it interacting with the Bounded Contexts it depends on. That's one kind of eventual consistency that you want to avoid.

It's not always the messaging mechanism that is the source of message-based problems. Consider this situation. Your Bounded Context becomes unavailable for some lengthy period of time. When it becomes available again, the durable message exchanges/queues that it subscribes to have collected a lot of undelivered messages. Once your Bounded Context starts up again and registers its consumers, it could require a considerable amount of time to receive and process all the available notifications. There may not be much that you can do about this situation other than doggedly pursue limited downtime goals, develop a "live" deployment scheme, and design with redundant nodes (a cluster) so that losing one node doesn't make your system unavailable. Still, there may be times when you can't avoid some downtime. For example, if changes to your application's code require changes to the database and you can't patch in changes without causing problems, you will need some system downtime. In such cases your message consumption processing may simply have to play catch-up. Clearly it's a situation that we need to be aware of and plan to avoid or deal with if it could be a problem.

Wrap-Up

In this chapter we've examined various ways to successfully integrate multiple Bounded Contexts.

- We reviewed the basic mindset necessary to succeed with integration in a distributed computing environment.

- We considered how we can integrate multiple Contexts by means of RESTful resources.

- You got to see several examples of integration with messaging, including how to develop and manage Long-Running Processes, from simple to complex.

- You learned the challenges faced when you decide to duplicate information across Bounded Contexts, and how to manage it and also how to avoid it.

- You benefited from considering simple examples, and then progressed to the more complex ones that employed increasing design maturity.

Now that we've seen how to integrate multiple Bounded Contexts, let's focus back on the single Bounded Context and how to design the parts of the application that surround the domain model.

Chapter 14

Application

Any program is only as good as it is useful.
—*Linus Torvalds*

A domain model often lives at the heart of an *application*. The application may have a user interface that presents concepts of the domain model and allows the user to perform various actions on the model. The user interface will make use of application-level services that coordinate use case tasks, manage transactions, and assert necessary security authorizations. Further, the user interface, **Application Services**, and domain model will rely on enterprise platform-specific infrastructural support. The infrastructure implementation details will generally include the facilities of a component container, application management, messaging, and database.

Road Map to This Chapter

- Learn several ways to provide domain model data for the user interface to render.
- See how Application Services are implemented, and the kinds of operations they perform.
- Study ways to decouple output from Application Services and disparate client types.
- Consider why you might need to compose multiple models in the user interface, and how it's done.
- Learn ways to use the infrastructure to provide the application's technical implementations.

Sometimes we work on models that exist to support applications. This is true of the *Identity and Access Context*. SaaSOvation has seen the need to break off identity and access management concerns and form a supporting model that will also serve as a subscription-based product of its own. Even in the case of IdOvation, it will of necessity have its own administrative and self-service user interface. It's true that **Generic** and **Supporting Subdomains** (2) will sometimes lack all the extras associated with a full application, and that's fine. When a model exists to support another model, the supporting model may be as simple as a set of classes in a separate **Module (9)** that address a specialty concept and provide some algorithms.[1] Other models will require at least some human user experience and application components. This chapter focuses on the latter, more complex variety.

We are here using the term *application* somewhat interchangeably with *system* and *business service*. I won't attempt to formally analyze at what point an application becomes a system, but I'd say when an application depends on other applications or services through integration, the whole solution could be called a system. Sometimes the terms *application* and *system* are used interchangeably to mean one and the same thing, where *system* really describes what we'd normally call an application. And a single business service that provides several or many technical service endpoints might also be called a system in a general sense. While I don't want to muddy the waters of what makes each of these three concepts distinct, I do want to use a single term that allows me to discuss concerns and responsibilities that are common to all three.

> **What's an Application?**
>
> To boil it down, I am using the term *application* to mean the finest set of components that are assembled to interact with and support a **Core Domain (2)** model. This generally means the domain model itself, a user interface, internally used Application Services, and infrastructural components. What exactly fits into each of those compartments will vary from application to application and will depend on the specific **Architectures (4)** in use.

When an application opens up its services programmatically, the user interface is broader and includes a kind of application programming interface (API). There are different ways to open its services, but the interface is not meant for human consumption. This kind of user interface is discussed in **Integrating Bounded Contexts (13)**. In this chapter I cover aspects of human user interfaces that are typically of the graphical variety.

For this topic I try to avoid leaning toward any specific Architecture. I reflect that departure in the odd-looking diagram of Figure 14.1, which purposely adheres to no typical architecture. Dashed lines with clear arrowheads depict implementation per UML, which is a reflection of **Dependency Inversion Principle (4)**, or DIP. Solid lines with open arrowheads indicate operation dispatching. For example, the infrastructure implements interface abstractions from the user interface, Application Services, and the domain model. It also dispatches operations to Application Services, the domain model, and the data store.

---

1. For an example Generic Subdomain that is a stand-alone model, see Eric Evans's "Time and Money Code Library": http://timeandmoney.sourceforge.net/.

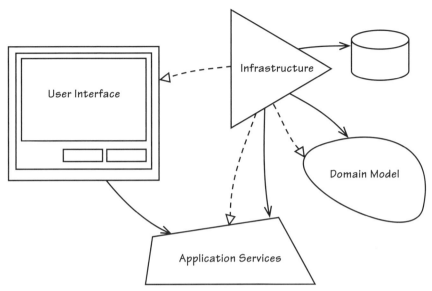

Figure 14.1 The primary application areas of concern, but without ties to any one architecture. These areas still emphasize the DIP with infrastructure dependent on abstractions of every other area.

Although it is inevitable that there will be some overlap with some architectural styles, our interest in this chapter is on what most any architecture would need to do to sustain the goals of the application. Where a specific architecture does enter the picture, I provide an acknowledgment.

It is difficult not to use the term *layer*, as in **Layers Architecture** (4). It is a useful term no matter what architectural style is being discussed. For example, consider the place where Application Services live. Whether you think of the Application Services as being in a ring around the domain model, in a hexagon encompassing the model, in a capsule hanging off a message bus, or in a layer below the user interface and above the model, it should be acceptable to use the term *Application Layer* to describe that conceptual place. While I try to refrain from overusing the term in this chapter, *layer* is helpful in labeling where components reside. This certainly does not imply that DDD is limited to existing only in a Layers Architecture.[2]

I start with the user interface, move on to Application Services, and then to infrastructure. Through each of the subjects I cover where the model fits in, but I don't delve into the model proper since that would be redundant with the remainder of the book.

---

2. See Chapter 4 for details.

User Interface

On the Java platform, the .NET platform, and others, there are so many human user interface frameworks that it seems neither interesting nor productive to study their advantages here.

What seems best is to understand the broader categories, which fall mainly under those described in the following list. They are listed in order of "heaviness" factors, not popularity. At the time of this writing it must almost certainly be the case that the second category of Web-based rich user interface is the direction of greatest choice and will soon be influenced by HTML5. Applications of the first category, pure request-response Web user interfaces, may still be more prolific as legacy applications than Web 2.0.

- Pure request-response Web user interfaces, perhaps best known as Web 1.0. Frameworks such as Struts, Spring MVC and Web Flow, and ASP.NET support this category.

- Web-based rich Internet application (RIA) user interfaces, including those that use DHTML and Ajax, known as Web 2.0. Google's GWT, Yahoo!'s YUI, Ext JS, Adobe's Flex, and Microsoft's Silverlight fall into this category.

- Native client GUIs (for example, Windows, Mac, and Linux desktop user interfaces) that may include the use of abstraction libraries (such as Eclipse SWT, Java Swing, or WinForms and WPF on Windows). This does not necessarily imply a heavy desktop application, but it is possible that it does. The native client GUI may access services over HTTP, for example, making the user interface the only client installed component.

With any of these user interface categories, a few priority questions must be answered: How do we render domain objects onto the glass? And how do we communicate user gestures back to the model?

Rendering Domain Objects

There is a fair amount of controversy and disagreement on how best to render objects of the domain model onto the user interface. The user interface regularly benefits from views of data richer than is required to accomplish the direct task. The display of extra data is necessary because it provides supporting information that users need in order to make intelligent decisions to carry out their immediate task. The extra data may also include selection options. Thus, the user interface will often need to render properties of multiple **Aggregate (10)** instances. This is despite the fact that in most cases a user should be

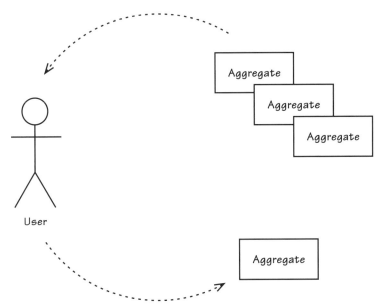

Figure 14.2   The user interface may need to render properties of multiple Aggregate instances but submit a request to modify only a single instance at a time.

performing a state-mutating task that is to be applied to just one instance of a single type of Aggregate. This situation is illustrated in Figure 14.2.

Render Data Transfer Object from Aggregate Instances

A popular way to tackle the problem of rendering multiple Aggregate instances to a single view is to use **Data Transfer Objects** [Fowler, P of EAA], or DTOs. The DTO is designed to hold the entire number of attributes that need to be displayed in a view. The Application Service (see "Application Services") will use **Repositories (12)** to read the necessary Aggregate instances and then delegate to a **DTO Assembler** [Fowler, P of EAA] to map the attributes of the DTO. The DTO thus carries the full complement of information that needs to be rendered. The user interface component accesses each individual DTO attribute and renders it onto the view.

    With this approach both reads and writes are performed through Repositories. It has the advantage of resolving any lazy-loaded collections because the DTO Assembler will directly access every part of the Aggregates that it needs to build the DTO. It also solves the specific problem where the presentation tier is physically separated from the business tier and you need to serialize data holders and transfer them over the network to another tier.

Interestingly, the DTO pattern was originally designed to deal with a remote presentation tier that consumes the DTO instances. The DTO is built on the business tier, serialized, sent over the wire, and deserialized on the presentation tier. If your presentation tier is not remote, this pattern many times leads to accidental complexity in the application's design, as in YAGNI ("You Ain't Gonna Need It"). This includes the disadvantage of requiring the creation of classes that sometimes closely resemble the shape of domain objects but are not quite the same. It also has the downside of instantiating additional potentially large objects that must be managed by the virtual machine (for example, JVM) when in fact they are mismatched for a single virtual machine application architecture.

Your Aggregates will need to be designed so that DTO Assemblers can query for necessary data. Think carefully about how to reveal state without revealing too much about the internal shape or structure of the Aggregates. Try to eliminate a client's coupling to all internal parts of an Aggregate. Should you allow clients—the Assemblers in this case—to navigate deeply into Aggregates? That can be a bad idea since it tightly couples each client to a specific Aggregate implementation.

Use a Mediator to Publish Aggregate Internal State

To work around the problem of tight coupling between the model and its clients, you may choose to design **Mediator** [Gamma et al.] (aka **Double-Dispatch** and **Callback**) interfaces to which the Aggregate publishes its internal state. Clients would implement the Mediator interface, passing the implementer's object reference to the Aggregate as a method argument. The Aggregate would then double-dispatch to that Mediator to publish the requested state, all without revealing its shape or structure. The trick is to not wed the Mediator's interface to any sort of view specification, but to keep it focused on rendering Aggregate states of interest:

```
public class BacklogItem ... {
    ...
    public void provideBacklogItemInterest(
            BacklogItemInterest anInterest) {
        anInterest.informTenantId(this.tenantId().id());
        anInterest.informProductId(this.productId().id());
        anInterest.informBacklogItemId(this.backlogItemId().id());
        anInterest.informStory(this.story());
        anInterest.informSummary(this.summary());
        anInterest.informType(this.type().toString());
        ...
    }
```

```
public void provideTasksInterest(TasksInterest anInterest) {
    Set<Task> tasks = this.allTasks();
    anInterest.informTaskCount(tasks.size());
    for (Task task : tasks) {
        ...
    }
}
...
}
```

The various interest providers may be implemented by other classes, much the same way that **Entities (5)** describe the way validation is delegated to separate validator classes.

Be aware that some will consider this approach completely outside the responsibility of an Aggregate. Others will consider it a completely natural extension of a well-designed domain model. As always, such trade-offs must be discussed by your technical team members.

Render Aggregate Instances from a Domain Payload Object

There is an approach that provides a possible improvement when DTOs are unnecessary. This one gathers multiple whole Aggregate instances for view rendition into a single **Domain Payload Object** [Vernon, DPO]. DPO has motivations similar to DTO but takes advantage of the single virtual machine application architecture. It is designed to contain references to whole Aggregate instances, not individual attributes. Clusters of Aggregate instances can be transferred between logical tiers or layers by a simple Payload container object. The Application Service (see "Application Services") uses Repositories to retrieve the necessary Aggregate instances and then instantiates the DPO to hold references to each. The presentation components ask the DPO object for the Aggregate instance references, and then ask the Aggregates for viewable attributes.

Cowboy Logic

LB: "If you haven't fallen off a horse, you haven't been ridin' long enough."

This approach has the advantage of simplifying the design of objects to move clusters of data between logical tiers. The DPOs tend to be much easier to design and have a smaller memory footprint. Since the Aggregate instances must be read into memory anyway, we leverage that they already exist.

There are a few potential negative consequences to consider. Because of the similarity to DTOs, this approach also requires Aggregates to provide a means to read their state. To avoid tightly coupling the user interface to the model, the same Mediator, Double-Dispatch, or Aggregate Root query interface, suggested previously for use by DTO Assemblers, may be employed here as well.

There's still another situation to deal with. Since the DPO holds references to whole Aggregate instances, any lazy-loaded objects/collections are not yet resolved. There is no reason to access all needed Aggregate properties to create the Domain Payload Object. Since even read-only transactions are generally committed when the Application Service method ends, any presentation component that references unresolved lazy-loaded objects will cause an exception.[3]

To fix up necessary lazy loads we might choose an eager loading strategy, or we can use a **Domain Dependency Resolver** [Vernon, DDR]. This is a form of **Strategy** [Gamma et al.], usually employing one Strategy per use case flow. Each Strategy forces access of all Aggregate lazy-loaded properties consumed by the specific use case flow. The forced access occurs before the Application Service commits the transaction and returns the Domain Payload Object to its client. The Strategy may be hard-coded to manually access the lazy-loaded properties, or it may employ a simple expression language that describes how to introspectively and reflectively navigate through the Aggregate instances. The reflection-based navigation crawler has the advantage that it can be made to work on hidden attributes. Still, you may be happier customizing your queries to eagerly fetch objects that are normally lazy loaded, if the option is available.

State Representations of Aggregate Instances

If your application provides REST-based resources as discussed in **REST (4)**, these will need to produce state representations of domain objects for clients. It is very important to create representations that are based on use case, not on Aggregate instances. This has very similar motivations as DTOs, which also are tuned for use cases. However, it may be more accurate to think of a set of RESTful resources as a separate model in their own right—a **View Model** or **Presentation Model** [Fowler, PM]. Resist the temptation to produce representations that are a one-to-one reflection of your domain model Aggregate states, possibly with links to navigate to deeper state. Otherwise your clients will have to understand your domain model as well as the Aggregates themselves. Clients

---

3. Some like to use Open Session In View (OSIV) to control transactions at the request-response level, high in the user interface. For various reason I consider OSIV harmful, but YMMV ("Your Mileage May Vary").

will have to be fully aware of subtleties in behaviors and state transitions, and you will lose all benefits of abstraction.

Use Case Optimal Repository Queries

Rather than reading multiple whole Aggregate instances of various types and then programmatically composing them into a single container (DTO or DPO), you might instead use what is called a *use case optimal query*. This is where you design your Repository with finder query methods that compose a custom object as a superset of one or more Aggregate instances. The query dynamically places the results into a **Value Object** (6) specifically designed to address the needs of the use case. You design a Value Object, not a DTO, because the query is domain specific, not application specific (as are DTOs). The custom use case optimal Value Object is then consumed directly by the view renderer.

The use case optimal query approach has motivations similar to **CQRS** (4). However, the use case optimal query uses a Repository against the unified domain model persistence store rather than a raw database (such as SQL) query against a separate query/read store. To understand the trade-offs of this approach versus CQRS, see the related discussion under **Repositories** (12). Still, once you start to go down this use case optimal query path, you are so close to CQRS that it may be worth going that route instead.

Dealing with Multiple, Disparate Clients

What will you do if your application must support multiple, disparate clients? This may include an RIA, a graphical thick client, REST-based services, and messaging too. You probably also consider various test drivers as being different client types. Discussed in more detail a bit later, you may design your Application Services to accept **Data Transformer**, where each client specifies the Data Transformer type. The Application Service would double-dispatch on the Data Transformer parameter, which would produce the required data format. Here's how the user interface side might look for a REST-based client:

```
...
CalendarWeekData calendarWeekData =
    calendarAppService
        .calendarWeek(date, new CalendarWeekXMLDataTransformer());

Response response =
    Response.ok(calendarWeekData.value())
        .cacheControl(this.cacheControlFor(30)).build();

return response;
```

Method `calendarWeek()` of the `CalendarApplicationService` accepts a `Date` within a given week and an implementation of interface `Calendar-WeekDataTransformer`. The chosen implementer is class `Calendar-WeekXMLDataTransformer`, which creates an XML document as a state representation of the `CalendarWeekData`. Method `value()` on `Calendar-WeekData` answers the preferred type of the given data format, which in this case is an XML document `String`.

Admittedly the example could benefit from having the Data Transformer instance *dependency injected*. It's hard-coded here to make the example easier to understand.

Among the possible implementers of `CalendarWeekDataTransformer` could be, for example:

- `CalendarWeekCSVDataTransformer`

- `CalendarWeekDPODataTransformer`

- `CalendarWeekDTODataTransformer`

- `CalendarWeekJSONDataTransformer`

- `CalendarWeekTextDataTransformer`

- `CalendarWeekXMLDataTransformer`

There is another possible approach to abstracting application output types to disparate clients that I discuss later under "Application Services."

Rendition Adapters and Handling User Edits

When you get to the point where you have your domain data and it needs to be viewed and edited by a user, there are patterns that can help you separate responsibilities. Again, there are simply too many frameworks out there and too many ways to deal with them to recommend a surefire way to deal with all of them. With some user interface frameworks you must adhere to the specific patterns that are supported. Sometimes those are good, and sometimes not so good. With others you have a bit more flexibility.

In whatever way your domain data is provided from Application Services—through DTOs, DPOs, or state representations—and whatever presentation framework you use, you may be able to benefit from Presentation Model.[4] Its goal is to separate responsibilities between presentation and view. While it

---

4. See also **Model-View-Presenter** [Dolphin], which [Fowler, PM] calls **Supervising Controller** and **Passive View**.

could be made to work with Web 1.0 applications, I think its strengths tend to be in favor of Web 2.0 RIA, or those with desktop clients, as described in the second and third categories listed earlier.

Using this pattern, we want to make views passive in that they only manage display of data and user interface controls and do little else. There are two possible ways of view rendering:

1. Views render themselves based on the Presentation Model. I think this is a more natural way and eliminates coupling from the Presentation Model to the view.

2. Views are rendered by the Presentation Model. This way has test advantages but requires the Presentation Model to couple to the view.

The Presentation Model acts as an **Adapter** [Gamma et al.]. It masks the details of the domain model by providing properties and behaviors that are designed in terms of the needs of the view. This means that there is more than a thin veneer around attributes on domain objects or DTOs. It means that decisions are made in the Adapter based on the state of the model as it applies to the view. For example, enabling a specific control on the view may not have a direct relationship to any one property of the domain model but can still be derived from one or more such. Rather than requiring the domain model to specifically support the necessary view properties, it is the responsibility of the Presentation Model to derive the view-specific indicators and properties from the state of the domain model.

A further, yet perhaps subtle, benefit of using a Presentation Model is that it can adapt Aggregates that don't support a JavaBean interface of getters to user interface frameworks that require getters. Many, if not all, of the Java-based Web frameworks require objects to provide public getters, such as getSummary() and getStory(), while the domain model design favors fluent, domain-specific expressions that closely reflect the **Ubiquitous Language** (**1**). The difference may be as simple as summary() and story() but produces a user interface framework impedance mismatch. Yet, a Presentation Model can be used to easily adapt summary() to getSummary() and story() to getStory(), eliminating tension between model and view:

```
public class BacklogItemPresentationModel
        extends AbstractPresentationModel {

    private BacklogItem backlogItem;

    public BacklogItemPresentationModel(BacklogItem aBacklogItem) {
        super();
        this.backlogItem = backlogItem;
    }
```

```
    public String getSummary() {
        return this.backlogItem.summary();
    }

    public String getStory() {
        return this.backlogItem.story();
    }
    ...
}
```

Of course, a Presentation Model can adapt between any number of the previously discussed approaches, including the use of a DTO or DPO, or using a Mediator through which Aggregate internal state is published.

Additionally, edits performed by the user are tracked by the Presentation Model. This is not a case of placing overloaded responsibilities on the Presentation Model, since it is meant to adapt in both directions, model to view and view to model.

One important point to keep in mind is that a Presentation Model is not a heavy-lifting **Facade** [Gamma et al.] around the Application Services or the domain model. Granted, once users have completed a task with the user interface, they will usually invoke an "apply" or "cancel" type of action, or preferably an explicit command. This will require the Presentation Model to reflect the user's action to the application, which in essence represents a minimal Facade around an Application Service:

```
public class BacklogItemPresentationModel
        extends AbstractPresentationModel {

    private BacklogItem backlogItem;
    private BacklogItemEditTracker editTracker;
    // following is injected
    private BacklogItemApplicationService backlogItemAppService;

    public BacklogItemPresentationModel(BacklogItem aBacklogItem) {
        super();
        this.backlogItem = backlogItem;
        this.editTracker = new BacklogItemEditTracker(aBacklogItem);
    }
    ...
    public void changeSummaryWithType() {
        this.backlogItemAppService
            .changeSummaryWithType(
                this.editTracker.summary(),
                this.editTracker.type());
    }
    ...
}
```

The user clicks a command button on the view that causes `change-SummaryWithType()` to be invoked. It is the responsibility of `BacklogItemPresentationModel` to interact with an Application Service to apply the edits that occurred on `editTracker`. There is no other bystander waiting to take the user's edits and do something with them. So we might say that the Presentation Model is a minimal Facade to the Application Services on behalf of the view, but just because `changeSummaryWithType()` is a higher-level interface that makes `BacklogItemApplicationService` easier to use. However, we would not want to see several lines of code in the Presentation Model class manage detailed use of the Application Service, or worse yet, to itself act as the Application Service to the domain model. That would go well beyond the responsibility of the Presentation Model. Instead, we want to see a simple delegation to the more complex and heavy-lifting Facade, `BacklogItemApplicationService`.

This is a powerful approach to coordinating the domain model and UI. It may even receive your vote for the most versatile UI management pattern. Using any of the view management techniques, however, we still often interact with an Application Services API.

Application Services

In some cases your user interface will aggregate multiple **Bounded Contexts (2)** using independent Presentation Model components, all composed on a single view. Whether your user interface renders a single model or composes multiple models, it will likely interact with Application Services, so let's consider those now.

The Application Services are the direct clients of the domain model. For options on the logical location of Application Service, see **Architecture (4)**. These are responsible for task coordination of use case flows, one service method per flow. When using an ACID database, the Application Services also control transactions, ensuring that model state transitions are atomically persisted. I discuss transaction control here briefly, but see **Repositories (12)** for a broader perspective. Security is also commonly cared for by Application Services.

It is a mistake to consider Application Services to be the same as **Domain Services (7)**. They are not. The contrast should be stark, which is clearly demonstrated in the next section. We should strive to push all business domain logic into the domain model, whether that be in Aggregates, Value Objects, or Domain Services. *Keep Application Services thin, using them only to coordinate tasks on the model.*

Sample Application Service

Let's take a look at the partial sample interface and implementation class for an Application Service. This is the service that provides use case task management for tenants of the *Identity and Access Context*. It is just a sample and not meant to be taken as the final say. Trade-offs will be apparent.

First consider the basic interface:

```
package com.saasovation.identityaccess.application;

public interface TenantIdentityService {

    public void activateTenant(TenantId aTenantId);

    public void deactivateTenant(TenantId aTenantId);

    public String offerLimitedRegistrationInvitation(
            TenantId aTenantId,
            Date aStartsOnDate,
            Date anUntilDate);

    public String offerOpenEndedRegistrationInvitation(
            TenantId aTenantId);

    public Tenant provisionTenant(
            String aTenantName,
            String aTenantDescription,
            boolean isActive,
            FullName anAdministratorName,
            EmailAddress anEmailAddress,
            PostalAddress aPostalAddress,
            Telephone aPrimaryTelephone,
            Telephone aSecondaryTelephone,
            String aTimeZone);

    public Tenant tenant(TenantId aTenantId);
    ...
}
```

These six Application Service methods are used to create or provision a tenant, to activate and deactivate an existing one, to offer limited and open-ended registration invitations to future users, and to query for a specific tenant.

Some types from the domain model are used in these method signatures. That will require the user interface to be aware of these types and depend on them. Sometimes the Application Services are designed to completely shield the user interface from all such domain knowledge. Doing so, the Application Service method signatures use only primitive types (int, long, double),

Strings, and possibly DTOs. As an alternative to these approaches, however, a better approach may be to design **Command** [Gamma et al.] objects instead. There is not necessarily a right or wrong way. It mostly depends on your tastes and goals. This book presents each of these styles in various examples.

Consider the trade-offs. If you eliminate types from the model, you avoid dependency and coupling, but you lose out on strong type checking and basic validations (guards) that you get for free from Value Object types. If you don't expose domain objects as return types, you will need to provide DTOs. If you provide DTOs, there may be accidental complexity in your solution from the extra overhead of the additional types. Then there is also the aforementioned memory overhead in high-traffic applications that is caused by the possibly unnecessary DTOs constantly being created and garbage collected.

Of course, if you expose domain objects to disparate clients, each client type will need to deal with them separately. Again, coupling is higher and with more client types this becomes a bigger issue. Given that, at least a few of these methods could be better designed to deal with return types. As discussed previously, we might instead use Data Transformers:

```
package com.saasovation.identityaccess.application;

public interface TenantIdentityService {
    ...
    public TenantData provisionTenant(
            String aTenantName,
            String aTenantDescription,
            boolean isActive,
            FullName anAdministratorName,
            EmailAddress anEmailAddress,
            PostalAddress aPostalAddress,
            Telephone aPrimaryTelephone,
            Telephone aSecondaryTelephone,
            String aTimeZone,
            TenantDataTransformer aDataTransformer);

    public TenantData tenant(
            TenantId aTenantId,
            TenantDataTransformer aDataTransformer);
    ...
}
```

For now I will stick with exposing domain objects to the client and assume that we have only one user interface that is Web based. It will help to simplify the examples. Later I'll go back to the Data Transformers approach.

Consider how the Application Service interface is implemented. Taking a look at a few of the more trivial methods to implement it helps highlight some basic points. Note that there may be no advantage to having a **Separated Interface** [Fowler, P of EAA]. Here is an example where we will just define the interface with the implementation class:

```
package com.saasovation.identityaccess.application;

public class TenantIdentityService {

    @Transactional
    public void activateTenant(TenantId aTenantId) {
        this.nonNullTenant(aTenantId).activate();
    }

    @Transactional
    public void deactivateTenant(TenantId aTenantId) {
        this.nonNullTenant(aTenantId).deactivate();
    }

    ...

    @Transactional(readOnly=true)
    public Tenant tenant(TenantId aTenantId) {
        Tenant tenant =
            this
                .tenantRepository()
                .tenantOfId(aTenantId);

        return tenant;
    }

    private Tenant nonNullTenant(TenantId aTenantId) {
        Tenant tenant = this.tenant(aTenantId);

        if (tenant == null) {
            throw new IllegalArgumentException(
                    "Tenant does not exist.");
        }

        return tenant;
    }
}
```

A client requests to deactivate an existing Tenant using deactivateTenant(). To interact with the actual Tenant object we need to retrieve it from its Repository using its TenantId. Here we have created an internal helper method named nonNullTenant(), which itself delegates to tenant(). The helper exists to guard against nonexistent Tenant instances and is used by all service methods that need to get an existing Tenant.

Methods `activateTenant()` and `deactivateTenant()` are marked write transactional by a Spring `Transactional` annotation. Method `tenant()` is marked read-only transactional. In all three cases, when a client obtains this bean through its Spring context and invokes a service method, a transaction is started. When the method completes by normal return, the transaction is committed. Depending on configuration, exceptions thrown within the scope of the method will cause the transaction to roll back.

But how would we prevent the misuse of these methods, say, by a malicious intruder? When we are talking about deactivating or reactivating a tenant, it's an operation that should actually be permitted only by an SaaSOvation employee authorized user. The same goes for provisioning a new tenant subscriber.

What if we were to leverage something like Spring Security? We could use another annotation, `PreAuthorize`:

```
public class TenantIdentityService {

    @Transactional
    @PreAuthorize("hasRole('SubscriberRepresentative')")
    public void activateTenant(TenantId aTenantId) {
        this.nonNullTenant(aTenantId).activate();
    }

    @Transactional
    @PreAuthorize("hasRole('SubscriberRepresentative')")
    public void deactivateTenant(TenantId aTenantId) {
        this.nonNullTenant(aTenantId).deactivate();
    }

    ...

    @Transactional
    @PreAuthorize("hasRole('SubscriberRepresentative')")
    public Tenant provisionTenant(
            String aTenantName,
            String aTenantDescription,
            boolean isActive,
            FullName anAdministratorName,
            EmailAddress anEmailAddress,
            PostalAddress aPostalAddress,
            Telephone aPrimaryTelephone,
            Telephone aSecondaryTelephone,
            String aTimeZone) {

        return
            this
                .tenantProvisioningService
```

```
            .provisionTenant(
                aTenantName,
                aTenantDescription,
                isActive,
                anAdministratorName,
                anEmailAddress,
                aPostalAddress,
                aPrimaryTelephone,
                aSecondaryTelephone,
                aTimeZone);
    }
    ...
}
```

This is declarative method-level security and prevents unauthorized users from accessing Application Services. Of course, the user interface would be designed to hide any navigation access to such facilities if the user were not authorized. That wouldn't stop a malicious attacker, however, but the security declaration will.

This declarative method security is different from what IdOvation is providing. SaaSOvation employees would log in to IdOvation differently from tenant users. Particularly those with the special role SubscriberRepresentative would be permitted to execute these sensitive methods, and no subscriber user would ever be permitted to. This, of course, would require integration between IdOvation and Spring Security.

Now, when we look at the implementation of provisionTenant(), we see that it delegates to a Domain Service. This highlights the difference between the two kinds of services, especially when we peek inside the domain Tenant-ProvisioningService. There is significant domain logic inside this Domain Service, but very little in the Application Service. Consider what the Domain Service does (although I don't present the code here):

1. Instantiates a new Tenant Aggregate and adds it to its Repository.

2. Assigns a new administrator for the new Tenant. This includes provisioning the Administrator role for the new Tenant and publishing Event TenantAdministratorRegistered.

3. Publishes the Event TenantProvisioned.

If the Application Service were to do more than step 1, we would be seriously leaking domain logic out of the model. Since there are two additional steps that are not the responsibility of the Application Service, we instead place all three inside the Domain Service. Using the Domain Service, we place this "significant process . . . in the domain" [Evans].[5] We also properly follow the definition of Application Service by managing the transaction, security, and the task of delegating this significant tenant provisioning process to the model.

But consider for a moment the noise caused by the `provisionTenant()` parameter list. There is a total of nine parameters, and that's probably at least a few too many. We can prevent this situation by designing simple **Command** [Gamma et al.] objects instead: "Encapsulate a request as an object, thereby letting you parameterize clients with different requests, queue or log requests, and support undoable operations." In other words, we might think of a Command object as a serialized method invocation, and in our case we are interested in everything a Command can help with except for undo operations. This is how simple a Command class is to design:

```java
public class ProvisionTenantCommand {
    private String tenantName;
    private String tenantDescription;
    private boolean isActive;
    private String administratorFirstName;
    private String administratorLastName;
    private String emailAddress;
    private String primaryTelephone;
    private String secondaryTelephone;
    private String addressStreetAddress;
    private String addressCity;
    private String addressStateProvince;
    private String addressPostalCode;
    private String addressCountryCode;
    private String timeZone;

    public ProvisionTenantCommand(...) {
        ...
    }

    public ProvisionTenantCommand() {
        super();
    }

    public String getTenantName() {
        return tenantName;
    }

    public void setTenantName(String tenantName) {
        this.tenantName = tenantName;
    }
    ...
}
```

---

5. See Chapter 7.

The `ProvisionTenantCommand` doesn't use model objects, just basic types. It has a multi-argument constructor and also a zero-argument constructor. Along with the zero-argument constructor, having public setters allows the Command to be populated by UI form-field-to-object mappers (for example, assuming a JavaBean, or .NET CLR properties). You might think of the Command as a DTO, but it is truly more than that. Since the Command object is named for the operation that is to be carried out, it is more explicit. The Command instance may be passed to an Application Service method:

```
public class TenantIdentityService {
    ...
    @Transactional
    public String provisionTenant(ProvisionTenantCommand aCommand) {
        ...
        return tenant.tenantId().id();
    }
    ...
}
```

Besides this approach of dispatching to an Application Service API method, as the pattern states we could instead or in addition to send Commands to a queue to be dispatched to a Command Handler. Consider a Command Handler to be semantically equivalent to an Application Service method, but temporally decoupled. As discussed in Appendix A, this enables greater throughput and scalability of Command handling.

Decoupled Service Output

A couple of times earlier I discussed the use of Data Transformers as a way to accommodate disparate client types with the specific data type they require. That approach uses Transformers to produce the data in a specific type that implements an abstract interface that all related types share. Again, from the client's perspective it might look like this:

```
TenantData tenantData =
    tenantIdentityService.provisionTenant(
            ..., myTenantDataTransformer);

TenantPresentationModel tenantPresentationModel =
    new TenantPresentationModel(tenantData.value());
```

The Application Services are designed as an API, with input and output. The reason for passing in a Data Transformer is to produce the specific output type needed by the client.

What if we took an entirely different course and made the rule that Application Services are always declared void and, thus, never return data to clients? How would that work? The answer lies in a mentality that the **Hexagonal Architecture** (4) promotes, the use of the **Ports and Adapters** style. In this instance we would use a single standard output Port with any number of adapters, one for each client type. Doing so would yield a `provisionTenant()` Application Service method like this one:

```
public class TenantIdentityService {
    ...

    @Transactional
    @PreAuthorize("hasRole('SubscriberRepresentative')")
    public void provisionTenant(
            String aTenantName,
            String aTenantDescription,
            boolean isActive,
            FullName anAdministratorName,
            EmailAddress anEmailAddress,
            PostalAddress aPostalAddress,
            Telephone aPrimaryTelephone,
            Telephone aSecondaryTelephone,
            String aTimeZone) {

        Tenant tenant =
            this
                .tenantProvisioningService
                .provisionTenant(
                        aTenantName,
                        aTenantDescription,
                        isActive,
                        anAdministratorName,
                        anEmailAddress,
                        aPostalAddress,
                        aPrimaryTelephone,
                        aSecondaryTelephone,
                        aTimeZone);

        this.tenantIdentityOutputPort().write(tenant);
    }
    ...
}
```

The output Port here is a specific named Port at the edge of the application. Using Spring, it would be a bean injected into the service. The only thing that `provisionTenant()` needs to know is that it must `write()` to the Port the `Tenant` instance it gets from the Domain Service. This Port would have any number of readers, which register themselves ahead of using the Application

Service. When a `write()` occurs, each of the registered readers is signaled to read the output as its input. At that point the readers may transform the output using the established mechanism, such as a Data Transformer.

This isn't just a fancy artifice to add complexity to your architecture. The strength is the same as with any Ports and Adapters architecture, whether for a software system or a hardware device. Each component only needs to understand the input it reads, its own behavior, and the Port to which it writes output.

Writing to a Port is roughly the same thing that an Aggregate pure command method does when it produces no return value, but it does publish a **Domain Event** (8). In the case of the Aggregate the **Domain Event Publisher** (8) is an Aggregate output Port. Further, if we solve querying the state of an Aggregate by using a Double-Dispatch on a Mediator, it is similar to using Ports and Adapters.

One downside of the Ports and Adapters approach is that it may make it more difficult to name Application Service methods that perform queries. Consider method `tenant()` from the sample service. That name now seems inappropriate because it no longer answers the `Tenant` that it queries. The name `provisionTenant()` still works for the provisioning API because it actually becomes a pure command method, no longer returning a value. But we might want to think of a better name for `tenant()`. The following may improve things a bit:

```
...
@Override
@Transactional(readOnly=true)
public void findTenant(TenantId aTenantId) {
    Tenant tenant =
        this
            .tenantRepository
            .tenantOfId(aTenantId);

    this.tenantIdentityOutputPort().write(tenant);
}
...
}
```

The name `findTenant()` might work because finding doesn't necessarily imply the need to answer a result. Whatever name is chosen, the situation confirms that each architectural decision we make leads to positive and negative consequences.

Composing Multiple Bounded Contexts

The examples I have provided don't address the possibility that a single user interface may need to compose two or more domain models. In my examples, concepts from upstream models are integrated into downstream models by translating them into terms of the downstream model.

That's different from the need to compose multiple models into one unified presentation, as seen in Figure 14.3. The foreign models, in this example, are *Products Context*, *Discussions Context*, and *Reviews Context*. The user interface should not be aware that it is composing multiple models. When a similar situation occurs in your application, you should give thought to how **Module (9)** structure and naming support your needs, and how Application Services can smooth out the probable disconnect between different models.

One solution uses multiple Application Layers, which is unlike that shown in Figure 14.3. With multiple Application Layers you would need to supply independent user interface components with each, where the user interface components would have some affinity to a specific underlying domain model. This is basically the portal-portlet style. Still, it could be more difficult to get the disparate Application Layers and independent user interface components to harmonize along use case flows, which is what the user interface is concerned with.

Since the Application Layer manages use cases, it may be easiest to create a single Application Layer as the actual source of model composition, which is the approach shown in Figure 14.3. Services in that single layer are devoid of business domain logic. It will only serve to aggregate objects from each model into cohesive ones that the user interface needs. Likely in this case you would

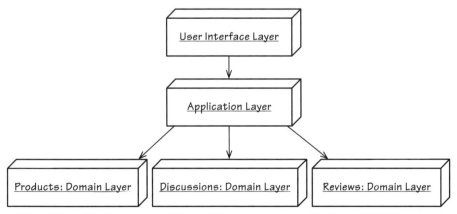

Figure 14.3 There are times when a UI must compose multiple models. Here three models are composed using a single Application Layer.

name Modules in the User Interface and Application Layers according to the purpose of the composition, a named context:

```
com.consumerhive.productreviews.presentation

com.consumerhive.productreviews.application
```

Consumer Hive provides consumer product reviews and discussions. It has separated the *Products Context* from the *Discussions Context* and *Reviews Context*. Yet, the presentation and application Modules reflect the unification under one user interface. Likely it gets its product catalog from one or more external sources, whereas the discussions and reviews are its Core Domain.

And speaking of Core Domain . . . Strangely enough, what do you detect here? Isn't this Application Layer really serving as a new domain model with a built-in **Anticorruption Layer (3)**? Yes, it is basically a new bargain-basement Bounded Context. Here the Application Services manage a merger of various DTOs, which mimic a sort of **Anemic Domain Model (1)**. It is a bit of a **Transaction Script (1)** approach that models the Core Domain.

If you were to decide that Consumer Hive's three-model composition is crying for a new **Domain Model (1)** that is a unified object model in a single Bounded Context, you might name the Modules of the new model as follows:

```
com.consumerhive.productreviews.domain.model.product

com.consumerhive.productreviews.domain.model.discussion

com.consumerhive.productreviews.domain.model.review
```

In the end you will have to decide how to model this situation. Will you decide to use strategic design and even tactical design to create a new model? At a minimum, this situation begs the question: Where do we draw the line between composing multiple Bounded Contexts into a single user interface, and creating a new, clean Bounded Context with a unified domain model? Each case must be considered carefully. A less significant system would have other influences and priorities. Still, we must not treat such decisions arbitrarily. Consideration should be given to the criteria provided in Bounded Contexts. In the end the best approach is the one that benefits the business the most.

Infrastructure

The job of the infrastructure is to provide technical capabilities for other parts of your application. While avoiding a discussion about **Layers (4)**, it is still useful to maintain a Dependency Inversion Principle mentality. So wherever

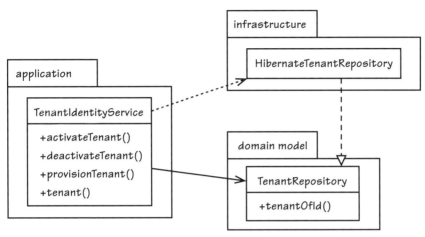

Figure 14.4 The Application Service depends on the Repository interface from the domain model but uses the implementation class from infrastructure. The packages encapsulate broad responsibilities.

your infrastructure lives architecturally, it works out very well if its components depend on the interfaces from the user interface, Application Services, and domain model that require special technical capabilities. That way, when an Application Service looks up a Repository, it will be dependent only on the interface from the domain model, but using the implementation from the infrastructure. Figure 14.4 provides the UML static structure diagram to illustrate how that works.

The lookup may be implicit through **Dependency Injection** [Fowler, DI] or using a **Service Factory**. The final section of this chapter, "Enterprise Component Containers," discusses these options. Repeating a portion of the Application Service used as a running example, you can see again here how the Service Factory is used to look up the Repository:

```
package com.saasovation.identityaccess.application;

public class TenantIdentityService {
    ...
    @Override
    @Transactional(readOnly=true)
    public Tenant tenant(TenantId aTenantId) {
        Tenant tenant =
            DomainRegistry
                .tenantRepository()
                .tenantOfId(aTenantId);
```

```
        return tenant;
    }
    ...
}
```

This Application Service could have instead injected the Repository, or we could have set up the inbound dependencies by way of constructor parameters.

Implementations of Repositories are kept in the infrastructure because they deal with storage, which is not a responsibility that the model should take on. You would use the infrastructure to implement interfaces that require use of messaging, such as message queues and e-mail. If there are special user interface components that feature generated graphical charts, maps, and the like, these would also be implemented in the infrastructure.

Enterprise Component Containers

These days, enterprise application servers are a commodity. There seems to be little innovation in the servers themselves and in the component containers that run inside them. We can use Enterprise JavaBeans (EJB) as **Session Facades** [Crupi et al.] or simple JavaBeans hosted by inversion-of-control containers, such as Spring, to facilitate the use of Application Services. There are arguments about which is better, but there has also been a lot of convergence among the frameworks. In fact, a peek inside some JEE servers reveals that some are implemented using Spring.

> **Is It WebLogic or Spring?**
>
> If you were to view a stack trace from the Oracle WebLogic Server, you'd likely see references to classes from Spring Framework. They aren't part of your application's deployment. In this case you are using only standard JEE with EJB Session Beans. The Spring classes you are seeing are part of WebLogic's EJB container implementation. Is this a case of "if you can't beat them, join them"?

I have chosen to implement the three sample Bounded Contexts I have provided using Spring Framework. Yet, these examples would easily carry over to other enterprise container platforms. So there's nothing lost if you don't use Spring on your projects, and you should still feel quite comfortable reading through the examples. There are minimal logical differences among the various containers.

In **Repositories (12)** is seen the Spring configuration used to wire up transactional support for Application Services that is used for persisting domain objects. Here let's look at other parts of the Spring configuration. Two files of interest are

```
config/spring/applicationContext-application.xml

config/spring/applicationContext-domain.xml
```

As the filenames indicate, Application Services and domain model components are wired in these. Consider a few from the application wiring:

```
<beans ...>
    <aop:aspectj-autoproxy/>

    <tx:annotation-driven transaction-manager="transactionManager"/>
    ...
    <bean
        id="applicationServiceRegistry"
        class="com.saasovation.identityaccess.application↵
.ApplicationServiceRegistry"
        autowire="byName">
    </bean>
    ...
    <bean
        id="tenantIdentityService"
        class="com.saasovation.identityaccess.application↵
.TenantIdentityService"
        autowire="byName">
    </bean>
    ...
</beans>
```

The bean `tenantIdentityService` is the one reviewed earlier. This bean can be wired into other Spring beans, such as in the user interface. If you prefer a Service Factory rather than injecting bean instances into others, we can use the other bean in the configuration, `applicationServiceRegistry`. This bean provides lookup access to all Application Services. You'd use it like this:

```
...
ApplicationServiceRegistry
    .tenantIdentityService()
    .deactivateTenant(tenantId);
```

We can do so because it is itself injected with the Spring `Application-Context` when the bean is newly created.

The same kind of registry bean is provided for access to components of the domain model, such as Repositories and Domain Services. Here is the Registry, Repository, and Domain Service bean configuration for the domain model:

```
<beans ...>
    ...
    <bean
        id="authenticationService"
        class="com.saasovation.identityaccess.infrastructure↵
.services.DefaultEncryptionAuthenticationService"
        autowire="byName">
    </bean>

    <bean
        id="domainRegistry"
        class="com.saasovation.identityaccess.domain.model↵
.DomainRegistry"
        autowire="byName">
    </bean>

    <bean
        id="encryptionService"
        class="com.saasovation.identityaccess.infrastructure↵
.services.MessageDigestEncryptionService"
        autowire="byName">
    </bean>

    <bean
        id="groupRepository"
        class="com.saasovation.identityaccess.infrastructure↵
.persistence.HibernateGroupRepository"
        autowire="byName">
    </bean>

    <bean
        id="roleRepository"
        class="com.saasovation.identityaccess.infrastructure↵
.persistence.HibernateRoleRepository"
        autowire="byName">
    </bean>

    <bean
        id="tenantProvisioningService"
        class="com.saasovation.identityaccess.domain.model↵
.identity.TenantProvisioningService"
        autowire="byName">
    </bean>

    <bean
        id="tenantRepository"
        class="com.saasovation.identityaccess.infrastructure↵
.persistence.HibernateTenantRepository"
        autowire="byName">
    </bean>
```

```
    <bean
        id="userRepository"
        class="com.saasovation.identityaccess.infrastructure↵
.persistence.HibernateUserRepository"
        autowire="byName">
    </bean>
</bcans>
```

Using the `DomainRegistry`, we can access any of these Spring registered beans. All of the beans are also available for dependency injection into other Spring beans. Thus, the Application Services could choose to use the Service Factory or Dependency Injection. See **Services** (7) for a more in-depth discussion of using these two approaches versus a constructor-based dependency setup.

Wrap-Up

In this chapter we've looked into how the application works outside the domain model.

- You've considered several techniques for rendering the model's data into user interfaces.

- You saw ways of accepting user input that is applied to the domain model.

- You've learned a variety of options for transferring model data, even when there are possibly many different kinds of user interface types.

- You have looked into Application Services and what they are responsible for.

- You were introduced to an option for decoupling output from specific client types.

- You've learned ways to use the infrastructure to keep technical implementations out of the domain model.

- You considered how, using DIP, to make clients of every aspect of the application depend on abstractions rather than implementation details, which promotes loose coupling.

- Finally, you saw how commodity application servers and enterprise component containers can give legs to your applications.

You should now be on solid footing to implement DDD from the carefully crafted domain model through to the components of the entire application.

Appendix A

Aggregates and Event Sourcing: A+ES

Contributed by Rinat Abdullin

The concept of **Event Sourcing** has been used for decades but has more recently been popularized by Greg Young by applying it to DDD [Young, ES].

Event Sourcing can be used to represent the entire state of an **Aggregate** (10) as a sequence of **Events** (8) that have occurred since it was created. The Events are used to rebuild the state of the Aggregate by replaying them in the same order in which they occurred. The premise is that this approach simplifies persistence and allows capturing concepts with complex behavioral properties.

The set of Events representing the state of each Aggregate is captured in an append-only Event Stream. This Aggregate state is further mutated by successive operations that append new Events to the end of the Event Stream, as illustrated in Figure A.1. (In this appendix Events are shown as light gray rectangles to make them stand out from other concepts.)

The Event Stream of each Aggregate is usually persisted in **Event Stores** (8), where they are uniquely distinguished, usually by the identity of the root **Entity** (5). How to build an Event Store specifically for use with Event Sourcing is addressed in more detail later in the appendix.

From here forward, let's refer to this approach of using Event Sourcing to maintain the state of Aggregates and persist them as **A+ES**.

Some of the primary benefits of A+ES are:

- Event Sourcing guarantees that the reason for each change to an Aggregate instance will not be lost. When using the traditional approach of

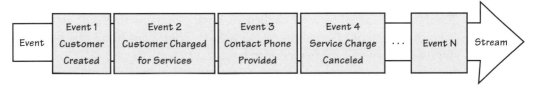

Figure A.1 An Event Stream with Domain Events in order of occurrence

serializing the current state of an Aggregate to a database, we are always overwriting the previous serialized state, never to be recovered. However, retaining the reason for every change from the creation of an Aggregate instance through its entire lifetime can be invaluable for the business. As discussed in **Architecture (4)**, the benefits can be far-reaching: reliability, near- and far-term business intelligence, analytic discoveries, full audit log, the ability to look back in time for debugging purposes.

- The append-only nature of Event Streams performs outstandingly well and supports an array of data replication options. Using similar approaches has allowed companies such as LMAX to facilitate very low-latency equities trading systems.

- The Event-centric approach to Aggregate design can allow developers to focus more of their attention on behaviors expressed by the **Ubiquitous Language (1)** by avoiding the potential impedance mismatch of object-relational mapping and can lead to systems that are more robust and tolerant to change.

That said, make no mistake: A+ES is not a silver bullet. Consider a few realistic drawbacks:

- Defining Events for A+ES requires a deep understanding of the business domain. As in any DDD project, this level of effort is usually justifiable only for complex models from which the organization will derive competitive advantage.

- At the time of writing, there is a lack of tooling and a consistent body of knowledge in this field. This increases costs and the risks of introducing the approach to inexperienced teams.

- The number of experienced developers is limited.

- Implementing A+ES almost certainly requires some form of Command-Query Responsibility Segregation, or **CQRS (4)**, since Event Streams are hard to query. This increases developer cognitive load and learning curve.

For those undaunted by these challenges, implementing with A+ES can provide a lot of benefits. Let's examine some ways to implement using this powerful approach in the object-oriented world.

Inside an Application Service

Looking at A+ES inside an **Application Service (4, 14)** demonstrates the big picture. It's common for Aggregates to reside inside a domain model behind Application Services, which serve as the direct clients of the domain model.

When an Application Service receives control, it loads an Aggregate and retrieves any supporting **Domain Services (7)** needed by the Aggregate's business operation. When the Application Service delegates to the Aggregate business operation, the Aggregate's method produces Events as the outcome. Those Events mutate the state of the Aggregate and are also published as notifications to all subscribers. The Aggregate's business method may require passing one or more Domain Services as parameters. The use of any such Domain Services could compute values used to cause side effects to the Aggregate's state. Some such Domain Service operations could include calling a payment gateway, requesting a unique identity, or querying data from a remote system. Figure A.2 illustrates how this works.

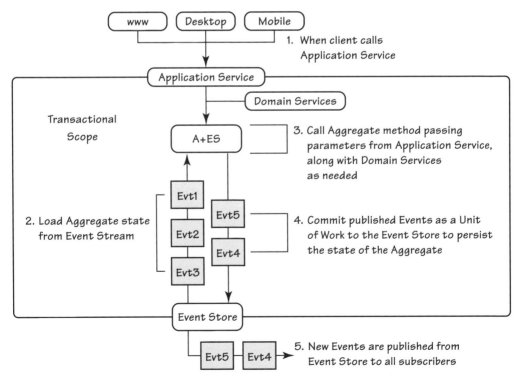

Figure A.2 An Application Service controls access to and use of the Aggregate.

The following Application Service implemented in C# shows how the steps of Figure A.2 might be supported:

```csharp
public class CustomerApplicationService
{
  // event store for accessing event streams
  IEventStore _eventStore;

  // domain service that is neeeded by aggregate
  IPricingService _pricingService;

  // pass dependencies for this application service via constructor
  public CustomerApplicationService(
    IEventStore eventStore,
    IPricingService pricing)
  {
    _eventStore = eventStore;
    _pricingService = pricing;
  }

  // Step 1: LockForAccountOverdraft method of
  // Customer Application Service is called
  public void LockForAccountOverdraft(
    CustomerId customerId, string comment)
  {
    // Step 2.1: Load event stream for Customer, given its id
    var stream = _eventStore.LoadEventStream(customerId);
    // Step 2.2: Build aggregate from event stream
    var customer = new Customer(stream.Events);
    // Step 3: Call aggregate method, passing it arguments and
    // pricing domain service
    customer.LockForAccountOverdraft(comment, _pricingService);
    // Step 4: Commit changes to the event stream by id
    _eventStore.AppendToStream(
      customerId, stream.Version, customer.Changes);
  }

  public void LockCustomer(CustomerId customerId, string reason)
  {
    var stream = _eventStore.LoadEventStream(customerId);
    var customer = new Customer(stream.Events);
    customer.Lock(reason);
    _eventStore.AppendToStream(
      customerId, stream.Version, customer.Changes);
  }

  // other methods on this application service
}
```

The `CustomerApplicationService` is initialized with two dependencies through the constructor, the `IEventStore`, and `IPricingService`.

Constructor-based initialization is a worthy means to fulfill the dependencies, but they could have been retrieved by means of a Service Factory or using dependency injection. Your team standards and practices reign.

> **Where Can I Find the Sample Code?**
> All source code for the A+ES examples is available for download here:
> http://lokad.github.com/lokad-iddd-sample/.

Our `IEventStore` can have a simple interface definition, and our `Event-Stream` follows suit:

```
public interface IEventStore
{
    EventStream LoadEventStream(IIdentity id);

    EventStream LoadEventStream(
        IIdentity id, int skipEvents, int maxCount);

    void AppendToStream(
        IIdentity id, int expectedVersion, ICollection<IEvent> events);
}

public class EventStream
{
    // version of the event stream returned
    public int Version;

    // all events in the stream
    public List<IEvent> Events;
}
```

This Event Store can be implemented quite easily with a relational database (Microsoft SQL, Oracle, or MySQL) or with a NoSQL store that has strong consistency guarantees (file system, MongoDB, RavenDB, or Azure Blob storage).

We load Events from the Event Store using the unique identity of the Aggregate instance to be reconstituted. Let's see how this can be done for an Aggregate named `Customer`. Although the unique identity could have any type, for expressiveness let's use an `IIdentity` interface implemented by `CustomerId`.

We need to load the Events belonging to the specific `Customer`, and the Events are passed to the `Customer`'s constructor to instantiate the Aggregate:

```
var eventStream = _eventStore.LoadEventStream(customerId);

var customer = new Customer(eventStream.Events);
```

As seen in Figure A.3, the Aggregate applies Events by replaying them through method Mutate(). Here's how it works:

```
public partial class Customer
{
  public Customer(IEnumerable<IEvent> events)
  {
    // reinstate this aggregate to the latest version
    foreach (var @event in events)
    {
      Mutate(@event);
    }
  }

  public bool ConsumptionLocked { get; private set; }

  public void Mutate(IEvent e)
  {
    // .NET magic to call one of 'When' handlers with
    // matching signature
    ((dynamic) this).When((dynamic)e);
  }

  public void When(CustomerLocked e)
  {
    ConsumptionLocked = true;
  }

  public void When(CustomerUnlocked e)
  {
    ConsumptionLocked = false;
  }

  // etc.
```

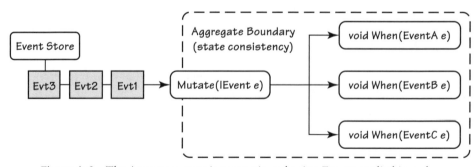

Figure A.3 The Aggregate state is reconstituted using Events applied in order of occurrence.

Mutate() just locates (via .NET dynamics) the appropriate overloaded When() method by the specific Event parameter type, and then executes the method by passing in the Event. After Mutate() has completed, the Customer instance has a completely reconstituted state.

We can make a reusable query operation for reconstituting an Aggregate instance from the Event Store:

```
public Customer LoadCustomerById(CustomerId id)
{
    var eventStream = _eventStore.LoadEventStream(id);
    var customer = new Customer(eventStream.Events);
    return customer;
}
```

After considering how an Aggregate instance can be reconstituted from a Stream of historic Events, it's easy to imagine other uses for the historical record. We can use them to look back in time just to view what happened, and when. The view capability becomes even more powerful when considering the need to debug production deployments.

How are business operations performed? Once the Aggregate is reconstituted from the Event Store, the Application Service delegates to a command operation on the Aggregate instance. It uses its current state and any Domain Services required by the contract to carry out the operation. As a behavior is executed, changes to the state are expressed as new Events. Each new Event is passed to the Aggregate's Apply() method, as pictured in Figure A.4.

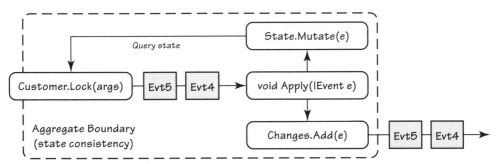

Figure A.4   Aggregate state is based on past Events, and outcome of behavior produces new Events.

As seen in the following code, new Events are accumulated in the `Changes` collection and then used to mutate the current state of the Aggregate:

```
public partial class Customer
{
  ...
  void Apply(IEvent event)
  {
    // append event to change list for further persistence
    Changes.Add(event);

    // pass each event to modify current in-memory state
    Mutate(event);
  }
  ...
}
```

All Events added to the `Changes` collection will be persisted as newly appended. Since each Event is also used to immediately mutate the Aggregate's state, if a behavior has multiple steps, each subsequent step has up-to-date state to operate on.

Next, take a look at some of the business behavior of the `Customer` Aggregate:

```
public partial class Customer
{
  // Second part of aggregate class
  public List<IEvent> Changes = new List<IEvent>();

  public void LockForAccountOverdraft(
    string comment, IPricingService pricing)
  {
    if (!ManualBilling)
    {
      var balance = pricing.GetOverdraftThreshold(Currency);
      if (Balance < balance)
      {
        LockCustomer("Overdraft. " + comment);
      }
    }
  }

  public void LockCustomer(string reason)
  {
    if (!ConsumptionLocked)
    {
      Apply(new CustomerLocked(_state.Id, reason));
    }
  }
}
```

```
// Other business methods are not shown ...

void Apply(IEvent e)
{
    Changes.Add(e);
    Mutate(e);
}
}
```

Consider Using Two Implementation Classes

To make your code clearer, you can split the A+ES implementation into two distinct classes, one for state and one for behavior, with the state object being held by the behavioral. The two objects would collaborate exclusively through the `Apply()` method. This ensures that state is mutated only by means of Events.

Once the mutating behaviors have completed, we must commit the `Changes` collection to the Event Store. We append all new changes, ensuring that there are no concurrency conflicts with other writing threads. This check is possible because we pass a concurrency version variable from the `Load()` to the `Append()` methods.

In the simplest implementation, there will be a background processor that catches up with newly appended Events and publishes them to a messaging infrastructure (such as RabbitMQ, JMS, MSMQ, or cloud queues), delivering them to all interested parties. See Figure A.5.

This simple implementation can be replaced by more elaborate ones. One such immediately or eventually replicates Events to one or more clones, increasing fault tolerance. Figure A.6 shows immediate Event replication to one clone.

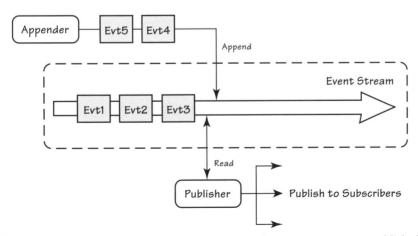

Figure A.5 Newly appended Aggregate behavioral outcome Events are published to subscribers.

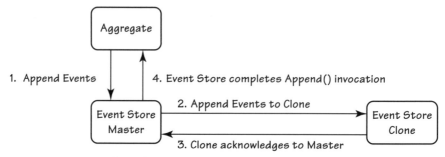

Figure A.6   Write through: A Master Event Store immediately replicates all newly appended Events to a Clone Event Store.

In this case, the Master Event Store considers its own Events to be saved only after it has successfully replicated them to the Clone Event Store, which is a write-through strategy.

An alternative is to replicate Events to the Clone after changes are saved by the Master using a separate thread, which is a write-behind strategy. This approach is illustrated in Figure A.7. In this case the Clone could be inconsistent with the Master, which is especially true if a server crashes or if partitioning is impacted by network latency.

To summarize what has been discussed so far, let's walk through the execution sequence that begins with the invocation of an operation on an Application Service:

1. A client invokes a method on an Application Service.

2. Obtain any Domain Services needed to carry out the business operation.

3. With the client-supplied Aggregate instance identity, retrieve its Event Stream.

Figure A.7   Write behind: A Master Event Store eventually replicates all newly appended Events to a Clone Event Store.

4. Reconstitute the Aggregate instance by applying to it all Events from the Stream.

5. Execute a business operation provided by the Aggregate, passing in all parameters required by the interface's contract.

6. The Aggregate may double-dispatch to any provided Domain Services, instances of other Aggregates, and so on and will generate new Events as the outcome of the operation.

7. Assuming no failed business operations, append all newly generated Events to the Stream using the Stream version to guard against concurrency conflicts.

8. Publish newly appended Events from the Event Store to subscribers using your choice of messaging infrastructure.

We could enhance our A+ES implementation using various options. For example, we could use a **Repository (12)** to encapsulate access to the Event Store and the details of reconstitution of the Aggregate instances. Given the preceding code snippets, it would be easy for you to create a reusable Repository base class. Let's focus on just two practical optional enhancements that help a lot with A+ES designs: *Command Handlers* and *lambdas*.

Command Handlers

Let's consider the advantages of using **Commands (4, 14)** and Command Handlers to control the task management of our application. To start, first take another look at our Application Service and its `LockCustomer()` method:

```
public class CustomerApplicationService
{
  ...
  public void LockCustomer(CustomerId id, string reason)
  {
    var eventStream = _eventStore.LoadEventStream(id);
    var customer = new Customer(stream.Events);
    customer.LockCustomer(reason);
    _store.AppendToStream(id, eventStream.Version, customer.Changes);
  }
  ...
}
```

Now imagine creating a serialized representation of the method name and its parameters. How might that look? We could create a class named for the application operation and create instance properties to match the parameters to the service method. This class forms a Command:

```
public sealed class LockCustomerCommand
{
  public CustomerId { get; set; }
  public string Reason { get; set; }
}
```

Command contracts follow the same semantics as Events and can be shared across systems in a similar fashion. This Command could then be passed to a method on the Application Service:

```
public class CustomerApplicationService
{
  ...
  public void When(LockCustomerCommand command)
  {
    var eventStream = _eventStore.LoadEventStream(command.CustomerId);
    var customer = new Customer(stream.Events);
    customer.LockCustomer(command.Reason);
    _eventStore.AppendToStream(
      command.CustomerId, eventStream.Version, customer.Changes);
  }
  ...
}
```

This simple refactoring could have a few long-term benefits for the system. Let's see how.

Since the Command objects can be serialized, we can send the textual or binary representations as messages over a message queue. The object that the message is delivered to is a message handler and is to us a Command Handler. The Command Handler effectively replaces the Application Service method, although it is roughly equivalent and may still be referred to as such. Anyway, decoupling the client from the Service can *enhance load balancing, enable competing consumers, and support system partitioning.* Take load balancing for one. We can spread the load by starting the same Command Handler (semantically an Application Service) on any number of servers. As Commands are put on the message queue, the Command messages can be delivered to one of the several Command Handlers that are listening for them. This is depicted

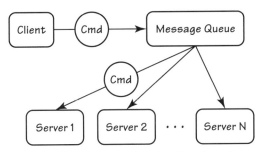

Figure A.8   Application Commands being distributed to any number
of Command Handlers

in Figure A.8. (In this appendix Commands are shown as circular objects.) The
actual distribution might be done using a simple round-robin style or some
more sophisticated delivery algorithm, any of which are provided by the messaging infrastructure.

This approach creates *temporal decoupling* between clients and the Application Service, leading toward more robust systems. For one, the client will no
longer be blocked if the Application Service is unavailable for a short period
of time (for example, for maintenance or upgrade). Instead, Commands will
be put into a persistent queue, which will be processed by the Command Handlers (Application Service) when its server comes back online, as indicated in
Figure A.9.

Another advantage is the ability to chain additional aspects before Command dispatching as needed. For example, we could easily patch in auditing,
logging, authorization, and validation.

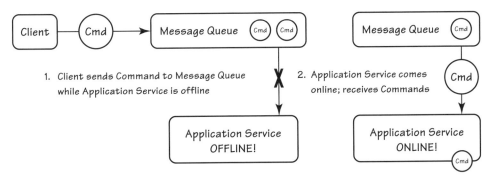

Figure A.9   The temporal decoupling characteristics of message-based Commands and
their Command Handlers allow for flexible system availability options.

Consider how we might patch in logging. We first define a standard interface and implement the interface in an Application Service class:

```
public interface IApplicationService
{
    void Execute(ICommand cmd);
}

public partial class CustomerApplicationService : IApplicationService
{
  public void Execute(ICommand command)
  {
    // pass command to a specific method When()
    // that can handle the command
    ((dynamic)this).When((dynamic)command);
  }
}
```

> **Execute and Mutate Have Similar Implementations**
> Note that the way this Execute() method is implemented has some characteristics similar to the Mutate() method described previously as part of an A+ES Aggregate's design.

Once we have a standard interface for all Command Handlers (Application Services), we can patch in any kind of standard pre- and post-execution features, such as generic logging:

```
public class LoggingWrapper : IApplicationService
{
  readonly IApplicationService _service;

  public LoggingWrapper(IApplicationService service)
  {
    _service = service;
  }

  public void Execute(ICommand cmd)
  {
    Console.WriteLine("Command: " + cmd);
    try
    {
      var watch = Stopwatch.StartNew();
      _service.Execute(cmd);
      var ms = watch.ElapsedMilliseconds;
      Console.WriteLine("  Completed in {0} ms", ms);
    }
```

```
  catch( Exception ex)
  {
    Console.WriteLine("Error: {0}", ex);
  }
}
}
```

Because all Application Services have a standard interface, we can patch in any number of generic utilities that operate before and/or after the actual Command Handler functions. Here's how the `CustomerApplicationService` is initialized with pre- and post-execution logging:

```
var customerService =
  new CustomerApplicationService(eventStore, pricingService);
var customerServiceWithLogging = new LoggingWrapper(customerService);
```

Of course, the fact that Commands are serialized objects dispatched to Command Handlers enables us to deal with various failures and error conditions in a single location. Given a certain class of error, such as resource contention over concurrency issues, we could choose a standard recovery action, such as retrying the operation X number of times. The retries could be based on a Capped Exponential Back-off strategy, making all retries uniform, reliable, and maintained in a single class.

Lambda Syntax

If your language supports lambda expressions, it is possible to make otherwise repetitive code more compact by avoiding repetitive Event Stream management. To demonstrate this fact, here we introduce a helper method within our Application Service:

```
public class CustomerApplicationService
{
  ...
  public void Update(CustomerId id, Action<Customer> execute)
  {
    EventStream eventStream = _eventStore.LoadEventStream(id);
    Customer customer = new Customer(eventStream.Events);
    execute(customer);
    _eventStore.AppendToStream(
      id, eventStream.Version, customer.Changes);
  }
  ...
}
```

In this method the parameter `Action<Customer>` execute references an anonymous function (C# delegate) that can operate on any `Customer` instance. The conciseness of the lambda expression can be seen in the parameter passed to `Update()`:

```
public class CustomerApplicationService
{
  ...
  public void When(LockCustomer c)
  {
    Update(c.Id, customer => customer.LockCustomer(c.Reason));
  }
  ...
}
```

In actuality the C# compiler generates something similar to the following code that fulfills the intent of the lambda expression:

```
public class AnonymousClass_X
{
    public string Reason;
    public void Execute(Customer customer);
    {
        Customer.LockCustomer(Reason);
    }
}

public delegate void Action<T>(T argument);

public void When(LockCustomer c)
{
  var x = new AnonymousClass_X();
  x.Reason = c.Reason
  Update(c.Id, new Action<Customer>(customer => x.Execute(customer)));
}
```

Since this generated function takes a `Customer` instance as an argument, it can actually be used to capture the behavior in the code and execute it multiple times on different `Customer` instances. The power of using lambdas is highlighted in the following section.

Concurrency Control

Aggregate Event Streams can be accessed and read by multiple threads simultaneously. This opens up the real potential for concurrency conflicts that, if

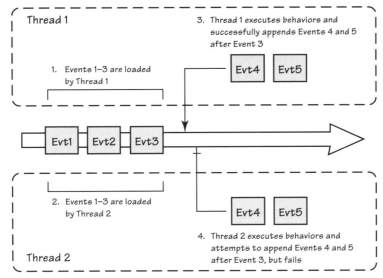

Figure A.10 Two threads contending for the same instance of an Aggregate designed using A+ES

left unchecked, could result in a random number of invalid Aggregate states. Consider a scenario when two threads attempt to modify the Event Stream at the same time, as shown in Figure A.10.

The simplest resolution to this situation is to use `EventStoreConcurrencyException` at step 4, allowing it to propagate all the way up to the ultimate client:

```
public class EventStoreConcurrencyException : Exception
{
    public List<IEvent> StoreEvents { get; set; }
    public long StoreVersion { get; set; }
}
```

Upon catching this exception in the ultimate client, the user would probably be instructed to retry the operation manually.

Instead of taking that approach first, you would probably agree that a standardized retry approach might be best. So when our Event Store throws `EventStoreConcurrencyException`, we can immediately attempt recovery:

```
void Update(CustomerId id, Action<Customer> execute)
{
  while(true)
  {
```

```
        EventStream eventStream = _eventStore.LoadEventStream(c.Id);
        var customer = new Customer(eventStream.Events);
        try
        {
          execute(customer);
          _eventStore.AppendToStream(
            c.Id, eventStream.Version, customer.Changes);
          return;
        }
        catch (EventStoreConcurrencyException)
        {
          // fall through and retry, with optional brief delay
        }
      }
    }
```

In the case where a concurrency conflict occurs, we would add these additional steps to overcome the problem:

1. Thread 2 catches the exception and falls through, with control going to the beginning of the `while` loop. Now Events 1–5 are loaded into a new `Customer` instance.

2. Thread 2 reexecutes the delegate on the reloaded `Customer`, which now creates Events 6–7, which will be successfully appended after Event 5.

If the required Aggregate behavior reexecution is too expensive or for some reason not feasible (for example, requires costly third-party system integration to place an order or to charge a credit card), we might want to employ a different strategy.

As is illustrated in Figure A.11, one such strategy is Event conflict resolution, which is employed to reduce the number of actual concurrency exceptions. Here's how a very simple use of conflict resolution can work:

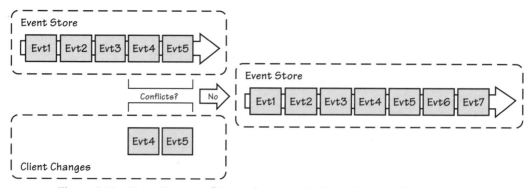

Figure A.11   Using Event conflict resolution on the Event Stream of an Aggregate

```
void UpdateWithSimpleConflictResolution(
  CustomerId id, Action<Customer> execute)
{
  while (true)
  {
    EventStream eventStream = _eventStore.LoadEventStream(id);
    Customer customer = new Customer(eventStream.Events);
    execute(customer);

    try
    {
      _eventStore.AppendToStream(
        id, eventStream.Version, customer.Changes);
      return;
    }
    catch (EventStoreConcurrencyException ex)
    {
      foreach (var failedEvent in customer.Changes)
      {
        foreach (var succeededEvent in ex.ActualEvents)
        {
          if (ConflictsWith(failedEvent, succeededEvent))
          {
            var msg = string.Format("Conflict between {0} and {1}",
              failedEvent, succeededEvent);
            throw new RealConcurrencyException(msg, ex);
          }
        }
      }
      // there are no conflicts and we can append
      _eventStore.AppendToStream(
        id, ex.ActualVersion, customer.Changes);
    }
  }
}
```

In this case the conflict detection method ConflictsWith() is used to compare each of the Aggregate Events for conflicts with Events that were concurrently appended to the Event Store (as reported in the exception).

This conflict resolution method is usually defined per Aggregate Root, depending on the specific kinds of behaviors it supports. Yet, there is a ConflictsWith() implementation that would work for the majority of Aggregates:

```
bool ConflictsWith(IEvent event1, IEvent event2)
{
  return event1.GetType() == event2.GetType();
}
```

This majority-case conflict resolution is based on a simple rule: Events of the same type always conflict with each other, but Events of different types do not.

Structural Freedom with A+ES

One of the biggest practical advantages of A+ES is the simplicity of persistence and the versatility it provides. No matter how complex the structure of a given Aggregate is, it can always be represented with a sequence of serialized Events that can be used to reconstitute it. Many domains influence changes to the model over time, with new behaviors or modeling subtleties that arise from changing requirements of an evolving system. Even if we must restructure the internal implementation of a given Aggregate in order to deal with significant changes, A+ES can most times facilitate such changes with lower risks and little frustration to developers.

The sequence of Events associated with a specific identity is usually referred to as an Event Stream. In essence, it is just an append-only list of messages serialized into byte blocks with the serializer of your choice. As such, an Event Stream can be persisted with equal success using relational databases, NoSQL persistence, plain file systems, or cloud storage, as long as any chosen store has strong consistency guarantees.

Here are three major advantages of A+ES persistence, which are especially important for **Bounded Contexts** (2) with a long life:

- The ability to adapt the internal implementations of an Aggregate to any practical structural representation necessary to express new behaviors encountered by domain experts

- The ability to move the entire infrastructure between various hosting solutions, which enables us to deal with cloud outages and provide sound fail-over options

- The ability of an Event Stream for any Aggregate instance to be downloaded to a development machine and replayed to debug an error condition

Performance

Sometimes loading Aggregates from large Streams can cause performance problems, especially when individual Streams go beyond hundreds of thousands of

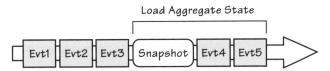

Figure A.12   An Aggregate's Event Stream with a snapshot of its state followed by two Events that occurred after the snapshot was taken

Events. There are a couple of simple patterns that could be applied in individual cases to solve this problem:

- Cache Event Streams in server memory, leveraging the fact that Events are immutable once written to an Event Store. While querying the Event Store for any changes, we could supply a version of the last known Event and ask only for those that occurred since then, if any. This can improve performance at the cost of memory consumption.

- Avoid loading and replaying a large portion of an Event Stream by taking a *snapshot* of each Aggregate instance. This way, while loading any Aggregate instance, you just need to find its latest snapshot and then replay any Events that were appended to the Event Stream since it was taken.

As seen in Figure A.12, snapshots are just serialized copies of an Aggregate's full state, taken at certain moments in time, that reside in the Event Stream as specific versions. They can be persisted in a Repository encapsulated behind a simple interface like this:

```
public interface ISnapshotRepository
{
  bool TryGetSnapshotById<TAggregate>(
    IIdentity id, out TAggregate snapshot, out int version);
  void SaveSnapshot(IIdentity id, TAggregate snapshot, int version);
}
```

We must record the Stream's version along with each snapshot. With the version we can load the snapshot along with only the Events that have occurred since the moment the snapshot was recorded. We first retrieve the snapshot as the base state of the Aggregate instance, and then we load and replay all Events that occurred since the snapshot was taken:

```
// simple document storage interface
ISnapshotRepository _snapshots;
```

```
// our event store
IEventStore _store;

public Customer LoadCustomerAggregateById(CustomerId id)
{
  Customer customer;
  long snapshotVersion = 0;
  if (_snapshots.TryGetSnapshotById(
        id, out customer, out snapshotVersion))
  {
    // load any events since snapshot was taken
    EventStream stream = _store.LoadEventStreamAfterVersion(
      id, snapshotVersion);
    // replay these events to update snapshot
    customer.ReplayEvents(stream.Events);
    return customer;
  }
  else // we don't have any persisted snapshot
  {
    EventStream stream = _store.LoadEventStream(id);
    return new Customer(stream.Events);
  }
}
```

The method `ReplayEvents()` must be used to bring the Aggregate
instance state up-to-date with the Events that occurred since the latest snapshot. Remember that the Aggregate instance state is mutated from the point of
the latest snapshot forward. Thus, we will not be instantiating the `Customer`
(in this example) using an Event Stream only. And we can't just use `Apply()`
because it not only mutates the current state with the given Event, it also saves
each Event it receives to the `Changes` collection. Saving Events to `Changes`
that are already in the Event Stream would cause serious bugs. Thus, we simply
need to implement the new method `ReplayEvents()`:

```
public partial class Customer
{
  ...
  public void ReplayEvents(IEnumerable<IEvent> events)
  {
    foreach (var event in events)
    {
      Mutate(event);
    }
  }
  ...
}
```

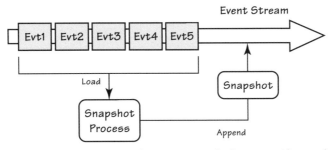

Figure A.13 An Aggregate's snapshot is generated after a specific number of new Events have occurred.

Here's some simple code for generating `Customer` snapshots:

```
public void GenerateSnapshotForCustomer(IIdentity id)
{
  // load all events from the start
  EventStream stream = _store.LoadEventStream(id);
  Customer customer = new Customer(stream.Events);
  _snapshots.SaveSnapshot(id, customer, stream.Version);
}
```

Snapshot generation and persistence can be delegated to a background thread. New snapshots would be produced only after some set number of Events have occurred since the latest snapshot. These steps are indicated in Figure A.13. Since the characteristics of each Aggregate type could be quite different, the snapshot threshold for each type can be tuned for specific performance needs.

One additional way to address performance concerns with A+ES Aggregates is to partition Aggregates among multiple processes or machines by Aggregate identity. This partitioning can be accomplished using identity hashing or other algorithms and can be combined with both Aggregate instance memory caching and Aggregate snapshots.

Implementing an Event Store

Let's now actually implement a few different Event Stores that are suitable for use with A+ES. The Stores here are simple and aren't designed for extremely high performance, yet they will be good enough for most domains.

While the implementation for each of the various Event Stores is different, the contracts are the same:

```
public interface IEventStore
{
  // loads all events for a stream
  EventStream LoadEventStream(IIdentity id);
  // loads subset of events for a stream
  EventStream LoadEventStream(
    IIdentity id, int skipEvents, int maxCount);
  // appends events to a stream, throwing
  // OptimisticConcurrencyException another appended
  // new events since expectedversion
  void AppendToStream(
    IIdentity id, int expectedVersion, ICollection<IEvent> events);
}

public class EventStream
{
    // version of the event stream returned
    public int Version;
    // all events in the stream
    public IList<IEvent> Events = new List<IEvent>();
}
```

As illustrated in Figure A.14, the class implementing `IEventStore` is a project-specific wrapper around the more generic and reusable `IAppend-OnlyStore`. While the `IEventStore` implementation deals with serialization and strong typing, the `IAppendOnlyStore` implementations provide low-level access to various storage engines.

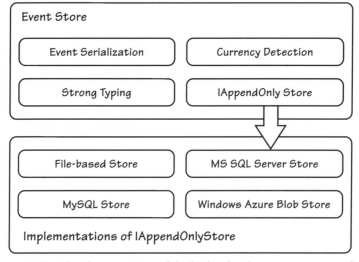

Figure A.14 The characteristics of the higher-level `IEventStore` and the lower-level `IAppendOnlyStore`

Event Store Source Code

Full source code for the range of Event Stores with multiple storage implementations is available for download as part of an A+ES sample project: http://lokad.github.com/lokad-iddd-sample/.

Here is the lower-level `IAppendOnlyStore` interface:

```
public interface IAppendOnlyStore : IDisposable
{
  void Append(string name, byte[] data, int expectedVersion = -1);
  IEnumerable<DataWithVersion> ReadRecords(
    string name, int afterVersion, int maxCount);
  IEnumerable<DataWithName> ReadRecords(
    int afterVersion, int maxCount);

  void Close();
}

public class DataWithVersion
{
  public int Version;
  public byte[] Data;
}

public sealed class DataWithName
{
  public string Name;
  public byte[] Data;
}
```

As you can see, `IAppendOnlyStore` deals with arrays of bytes instead of Event collections, and string names instead of strongly typed identities. Class `EventStore` handles conversions between the two types of data.

The `IAppendOnlyStore` declares two distinct `ReadRecords()` methods. The first one listed is used to read Events within a single Stream by their names, and the second one to read all Events in the Store. Both method implementations must always read Events in the order in which they were persisted. As you have probably deduced, the first overloaded method is required for rebuilding the state of a single Aggregate. The second `ReadRecords()` is used by the infrastructure to replicate Events, to publish them without the need for two-phase commit, and to rebuild persistent read models such as are needed for CQRS-based user interfaces.

A simple approach to serialization and deserialization—conversion between bytes and strongly typed Event objects—could use the .NET `BinaryFormatter`:

```csharp
public class EventStore : IEventStore
{
  readonly BinaryFormatter _formatter = new BinaryFormatter();

  byte[] SerializeEvent(IEvent[] e)
  {
    using (var mem = new MemoryStream())
    {
      _formatter.Serialize(mem, e);
      return mem.ToArray();
    }
  }

  IEvent[] DeserializeEvent(byte[] data)
  {
    using (var mem = new MemoryStream(data))
    {
      return (IEvent[])_formatter.Deserialize(mem);
    }
  }
}
```

Here's how we can use serialization and deserialization to load an Event Stream:

```csharp
readonly IAppendOnlyStore _appendOnlyStore;
...
public EventStream LoadEventStream(IIdentity id, int skip, int take)
{
  var name = IdentityToString(id);
  var records = _appendOnlyStore.ReadRecords(name, skip, take).ToList();
  var stream = new EventStream();

  foreach (var tapeRecord in records)
  {
    stream.Events.AddRange(DeserializeEvent(tapeRecord.Data));
    stream.Version = tapeRecord.Version;
  }
  return stream;
}

string IdentityToString(IIdentity id)
{
  // in this project all identities produce proper name
  return id.ToString();
}
```

Here we see how to append new Events to the Event Store by way of the `IAppendOnlyStore`:

```
public void AppendToStream(
  IIdentity id, int originalVersion, ICollection<IEvent> events)
{
  if (events.Count == 0)
    return;
  var name = IdentityToString(id);
  var data = SerializeEvent(events.ToArray());
  try
  {
    _appendOnlyStore.Append(name, data, originalVersion);
  }
  catch(AppendOnlyStoreConcurrencyException e)
  {
    // load server events
    var server = LoadEventStream(id, 0, int.MaxValue);
    // throw a real problem
    throw OptimisticConcurrencyException.Create(
      server.Version, e.ExpectedVersion, id, server.Events);
  }
}
```

Relational Persistence

The capabilities and strong consistency guarantees provided by relational databases make for the simplest approach to implementing append-only persistence. The fact that many enterprises have already standardized on one or more relational database products means there is little to no cost or learning curve to using them for Event Stores.

Since the MySQL database is a popular open source relational database server that is available on several platforms, we will use it to implement an Event Store. The `MySQLAppendOnlyStore` implements `IAppendOnlyStore`, acting as an access layer. It will be used to save Events as binary data into an `ES_Events` table, and to subsequently load those persisted Events.

Here's the table definition, which manages an Event Stream for each Aggregate type in a Bounded Context:

```
CREATE TABLE IF NOT EXISTS `ES_Events` (
  `Id` int NOT NULL AUTO_INCREMENT,       -- unique id
  `Name` nvarchar(50) NOT NULL,           -- name of the stream
```

```
  `Version` int NOT NULL,              -- incrementing stream version
  `Data` LONGBLOB NOT NULL             -- data payload
)
```

To append an Event to a specific Stream using a transaction, use the following steps:

1. Begin a transaction.

2. Check if the Event Store changed from the expected version; if so, throw an exception.

3. If there are no concurrency conflicts, append the Events.

4. Commit the transaction.

Here is the source code for method `Append()`:

```
public void Append(string name, byte[] data, int expectedVersion)
{
  using (var conn = new MySqlConnection(_connectionString))
  {
    conn.Open();
    using (var tx = conn.BeginTransaction())
    {
      const string sql =
        @"SELECT COALESCE(MAX(Version),0)
          FROM `ES_Events`
          WHERE Name=?name";
      int version;
      using (var cmd = new MySqlCommand(sql, conn, tx))
      {
        cmd.Parameters.AddWithValue("?name", name);
        version = (int)cmd.ExecuteScalar();
        if (expectedVersion != -1)
        {
          if (version != expectedVersion)
          {
            throw new AppendOnlyStoreConcurrencyException(
              version, expectedVersion, name);
          }
        }
      }

      const string txt =
          @"INSERT INTO `ES_Events` (`Name`, `Version`, `Data`)
            VALUES(?name, ?version, ?data)";

      using (var cmd = new MySqlCommand(txt, conn, tx))
      {
        cmd.Parameters.AddWithValue("?name", name);
```

```
        cmd.Parameters.AddWithValue("?version", version+1);
        cmd.Parameters.AddWithValue("?data", data);
        cmd.ExecuteNonQuery();
      }
      tx.Commit();
    }
  }
}
```

Reading from the `IAppendOnlyStore` is quite simple, requiring only a basic query. For example, this is how we get a list of records for an Aggregate's Event Stream:

```
public IEnumerable<DataWithVersion> ReadRecords(
  string name, int afterVersion, int maxCount)
{
  using (var conn = new MySqlConnection(_connectionString))
  {
    conn.Open();
    const string sql =
      @"SELECT `Data`, `Version` FROM `ES_Events`
        WHERE `Name` = ?name AND `Version`>?version
        ORDER BY `Version`
        LIMIT 0,?take";
    using (var cmd = new MySqlCommand(sql, conn))
    {
      cmd.Parameters.AddWithValue("?name", name);
      cmd.Parameters.AddWithValue("?version", afterVersion);
      cmd.Parameters.AddWithValue("?take", maxCount);
      using (var reader = cmd.ExecuteReader())
      {
        while (reader.Read())
        {
          var data = (byte[])reader["Data"];
          var version = (int)reader["Version"];
          yield return new DataWithVersion(version, data);
        }
      }
    }
  }
}
```

You will find the full source code for this MySQL-based Event Store with the rest of the sample code. A similar implementation is provided for Microsoft SQL Server.

BLOB Persistence

Leveraging a database server (such as MySQL or MS SQL Server) will save you a lot of work. It saves significant effort in dealing with concurrency management, file fragmentation, caching, and data consistency. Obviously, then, not using a database product would require us to handle many of those concerns on our own.

However, if we did choose to brave a rougher road to Event Stores, we do have some help. For example, Windows Azure Blob storage and simple file system storage are at our disposal, and the sample project includes implementations of both.

Let's consider some design guidelines for building an Event Store without a database, some of which are summarized by Figure A.15:

1. Our custom storage is composed of a set of one or more append-only binary large object (BLOB) files or their equivalents. The component that writes to the storage locks it exclusively as it appends but allows for concurrent reads.

2. Depending on your strategy, you could use just one BLOB store for all Aggregate types and instances for a Bounded Context. Alternatively you could create one BLOB store for each Aggregate type, where all instances of a given type would be stored. Or you could split up the BLOB stores for each Aggregate type by instance, where the Event Stream for a single instance would be stored on its own.

3. When the writer component appends, it opens the appropriate BLOB store, writes to it, and maintains an index into the store.

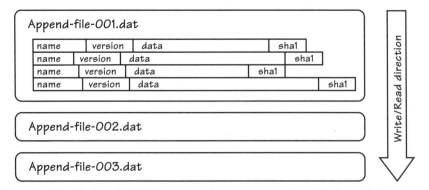

Figure A.15   File-based BLOB storage using a strategy of one file for each Aggregate instance, containing one record for each Event

4. Regardless of the BLOB storage strategy in use, all new Events are appended to the end. Each record is composed of a name, version, and binary data fields. This is similar to the way we store Event records to a relational database. However, with a BLOB store we must prefix variable-length fields with the byte count length, and we also append a hash code or cyclic redundancy check (CRC) to verify data integrity when the records are read.

5. BLOB-based append-only storage allows for enumeration of all Events across all Event Streams simply by enumerating all files and their contents. In order to speed up disk seeks and reading Events for a specific Stream, we would need to maintain a dedicated in-memory index and/or cache the Event Streams in memory. If memory caching is used, each append would require the cache to be refreshed. Further, Aggregate state snapshots and file defragmentation can also help to improve performance.

6. Of course, we can avoid many of the file system disk fragmentation issues by preallocating large regions of BLOB file space as each file-based Event Stream is created.

This design is inspired by the Riak Bitcask model. You can read more details and explanations in the Riak Bitcask architecture paper: http://downloads.basho.com/papers/bitcask-intro.pdf.

Focused Aggregates

While developing Aggregates with traditional persistence (for example, relational database without the use of Event Sourcing), development friction from introducing a new Entity into the system or enriching an existing one can be noticeable. We need to create new tables and define new mapping schemata and Repository methods. If our tendency is to resist such development overhead, it can cause us to grow Aggregates as we concentrate more state structure and behaviors on each. It can be much easier to add onto an existing Aggregate rather than to create a new one.

However, our bias can shift if Aggregates are more easily designed anew, and I assert that this is true when Event Sourcing is in use. In my experience, Aggregates designed using A+ES tend to be smaller, which is one of the primary Aggregate Rules of Thumb.

For example, for a company providing software as a service, a real-world customer might be represented with distinct Aggregates focusing on different behavioral aspects:

- `Customer:505` hosts behaviors for billing, invoicing, and general account management.

- `Security-Account:505` maintains multiple users with access permissions for each.

- `Consumer:505` tracks actual service consumption.

Each of these Aggregate types may be implemented in a different Bounded Context, each Bounded Context using different technologies and architectural approaches. For example, the `Consumer` aspect might need to provide high scalability and deal with consuming thousands of messages for customers each second. Assuming that is so, such an Event Stream should be hosted in auto-scaling cloud fabric. Other aspects might be less demanding, allowing them to be hosted in a less demanding environment.

Of course, Aggregates should never be designed to be arbitrarily small. We always want to design Aggregates to protect true business invariants, and doing so may cause any given Aggregate to be composed of multiple Entities and a number of Value Objects. Yet, the ease of using A+ES provides us with greater opportunity to strive for simple and efficient designs. This is an advantage that should be embraced whenever possible.

In fact, sometimes it can be helpful to start domain modeling by defining the core of your Ubiquitous Language by defining the primary incoming Commands and outgoing Events, as well as the behaviors that are performed. Only at a later stage would we actually group some concepts as Aggregates, based on similarity, relevance, and business rules. Such an approach—even if it is just a temporary development spike used as a part of a domain modeling exercise—can lead to a deeper understanding of our core business concepts.

Read Model Projections

One of the common concerns of the A+ES design approach is how to query the Aggregates by their properties. Event Sourcing does not provide a simple way to answer a question such as "What is the total amount of all customer orders within the last month?" We would actually need to load every `Customer` instance, enumerate all of the `Order` instances within the last month for each one, and calculate their total, which would be extremely inefficient.

This is where **Read Model Projections** can help. Read Model Projections can be realized through a simple set of Domain Event subscribers that are used to generate and update a persistent Read Model. In other words, they *project Events to a persistent Read Model*. When Event subscribers receive new

Events, they calculate some query results and store them in the Read Model for later consumption.

In a nutshell, a Projection is very similar to an Aggregate instance. As Events are received and handled, we use the data from them to build the Projection's state. Read Model Projections are persisted after each update and can be accessed by many readers, both inside and outside the Bounded Context.

> **Projection Samples Are Available**
>
> More information about using Projections, including source code for various persistence scenarios and automatic rebuilding of Read Models, is available in the sample project: http://lokad.github.com/lokad-cqrs/.

This is how we could define a Projection to capture all transactions for each `Customer`:

```
public class CustomerTransactionsProjection
{
  IDocumentWriter<CustomerId, CustomerTransactions> _store;

  public CustomerTransactionsProjection(
    IDocumentWriter<CustomerId, CustomerTransactions> store)
  {
    _store = store;
  }

  public void When(CustomerCreated e)
  {
    _store.Add(e.Id, new CustomerTransactions());
  }

  public void When(CustomerChargeAdded e)
  {
    _store.UpdateOrThrow(e.Id,
      v => v.AddTx(e.ChargeName, -e.Charge, e.NewBalance, e.TimeUtc));
  }

  public void When(CustomerPaymentAdded e)
  {
    _store.UpdateOrThrow(e.Id,
      v => v.AddTx(e.PaymentName, e.Payment, e.NewBalance, e.TimeUtc));
  }
}
```

This Projection class is similar to an Application Service designed for A+ES that uses lambdas. However, our Projection reacts to Events rather than Commands and updates documents using `IDocumentWriter`, rather than updating Aggregate instances.

The underlying Read Model is actually just a simple **Data Transfer Object** (DTO) [Fowler] that can be serialized and persisted to some underlying storage by means of an `IDocumentWriter`:

```
[Serializable]
public class CustomerTransactions
{
  public IList<CustomerTransaction> Transactions =
    new List<CustomerTransaction>();

  public void AddTx(
    string name, CurrencyAmount change,
    CurrencyAmount balance, DateTime timeUtc)
  {
    Transactions.Add(new CustomerTransaction()
    {
        Name = name,
        Balance = balance,
        Change = change,
        TimeUtc = timeUtc
    });
  }
}

[Serializable]
public class CustomerTransaction
{
  public CurrencyAmount Change;
  public CurrencyAmount Balance;
  public string Name;
  public DateTime TimeUtc;
}
```

It is common practice to persist Read Models in a document database, although other options can be used. We may cache Read Models in memory (for example, memcached instance), push them as documents into a content-delivery network, or persist them in relational database tables.

In addition to scalability, one of the major advantages of Projections is that they are completely disposable. They can be added, modified, or completely replaced at any time during the application's lifetime. To replace the whole Read Model, discard all existing Read Model data and generate new data by running your entire Event Stream through your Projection classes. This process can be automated. It's even possible to prevent any downtime while effecting full Read Model replacement.

Use with Aggregate Design

Such Read Model Projections are frequently used to expose information to various clients (such as desktop and Web user interfaces), but they are also quite useful for sharing information between Bounded Contexts and their Aggregates. Consider the scenario where an `Invoice` Aggregate needs some `Customer` information (for example, name, billing address, and tax ID) in order to calculate and prepare a proper `Invoice`. We can capture this information in an easy-to-consume form via `CustomerBillingProjection`, which will create and maintain an exclusive instance of `CustomerBilling-View`. This Read Model is available to the `Invoice` Aggregate through the Domain Service named `IProvideCustomerBillingInformation`. Under the covers this Domain Service just queries the document store for the appropriate instance of the `CustomerBillingView`.

Projections also enable us to share information between Aggregate instances in a loosely coupled and more maintainable way. If at any point in time we need to change information returned by `IProvideCustomerBillingView`, we can do so without modifying the `Customer` Aggregate. We only need to change the Projection implementation and rebuild the Read Models by replaying all Events.

Events Enrichment

One of the more common problems with A+ES designs comes from their dual purpose. Events are used both for Aggregate persistence and to communicate domain-level happenings around the enterprise by means of Event publishing.

For example, consider the following: A project management system allows customers to create new projects and archive completed projects. Imagine that we publish a `ProjectArchived` Event each time a user archives a project. This Domain Event could have this design:

```
public class ProjectArchived {
  public ProjectId Id { get; set; }
  public UserId ChangeAuthorId { get; set; }
  public DateTime ArchivedUtc { get; set; }
  public string OptionalComment { get; set; }
}
```

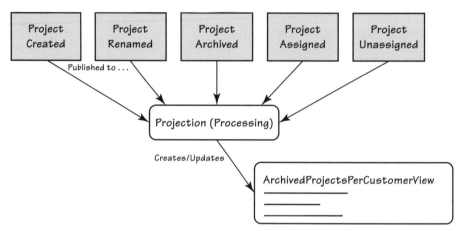

Figure A.16   Multiple Domain Events are consumed by a Projection and used to build up a view of a Read Model.

This information is rich enough to be used to reconstitute an archived `Project` using A+ES. However, designed in this way, our Event could be rather problematic for publishers to consume.

Why? Consider the Projection for the `ArchivedProjectsPerCustomer` view, as illustrated in Figure A.16. It subscribes to Events and maintains a list of archived projects per customer. In order to get the job done, this Projection will need the latest information about things like

- Project names

- Names of customers

- Assignments of projects to customers

- Project archival Events

We can simplify this Projection significantly by enriching our `Project-Archived` Event with additional data members to push relevant information. The additional data members would not be essential for reconstituting the state of the corresponding Aggregate but would noticeably simplify our Event consumers. Consider this alternative Event contract:

```
public class ProjectArchived {
  public ProjectId Id { get; set; }
  public string ProjectName { get; set; }
  public UserId ChangeAuthorId { get; set; }
  public DateTime ArchivedUtc { get; set; }
```

```
  public string OptionalComment { get; set; }
  public CustomerId Customer { get; set; }
  public string CustomerName { get; set; }
}
```

Given this newly enriched Event, our `ArchivedProjectsPerCustomer-View` generated by the Projection can be simplified as seen in Figure A.17.

A Domain Event rule of thumb says to design them with enough information to satisfy 80 percent of subscribers, even though doing so would require Events to have more information than needed by a good number of subscribers. Remembering that we want to ensure that view Projection processors have a rich set of Event data, we usually include

- Entity identifiers, which are the Event owners/masters, such as `CustomerId` is to `Customer`

- Names and other properties that are generally used for display purposes, such as `ProjectName`, `CustomerName`, and the like

These are recommendations, not rules. They usually work well for enterprises that have a lot of different Bounded Contexts. Monolithic Bounded Contexts benefit less from these suggestions, since they tend to maintain secondary lookup tables and Entity maps. Of course, you are in the best position to know which properties should be included in your Events. Sometimes it's obvious just which properties belong in a given Event type, and for those refactoring is seldom required.

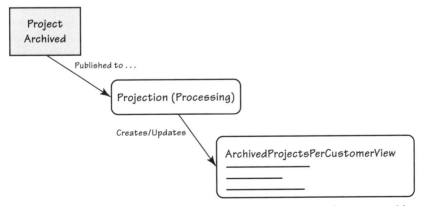

Figure A.17 Domain Events such as `ProjectArchived` can be consumed by Projection processors that generate view- and report-specific Read Models.

Supporting Tools and Patterns

Developing, building, deploying, and maintaining systems using A+ES require a set of patterns that can differ somewhat from those of traditional systems. This section presents some patterns, tools, and practices that have proven quite useful when using A+ES.

Event Serializers

It's wise to choose a serializer that favors versioning and renaming Events. This is especially true early on in an A+ES project as the domain model tends to evolve rapidly. Consider this Event, which is declared using a .NET implementation of **Protocol Buffers**[1] annotations:

```
[DataContract]
public class ProjectClosed {
  [DataMember(Order=1)] public long ProjectId { get; set; }
  [DataMember(Order=2)] public DateTime Closed { get; set; }
}
```

Now, if we were to serialize `ProjectClosed` using `DataContract-Serializer` or `JsonSerializer` rather than Protocol Buffers, any renamed members could easily break dependent consumers. For example, assume you rename the `Closed` property `ClosedUtc`. Unless you take special care to map the renamed property in a consuming Bounded Context, you'd produce a confusing error or produce buggy data:

```
[DataContract]
public class ProjectClosed {
  [DataMember] public long ProjectId { get; set; }
  [DataMember(Name="Closed")] public DateTime ClosedUtc { get; set; }
}
```

Protocol Buffers accommodates evolving serialization situations because it tracks contract members by integral tags, not names. As can be seen in the following code, clients may successfully use either `Close` or `CloseUtc` as the property name. It serializes objects extremely quickly and produces a very compact binary representation. Using Protocol Buffers, we can rename Event properties without worrying about backward compatibility, reducing development friction in an evolving domain model.

---

1. Protocol Buffers was originated by Google. Others have created .NET implementations.

```
[DataContract]
public class ProjectClosed {
  [DataMember(Order=1)] public long ProjectId { get; set; }
  [DataMember(Order=2)] public DateTime ClosedUtc { get; set; }
}
```

Some additional cross-platform serialization tools include Apache Thrift, Avro, and MessagePack, giving a variety of worthy options.

Event Immutability

Event Streams are considered to be immutable by nature. In order to keep the development model consistent with this concept (and avoid undesirable side effects), Event contracts should be implemented as immutable. To do that with C# on .NET, we mark fields as read-only and set values only via the constructor. Given the previous `ProjectClosed` Event, we can make it an immutable implementation:

```
[DataContract]
public class ProjectClosed {
  [DataMember(Order=1)] public long ProjectId { get; private set }
  [DataMember(Order=2)] public DateTime ClosedUtc { get; private set; }
  public ProjectClosed(long projectId, DateTime closedUtc)
  {
    ProjectId  = projectId;
    ClosedUtc = closedUtc;
  }
}
```

Value Objects

As discussed thoroughly in **Value Objects (6)**, this is a pattern that can greatly simplify development and the evolution of rich domain models. Using Value Objects, we compose cohesive primitive types into an explicitly named immutable type. For instance, instead of declaring the identity of a project as a `long`, we would model an explicit `ProjectId`:

```
public struct ProjectId
{
  public readonly long Id { get; private set; }
  public ProjectId(long id)
  {
    Id = id
  }
```

```
public override ToString() {
  return string.Format("Project-{0}", Id);
  }
}
```

We still use a `long` type to hold the actual identity number, but we use the `ProjectId` type to distinguish it from all others. Value types are certainly not limited to unique identities. Other appropriate Value types include money objects (especially in multicurrency systems), addresses, e-mails, measurements, and so on.

In addition to enrichment and expressiveness of Event and Command contracts, domain Value Objects bring more practical benefits to A+ES implementations, like static type checking and IDE support. Consider the following scenario, where a developer can accidentally misplace parameters of a simple Event constructor by passing them in the wrong order:

```
long customerId = ...;
long projectId = ...;
var event = new ProjectAssignedToCustomer(customerId, projectId);
```

This is an error that would not be caught by the compiler but might be found only through much debugging and frustration. However, if you use Value Objects as identifiers, the compiler (and thus the IDE editor) would catch the error in passing the `CustomerId` first and the `ProjectId` second:

```
CustomerId customerId = ...;
ProjectId projectId = ...;
var event = new ProjectAssignedToCustomer(customerId, projectId);
```

Benefits become even more apparent when you have flat contract classes with a large number of fields. For instance, consider this Event (simplified from the actual production version):

```
public class CustomerInvoiceWritten {
  public InvoiceId Id { get; private set; }
  public DateTime CreatedUtc { get; private set; }
  public CurrencyType Currency { get; private set; }
  public InvoiceLine[] Lines { get; private set; }
  public decimal SubTotal { get; private set; }

  public CustomerId Customer { get; private set; }
  public string CustomerName { get; private set; }
  public string CustomerBillingAddress { get; private set; }
```

```
  public float OptionalVatRatio { get; private set; }
  public string OptionalVatName { get; private set; }
  public decimal VatTax { get; private set; }
  public decimal Total { get; private set; }
}
```

As you can imagine, dealing with a class having so many properties[2] can be a bit complicated. We can refactor this large Event to be more explicit and readable by refining its model according to existing domain concepts:

```
public class CustomerInvoiceWritten {
  public InvoiceId Id { get; private set; }
  public InvoiceHeader Header { get; private set; }
  public InvoiceLine[] Lines { get; private set; }
  public InvoiceFooter Footer { get; private set; }
}
```

The `InvoiceHeader` and `InvoiceFooter` constitute cohesive properties:

```
public class InvoiceHeader {
  public DateTime CreatedUtc { get; private set; }
  public CustomerId Customer { get; private set; }
  public string CustomerName { get; private set; }
  public string CustomerBillingAddress { get; private set; }
}

public class InvoiceFooter {
  public CurrencyAmount SubTotal { get; private set; }
  public VatInformation OptionalVat { get; private set; }
  public CurrencyAmount VarAmount { get; private set; }
  public CurrencyAmount Total { get; private set; }
}
```

We replaced the separate `CurrencyType Currency` and `decimal SubTotal` properties with a `CurrencyAmount` Value Object. An added benefit is that this class could be enhanced with sanity check logic that prevents operations between amounts expressed in different currencies and other inappropriate operations. The same goes for joining VAT information into a separate Value Object that is then composed on the `InvoiceFooter`, along with the other invoice totals.

Wherever possible we should strive to employ Value Objects, whether for Command objects, Events, or Aggregate parts.

---

2. Empirical data proves an appropriate rule of thumb: There should be no more than five to seven property members per class.

Obviously, using Value Objects in Commands and/or Events would require deploying them together, or even creating a **Shared Kernel** (3). However, some deeply complex domains might require designing some Value Objects with extremely involved business logic. In such cases, placing such Value Objects in a Shared Kernel merely for type-safe deserialization would likely result in a brittle design. It could help to distinguish between simple shared classes used to deserialize Command and Event data in a type-safe way from the more complex ones required by the **Core Domain** (2). That would mean creating two sets of Value Object classes, those used exclusively by the Core Domain and those that are deployed with Command and Event classes. The data held by the two is converted from one to the other as needed.

Depending on your taste, duplicating classes may seem more complex than necessary, leading you down the path of creating accidental complexity in your systems. If that's your opinion, it may be worth considering a different approach. One alternative is to standardize serialized Events as a **Published Language** (3). As explained in **Integrating Bounded Contexts** (13), you may choose to consume Event notifications using a dynamic typing approach. Doing so would eliminate the need for Event and Value Object types being deployed to the consuming subscribers. As with all approaches, this one has trade-offs that must be weighed.

Contract Generation

Maintaining hundreds of Event (and Command) contracts manually is both tedious and error prone. It's usually more efficient to express their definitions in some compact domain-specific language (DSL) that can be used for simple code generation, by building correct classes at build time. There are several ways to formulate a DSL syntax, and we might consider the Protocol Buffer `.proto` format or a similar one to be the way to go. For example, you may find this approach useful:

```
CustomerInvoiceWritten!(InvoiceId Id, InvoiceHeader header,
    InvoiceLine[] lines, InvoiceFooter footer)
```

A simple code generator can use the parsed DSL to generate code for each source line. Note one example here, where the `CustomerInvoiceWritten` is generated from the preceding DSL:

```
[DataContract]
public sealed class CustomerInvoiceWritten : IDomainEvent {
  [DataMember(Order=1)] public InvoiceId Id
    { get; private set; }
  [DataMember(Order=2)] public InvoiceHeader Header
    { get; private set; }
  [DataMember(Order=3)] public InvoiceLine[] Lines
    { get; private set; }
  [DataMember(Order=4)] public InvoiceFooter Footer
    { get; private set; }
  public CustomerInvoiceWriter(
    InvoiceId id, InvoiceHeader header, InvoiceLine[] lines,
    InvoiceFooter footer)
  {
    Id = id;
    Header = header;
    Lines = lines;
    Footer = footer;
  }

  // required by serializer
  ProjectClosed() {
    Lines = new InvoiceLine[0];
  }
}
```

This has the following practical benefits:

- It reduces development friction by enabling faster domain modeling iterations.

- It reduces the probability of human errors common with manual labor.

- The compact representation allows us to keep all Event definitions on a single screen, providing a big-picture view for improved insight. This can even serve as a terse glossary to the Ubiquitous Language.

- We can version and distribute Event contracts as compact definitions instead of requiring source or binary code. This might even serve to enhance collaboration between various teams.

The same can be applied to Command contracts as well. The open source implementation of a DSL-based code generation tool along with examples is available within the sample project.

Unit Testing and Specifications

Consider an added benefit of using Event Sourcing as we create unit tests. We can easily specify our tests in the form *Given-When-Expect*, as follows:

1. *Given* Events in the past

2. *When* Aggregate method is called

3. *Expect* the following Events *or* an exception

Here's how it works. Past Events are used to set up the state of an Aggregate at the beginning of the unit test. We then execute the Aggregate method being tested, supplying test arguments and mock implementations of Domain Services as needed. Finally, we assert the expected results by comparing Events produced by an Aggregate with expected Events.

This approach allows us to capture and verify behaviors associated with each Aggregate. At the same time, we stay decoupled from the internals of the Aggregate state. This helps to reduce test *fragility* because development teams can change and optimize each Aggregate implementation in any way, as long as the behavioral contracts are fulfilled as confirmed by the unit tests.

It is possible to take this approach one step further by expressing the *When* clause directly using a Command, which is passed to the appropriate Application Service hosting the Aggregate under test. This allows us to express the unit test as a *specification* expressed completely in the terms of our Ubiquitous Language, either through code or by creating a DSL.

With just a little bit of code, such specifications can be automatically printed out as human-readable use cases that domain experts can comprehend. These use case definitions can help project teams communicate better over domains with complex behaviors, which enhances their modeling efforts.

Here's a simple specification defined by a text document:

```
[Passed] Use case 'Add Customer Payment - Unlock On Payment'.

Given:
 1. Created customer 7 Eur 'Northwind' with key c67b30 ...
 2. Customer locked

When:
  Add 'unlock' payment 10 EUR via unlock

Expectations:
  [ok] Tx 1: payment 10 EUR 'unlock' (none)
  [ok] Customer unlocked
```

If this approach interests you, performing a Web search for "Event Sourcing Specifications" will result in detailed guidance.

Event Sourcing in Functional Languages

The implementation patterns outlined previously focused on an object-oriented approach, which is a good fit for programming languages such as Java and C#. However, Event Sourcing is inherently functional in nature. Thus, it can be successfully implemented with functional languages such as F# and Clojure. Doing so could potentially lead to more concise code that performs optimally.

Here are some peculiarities of switching from an object-oriented to a functional approach for Aggregate implementations:

- We must switch from using a mutable object-oriented Aggregate state object to designing a simple immutable state record with a collection of mutating functions. The mutating functions simply take a state record and Event arguments, returning a new state record as the result. This is quite like the design of an immutable Value Object, where its Side-Effect-Free Functions only produce new Values based on its own state and function arguments. Such functions take the form `Func<State, Event, State>`.

- The current Aggregate state can be defined as a left fold of all past Events that are passed to the mutating functions.

- Aggregate methods can also be transformed into a collection of stateless functions, which take Command parameters, Domain Services, and a state. Such functions return zero or more Events and take the form `Func<TArg1, TArg2..., State, Event[]>`.

- An Event Store can be perceived and communicated as a *functional database*, because it persists the arguments to functions that mutate Aggregate state. Supporting snapshots in a functional Event Store is familiar to functional programmers under the name *memoization*.

A development spike that captures core business concepts by means of A+ES in a functional programming language can accelerate our domain modeling efforts. What is more, it forces us to shift our domain exploration focus away from Aggregate structure toward a strict reflection of our domain's Ubiquitous Language expressed by its behaviors. Anything that can help us give more emphasis to the Core Domain and less to technology will likely drive out more value for the business and help it achieve an even greater competitive advantage.

Bibliography

[Appleton, LoD] Appleton, Brad. n.d. "Introducing Demeter and Its Laws."
www.bradapp.com/docs/demeter-intro.html.

[Bentley] Bentley, Jon. 2000. *Programming Pearls, Second Edition*. Boston,
MA: Addison-Wesley.
http://cs.bell-labs.com/cm/cs/pearls/bote.html.

[Brandolini] Brandolini, Alberto. 2009. "Strategic Domain-Driven Design
with Context Mapping."
www.infoq.com/articles/ddd-contextmapping.

[Buschmann et al.] Buschmann, Frank, et al. 1996. *Pattern-Oriented Software Architecture, Volume 1: A System of Patterns*. New York: Wiley.

[Cockburn] Cockburn, Alastair. 2012. "Hexagonal Architecture."
http://alistair.cockburn.us/Hexagonal+architecture.

[Crupi et al.] Crupi, John, et al. n.d. "Core J2EE Patterns."
http://corej2eepatterns.com/Patterns2ndEd/DataAccessObject.htm.

[Cunningham, Checks] Cunningham, Ward. 1994. "The CHECKS Pattern
Language of Information Integrity."
http://c2.com/ppr/checks.html.

[Cunningham, Whole Value] Cunningham, Ward. 1994. "1. Whole Value."
http://c2.com/ppr/checks.html#1.

[Cunningham, Whole Value aka Value Object] Cunningham, Ward. 2005.
"Whole Value."
http://fit.c2.com/wiki.cgi?WholeValue.

[Dahan, CQRS] Dahan, Udi. 2009. "Clarified CQRS."
www.udidahan.com/2009/12/09/clarified-cqrs/.

[Dahan, Roles] Dahan, Udi. 2009. "Making Roles Explicit."
www.infoq.com/presentations/Making-Roles-Explicit-Udi-Dahan.

[Deutsch] Deutsch, Peter. 2012. "Fallacies of Distributed Computing."
http://en.wikipedia.org/wiki/Fallacies_of_Distributed_Computing.

[Dolphin] Object Arts. 2000. "Dolphin Smalltalk; Twisting the Triad."
www.object-arts.com/downloads/papers/TwistingTheTriad.PDF.

[Erl] Erl, Thomas. 2012. "SOA Principles: An Introduction to the Service-
Oriented Paradigm."
http://serviceorientation.com/index.php/serviceorientation/index.

[Evans] Evans, Eric. 2004. *Domain-Driven Design: Tackling the Complexity in the Heart of Software.* Boston, MA: Addison-Wesley.

[Evans, Ref] Evans, Eric. 2012. "Domain-Driven Design Reference." http://domainlanguage.com/ddd/patterns/DDD_Reference_2011-01-31.pdf.

[Evans & Fowler, Spec] Evans, Eric, and Martin Fowler. 2012. "Specifications." http://martinfowler.com/apsupp/spec.pdf.

[Fairbanks] Fairbanks, George. 2011. *Just Enough Software Architecture.* Marshall & Brainerd.

[Fowler, Anemic] Fowler, Martin. 2003. "AnemicDomainModel." http://martinfowler.com/bliki/AnemicDomainModel.html.

[Fowler, CQS] Fowler, Martin. 2005. "CommandQuerySeparation." http://martinfowler.com/bliki/CommandQuerySeparation.html.

[Fowler, DI] Fowler, Martin. 2004. "Inversion of Control Containers and the Dependency Injection Pattern." http://martinfowler.com/articles/injection.html.

[Fowler, P of EAA] Fowler, Martin. 2003. *Patterns of Enterprise Application Architecture.* Boston, MA: Addison-Wesley.

[Fowler, PM] Fowler, Martin. 2004. "Presentation Model." http://martinfowler.com/eaaDev/PresentationModel.html.

[Fowler, Self Encap] Fowler, Martin. 2012. "SelfEncapsulation." http://martinfowler.com/bliki/SelfEncapsulation.html.

[Fowler, SOA] Fowler, Martin. 2005. "ServiceOrientedAmbiguity." http://martinfowler.com/bliki/ServiceOrientedAmbiguity.html.

[Freeman et al.] Freeman, Eric, Elisabeth Robson, Bert Bates, and Kathy Sierra. 2004. *Head First Design Patterns.* Sebastopol, CA: O'Reilly Media.

[Gamma et al.] Gamma, Erich, Richard Helm, Ralph Johnson, and John Vlissides. 1994. *Design Patterns.* Reading, MA: Addison-Wesley.

[Garcia-Molina & Salem] Garcia-Molina, Hector, and Kenneth Salem. 1987. "Sagas." ACM, Department of Computer Science, Princeton University, Princeton, NJ. www.amundsen.com/downloads/sagas.pdf.

[GemFire Functions] 2012. VMware vFabric 5 Documentation Center. http://pubs.vmware.com/vfabric5/index.jsp?topic=/com.vmware.vfabric .gemfire.6.6/developing/function_exec/chapter_overview.html.

[Gson] 2012. A Java JSON library hosted on Google Code. http://code.google.com/p/google-gson/.

[Helland] Helland, Pat. 2007. "Life beyond Distributed Transactions: An Apostate's Opinion." Third Biennial Conference on Innovative DataSystems Research (CIDR), January 7–10, Asilomar, CA. www.ics.uci.edu/~cs223/papers/cidr07p15.pdf.

[Hohpe & Woolf] Hohpe, Gregor, and Bobby Woolf. 2004. *Enterprise Integration Patterns: Designing, Building, and Deploying Messaging Systems.* Boston, MA: Addison-Wesley.

[Inductive UI] 2001. Microsoft Inductive User Interface Guidelines. http://msdn.microsoft.com/en-us/library/ms997506.aspx.

[Jezequel et al.] Jezequel, Jean-Marc, Michael Train, and Christine Mingins. 2000. *Design Patterns and Contract.* Reading, MA: Addison-Wesley.

[Keith & Stafford] Keith, Michael, and Randy Stafford. 2008. "Exposing the ORM Cache." *ACM*, May 1. http://queue.acm.org/detail.cfm?id=1394141.

[Liskov] Liskov, Barbara. 1987. Conference Keynote: "Data Abstraction and Hierarchy." http://en.wikipedia.org/wiki/Liskov_substitution_principle. "The Liskov Substitution Principle." www.objectmentor.com/resources/articles/lsp.pdf.

[Martin, DIP] Martin, Robert. 1996. "The Dependency Inversion Principle." www.objectmentor.com/resources/articles/dip.pdf.

[Martin, SRP] Martin, Robert. 2012. "SRP: The Single Responsibility Principle." www.objectmentor.com/resources/articles/srp.pdf.

[MassTransit] Patterson, Chris. 2008. "Managing Long-Lived Transactions with MassTransit.Saga." http://lostechies.com/chrispatterson/2008/08/29/managing-long-lived-transactions-with-masstransit-saga/.

[MSDN Assemblies] 2012. http://msdn.microsoft.com/en-us/library/51ket42z%28v=vs.71%29.aspx.

[Nilsson] Nilsson, Jimmy. 2006. *Applying Domain-Driven Design and Patterns: With Examples in C# and .NET.* Boston, MA: Addison-Wesley.

[Nijof, CQRS] Nijof, Mark. 2009. "CQRS à la Greg Young." http://cre8ivethought.com/blog/2009/11/12/cqrs--la-greg-young.

[NServiceBus] 2012. www.nservicebus.com/.

[Öberg] Öberg, Rickard. 2012. "What Is Qi4j™?" http://qi4j.org/.

[Parastatidis et al., RiP] Webber, Jim, Savas Parastatidis, and Ian Robinson. 2011. *REST in Practice*. Sebastopol, CA: O'Reilly Media.

[PragProg, TDA] The Pragmatic Programmer. "Tell, Don't Ask." http://pragprog.com/articles/tell-dont-ask.

[Quartz] 2012. Terracotta Quartz Scheduler. http://terracotta.org/products/quartz-scheduler.

[Seović] Seović, Aleksandar, Mark Falco, and Patrick Peralta. 2010. *Oracle Coherence 3.5: Creating Internet-Scale Applications Using Oracle's High-Performance Data Grid*. Birmingham, England: Packt Publishing.

[SOA Manifesto] 2009. SOA Manifesto. www.soa-manifesto.org/.

[Sutherland] Sutherland, Jeff. 2010. "Story Points: Why Are They Better than Hours?" http://scrum.jeffsutherland.com/2010/04/story-points-why-are-they-better-than.html.

[Tilkov, Manifesto] Tilkov, Stefan. 2009. "Comments on the SOA Manifesto." www.innoq.com/blog/st/2009/10/comments_on_the_soa_manifesto.html.

[Tilkov, RESTful Doubts] Tilkov, Stefan. 2012. "Addressing Doubts about REST." www.infoq.com/articles/tilkov-rest-doubts.

[Vernon, DDR] Vernon, Vaughn. n.d. "Architecture and Domain-Driven Design." http://vaughnvernon.co/?page_id=38.

[Vernon, DPO] Vernon, Vaughn. n.d. "Architecture and Domain-Driven Design." http://vaughnvernon.co/?page_id=40.

[Vernon, RESTful DDD] Vernon, Vaughn. 2010. "RESTful SOA or Domain-Driven Design—A Compromise?" QCon SF 2010. www.infoq.com/presentations/RESTful-SOA-DDD.

[Webber, REST & DDD] Webber, Jim. "REST and DDD." http://skillsmatter.com/podcast/design-architecture/rest-and-ddd.

[Wiegers] Wiegers, Karl E. 2012. "First Things First: Prioritizing Requirements." www.processimpact.com/articles/prioritizing.html.

[Wikipedia, CQS] 2012. "Command-Query Separation." http://en.wikipedia.org/wiki/Command-query_separation.

[Wikipedia, EDA] 2012. "Event-Driven Architecture." http://en.wikipedia.org/wiki/Event-driven_architecture.

[Young, ES] Young, Greg. 2010. "Why Use Event Sourcing?" http://codebetter.com/gregyoung/2010/02/20/why-use-event-sourcing/.

Index

A

Abstract classes, in modules, 338
Abstract Factory pattern, 389
Abstraction, Dependency Inversion Principle and, 123
Access management, identity and, 91–92
ACID databases, 521
ACL. *See* Anticorruption Layer (ACL)
Active Record, in Transaction Scripts, 441
ActiveMQ, as messaging middleware, 303
Actor Model, 295
Adapters. *See also* Hexagonal Architecture
 Domain Services use for integration, 280
 handling client output types, 529–530
 Hexagonal Architecture and, 126–127
 Presentation Model as, 519
 for REST client implementation, 465–466
Aggregate Root query interface, 516
Aggregate Stores
 distributed caches of Data Fabrics as, 164
 persistence-oriented repositories and, 418
Aggregate-Oriented Databases, 418
Aggregates. *See also* A+ES (Aggregates and Event Sourcing)
 Application Services and, 120–121
 avoiding dependency Injection, 387
 behavioral focus of, 569–570
 Context Maps and, 90
 cost estimates of memory overhead, 372–373
 creating and publishing Events, 287
 decision process in designing, 379–380
 designing, 573
 designing based on usage scenarios, 375–376
 Domain Events with Aggregate characteristics, 294–295
 Event Sourcing and, 160–162, 539
 eventual consistency, 364–367, 376–378
 executives and trackers merged in, 156
 factories on Aggregate Root, 391–392
 global transactions as reason to break design rules, 369
 implementing, 380

information hiding (Law of Demeter and Tell, Don't Ask), 382–384
invariant determination in creating clusters, 353–355
lack of technical mechanisms as reason to break design rules, 368–369
local identity of Entities and, 177
mediators publishing internal state of, 514–515
memory consumption and, 374–375
model navigation and, 362–363
motivations for Factory use, 389
as object collections, 203
optimistic concurrency, 385–387
organizing into large clusters, 349–351
organizing into smaller units, 351–353
overview of, 347–348
placing in repository, 401
query performance as reason to break design rules, 369–370
querying repositories and, 138
references between, 359–362
removing from repository, 409
rendering Data Transfer Objects, 513–514
rendering Domain Payload Objects, 515–516
rendering properties of multiple instances, 512–513
rethinking design, 370–372
review, 388
Root Entity and, 380–382
scalability and distribution of, 363–364
in Scrum Core Domain, 348–349
single-aggregate-instance-in-single-transaction rule of thumb, 302
size of Bounded Contexts and, 68
small Aggregate design, 355–358
snapshots of, 559–561
as Standard Type, 237
state of, 516–517
storing in Data Fabrics, 164
synchronizing instances in local Bounded Context, 287